Measurement and Assessment in Education

Measurement and Assessment in Education

Cecil R. Reynolds
Texas A&M University

Ronald B. Livingston
University of Texas at Tyler

Victor Willson
Texas A&M University

Boston ■ New York ■ San Francisco
Mexico City ■ Montreal ■ Toronto ■ London ■ Madrid ■ Munich ■ Paris
Hong Kong ■ Singapore ■ Tokyo ■ Cape Town ■ Sydney

Cecil: To Julia for the many sacrifices she makes for me and my work.

Ron: To Kim—thank you for your love, support, and companionship!

Senior Editor: *Arnis E. Burvikovs*
Editorial Assistant: *Kelly Hopkins*
Marketing Manager: *Tara Kelly*
Composition and Prepress Buyer: *Linda Cox*
Manufacturing Buyer: *Andrew Turso*
Cover Administrator: *Kristina Mose-Libon*
Editorial-Production Service: *Omegatype Typography, Inc.*
Electronic Composition: *Omegatype Typography, Inc.*

For related titles and support materials, visit our online catalog at www.ablongman.com.

Between the time website information is gathered and then published, it is not unusual for some sites to have closed. Also, the transcription of URLs can result in unintended typographical errors. The publisher would appreciate notification where these errors occur so that they may be corrected in subsequent editions.

Many of the designations used by manufacturers and sellers to distinguish their products are claimed as trademarks. Where those designations appear in this book, and Allyn and Bacon was aware of a trademark claim, the designations have been printed in initial or all caps.

Library of Congress Cataloging-in-Publication Data

Reynolds, Cecil R.
    Measurement & assessment in education / Cecil R. Reynolds, Ronald B. Livingston, and Victor Willson.
      p. cm.
    Includes bibliographical references and index.
    ISBN 0-205-37602-9 (alk. paper)
    1. Educational tests and measurements—Handbooks, manuals, etc.   I. Title: Measurement and assessment in education.   II. Livingston, Ronald B.   III. Willson, Victor L.   IV. Title.
LB3051.R45 2005
371.26—dc22

                                            2004063385

Printed in the United States of America

10 9 8 7 6 5 4 3 2   09 08 07 06

CONTENTS

PREFACE

When we meet someone for the first or first few times, we engage inescapably in some form of evaluation. Funny, personable, intelligent, witty, arrogant, and rude are just some of the descriptors we might apply to people we meet. This happens in classrooms as well. As university professors, just as other classroom teachers do, we meet new students each year and form impressions about them from our interactions. These impressions are forms of evaluation or assessment of characteristics we observe or determine from our interactions with these new students. We all do this, and we do it informally, and at times we realize, once we have had more experience with someone, that our early evaluations were in error. There are times, however, when our evaluations must be far more formal and hopefully more precise. This is a book about those times and how to make our appraisals more accurate and meaningful.

We must, for example, assign grades and determine a student's suitability for advancement. Psychologists need to determine accurately proper diagnoses of various forms of psychopathology such as mental retardation, learning disabilities, schizophrenia, depression, anxiety disorders, and the like. These types of evaluations are best accomplished through more rigorous means than casual interaction and more often than not are accomplished best via the use of some formal measurement procedures. Just as a carpenter can estimate the length of a board needed for some construction project, we can estimate student characteristics—but neither is satisfactory when it is time for the final construction or decision. We both must measure.

Educational and psychological tests are the measuring devices we use to address such questions as the degree of mastery of a subject matter area, the achievement of educational objectives, the degree of anxiety a student displays over taking a test, or even the ability of a student to pay attention in a classroom environment. Some tests are more formal than others, and the degree of formality of our measuring techniques varies on a continuum from the typical classroom, teacher-made test on a specific assignment to commercially prepared, carefully standardized procedures with large, nationally representative reference samples for standard setting.

The purposes of this book include educating the reader about the different ways in which we can measure constructs of interest to us in schools and the ways to ensure that we do the best job possible in designing our own classroom assessments. We also provide detailed information on a variety of assessments used by other professionals in schools, such as school psychologists, so the reader can interact with these other professionals more intelligently and use the results of the many assessments that occur in schools to do a better job with the students.

Not only is the classroom assessment process covered in detail, but the use of various standardized tests is also covered. The regular or general education classroom is emphasized, but special applications of the evaluation and measurement processes to students with disabilities are also noted and explained. Whenever possible, we have tried to illustrate the principles taught through application to everyday problems in the schools. Through an integrated approach to presentation and explanation of principles of tests and measurement with an emphasis on applications to classroom issues, we hope we will have prepared the reader for the changing face of assessment and evaluation in the schools. The fundamental principles taught may change little, but actual practice in the schools is sure to change.

This book is targeted primarily at individuals who are in teacher preparation programs or preparing for related educational positions such as school administrators. Others who may pursue work in educational settings will also find the content informative and at all times, we hope, practical. In preparing this text, we repeatedly asked ourselves two questions. First, what do teachers really need to know to perform their jobs? We recognize that most teachers do not aspire to become assessment experts so we have tried to focus on the essential knowledge and skills and avoid esoteric information. Second, what does the empirical research tell us about educational assessment and measurement? At times it might be easier to go with educational fads and popular trends and disregard what years of research have shown us. While this may be enticing, it is not acceptable! We owe you, our readers, the most accurate information available that is based on the current state of scientific knowledge. We also owe this to the many students you will be evaluating during your careers.

The authors have developed several indispensable supplements to augment the textbook. Students will find many useful resources in the free Student Activities Manual, which correlates closely with the text content and is available as a special package. Instructor resources include an Instructor's Manual with Test Bank and PowerPoint™ presentations, which are available electronically by contacting your local representative.

Acknowledgments

We would like to express our appreciation to our editor, Arnis Burvikovs, for his leadership in helping us bring this volume to closure. His work in obtaining so many high-quality reviews and guiding us in choosing the right revisions to make based thereon was of tremendous benefit to us in our writing assignments. Our thanks to the reviewers: William M. Bart, University of Minnesota; Boyd Dressler, Montana State University; Beverly M. Klecker, Morehead State University; Marie Kraska, Auburn University; John R. McClure, Northern Arizona University; and James Tate, Southwestern Oklahoma State University. To our respective families, we owe a continual debt of gratitude for the warm reception they give our work, for their encouragement, and for their allowances for our work schedules. Hopefully, this volume will be of use to those who toil in the classrooms of our nation and will assist them in conducting better evaluations of students, enabling even better teaching to occur. This will be our thanks.

1 Introduction to Educational Assessment

Why do I need to learn about testing and assessment?

CHAPTER HIGHLIGHTS

The Language of Assessment

Assumptions of Educational Assessment

Participants in the Assessment Process

Common Applications
of Educational Assessments

What Teachers Need to Know
about Assessment

Educational Assessment
in the Twenty-First Century

LEARNING OBJECTIVES

After reading and studying this chapter, students should be able to:

1. Define test, measurement, and assessment.
2. Describe and give examples of different types of tests.
3. Describe and give examples of different types of score interpretations.
4. Describe and explain the assumptions underlying educational assessment.
5. Describe the major participants in the assessment process.
6. Describe and explain the major applications of assessment in schools.
7. Describe and explain the competencies teachers should demonstrate
   in educational assessment.
8. Describe some major trends in assessment.

Students in teacher preparation programs want to teach, but our combined experience of more than sixty years in colleges of education suggests that they are generally not very interested in testing and assessment. Yes, they know that teachers do test, but testing is not what led them to select a career in teaching. Teachers love children and love teaching, but they often have a negative or at best neutral view of testing. This predisposition is not limited to education students. Undergraduate psychology students are typically drawn to psychology because they want to work with and help people. Most aspire to be counselors or

Assessment is an integral component of the teaching process. Assessment can and should provide information that both enhances instruction and promotes learning.

therapists, and relatively few want to specialize in assessment. When we teach undergraduate education or psychology test and measurement courses, we recognize that it is important to spend some time explaining to our students why they need to learn about testing and assessment. This is one of the major goals of this chapter. We want to explain to you why you need to learn about testing and assessment, and hopefully convince you that this is a worthwhile endeavor.

Teaching is often conceptualized as a straightforward process whereby teachers provide instruction and students learn. With this perspective, teaching is seen as a simple instruction–learning process. In actual practice, it is more realistic to view assessment as an integral component of the teaching process. In fact it has been estimated that teachers devote at least one-third of their professional time to assessment-related activities (Stiggins & Conklin, 1992). Assessment can and should provide relevant information that both enhances instruction and promotes learning. In other words, there should be a close reciprocal relationship between instruction, learning, and assessment. With this expanded conceptualization of teaching, instruction and assessment are integrally related, with assessment providing objective feedback about what the students have learned, how well they have learned it, how effective the instruction has been, and what information, concepts, and objectives require more attention. Instead of teaching being limited to an instruction–learning process, it is conceptualized more accurately as an instruction–learning–assessment process. In this model, the goal of assessment, like that of instruction, is to facilitate student achievement (e.g., Gronlund, 1998). In the real world of education, it is difficult to imagine effective teaching that does not involve some form of assessment. The better job teachers do in assessing student learning, the better their teaching will be.

The following quote from Stiggins and Conklin (1992) illustrates the important role teachers play in the overall process of educational assessment.

> As a nation, we spend billions of dollars on educational assessment, including hundreds of millions for international and national assessments, and additional hundreds of millions for statewide testing programs. On top of these, the standardized tests that form the basis of district-wide testing programs represent a billion dollar industry. If we total all of these expensive, highly visible, politically important assessments, we still account for less than 1 percent of all the assessments conducted in America's schools. The other 99 percent are conducted by teachers in their classrooms on a moment-to-moment, day-to-day, and week-to-week basis. (back cover)

In summary, if you want to be an effective teacher, you need to be knowledgeable about testing and assessment. Instruction and assessment are both instrumental parts of the teaching process, and assessment is a major component of a teacher's day-to-day job. We hope that by the time you finish this chapter you will have a better understanding of the role of assessment in education and recognize that although you may never want to specialize in testing and assessment, you will appreciate the important role assessment plays in the overall educational process.

The Language of Assessment

In our brief introduction we have already used a number of relatively common but somewhat technical terms. Before we go any further it would be beneficial to define them for you.

Tests, Measurement, and Assessment

A *test* is a procedure in which a sample of an individual's behavior is obtained, evaluated, and scored using standardized procedures (AERA et al., 1999).

■ *Test.* A **test** is a device or procedure in which a sample of an individual's behavior is obtained, evaluated, and scored using standardized procedures (AERA, APA, & NCME, 1999). This is a rather broad or general definition, but at this point in our discussion we will be best served with this generic definition. Rest assured that we will provide more specific information on different types of tests in due time. Before proceeding, however, it should be noted that a specific aspect of our definition of a test deserves mentioning. Because a test is only a sample of behavior, it is imperative that tests reflect a representative sample of the behavior you are interested in learning about. Your assessments should assess content areas in accordance with the relative importance you have assigned to them. The importance of the concept of a representative sample will become more apparent as we proceed with our study of testing and assessment, and we will touch on it in more detail in later chapters when we address the technical properties of tests.

Measurement is a set of rules for assigning numbers to represent objects, traits, attributes, or behaviors.

■ *Measurement.* **Measurement** can be defined as a set of rules for assigning numbers to represent objects, traits, attributes, or behaviors. An educational test is a measuring device and therefore involves rules (e.g., administration guidelines and scoring criteria) for assigning numbers that represent an individual's performance. In turn, these numbers are interpreted as reflecting characteristics of the test taker. For example, the number of words spelled correctly on a spelling test might be interpreted as reflecting a student's spelling skills.

Assessment is any systematic procedure for collecting information that can be used to make inferences about the characteristics of people or objects (AERA et al., 1999).

■ *Assessment.* **Assessment** is any systematic procedure for collecting information that can be used to make inferences about the characteristics of people or objects (AERA et al., 1999). Assessment should lead to an increased understanding of these characteristics. Tests are obviously one systematic method of collecting information and are therefore one set of tools for assessment. Reviews of historical records, interviews, and observations are also legitimate assessment techniques and all are maximally useful when they are integrated. Therefore, assessment is a broader, more comprehensive process than testing.

Now that we have defined these common terms, with some reluctance we acknowledge that in actual practice many educational professionals use *testing, measurement,* and *assessment* interchangeably. Recognizing this, Popham (2000) noted that in contemporary educational circles, *assessment* has become the preferred term. *Measurement* sounds rather rigid and sterile when applied to students and tends to be avoided. *Testing* has its own negative connotations. For example, hardly a week goes by when newspapers don't contain articles about "teaching to the test" or "high-stakes testing," typically with negative connotations. Additionally, when people hear the word *test* they usually think of paper-and-pencil tests. In recent years, as a result of growing dissatisfaction with traditional paper-and-pencil tests, alternative testing procedures have been developed (e.g., performance assessments and portfolios). As a result, *testing* is not seen as particularly descriptive of modern educational practices. That leaves us with *assessment* as the current buzzword among educators.

Before proceeding, we should define some other terms. **Psychometrics** is the science of psychological measurement, and a *psychometrician* is a psychological or educational professional who has specialized in the area of testing, measurement, and assessment. You will likely hear people refer to the psychometric properties of a test, and by this they mean the measurement or statistical characteristics of a test. These measurement characteristics include reliability and validity. **Reliability** refers to the stability or consistency of test scores. On a more theoretical level, reliability refers to the degree to which test scores are free from measurement errors (AERA et al., 1999). Scores that are relatively free from measurement errors will be stable or consistent (i.e., reliable). **Validity,** in simplest terms, refers to the appropriateness or accuracy of the interpretations of test scores. If test scores are interpreted as reflecting intelligence, do they actually reflect intellectual ability? If test scores are used to predict success on a job, can they accurately predict who will be successful on the job?

Reliability **refers to the stability or consistency of the test scores.**

Validity **refers to the accuracy of the interpretations of test scores.** *tests what it is suppose to test*

Types of Tests

We defined a *test* as a device or procedure in which a sample of an individual's behavior is obtained, evaluated, and scored using standardized procedures (AERA et al., 1999). You have probably taken a large number of tests in your life, and it is likely that you have noticed that all tests are not alike. For example, people take tests in schools that help determine their grades, a test to obtain a driver's license, interest inventories to help make educational and vocational decisions, admissions tests when applying for college, exams to obtain professional certificates and licenses, and personality tests to gain personal understanding. This brief list is clearly not exhaustive!

Cronbach (1990) notes that tests can generally be classified as measures of either *maximum performance* or *typical response*. Maximum performance tests are also often referred to as ability tests, but achievement tests are included here as well. On maximum performance tests items may be scored as either "correct" or "incorrect," and examinees are encouraged to demonstrate their very best performances. **Maximum performance tests** are designed to assess the upper limits of the examinee's knowledge and abilities. For example, maximum performance tests can be designed to assess how well a student performs selected tasks or has mastered a specified content domain. Intelligence tests and classroom achievement tests are common examples of maximum performance tests. In contrast, typical response tests attempt to measure the typical behavior and characteristics of examinees. Often, typical response tests are referred to as personality tests, and in this context *personality* is used broadly to reflect a whole host of noncognitive characteristics such as attitudes, behaviors, emotions, and interests (Anastasi & Urbina, 1997). Some individuals reserve the term *test* for maximum performance measures, while using terms such as *scale* and inventory when referring to typical performance instruments (AERA et al., 1999). In this textbook we will use the term *test* in its broader sense, applying to both maximum performance and typical response procedures.

Maximum Performance Tests. As we noted, maximum performance tests are designed to assess the upper limits of the examinee's knowledge and abilities. Within the broad category of maximum performance tests, a number of subcategories are often employed. First, maximum performance tests are often classified as either achievement tests or aptitude tests.

Maximum performance tests are designed to assess the upper limits of the examinee's knowledge and abilities.

Second, maximum performance tests are often described as either speed or power tests. Finally, maximum performance tests can be classified as either objective or subjective. These distinctions, while not absolute in nature, have a long historical basis and provide some useful descriptive information.

Achievement and Aptitude. Maximum performance tests are often classified as either achievement tests or aptitude tests. **Achievement tests** are designed to assess the knowledge or skills of an individual in a content domain in which he or she has received instruction (AERA et al., 1999). In contrast, **aptitude tests** are broader in scope and are designed to measure the cognitive skills, abilities, and knowledge that an individual has accumulated as the result of overall life experiences. In other words, achievement tests are linked or tied to a specific program of instructional objectives, whereas aptitude tests reflect the cumulative impact of life experiences as a whole. This distinction, however, is not absolute and is actually a matter of degree or emphasis. Most testing experts today conceptualize both achievement and aptitude tests as measures of developed cognitive abilities that can be ordered along a continuum in terms of how closely linked the assessed abilities are to specific learning experiences.

Achievement tests measure knowledge and skills in an area in which instruction has been provided (AERA et al., 1999).

Aptitude tests measure cognitive abilities and skills that are accumulated as the result of overall life experiences (AERA et al., 1999). — cognitive abilities

Another distinction between achievement and aptitude tests involves the ways their results are used or interpreted. Achievement tests typically are used to measure what has been learned or "achieved" at a specific point in time. In contrast, aptitude tests usually are used to predict future performance or reflect an individual's potential in terms of academic or job performance. However, this distinction is not absolute either. As an example, a test given at the end of high school to assess achievement might also be used to predict success in college. Although it is important to recognize that the distinction between achievement and academic tests is not absolute, the achievement/aptitude distinction is also useful when discussing different types of student abilities.

Speed and Power Tests. Maximum performance tests often are categorized as either speed or power tests. On a pure **speed test**, performance only reflects differences in the speed of performance. A speed test generally contains items that are relatively easy and has a strict time limit that prevents any examinees from successfully completing all the items. On a pure **power test**, the speed of performance is not an issue. Everyone is given plenty of time to attempt all the items, but the items are ordered according to difficulty, and the test contains some items that are so difficult that no examinee is expected to answer them all. As a result, performance on a power test primarily reflects the difficulty of the items the examinee is able to answer correctly. Well-developed speed and power tests are

On *speed tests,* performance reflects differences in the speed of performance.

On *power tests,* performance reflects the difficulty of the items the examinee is able to answer correctly.

designed so no one will obtain a perfect score. They are designed this way because perfect scores are "indeterminate." That is, if someone obtains a perfect score on a test, the test failed to assess the very upper limits of that person's ability. To access adequately the upper limits of ability, tests need to have what test experts refer to as an "adequate ceiling"; that is, the tests are difficult enough that no examinee will be able to obtain a perfect score. As you might expect, this distinction between speed and power tests is also one of degree rather than being absolute. Most often a test is not a *pure* speed test or a *pure* power test, but incorporates some combination of the two approaches. For example, the Scholastic Assessment Test (SAT) and Graduate Record Examination (GRE) are considered power tests, but both have time limits. When time limits are set such that 95 percent or more of examinees will have the opportunity to respond to all items, the test is still considered to be a power test and not a speed test.

Objective and Subjective Maximum Performance Tests.   Objectivity typically implies impartiality or the absence of personal bias. Cronbach (1990) notes that the less test scores are influenced by the subjective judgment of the person grading or scoring the test, the more objective the test is. In other words, objectivity refers to the extent that trained examiners who score a test will be in agreement and score responses in the same way. Tests with selected-response items (e.g., multiple choice, true–false, and matching) that can be scored using a fixed key and that minimize subjectivity in scoring are often referred to as "objective" tests. In contrast, subjective tests are those that rely on the personal judgment of the individual grading the test. For example, essay tests are considered subjective because test graders rely to some extent on their own subjective judgment when scoring the essays. Most students are well aware that different teachers might assign different grades to the same essay item. It is common, and desirable, for those developing subjective tests to provide explicit scoring rubrics in an effort to reduce the impact of the subjective judgment of the person scoring the test.

Typical response tests are designed to measure the typical behavior and characteristics of examinees.

Typical Response Tests.   As we indicated, **typical response tests** are designed to measure the typical behavior and characteristics of examinees. Typical response tests measure constructs such as personality, behavior, attitudes, or interests. In conventional assessment terminology, the general term *personality* broadly encompasses a wide range of emotional, interpersonal, motivational, attitudinal, and other personal characteristics (Anastasi & Urbina, 1997). In terms of personality testing, most testing experts distinguish between objective and projective techniques. Although there are some differences, this distinction largely parallels the separation of maximum performance tests into objective or subjective tests. These two approaches are described next.

Objective Personality Tests.   As with maximum performance tests, in the context of typical response assessment objectivity also implies impartiality or the absence of personal bias. **Objective personality tests** are those that use selected-response items (e.g., true–false) and are

Objective personality tests use items that are not influenced by the subjective judgment of the person scoring the test.

scored in an objective manner. For example, a personality test that includes true–false items such as "I enjoy parties" is considered objective. The test takers simply respond *true* if the statement describes them and *false* if it does not. By using a scoring key, there should be no disagreement among scorers regarding how to score the items.

***Projective personality tests
involve the presentation of
ambiguous material that elicits
an almost infinite range of
responses. Most projective tests
involve subjectivity in scoring.***

Projective Personality Tests. **Projective personality tests** typically involve the presentation of unstructured or ambiguous materials that can elicit an almost infinite range of responses from the examinee. For example, the clinician may show the examinee an inkblot and ask: "What might this be?" Instructions to the examinee are minimal, there are essentially no restrictions on the examinee's response, and there is considerable subjectivity when scoring the response. Elaborating on the distinction between objective and projective tests, Reynolds (1998b) noted:

> It is primarily the agreement on scoring that differentiates objective from subjective tests. If trained examiners agree on how a particular answer is scored, tests are considered objective; if not, they are considered subjective. Projective is not synonymous with subjective in this context but most projective tests are closer to the subjective than objective end of the continuum of agreement on scoring. (p. 49)

Exclusive to projective tests is what is referred to as the "projective hypothesis." In summary, the projective hypothesis holds that when examinees respond to ambiguous stimuli, they respond in a manner that reflects their genuine unconscious desires, motives, and drives without interference from the ego or conscious mind (Reynolds, 1998b). Projective techniques are extremely popular, but they are the focus of considerable controversy. This controversy focuses on the subjective nature of this approach and the lack of empirical evidence supporting the technical qualities of the instruments. In other words, although the tests are popular there is little evidence they provide reliable and valid information.

Table 1.1 depicts the major categories of tests we have discussed. Although we have introduced you to the major types of tests, this brief introduction clearly is not exhaustive. Even though essentially all tests can be classified according to this scheme, other distinctions are possible. For example, a common distinction is made between standardized tests and nonstandardized tests. **Standardized tests** are professionally developed tests that are administered, scored, and interpreted in a standard manner. The goal of standardization is to make sure that testing conditions are the same for all the individuals taking the test (AERA et al., 1999). Part of the process of standardizing most tests involves administering them to large, representative samples that represent the types of individuals who will take the test. This group, typically referred to as the **standardization sample**, is used to establish "norms" that facilitate the interpretation of test results (Anastasi & Urbina, 1997). Examples of standardized tests include the Scholastic Assessment Test (SAT) and the American College Test (ACT), popular admission tests used by colleges to help select students. **Nonstandardized tests** are developed in a less formal manner. The most common type of nonstandardized tests is the classroom achievement tests with which we are all familiar. Practically every day of the academic year teachers are developing and administering classroom tests.

Finally, it is common to distinguish between individual tests (i.e., tests designed to be administered to one examinee at a time) and group tests (i.e., tests administered to more than one examinee at a time). This is an important distinction that applies to the administration of the test rather than the type of the test. For example, individual aptitude tests and group aptitude tests are both aptitude tests; they simply differ in how they are administered. This

TABLE 1.1   Major Categories of Tests

I. Maximum Performance Tests

  a. *Achievement tests:* assess knowledge and skills in an area in which the student has received instruction.

  1. *Speed tests:* e.g., a timed typing test.

  2. *Power tests:* e.g., a spelling test containing words of increasing difficulty.

  b. *Aptitude tests:* assess knowledge and skills accumulated as the result of overall life experiences.

  1. *Speed tests:* e.g., a timed test whereby the test taker quickly scans groups of symbols and marks symbols that meet predetermined criteria.

  2. *Power tests:* e.g., a test of nonverbal reasoning and problem solving that requires the test taker to solve problems of increasing difficulty.

  c. Maximum performance tests are often classified as either objective or subjective. When the scoring of a test does not rely on the subjective judgment of the individual scoring it, it is said to be objective. If the scoring of a test does rely on subjective judgment, it is said to be subjective.

II. Typical Response Tests

  a. *Objective personality tests:* e.g., a test whereby the test taker answers true–false items referring to personal beliefs and preferences.

  b. *Projective personality tests:* e.g., a test whereby the test taker looks at an inkblot and describes what he or she sees.

---

is true in the personality domain as well wherein some tests require one-on-one administration but others can be given to groups.

Types of Score Interpretations

Practically all tests produce scores that reflect or represent the performance of the individuals taking the tests. There are two fundamental approaches to understanding scores: the norm-referenced approach and the criterion-referenced approach. With **norm-referenced score** interpretations, an examinee's performance is compared to the performance of other people, often those in a standardization sample. For example, if you say that a student scored better than 95% of his or her peers, this is a norm-referenced interpretation. The standardization sample serves as the reference group against which performance is judged. With **criterion-referenced score** interpretations, the examinee's performance is not compared to that of other people, but to a specified level of performance. With criterion-referenced interpretations, the emphasis is on what the examinees know or what they can do, not their standing relative to other people. One of the most common examples of criterion-referenced scoring is the percentage of correct responses on a classroom examination. For example, if you report that a student correctly answered 95% of the items on a classroom test, this is a criterion-referenced interpretation. In addition to percent correct, another type of criterion-referenced interpretation

Norm-referenced score **interpretations compare an examinee's performance to the performance of other people.**

Criterion-referenced score **interpretations compare an examinee's performance to a specified level of performance.**

is referred to as **mastery testing.** Mastery testing involves determining whether the examinee has achieved a specified level of mastery designated by a *cut score,* and performance is usually reported with an all-or-none score such as a pass–fail designation (AERA et al., 1999). For example, on a licensing exam for teachers the cut score might be 70%, and all examinees earning a score of 70% or greater will receive a designation of "pass."

Norm-referenced interpretations are relative (i.e., relative to the performance of other examinees) whereas criterion-referenced interpretations are absolute (i.e., compared to an absolute standard). People often refer to norm-referenced and criterion-referenced tests; but this is not technically accurate. Actually, the terms *norm-referenced* and *criterion-referenced* refer to the interpretation of test scores. Although it is more common for tests to produce either norm-referenced or criterion-referenced scores, it is possible for a test to produce both norm- and criterion-referenced scores. Table 1.2 depicts salient information about norm- and criterion-referenced scores.

Assumptions of Educational Assessment

Now that we have introduced you to some of the basic concepts of educational assessment, this is an opportune time to discuss some basic assumptions that underlie educational assessment. These assumptions were adopted in part from Cohen and Swerdlik (2002), who note, appropriately, that these assumptions actually represent a simplification of some very complex issues. As you progress through this text, you will develop a better understanding of these complex and interrelated issues.

Psychological and Educational Constructs Exist

In assessment terminology, a **construct** is simply the trait or characteristic that a test is designed to measure. For example, achievement is a construct that reflects an individual's

TABLE 1.2 Norm- and Criterion-Referenced Scores

Type of Score	Description	Example
Norm-referenced scores	An examinee's performance is compared to that of other people. Interpretation is relative to that of other people.	An examinee earns a percentile rank score of 50, meaning that the score was better than 50% of the individuals in the standardization sample.
Criterion-referenced scores	An examinee's performance is compared to a specified level of performance. Interpretation is absolute (not relative).	A student correctly answers 50% of the items on a test. On a licensing exam, an examinee obtains a score greater than the cut score and receives a passing score.

Constructs **are the traits or characteristics a test is designed to measure (AERA et al., 1999).**

knowledge or accomplishments in areas in which they have received instruction (AERA et al., 1999). In schools we are often interested in measuring a number of constructs, such as a student's intelligence, achievement in a specific content area, or attitude toward learning. This assumption simply acknowledges that constructs such as intelligence, achievement, or attitudes exist.

Psychological and Educational Constructs Can Be Measured

Cronbach (1990) notes that an old, often-quoted adage among measurement professional goes "If a thing exists, it exists in some amount. If it exists in some amount, it can be measured" (p. 34). If we accept the assumption that psychological constructs exist, the next natural question is "Can these constructs be measured?" As you might predict, assessment experts believe psychological and educational constructs can be measured.

Although We Can Measure Constructs, Our Measurement Is Not Perfect

Although assessment experts believe they can measure psychological constructs, they also acknowledge the measurement process is not perfect. This is usually framed in terms of measurement error and its effects on the reliability of scores. Some degree of **error** is inherent in all measurement, and measurement error reduces the usefulness of measurement. As you will learn, assessment experts make considerable efforts to estimate and minimize the effects of measurement error.

Some degree of *error* is inherent in all measurement.

There Are Different Ways to Measure Any Given Construct

There are *multiple approaches* to measuring any given construct, and these different approaches have their own unique strengths and weaknesses.

As you will learn in this text, there are multiple approaches to measuring any given construct. Consider the example of academic achievement. A student's achievement in a specific area can be measured using a number of different approaches. For example, a teacher might base a student's grade in a course on a variety of components including traditional paper-and-pencil tests (e.g., multiple-choice, short-answer, and essay items), homework assignments, class projects, performance assessments, and portfolios. Although all of these different approaches typically are aimed at measuring the knowledge, skills, and abilities of students, each has its own unique characteristics.

All Assessment Procedures Have Strengths and Limitations

While acknowledging that there are a number of different approaches to measuring any construct, assessment experts also acknowledge that all assessment procedures have their own specific set of strengths and limitations. One assessment approach might produce highly reliable scores, but not measure some aspects of a construct as well as another approach, which produces less reliable scores. As a result, it is important that test users understand the specific strengths and weaknesses of the procedures they use. The relatively simple idea that professionals should be aware of the limitations of their assessment procedures and the information obtained from them is a key issue in ethical assessment practice (e.g., Cohen & Swerdlik, 2002).

Multiple Sources of Information Should Be Part of the Assessment Process

Given that there are different approaches to measuring any given construct and that each approach has its own strengths and weaknesses, it only follows that assessment should incorporate information from different approaches. Important decisions *should not be based on the results of a single test or other assessment procedure.* For example, when deciding which applicants should be admitted to a college or university, information such as performance on an admissions test (e.g., SAT or ACT), high school grade point average (GPA), letters of recommendation, evidence of extracurricular activities, and a written statement of purpose should be considered. It would be inappropriate to base this decision on any one source of information.

Important decisions should not be based on the result of a single test or other assessment procedure.

Performance on Tests Can Be Generalized to Nontest Behaviors

Typically when we give a test we are not simply interested in the individual's performance on the test, but in the ability to generalize from test performance to nontest behaviors. For example, it is not an individual's score on the SAT that is in itself important to a college admissions officer, but the fact that the score can be used to help predict performance in college. The same applies to a 20-item test measuring multiplication skills. It is not really the student's ability to answer those specific multiplication problems correctly that is of primary importance, but that the performance on those 20 items reflects the ability to perform multiplication problems in general. This assumption holds that test performance is important, not in and of itself, but because of what it tells us about the test taker's standing on the measured construct or ability to perform certain tasks or jobs.

Assessment Can Provide Information That Helps Educators Make Better Educational Decisions

The widespread use of assessment procedures in educational settings is based on the premise that the information obtained from assessment procedures can help educators make better decisions. These decisions range from the specific grade a student should receive in a course to the effectiveness of the curriculum used in a state or school district.

Information obtained from assessment procedures can help educators make better decisions.

Educational assessments are not perfect, but they can provide useful information.

Assessments Can Be Conducted in a Fair Manner

Although many critics of testing might argue against this assumption, contemporary assessment experts spend considerable time and energy developing instruments that, when administered and interpreted

Well-made tests that are appropriately administered and interpreted are among the most equitable methods of evaluating people.

according to guidelines, are fair and minimize bias. Nevertheless, tests can be used inappropriately, and when they are it discredits or stigmatizes assessment procedures in general. However, in such circumstances the culprit is the person using the test, not the test itself. At times, people criticize assessments because they do not like the results obtained. In many instances, this is akin to "killing the messenger."

Testing and Assessment Can Benefit Our Educational Institutions and Society as a Whole

Although many people might initially argue that the elimination of all tests would be a positive event, on closer examination most will agree that tests and other assessment procedures make significant contributions to education and society as a whole. Consider a world without tests. People would be able to present themselves as surgeons without ever having their ability to perform surgery competently assessed. People would be given drivers' licenses without having their ability to drive assessed. Airline pilots would be flying commercial jets without having to demonstrate their competence as pilots. All of these examples should give you reasons to consider the value of tests. Although it is typically not a matter of life and death, the use of tests in schools also has important implications. How comfortable would you be if your instructors simply assigned your grades based exclusively on their subjective impressions of you? In this situation it is likely that each instructor's personal biases and preferences would play important roles in determining one's grades. If the instructor felt you were a "good student," you would likely receive a good grade. However, if the instructor had a negative impression of you for any reason, you might not be so lucky. Most people would prefer to be evaluated based on their demonstrated skills and abilities rather than on subjective judgment. The same principle applies to admissions decisions made by universities. Without tests admission officers might make arbitrary decisions based solely on their personal likes and dislikes. In fact, the SAT was developed to increase the objectivity of college admissions, which in the first quarter of the twentieth century depended primarily on family status. When used appropriately tests can provide objective information that is free from personal biases and other subjective influences.

These assumptions are listed in Table 1.3. As we noted, these seemingly simple assumptions represent some complex and controversial issues, and there is considerable debate regarding the pros and cons of testing and assessment. Many of the controversies surrounding the use of tests are the results of misunderstandings and misuses of tests. As noted in assumption 3 in Table 1.3, tests and all other assessment procedures contain some degree of measurement error. Tests are not perfect and they should not be interpreted as if they were perfect. However, this limitation is not limited to psychological and educational measurement; all measurement is subject to error. Chemistry, physics, and engineering all struggle with imperfect, error-laden measurement that is always, to some extent, limiting the advancement of the discipline. An example most of us can relate to involves the medical profession. There is error in medical assessment procedures such as blood pressure tests or tests of blood cholesterol level, but they still provide useful information. The same is true of educational assessment procedures. They are not perfect, but they still provide useful information. While you probably will not hear anyone proclaim that there should be a ban on the use

TABLE 1.3   Assumptions of Educational Assessment

1. Psychological and educational constructs exist.
2. Psychological and educational constructs can be measured.
3. Although we can measure constructs, our measurement is not perfect.
4. There are different ways to measure any given construct.
5. All assessment procedures have strengths and limitations.
6. Multiple sources of information should be part of the assessment process.
7. Performance on tests can be generalized to nontest behaviors.
8. Assessment can provide information that helps educators make better educational decisions.
9. Assessments can be conducted in a fair manner.
10. Testing and assessment can benefit our educational institutions and society as a whole.

of medical tests, you will hear critics of educational and psychological testing call for a ban on, or at least a significant reduction in, the use of tests. Although educational tests are not perfect (and never will be), testing experts spend considerable time and effort studying the measurement characteristics of tests. This process allows us to determine how accurate and reliable tests are, can provide guidelines for their appropriate interpretation and use, and can result in the development of more accurate assessment procedures (e.g., Friedenberg, 1995).

Assumption 9 in Table 1.3 suggests that tests can be used in a fair manner. Many people criticize tests, claiming that they are biased, unfair, and discriminatory against certain groups of people. Although it is probably accurate to say that no test is perfectly fair to all examinees, neither is any other approach to selecting, classifying, or evaluating people. The majority of professionally developed tests are carefully constructed and scrutinized to minimize bias, and when used properly actually promote fairness and equality. In fact, it is probably safe to say that well-made tests that are appropriately administered and interpreted are among the most equitable methods of evaluating people. Nevertheless, the improper use of tests can result in considerable harm to individual test takers, institutions, and society (AERA et al., 1999).

Participants in the Assessment Process

A large number of individuals are involved in different aspects of the assessment process. Brief descriptions follow of some of the major participants in the assessment process (e.g., AERA et al., 1999).

People Who Develop Tests

Can you guess how many new tests are developed in a given year? Although the exact number is unknown, it is probably much larger than you might imagine. The American Psychological Association (1993) estimated that up to 20,000 new psychological, behavioral, and cognitive tests are developed every year. This number includes tests published by commercial test publishers, tests developed by professionals hoping to have their instruments published, and tests developed by researchers to address specific research questions. However, even this rather daunting figure does not include the vast number of tests developed by classroom teachers to assess the achievement or progress of their students. There are minimal standards that all of these tests should meet, whether they are developed by an assessment professional, a graduate student completing a thesis, or a teacher assessing the math skills of 3rd graders. To provide standards for the development and use of psychological and educational tests and other assessment procedures, numerous professional organizations have developed guidelines. The most influential and comprehensive set of guidelines is the *Standards for Educational and Psychological Testing,* published by the American Educational Research Association, the American Psychological Association, and the National Council on Measurement in Education (1999). We have referenced this document numerous times earlier in this chapter and will continue to do so throughout this text.

Standards for Educational and Psychological Testing **is the most influential and comprehensive set of guidelines for developing and using psychological and educational tests.**

People Who Use Tests

The list of people who use tests includes those who select, administer, score, interpret, and use the results of tests and other assessment procedures. Tests are utilized in a wide span of settings by a wide range of individuals. For example, teachers use tests in schools to assess their students' academic progress. Psychologists and counselors use tests to understand their clients better and to help refine their diagnostic impressions. Employers use tests to help select and hire skilled employees. States use tests to determine who will be given drivers' licenses. Professional licensing boards use tests to determine who has the knowledge and skills necessary to enter professions ranging from medicine to real estate. This is only a small sampling of the many settings in which tests are used. As with the development of tests, some of the people using these tests are assessment experts whose primary responsibility is administering, scoring, and interpreting tests. However, many of the people using tests are trained in other professional areas, and assessment is not their primary area of training. As with test development, the administration, scoring, and interpretation of tests involves professional and ethical standards and responsibilities. In addition to the *Standards for Educational and Psychological Testing* (AERA et al., 1999) already mentioned, *The Student Evaluation Standards* (JCSEE, 2003), *Code of Professional Responsibilities in Educational Measurement* (NCME, 1995), and *Code of Fair Testing Practices in Education* (JCTP, 1988) provide guidelines for the ethical and responsible use of tests. These last three documents are included in Appendixes A, B, and C, respectively.

People Who Take Tests

We have all been in this category at many times in our life. In public school we take an untold number of tests to help our teachers evaluate our academic progress, knowledge, and skills. You probably took the SAT or ACT test to gain admission to college. When you graduate from college and are ready to obtain a teacher's license or certificate, you will probably be given another test to evaluate how well prepared you are to enter the teaching profession. While the other participants in the assessment process have professional and ethical responsibilities, test takers have a number of rights. The Joint Committee

The most fundamental right of test takers is to be tested with tests that meet high professional standards and are valid for the intended purpose.

on Testing Practices (JCTP, 1998) notes that the most fundamental right test takers have is to be tested with tests that meet high professional standards and that are valid for the intended purposes. Other rights of test takers include the following:

- Test takers should be given information about the purposes of the testing, how the results will be used, who will receive the results, the availability of information regarding accommodations available for individuals with disabilities or language differences, and any costs associated with the testing.
- Test takers have the right to be treated with courtesy, respect, and impartiality.
- Test takers have the right to have tests administered and interpreted by adequately trained individuals who follow professional ethics codes.
- Test takers have the right to receive information about their test results.
- Test takers have the right to have their test results kept confidential.

Appendix D contains the Joint Committee on Testing Practices' *Rights and Responsibilities of Test Takers: Guidelines and Expectations.*

Other People Involved in the Assessment Process

Although the preceding three categories probably encompass most participants in the assessment process, they are not exhaustive. For example, there are individuals who market and sell assessment products and services, those who teach others about assessment practices, and those who conduct research on assessment procedures and evaluate assessment programs (NCME, 1995).

Common Applications of Educational Assessments

Now that we have introduced you to some of the basic terminology, assumptions, and types of individuals involved in educational testing and assessment, we will explain further why testing and assessment play such prominent roles in educational settings. Tests and assessments have many uses in educational settings, but underlying practically all of these uses is the belief that tests can provide valuable information that facilitates student learning and helps educators make better decisions. It would be difficult, if not impossible, to provide a comprehensive listing of all the educational applications of tests and other assessment procedures, so what follows is a listing of the prominent uses commonly identified in the literature (e.g., AFT, NCME, & NEA, 1990; Gronlund, 1998, 2003; Nitko, 2001; Popham, 2000).

Student Evaluations

The appropriate use of tests and other assessment procedures allows educators to monitor the progress of their students. In this context, probably the most common use of educational assessments involves assigning grades to students to reflect their academic progress or achievement. This type of evaluation is typically referred to as summative evaluation. **Summative evaluation** involves the determination of the value or quality of an outcome. In the classroom, summative evaluation typically involves the formal evaluation of student performance,

Summative evaluation **involves the determination of the value or quality of an outcome.**

commonly taking the form of a numerical or letter grade (e.g., A, B, C, D, or F). Summative evaluation is often designed to communicate information about student progress, strengths, and weaknesses to parents and other involved adults. Another prominent application of student assessments is to provide specific feedback to students in order to facilitate or guide their learning. Optimally, students need to know both what they have and have not mastered. This type of feedback serves to facilitate and guide learning activities and can help motivate students. It is often very frustrating to students to receive a score on an assignment without also receiving feedback about what they can do to improve their performance in the future. This type of evaluation is referred to as formative evaluation. **Formative evaluation** involves evaluative activities aimed at providing feedback to students.

Formative evaluation **involves activities designed to provide feedback to students.**

Instructional Decisions

Educational assessments also can provide important information that helps teachers adjust and enhance their teaching practices. For example, assessment information can help teachers determine what to teach, how to teach it, and how effective their instruction has been. Gronlund (2003) delineated a number of ways in which assessment can be used to enhance instructional decisions. For example, in terms of providing information about what to teach, teachers should routinely assess the skills and knowledge that students bring to their classroom in order to establish appropriate learning objectives (sometimes referred to as "sizing up" students).

Educational assessments can provide important information that helps teachers adjust and enhance their teaching practices.

Teachers do not want to spend an excessive amount of time covering material that the students have already mastered, nor do they want to introduce material for which the students are ill prepared. Assessment done at the beginning of instruction is often referred to as **placement assessment.** In addition to decisions about the content of instruction, student assessments can help teachers tailor learning activities to match the individual strengths and weaknesses of their students. Understanding the cognitive strengths and weaknesses of students facilitates this process, and certain diagnostic tests provide precisely this type of information. This type of assessment is frequently referred to as **diagnostic assessment.** Finally, educational assessment can (and should) provide feedback to teachers about how effective their instructional practices are. Teachers can use assessment information to determine whether the learning objectives were reasonable, which instructional activities were effective, and which activities need to be modified or abandoned. Special Interest Topic 1.1 provides a brief commentary on some recent efforts to further integrate assessment and instruction.

Selection, Placement, and Classification Decisions

The terms *selection, placement,* and *classification* are often used interchangeably, but technically they have different meanings. Nitko (2001) notes that *selection* refers to decisions by a school, college, or other institution to either accept or reject a student. With **selection decisions,** the key factor is that some individuals are selected while others are "rejected." A

SPECIAL INTEREST TOPIC   **1.1**

Cognitive Diagnostic Assessment—Another Step toward Unifying Assessment and Instruction

Chipman, Nichols, and Brennan (1995) note that most contemporary high-quality educational assessments do a good job of ranking students in terms of their acquired knowledge and skills. However, they are typically less effective when it comes to providing diagnostic information about the specific knowledge and processing skills that need to be taught to help students improve their academic performance. An innovative approach, known as "Cognitive Diagnostic Assessment," is evolving that combines cognitive science with psychometrics in an effort to enhance the integration of assessment and instruction. Recent developments in cognitive science have provided a growing understanding of the basic nature of knowledge and cognitive processing to the point that these "cognitive models" can serve as a guide for assessment. Although much of the literature in this area is rather advanced, in simplest terms the goal is to diagnose the specific type of cognitive errors a student is making in his or her academic work. By doing so one is then better prepared to tailor instruction to meet the student's specific needs. Although teachers have been doing their own cognitive diagnostic assessment since time immemorial, this new approach uses computer technology and intricate mathematical models to facilitate the process. The results are promising. For example, Tatsuoka and Tatsuoka (1997) describe the use of computerized cognitive diagnostic assessment to diagnose student errors in addition problems involving fractions. The results indicate that the program can successfully identify students' misconceptions and suggest ways of remediating their errors effectively and efficiently.

common example of selection involves universities making admissions decisions. In this situation, some applicants are rejected and are no longer a concern of the university. In contrast, **placement decisions** involve situations in which students are assigned to various categories that represent different educational tracks or levels that are ordered in some way. With placement, all students are placed and there are no actual rejections. For example, if all the students in a secondary school are assigned to one of three instructional programs (e.g., remedial, regular, and honors), this is a placement decision. Finally, **classification decisions** refer to situations in which students are assigned to different categories that are not ordered in any way. For example, special education students may be classified as learning disabled, emotionally disturbed, speech handicapped, or some other category of handicapping conditions, but these categories are not ordered in any particular manner; they are simply descriptive. Psychological and educational tests often provide important diagnostic information that is used when making classification decisions. In summary, although selection, placement, and classification decisions are technically different, educational tests and assessments provide valuable information that can help educators make better decisions.

Policy Decisions

We use the category of "policy decisions" to represent a wide range of administrative decisions made at the school, district, state, or national level. These decisions involve issues such

Instruction and assessment are two important and integrated aspects of the teaching process. as evaluating the curriculum and instructional materials employed, determining which programs to fund, and even deciding which employees receive merit raises and/or promotions. We are currently in an era of increased accountability in which parents and politicians are setting higher standards for students and schools, and there is a national trend to base many administrative policies and decisions on information garnered from state or national assessment programs.

Counseling and Guidance Decisions

Educational assessments can also provide information that promotes self-understanding and helps students plan for the future. For example, parents and students can use assessment information to make educational plans and select careers that best match a student's abilities and interests.

Although this listing of common applications of testing and assessment is clearly not exhaustive, it should give you an idea of some of the most important applications of assessment procedures. Again, we want to emphasize that instruction and assessment are two important and integrated aspects of the teaching process. Table 1.4 outlines these major applications of assessment in education.

What Teachers Need to Know about Assessment

So far in this chapter we have discussed the central concepts related to educational assessment and some of the many applications of assessment in today's schools. We will now elaborate on what teachers need to know about educational testing and assessment. First

TABLE 1.4   Common Applications of Educational Assessments

Type of Application	Examples
Student evaluations	Summative evaluation (e.g., assigning grades) Formative evaluation (e.g., providing feedback)
Instructional decisions	Placement assessment (e.g., sizing up) Diagnostic assessment (detecting cognitive strengths and weaknesses) Feedback on effectiveness of instruction
Selection, placement, and classification decisions	College admission decisions Assigning students to remedial, regular, or honors programs Determining eligibility for special education services
Policy decisions	Evaluating curriculum and instructional practices
Counseling and guidance decisions	Promote self-understanding and help students plan for the future

we want to emphasize that we recognize that most teachers will not make psychometrics their focus of study. However, because assessment plays such a prominent role in schools and teachers devote so much of their time to assessment-related activities, there are some basic competencies that all teachers should master. In fact in 1990 the American Federation of Teachers, the National Council on Measurement in Education, and the National Education Association collaborated to develop a document titled *Standards for Teacher Competence in Educational Assessment of Students.* In the following section we will briefly review these competencies (this document is reproduced in its entirety in Appendix E). Where appropriate, we will identify which chapters in this text are most closely linked to specific competencies.

Teachers Should Be Proficient in Selecting Professionally Developed Assessment Procedures Appropriate for Making Instructional Decisions

This competency requires that teachers be able to select professionally developed tests and other assessment procedures that are appropriate for their situation, technically adequate, fair, and that provide useful information. This requires that teachers be familiar with the wide range of assessment procedures available for use in schools and the type of information the different procedures provide (addressed primarily in Chapters 1, 12, 13, and 14). To evaluate the technical merits of tests, teachers need to be familiar with the concepts of reliability and validity and be able to make evaluative decisions about the quality and suitability of different assessment procedures (addressed primarily in Chapters 4, 5, 6, and 17). In order to make informed decisions about the quality of assessment procedures, teachers need to be able to locate, interpret, and use technical information and critical reviews of professionally developed tests (addressed primarily in Chapter 15).

Teachers Should Be Proficient in Developing Assessment Procedures Appropriate for Making Instructional Decisions

In addition to being able to select among the professionally developed assessment procedures that are available, teachers need to be able to develop their own technically adequate assessment procedures. In fact, the vast majority of the assessment information teachers collect and use on a daily basis comes from teacher-made tests. As a result, teachers need to be proficient in planning, developing, and using classroom tests. To accomplish this, teachers must be familiar with the principles and standards for developing a wide range of assessment techniques including selected-response items, constructed-response items, performance assessments, and portfolios (addressed primarily in Chapters 7, 8, 9, and 10). Teachers must also be able to evaluate the technical quality of the instruments they develop (addressed primarily in Chapters 4, 5, and 6).

> **The vast majority of the assessment information teachers collect and use comes from teacher-made tests.**

Teachers Should Be Proficient in Administering, Scoring, and Interpreting Professionally Developed and Teacher-Made Assessment Procedures

In addition to being able to select and develop good assessment procedures, teachers must be able to use them appropriately. Teachers need to understand the principles of standardization and be prepared to administer tests in a standardized manner (addressed primarily in Chapters 3 and 12). They should be able reliably and accurately to score a wide range of assessment procedures including selected-response items, constructed-response items, performance assessments, and portfolios (addressed primarily in Chapters 8, 9, and 10). Teachers need to be able to interpret the scores reported on standardized assessment procedures such as percentile ranks and standard scores (addressed primarily in Chapter 3). The proper interpretation of scores also requires that teachers have a practical knowledge of basic statistical (e.g., measures of central tendency, dispersion, correlation) and psychometric concepts (e.g., reliability, errors of measurement, validity) (addressed primarily in Chapters 2, 4, and 5).

Teachers Should Be Proficient in Using Assessment Results When Making Educational Decisions

As we have noted, assessment results are used to make a wide range of consequential educational decisions (e.g., student evaluations, instructional planning, curriculum development, and educational policies). Because teachers play such a pivotal role in using assessment information in the schools, they must be able to interpret assessment results accurately and use them appropriately. They need to understand the concepts of reliability and validity and be prepared to interpret test results in an appropriately cautious manner. Teachers should understand and be able to describe the implications and limitations of assessment results and use them to enhance the education of their students and society in general (addressed primarily in Chapters 1, 4, 5, and 11).

Teachers must be able to interpret assessment results accurately and use them appropriately.

Teachers Should Be Proficient in Developing Valid Grading Procedures That Incorporate Assessment Information

Assigning grades to students is an important aspect of teaching. Teachers must be able to develop and apply fair and valid procedures for assigning grades based on the performance of students on tests, homework assignments, class projects, and other assessments procedures (addressed primarily in Chapters 11 and 15).

Teachers Should Be Proficient in Communicating Assessment Results

Teachers are routinely called on to interpret and report assessment results to students, parents, and other invested individuals. As a result, teachers must be able to use assessment terminology correctly, understand different score formats, and explain the meaning and implications of assessment results. Teachers must be able to explain, and often defend, their own assessment and grading practices (addressed primarily in Chapters 1, 11, and 15). They should be able to describe the strengths and limitations of different assessment methods (addressed primarily in Chapters 8, 9, and 10). In addition to explaining the results of their own classroom assessments, they must be able to explain the results of professionally developed standardized tests (addressed primarily in Chapters 12, 13, and 14).

Teachers Should Be Proficient in Recognizing Unethical, Illegal, and Other Inappropriate Uses of Assessment Procedures or Information

It is essential that teachers be familiar with the ethical codes and laws that apply to educational assessment practices.

It is essential that teachers be familiar with the ethical codes and laws that apply to educational assessment practices. Teachers must ensure that their assessment practices are consistent with these professional ethical and legal standards, and if they become aware of inappropriate assessment practices by other professionals they should take steps to correct the situation (addressed primarily in Chapters 15, 16, and 17). Table 1.5 outlines these standards for teacher competence in educational assessments.

Educational Assessment in the Twenty-First Century

The field of educational assessment is dynamic and continuously evolving. There are some aspects of the profession that have been stable for many years. For example, classical test theory (discussed in some detail in Chapter 4) has been around for almost a century and is still very influential today. However, many aspects of educational assessment are almost constantly evolving as the result of a number of external and internal factors. Some of these changes are the result of theoretical or technical advances, some reflect philosophical

---

TABLE 1.5   Teacher Competencies in Educational Assessment

Teachers should be proficient in the following:

1. Selecting professionally developed assessment procedures appropriate for making instructional decisions.
2. Developing assessment procedures that are appropriate for making instructional decisions.
3. Administering, scoring, and interpreting professionally developed and teacher-made assessment procedures.
4. Using assessment results when making educational decisions.
5. Developing valid grading procedures that incorporate assessment information.
6. Communicating assessment results.
7. Recognizing unethical, illegal, and other inappropriate uses of assessment procedures or information.

changes within the profession, and some are the result of external societal or political influences. It is important for assessment professionals to stay informed regarding new developments in the field and to consider them with an open mind. To illustrate some of the developments the profession is dealing with today, we will briefly highlight a few contemporary trends that are likely to continue to impact assessment practices as you enter the teaching profession.

Computerized Adaptive Testing (CAT) and Other Technological Advances

The widespread availability of fairly sophisticated and powerful tabletop computers has had a significant impact on many aspects of our society, and the field of assessment is no exception. One of the most dramatic and innovative uses of computer technology has been the emergence of **computerized adaptive testing** (CAT). In CAT the test taker is initially given an item that is of medium difficulty. If the test taker correctly responds to that item, the computer selects and administers a slightly more difficult item. If the examinee misses the initial item, the computer selects a somewhat easier item. As the testing proceeds the computer continues to select items on the basis of the test taker's performance on previous items. CAT continues until a specified level of precision is reached. Research suggests that CAT can produce the same levels of reliability and validity as conventional paper-and-pencil tests, but because it requires the administration of fewer test items, assessment efficiency can be enhanced (e.g., Weiss, 1982, 1985, 1995).

CAT is not the only innovative application of computer technology in the field of assessment. Some of the most promising applications of technology in assessment involve the use of technology to present problem simulations that cannot be realistically addressed with paper-and-pencil tests. For example, flight-training programs routinely use sophisticated flight simulators to assess the skills of pilots. This technology allows programs to assess how pilots will handle emergency and other low-incidence situations, assessing skills that were previously difficult if not impossible to assess accurately. Another innovative use of technology is the commercially available instrumental music assessment systems that allow students to perform musical pieces and have their performances analyzed and graded in terms of pitch and rhythm. Online versions of these programs allow students to practice at home and have their performance results forwarded to their instructors at school. Although it is difficult to anticipate the many ways technology will change assessment practices in the twenty-first century, it is safe to say that they will be dramatic and sweeping. Special Interest Topic 1.2 provides information on the growing use of technology to enhance assessment in contemporary schools.

"Authentic" or Complex-Performance Assessments

Although advances in technology are driving some of the current trends in assessment, others are the result of philosophical changes among members of the assessment profession. This is exemplified in the current emphasis on performance assessments and portfolios in education. Performance assessments and portfolios are not new creations, but have been around for many years (e.g., performance assessments have been used in industrial and organizational psy-

SPECIAL INTEREST TOPIC **1.2**

Technology and Assessment in the Schools

According to a report in *Education Week* (May 8, 2003), computer- and Web-based assessments are starting to find strong support in the schools. For example, the No Child Left Behind Act of 2001, which requires states to test all students in the 3rd through 8th grades in reading and mathematics every year, has caused states to start looking for more efficient and economical forms of assessment. Assessment companies believe they have the answer: switch to computer or online assessments. Although the cost of developing a computerized test is comparable to that of a traditional paper-and-pencil test, once the test is developed the computer test is far less expensive. Some experts estimate that computerized tests can be administered for as little as 25% of the cost of a paper-and-pencil test. Another positive feature of computer-based assessment is that the results can often be available in a few days as opposed to the months educators and students are used to waiting.

Another area in which technology is having a positive impact on educational assessment practices involves preparing students for tests. More and more states and school districts are developing online test-preparation programs to help students improve their performance on high-stakes assessments. The initial results are promising! For example, a pilot program in Houston, Texas, found that 75% of the high school students who had initially failed the mandatory state assessment improved their reading scores by 29% after using a computer-based test-preparation program. In addition to being effective, these computer-based programs are considerably less expensive for the school districts than face-to-face test-preparation courses.

While it is too early to draw any firm conclusions about the impact of technology on school assessment practices, the early results are very promising. It is likely that by the year 2010 school-based assessments will be very different than they are today. This is an exciting time to work in the field of educational assessment!

chology for decades). However, the use of performance assessments and portfolios in schools has increased appreciably in recent years. Traditional testing formats, particularly multiple-choice and other selected-response formats (e.g., true–false, matching), have always had their critics, but their opposition has become more vocal in recent years. Opponents of traditional test formats complain that they emphasize rote memorization and other low-level cognitive skills and largely neglect higher-order conceptual and problem-solving skills. To address these and related shortcomings, many educational assessment experts have promoted the use of more "authentic" or complex-performance assessments, typically in the form of performance assessments and portfolios. Performance assessments require test takers to complete a process or produce a product in a context that closely resembles real-life situations. For example, a medical student might be required to interview a mock patient, select tests and other assessment procedures, arrive at a diagnosis, and develop a treatment plan (AERA et al., 1999). Portfolios, a form of performance assessment, involve the systematic collection of student work products over a certain period of time according to a specific set of guidelines (AERA et al., 1999). Artists, architects, writers, and others have long used portfolios to represent their work, and in the last decade portfolios have become increasingly popular in the assessment of students. Although performance assessments have their own set of strengths and weaknesses, they do represent a significant addition to the assessment options available to teachers.

Educational Accountability and High-Stakes Assessment

So far we have described how technological and philosophical developments within the profession have influenced current assessment practices. Other changes are the result of societal and political influences, such as the increasing emphasis on educational accountability and high-stakes testing. Although parents and politicians have always closely scrutinized the public schools, over the last three decades the public demands for increased **educational accountability** in the schools have reached an all-time high. To help ensure that teachers are teaching what they are supposed to be teaching and students are learning what they are supposed to be learning, all fifty states and the District of Columbia have implemented statewide testing programs (Doherty, 2002). These testing programs are often referred to as **high-stakes testing** because they produce results that have direct and substantial consequences for both the students and schools (AERA et al., 1999). Students who do not pass the tests may not be promoted to the next grade or allowed to graduate. However, the high stakes are not limited to students. Many states publish "report cards" that reflect the performance of school districts and individual schools. In some states low-performing schools can be closed, reconstituted, or taken over by the state, and administrators and teachers can be terminated or replaced (Amrein & Berliner, 2002).

Proponents of these testing programs maintain that they ensure that public school students are acquiring the knowledge and skills necessary to succeed in society. To support their position, they refer to data showing that national achievement scores have improved since these testing programs were implemented. Opponents of high-stakes testing programs argue that the tests emphasize rote learning and generally neglect critical thinking, problem solving, and communication skills. Additionally, these critics feel that too much instructional time is spent "teaching to the test" instead of teaching the vitally important skills teachers would prefer to focus on (Doherty, 2002). This debate is likely to continue for the foreseeable future, but in the meantime accountability and the associated testing programs are likely to play a major role in our public schools. In fact the trend is toward more, rather than less, standardized testing in public schools. For example, the Elementary and Secondary Education Act of 2001 (No Child Left Behind Act) requires that states test students annually in grades 3 through 8. Because many states typically administer standardized achievement tests in only a few of these grades, this new law will require even more high-stakes testing than is currently in use (Kober, 2002). Special Interest Topic 1.3 provides a discussion of a recent national review of state accountability systems. Special Interest Topic 1.4 provides a brief description of the National Assessment of Educational Progress (NAEP), commonly referred to as the "Nation's Report Card."

Trends in the Assessment of Students with Disabilities

Recent amendments to the Individuals with Disability Education Act (IDEA) have significantly impacted the assessment and instruction of children with disabilities. In summary, current laws require that students with disabilities, with few exceptions, be included in regular education classes and participate in all state and district assessment programs. The effect of this for regular education teachers is far reaching. In the past the instruction and assessment of students with disabilities was largely the responsibility of special education teachers, but now regular education teachers play a prominent role. Regular education teachers will have

SPECIAL INTEREST TOPIC   **1.3**

Princeton Review's Rankings of High-Stakes Testing Programs

In the spring of 2003 the Princeton Review released *Testing the Testers 2003* based on data collected from all 50 states and the District of Columbia regarding high-stakes accountability systems for students and schools. It evaluated each state based on the following criteria (percentage in parentheses indicates weighting):

Academic Alignment (20%): Is the content of the test aligned with state's curriculum?
Test Quality (15%): Are the tests valid for the intended purposes?
Sunshine (30%): Are the details of the assessment programs open to public scrutiny?
Policy (35%): Does the accountability system have the desired effects on the public schools?

State Rankings

Rank	State	Rank	State
1	NY	26	MI
2	MA	27	ID
3	TX	28	NJ
4	NC	29	AR
5	VA	30	CT
6	LA	31	NE
6	FL	32	VT
8	AZ	33	AL
8	OK	34	MO
10	CA	35	MD
11	SC	36	DE
12	MS	37	NM
13	PA	38	NH
14	UT	39	DC
15	MN	40	GA
16	CO	41	KS
17	NV	42	IN
17	TN	43	HI
19	IL	44	WY
20	ME	45	ND
20	OR	46	WI
22	OH	47	WV
23	KY	48	SD
24	WA	49	RI
25	AK	50	MT

Note: Adopted from *Testing the Testers 2003* by The Princeton Review. States with the same weighted scores received the same rankings. Iowa was excluded from the rankings because the state largely leaves accountability to the local schools.

The "Nation's Report Card"

The National Assessment of Educational Progress (NAEP), also referred to as the "Nation's Report Card," is the only ongoing nationally administered assessment of academic achievement in the United States. NAEP provides a comprehensive assessment of our students' achievement at critical periods in their academic experience (i.e., grades 4, 8, and 12). NAEP assesses performance in mathematics, science, reading, writing, world geography, U.S. history, civics, and the arts. New assessments in world history, economics, and foreign language are currently being developed. NAEP has been administered regularly since 1969. It does not provide information on the performance of individual students or schools, but presents aggregated data reflecting achievement in specific academic areas, instructional practices, and academic environments for broad samples of students and specific subgroups. The NAEP has an excellent Web site that can be accessed at http://nces.ed.gov/nationsreportcard.

Of particular interest to teachers is the NAEP *Questions Tool.* This tool provides access to NAEP questions, student responses, and scoring guides that have been released to the public. This tool can be accessed at http://nces.ed.gov/nationsreportcard/itmrls.

Teachers may also find the NAEP *Data Tool* to be very interesting. This tool provides access to tables of data from NAEP's national and state assessments. These data are based on information garnered from students, teachers, and schools. This tool can be accessed at http://nces.ed.gov/nations reportcard/naepdata.

more students receiving special education services in their classroom and, as a result, will be integrally involved in their instruction and assessment. Regular education teachers are increasingly being required to help develop and implement Individual Education Programs (IEP) for these students and assess their progress toward goals and objectives specified in the IEP.

This has been a brief and clearly incomplete discussion of some current trends in the field of assessment. Special Interest Topic 1.5 provides a commentary by a respected assessment expert about what she expects to evolve during the next century.

Summary

This chapter is a broad introduction to the field of educational assessment. We started by emphasizing that assessment should be seen as an integral part of the teaching process. When appropriately used, assessment can and should provide information that both enhances instruction and promotes learning. We then defined some common terms used in the educational assessment literature, including:

- A *test* is a procedure in which a sample of an individual's behavior is obtained, evaluated, and scored using standardized procedures (AERA et al., 1999).
- *Measurement* is a set of rules for assigning numbers to represent objects, traits, attributes, or behaviors.

SPECIAL INTEREST TOPIC **1.5**

What Does the Twenty-First Century Hold for the Assessment Profession?

In 2001 Dr. Susan Embretson presented a lecture titled "The Second Century of Ability Testing: Some Predictions and Speculations" at the Educational Testing Service (ETS) in Princeton, New Jersey. She started by reviewing the history of ability testing, which dates back approximately one hundred years. She noted that by 1930 most of the key psychometric principles were firmly established and that the remainder of the twentieth century was largely spent applying and refining those principles. As the profession enters its second century, she predicts changes in the way tests are developed, the way abilities are measured, and the aspects of ability that are measured. Here is a brief summary of some of her key points.

The Way Tests Are Developed
Dr. Embretson believes that technological advances will significantly impact the way tests are developed. For example, test revision is currently an expensive and labor-intensive process with tests revised and renormed every few years. In the future she anticipates tests will undergo continuous test revisions. As more assessments are administered via computers and data collection is centralized, test developers will be able to try out new items and update normative data on an ongoing basis. Computer-administered tests and centralized data collection will also facilitate automated validity studies and even allow items to be developed through the use of artificial intelligence.

The Way Abilities Are Measured
Based on technological and theoretical advances, Dr. Embretson predicts ability tests will become both shorter and more reliable. She also predicts a broader conceptualization of test items. For example, ability testing will incorporate more essays and other work products that had previously been difficult to evaluate in a reliable and economical manner. In recent years computer programs have been developed that can score written essays and graphical problems, and these initial efforts show considerable potential.

The Aspects of Ability That Are Measured
During the twentieth century normative interpretations of ability predominated, but Dr. Embretson expects new interpretive models to become increasingly popular. For example, she believes domain-referenced interpretations will emerge whereby abilities will be interpreted in reference to the cognitive processes and structures that are required to solve the assessment problems or tasks. Instead of focusing almost exclusively on quantitative aspects of performance, future assessments will focus more on the qualitative aspects of test performance. Finally, she believes dynamic testing will become an increasingly important force in ability testing. Dynamic testing measures how responsive the examinee's performance is to changes in conditions as the assessment proceeds.

   Although Dr. Embretson expects changes to occur rapidly over the next few decades, she also believes that the basic psychometric principles that have been with us for almost a century will still be important. Therefore, while some exciting changes are in store for the assessment profession, the basic principles and concepts presented in this textbook will continue to be fundamental aspects of the profession.

   If you are interested in reading this intriguing paper, it can be accessed at www.ets.org/research/pic/angoff7.pdf, or you can purchase a copy for $3.00 by contacting the ETS Policy Information Center, MS-04R, Rosedale Road, Princeton, NJ 08651-0001.

- *Assessment* is any systematic procedure for collecting information that can be used to make inferences about the characteristics of people or objects (AERA et al., 1999).
- *Reliability* refers to the stability, accuracy, or consistency of test scores.
- *Validity* refers to the accuracy of the interpretations of test scores.

Our discussion then turned to a description of different types of tests. Most tests can be classified as either *maximum performance* or *typical response.* Maximum performance tests are designed to assess the upper limits of the examinee's knowledge and abilities whereas typical response tests are designed to measure the typical behavior and characteristics of examinees. Maximum performance tests are often classified as *achievement* tests or *aptitude* tests. Achievement tests measure knowledge and skills in an area in which the examinee has received instruction. In contrast, aptitude tests measure cognitive abilities and skills that are accumulated as the result of overall life experiences (AERA et al., 1999). Maximum performance tests can also be classified as either *speed* tests or *power* tests. On pure speed tests, performance reflects only differences in the speed of performance whereas on pure power tests, performance reflects only the difficulty of the items the examinee is able to answer correctly. In most situations a test is not a measure of pure speed or pure power, but reflects some combination of both approaches. Finally, maximum performance tests are often classified as objective or subjective. When the scoring of a test does not rely on the subjective judgment of the person scoring the test, it is said to be objective. For example, multiple-choice tests can be scored using a fixed scoring key and are considered objective (multiple-choice tests are often scored by a computer). If the scoring of a test does rely on the subjective judgment of the person scoring the test, it is said to be subjective. Essay exams are examples of subjective tests.

Typical response tests measure constructs such as personality, behavior, attitudes, or interests, and are often classified as being either *objective* or *projective.* Objective tests use selected-response items (e.g., true–false, multiple-choice) that are not influenced by the subjective judgment of the person scoring the test. Projective tests involve the presentation of ambiguous material that can elicit an almost infinite range of responses. Most projective tests involve some subjectivity in scoring, but what is exclusive to projective techniques is the belief that these techniques elicit unconscious material that has not been censored by the conscious mind.

Most tests produce scores that reflect the test takers' performance. *Norm-referenced* score interpretations compare an examinee's performance to the performance of other people. *Criterion-referenced* score interpretations compare an examinee's performance to a specified level of performance. Typically tests are designed to produce either norm-referenced or criterion-referenced scores, but it is possible for a test to produce both norm- and criterion-referenced scores.

Next we discussed the basic assumptions that underlie educational assessment. These include:

- Psychological and educational constructs exist.
- Psychological and educational constructs can be measured.
- Although we can measure constructs, our measurement is not perfect.
- There are different ways to measure any given construct.
- All assessment procedures have strengths and limitations.

- Multiple sources of information should be part of the assessment process.
- Performance on tests can be generalized to nontest behaviors.
- Assessment can provide information that helps educators make better educational decisions.
- Assessments can be conducted in a fair manner.
- Testing and assessment can benefit our educational institutions and society as a whole.

We described the major participants in the assessment process, including those who develop tests, use tests, and take tests. We noted that the use of assessments in schools is predicated on the belief that they can provide valuable information that promotes student learning and helps educators make better decisions. Prominent uses include:

- *Student evaluations:* Appropriate assessment procedures allow teachers to monitor student progress and provide constructive feedback.
- *Instructional decisions:* Appropriate assessment procedures can provide information that allows teachers to modify and improve their instructional practices.
- *Selection, placement, and classification decisions:* Educational tests and assessments provide useful information to help educators select, place, and classify students.
- *Policy decisions:* We are in an era of increased accountability, and policy makers and educational administrators are relying more on information from educational assessments to guide policy decisions.
- *Counseling and guidance decisions:* Educational assessments also provide information that promotes self-understanding and helps students plan for the future.

Next we elaborated on what teachers need to know about educational testing and assessment. These competencies include proficiency in the following:

- Selecting professionally developed assessment procedures appropriate for making instructional decisions.
- Developing assessment procedures that are appropriate for making instructional decisions.
- Administering, scoring, and interpreting professionally developed and teacher-made assessment procedures.
- Using assessment results when making educational decisions.
- Developing valid grading procedures that incorporate assessment information.
- Communicating assessment results.
- Recognizing unethical, illegal, and other inappropriate uses of assessment procedures or information.

We concluded this chapter by describing some of the trends in educational assessment at the beginning of the twenty-first century. These included the influence of computerized adaptive testing (CAT) and other technological advances, the growing emphasis on authentic or complex-performance assessments, the national emphasis on educational accountability and high-stakes assessment, and recent developments in the assessment of students with disabilities.

KEY TERMS AND CONCEPTS

Achievement tests, p. 5

Aptitude tests, p. 5

Assessment, p. 3

Classification decisions, p. 17

Computerized adaptive testing, p. 22

Construct, p. 9

Criterion-referenced score, p. 8

Diagnostic assessment, p. 16

Educational accountability, p. 24

Error, p. 10

Formative evaluation, p. 16

High-stakes testing, p. 24

Mastery testing, p. 9

Maximum performance tests, p. 4

Measurement, p. 3

Nonstandardized tests, p. 7

Norm-referenced score, p. 8

Objective personality tests, p. 6

Placement assessment, p. 16

Placement decisions, p. 17

Power tests, p. 5

Projective personality tests, p. 7

Psychometrics, p. 4

Reliability, p. 4

Selection decisions, p. 16

Speed tests, p. 5

Standardization sample, p. 7

Standardized tests, p. 7

Summative evaluation, p. 15

Test, p. 3

Typical response tests, p. 6

Validity, p. 4

RECOMMENDED READINGS

American Educational Research Association, American Psychological Association, & National Council on Measurement in Education (1999). *Standards for educational and psychological testing.* Washington, DC: American Educational Research Association. In practically every content area this resource is indispensable!

Joint Committee on Standards for Educational Evaluation (2003). *The student evaluation standards.* Thousand Oaks, CA: Corwin Press. This text presents the JCSEE guidelines as well as illustrative vignettes intended to help educational professionals implement the standards. The classroom vignettes cover elementary, secondary, and higher education settings.

Shepard, L. A. (2000). *The role of classroom assessment in teaching and learning.* (CSE Technical Report 517). Los Angeles, CA: Center for the Study of Evaluation. This outstanding report conceptualizes classroom assessment as an integral part of teaching and learning. It is advanced reading at times, but well worth it.

Weiss, D. J. (1995). Improving individual difference measurement with item response theory and computerized adaptive testing. In D. Lubinski & R. Dawis (Eds.), *Assessing individual differences in human behavior: New concepts, methods, and findings* (pp. 49–79). Palo Alto, CA: Davies-Black. This chapter provides a good introduction to IRT and CAT.

Zenisky, A., & Sierci, S. (2002). Technological innovations in large-scale assessment. *Applied Measurement in Education, 15,* 337–362. This article details some of the ways computers have affected and likely will impact assessment practices.

INTERNET SITES OF INTEREST

www.aft.org

This is the Web site for the American Federation of Teachers, an outstanding resource for all interested in education.

http://edweek.org

Education Week is a weekly newsletter that is available online. This very valuable resource allows teachers to stay informed about professional events across the nation. You can sign up for a weekly alert and summary of articles. This is really worth checking out!

www.ncme.org

This Web site for the National Council on Measurement in Education is an excellent resource for those interested in finding scholarly information on assessment in education.

2 The Basic Mathematics of Measurement

One does not need to be a statistical wizard to grasp the basic mathematical concepts needed to understand major measurement issues.

CHAPTER HIGHLIGHTS

The Role of Mathematics in Assessment

Scales of Measurement

The Description of Test Scores

Correlation Coefficients

LEARNING OBJECTIVES

After reading and studying this chapter, students should be able to:

1. Define measurement.
2. Describe the different scales of measurement and give examples.
3. Describe the measures of central tendency and their appropriate use.
4. Describe the measures of variability and their appropriate use.
5. Explain the meaning of correlation coefficients and how they are used.
6. Explain how scatterplots are used to describe the relationships between two variables.
7. Describe how linear regression is used to predict performance.
8. Describe major types of correlation coefficients.
9. Distinguish between correlation and causation.

The Role of Mathematics in Assessment

Every semester, whenever one of us teaches a course in tests and measurement for undergraduate students in psychology and education, we inevitably hear a common moan. Students are quick to say they fear this course because they hear it involves "a lot of statistics" and they are not good at math, much less statistics. As stated in the opening quotation, you do not have to be a statistical wizard to comprehend the mathematical concepts needed to understand major measurement issues. In fact Kubiszyn and Borich (2003) estimate that less than 1% of the students in their testing and assessment courses performed poorly entirely because of insufficient math skills. Nevertheless, all measurements in education and psychology have mathematical properties, and those who use tests and other assessments, whether teacher-made or standardized commercial procedures, need to have an understanding of the basic mathematical and statistical concepts on which these assessments are predicated. In this chapter we will introduce these mathematical concepts. Generally we will emphasize the development of a conceptual understanding of these issues rather than focusing on mathematical computations. In a few instances we will present mathematical formulas and demonstrate their application, but we will keep the computational aspect to a minimum. To guard against becoming overly technical in this chapter, we asked undergraduate students in nonmath majors to review it. Their consensus was that it was readable and "user friendly." We hope you will agree!

In developing this textbook our guiding principle has been to address only those concepts that teachers *really* need to know to develop, administer, and interpret assessments in educational settings. We recognize that most teachers do not desire to become test development experts, but because teachers routinely develop, use, and interpret assessments, they need to be competent in their use. In this chapter, we will first discuss scales of measurement and show you how different scales have different properties or characteristics. Next we will introduce the concept of a collection or distribution of scores and review the different statistics available to describe distributions. Finally we will introduce the concept of correlation, how it is measured, and what it means.

Scales of Measurement

What Is Measurement?

Measurement is a set of rules for assigning numbers to represent objects, traits, attributes, or behaviors. An educational or psychological test is a measuring device, and as such it involves rules (e.g., specific items, administration, and scoring instructions) for assigning numbers to an individual's performance that are interpreted as reflecting characteristics of the individual. For example, the number of math questions students answer correctly on a particular math quiz may be interpreted as reflecting their understanding of two-digit multiplication. Another example is that your responses to questions about how often you worry about aspects of your life and are distracted by small inconveniences may be interpreted as revealing your relative level of anxiety. When we measure something, the units of measurement have a mathematical property called the **scale of measurement.** A scale is a system or scheme for assigning values or scores to the characteristic being measured (e.g., Sattler, 1992). There are four scales of measurement, and these different scales have distinct properties and convey unique types of information. The four scales of measurement are nominal, ordinal, interval, and ratio. The scales form a hierarchy, and as we progress from nominal to ratio scales we are able to perform increasingly sophisticated measurements that capture more detailed information.

> *Measurement* is a set of rules for assigning numbers to represent objects, traits, attributes, or behaviors.

Nominal Scales

Nominal scales are the simplest of the four scales. **Nominal scales** provide a qualitative system for categorizing people or objects into categories, classes, or sets. In most situations, these categories are mutually exclusive. For example, gender is an example of a nominal scale that assigns individuals to mutually exclusive categories. Another example is assigning people to categories based on their college academic majors (e.g., education, psychology, chemistry). You may have noticed that in these examples we did not assign numbers to the categories. In some situations we do assign numbers in nominal scales simply to identify or label the categories; however, the categories are not ordered in a meaningful manner. For example, we might use the number one to represent a category of students who list their academic major as education, the number two for the academic major of psychology, the number three for the academic major of chemistry, and so forth. Notice that no attempt is made to order the categories. Three is not greater than two, and two is not greater than one. The assignment of numbers is completely arbitrary. We could just as easily call them red, blue, green, and so on. Another individual might assign a new set of numbers, which would be just as useful as ours. Because of the arbitrary use of numbers in nominal scales, nominal scales do not actually quantify the variables under examination. Numbers assigned to nominal scales should not be added, subtracted, ranked, or otherwise manipulated. As a result, many common statistical procedures cannot be used with these scales so their usefulness is limited.

Nominal scales **classify people or objects into categories, classes, or sets.**

Ordinal Scales

Ordinal scale measurement allows you to rank people or objects according to the amount or quantity of a characteristic they display or possess. As a result, **ordinal scales** enable us to quantify the variables under examination and provide substantially more information than nominal scales. For example, ranking the children in a classroom according to height from the tallest to the shortest is an example of ordinal measurement. Traditionally the ranking is ordered from the "most" to the "least." In our example the tallest person in the class would receive the rank of 1, the next tallest a rank of 2, and the like. Although ordinal scale measurement provides quantitative information, it does not ensure that the intervals between the ranks are consistent. That is, the difference in height between the children ranked 1 and 2 might be three inches while the difference between those ranked 3 and 4 might be one inch. Ordinal scales indicate the rank-order position among individuals or objects, but they do not indicate the extent by which they differ. All the ordinal scale tells us then is who is taller, number 5 or number 7; it tells us nothing about how much taller. As a result, these scales are somewhat limited in both the measurement information they provide and the statistical procedures that can be applied. Nevertheless, the use of these scales is fairly common in educational settings. Percentile rank, age equivalents, and grade equivalents are all examples of ordinal scales.

Ordinal scales **rank people or objects according to the amount of a characteristic they display or possess.**

Interval Scales

Interval scales rank people or objects like an ordinal scale, but on a scale with equal units.

Interval scales provide more information than either nominal or ordinal scales. Interval scale measurement allows you to rank people or objects like an ordinal scale, but on a scale with equal units. By equal scale units, we mean the difference between adjacent units on the scale is equivalent. The difference between scores of 70 and 71 is the same as the difference between scores of 50 and 51 (or 92 and 93; 37 and 38; etc.). Many educational and psychological tests are designed to produce interval level scores. Let's look at an example of scores for three people on an aptitude test. Assume individual A receives a score of 100, individual B a score of 110, and individual C a score of 120. First, we know that person C scored the highest followed by B then A. Second, given that the scores are on an interval scale, we also know that the difference between individuals A and B (i.e., 10 points) is equivalent to the difference between B and C (i.e., 10 points). Finally, we know the difference between individuals A and C (i.e., 20 points) is twice as large as the difference between individuals A and B (i.e., 10 points). Interval level data can be manipulated using common mathematical operations (e.g., addition, subtraction, multiplication, and division) whereas lesser scales (i.e., nominal and ordinal) cannot. A final advantage is that most statistical procedures can be used with interval scale data.

As you can see, interval scales represent a substantial improvement over ordinal scales and provide considerable information. Their one limitation is that interval scales do not have a true zero point. That is, on interval scales a score of zero does not reflect the total absence of the attribute. For example, if an individual were unable to answer any questions correctly on an intelligence test and scored a zero, it would not indicate the complete lack of intelligence, but only that he or she were unable to respond correctly to any questions on this test. (Actually intelligence tests are designed so no one actually receives a score of zero. We just use this example to illustrate the concept of an arbitrary zero point.) Likewise, even though an IQ of 100 is twice as large as an IQ of 50, it does not mean that the person with an IQ of 100 is twice as intelligent as the person with an IQ of 50. In educational settings, interval scale scores are most commonly seen in the form of standard scores (there are a number of standard scores used in education, which will be discussed in the next chapter).

Ratio Scales

Ratio scales have the properties of interval scales plus a true zero point.

Ratio scales have the properties of interval scales plus a true zero point that reflects the complete absence of the characteristic being measured. Miles per hour, length, and weight are all examples of ratio scales. As the name suggests, with these scales we can interpret ratios between scores. For example, 60 miles per hour is twice as fast as 30 miles per hour, 20 feet is twice as long as 10 feet, and 60 pounds is three times as much as 20 pounds. Ratios are not meaningful or interpretable with interval scales. As we noted, a child with an intelligence quotient (IQ) of 100 is not twice as intelligent as one with an IQ of 50; a child with a standardized math achievement test score of 100 does not know twice as much as one with a score of 50. With the exception of percent correct on classroom achievement tests and the measurement of behavioral responses (e.g., reaction time), there are relatively few ratio scales in educational and psychological measurement. Fortunately, we are able to address most of the measurement issues in education adequately using interval scales.

Table 2.1 gives examples of common nominal, ordinal, interval, and ratio scales found in educational and psychological measurement. As we noted, there is a hierarchy among the scales with nominal scales being the least sophisticated and providing the least information

TABLE 2.1   Common Nominal, Ordinal, Interval, and Ratio Scales

Scale	Example	Sample Scores
Nominal	Gender of participant	Female = 1 Male = 2
	Ethnicity	African American = 1 Caucasian = 2 Hispanic American = 3 Native American = 4 Oriental American = 5
	Place of birth	Northeast = 1 Southeast = 2 Midwest = 3 Southwest = 4 Northwest = 5 Pacific = 6
Ordinal	Preference for activity	1 = Most preferred 2 = Intermediate preferred 3 = Least preferred
	Graduation class rank	1 = Valedictorian 2 = Salutatorian 3 = Third Rank Etc.
	Percentile rank	99th Percentile 98th Percentile 97th Percentile Etc.
Interval	Intelligence scores	Intelligence quotient of 100
	Personality test scores	Depression score of 75
	Graduate Record Exam	Verbal score of 550
Ratio	Height in inches	60 inches tall
	Weight in pounds	100 pounds
	Percent correct on classroom test	100%

and ratio scales being the most sophisticated and providing the most information. Nominal scales allow you to assign a number to a person that associates that person with a set or category, but other useful quantitative properties are missing. Ordinal scales have all the positive properties of nominal scales with the addition of the ability to rank people according to the amount of a characteristic they possess. Interval scales have all the positive properties of ordinal scales and also incorporate equal scale units. The inclusion of equal scale units allows one to make relative statements regarding scores (e.g., the difference between a score of 82 and a score of 84 is the same as the difference between a score of 92 and 94). Finally, ratio scales have all of the positive properties of an interval scale with the addition of an absolute zero point. The inclusion of an absolute zero point allows us to form meaningful ratios between scores (e.g., a score of 50 reflects twice the amount of the characteristic as a score of 25). Although these scales do form a hierarchy, this does not mean the lower scales are of little or no use. If you want to categorize students according to their academic major, a nominal scale is clearly appropriate. Accordingly, if you simply want to rank people according to height, an ordinal scale would be adequate and appropriate. However, in most measurement situations you want to use the scale that provides the most information.

The Description of Test Scores

An individual's test score in isolation provides very little information, even if we know its scale of measurement. For example, if you know that an individual's score on a test of reading achievement is 79, you know very little about that student's reading ability. Even if you know the scale of measurement represented by the test (e.g., an interval scale), you still know very little about the individual's reading ability. To meaningfully interpret or describe test scores you need to have a frame of reference. Often the frame of reference is how other people performed on the test. For example, if you knew that in a class of 25 children, a score of 79 were the highest score achieved, you would describe it as reflecting above average (or possibly superior) performance. In contrast, if 79 were the lowest score, you would know that the score reflects below average performance. The following sections provide information about score distributions and the statistics used to describe them. In the next chapter we will use many of these concepts and procedures to help you learn how to describe and interpret test scores.

Distributions

A **distribution** is simply a set of scores. These can be scores earned on a reading test, scores on an intelligence test, or scores on a measure of depression. We can also have distributions reflecting physical characteristics such as weight, height, or strength. Distributions can be represented in a number of ways, including tables and graphs. Table 2.2 presents scores for 20 students on a homework assignment similar to what might be recorded in a teacher's grade book. Table 2.3 presents an ungrouped frequency distribution of the same 20 scores. Notice that in this example there are only 7 possible measurement categories or scores (i.e., 4, 5, 6, 7, 8, 9, and 10). In some situations there are so many possible scores that it is not practical to list each potential score individually. In these situations it is common to use a grouped frequency distribution. In

A *distribution* is a set of scores.

TABLE 2.2   Distribution of Scores for 20 Students

Student	Homework Scores
Cindy	7
Tommy	8
Paula	9
Steven	6
Angela	7
Robert	6
Kim	10
Kevin	8
Randy	5
Charles	9
Julie	9
Shawn	9
Karen	8
Paul	4
Teresa	5
Freddie	6
Tammy	7
Shelly	8
Carol	8
Johnny	7

Mean = 7.3
Median = 7.5
Mode = 8

TABLE 2.3   Ungrouped Frequency Distribution

Score	Frequency
10	1
9	4
8	5
7	4
6	3
5	2
4	1

Note: This reflects the same distribution of scores depicted in Table 2.2.

grouped frequency distributions the possible scores are "combined" or "grouped" into class intervals that encompass a range of possible scores. Table 2.4 presents a grouped frequency distribution of 250 hypothetical scores that are grouped into class intervals that incorporate 5 score values.

Frequency graphs are also popular and provide a visual representation of a distribution. When reading a frequency graph, scores are traditionally listed on the horizontal axis and the frequency of scores is listed on the vertical axis. Figure 2.1 presents a graph of the set of homework scores listed in Tables 2.2 and 2.3. In examining this figure you see that there was only one score of 10 (reflecting perfect performance) and there was only one score of 4 (reflecting correctly responding to only 4 questions). Most of the students received scores between 7 and 9. Figure 2.2 presents a graph of a distribution that might reflect a large standardization sample. Examining this figure reveals that the scores tend to accumulate around the middle with their frequency, diminishing as we move further away from the middle.

Another characteristic of the distribution depicted in Figure 2.2 is that it is symmetrical, which means that if you divide the distribution into two halves, they will mirror each other. Not all distributions are **symmetrical.** When a distribution is not symmetrical it is referred to as skewed. Skewed distributions can be either negatively or positively skewed. A **negatively skewed distribution** is one with few scores at the low end, as illustrated in Figure 2.3. When a test produces scores that are negatively skewed, it is probable that the test is too easy because there are many high scores and relatively few low scores. A **positively skewed distribution** is one with few scores at the high end, as illustrated in Figure 2.4. If a

TABLE 2.4   Grouped Frequency Distribution

Class Interval	Frequency
125–129	6
120–124	14
115–119	17
110–114	23
105–109	27
100–104	42
95–99	39
90–94	25
85–89	22
80–84	17
75–79	13
70–74	5

Note: This presents a grouped frequency distribution of 250 hypothetical scores that are grouped into class intervals that incorporate 5 score values.

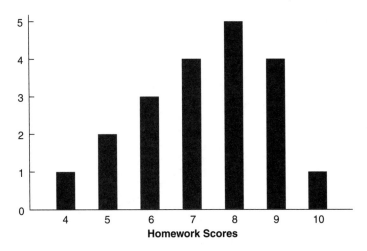

FIGURE 2.1   Graph of the Homework Scores

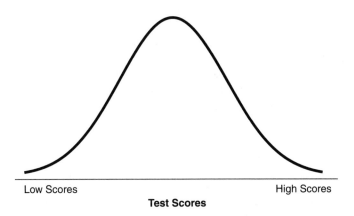

FIGURE 2.2   Hypothetical Distribution
of Large Standardization Sample

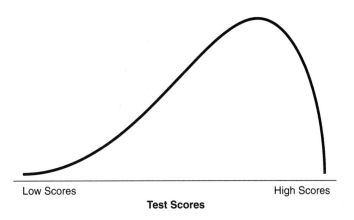

FIGURE 2.3   Negatively Skewed Distribution

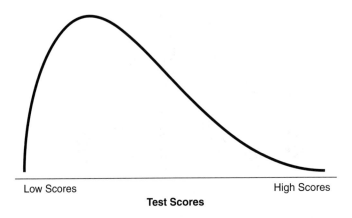

Low Scores   High Scores

Test Scores

FIGURE 2.4   Positively Skewed Distribution

test produces scores that are positively skewed, it is likely that the test is too difficult because there are many low scores and few high scores. In the next chapter we will introduce a special type of distribution referred to as the normal distribution and describe how it is used to help interpret test scores. First, however, we will describe two important characteristics of distributions and the methods we have for describing them. The first characteristic is central tendency and the second is variability.

Measures of Central Tendency

The scores in many distributions tend to concentrate around a center (hence the term *central tendency*) and there are three common descriptive statistics used to summarize this tendency. The three **measures of central tendency** are the mean, median, and mode. These statistics are frequently referenced in mental and in physical measurement and all teachers should be familiar with them. It is likely that you have heard of all of these statistics, but we will briefly discuss them to ensure that you are familiar with the special characteristics of each.

The *mean* is the arithmetic average of a distribution.

Mean.   Most people are familiar with the **mean** as the simple arithmetic average. Practically every day you will hear multiple discussions involving the concept of the average amount of some entity. Meteorologists give you information about the average temperature and amount of rain, politicians and economists discuss the average hourly wage, educators talk about the grade point average, health professionals talk about the average weight and average life expectancy, and the list goes on. Formally, the mean of a set of scores is defined by the equation:

Mean = Sum of Scores / Number of Scores

The mean of the homework scores listed in Table 2.2 is calculated by summing the 20 scores in the distribution and dividing by 20. This results in a mean of 7.3. Note that the mean is near the middle of the distribution (see Figure 2.1). Although no student obtained a score of 7.3, the mean is useful in providing a sense of the central tendency of the group of scores. Several important mathematical characteristics of the mean make it useful as a measure of central tendency. First, the mean is meaningful for distributions containing ordinal, interval, and ratio level scores (though it is not applicable for nominal scores). Second, the mean of a sample is a good estimate of the mean for the population from which the sample was drawn. This is useful when developing standardized tests in which standardization samples are tested and the resulting distribution is believed to reflect characteristics of the entire population of people with whom the test is expected to be used (see Special Interest Topic 2.1 for more information on this topic). Another positive characteristic of the mean is

SPECIAL INTEREST TOPIC   **2.1**

Population Parameters and Sample Statistics

Although we try to minimize the use of statistical jargon whenever possible, at this point it is useful to highlight the distinction between population parameters and sample statistics. Statisticians differentiate between populations and samples. A population is the complete group of people, objects, or other things of interest. An example of a population is all of the secondary students in the United States. Because this is a very large number of students, it would be extremely difficult to study such a group. Due to these types of constraints, researchers often are unable to study entire populations. Instead they study samples. A sample is just a subset of the larger population that is thought to be representative of the population. By studying samples researchers are able to make generalizations about populations. For example, although it might not be practical to administer a questionnaire to all secondary students in the United States, it would be possible to select a random sample of secondary students and administer the questionnaire to them. If we are careful in selecting this sample and it is of sufficient size, the information garnered from the sample may allow us to draw some conclusions about the population.

Now we will address the distinction between parameters and statistics. Population values are referred to as parameters and are typically represented with Greek symbols. For example, statisticians use *mu* (μ) to indicate a population mean and *sigma* (σ) to indicate a population standard deviation. Because it is often not possible to study entire populations, we do not know population parameters and have to estimate them using statistics. A statistic is a value that is calculated based on a sample. Statistics are typically represented with Roman letters. For example, statisticians use X to indicate the sample mean (some statisticians use M to indicate the mean) and SD (or S) to indicate the sample standard deviation. Sample statistics can provide information about the corresponding population parameters. For example, the sample mean (X) may serve as an estimate of the population mean (μ). Of course the information provided by a sample statistic is only as good as the sample the statistic is based on. Large representative samples can provide good information whereas small or biased samples will provide poor information. Without going into detail about sampling and inferential statistics at this point, we do want to make you aware of the distinction between parameters and statistics. In this and other texts you will see references to both parameters and statistics and understanding this distinction will help you avoid a misunderstanding. Remember, as a general rule if the value is designated with a Greek symbol it refers to a population parameter, but if it is designated with a Roman letter it is a sample statistic.

that it is essential to the definition and calculation of other descriptive statistics that are useful in the context of measurement.

An undesirable characteristic of the mean is that it is sensitive to unbalanced extreme scores. By this we mean a score that is either extremely high or extremely low relative to the rest of the scores in the distribution. An extreme score, either very large or very small, tends to "pull" the mean in its direction. This might not be readily apparent so let's look at an example. In the set of scores 1, 2, 3, 4, 5, and 38, the mean is 8.8. Notice that 8.8 is not near any score that actually occurs in the distribution. The extreme score of 38 pulls the mean in its direction. The tendency for the mean to be affected by extreme scores is particularly problematic when there is a small number of scores. The influence of an extreme score decreases as the total number of scores in the distribution increases. For example, the mean of 1, 1, 1, 1, 2, 2, 2, 2, 3, 3, 3, 3, 4, 4, 4, 4, 5, 5, 5, 5, and 38 is 4.6. In this example the influence of the extreme score is reduced by the presence of a larger number of scores.

The *median* is the score or potential score that divides a distribution in half.

Median. The **median** is the score or potential score that divides a distribution in half. In the distribution of scores depicted in Table 2.3, half the scores are 8 or above and half the scores are 7 or below. Therefore, the point that divides the distribution in half is between 8 and 7, or 7.5. When the number of scores in a distribution is an odd number, the median is simply the score that is in the middle of the distribution. Consider the following set of scores: 9, 8, 7, 6, 5. In this example the median is 7 because two scores fall above it and two fall below it. In actual practice a process referred to as interpolation is often used to compute the median (because interpolation is illustrated in practically every basic statistics textbook, we will not go into detail about the process). Like the mean, the median can be calculated for distributions containing ratio, interval, or ordinal level scores, but it is not appropriate for nominal level scores. The median is a useful and versatile measure of central tendency.

The *mode* is the most frequently occurring score in a distribution.

Mode. The **mode** of a distribution is the most frequently occurring score. Refer back to Table 2.3, which presents the ungrouped frequency distribution of 20 students on a homework assignment. By examining these scores you will see that the most frequently occurring score is 8. These scores are graphed in Figure 2.1, and by locating the highest point in the graph you are also able to identify the mode (i.e., 8). An advantage of the mode is that it can be used with nominal data (e.g., the most frequent college major selected by students) as well as ordinal, interval, and ratio data (Hays, 1994). However, the mode does have significant limitations as a measure of central tendency. First, some distributions have two scores that are equal in frequency and higher than other scores (see Figure 2.5). This is referred to as a "bimodal" distribution and the mode is ineffective as a measure of central tendency. Second, the mode is not a very stable measure of central tendency, particularly with small samples. For example, in the distribution depicted in Table 2.3, if one student who earned a score 8 had earned a score of either 7 or 9, the mode would have shifted from 8 to 7 or 9. As a result of these limitations, the mode is often of little utility as a measure of central tendency.

Choosing between the Mean, Median, and Mode. A natural question is, Which measure of central tendency is most useful or appropriate? As you might expect, the answer de-

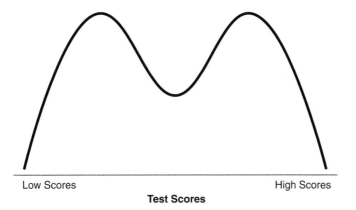

Low Scores   High Scores

Test Scores

FIGURE 2.5   Bimodal Distribution

pends on a number of factors. First, as we noted when discussing the mean, it is essential when calculating other useful statistics. For this and other rather technical reasons (see Hays, 1994), the mean has considerable utility as a measure of central tendency. However, for purely descriptive purposes the median is often the most versatile and useful measure of central tendency. When a distribution is skewed, the influence of unbalanced extreme scores on the mean tends to undermine its usefulness. Figure 2.6 illustrates the expected relationship between the mean and the median in skewed distributions. Note that the mean is "pulled" in the direction of the skew: that is, lower than the median in negatively skewed distributions; higher than the median in positively skewed distributions. To illustrate how the mean can be misleading in skewed distributions, Hopkins (1998) notes that due to the influence of extremely wealthy individuals, about 60% of the families in the United States have incomes below the national mean. In this situation, the mean is pulled in the direction of the extreme high scores and is somewhat misleading as a measure of central tendency. Finally, if you are dealing with nominal level data, the mode is the only measure of central tendency that provides useful information.

At this point you should have a good understanding of the various measures of central tendency and be able to interpret them in many common applications. You might be surprised how often individuals in the popular media demonstrate a fundamental misunderstanding of these measures. See Special Interest Topic 2.2 for a rather humorous example of how a journalist misinterpreted information based on measures of central tendency.

Measures of Variability

Two distributions can have the same mean, median, and mode yet differ considerably in the way the scores are distributed around the measures of central tendency. Therefore, it is not sufficient to characterize a set of scores solely by measures of central tendency. Figure 2.7 presents graphs of three distributions with identical means but different degrees

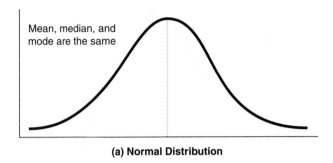

(a) Normal Distribution

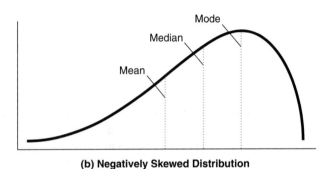

(b) Negatively Skewed Distribution

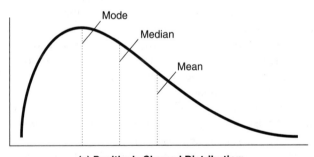

(c) Positively Skewed Distribution

FIGURE 2.6   Relationship between Mean, Median, and Mode in Normal and Skewed Distributions

Source: From *Psychological Testing: Theory and Applications* (Fig. 2.1, p. 28), by L. H. Janda, 1998, Boston: Allyn & Bacon. Copyright 1998 by Pearson Education. Reprinted with permission.

of variability. A measure of the dispersion, spread, or variability of a set of scores will help us describe the distribution more fully. We will examine three **measures of variability** commonly used to describe distributions: range, standard deviation, and variance.

A Public Outrage: Physicians Overcharge Their Patients

Half of all professionals charge above the median fee for their services. Now that you understand the mean, median, and mode, you will recognize how obvious this statement is. However, a few years back a local newspaper columnist in Texas, apparently unhappy with his physician's bill for some services, conducted an investigation of charges for various medical procedures in the county in which he resided. In a somewhat angry column he revealed to the community that "fully half of all physicians surveyed charge above the median fee for their services."

We would like him to know that "fully half" of all professionals, plumbers, electricians, painters, lawn services, hospitals, and everyone else we can think of also charge above the median for their services. We wouldn't have it any other way!

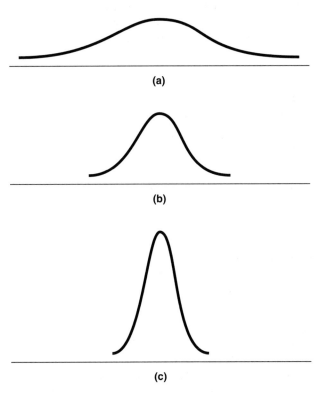

(a)

(b)

(c)

FIGURE 2.7   Three Distributions with Different Degrees of Variability

Source: From *Psychological Testing: History, Principles, and Applications,* 3rd ed. (Fig 3.2, p. 60), by Robert J. Gregory, 2000, Boston: Allyn & Bacon. Copyright 2000 by Pearson Education. Reprinted with permission.

The *range* is the distance between the smallest and largest score in a distribution.

Range.   The **range** is the distance between the smallest and largest score in a distribution. The range is calculated:

Range = Highest Score − Lowest Score

For example, in referring back to the distribution of scores listed in Table 2.3, you see that the largest score is 10 and the smallest score is 4. By simply subtracting 4 from 10 you determine the range is 6. The range considers only the two most extreme scores in a distribution and tells us about the limits or extremes of a distribution. However, it does not provide information about how the remaining scores are spread out or dispersed within these limits. We need other descriptive statistics, namely the standard deviation and variance, to provide information about the spread or dispersion of scores within the limits described by the range.

The *standard deviation* is a measure of the average distance that scores vary from the mean of the distribution.

Standard Deviation.   The mean and standard deviation are the most widely used statistics in educational and psychological testing as well as research in the social and behavioral sciences. The **standard deviation** is computed with the following steps:

Step 1: Compute the mean of the distribution.

Step 2: Subtract each score in the distribution from the mean. This will yield some negative numbers, and if you add all of these differences, the sum will be zero. To overcome this difficulty, we simply square each difference score because the square of any number is always positive.

Step 3: Sum all the squared difference scores.

Step 4: Divide this sum by the number of scores to derive the average of the squared deviations from the mean. This value is the variance and is designated by σ^2 (we will return to this value briefly).

Step 5: The standard deviation (σ) is the positive square root of the variance (σ^2). It is the square root because we first squared all the scores before adding them. To now get a true look at the standard distance between key points in the distribution, we have to undo our little trick that eliminated all those negative signs.

These steps are illustrated in Table 2.5 using the scores listed in Table 2.2. This example illustrates the calculation of the population standard deviation, designated with the Greek symbol *sigma* (σ). You will also see the standard deviation designated with SD or S. This is appropriate when you are describing the standard deviation of a sample rather than a population (refer back to Special Interest Topic 2.1 for information on the distinction between population parameters and sample statistics).[1]

---

[1] The discussion and formulas provided in this chapter are those used in descriptive statistics. In inferential statistics when the population variance is estimated from a sample, the N in the denominator is replaced with $N-1$.

TABLE 2.5 Calculating the Standard Deviation and Variance

Student Scores	Difference (Score – Mean)	Difference Squared
7	(7 – 7.3) = –0.3	0.09
8	(8 – 7.3) = 0.7	0.49
9	(9 – 7.3) = 1.7	2.89
6	(6 – 7.3) = –1.3	1.69
7	(7 – 7.3) = –0.3	0.09
6	(6 – 7.3) = –1.3	1.69
10	(10 – 7.3) = 2.7	7.29
8	(8 – 7.3) = 0.7	0.49
5	(5 – 7.3) = –2.3	5.29
9	(9 – 7.3) = 1.7	2.89
9	(9 – 7.3) = 1.7	2.89
9	(9 – 7.3) = 1.7	2.89
8	(8 – 7.3) = 0.7	0.49
4	(4 – 7.3) = –3.3	10.89
5	(5 – 7.3) = –2.3	5.29
6	(6 – 7.3) = –1.3	1.69
7	(7 – 7.3) = –0.3	0.09
8	(8 – 7.3) = 0.7	0.49
8	(8 – 7.3) = 0.7	0.49
7	(7 – 7.3) = –0.3	0.09

Sum = 146

Mean = 7.3

Sum = 48.2

Variance = $48.2/(n)$
= 48.2/20
= 2.41

Standard Deviation = $\sqrt{\text{Variance}}$
= $\sqrt{2.41}$
= 1.55

The standard deviation is a measure of the average distance that scores vary from the mean of the distribution. The larger the standard deviation, the more scores differ from the mean and the more variability there is in the distribution. If scores are widely dispersed or spread around the mean, the standard deviation will be large. If there is relatively little dispersion or spread of scores around the mean, the standard deviation will be small.

SPECIAL INTEREST TOPIC   **2.3**

Is the Variance Always Larger than the Standard Deviation?

In this chapter we show that the standard deviation is the positive square root of the variance. For example, if a distribution has a variance of 100, the standard deviation is 10. If the variance is 25, the standard deviation is 5. Can you think of any situations in which the variance is not larger than the standard deviation?

It might surprise you, but in certain situations the variance is not larger than the standard deviation. If the variance is 1.0, the standard deviation is also 1.0. In the next chapter you will learn about z-scores that have a mean of 0 and a standard deviation of 1.0. It is also possible for the standard deviation actually to be larger than the variance. For example, if the variance is 0.25, the standard deviation is 0.50. Although it is not common to find situations in which the variance and standard deviation are decimals in educational assessment, you should be aware of the possibility.

The *variance* is a measure of variability that has special meaning as a theoretical concept in measurement theory and statistics.

Variance.   In calculating the standard deviation we actually first calculate the variance (σ^2). As illustrated in Table 2.5, the standard deviation is actually the positive square root of the variance. Therefore, the **variance** is also a measure of the variability of scores. The reason the standard deviation is more frequently used when interpreting individual scores is that the variance is in squared units of measurement, which complicates interpretation. For example, we can easily interpret weight in pounds, but it is more difficult to interpret and use weight reported in squared pounds. While the variance is in squared units, the standard deviation (i.e., the square root of the variance) is in the same units as the scores and so is more easily understood. Although the variance is difficult to apply when describing individual scores, it does have special meaning as a theoretical concept in measurement theory and statistics. For now, simply remember that the variance is a measure of the degree of variability in scores.

Choosing between the Range, Standard Deviation, and Variance.   As we noted, the range conveys information about the limits of a distribution, but does not tell us how the scores are dispersed within these limits. The standard deviation indicates the average distance that scores vary from the mean of the distribution. The larger the standard deviation, the more variability there is in the distribution. The standard deviation is very useful in describing distributions and will be of particular importance when we turn our attention to the interpretation of scores in the next chapter. The variance is another important and useful measure of variability. Because the variance is expressed in terms of squared measurement units, it is not as useful in interpreting individual scores as is the standard deviation. However, the variance is important as a theoretical concept, and we will return to it when discussing reliability and validity in later chapters.

Correlation Coefficients

Most students are somewhat familiar with the concept of correlation. When people speak of a correlation, they are referring to the relationship between two variables. The variables can be physical such as weight and height or psychological such as intelligence and academic achievement. For example, it is reasonable to expect height to demonstrate a relationship with weight. Taller individuals tend to weigh more than shorter individuals. This relationship is not perfect because there are some short individuals who weigh more than taller individuals, but the tendency is for taller people to outweigh shorter people. You might also expect more intelligent people to score higher on tests of academic achievement than less intelligent people, and this is what research indicates. Again, the relationship is not perfect, but as a general rule more intelligent individuals perform better on tests of academic achievement than their less intelligent peers.

A *correlation coefficient* is a quantitative measure of the relationship between two variables.

A **correlation coefficient** is a quantitative measure of the relationship between two variables. The correlation coefficient was developed by Karl Pearson (1857–1936) and is designated by the letter r. Correlation coefficients can range from –1.0 to +1.0. When interpreting correlation coefficients, there are two parameters to consider. The first parameter is the sign of the coefficient. A positive correlation coefficient indicates that an increase on one variable is associated with an increase on the other variable. For example, height and weight demonstrate a positive correlation with each other. As noted earlier, taller individuals tend to weigh more than shorter individuals. A negative correlation coefficient indicates that an increase on one variable is associated with a decrease on the other variable. For example, because lower scores denote superior performance in the game of golf, there is a negative correlation between the amount of tournament prize money won and a professional's average golf score. Professional golfers with the lowest average scores tend to win the most tournaments.

The second parameter to consider when interpreting correlation coefficients is the magnitude or absolute size of the coefficient. The magnitude of a coefficient indicates the strength of the relationship between two variables. A value of 0 indicates the absence of a relationship between the variables. As coefficients approach a value of 1.0, the strength of the relationship increases. A coefficient of 1.0 (either positive or negative) indicates a perfect correlation, one in which change in one variable is accompanied by a corresponding and proportionate change in the other variable, without exception. Perfect correlation coefficients are rare in psychological and educational measurement, but they might occur in very small samples simply by chance.

There are numerous qualitative and quantitative ways of describing correlation coefficients. A qualitative approach to describe correlation coefficients is as weak, moderate, or strong. Although there are no universally accepted standards for describing the strength of correlations, we offer the following guidelines: <0.30 weak; 0.30–0.70 moderate; and >0.70 strong (these are just guidelines and should not be applied in a rigid manner). This approach is satisfactory in many situations, but in other contexts it may be more important to determine whether a correlation is "statistically significant." Statistical significance is determined by both the size of the correlation coefficient and the size of the sample. A discussion of statistical significance would lead us into the realm of inferential statistics and is beyond the scope of this text. However, most introductory statistics texts address this concept in considerable detail and contain tables that allow you to determine whether a correlation coefficient is significant given the size of the sample.

Another way of describing correlation coefficients is by squaring it to derive the coefficient of determination (i.e., r^2). The **coefficient of determination** is interpreted as the amount of variance shared by the two variables. In other words, the

The *coefficient of determination* is interpreted as the amount of variance shared by two variables.

coefficient of determination reflects the amount of variance in one variable that is predictable from the other variable, and vice versa. This might not be clear so let's look at an example. Assume a correlation between an intelligence test and an achievement test of 0.60 (i.e., $r = 0.60$). By squaring this value we derive the coefficient of determination is 0.36 (i.e., $r^2 = 0.36$). This indicates that 36% of the variance in one variable is predictable from the other variable.

Scatterplots

As noted, a correlation coefficient is a quantitative measure of the relationship between two variables. Examining scatterplots may enhance our understanding of the relationship between variables. A **scatterplot** is simply a graph that visually dis-

A *scatterplot* is a graph that visually displays the relationship between two variables.

plays the relationship between two variables. To create a scatterplot you need to have two scores for each individual. For example, you could graph each individual's weight and height. In the context of educational testing, you could have scores for the students in a class on two different homework assignments. In a scatterplot the X-axis represents one variable and the Y-axis the other variable. Each mark in the scatterplot actually represents two scores, an individual's scores on the X variable and the Y variable.

Figure 2.8 shows scatterplots for various correlation values. First, look at Figure 2.8a, which shows a hypothetical perfect positive correlation (+1.0). Notice that with a perfect correlation all of the marks will fall on a straight line. Because this is a **positive correlation** an increase on one variable is associated with a corresponding increase on the other variable. Because it is a perfect correlation, if you know an individual's score on one variable you can predict the score on the other variable with perfect precision. Next examine Figure 2.8b, which illustrates a perfect **negative correlation** (−1.0). Being a perfect correlation all the marks fall on a straight line, but because it is a negative correlation an increase on one variable is associated with a corresponding decrease on the other variable. Given a score on one variable, you can still predict the individual's performance on the other variable with perfect precision. Now examine Figure 2.8c, which illustrates a correlation of 0.0. Here there is not a relationship between the variables. In this situation, knowledge about performance on one variable does not provide any information about the individual's performance on the other variable or enhance prediction.

So far we have examined only the scatterplots of perfect and zero correlation coefficients. Examine Figure 2.8d which depicts a correlation of +0.90. Notice that the marks clearly cluster along a straight line. However, they no longer all fall on the line, but rather around the line. As you might expect, in this situation knowledge of performance on one variable helps us predict performance on the other variable, but our ability to predict performance is not perfect as it was with a perfect correlation. Finally, examine Figures 2.8e and 2.8f which illustrate coefficients of 0.60 and 0.30, respectively. As you can see a correlation of 0.60 is

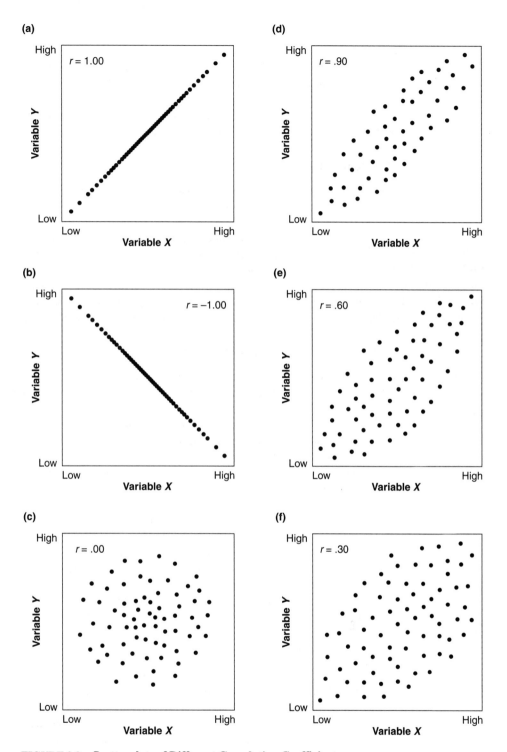

FIGURE 2.8   Scatterplots of Different Correlation Coefficients

Source: From *Educational and Psychological Measurement and Evaluation,* 8th ed. (Fig. 4.3, p. 85), by D. Hopkins, 1998, Boston: Allyn & Bacon. Copyright 1998 by Pearson Education. Reprinted with permission.

characterized by marks that still cluster along a straight line, but there is more variability around this line than there was with a correlation of 0.90. Accordingly, with a correlation of .30 there is still more variability of marks around a straight line. In these situations knowledge of performance on one variable will help us predict performance on the other variable, but as the correlation coefficients decrease so does our ability to predict performance.

Correlation and Prediction

Linear regression **is a mathematical procedure that allows you to predict values on one variable given information on another variable.**

In the previous section we mentioned that when variables are correlated, particularly when there is a strong correlation, knowledge about performance on one variable provides information that can help predict performance on the other variable. A special mathematical procedure referred to as linear regression is designed precisely for this purpose. **Linear regression** allows you to predict values on one variable given information on another variable. We will not be going into detail about its computation, but linear regression has numerous applications in developing and evaluating tests, and so we will come back to linear regression in later chapters.

Types of Correlation Coefficients

Specific correlation coefficients are appropriate for specific situations.

Specific correlation coefficients are appropriate for specific situations. The most common coefficient is the Pearson product-moment correlation. The Pearson coefficient is appropriate when the variables being correlated are measured on an interval or ratio scale. Table 2.6 illustrates the calculation of the Pearson correlation coefficient. Although the formula for calculating a Pearson correlation may appear rather intimidating, it is not actually difficult, and we encourage you to review this section if you are interested in how these coefficients are calculated (or if your professor wants you to be familiar with the process). Spearman's rank correlation coefficient, another popular coefficient, is used when the variables are measured on an ordinal scale. The point-biserial correlation coefficient is also widely used in test development when one variable is dichotomous (meaning only two scores are possible, e.g., pass or fail, 0 or 1, etc.) and the other variable is measured on an interval or ratio scale. A common application of the point-biserial correlation is in calculating an item-total test score correlation. Here the dichotomous variable is the score on a single item (e.g., right or wrong) and the variable measured on an interval scale is the total test score. A large item-total correlation is taken as evidence that an item is measuring the same construct as the overall test measures.

Correlation versus Causality

Correlation analysis does allow one to establish causality.

Our discussion of correlation has indicated that when variables are correlated, information about an individual's performance on one variable enhances our ability to predict performance on the other variable. We have also seen that by squaring a correlation coefficient to get the coefficient of determination, we can make statements about the amount of variance shared by two variables. In later chapters we will show how correlation coefficients are used in developing and evaluating tests. *It is, however, a common misconception to believe that if two variables are*

TABLE 2.6 Calculating a Pearson Correlation Coefficient

There are different formulas for calculating a Pearson correlation coefficient and we will illustrate one of the simpler ones. For this illustration we will use the homework assignment scores we have used before as the X variable, and another set of 20 hypothetical scores as the Y variable. The formula is:

$$r_{xy} = \frac{N\sum XY - (\sum X)(\sum Y)}{\sqrt{N\sum X^2 - (\sum X)^2}\sqrt{N\sum Y^2 - (\sum Y)^2}}$$

XY = sum of the XY products
X = sum of X scores
Y = sum of Y scores
X^2 = sum of squared X scores
Y^2 = sum of squared Y scores

Homework 1 (X)	X^2	Homework 2 (Y)	Y^2	$(X)(Y)$
7	49	8	64	56
8	64	7	49	56
9	81	10	100	90
6	36	5	25	30
7	49	7	49	49
6	36	6	36	36
10	199	9	81	90
8	64	8	64	64
5	25	5	25	25
9	81	9	81	81
9	81	8	64	72
9	81	7	49	63
8	64	7	49	56
4	16	4	16	16
5	25	6	36	30
6	36	7	49	42
7	49	7	49	49
8	64	9	81	72
8	64	8	64	64
7	49	6	36	42
X = 146	X^2 = 1,114	Y = 143	Y^2 = 1,067	XY = 1,083

$$r_{xy} = \frac{20(1,083) - (146)(143)}{\sqrt{20(1,114) - (146)^2}\sqrt{20(1,067) - (143)^2}}$$

$$\frac{21,660 - 20,878}{\sqrt{22,280 - 21,316}\sqrt{21,340 - 20,449}} = \frac{782}{\sqrt{964}\sqrt{891}}$$

$$\frac{782}{(31.048)(29.849)} = 0.843$$

correlated one is causing the other. It is possible that the variables are causally related, but it is also possible that a third variable explains the relationship. Let's look at an example. Assume we found a correlation between the amount of ice cream consumed in New York and the number of deaths by drowning in Texas. If you were to interpret this correlation as inferring causation, you would either believe that people eating ice cream in New York caused people to drown in Texas or that people drowning in Texas caused people to eat ice cream in New York. Obviously neither would be correct! How would you explain this relationship? The answer is that the seasonal change in temperature accounts for the relationship. In late spring and summer people in New York consume more ice cream and people in Texas engage in more water-related activities (i.e., swimming, skiing, boating) and consequently drown more frequently. This is a fairly obvious case of a third variable explaining the relationship; however, identifying the third variable is not always so easy. It is fairly common for individuals or groups in the popular media to attribute causation on the basis of a correlation. So the next time you hear on television or read in the newspaper that researchers found a correlation between variable A and variable B, and that this correlation means that A causes B, you will not be fooled. Although correlation analysis does not allow us to establish causality, certain statistical procedures are specifically designed to allow us to infer causality. These procedures are referred to as inferential statistics and are covered in statistical courses. Special Interest Topic 2.4 presents a historical example of when interpreting a relationship between variables as indicating causality resulted in an erroneous conclusion.

SPECIAL INTEREST TOPIC   **2.4**

Caution: Drawing Conclusions of Causality

Reynolds (1999) related this historical example of how interpreting a relationship between variables as indicating causality can lead to an erroneous conclusion. He noted that in the 1800s a physician realized that a large number of women were dying of "childbed fever" (i.e., puerperal fever) in the prestigious Vienna General Hospital. Curiously more women died when they gave birth in the hospital than when the birth was at home. Childbed fever was even less common among women who gave birth in unsanitary conditions on the streets of Vienna. A commission studied this situation and after careful observation concluded that priests who came to the hospital to administer last rites were the cause of the increase in childbed fever in the hospital. The priests were present in the hospital, but were not present if the birth were outside of the hospital. According to the reasoning of the commission, when priests appeared in this ritualistic fashion the women in the hospital were frightened, and this stress made them more susceptible to childbed fever.

Eventually, experimental research debunked this explanation and identified what was actually causing the high mortality rate. At that time the doctors who delivered the babies were the same doctors who dissected corpses. The doctors would move from dissecting diseased corpses to delivering babies without washing their hands or taking other sanitary procedures. When hand washing and other antiseptic procedures were implemented, the incidence of childbed fever dropped dramatically.

In summary, it was the transmission of disease from corpses to new mothers that caused childbed fever, not the presence of priests. Although the conclusion of the commission might sound foolish to us now, if you listen carefully to the popular media you are likely to hear contemporary "experts" establishing causality based on observed relationships between variables. However, now you know to be cautious when evaluating this information.

Summary

In this chapter we surveyed the basic mathematical concepts and procedures essential to understanding measurement. We defined measurement as a set of rules for assigning numbers to represent objects, traits, or other characteristics. Measurement can involve four different scales—nominal, ordinal, interval, and ratio—that have distinct properties.

Nominal scale: a qualitative system for categorizing people or objects into categories. In nominal scales the categories are not ordered in a meaningful manner and do not convey quantitative information.

Ordinal scale: a quantitative system that allows you to rank people or objects according to the amount of a characteristic possessed. Ordinal scales provide quantitative information, but they do not ensure that the intervals between the ranks are consistent.

Interval scale: a system that allows you to rank people or objects like an ordinal scale but with the added advantage of equal scale units. Equal scale units indicate that the intervals between the units or ranks are the same size.

Ratio scale: a system with all the properties of an interval scale with the added advantage of a true zero point.

These scales form a hierarchy, and we are able to perform more sophisticated measurements as we move from nominal to the ratio scales.

We next turned our attention to distributions. A distribution is simply a set of scores, and distributions can be represented in a number of ways, including tables and graphs. Descriptive statistics have been developed that help us summarize and describe major characteristics of distributions. For example, measures of central tendency are frequently used to summarize distributions. The major measures of central tendency are:

Mean: the simple arithmetic average of a distribution. Formally, the mean is defined by this equation: Mean = Sum of Score / Number of Scores.

Median: the score or potential score that divides a distribution in half.

Mode: the most frequently occurring score in a distribution.

Measures of variability (or dispersion) comprise another set of descriptive statistics used to characterize distributions. These measures provide information about the way scores are spread out or dispersed. They include:

Range: the distance between the smallest and largest score in a distribution.

Standard deviation: a popular index of the average distance that scores vary from the mean.

Variance: another measure of the variability of scores, expressed in squared score units. Less useful when interpreting individual scores, but important as a theoretical concept.

Finally we discussed correlation coefficients. A correlation coefficient is a quantitative measure of the relationship between two variables. We described how correlation coefficients provide information about both the direction and strength of a relationship. The sign of the coefficient (i.e., + or –) indicates the direction of the relationship while the magnitude of the coefficient indicates the strength of the relationship. Correlation coefficients also have important implications in the context of predicting performance. The stronger the correlation between two variables, the better we can predict performance on one variable given information about performance on the other variable. When there is a perfect correlation between two variables (either positive or negative), you can predict performance with perfect precision. We also described the use of scatterplots to illustrate correlations and cautioned that although correlations are extremely useful, they do not imply a causal relationship.

KEY TERMS AND CONCEPTS

Coefficient of determination, p. 50
Correlation coefficient, p. 49
  Negative correlation, p. 50
  Positive correlation, p. 50
Correlation versus causality, p. 52
Distribution, p. 36
  Positively skewed distributions, p. 38
  Negatively skewed distributions, p. 38

Symmetrical distributions, p. 38
Linear regression, p. 52
Measures of central tendency, p. 40
  Mean, p. 40
  Median, p. 42
  Mode, p. 42
Measures of variability, p. 44
  Range, p. 46
  Standard deviation, p. 46
  Variance, p. 48

Scales of measurement, p. 32
  Interval scales, p. 34
  Nominal scales, p. 33
  Ordinal scales, p. 33
  Ratio scales, p. 34
Scatterplot, p. 50

RECOMMENDED READINGS

Hays, W. (1994). *Statistics* (5th ed.). New York: Harcourt Brace. This is an excellent advanced statistics text. It covers the information covered in this chapter in greater detail and provides comprehensive coverage of statistics in general.

Nunnally, J. C., & Bernstein, I. H. (1994). *Psychometric theory* (3rd ed.). New York: McGraw-Hill. An excellent advanced psychometric text. Chapters 2 and 4 are particularly relevant to students wanting a more detailed discussion of issues introduced in this chapter.

Reynolds, C. R. (1999). Inferring causality from relational data and design: Historical and contemporary lessons for research and clinical practice. *The Clinical Neuropsychologist, 13,* 386–395. An entertaining and enlightening discussion of the need for caution when inferring causality from relational data.

INTERNET SITES OF INTEREST

www.fedstats.gov
  This site provides easy access to statistics and information provided by over one hundred U.S. federal agencies.

ncaa.org/stats
  This site is great for sports enthusiasts! It provides access to statistics compiled by the National Collegiate Athletic Association for sports ranging from baseball to lacrosse.

http://nces.ed.govt
  This is the site for the National Center for Education Statistics, the primary federal agency responsible for collecting and analyzing data related to education. It contains interesting information for public school teachers and administrators.

www.statistics.com

This site provides access to statistical information ranging from governmental, military, educational, medical, sports, and other sources. It has discussion boards that provide forums for discussing statistics and related issues and a section tailored to teachers and students.

www.xist.org

This is the Global Statistics Homepage. It contains information on the population and demographics of regions, countries, and cities.

PRACTICE ITEMS

1. Calculate the mean, variance, and standard deviation for the following score distributions. For these exercises, use the formulas listed in Table 2.5 for calculating variance and standard deviation.

Distribution 1	Distribution 2	Distribution 3
10	10	9
10	9	8
9	8	7
9	7	7
8	6	6
8	6	6
8	6	6
7	5	5
7	5	5
7	5	5
7	4	4
6	4	4
5	3	3
4	2	2
4	2	1

2. Calculate the Pearson correlation coefficient for the following pairs of scores.

Sample 1		Sample 2		Sample 3	
Variable X	Variable Y	Variable X	Variable Y	Variable X	Variable Y
9	10	9	10	9	7
10	9	9	9	9	7
9	8	8	8	8	8
8	7	8	7	8	5
9	6	7	5	7	4
5	6	7	5	7	5
3	6	6	4	6	5
7	5	6	3	6	5
5	5	5	4	5	4
4	5	5	5	5	4
7	4	4	4	4	7
3	4	4	3	4	8
5	3	3	2	3	5
6	2	2	3	2	5
5	2	2	2	2	5

3

The Meaning of Test Scores

Scores are the keys to understanding a student's performance on tests and other assessments. As a result, thoroughly understanding the meaning of test scores and how they are interpreted is of utmost importance.

CHAPTER HIGHLIGHTS

**Norm-Referenced and Criterion-Referenced
    Score Interpretations**
Norm-Referenced, Criterion-Referenced, or Both?
Qualitative Description of Scores

LEARNING OBJECTIVES

After reading and studying this chapter, students should be able to:

1. Describe raw scores and explain their limitations.
2. Define norm-referenced and criterion-referenced score interpretations and explain their major characteristics.
3. List and explain the important criteria for evaluating standardization data.
4. Describe the normal curve and explain its importance in interpreting test scores.
5. Describe the major types of standard scores.
6. Transform raw scores to standard scores.
7. Convert standard scores from one format to another.
8. Define normalized standard scores and describe the major types of normalized standard scores.
9. Define percentile rank and explain its interpretation.
10. Define grade equivalents and explain their limitations.
11. Describe some common applications of criterion-referenced score interpretations.
12. Explain how tests can be developed that produce both norm-referenced and criterion-referenced interpretations.
13. Explain and give an example of a qualitative score description.

Test scores reflect the performance or ratings of the individuals completing a test. Because test scores are the keys to interpreting and understanding the examinees' performance, their meaning and interpretation are extremely important topics and deserve careful attention. As you will see, there is a wide assortment of scores available for our use and each format has its own unique characteristics. Possibly the simplest type of score is a raw score. A **raw score** is simply the number of items scored or coded in a specific manner such as correct/incorrect, true/false, and so on. For example, the raw score on a classroom math test might be the number of items the student answered correctly. The calculation of raw scores is usually fairly straightforward, but raw scores are often of limited use to those interpreting the test results; they tend to offer very little useful information. Let's say a student's score on a classroom math test is 50. Does a raw score of 50 represent poor, average, or superior performance? The answer to this question depends on a number of factors such as how many items are on the test, how difficult the items are, and the like. For example, if the test contained only 50 items and the student's raw score were 50, the student demonstrated perfect performance. If the test contained 100 items and the student's raw score were 50, he or she answered only half of the items correctly. However, we still do not know what that really means. If the test contained 100 extremely difficult items and a raw score of 50 were the highest score in the class, this would likely reflect very good performance. Because raw scores in most situations have little interpretative meaning, we need to transform or convert them into another format to facilitate their interpretation and give them meaning. These transformed scores, typically referred to as derived scores, standard scores, or scaled scores, are pivotal in helping us interpret test results. There are a number of different derived scores, but they all can be classified as either norm-referenced or criterion-referenced. We will begin our discussion of scores and their interpretation by introducing you to these two different approaches to deriving and interpreting test scores.

> A *raw score* is simply the number of items scored or coded in a specific manner such as correct/incorrect, true/false, and so on.

Norm-Referenced and Criterion-Referenced Score Interpretations

To help us understand and interpret test results we need a frame of reference. That is, we need to compare the examinee's performance to "something." Score interpretations can be classified as either norm-referenced or criterion-referenced, and this distinction refers to the "something" to which we compare the examinee's performance. With **norm-referenced** score interpretations, the examinee's performance is compared to the performance of other people (a reference group). For example, scores on tests of intelligence are norm-referenced. If you report that an examinee has an IQ of 100, this indicates he or she scored higher than 50% of the people in the standardization sample. This is a norm-referenced interpretation. The examinee's performance is being compared with that of other test takers. Personality tests are also typically reported as norm-referenced scores. For example, it might be reported that an examinee scored higher than 98% of the

> With *norm-referenced* score interpretations, the examinee's performance is compared to the performance of other people.

standardization sample on some trait such as extroversion or sensation seeking. With all norm-referenced interpretations the examinee's performance is compared to that of others.

With *criterion-referenced* score interpretations, the examinee's performance is compared to a specified level of performance.

With **criterion-referenced** score interpretations, the examinee's performance is not compared to that of other people; instead it is compared to a specified level of performance (i.e., a criterion). With criterion-referenced interpretations, the emphasis is on what the examinees know or what they can do, not their standing relative to other test takers. Possibly the most common example of a criterion-referenced score is the percentage of correct responses on a classroom examination. If you report that a student correctly answered 85% of the items on a classroom test, this is a criterion-referenced interpretation. Notice that you are not comparing the student's performance to that of other examinees; you are comparing it to a standard, in this case perfect performance on the test.

Norm-referenced interpretations are relative whereas criterion-referenced interpretations are absolute.

Norm-referenced interpretations are relative (i.e., relative to the performance of other examinees) whereas criterion-referenced interpretations are absolute (i.e., compared to an absolute standard). Norm-referenced score interpretations have many applications, and the majority of published standardized tests produce norm-referenced scores. Nevertheless, criterion-referenced tests also have important applications, particularly in educational settings. Although people frequently refer to norm-referenced and criterion-referenced tests, this is not technically accurate. The terms *norm-referenced* and *criterion-referenced* actually refer to the interpretation of test scores. Although it is most common for tests to produce either norm-referenced or criterion-referenced scores, it is actually possible for a test to produce both norm- and criterion-referenced scores. We will come back to this topic later. First, we will discuss norm-referenced and criterion-referenced score interpretations and the types of derived scores associated with each approach.

Norm-Referenced Interpretations

Norms and Reference Groups. To understand performance on a psychological or educational test, it is often useful to compare an examinee's performance to the performance of some preselected group of individuals. Raw scores on a test, such as the number correct, take on special meaning when they are evaluated against the performance of a normative or reference group. To accomplish this, when using a norm-referenced approach to interpreting test scores, raw scores on the test are typically converted to derived scores based on information about the performance of a specific normative or reference group. Probably the most important consideration when making norm-referenced interpretations involves the relevance of the group of individuals to whom the examinee's performance is compared. The reference group from which the norms are derived should be representative of the type of individuals expected to take the test and should be defined prior to the standardization of the test. When you interpret a student's performance on a test or other assessment, you should ask yourself, "Are these norms appropriate for this student?" For example, it would be reasonable to compare a student's performance on a test of academic achievement to other students of the same age, grade, and educational background. However, it would probably not be particularly useful to compare a student's performance to younger students who had not been exposed to the same curriculum, or to older students who have received additional instruction, training, or experience. For norm-referenced interpretations to be meaningful, you need to compare the examinee's performance to that of a relevant reference group or sample. Therefore, the first step in developing good normative data is to define clearly the population for whom the test is designed.

Once the appropriate reference population has been defined clearly, a random sample is selected and tested. The normative reference group most often used to derive scores is called the **standardization sample,** a sample of the target population drawn using a specific set of procedures. Most test publishers and developers select a standardization sample using a procedure known as population proportionate stratified random sampling. This means that samples of people are selected in such a way as to ensure that the national population as a whole is proportionately represented on important variables. In the United States, for example, tests are typically standardized using a sampling plan that stratifies the sample by gender, age, education, ethnicity, socioeconomic background, region of residence, and community size based on population statistics provided by the U.S. Census Bureau. If data from the Census Bureau indicate that 1% of the U.S. population consists of African American males in the middle range of socioeconomic status residing in urban centers of the southern region, then 1% of the standardization sample of the test is drawn to meet this same set of characteristics. Once the standardization sample has been selected and tested, tables of derived scores are developed. These tables are based on the performance of the standardization sample and are typically referred to as normative tables or "norms." Because the relevance of the standardization sample is so important when using norm-referenced tests, it is the responsibility of test publishers to provide adequate information about the standardization sample. Additionally, it is the responsibility of every test user to evaluate the adequacy of the sample and the appropriateness of comparing the examinee's score to this particular group. In making this determination, you should consider the following factors:

Standardization samples **should be representative of the types of individuals expected to take the tests.**

- Is the standardization sample representative of the examinees with whom you will be using the test? Are demographic characteristics of the sample (e.g., age, race, sex, education, geographical location, etc.) similar to those who will take the test? In lay terms, are you comparing apples to apples and oranges to oranges?

- Is the sample current? Participants in samples from twenty years ago may have responded quite differently from a contemporary sample. Attitudes, beliefs, behaviors, and even cognitive abilities change over time, and to be relevant the normative data need to be current (see Special Interest Topic 3.1 for information on the "Flynn Effect" and how intelligence changes over time).

Normative data need to be current and the samples should be large enough to produce stable statistical information.

- Is the sample size large enough to provide stable statistical information? Although there is no magic number, if a test covers a broad age range it is common for standardization samples to exceed 1,000 participants. Otherwise, the number of participants at each age or grade level may be too small to produce stable estimation of means, standard deviations, and the more general distribution of scores. For example, the *Wechsler Individual Achievement Test—Second Edition* (WIAT-II; The Psychological Corporation,

SPECIAL INTEREST TOPIC   **3.1**

The "Flynn Effect"

Research has shown that there were significant increases in IQ during the twentieth century. This phenomenon has come to be referred to as the "Flynn Effect" after the primary research credited with its discovery, James Flynn. In discussing his research, Flynn (1998) notes:

> Massive IQ gains began in the 19th century, possibly as early as the industrial revolution, and have affected 20 nations, all for whom data exist. No doubt, different nations enjoyed different rates of gains, but the best data do not provide an estimate of the differences. Different kinds of IQ tests show different rates of gains: Culture-reduced tests of fluid intelligence show gains of as much as 20 points per generation (30 years); performance tests show 10–20 points; and verbal tests sometimes show 10 points or below. Tests closest to the content of school-taught subjects, such as arithmetic reasoning, general information, and vocabulary, show modest or nil gains. More often than not, gains are similar at all IQ levels. Gains may be age specific, but this has not yet been established and they certainly persist into adulthood. The fact that gains are fully present in young children means that causal factors are present in early childhood but not necessarily that they are more potent in young children than older children or adults. (p. 61)

So what do you think is causing these gains in IQ? When we ask our students some initially suggest that these increases in IQ reflect the effects of evolution or changes in the gene pool. However, this is not really a plausible explanation because it is happening much too fast. Summarizing the current thinking on this topic, Kamphaus (2001) notes that while there is not total agreement, most investigators believe it is the result of environmental factors such as better prenatal care and nutrition, enhanced education, increased test wiseness, urbanization, and higher standards of living.

Consider the importance of this effect in relation to our discussion of the development of test norms. When we told you that it is important to consider the date of the normative data when evaluating its adequacy, we were concerned with factors such as the Flynn Effect. Due to the gradual but consistent increase in IQ, normative data become more demanding as time passes. In other words, an examinee must obtain a higher raw score (i.e., correctly answer more items) each time a test is renormed in order for his or her score to remain the same. Kamphaus suggests that as a rule of thumb, IQ norms increase in difficulty by about 3 points every 10 years (based on a mean of 100 and a standard deviation of 15). For example, the same performance on IQ tests normed 10 years apart would result in IQs about 3 points apart, with the newer test producing the lower scores. As a result, he recommends that if the normative data for a test are more than 10 years old one should be concerned about the accuracy of the norms. This is a reasonable suggestion, and test publishers are becoming better at providing timely revisions. For example, the *Wechsler Intelligence Scale for Children—Revised* (WISC-R) was published in 1974, but the next revision, the WISC-III, was not released until 1991, a 17-year interval. The most current revision, the WISC-IV, was released in 2003, only 12 years after its predecessor.

2002) has 3,600 participants in the standardization, with a minimum of 150 at each grade level (i.e., pre-kindergarten through grade 12).

A final consideration regarding norm-referenced interpretations is the importance of standardized administration. The normative sample should be administered the test under the same conditions and with the same administrative procedures that will be used in actual practice. Accordingly, when the test is administered in clinical or educational settings, it is important that the test user follow the administrative procedures precisely. For example, if you are administering standardized tests you need to make sure that you are reading the directions verbatim and closely adhering to time limits. It obviously would not be reasonable to compare your students' performance on a timed mathematics test to the performance of a standardization sample that was given either more or less time to complete the items. (The need to follow standard administration and scoring procedures actually applies to all standardized tests, both norm-referenced and criterion-referenced.)

Many types of derived scores or units of measurement may be reported in "norms tables," and the selection of which derived score to employ can influence the interpretation of scores. Before starting our discussion of common norm-referenced derived scores, we need to introduce the concept of a normal distribution.

The Normal Curve. The normal distribution is a special type of distribution that is very useful when interpreting test scores. Figure 3.1 depicts a normal distribution. The normal distribution, which is also referred to as the Gaussian or bell-shaped curve, is a distribution that characterizes many variables that occur in nature (see Special Interest Topic 3.2 for information on Carl Frederich Gauss, who is credited with discovering the bell curve). Gray (1999) indicates that the height of individuals of a given age and gender is an example of a variable that is distributed normally. He notes that numerous genetic and nutritional factors influence an individual's height, and in most cases these various factors average out so that people of a given age and gender tend to be of approximately the same height. This accounts for the peak frequency in the normal distribution. In referring to Figure 3.1 you will see that a large number of scores tend to "pile up" around the middle of the distribution. However,

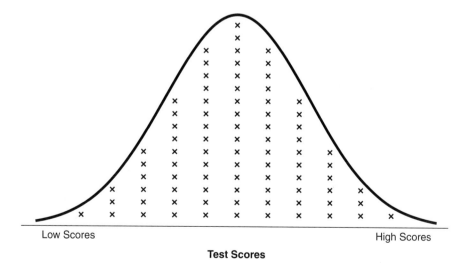

Low Scores   High Scores

Test Scores

FIGURE 3.1 **Illustration of the Normal Distribution**

SPECIAL INTEREST TOPIC **3.2**

Whence the Normal Curve?

Carl Frederich Gauss (1777–1855) was a noted German mathematician who is generally credited with being one of the founders of modern mathematics. Born in Brunswick, he turned his scholarly pursuits toward the field of astronomy around the turn of the nineteenth century. In the course of tracking star movements and taking other forms of physical survey measurements (at times with instruments of his own invention), Gauss found to his annoyance that students and colleagues who were plotting the location of an object at the same time, noted it to be in somewhat different places! He began to plot the frequency of the observed locations systematically and found the observations to take the shape of a curve. He determined that the best estimate of the true location of the object was the mean of the observations and that each independent observation contained some degree of error. These errors formed a curve that was in the shape of a bell. This curve or distribution of error terms has since been demonstrated to occur with a variety of natural phenomena and indeed has become so commonplace that it is most often known as the "normal curve" or the normal distribution. Of course, you may know it as the bell curve as well due to its shape, and mathematicians and others in the sciences sometimes refer to it as the Gaussian curve after its discoverer and the man who described many of its characteristics. Interestingly, Gauss was a very prolific scholar and the Gaussian curve is not the only discovery to bear his name. He did groundbreaking research on magnetism and the unit of magnetic intensity is called a gauss.

for a relatively small number of individuals a unique combination of factors results in them being either much shorter or much taller than the average. This accounts for the distribution trailing off at both the low and high ends.

Although the previous discussion addressed only observable characteristics of the normal distribution, certain mathematical properties make it particularly useful when interpreting scores. For example, the **normal distribution** is a symmetrical, unimodal distribution in which the mean, median, and mode are all equal. It is also symmetrical, meaning that if you divide the distribution into two halves, they will mirror each other. Probably the most useful characteristic of the normal distribution is that predictable proportions of scores occur at specific points in the distribution. Referring to Figure 3.2 you find a normal distribution with the mean and standard deviations (σ) marked. Figure 3.2 also indicates percentile rank (PR), which will be discussed later in this chapter. Because we know that the mean equals the median in a normal distribution, we know that an individual who scores at the mean scored better than 50% of the sample of examinees (remember, earlier we defined the median as the score that divides the distribution in half). Because approximately 34% of the scores fall between the mean and 1 standard deviation above the mean, an individual whose score falls 1 standard deviation above the mean performs at a level exceeding approximately 84% (i.e., 50% + 34%) of the population. A score 2 standard deviation above the mean will be above 98% of the population. Because the distribution is symmetrical, the relationship is the same

> The *normal distribution* is a symmetrical, unimodal distribution in which the mean, median, and mode are all equal.

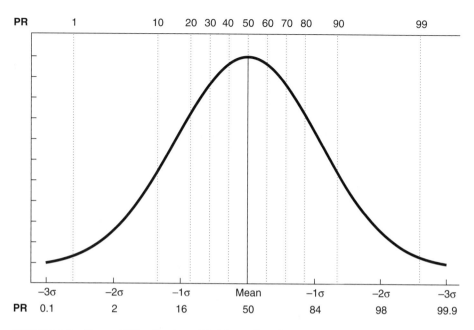

FIGURE 3.2   Normal Distribution with Mean, Standard Deviations, and Percentages

Source: From *Psychological Testing: Theory and Applications* (Fig. 3.1, p. 45), by L. H. Janda, 1998, Boston, MA: Allyn & Bacon. Copyright 1998 by Pearson Education. Reprinted with permission.

in the inverse below the mean. A score 1 standard deviation *below* the mean indicates that the individual exceeds only about 16% (i.e., 50% − 34%) of the population on the attribute in question. Approximately two-thirds (i.e., 68%) of the population will score within 1 standard deviation above and below the mean on a normally distributed variable.

We have reproduced in Appendix F a table that allows you to determine what proportion of scores are below any given point in a distribution by specifying standard deviation units. For example, you can use these tables to determine that a score 1.96 SD *above* the mean exceeds 97.5% of the scores in the distribution whereas a score 1.96 SD *below* the mean exceeds only 2.5% of the scores. Although we do not feel it is necessary for you to become an expert in using these statistical tables, we do encourage you to examine Figure 3.2 carefully to ensure you have a good grasp of the basic properties of the normal distribution before proceeding.

Although many variables closely approximate the normal distribution, not all educational or psychological variables are distributed normally.

Although many variables of importance in educational settings such as achievement and intelligence are very close to conforming to the normal distribution, not all educational, psychological, or behavioral variables are normally distributed. For example, aggressive behavior and psychotic behavior are two variables of interest to psychologists and educators that are distinctly different from the normal curve in their distributions. Most children are not aggressive toward their peers, so on measures of aggression, most children pile up at the left side of the distribution whereas children who are only slightly aggressive may score relatively far to the right. Likewise, few people ever experience psychotic symptoms such as hearing voices of people who are not there or seeing things no one else can see. Such variables will each have their own unique distribution, and even though one can, via statistical manipulation, force these score distributions into the shape of a normal curve, it is not always desirable to do so. We will return to this issue later, but at this point it is important to refute the common myth that all human behaviors or attributes conform to the normal curve; clearly they do not!

Standard scores **are the transformation of raw scores to a desired scale with a predetermined mean and standard deviation.**

Derived Scores Used with Norm-Referenced Interpretations

Standard Scores.   As we have noted, raw scores such as the number of items correct are difficult to work with and interpret. Raw scores therefore are typically transformed to another unit of measurement or derived score. With norm-referenced score interpretations, **standard scores** (sometimes called scaled scores) are often the preferred type of derived score. Transforming raw scores into standard scores involves creating a set of scores with a predetermined mean and standard deviation that remains constant across some preselected variable such as age. Although we are going to describe a number of different standard score formats, they all share numerous common characteristics. All standard scores use standard deviation units to indicate where an examinee's score is located relative to the mean of the distribution. Standard scores are typically linear transformations of raw scores to a desired scale with a predetermined mean and standard deviation. In a linear transformation, the following generic equation is applied to each score:

$$\text{Standard Score} = X_{ss} + SD_{ss} \times \frac{(X_i - X)}{SD_x}$$

where
X_i = raw score of any individual taking the test i
X = mean of the raw scores
SD_x = standard deviation of the raw scores
SD_{ss} = desired standard deviation of the derived standard scores
X_{ss} = desired mean of the derived or standard scores

Standard scores calculated using *linear transformations* retain a direct relationship with raw scores and the distribution retains its original shape.

This transformation is known as a **linear transformation,** and standard scores computed using it retain a direct relationship with the raw scores and the distribution retains its original shape (the importance of this statement will become more evident when we discuss normalized standard scores). Table 3.1 provides an example of how this formula is applied to raw scores to transform them into standard scores.

As we noted, there are different standard score formats that have common characteristics. They differ in means and standard deviations. Here are brief descriptions of some of the more common standard score formats. This is not an exhaustive list, and it is possible to create a new format with virtually any mean and standard deviation you desire. However, test authors and publishers typically use these common standard score formats because educators and psychologists are most familiar with them.

TABLE 3.1   Transforming Raw Scores to Standard Scores

In this chapter we provided the following formula for transforming raw scores to z-scores.

$$z\text{-score} = \frac{(X_i - X)}{SD_x}$$

where X_i = raw score of any individual i
  X = mean of the raw scores
  SD = standard deviation of the raw scores

Consider the situation in which the mean of the raw scores (X) is 75, the standard deviation of raw scores (SD) is 10, and the individual's raw score is a 90.

$$z\text{-score} = \frac{(90 - 75)}{10}$$
$$= 15/10$$
$$= 1.5$$

If you wanted to convert the individual's score to a T-score, you would use the generic formula:

$$\text{Standard Score} = X_{ss} + SD_{ss} \times \frac{X_i - X}{SD_x}$$

where X_i = raw score of any individual taking the test i
  X = mean of the raw scores
  SD_x = standard deviation of the raw scores
  SD_{ss} = desired standard deviation of the derived standard scores
  X_{ss} = desired mean of the derived or standard scores

In this case the calculations are:

$$T\text{-score} = 50 + 10 \times \frac{(90 - 75)}{10}$$
$$= 50 + 10 \times 1.5$$
$$= 50 + 15$$
$$= 65$$

---

z-scores are the simplest of the standard scores and indicate how far above or below the mean of the distribution the raw score is in standard deviation units.

■ z-scores. *z-scores* are the simplest of the standard score formats and indicate how far above or below the mean of the distribution the raw score is in standard deviation units. z-scores are simple to calculate and a simplified equation can be used (equation 2):

$$z\text{-score} = \frac{X_i - X}{SD}$$

where X_i = raw score of any individual i
  X = mean of the raw scores
  SD = standard deviation of the raw scores

z-scores have a mean of 0 and a standard deviation of 1. As a result all scores above the mean will be positive and all scores below the mean will be negative. For example, a *z*-score of 1.6 is 1.6 standard deviation above the mean (i.e., exceeding 95% of the scores in the distribution) and a score of –1.6 is 1.6 standard deviation *below* the mean (i.e., exceeding only 5% of the scores in the distribution). As you see, in addition to negative scores, *z*-scores involve decimals. This results in scores that many find difficult to use and interpret. As a result, few test publishers routinely report *z*-scores for their tests. However, researchers commonly use *z*-scores because scores with a mean of 0 and a standard deviation of 1 make statistical formulas easier to calculate.

- *T-scores:* **T-scores** have a mean of 50 and a standard deviation of 10. Relative to *z*-scores they have the advantage of all scores being positive and without decimals. For example, a score of 66 is 1.6 standard deviation above the mean (i.e., exceeding 95% of the scores in the distribution) and a score of 34 is 1.6 standard deviation *below* the mean (i.e., exceeding only 5% of the scores in the distribution).

- *Wechsler IQs (and many others):* The Wechsler intelligence scales use a standard score format with a mean of 100 and a standard deviation of 15. Like *T*-scores, the **Wechsler IQ** format avoids decimals and negative values. For example, a score of 124 is 1.6 standard deviation above the mean (i.e., exceeding 95% of the scores in the distribution) and a score of 76 is 1.6 standard deviation *below* the mean (i.e., exceeding only 5% of the scores in the distribution). This format has become very popular, and most aptitude and individually administered achievement tests report standard scores with mean of 100 and standard deviation of 15.

- *Stanford-Binet IQs:* The Stanford-Binet intelligence scales until recently used a standard score format with a mean of 100 and a standard deviation of 16. This is similar to the format adopted by the Wechsler scales, but instead of a standard deviation of 15 there is a standard deviation of 16 (see Special Interest Topic 3.3 for an explanation). This may appear to be a negligible difference, but it was enough to preclude direct comparisons between the scales. With the Stanford-Binet scales, a score of 126 is 1.6 standard deviation above the mean (i.e., exceeding 95% of the scores in the distribution) and a score of 74 is 1.6 standard deviation *below* the mean (i.e., exceeding only 5% of the scores in the distribution). The most recent edition of the Stanford-Binet (the fifth edition) adopted a mean of 100 and a standard deviation of 15 to be consistent with the Wechsler and other popular standardized tests.

- *CEEB Scores (SAT/GRE):* This format was developed by the College Entrance Examination Board and used with tests including the Scholastic Assessment Test (SAT) and the Graduate Record Examination (GRE). **CEEB scores** have a mean of 500 and a standard deviation of 100. With this format, a score of 660 is 1.6 standard deviation above the mean (i.e., exceeding 95% of the scores in the distribution) and a score of 340 is 1.6 standard deviation below the mean (i.e., exceeding only 5% of the scores in the distribution).

As we noted, standard scores can be set to any desired mean and standard deviation, with the fancy of the test author frequently being the sole determining factor. Fortunately, the few standard score formats we just summarized will account for the majority of standardized

Why Do IQ Tests Use a Mean of 100 and a Standard Deviation of 15?

When Alfred Binet and Theodore Simon developed the first popular IQ test in the late 1800s, items were scored according to the age at which half the children got the answer correct. This resulted in the concept of a "mental age" for each examinee. This concept of a mental age (MA) gradually progressed to the development of the IQ, which at first was calculated as the ratio of the child's MA to actual or chronological age multiplied by 100 to remove all decimals. The original form for this score, known as the Ratio IQ, was:

$$MA/CA \times 100$$

where   MA = mental age
          CA = chronological age

This score distribution has a mean fixed at 100 at every age. However, due to the different restrictions on the range of mental age possible at each chronological age (e.g., a 2-year-old can range in MA only 2 years below CA but a 10-year-old can range 10 years below the CA), the standard deviation of the distribution of the Ratio IQ changes at every CA! At younger ages it tends to be small and it is typically larger at upper ages. The differences are quite large, often with the standard deviation from large samples varying from 10 to 30! Thus, at one age a Ratio IQ of 110 is 1 standard deviation above the mean, whereas at another age the same Ratio IQ of 110 is only 0.33 standard deviation above the mean. Across age, the average standard deviation of the now archaic Ratio IQ is about 16. This value was then adopted as *the* standard deviation for the Stanford-Binet IQ tests and continued until David Wechsler scaled his first IQ measure in the 1930s to have a standard deviation of 15, which he felt would be easier to work with. Additionally, he selected a standard deviation of 15 to help distinguish his test from the then dominant Stanford-Binet test. The Stanford-Binet tests have long abandoned the Ratio IQ in favor of a true standard score, but remained tethered to the standard deviation of 16 until Stanford-Binet's fifth edition was published in 2003. With the fifth edition Standford-Binet's new primary author, Gale Roid, converted to the far more popular scale with a mean of 100 and a standard deviation of 15.

tests in education and psychology. Figure 3.3 and Table 3.2 illustrate the relationship between various standard score formats. If reference groups are comparable, Table 3.2 can also be used to help you equate scores across tests to aid in the comparison of a student's performance on tests of different attributes using different standard scores. Table 3.3 illustrates a simple formula that allows you to convert standard scores from one format to another (e.g., z-scores to T-scores).

It is important to recognize that not all authors, educators, or clinicians are specific when it comes to reporting or describing scores. That is, they may report "standard scores," but not specify exactly what standard score format they are using. Obviously the format is extremely important. Consider a standard score of 70. If this is a T-score it represents a score 2 standard deviation *above* the mean (exceeding approximately 98% of the scores in

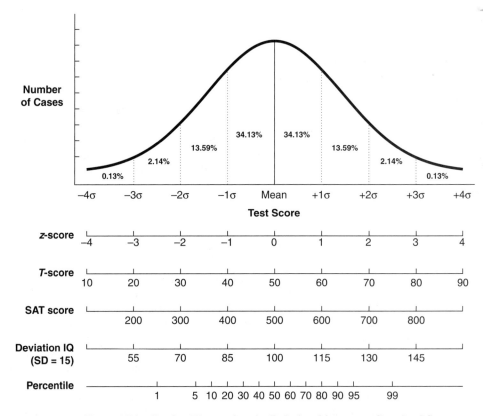

FIGURE 3.3   Normal Distribution Illustrating the Relationship among Standard Scores

Source: From *Psychological Testing: Theory and Applications* (Fig. 3.2, p. 49), by L. H. Janda, 1998, Boston, MA: Allyn & Bacon. Copyright 1998 by Pearson Education. Reprinted with permission.

the distribution). If it is a Wechsler IQ (or comparable score) it is 2 standard deviation *below* the mean (exceeding only approximately 2% of the scores in the distribution). In other words, be sure to know what standard score format is being used so you will be able to interpret the scores accurately.

Normalized standard scores are standard scores based on underlying distributions that were not originally normal, but were transformed into normal distributions.

Normalized Standard Scores.   Discussion about standard scores thus far applies primarily to scores from distributions that are normal (or that at least approximate normality) and were computed using a linear transformation. As noted earlier, although it is commonly held that psychological and educational variables are normally distributed, this is not always the case. Many variables such as intelligence, memory skills, and academic achievement will closely approximate the normal distribution when well measured. However, many variables of interest in psychology and education, especially behavioral ones (e.g., aggression, attention, and hyperactivity), may deviate substantially from the normal distribution. As a result it is not

TABLE 3.2   Relationship of Different Standard Score Formats

z-scores X = 0 SD = 1	T-scores X = 50 SD = 10	Wechsler IQ X = 100 SD = 15	CEEB Scores X = 500 SD = 100	Percentile Rank
2.6	76	139	760	>99
2.4	74	136	740	99
2.2	72	133	720	99
2.0	70	130	700	98
1.8	68	127	680	96
1.6	66	124	660	95
1.4	64	121	640	92
1.2	62	118	620	88
1.0	60	115	600	84
0.8	58	112	580	79
0.6	56	109	560	73
0.4	54	106	540	66
0.2	52	103	520	58
0.0	50	100	500	50
−0.2	48	97	480	42
−0.4	46	94	460	34
−0.6	44	91	440	27
−0.8	42	88	420	21
−1.0	40	85	400	16
−1.2	38	82	380	12
−1.4	36	79	360	8
−1.6	34	76	340	5
−1.8	32	73	320	4
−2.0	30	70	300	2
−2.2	28	67	280	1
−2.4	26	64	260	1
−2.6	24	61	240	1

Note: X = mean, SD = standard deviation.

Source: Adapted from Reynolds (1998b).

TABLE 3.3   Converting Standard Scores from One Format to Another

You can easily convert standard scores from one format to another using the following formula:

$$\text{New Standard Score} = X_{ss2} + SD_{ss2} \times \frac{X - X_{ss1}}{SD_{ss1}}$$

where
X = original standard score
X_{ss1} = mean of the original standard score format
SD_{ss1} = standard deviation of the original standard score format
X_{ss2} = mean of the new standard score format
SD_{ss2} = standard deviation of the new standard score format

For example, consider the situation in which you want to convert a z-score of 1.0 to a T-score. The calculations are:

$$T\text{-score} = 50 + 10 \times \frac{(1 - 0)}{1}$$
$$= 50 + 10 \times (1/1)$$
$$= 50 + 10 \times 1$$
$$= 50 + 10$$
$$= 60$$

If you want to convert a T-score of 60 to a CEEB score, the calculations are:

$$\text{CEEB score} = 500 + 100 \times \frac{(60 - 50)}{10}$$
$$= 500 + 100 \times (10/10)$$
$$= 500 + 100 \times 1$$
$$= 500 + 100$$
$$= 600$$

---

unusual for test developers to end up with distributions that deviate from normality enough to cause concern. In these situations test developers may elect to develop normalized standard scores. **Normalized standard scores** are standard scores based on underlying distributions that were not originally normal, but were transformed into normal distributions. The transformations applied in these situations are often nonlinear transformations. Whereas standard scores calculated with linear transformations retain a direct relationship with the original raw scores and the distribution retains its original shape, this is not necessarily so with normalized standard scores based on nonlinear transformations. This does not mean that normalized standard scores are undesirable. In situations in which the obtained distribution is not normal because the variable is not normally distributed, normalization is not generally useful and indeed may be misleading. However, in situations in which the obtained distribution is not normal because of sampling error or choice of subjects, normalization can enhance the usefulness and interpretability of the scores. Nevertheless, it is desirable to know what type of scores you are working with and how they were calculated.

In most situations, normalized standard scores are interpreted in a manner similar to other standard scores. In fact, they often look strikingly similar to standard scores. For example, they may be reported as normalized *z*-scores or normalized *T*-scores and often reported without the prefix *normalized* at all. In this context, they will have the same mean and standard deviation as their counterparts derived with linear transformations. However, several types of scores that have traditionally been based on nonlinear transformations are normalized standard scores. These include:

- *Stanine scores:* Stanine (i.e., *sta*ndard *nine*) scores divide the distribution into nine bands (1 through 9). **Stanine scores** have a mean of 5 and a standard deviation of 2. Because stanine scores use only nine values to represent the full range of scores, they are not a particularly precise score format. As a result, some professionals avoid their use. However, certain professionals prefer them *because* of their imprecision. These professionals, concerned with the imprecision inherent in all psychological and educational measurement, choose stanine scores because they do not misrepresent the precision of measurement (e.g., Popham, 2000). Special Interest Topic 3.4 briefly describes the history of stanine scores.
- *Wechsler scaled scores:* The subtests of the *Wechsler Intelligence Scale for Children— Fourth Edition* (WISC-IV; Wechsler, 2003) and predecessors are reported as normalized standard scores referred to as scaled scores. The **Wechsler scaled scores** have a mean of 10 and a standard deviation of 3. This transformation was performed so the subtest scores would be comparable, even though their underlying distributions may have deviated from the normal curve and each other.
- *Normal Curve Equivalent (NCE):* The **normal curve equivalent (NCE)** is a normalized standard score with a mean of 50 and a standard deviation of 21.06. NCEs are not usually used for evaluating individuals, but are primarily used to assess the progress of groups (e.g., The Psychological Corporation, 2002). Because school districts must report NCE scores to meet criteria as part of certain federal education programs, many test publishers report these scores for tests used in education.

SPECIAL INTEREST TOPIC   **3.4**
The History of Stanine Scores

Stanines have a mean of 5 and a standard deviation of 2. Stanines have a range of 1 to 9 and are a form of standard score. Because they are standardized and have nine possible values, the contrived, contracted name of *stanines* was given to these scores (*sta*ndard *nine*). A stanine is a conversion of the percentile rank that represents a wide range of percentile ranks at each score point. The U.S. Air Force developed this system during World War II because a simple score system was needed that could represent scores as a single digit. On older computers, which used cards with holes punched in them for entering data, the use of stanine scores not only saved time by having only one digit to punch but also increased the speed of the computations made by computers and conserved computer memory. Stanines are now used only occasionally and usually only in statistical reporting of aggregated scores (from Reynolds, 2002).

One of the most popular and easily understood ways to interpret and report a test score is the *percentile rank*. Percentile ranks reflect the percentage of individuals scoring below a given point in a distribution.

Percentile Rank. One of the most popular and easily understood ways to interpret and report a test score is the **percentile rank.** Like all norm-referenced scores, the percentile rank simply reflects an examinee's performance relative to a specific group. Although there are some subtle differences in the ways percentile ranks are calculated and interpreted, the typical way of interpreting them is as reflecting the percentage of individuals scoring below a given point in a distribution. For example, a percentile rank of 80 indicates that 80% of the individuals in the standardization sample scored below this score. A percentile rank of 20 indicates that only 20% of the individuals in the standardization sample scored below this score. Percentile ranks range from 1 to 99, and a rank of 50 indicates the median performance (in a perfectly normal distribution it is also the mean score). As you can see, percentile ranks can be easily explained to and understood by individuals without formal training in psychometrics. Whereas standard scores might seem somewhat confusing, a percentile rank might be more understandable. For example, a parent might believe an IQ of 75 is in the average range, generalizing from experiences with classroom tests whereby 70 to 80 is often interpreted as representing average or perhaps "C-level" performance. However, explaining that the child's score exceeded only approximately 5% of the standardization sample or scores of other children at the same age level might clarify the issue. One common misunderstanding may arise when using percentile ranks: It is important to ensure that results in terms of percentile rank are not misinterpreted as "percent correct" (Kamphaus, 1993). That is, a percentile rank of 60 means that the examinee scored better than 60% of the standardization sample, not that the examinee correctly answered 60% of the items.

Although percentile ranks can be easily interpreted, they do not represent interval level measurement. That is, percentile ranks are not equal across all parts of a distribution. Percentile ranks are compressed near the middle of the distribution, where there are large numbers of scores, and spread out near the tails, where there are relatively few scores (you can see this in Figure 3.3 by examining the line that depicts percentiles). This implies that small differences in percentile ranks near the middle of the distribution might be of little importance, whereas the same difference at the extremes might be substantial. However, because the pattern of inequality is predictable, this can be taken into consideration when interpreting scores and it is not particularly problematic.

There are two formats based on percentile ranks that you might come across in educational settings. Some publishers report quartile scores that divide the distribution of percentile ranks into four equal units. The lower 25% receives a quartile score of 1, 26% to 50% a quartile score of 2, 51% to 75% a quartile score of 3, and the upper 25% a quartile score of 4. Similarly, some publishers report decile-based scores, which divide the distribution of percentile ranks into 10 equal parts. The lowest decile-based score is 1 and corresponds to scores with percentile ranks between 0% and 10%. The highest decile-based score is 10 and corresponds to scores with percentile ranks between 90% and 100% (e.g., The Psychological Corporation, 2002).

Grade Equivalents. **Grade equivalents** are norm-referenced derived scores that identify the academic grade level achieved by the examinee. Although grade equivalents are very

Grade equivalents **are norm-referenced scores that identify the academic grade level achieved by the examinee. Although grade equivalents are very popular and appear to be easy to interpret, they actually need to be interpreted with considerable caution.**

popular in school settings and *appear* to be easy to interpret, they actually need to be interpreted with considerable caution. To understand grade equivalents, it is helpful to be familiar with how they are calculated. When a test is administered to a group of children, the mean raw score is calculated at each grade level, and this mean raw score is called the grade equivalent for raw scores of that magnitude. For example, if the mean raw score for beginning 3rd graders on a reading test is 50, then any examinee earning a score of 50 on the test is assigned a grade equivalent of 3.0 regardless of age. If the mean score for 4th graders is 60, then any examinee earning a score of 60 is assigned a grade equivalent of 4.0. It becomes a little more complicated when raw scores fall between two median grade scores. In these situations intermediate grade equivalents are typically calculated using a procedure referred to as **interpolation.** To illustrate this procedure with a straightforward example, consider a score of 55 on our imaginary reading test. Here, the difference between a grade equivalent of 3.0 (i.e., raw score of 50) and a grade equivalent of 4.0 (i.e., raw score of 60) is divided into 10 equal units to correspond to 10 months of academic instruction. In this example, because the difference is 10 ($40 - 30 = 10$), each raw score unit corresponds to one-tenth (i.e., one month), and a raw score of 55 would be assigned a grade equivalent of 3.5. In actual practice, interpolation is not always this straightforward. For example, if the difference between a grade equivalent of 3.0 and 4.0 had been 6 points (instead of 10), the calculations would have been somewhat more complicated.

Much has been written about the limitations of grade equivalents, and the following list highlights some major concerns summarized from several sources (Anastasi & Urbina, 1997; Psychological Corporation, 2002; Popham, 2000; Reynolds, 1998b):

- The use of interpolation to calculate intermediate grade equivalents assumes that academic skills are achieved at a constant rate and that there is no gain or loss during the summer vacation. This tenuous assumption is probably not accurate in many situations.
- Grade equivalents are not comparable across tests or even subtests of the same battery of tests. For example, grade equivalents of 6.0 on a test of reading comprehension and a test of math calculation do not indicate that the examinee has the same level of proficiency in the two academic areas. Additionally, there can be substantial differences between the examinee's percentile ranks on the two tests.
- Grade equivalents reflect an ordinal level scale of measurement, not an interval scale. As discussed in the previous chapter, ordinal level scales do not have equal scale units across the scale. For example, the difference between grade equivalents of 3.0 and 4.0 is not necessarily the same as the difference between grade equivalents of 5.0 and 6.0. Statistically, one should not add, subtract, multiply, or divide such scores because their underlying metrics are different. It is like multiplying feet by meters—you can multiply 3 feet by 3 meters and get 9, but what does it mean?
- There is not a predictable relationship between grade equivalents and percentile ranks. For example, examinees may have a higher grade equivalent on a test of reading comprehension than of math calculations, but their percentile rank and thus their skill relative to age peers on the math test may actually be higher.

- A common misperception is that children should receive instruction at the level suggested by their grade equivalents. Parents may ask, "Johnny is only in the 4th grade but has a grade equivalent of 6.5 in math. Doesn't that mean he is ready for 6th-grade math instruction?" The answer is clearly "No!" Although Johnny correctly answered the same number of items as an average 6th grader, this does not indicate that he has mastered the necessary prerequisites to succeed at the 6th-grade level.
- Unfortunately, grade equivalents tend to become standards of performance. For example, lawmakers might decide that all students entering the 6th grade should achieve grade equivalents of 6.0 or better on a standardized reading test. If you will recall how grade equivalents are calculated, you will see how ridiculous this is. Because the mean raw score at each grade level is designated the grade equivalent, 50% of the standardization sample scored below the grade equivalent. As a result, it would be expected that a large number of students with average reading skills would enter the 6th grade with grade equivalents below 6.0. It is a law of mathematics that not everyone can score above the average! (See Special Interest Topic 3.5 for more on this topic.)

We recommend that you avoid using grade equivalents.

As the result of these and other limitations, we recommend that you avoid using grade equivalents. **Age equivalents** are another derived score format that indicates the age, typically in years and months, at which a raw score is the mean or median. Age equivalents have the same limitations as grade equivalents and we again recommend that you avoid using them. Many test publishers report grade and age equivalents and occasionally you will find a testing expert that favors them (at least at the lower grade levels). Nevertheless, they are subject to misinterpretation and should be avoided when possible. If you are required to use them, we recommend that you also report standard scores and percentile ranks and emphasize these more precise derived scores when explaining test results.

Criterion-Referenced Interpretations

Criterion-referenced interpretations emphasize what the examinees know or what they can do, not their standing relative to other test takers.

As noted previously, with criterion-referenced interpretations the examinee's performance is not compared to that of other people, but to a specified level of performance (i.e., a criterion). Criterion-referenced interpretations emphasize what the examinees know or what they can do, not their standing relative to other test takers. Although some authors appear to view criterion-referenced score interpretations as a relatively new approach dating back to only the 1960s or 1970s, criterion-referenced interpretations actually predate norm-referenced interpretations. For example, educators were evaluating their students' performance in terms of "percentage correct" or letter grades to reflect mastery (i.e., A, B, C, D, and F) long before test developers started developing norm-referenced scores. Nevertheless, since the 1960s there has been renewed interest in and refinement of criterion-referenced score interpretations. A number of different labels have been applied to this type of score interpretation in the last forty years, including content-referenced, domain-referenced, and objective-referenced (e.g., Anastasi & Urbina, 1997). In this text we will be using the term *criterion-referenced* because it is probably the broadest and most common label.

SPECIAL INTEREST TOPIC 3.5

Every Child on Grade Level?

As one component of the federal initiative generally known as "No Child Left Behind," state education agencies have been asked to adopt a goal of having every child perform on or above grade level. This is a laudable goal, but for it to be successful it would be helpful for the administration to define precisely what is meant by "grade level." Leaving it to the individual states is likely to result in a hodgepodge of definitions, some good and some not so good. If grade level is defined as the criterion for passing the state-mandated achievement tests, the goal is clearly challenging, but theoretically feasible. On the other hand, if grade level is interpreted to mean the same thing as grade equivalent (as in grade equivalent scores), we have problems. A grade equivalent is defined as the average level of performance of children in a particular grade. Thus, if students in grade 3 are tested in September the grade equivalent is 3.0, but if they are tested in January the average test score has a grade equivalent of 3.4. The average score, in a normal distribution, is at the exact center of the score distribution, such that half the scores are below average and half are above average. Achievement in the classroom on academic subjects approximates the normal distribution, or bell curve as it is often called. Because of the way grade equivalents are calculated, it is not possible for every child to be on grade level (if this definition is used) except under the very unusual circumstance whereby every child performs at exactly the same level; that is, no child is above or below the average level of performance—if all children are at least on grade level, then all children will be exactly at grade level, none above and none below!!

Although the ideology behind the concept of all children at or above grade level sounds wonderful and is very democratic, it is a mathematical near impossibility. This is reminiscent of what some refer to as the "Lake Wobegon Effect." Lake Wobegon is a fictional community described in a popular radio show in which ". . . all of the children are above average." This is a desirable, but unrealistic situation. As is so often the case when interpreting scores, it comes down to your frame of reference. An achievable goal would be to establish performance standards that lead to success in life and create a curriculum wherein the maximum number of children acquire these specific skills—grade level can be defined as a relative standard with regard to the average level of performance or an absolute standard. What is required for the program to have any hope of effectiveness is an absolute standard that depends on the performance of the individual pupil, not the relative performance of the entire group. Let's hope the various state education agencies set absolute or criterion-referenced standards and do not fall into the trap of defining grade level the same as grade equivalent scores.

Probably the most common example of a criterion-referenced score is percent correct. For example, when a teacher reports that a student correctly answered 85% of the problems on a classroom test assessing the student's ability to multiply double digits, this is a criterion-referenced interpretation. Although there is a variety of criterion-referenced scoring systems, they all involve an absolute evaluation of examinees' performances as opposed to a relative evaluation. That is, instead of comparing their performances to the performances of others (a relative interpretation), a criterion-referenced interpretation attempts to describe what they know or are capable of doing—the absolute level of performance.

Mastery testing **involves determining whether the examinee has achieved a specific level of mastery of the knowledge and skills domain and is usually reported in an all-or-none score such as a pass/fail designation.**

In addition to percent correct, another type of criterion-referenced interpretation is referred to as mastery testing. **Mastery testing** involves determining whether the examinee has achieved a specific level of mastery of the knowledge or skills domain and is usually reported in an all-or-none score such as a pass/fail designation (AERA et al., 1999). Most of us have had experience with mastery testing in obtaining a driver's license. The written exam required to obtain a driver's license is designed to determine whether the applicant has acquired the basic knowledge necessary to operate a motor vehicle successfully and safely (e.g., state motoring laws and standards). A **cut score** had been previously established, and all scores equal to or above this score are reported as "pass" whereas scores below it are reported as "fail." If the cut score requires correctly answering 85% of the items, all examinees with scores of 84% or below fail and all with 85% and above pass. There is no practical distinction in such a decision between an examinee answering 85% of the items correctly and one who answered 100% correctly. They both pass! For many educators, mastery testing is viewed as the preferred way of assessing mastery or proficiency of basic educational skills. For example, a teacher can develop a test to assess students' mastery of multiplication of fractions or addition with decimals. Likewise, a teacher can develop a test to assess students' mastery of spelling words on a 3rd-grade reading list. In both of these situations, the teacher may set the cut score for designating mastery at 85%, and all students achieving a score of 85% or higher will be considered to have mastered the relevant knowledge or skills domain.

Another common criterion-referenced interpretative approach is referred to as "standards-based interpretations." Whereas mastery testing typically results in an all-or-none interpretation (i.e., the student either passes or fails), standards-based interpretations usually involve three to five performance categories. For example, the results of an achievement test might be reported as not proficient, partially proficient, proficient, or advanced performance (e.g., Linn & Gronlund, 2000). An old variant of this approach is the assignment of letter grades to reflect performance on classroom achievement tests. For example, many teachers assign letter grades based on the percentage of items correct on a test, which is another type of criterion-referenced interpretation. For example, As might be assigned for percentage correct scores between 90% and 100%, Bs for scores between 80% and 89%, Cs for scores between 70% and 79%, Ds for scores between 60% and 69%, and Fs for scores below 60%. Note that with this system a student with a score of 95% receives an A regardless of how other students scored. If all of the students in the class correctly answered 90% or more of the items correctly, they would all receive As on the test.

As noted previously, with norm-referenced interpretations the most important consideration is the relevance of the group that the examinee's performance is compared to.

The most important consideration with criterion-referenced interpretations is how clearly the knowledge or skill domain is specified or defined.

However, with criterion-referenced interpretations, there is no comparison group, and the most important consideration is how clearly the knowledge or skill domain being assessed is specified or defined (e.g., Popham, 2000). For criterion-referenced interpretations to provide useful information about what students know or what skills they possess, it is important that the knowledge or skill domain assessed by the test be clearly defined. To facilitate this, it is common for tests specifically designed to produce criterion-referenced interpretations to assess more limited or narrowly focused content domains than those designed to produce norm-referenced interpretations. For example, a test designed to produce norm-referenced interpretations might be developed to assess broad achievement in mathematics (e.g., ranging from simple number recognition to advanced algebraic computations). In contrast, a math test designed to produce criterion-referenced interpretations might be developed to assess the students' ability to add fractions. In this situation, the criterion-referenced domain is much more focused, which allows for more meaningful criterion-based interpretations. For example, if a student successfully completed 95% of the fractional addition problems, you would have a good idea of his or her math skills in this limited, but clearly defined area. In contrast, if a student scored at the 50th percentile on the norm-referenced broad mathematics achievement test, you would know that the performance was average for that age. However, you would not be able to make definitive statements about the specific types of math problems the student is able to perform. Although criterion-referenced interpretations are most applicable to narrowly defined domains, they are often applied to broader, less clearly defined domains. For example, most tests used for licensing professionals such as physicians, lawyers, teachers, or psychologists involve criterion-referenced interpretations.

Norm-Referenced, Criterion-Referenced, or Both?

It is not technically accurate to refer to norm-referenced or criterion-referenced tests. It is the interpretation of performance on a test that is either norm-referenced or criterion-referenced.

Early in this chapter we noted that it is not technically accurate to refer to norm-referenced tests or criterion-referenced tests. It is the interpretation of performance on a test that is either norm-referenced or criterion-referenced. As a result, it is possible for a test to produce both norm-referenced and criterion-referenced interpretations. That being said, for several reasons it is usually optimal for tests to be designed to produce either norm-referenced or criterion-referenced scores. Norm-referenced interpretations can be applied to a larger variety of tests than criterion-referenced interpretations. We have made the distinction between maximum performance tests (e.g., aptitude and achievement) and typical response tests (e.g., interest, attitudes, and behavior). Norm-referenced interpretations can be applied to both categories, but criterion-referenced interpretations are typically applied only to maximum performance tests. That is, because criterion-referenced scores reflect an examinee's knowledge or skills in a specific domain, it is not logical to apply them to measures of personality. Even in the broad category of maximum performance tests, norm-referenced interpretations tend to have broader applications. Consistent with their focus on well-defined knowledge and skills domains, criterion-referenced interpretations are most often applied to educational achievement tests or other tests designed to assess mastery of a clearly defined set of skills and abilities. Constructs such as aptitude and intelligence are typically broader and lend themselves best to norm-referenced interpretations. Even in the context of achievement testing we have alluded to the fact that tests designed for norm-referenced interpretations often cover broader knowledge and skill domains than those designed for criterion-referenced interpretations.

Tests can be developed that provide both norm-referenced and criterion-referenced interpretations.

In addition to the breadth or focus of the knowledge or skills domain being assessed, test developers consider other factors when developing tests intended primarily for either norm-referenced or criterion-referenced interpretations. For example, because tests designed for criterion-referenced interpretations typically have a narrow focus, they are able to devote a large number of items to measuring each objective or skill. In contrast, because tests designed for norm-referenced interpretations typically have a broader focus they may devote only a few items to measuring each objective or skill. When developing tests intended for norm-referenced interpretations, test developers will typically select items of average difficulty and eliminate extremely difficult or easy items. When developing tests intended for criterion-referenced interpretations, test developers match the difficulty of the items to the difficulty of the knowledge or skills domain being assessed.

Although our discussion to this point has emphasized differences between norm-referenced and criterion-referenced interpretations, they are not mutually exclusive. Tests can be developed that provide both norm-referenced and criterion-referenced interpretations. Both interpretative approaches have positive characteristics and provide useful information (see Table 3.4). Whereas norm-referenced interpretations provide important information about how an examinee performed relative to a specified reference group, criterion-referenced interpretations provide important information about how well an examinee has mastered a specified knowledge or skills domain. It is possible, and sometimes desirable, for a test to produce both norm-referenced and criterion-referenced scores. For example, it would be possible to interpret a student's test performance as "by correctly answering 75% of the multiplication problems, the student scored better than 60% of the students in the class." Although the development of a test to provide both norm-

TABLE 3.4   Characteristics of Norm-Referenced and Criterion-Referenced Scores

Norm-Referenced Interpretations	Criterion-Referenced Interpretations
Compare performance to a specific reference group—a relative interpretation.	Compare performance to a specific level of performance—an absolute interpretation.
Useful interpretations require a relevant reference group.	Useful interpretations require a carefully defined knowledge or skills domain.
Usually assess a fairly broad range of knowledge or skills.	Usually assess a limited or narrow domain of knowledge or skills.
Typically have only a limited number of items to measure each objective or skill.	Typically have several items to measure each test objective or skill.
Items are selected that are of medium difficulty and maximize variance; very difficult and very easy items are usually deleted.	Items are selected that provide good coverage of content domain; the difficulty of the items matches the difficulty of content domain.
Example: Percentile rank—a percentile rank of 80 indicates that the examinee scored better than 80% of the subjects in the reference group.	Example: Percentage correct—a percentage correct score of 80 indicates that the examinee successfully answered 80% of the test items.

referenced and criterion-referenced scores may require some compromises, the increased interpretative versatility may justify these compromises (e.g., Linn & Gronlund, 2000). As a result, some test publishers are beginning to produce more tests that provide both interpretative formats. Nevertheless, most tests are designed for *either* norm-referenced or criterion-referenced interpretations. Although the majority of published standardized tests are designed to produce norm-referenced interpretations, tests producing criterion-referenced interpretations play an extremely important role in educational and other settings.

Qualitative Description of Scores

Qualitative descriptions **of test scores help professionals communicate results in written reports and other formats.**

Test developers commonly provide **qualitative descriptions** of the scores produced by their tests. These qualitative descriptors help professionals communicate results in written reports and other formats. For example, the *Stanford-Binet Intelligence Scales, Fifth Edition (SB5)* (Roid, 2003) provides the following qualitative descriptions:

IQ	Classification
145 and above	Very Gifted or Highly Advanced
130–144	Gifted or Very Advanced
120–129	Superior
110–119	High Average
90–109	Average
80–89	Low Average
70–79	Borderline Impaired or Delayed
55–69	Mildly Impaired or Delayed
40–54	Moderately Impaired or Delayed

These qualitative descriptors help professionals communicate information about an examinee's performance in an accurate and consistent manner. That is, professionals using the SB5 should consistently use these descriptors when describing test performance.

A similar approach is often used with typical response assessments. For example, the *Behavior Assessment System for Children* (BASC; Reynolds & Kamphaus, 1998) provides the following descriptions of the clinical scales such as the depression or anxiety scales:

T-Score Range	Classification
70 and above	Clinically Significant
60–69	At-Risk
41–59	Average
31–40	Low
30 and below	Very Low

Summary

This chapter provided an overview of different types of test scores and their meaning. We started by noting that raw scores, while easy to calculate, usually provide little useful information about an examinee's performance on a test. As a result, we usually transform raw scores into derived scores. The many different types of derived scores can be classified as either norm-referenced or criterion-referenced. Norm-referenced score interpretations compare an examinee's performance on a test to the performance of other people, typically the standardization sample. When making norm-referenced interpretations, it is important to evaluate the adequacy of the standardization sample. This involves determining if the standardization is representative of the examinees the test will be used with; if the sample is current; and if the sample is of adequate size to produce stable statistics.

When making norm-referenced interpretations it is useful to have a basic understanding of the normal distribution (also referred to as the bell-shaped curve). The normal distribution is a distribution that characterizes many naturally occurring variables and has several characteristics that psychometricians find very useful. The most useful of these characteristics is that predictable proportions of scores occur at specific points in the distribution. For example, if you know that an individual's score is one standard deviation above the mean on a normally distributed variable, you know that the individual's score exceeds approximately 84% of the scores in the standardization sample. This predictable distribution of scores facilitates the interpretation and reporting of test scores.

Standard scores are norm-referenced derived scores that have a predetermined mean and standard deviation. A variety of standard scores is commonly used today, including:

- z-scores: mean of 0 and standard deviation of 1
- T-scores: mean of 50 and standard deviation of 10
- Wechsler IQs: mean of 100 and standard deviation of 15
- Stanford-Binet IQs: mean of 100 and standard deviation of 16 (recently changed to 50 of 15)
- CEEB Scores (SAT/GRE): mean of 500 and standard deviation of 100

By combining an understanding of the normal distribution with the information provided by standard scores, you can easily interpret an examinee's performance relative to the specified reference group. For example, an examinee with a T-score of 60 scored 1 standard deviation above the mean. You know that approximately 84% of the scores in a normal distribution are below 1 standard deviation above the mean. Therefore, the examinee's score exceeded approximately 84% of the scores in the reference group.

When scores are *not* normally distributed (i.e., do not take the form of a normal distribution), test publishers often use normalized standard scores. These normalized scores often look just like regular standard scores, but they are computed in a different manner. Nevertheless, they are interpreted in a similar manner. For example, if a test publisher reports normalized T-scores, they will have a mean of 50 and standard deviation of 10, just like regular T-scores. There are some unique normalized standard scores, including:

- Stanine scores: mean of 5 and standard deviation of 2
- Wechsler Subtest Scaled scores: mean of 10 and standard deviation of 3
- Normal Curve Equivalent (NCE): mean of 50 and standard deviation of 21.06

Another common type of norm-referenced score is percentile rank. This popular format is one of the most easily understood norm-referenced derived scores. Like all norm-referenced scores, the percentile rank reflects an examinee's performance relative to a specific reference group. However, instead of using a scale with a specific mean and standard deviation, the percentile rank simply specifies the percentage of individuals scoring below a given point in a distribution. For example, a percentile rank of 80 indicates that 80% of the individuals in the reference group scored below this score. Percentile ranks have the advantage of being easily explained to and understood by individuals without formal training in psychometrics.

The final norm-referenced derived scores we discussed were grade and age equivalents. For numerous reasons, we recommend that you avoid using these scores. If you are required to report them, also report standard scores and percentile ranks and emphasize these when interpreting the results.

In contrast to norm-referenced scores, criterion-referenced scores compare an examinee's performance to a specified level of performance referred to as a criterion. Probably the most common criterion-referenced score is the percent correct score routinely reported on classroom achievement tests. For example, if you report that a student correctly answered 80% of the items on a spelling test, this is a criterion-referenced interpretation. Another type of criterion-referenced interpretation is mastery testing. On a mastery test you determine whether examinees have achieved a specified level of mastery on the knowledge or skill domain. Here, performance is typically reported as either pass or fail. If examinees score above the cut score they pass; if they score below the cut score they fail. Another criterion-referenced interpretation is referred to as standards-based interpretations. Instead of reporting performance as simply pass/fail, standard-based interpretations typically involve three to five performance categories.

With criterion-referenced interpretations, a prominent consideration is how clearly the knowledge or domain is defined. For useful criterion-referenced interpretations, the knowledge or skill domain being assessed must be clearly defined. To facilitate this, criterion-referenced interpretations are typically applied to tests that measure focused or narrow domains. For example, a math test designed to produce criterion-referenced scores might be limited to the addition of fractions. This way, if a student correctly answers 95% of the fraction problems, you will have useful information regarding the student's proficiency with this specific type of math problem. You are not able to make inferences about a student's proficiency in other areas of math, but you will know if this specific type of math problem was mastered. If the math test contained a wide variety of math problems (as is common with norm-referenced tests), it would be more difficult to specify exactly in which areas a student is proficient.

We closed the chapter by noting that the terms *norm-referenced* and *criterion-referenced* refer to the interpretation of test performance, not the test itself. Although it is often optimal to develop a test to produce either norm-referenced or criterion-referenced scores, it is possible and sometimes desirable for a test to produce both norm-referenced and criterion-referenced scores. This may require some compromises when developing the test, but the increased flexibility may justify these compromises. Nevertheless, most tests are designed for either norm-referenced or criterion-referenced interpretations, and most published standardized tests produce norm-referenced interpretations. That being said, tests that produce criterion-referenced interpretations have many important applications, particularly in educational settings.

KEY TERMS AND CONCEPTS

RECOMMENDED READINGS

American Educational Research Association, American Psychological Association, & National Council on Measurement in Education (1999). *Standards for educational and psychological testing.* Washington, DC: AERA. For the technically minded, Chapter 4, Scales, Norms, and Score Comparability, is must reading!

Lyman, H. B. (1998). *Test scores and what they mean.* Boston: Allyn & Bacon. This text provides a comprehensive and very readable discussion of test scores. An excellent resource!

INTERNET SITES OF INTEREST

www.teachersandfamilies.com/open/parent/scores1.cfm
Understanding Test Scores: A Primer for Parents is a user-friendly discussion of tests that is accurate and readable. Another good resource for parents.

http://childparenting.miningco.com/cs/learningproblems/a/wisciii.htm
This Parents' Guide to Understanding the IQ Test Scores contains a good discussion of the use of intelligence tests in schools and how they help in assessing learning disabilities. A good resource for parents.

PRACTICE ITEMS

1. Transform the following raw scores to the specified standard score formats. The raw score distribution has a mean of 70 and a standard deviation of 10.
   a. Raw score = 85 z-score = T-score =
   b. Raw score = 60 z-score = T-score =
   c. Raw score = 55 z-score = T-score =
   d. Raw score = 95 z-score = T-score =
   e. Raw score = 75 z-score = T-score =

2. Convert the following z-scores to T-scores and CEEB scores.
   a. z-score = 1.5 T-score =   CEEB score =
   b. z-score = −1.5 T-score =   CEEB score =
   c. z-score = 2.5 T-score =   CEEB score =
   d. z-score = −2.0 T-score =   CEEB score =
   e. z-score = −1.70 T-score =   CEEB score =

4

Reliability for Teachers

It is the user who must take responsibility for determining whether or not scores are sufficiently trustworthy to justify anticipated uses and interpretations.
—AERA et al., 1999, p. 31

CHAPTER HIGHLIGHTS

Errors of Measurement

Methods of Estimating Reliability

The Standard Error of Measurement

Reliability: Practical Strategies for Teachers

LEARNING OBJECTIVES

After reading and studying this chapter, students should be able to:

1. Define and explain the importance of reliability in educational assessment.
2. Define and explain the concept of measurement error.
3. Explain classical test theory and its importance to educational assessment.
4. Describe the major sources of measurement error and give examples.
5. Identify the major methods for estimating reliability and describe how these analyses are performed.
6. Identify the sources of measurement error that are reflected in different reliability estimates.
7. Explain how multiple scores can be combined in a composite to enhance reliability.
8. Describe the factors that should be considered when selecting a reliability coefficient for a specific assessment application.
9. Explain the factors that should be considered when evaluating the magnitude of reliability coefficients.
10. Describe steps that can be taken to improve reliability.
11. Discuss special issues in estimating reliability such as estimating the reliability of speed tests and mastery testing.
12. Define the standard error of measurement (SEM) and explain its importance.
13. Explain how SEM is calculated and describe its relation to reliability.
14. Explain how confidence intervals are calculated and used in educational and psychological assessment.
15. Describe and apply shortcut procedures for estimating the reliability of classroom tests.

In simplest terms, in the context of measurement, *reliability* refers to consistency or stability of assessment results.

Most dictionaries define reliability in terms of dependability, trustworthiness, or having a high degree of confidence in something. Reliability in the context of educational and psychological measurement is concerned to some extent with these same factors, but is extended to such concepts as stability and consistency. In simplest terms, in the context of measurement, **reliability** refers to consistency or stability of assessment results. Although it is common for people to refer to the "reliability of a test," in the new *Standards for Educational and Psychological Testing* (AERA et al., 1999) reliability is considered to be a characteristic of scores or assessment results, not tests themselves. Consider the following example: A teacher administers a 25-item math test in the morning to assess the students' skill in multiplying two-digit numbers. If the test had been administered in the afternoon rather than the morning, would Susie's score on the test have been the same? Because there are literally thousands of two-digit multiplication problems, if the teacher had asked a different group of 25 two-digit multiplication problems, would Susie have received the same score? What about the ambulance that went by, its siren wailing loudly, causing Johnny to look up and watch for a few seconds? Did this affect his score, and did it affect Susie's, who kept working quietly? Joey wasn't feeling well that morning but came to school because he felt the test was so important. Would his score have been better if he had waited to take the test when he was feeling better? Would the students have received the same scores if another teacher had graded the test? All of these questions involve issues of reliability. They all ask if the test produces consistent scores.

As you can see from these examples, numerous factors can affect reliability. The time the test is administered, the specific set of questions included on the test, distractions due to external (e.g., ambulances) or internal (e.g., illness) events, and the person grading the test are just a few of these factors. In this chapter you will learn to take many of the sources of unreliability into account when selecting or developing assessments and evaluating scores. You will also learn to estimate the degree of reliability in test scores with a method that best fits your particular situation. First, however, we will introduce the concept of measurement error as it is essential to developing a thorough understanding of reliability.

Errors of Measurement

Some degree of *measurement error* is inherent in all measurement.

Some degree of error is inherent in all measurement. Although **measurement error** has largely been studied in the context of psychological and educational tests, measurement error is clearly not unique to this context. In fact, as Nunnally and Bernstein (1994) point out, measurement in other scientific disciplines has as much, if not more, error than that in psychology and education. They give the example of physiological blood pressure measurement, which is considerably less reliable than many educational tests. Even in situations in which we generally believe measurement is exact, some error is present. If we asked a dozen people to time a 440-yard race using the same brand of stopwatch, it is extremely unlikely that they would all report precisely the same time. If we had a dozen people and a measuring tape graduated in millimeters, and required each person to measure independently the length of a 100-foot strip of land, it is unlikely all of them would report the same answer to the nearest millimeter. In the physical sciences the introduction of more technologically sophisticated measurement devices has reduced, but not eliminated, measurement error.

Different theories or models have been developed to address measurement issues, but possibly the most influential is classical test theory (also called true score theory). According to this theory, every score on a test is composed of two components: the **true score** (i.e., the score that would be obtained if there were no errors) and the **error score**: Obtained Score = True Score + Error. This can be represented in a very simple equation:

$$X_i + T + E$$

Here we use X_i to represent the obtained or observed score of an individual. X_i is the score the test taker received on the test. The symbol T is used to represent an individual's true score and reflects the test taker's true skills, abilities, knowledge, attitudes, or whatever the test measures. Finally, E represents measurement error.

Measurement error reduces the usefulness of measurement. It limits the extent to which test results can be generalized and reduces the confidence we have in test results (AERA et al., 1999). Practically speaking, when we administer a test we are interested in knowing the test taker's true score. Due to the presence of measurement error we can never know with absolute confidence what the true score is. However, if we have information about the reliability of measurement, we can establish intervals around an obtained score and calculate the probability that the true score will fall within the interval specified. We will come back to this with a more detailed explanation when we discuss the standard error of measurement later in this chapter. First, we will elaborate on the major sources of measurement error. It should be noted that we will limit our discussion to random measurement error. Some writers distinguish between random and systematic errors. Systematic error is much harder to detect and requires special statistical methods that are beyond the scope of this text. (Special Interest Topic 4.1 provides a brief introduction to Generalizability Theory, an extension of classical reliability theory.)

> **Measurement error limits the extent to which test results can be generalized and reduces the confidence we have in test results (AERA et al., 1999).**

Sources of Measurement Error

> **As educational professionals we should work to identify sources of measurement error and minimize their impact to the extent possible.**

Because measurement error is so pervasive, it is beneficial to be knowledgeable about its characteristics and aware of the methods that are available for estimating its magnitude. As educational professionals we should also work to identify sources of measurement error and minimize their impact to the extent possible. Generally, whenever you hear a discussion of reliability or read about the reliability of test scores, it is the score's relative freedom from measurement errors that is being discussed. Reliable assessment results are relatively free from measurement error whereas less reliable results are influenced to a larger degree by measurement error. A number of factors may introduce error into test scores and even though all cannot be assigned to distinct categories, it may be helpful to group these sources in some

SPECIAL INTEREST TOPIC **4.1**
Generalizability Theory

Lee Cronbach and colleagues developed an extension of classical reliability theory known as "generalizability theory" in the 1960s and 1970s. Cronbach was instrumental in the development of the general theory of reliability discussed in this chapter during and after World War II. The basic focus of generalizability theory is to examine various conditions that might affect the reliability of a test score. In classical reliability theory there are only two sources for variation in an observed test score: true score and random error. Suppose, however, that for different groups of people the scores reflect different things. For example, boys and girls might respond differently to career interest items. When the items for a particular career area are then grouped into a scale, the reliability of the scale might be quite different for boys and girls as a result. This gender effect becomes a limitation on the generalizability of the test's functioning with respect to reliability.

Generalizability theory extends the concept of reliability as the ratio of true score variance to total score variance by adding other possible sources of true score variation to both the numerator and the denominator of the reliability estimate. Because gender is a reliable indicator, if there is significant gender variation on a test scale due to gender differences, this additional variation will change the original true score variation. What originally appeared to be high true score variation might instead be a modest true score variation and large gender variation. In some instances the true score variation may be high within the boy's group but near zero within the girls' group. Thus, in this study, gender limits the generalizability of the test with respect to reliability.

The sources of variation that might be considered are usually limited to theoretically relevant characteristics of population, ecology, or time. For example, population characteristics may include gender, ethnicity, or region of residence. These are usually discussed as fixed sources, because typically all characteristics will be present in the data analysis (male and female, all ethnic groups of interest, or all regions to be considered). Sources are considered random when only a sample of the possible current or future population is involved in the analysis. Common random sources include raters or observers; classrooms, schools, or districts; clinics or hospitals; or other organized groupings in which respondents are placed. In a nursing school, for example, students may be evaluated in a series of activities that they are expected to have mastered (administering an injection, adjusting a drip, and determining medication levels). Several instructors might rate each activity. Because we are usually interested in how reliable the ratings are for raters like those in the study, but not just those specific raters, the rater source is considered a random source. Random sources are always included only in the denominator of the reliability ratio. That is, the variance associated with raters will be added to the error variance and true score variance only to the total variance term.

Although calculating generalizability coefficients is beyond the scope of this text, the general procedure is to use a statistical analysis program such as Statistical Package for the Social Sciences (SPSS) or Statistical Analysis System (SAS). These statistical programs have analysis options that will estimate the variance components (i.e., the variances of each source of variation specified by the analyst). A numerical value for each source is obtained, and the generalizability value is calculated from specific rules of computation that have been derived over the last several decades. Some psychometricians advocate simply examining the magnitude of the variances. For example, if true score variance in the gender study mentioned is 10, but gender variance is 50, while error variance per item is 2, it is clear that most of the apparent reliability of the test is due to gender differences rather than individual differences. Boy and girl studies might be conducted separately at this point. In the nursing study, if rater variance is 3 and individual true score variance is 40, it is clear without further study that raters will have little affect on the reliability of the nursing assessments.

manner and to discuss their relative contributions. The types of errors that are our greatest concern are errors due to content sampling and time sampling.

Content Sampling Error.   Tests rarely, if ever, include every possible question or evaluate every possible relevant behavior. Let's revisit the example we introduced at the beginning of this chapter. A teacher administers a math test designed to assess students' skill in multiplying two-digit numbers. We noted that there are literally thousands of two-digit multiplication problems. Obviously it would be impossible for the teacher to develop and administer a test that includes all possible items. Instead, a universe or domain of test items is defined based on the content of the material to be covered. From this domain a sample of test questions is taken. In this example, the teacher decided to select 25 items to measure students' ability. These 25 items are simply a sample and, as with any sampling procedure, may not be representative of the domain from which they are drawn. The error that results from differences between the sample of items (i.e., the test) and the domain of items (i.e., all the possible items) is referred to as **content sampling error**. Content sampling error is typically considered the largest source of error in test scores and therefore is the source that concerns us most. Fortunately, content sampling error is also the easiest and most accurately estimated source of measurement error.

The amount of measurement error due to content sampling is determined by how well we sample the total domain of items. If the items on a test are a good sample of the domain, the amount of measurement error due to content sampling will be relatively small. If the items on a test are a poor sample of the domain, the amount of measurement error due to content sampling will be relatively large. Measurement error resulting from content sampling is estimated by analyzing the degree of similarity among the items making up the test. In other words, we analyze the test items to determine how well they correlate with one another and with the test taker's standing on the construct being measured. We will explore a variety of methods for estimating measurement errors due to content sampling later in this chapter.

> **If the items on a test are a good sample of the domain, the amount of measurement error due to content sampling will be relatively small.**

Time Sampling Error.   Measurement error can also be introduced by one's choice of a particular time to administer the test. If Eddie did not have breakfast and the math test was just before lunch, he might be distracted or hurried and not perform as well as if he took the test after lunch. But Michael, who ate too much at lunch and was up a little late last night, was a little sleepy in the afternoon and might not perform as well on an afternoon test as he would have on the morning test. If during the morning testing session a neighboring class was making enough noise to be disruptive, the class might have performed better in the afternoon when the neighboring class was relatively quiet. These are all examples of situations in which random changes in the test taker (e.g., fatigue, illness, anxiety) or the testing environment (e.g., distractions, temperature) impact performance on the test. This type of measurement error is referred to as **time sampling error** and reflects random fluctuations in performance from one situation or time to another and limits our ability to generalize test results across different situations. Some assessment experts refer to this

> **Measurement error due to time sampling reflects random fluctuations in performance from one situation to another and limits our ability to generalize test scores across different situations.**

type of error as temporal instability. As you might expect, testing experts have developed methods of estimating error due to time sampling.

Other Sources of Error.   Although errors due to content sampling and time sampling account for the major proportion of random error in testing, administrative and scoring errors that do not affect all test takers equally will also contribute to the random error observed in scores. Clerical errors committed while adding up a student's score or an administrative error on an individually administered test are common examples. When the scoring of a test relies heavily on the subjective judgment of the person grading the test or involves subtle discriminations, it is important to consider differences in graders, usually referred to as inter-scorer or **inter-rater differences**. That is, would the test taker receive the same score if different individuals graded the test? For example, on an essay test would two different graders assign the same scores? These are just a few examples of sources of error that do not fit neatly into the broad categories of content or time sampling errors.

Methods of Estimating Reliability

You will note that we are referring to reliability as being *estimated*. This is because the absolute or precise reliability of assessment results cannot be known. Just as we always have some error in test scores, we also have some error in our attempts to measure reliability. Earlier in this chapter we introduced the idea that test scores are composed of two components, the true score and the error score. We represented this with the equation:

$$X_i = T + E$$

As you remember, X_i represents an individual's obtained score, T represents the true score, and E represents random measurement error. This equation can be extended to incorporate the concept of variance. This extension indicates that the variance of test scores is the sum of the **true score variance** plus the **error variance,** and is represented in the following equation:

$$\sigma_X^2 = \sigma_T^2 + \sigma_E^2$$

Here, σ_X^2 represents the variance of the total test, σ_T^2 represents true score variance, and σ_E^2 represents the variance due to measurement error. True score variance reflects differences in test takers due to real differences in skills, abilities, knowledge, attitudes, and so on, whereas the total score variance is made up of true score variance plus variance due to all the sources of random error we have previously described.

The general symbol for the reliability of assessment results is r_{xx} and is referred to as the **reliability coefficient.** We estimate the reliability of a test score as the ratio of true score variance to total score variance. Mathematically, reliability is written:

$$r_{xx} = \sigma_T^2 / \sigma_X^2$$

This equation defines the reliability of test scores as the proportion of test score variance due to true score differences. The reliability coefficient is considered to be the summary mathematical representation of this ratio or proportion.

Reliability coefficients can be classified into three broad categories (AERA et al., 1999). These include (1) coefficients derived from the administration of the same test on different occasions (i.e., test-retest reliability), (2) coefficients based on the administration of parallel forms of a test (i.e., alternate-form reliability), and (3) coefficients derived from a single administration of a test (internal consistency coefficients). A fourth type, inter-rater reliability, is indicated when scoring involves a significant degree of subjective judgment. The major methods of estimating reliability are summarized in Table 4.1. Each of these approaches produces a reliability coefficient (r_{xx}) that can be interpreted in terms of the proportion or percentage of test score variance attributable to true variance. For example, a reliability coefficient of 0.90 indicates that 90% of the variance in test scores is attributable to true variance. The remaining 10% reflects error variance. We will now consider each of these methods of estimating reliability.

> **Reliability can be defined as the proportion of test score variance due to true score differences.**

TABLE 4.1   Major Types of Reliability

Type of Reliability Estimate	Number of Test Forms	Number of Testing Sessions	Summary
Test-Retest	One form	Two sessions	Administer the same test to the same group at two different sessions.
Alternate forms			
Simultaneous administration	Two forms	One session	Administer two forms of the test to the same group in the same session.
Delayed administration	Two forms	Two sessions	Administer two forms of the test to the same group at two different sessions.
Split-half	One form	One session	Administer the test to a group one time. Split the test into two equivalent halves.
Coefficient alpha or KR-20	One form	One session	Administer the test to a group one time. Apply appropriate procedures.
Inter-rater	One form	One session	Administer the test to a group one time. Two or more raters score the test independently.

Test-Retest Reliability

Test-retest reliability is sensitive to measurement error due to time sampling and is an index of the stability of scores over time.

Probably the most obvious way to estimate the reliability of a test is to administer the same test to the same group of individuals on two different occasions. With this approach the reliability coefficient is obtained by simply calculating the correlation between the scores on the two administrations. For example, we could administer our 25-item math test one week after the initial administration and then correlate the scores obtained on the two administrations. This estimate of reliability is referred to as **test-retest reliability** and is sensitive to measurement error due to time sampling. It is an index of the stability of test scores over time. Because many tests are intended to measure fairly stable characteristics, we expect tests of these constructs to produce stable scores. Test-retest reliability reflects the degree to which test scores can be generalized across different situations or over time.

One important consideration when calculating and evaluating test-retest reliability is the length of the interval between the two test administrations.

One important consideration when calculating and evaluating test-retest reliability is the length of the interval between the two test administrations. If the test-retest interval is very short (e.g., hours or days), the reliability estimate may be artificially inflated by memory and practice effects from the first administration. If the test interval is longer, the estimate of reliability may be lowered not only by the instability of the scores but also by actual changes in the test takers during the extended period. In practice, there is no single "best" time interval, but the optimal interval is determined by the way the test results are to be used. For example, intelligence is a construct or characteristic that is thought to be fairly stable, so it would be reasonable to expect stability in intelligence scores over weeks or months. In contrast, an individual's mood (e.g., depressed, elated, nervous) is more subject to transient fluctuations, and stability across weeks or months would not be expected.

In addition to the construct being measured, the way the test is to be used is an important consideration in determining what is an appropriate test-retest interval. Because the SAT is used to predict performance in college, it is sensible to expect stability over relatively long periods of time. In other situations, long-term stability is much less of an issue. For example, the long-term stability of a classroom achievement test (such as our math test) is not a major concern because it is expected that the students will be enhancing existing skills and acquiring new ones due to class instruction and studying. In summary, when evaluating the stability of test scores, one should consider the length of the test–retest interval in the context of the characteristics being measured and how the scores are to be used.

The test-retest approach does have significant limitations, the most prominent being carryover effects from the first to second testing. Practice and memory effects result in different amounts of improvement in retest scores for different test takers. These carryover effects prevent the two administrations from being independent and as a result the reliability coefficients may be artificially inflated. In other instances, repetition of the test may change either the nature of the test or the test taker in some subtle way (Ghiselli, Campbell, & Zedeck, 1981). As a result, only tests that are not appreciably influenced by these carryover effects are suitable for this method of estimating reliability.

The test-retest approach does have significant limitations, the most prominent being carry-over effects from the first to second testing.

Alternate-Form Reliability

Another approach to estimating reliability involves the development of two equivalent or parallel forms of the test. The development of these alternate forms requires a detailed test plan and considerable effort because the tests must truly be parallel in terms of content, difficulty, and other relevant characteristics. The two forms of the test are then administered to the same group of individuals and the correlation is calculated between the scores on the two assessments. In our example of the 25-item math test, the teacher could develop a parallel test containing 25 new problems involving the multiplication of double digits. To be parallel the items would need to be presented in the same format and be of the same level of difficulty. Two fairly common procedures are used to establish **alternate-form reliability.** One is alternate-form reliability based on simultaneous administrations and is obtained when the two forms of the test are administered on the same occasion (i.e., back to back). The other, alternate form with delayed administration, is obtained when the two forms of the test are administered on two different occasions. Alternate-form reliability based on simultaneous administration is primarily sensitive to measurement error related to content sampling. Alternate-form reliability with delayed administration is sensitive to measurement error due to both content sampling and time sampling.

Alternate-form reliability **based on simultaneous administration is primarily sensitive to measurement error due to content sampling.**

Alternate-form reliability based on delayed administration is sensitive to measurement error due to content sampling and time sampling.

Alternate-form reliability has the advantage of reducing the carryover effects that are a prominent concern with test-retest reliability. However, although practice and memory effects may be reduced using the alternate-form approach, they are often not fully eliminated. Simply exposing test takers to the common format required for parallel tests often results in some carryover effects even if the content of the two tests is different. For example, a test taker given a test measuring nonverbal reasoning abilities may develop strategies during the administration of the first form that alter her approach to the second form, even if the specific content of the items is different. Another limitation of the alternate-form approach to estimating reliability is that relatively few tests, standardized or teacher made, have alternate forms. As we suggested, the development of alternate forms that are actually equivalent is a time-consuming process, and many test developers do not pursue this option. Nevertheless, at times it is desirable to have more than one form of a test, and when multiple forms exist, alternate-form reliability is an important consideration.

Internal-Consistency Reliability

Internal-consistency reliability estimates primarily reflect errors related to content sampling. These estimates are based on the relationship between items within a test and are derived from a single administration of the test.

Split-Half Reliability. Estimating **split-half reliability** involves administering a test and then dividing the test into two equivalent halves that are scored independently. The results on one-half the test are then correlated with results on the other half of the test by calculating the Pearson product-moment correlation. Obviously, there are many ways a test can be

Split-half reliability can be calculated from one administration of a test and reflects error due to content sampling.

divided in half. For example, one might correlate scores on the first half of the test with scores on the second half. This is usually not a good idea because the items on some tests get more difficult as the test progresses, resulting in halves that are not actually equivalent. Other factors, such as practice effects, fatigue, or declining attention that increases as the test progresses, can also make the first and second halves of the test not equivalent. A more acceptable approach would be to assign test items randomly to one half or the other. However, the most common approach is to use an odd–even split. Here all "odd" numbered items go into one half and all "even" numbered items go into the other half. A correlation is then calculated between scores on the odd-numbered and even-numbered items.

Before we can use this correlation coefficient as an estimate of reliability, there is one more task to perform. Because we are actually correlating two halves of the test, the reliability coefficient does not take into account the reliability of the test when the two halves are combined. In essence, this initial coefficient reflects the reliability of only a shortened, half test. As a general rule, longer tests are more reliable than shorter tests. If we have twice as many test items, then we are able to sample the domain of test questions more accurately. The better we sample the domain the lower the error due to content sampling and the higher the reliability of our test. To "put the two halves of the test back together" with regard to a reliability estimate, we use a correction formula commonly referred to as the **Spearman-Brown formula.** To estimate the reliability of the full test, the Spearman-Brown formula is generally applied as:

$$\text{Reliability of Full Test} = \frac{2 \times \text{Reliability of Half Test}}{1 + \text{Reliability of Half Test}}$$

Here is an example. Suppose the correlation between odd and even halves of your mid-term in this course were 0.74, the calculation using the Spearman-Brown formula would go as follows:

$$\text{Reliability of Full Test} = \frac{2 \times 0.74}{1 + 0.74}$$

$$\text{Reliability of Full Test} = \frac{1.48}{1.74} = .85$$

The reliability coefficient of 0.85 estimates the reliability of the full test when the odd–even halves correlated at 0.74. This demonstrates that the uncorrected split-half reliability coefficient presents an underestimate of the reliability of the full test. Table 4.2 provides examples of half-test coefficients and the corresponding full-test coefficients that were corrected with the Spearman-Brown formula. By looking at the first row in this table, you will see that a half-test correlation of 0.50 corresponds to a corrected full-test coefficient of 0.67.

Although the odd–even approach is the most common way to divide a test and will generally produce equivalent halves, certain situations deserve special attention. For example, if you have a test with a relatively small number of items (e.g., <8), it may be desirable to divide the test into equivalent halves based on a careful review of item characteristics such as content, format, and difficulty. Another situation that deserves special attention involves groups of items that deal with an integrated problem (this is referred to as a testlet). For ex-

TABLE 4.2   Half-Test Coefficients and Corresponding Full-Test
Coefficients Corrected with the Spearman-Brown Formula

Half-Test Correlation	Spearman-Brown Reliability
0.50	0.67
0.55	0.71
0.60	0.75
0.65	0.79
0.70	0.82
0.75	0.86
0.80	0.89
0.85	0.92
0.90	0.95
0.95	0.97

ample, if multiple questions refer to a specific diagram or reading passage, that whole set of questions should be included in the same half of the test. Splitting integrated problems can artificially inflate the reliability estimate (e.g., Sireci, Thissen, & Wainer, 1991).

An advantage of the split-half approach to reliability is that it can be calculated from a single administration of a test. However, because only one testing session is involved, this approach reflects errors due only to content sampling and is not sensitive to time sampling errors.

Coefficient alpha and Kuder-Richardson reliability **are sensitive to error introduced by content sampling, but also reflect the heterogeneity of test content.**

Coefficient Alpha and Kuder-Richardson Reliability.   Other approaches to estimating reliability from a single administration of a test are based on formulas developed by Kuder and Richardson (1937) and Cronbach (1951). Instead of comparing responses on two halves of the test as in split-half reliability, this approach examines the consistency of responding to all the individual items on the test. Reliability estimates produced with these formulas can be thought of as the average of all possible split-half coefficients. Like split-half reliability, these estimates are sensitive to measurement error introduced by content sampling. Additionally, they are also sensitive to the heterogeneity of the test content. When we refer to **content heterogeneity,** we are concerned with the degree to which the test items measure related characteristics. For example, our 25-item math test involving multiplying two-digit numbers would probably be more homogeneous than a test designed to measure both multiplication and division. An even more heterogeneous test would be one that involves multiplication and reading comprehension, two fairly dissimilar content domains.

While Kuder and Richardson's formulas and coefficient alpha both reflect item heterogeneity and errors due to content sampling, there is an important difference in terms of their application. In their original article Kuder and Richardson (1937) presented numerous formulas for estimating reliability. The most commonly used formula is known as the **Kuder-Richardson formula 20** (KR-20). KR-20 is applicable when test items are scored dichotomously, that is, simply right or wrong, as 0 or 1. **Coefficient alpha** (Cronbach, 1951) is a more general form of KR-20 that also deals with test items that produce scores with multiple values (e.g., 0, 1, or 2). Because coefficient alpha is more broadly applicable, it has become the preferred statistic for estimating internal consistency (Keith & Reynolds, 1990). Tables 4.3 and 4.4 illustrate the calculation of KR-20 and coefficient alpha, respectively.

TABLE 4.3   Calculating KR-20

KR-20 is sensitive to measurement error due to content sampling and is also a measure of item heterogeneity. KR-20 is applicable when test items are scored dichotomously, that is, simply right or wrong, as 0 or 1. The formula for calculating KR-20 is:

$$\text{KR-20} = k/k - 1\left(\frac{\text{SD}^2 - \sum p_i \times q_i}{\text{SD}^2}\right)$$

where

k = number of items
SD^2 = variance of total test scores
p_i = proportion of correct responses on item
q_i = proportion of incorrect responses on item

Consider these data for a five-item test administered to six students. Each item could receive a score of either 1 or 0.

	Item 1	Item 2	Item 3	Item 4	Item 5	Total Score
Student 1	1	0	1	1	1	4
Student 1	1	1	1	1	1	5
Student 3	1	0	1	0	0	2
Student 4	0	0	0	1	0	1
Student 5	1	1	1	1	1	5
Student 6	1	1	0	1	1	4
p_i	0.8333	0.5	0.6667	0.8333	0.6667	$\text{SD}^2 = 2.25$
q_i	0.1667	0.5	0.3333	0.1667	0.3333	
$p_i \times q_i$	0.1389	0.25	0.2222	0.1389	0.2222	

Note: When calculating SD^2, n was used in the denominator.

$$\sum p_i \times q_i = 0.1389 + 0.25 + 0.2222 + 0.1389 + 0.2222$$

$$\sum p_i \times q_i = 0.972$$

$$\text{KR-20} = 5/4\left(\frac{2.25 - 0.972}{2.25}\right)$$
$$= 1.25(1.278/2.25)$$
$$= 1.25(.568)$$
$$= 0.71$$

TABLE 4.4   Calculating Coefficient Alpha

Coefficient alpha is sensitive to measurement error due to content sampling and is also a measure of item heterogeneity. It can be applied to tests with items that are scored dichotomously or that have multiple values. The formula for calculating coefficient alpha is:

$$\text{Coefficient alpha} = \left(\frac{k}{k-1}\right)\left(1 - \frac{\sum SD_i^2}{SD^2}\right)$$

where
$$k = \text{number of items}$$
$$SD_i^2 = \text{variance of individual items}$$
$$SD^2 = \text{variance of total test scores}$$

Consider these data for a five-item test that was administered to six students. Each item could receive a score ranging from 1 to 5.

	Item 1	Item 2	Item 3	Item 4	Item 5	Total Score
Student 1	4	3	4	5	5	21
Student 2	3	3	2	3	3	14
Student 3	2	3	2	2	1	10
Student 4	4	4	5	3	4	20
Student 5	2	3	4	2	3	14
Student 6	2	2	2	1	3	10
SD_i^2	0.8056	0.3333	1.4722	1.5556	1.4722	$SD^2 = 18.81$

Note: When calculating SD_i^2 and SD^2, n was used in the denominator.

$$\text{Coefficient Alpha} = 5/4\left(1 - \frac{0.8056 + 0.3333 + 1.4722 + 1.5556 + 1.4722}{18.81}\right)$$
$$= 1.25(1 - 5.63889/18.81)$$
$$= 1.25(1 - 0.29978)$$
$$= 1.25(0.70)$$
$$= 0.875$$

Inter-rater Reliability

If the scoring of a test relies on subjective judgment, it is important to evaluate the degree of agreement when different individuals score the test. This is referred to as inter-scorer or **inter-rater reliability.** Estimating inter-rater reliability is a fairly straightforward process. The test is administered one time and two individuals independently score each test. A correlation is then calculated between the scores obtained by the two scorers. This estimate of reliability is not sensitive to error due to content or time sampling, but only reflects differences due to the individuals scoring the test. In addition to the correlational approach, inter-rater agreement can also be evaluated by calculating the percentage of

> If the scoring of an assessment relies on subjective judgment, it is important to evaluate the degree of agreement when different individuals score the test. This is referred to as *inter-rater reliability.*

Calculating Inter-rater Agreement

Performance assessments require test takers to complete a process or produce a product in a context that closely resembles real-life situations. For example, a student might engage in a debate, compose a poem, or perform a piece of music. The evaluation of these types of performances is typically based on scoring rubrics that specify what aspects of the student's performance should be considered when providing a score or grade. The scoring of these types of assessments obviously involves the subjective judgment of the individual scoring the performance, and as a result inter-rater reliability is a concern. As noted in the text one approach to estimating inter-rater reliability is to calculate the correlation between the scores that are assigned by two judges. Another approach is to calculate the percentage of agreement between the judges' scores.

Consider an example wherein two judges rated poems composed by 25 students. The poems were scored from 1 to 5 based on criteria specified in a rubric, with 1 being the lowest performance and 5 being the highest. The results are illustrated in the following table:

Ratings of Rater 2	Ratings of Rater 1				
	1	*2*	*3*	*4*	*5*
5	0	0	1	2	4
4	0	0	2	3	2
3	0	2	3	1	0
2	1	1	1	0	0
1	1	1	0	0	0

Once the data are recorded you can calculate inter-rater agreement with the following formula:

$$\text{Inter-rater Agreement} = \frac{\text{Number of Cases Assigned the Same Scores}}{\text{Total Number of Cases}} \times 100$$

In our example the calculation would be:

Inter-rater Agreement $= 12/25 \times 100$

Inter-rater Agreement $= 48\%$

This degree of inter-rater agreement might appear low to you, but this would actually be respectable for a classroom test. In fact the Pearson correlation between these judges' ratings is 0.80 (better than many, if not most performance assessments).

Instead of requiring the judges to assign the exact same score for agreement, some authors suggest the less rigorous criterion of scores being within one point of each other (e.g., Linn & Gronlund, 2000). If this criterion were applied to these data, the modified agreement percent would be 96 percent because only one of the judges' scores were not within one point of each other (Rater 1 assigned a 3 and Rater 2 a 5).

We caution you not to expect this high a rate of agreement should you examine the inter-rater agreement of your own performance assessments. In fact you will learn later that difficulty scoring performance assessments in a reliable manner is one of the major limitations of these procedures.

times that two individuals assign the same scores to the performances of students. This approach is illustrated in Special Interest Topic 4.2.

On some tests, inter-rater reliability is of little concern. For example, on a test with multiple-choice or true–false items, grading is fairly straightforward and a conscientious grader should produce reliable and accurate scores. In the case of our 25-item math test, a careful grader should be able to determine whether the students' answers are accurate and assign a score consistent with that of another careful grader. However, for some tests inter-rater reliability is a major concern. Classroom essay tests are a classic example. It is common for students to feel that a different teacher might have assigned a different score to their essays. It can be argued that the teacher's personal biases, preferences, or mood influenced the score, not only the content and quality of the student's essay. Even on our 25-item math test, if the teacher required that the students "show their work" and this influenced the students' grades, subjective judgment might be involved and inter-rater reliability could be a concern.

Reliability of Composite Scores

Reliability of *composite scores* is generally greater than the measures that contribute to the composite.

Psychological and educational measurement often yields multiple scores that can be combined to form a composite. For example, the assignment of grades in educational settings is often based on a composite of several tests and other assessments administered over a grading period or semester. Many standardized psychological instruments contain several measures that are combined to form an overall composite score. For example, the *Wechsler Adult Intelligence Scale—Third Edition* (Wechsler, 1997) is composed of eleven subtests used in the calculation of the Full Scale Intelligence Quotient (FSIQ). Both of these situations involve composite scores obtained by combining the scores on several different tests or subtests. The advantage of composite scores is that the reliability of composites is generally greater than that of the individual scores that contribute to the composite. More precisely, the reliability of a composite is the result of the number of scores in the composite, the reliability of the individual scores, and the correlation between those scores. The more scores in the composite, the higher the correlation between those scores, and the higher the individual reliabilities, the higher the composite reliability. As we noted, tests are simply samples of the test domain, and combining multiple measures is analogous to increasing the number of observations or the sample size.

Selecting a Reliability Coefficient

Table 4.5 summarizes the sources of measurement error reflected in different reliability coefficients. As we have suggested in our discussion of each approach to estimating reliability, different conditions call for different estimates of reliability. One should consider factors such as the nature of the construct and how the scores will be used when selecting an estimate of reliability. If a test is designed to be given more than one time to the same individuals, test-retest and alternate-form reliability with delayed administration are appropriate because they are sensitive to measurement errors resulting from time sampling. Accordingly, if a test is used to

One should consider factors such as the nature of the construct being measured and how the scores will be used when selecting an estimate of reliability.

TABLE 4.5   Sources of Error Variance Associated with the Major Types of Reliability

Type of reliability	Error variance
Test-retest reliability	Time sampling
Alternate-form reliability	
Simultaneous administration	Content sampling
Delayed administration	Time sampling and content sampling
Split-half reliability	Content sampling
Coefficient alpha and KR-20	Content sampling and item heterogeneity
Inter-rater reliability	Differences due to raters/scorers

predict an individual's performance on a criterion in the future, it is also important to use a reliability estimate that reflects errors due to time sampling.

When a test is designed to be administered only one time, an estimate of internal consistency is appropriate. As we noted, split-half reliability estimates error variance resulting from content sampling whereas coefficient alpha and KR-20 estimate error variance due to content sampling and content heterogeneity. Because KR-20 and coefficient alpha are sensitive to content heterogeneity, they are applicable when the test measures a homogeneous domain of knowledge or a unitary characteristic. For example, our 25-item test measuring the ability to multiply double digits reflects a homogeneous domain and coefficient alpha would provide a good estimate of reliability. However, if we have a 50-item test, 25 measuring multiplication with double digits and 25 measuring division, the domain is more heterogeneous and coefficient alpha and KR-20 would probably underestimate reliability. In the latter situation, in which we have a test with heterogeneous content (the heterogeneity is intended and not a mistake), the split-half method is preferred. Because the goal of the split-half approach is to compare two equivalent halves, it would be possible to ensure that each half has equal numbers of both multiplication and division problems.

We have been focusing on tests of achievement when providing examples, but the same principles apply to other types of tests. For example, a test that measures depressed mood may assess a fairly homogeneous domain, making the use of coefficient alpha or KR-20 appropriate. However, if the test measures depression, anxiety, anger, and impulsiveness, the content becomes more heterogeneous and the split-half estimate would be indicated. In this situation, the split-half approach would allow the construction of two equivalent halves with equal numbers of items reflecting the different traits or characteristics under investigation.

Naturally, if different forms of a test are available, it would be important to estimate alternate-form reliability. If a test involves subjective judgment by the person scoring the test, inter-rater reliability is important. Many contemporary test manuals report multiple estimates of reliability. Given enough information about reliability, one can partition the error variance into its components, as demonstrated in Figure 4.1.

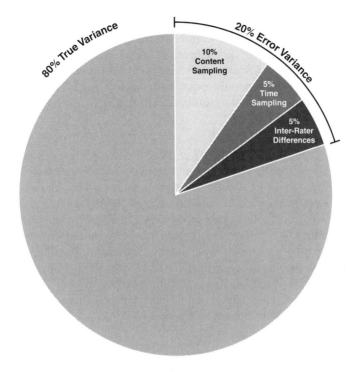

**FIGURE 4.1   Partitioning the Variance
to Reflect Sources of Variance**

Evaluating Reliability Coefficients

Another important question that arises when considering reliability coefficients is "How large do reliability coefficients need to be?" Remember, we said reliability coefficients can be interpreted in terms of the proportion of test score variance attributable to true variance.

What constitutes an acceptable reliability coefficient depends on several factors, including the construct being measured, the amount of time available for testing, the way the scores will be used, and the method of estimating reliability.

Ideally we would like our reliability coefficients to equal 1.0 because this would indicate that 100% of the test score variance is due to true differences between individuals. However, due to measurement error, perfectly reliable measurement does not exist. There is not a single, simple answer to our question about what is an acceptable level of reliability. What constitutes an acceptable reliability coefficient depends on several factors, including the construct being measured, the amount of time available for testing, the way the scores will be used, and the method of estimating reliability. We will now briefly address each of these factors.

Construct.   Some constructs are more difficult to measure than others simply because the item domain is more difficult to sample adequately. As a general rule, personality variables are more difficult to measure than academic knowledge. As a result, what might be an acceptable level of reliability for a measure of "dependency" might be regarded as unacceptable for a measure of reading comprehension. In evaluating the acceptability of a reliability coefficient one should consider the nature of the variable under investigation and how difficult it is to measure. By carefully reviewing and comparing the reliability estimates of different instruments available for measuring a construct, one can determine which is the most reliable measure of the construct.

Time Available for Testing.   If the amount of time available for testing is limited, only a limited number of items can be administered and the sampling of the test domain is open to greater error. This could occur in a research project in which the school principal allows you to conduct a study in his or her school but allows only twenty minutes to measure all the variables in your study. As another example, consider a district-wide screening for reading problems wherein the budget allows only fifteen minutes of testing per student. In contrast, a psychologist may have two hours to administer a standardized intelligence test individually. It would be unreasonable to expect the same level of reliability from these significantly different measurement processes. However, comparing the reliability coefficients associated with instruments that can be administered within the parameters of the testing situation can help one select the best instrument for the situation.

Test Score Use.   The way the test scores will be used is another major consideration when evaluating the adequacy of reliability coefficients. Diagnostic tests that form the basis for major decisions about individuals should be held to a higher standard than tests used with group research or for screening large numbers of individuals. For example, an individually administered test of intelligence that is used in the diagnosis of mental retardation would be expected to produce scores with a very high level of reliability. In this context, performance on the intelligence test provides critical information used to determine whether the individual meets the diagnostic criteria. In contrast, a brief test used to screen all students in a school district for reading problems would be held to less rigorous standards. In this situation, the instrument is used simply for screening purposes and no decisions are being made that cannot easily be reversed. It helps to remember that although high reliability is desirable with all assessments, standards of acceptability vary according to the way test scores will be used. High-stakes decisions demand highly reliable information!

Method of Estimating Reliability.   The size of reliability coefficients is also related to the method selected to estimate reliability. Some methods tend to produce higher estimates than other methods. As a result, it is important to take into consideration the method used to produce correlation coefficients when evaluating and comparing the reliability of different tests. For example, KR-20 and coefficient alpha typically produce reliability estimates that are smaller than ones obtained using the split-half method. As indicated in Table 4.5, alternate form reliability with delayed administration takes into account more sources of error than other methods do and generally produces lower reliability coefficients. In summary, some methods of estimating reliability are more rigorous and tend to produce smaller coefficients, and this variability should be considered when evaluating reliability coefficients.

General Guidelines. Although it is apparent that many factors deserve consideration when evaluating reliability coefficients, we will provide some general guidelines that can provide some guidance.

If a test is being used to make important decisions that are likely to impact individuals significantly and are not easily reversed, it is reasonable to expect reliability coefficients of 0.90 or even 0.95.

- If a test is being used to make important decisions that are likely to significantly impact individuals and are not easily reversed, it is reasonable to expect reliability coefficients of 0.90 or even 0.95. This level of reliability is regularly obtained with individually administered tests of intelligence. For example, the reliability of the *Wechsler Adult Intelligence Scale—Third Edition* (Wechsler, 1997), an individually administered intelligence test, is 0.98.
- Reliability estimates of 0.80 or more are considered acceptable in many testing situations and are commonly reported for group and individually administered achievement and personality tests. For example, the *California Achievement Test/5* (CAT/5)(CTB/Macmillan/McGraw-Hill, 1993), a set of group-administered achievement tests frequently used in public schools, has reliability coefficients that exceed 0.80 for most of its subtests.
- For teacher-made classroom tests and tests used for screening, reliability estimates of at least 0.70 are expected. Classroom tests are frequently combined to form linear composites that determine a final grade, and the reliability of these composites is expected to be greater than the reliabilities of the individual tests. Marginal coefficients in the 0.70s might also be acceptable when more thorough assessment procedures are available to address concerns about individual cases.

Some writers suggest that reliability coefficients as low as 0.60 are acceptable for group research, performance assessments, and projective measures, but we are reluctant to endorse the use of any assessment that produces scores with reliability estimates below 0.70. As you recall, a reliability coefficient of 0.60 indicates that 40% of the observed variance can be attributed to random error. How much confidence can you place in assessment results when you know that 40% of the variance is attributed to random error?

Possibly the most obvious way to improve the reliability of measurement is simply to increase the number of items on a test. If we increase the number of items while maintaining the same quality as the original items, we will increase the reliability of the test.

How to Improve Reliability

A natural question at this point is "What can we do to improve the reliability of our assessment results?" In essence we are asking what steps can be taken to maximize true score variance and minimize error variance. Probably the most obvious approach is simply to increase the number of items on a test. In the context of an individual test, if we increase the number of items while maintaining the same quality as the original items, we will increase the reliability of the test. This concept was introduced when we discussed split-half reliability and presented the Spearman-Brown formula. In fact, a variation of the Spearman-Brown formula can be used to predict the effects on reliability achieved by adding items. This equation is:

$$r = \frac{n \times r_{xx}}{1 + (n - 1)r_{xx}}$$

where r = estimated reliability on test with new items
         n = factor by which the test length is increased
         r_{xx} = reliability of the original test

For instance, consider the example of our 25-item math test. If the reliability of the test were 0.80 and we wanted to estimate the increase in reliability we would achieve by increasing the test to 30 items (a factor of 1.2), the formula would be:

$$r = \frac{1.2 \times 0.80}{1 + ((1.2 - 1).80)}$$
$$r = \frac{0.96}{1.16}$$
$$r = 0.83$$

Table 4.6 provides other examples illustrating the effects of increasing the length of our hypothetical test on reliability. By looking in the first row of this table you see that increasing the number of items on a test with a reliability of 0.50 by a factor of 1.25 results in a predicted reliability of 0.56. Increasing the number of items by a factor of 2.0 (i.e., doubling the length of the test) increases the reliability to 0.67.

TABLE 4.6   Reliability Expected when Increasing the Number of Items

Current Reliability	The Reliability Expected when the Number of Items Is Increased By:			
	× 1.25	× 1.50	× 2.0	× 2.5
0.50	0.56	0.60	0.67	0.71
0.55	0.60	0.65	0.71	0.75
0.60	0.65	0.69	0.75	0.79
0.65	0.70	0.74	0.79	0.82
0.70	0.74	0.78	0.82	0.85
0.75	0.79	0.82	0.86	0.88
0.80	0.83	0.86	0.89	0.91
0.85	0.88	0.89	0.92	0.93
0.90	0.92	0.93	0.95	0.96

In some situations various factors will limit the number of items we can include in a test. For example, teachers generally develop tests that can be administered in a specific time interval, usually the time allocated for a class period. In these situations, one can enhance reliability by using multiple measurements that are combined for an average or composite score. As noted earlier, combining multiple tests in a linear composite will increase the reliability of measurement over that of the component tests. In summary, anything we do to get a more adequate sampling of the content domain will increase the reliability of our measurement.

In a later chapter we will discuss a set of procedures collectively referred to as "item analyses." These procedures help us select, develop, and retain test items with good measurement characteristics. While it is premature to discuss these procedures in detail, it should be noted that selecting or developing good items is an important step in developing a good test. Selecting and developing good items will enhance the measurement characteristics of the assessments you use.

Another way to reduce the effects of measurement error is what Ghiselli, Campbell, and Zedeck (1981) refer to as "good housekeeping procedures." By this they mean test developers should provide precise and clearly stated procedures regarding the administration and scoring of tests. Examples include providing explicit instructions for standardized administration, developing high-quality rubrics to facilitate reliable scoring, and requiring extensive training before individuals can administer, grade, or interpret a test.

Special Problems in Estimating Reliability

When estimating the reliability of the results of speed tests, estimates derived from a single administration of a test are not appropriate.

Reliability of Speed Tests.   A speed test generally contains items that are relatively easy but has a time limit that prevents any test takers from correctly answering all questions. As a result, the test taker's score on a speed test primarily reflects the speed of performance. When estimating the reliability of the results of speed tests, estimates derived from a single administration of a test are not appropriate. Therefore, with speed tests, test-retest or alternate-form reliability is appropriate, but split-half, coefficient alpha, and KR-20 should be avoided.

Reliability as a Function of Score Level.   Though it is desirable, tests do not always measure with the same degree of precision throughout the full range of scores. If a group of individuals is tested for whom the test is either too easy or too difficult, we are likely to have additional error introduced into the scores. At the extremes of the distribution, at which scores reflect either all correct or all wrong responses, little accurate measurement has occurred. It would be inaccurate to infer that a child who missed every question on an intelligence test has "no" intelligence. Rather, the test did not adequately assess the low-level skills necessary to measure the child's intelligence. This is referred to as the test having an insufficient "floor." At the other end, it would be inaccurate to report that a child who answers all of the questions on an intelligence test correctly has an "infinite level of intelligence." The test is simply too easy to provide an adequate measurement, a situation referred to as a test having an insufficient "ceiling." In both cases we need a more appropriate test. Generally, aptitude and achievement tests are designed for use with individuals of certain ability levels. When a test is used with individuals who fall either at the extremes or outside this range, the scores might not be as accurate as the reliability estimates suggest. In these situations, further study of the test's reliability is indicated.

Range Restriction.   The values we obtain when calculating reliability coefficients are dependent on characteristics of the sample or group of individuals on which the analyses are based. One characteristic of the sample that significantly impacts the coefficients is the degree of variability in performance (i.e., variance). More precisely, reliability coefficients based on samples with large variances (referred to as heterogeneous samples) will generally produce higher estimates of reliability than those based on samples with small variances (referred to as homogeneous samples). When reliability coefficients are based on a sample with a restricted range of variability, the coefficients may actually underestimate the reliability of measurement. For example, if you base a reliability analysis on students in a gifted and talented class in which practically all of the scores reflect exemplary performance (e.g., > 90% correct), you will receive lower estimates of reliability than if the analyses are based on a class with a broader and more nearly normal distribution of scores.

The reliability estimates discussed in this chapter are usually not applicable to mastery tests. Because mastery tests emphasize classification, a recommended approach is to use an index that reflects the consistency of classification.

Mastery Testing.   Criterion-referenced tests are used to make interpretations relative to a specific level of performance. Mastery testing is an example of a criterion-referenced test by which a test taker's performance is evaluated in terms of achieving a cut score instead of the degree of achievement. The emphasis in this testing situation is on classification. Either test takers score at or above the cut score and are classified as having mastered the skill or domain, or they score below the cut score and are classified as having not mastered the skill or domain. Mastery testing often results in limited variability among test takers, and as we just described, limited variability in performance results in small reliability coefficients. As a result, the reliability estimates discussed in this chapter are typically inadequate for assessing the reliability of mastery tests. Given the emphasis on classification, a recommended approach is to use an index that reflects the consistency of classification (AERA et al., 1999). Special Interest Topic 4.3 illustrates a useful procedure for evaluating the consistency of classification when using mastery tests.

Reliability coefficients are useful when comparing the reliability of the scores produced by different tests, but when the focus is on interpreting the test scores of individuals the standard error of measurement is a more practical statistic.

The Standard Error of Measurement

Reliability coefficients are interpreted in terms of the proportion of observed variance attributable to true variance and are a useful way of comparing the reliability of scores produced by different assessment procedures. Other things being equal, you will want to select the test that produces scores with the best reliability. However, once a test has been selected and the focus is on interpreting scores, the **standard error of measurement** (SEM) is a more practical statistic. The SEM is the standard deviation of the distribution of scores that would be

SPECIAL INTEREST TOPIC **4.3**

Consistency of Classification with Mastery Tests

As noted in the text, the size of reliability coefficients is substantially affected by the variance of the test scores. Limited test score variance results in lower reliability coefficients. Because mastery tests often do not produce test scores with much variability, the methods of estimating reliability described in this chapter will often underestimate the reliability of these tests. To address this, reliability analyses of mastery tests typically focus on the consistency of classification. That is, because the objective of mastery tests is to determine if a student has mastered the skill or knowledge domain, the question of reliability can be framed as one of how consistent mastery–nonmastery classifications are. For example, if two parallel or equivalent mastery tests covering the same skill or content domain consistently produce the same classifications (i.e., mastery versus nonmastery), we would have evidence of consistency of classification. If two parallel mastery tests produced divergent classifications we would have cause for concern. In this case the test results are not consistent or reliable.

The procedure for examining the consistency of classification on parallel mastery tests is fairly straightforward. Simply administer both tests to a group of students and complete a table like the one that follows. For example, consider two mathematics mastery tests designed to assess students' ability to multiply fractions. The cut score is set at 80%, so all students scoring 80% or higher are classified as having mastered the skill while those scoring less than 80% are classified as not having mastered the skill. In the following example, data are provided for 50 students:

	Form B: Nonmastery (score < 80%)	Form B: Mastery (score of 80% or better)
Form A: Mastery (score of 80% or better)	4	32
Form A: Nonmastery (score < 80%)	11	3

Students classified as achieving mastery on both tests are denoted in the upper right-hand cell while students classified as not having mastered the skill are denoted in the lower left-hand cell. There were four students who were classified as having mastered the skills on Form A but not on Form B (denoted in the upper left-hand cell). There were three students who were classified as having mastered the skills on Form B but not on Form A (denoted in the lower right-hand cell). The next step is to calculate the percentage of consistency by using the following formula:

$$\text{Percent Consistency} = \frac{\text{Mastery on Both Forms} + \text{Nonmastery on Both Forms}}{\text{Total Number of Students}} \times 100$$

$$\text{Percent Consistency} = \frac{32 + 11}{50} \times 100$$

$$\text{Percent Consistency} = 0.86 \times 100$$

$$\text{Percent Consistency} = 86\%$$

(continued)

This approach is limited to situations in which you have parallel mastery tests. Another limitation is that there are no clear standards regarding what constitutes "acceptable" consistency of classification. Consistent with the evaluation of all reliability information, the evaluation of classification consistency should take into consideration the consequences of any decisions that are based on the test results (e.g., Gronlund, 2003). If the test results are used to make high-stakes decisions (e.g., awarding a diploma), a very high level of consistency is required. If the test is used only for low-stake decisions (e.g., failure results in further instruction and retesting), a lower level of consistency may be acceptable. Subkoviak (1984) provides a good discussion of several techniques for estimating the classification consistency of mastery tests, including some rather sophisticated approaches that require only a single administration of the test.

obtained by one person if he or she were tested on an infinite number of parallel forms of a test comprised of items randomly sampled from the same content domain. In other words, if we created an infinite number of parallel forms of a test and had the same person take them with no carryover effects, the presence of measurement error would prevent the person from earning the same score every time. Although each test might represent the content domain equally well, the test taker would perform better on some tests and worse on others simply due to random error. By taking the scores obtained on all of these tests, a distribution of scores would result. The mean of this distribution is the individual's true score (T) and the SEM is the standard deviation of this distribution of error score. Obviously, we are never actually able to follow these procedures and must estimate the SEM using information that is available to us.

Evaluating the Standard Error of Measurement

The greater the reliability of a test, the smaller the SEM and the more confidence we have in the precision of test scores.

The SEM is a function of the reliability (r_{xx}) and standard deviation (SD) of a test. When calculating the SEM, the reliability coefficient takes into consideration measurement errors present in test scores, and the SD reflects the variability of the scores in the distribution. The SEM is estimated using the following formula:

$$SEM = SD\sqrt{1 - r_{xx}}$$

where   SD = the standard deviation of the obtained scores
         r_{xx} = the reliability of the test

Let's work through two quick examples. First, let's assume a test with a standard deviation of 10 and reliability of 0.90.

Example 1: $SEM = 10\sqrt{1 - 0.90}$

$SEM = 10\sqrt{0.10}$

$SEM = 3.2$

Now let's assume a test with a standard deviation of 10 and reliability of 0.80. The SD is the same as in the previous example, but the reliability is lower.

Example 2 $\text{SEM} = 10\sqrt{1 - 0.80}$

                $\text{SEM} = 10\sqrt{0.20}$

                $\text{SEM} = 4.5$

Notice that as the reliability of the test decreases, the SEM increases. Because the reliability coefficient reflects the proportion of observed score variance due to true score variance and the SEM is an estimate of the amount of error in test scores, this inverse relationship is what one would expect. The greater the reliability of test scores, the smaller the SEM and the more confidence we have in the precision of test scores. The lower the reliability of a test, the larger the SEM and the less confidence we have in the precision of test scores. Table 4.7 shows the SEM as a function of SD and reliability. Examining the first row in the table shows that on a test with a standard deviation of 30 and a reliability coefficient of 0.95 the SEM is 6.7. In comparison, if the reliability of the test is 0.90 the SEM is 9.5; if the reliability of the test is 0.85 the SEM is 11.6; and so forth. The SEM is

TABLE 4.7   Standard Errors of Measurement for Values of Reliability and Standard Deviation

Standard Deviation	Reliability Coefficients					
	0.95	*0.90*	*0.85*	*0.80*	*0.75*	*0.70*
30	6.7	9.5	11.6	13.4	15.0	16.4
28	6.3	8.9	10.8	12.5	14.0	15.3
26	5.8	8.2	10.1	11.6	13.0	14.2
24	5.4	7.6	9.3	10.7	12.0	13.1
22	4.9	7.0	8.5	9.8	11.0	12.0
20	4.5	6.3	7.7	8.9	10.0	11.0
18	4.0	5.7	7.0	8.0	9.0	9.9
16	3.6	5.1	6.2	7.2	8.0	8.8
14	3.1	4.4	5.4	6.3	7.0	7.7
12	2.7	3.8	4.6	5.4	6.0	6.6
10	2.2	3.2	3.9	4.5	5.0	5.5
8	1.8	2.5	3.1	3.6	4.0	4.4
6	1.3	1.9	2.3	2.7	3.0	3.3
4	.9	1.3	1.5	1.8	2.0	2.2
2	.4	.6	.8	.9	1.0	1.1

used in calculating intervals or bands around observed scores in which the true score is expected to fall. We will now turn to this application of the SEM.

A *confidence interval* reflects a range of scores that will contain the individual's true score with a prescribed probability (AERA et al., 1999).

Calculating Confidence Intervals.   A **confidence interval** reflects a range of scores that will contain the individual's true score with a prescribed probability (AERA et al., 1999). We use the SEM to calculate confidence intervals. When introducing the SEM, we said it provides information about the distribution of observed scores around true scores. More precisely, we defined the SEM as the standard deviation of the distribution of error scores. Like any standard deviation, the SEM can be interpreted in terms of frequencies represented in a normal distribution. In the previous chapter we showed that approximately 68% of the scores in a normal distribution are located between one SD below the mean and one SD above the mean. As a result, approximately 68% of the time an individual's observed score would be expected to be within ±1 SEM of the true score. For example, if an individual had a true score of 70 on a test with a SEM of 3, then we would expect him or her to obtain scores between 67 and 73 two-thirds of the time. To obtain a 95% confidence interval we simply determine the number of standard deviations encompassing 95% of the scores in a distribution. By referring to a table representing areas under the normal curve (see Appendix F), you can determine that 95% of the scores in a normal distribution fall within ± 1.96 of the mean. Given a true score of 70 and SEM of 3, the 95% confidence interval would be 70 ± 3(1.96) or 70 ± 5.88. Therefore, in this situation an individual's observed score would be expected to be between 64.12 and 75.88 95% of the time.

You might have noticed a potential problem with this approach to calculating confidence intervals. So far we have described how the SEM allows us to form confidence intervals around the test taker's true score. The problem is that we don't know a test taker's true score, only the observed score. Although it is possible for us to estimate true scores (see Nunnally & Bernstein, 1994), it is common practice to use the SEM to establish confidence intervals around obtained scores (see Gulliksen, 1950). These confidence intervals are calculated in the same manner as just described, but the interpretation is slightly different. In this context the confidence interval is used to define the range of scores, which will contain the individual's true score. For example, if an individual obtains a score of 70 on a test with a SEM of 3.0, we would expect his or her true score to be between 67 and 73 68% of the time (obtained score ± 1 SEM). Accordingly, we would expect his or her true score to be between 64.12 and 75.88 95% of the time (obtained score ± 1.96 SEM).

It may help to make note of the relationship between the reliability of the test, the SEM, and confidence intervals. Remember that we noted that as the reliability of scores increase the SEM decreases. The same relationship exists between test reliability and confidence intervals. As the reliability of test scores increases (denoting less measurement error), the confidence intervals become smaller (denoting more precision in measurement).

A major advantage of the SEM and the use of confidence intervals is that they serve to remind us that measurement error is present in all scores and that we should interpret scores cautiously. A single numerical score is often interpreted as if it is precise and involves no error. For example, if you report that Susie has a Full Scale IQ of 113, her parents might

A major advantage of the SEM and the use of confidence intervals is that they serve to remind us that measurement error is present in all scores and that we should interpret scores cautiously.

interpret this as implying that Susie's IQ is exactly 113. If you are using a high-quality IQ test such as the *Wechsler Intelligence Scale for Children—4th Edition* or the *Stanford-Binet, 5th Edition*, the obtained IQ is very likely a good estimate of her true IQ. However, even with the best assessment instruments the obtained scores contain some degree of error and the SEM and confidence intervals help us illustrate this. This information can be reported in different ways in written reports. For example, Kaufman and Lichtenberger (1999) recommend the following format:

Susie obtained a full scale IQ of 113 (between 108 and 118 with 95% confidence).

Kamphaus (2001) recommends a slightly different format:

Susie obtained a full scale IQ in the High Average range, with a 95% probability that her true IQ falls between 108 and 118.

Regardless of the exact format used, the inclusion of confidence intervals highlights the fact that test scores contain some degree of measurement error and should be interpreted with caution. Most professional test publishers either report scores as bands within which the test taker's true score is likely to fall or provide information on calculating these confidence intervals.

Reliability: Practical Strategies for Teachers

Now that you are aware of the importance on the reliability of measurement, a natural question is "How can I estimate the reliability of scores on my classroom tests?" Most teachers have a number of options. First, if you use multiple-choice or other tests that can be scored by a computer scoring program, the score printout will typically report some reliability estimate (e.g., coefficient alpha or KR-20). If you do not have access to computer scoring, but the items on a test are of approximately equal difficulty and scored dichotomously (i.e., correct/incorrect), you can use an internal consistency reliability estimate known as the Kuder-Richardson formula 21 (KR-21). This formula is actually an estimate of the KR-20 discussed earlier and is usually adequate for classroom tests. To calculate KR-21 you need to know only the mean, variance, and number of items on the test. The formula is:

Most teachers have multiple options for estimating the reliability of scores produced by their classroom tests.

$$KR\text{-}21 = 1 - \frac{X(n-X)}{n\sigma^2}$$

where X = mean
σ^2 = variance
n = number of items

Consider the following set of 20 scores: 50, 48, 47, 46, 42, 42, 41, 40, 40, 38, 37, 36, 36, 35, 34, 32, 32, 31, 30, 28. Here the $X = 38.25$, $\sigma^2 = 39.8$, and $n = 50$. Therefore,

$$\text{KR-21} = 1 - \frac{38.25(50 - 38.25)}{50(39.8)}$$

$$= 1 - \frac{449.4375}{1990}$$

$$= 1 - .23 = 0.77$$

As you see, this is a fairly simple procedure. If you have access to a computer with a spreadsheet program or a calculator with mean and variance functions, you can estimate the reliability of a classroom test easily in a matter of minutes with this formula.

Special Interest Topic 4.4 presents a shortcut approach for calculating Kuder-Richardson formula 21 (KR-21). If you want to avoid even these limited computations, we prepared Table 4.8 which allows you to estimate the KR-21 reliability for dichotomously scored classroom tests if you know the standard deviation and number of items (this table was modeled after tables originally presented by Deiderich, 1973). This table is appropriate for tests with a mean of approximately 80% correct (we are using a mean of 80% correct because it is fairly representative of many classroom tests). To illustrate its application, consider the following example. If your test has 50 items and an SD of 8, select the "Number of Items" row for 50 items and the "Standard Deviation" column for $0.15n$, because $.15(50) = 7.5$, which is close to your actual SD of 8. The number at the intersection is 0.86, which is very respectable reliability for a classroom test (or a professionally developed test for that matter).

If you examine Table 4.8, you will likely detect a few fairly obvious trends. First, the more items on the test the higher the estimated reliability coefficients. We alluded to the beneficial impact of increasing test length previously in this chapter and the increase in reliability is due to enhanced sampling of the content domain. Second, tests with larger standard deviations (i.e., variance) produce more reliable results. For example, a 30-item test

TABLE 4.8   KR-21 Reliability Estimates for Tests with a Mean of 80%

Number of Items (n)	Standard Deviation of Test		
	0.10(n)	0.15(n)	0.20(n)
10	—	0.29	0.60
20	0.20	0.64	0.80
30	0.47	0.76	0.87
40	0.60	0.82	0.90
50	0.68	0.86	0.92
75	0.79	0.91	0.95
100	0.84	0.93	0.96

SPECIAL INTEREST TOPIC   **4.4**

A Quick Way to Estimate Reliability for Classroom Exams

Saupe (1961) provided a quick method for teachers to calculate reliability for a classroom exam in the era prior to easy access to calculators or computers. It is appropriate for a test in which each item is given equal weight and each item is scored either right or wrong. First, the standard deviation of the exam must be estimated from a simple approximation:

SD = [sum of top 1/6th of scores − sum of bottom 1/6th of scores] / [total # of scores − 1]/2

Then reliability can be estimated from:

Reliability = 1 − [0.19 × number of items] / SD^2

Thus, for example, in a class with 24 student test scores, the top one-sixth of the scores are 98, 92, 87, and 86, while the bottom sixth of the scores are 48, 72, 74, and 75. With 25 test items, the calculations are:

$$SD = [98 + 92 + 87 + 86 − 48 − 72 − 74 − 75] / 23/2$$
$$= [363 − 269] / 11.5$$
$$= 94 / 11.5 = 8.17$$

So,

$$Reliability = 1 − [0.19 × 25] / 8.17^2$$
$$= 1 − .07$$
$$= .93$$

A reliability coefficient of 0.93 for a classroom test is excellent! Don't be dismayed if your classroom tests do not achieve this high a level of reliability.

Source: Saupe, J. L. (1961). Some useful estimates of the Kuder-Richardson formula number 20 reliability coefficient. *Educational and Psychological Measurement, 2,* 63–72.

with an SD of 3 (i.e., 0.10[n]) results in an estimated reliability of 0.47, while one with a SD of 4.5 (i.e., 0.15[n]) results in an estimated reliability of 0.76. This reflects the tendency we described earlier that restricted score variance results in smaller reliability coefficients. We should note that while we include a column for standard deviations of 0.20(n), standard deviations this large are rare with classroom tests (Deiderich, 1973). In fact, from our experience it is more common for classroom tests to have standard deviations closer to 0.10(n). Before leaving our discussion of KR-21 and its application to classroom tests, we do want to caution you that KR-21 is only an approximation of KR-20 or coefficient alpha. KR-21 assumes the test items are of equal difficulty and it is usually slightly lower than KR-20 or coefficient alpha (Hopkins, 1998). Nevertheless, if the assumptions are not grossly violated it is probably a reasonably good estimate of reliability for many classroom applications.

Our discussion of shortcut reliability estimates to this point has been limited to tests that are dichotomously scored. Obviously, many of the assessments teachers use are not dichotomously scored and this makes the situation a little more complicated. If your items are not scored dichotomously, you can calculate coefficient alpha with relative ease using a commonly available spreadsheet such as Microsoft Excel. With a little effort you should be able to use a spreadsheet to perform the computations illustrated previously in Tables 4.3 and 4.4.

Summary

Reliability refers to consistency in test scores. If a test or other assessment procedure produces consistent measurements, its scores are reliable. Why is reliability so important? As we have emphasized, assessments are useful because they provide information that helps educators make better decisions. However, the reliability (and validity) of that information is of paramount importance. For us to make good decisions, we need reliable information. By estimating the reliability of our assessment results, we get an indication of how much confidence we can place in them. If we have highly reliable and valid information, it is probable that we can use that information to make better decisions. If the results are unreliable, they are of little value to us.

Errors of measurement undermine the reliability of measurement and therefore reduce the utility of the measurement. Although there are multiple sources of measurement error, the major ones are content sampling and time sampling errors. Content sampling errors are the result of less than perfect sampling of the content domain. The more representative tests are of the content domain, the less content sampling errors threaten the reliability of the test. Time sampling errors are the result of random changes in the test taker or environment over time. Experts in testing and measurement have developed methods of estimating errors due to these and other sources. The major approaches to estimating reliability include:

- *Test-retest reliability* involves the administration of the same test to a group of individuals on two different occasions. The correlation between the two sets of scores is the test-retest reliability coefficient and reflects errors due to time sampling.
- *Alternate-form reliability* involves the administration of parallel forms of a test to a group of individuals. The correlation between the scores on the two forms is the reliability coefficient. If the two forms are administered at the same time, the reliability coefficient reflects only content sampling error. If the two forms of the test are administered at different times, the reliability coefficient reflects both content and time sampling errors.
- *Internal-consistency reliability* estimates are derived from a single administration of a test. Split-half reliability involves dividing the test into two equivalent halves and calculating the correlation between the two halves. Instead of comparing performance on two halves of the test, coefficient alpha and the Kuder-Richardson approaches examine the consistency of responding among all of the individual items of the test. Split-half reliability reflects errors due to content sampling whereas coefficient alpha and the Kuder-Richardson approaches reflect both item heterogeneity and errors due to content sampling.
- *Inter-rater reliability* is estimated by administering the test once but having the responses scored by different examiners. By comparing the scores assigned by different examiners, one can determine the influence of different raters or scorers.

Inter-rater reliability is important to examine when scoring involves considerable subjective judgment.

We also discussed a number of issues important for understanding and interpreting reliability estimates. We provided some guidelines for selecting the type of reliability estimate most appropriate for specific assessment procedures, some guidelines for evaluating reliability coefficients, and some suggestions on improving the reliability of measurement. Although reliability coefficients are useful when comparing the reliability of different tests, the standard error of measurement (SEM) is more useful when interpreting scores. The SEM is an index of the amount of error in test scores and is used in calculating confidence intervals within which we expect the true score to fall. An advantage of the SEM and the use of confidence intervals is that they serve to remind us that measurement error is present in all scores and that we should use caution when interpreting scores. We closed the chapter by illustrating some shortcut procedures that teachers can use to estimate the reliability of their classroom tests.

KEY TERMS AND CONCEPTS

Alternate-form reliability, p. 93
Coefficient alpha, p. 95
Composite score, p. 99
Confidence interval, p. 110
Content heterogeneity, p. 95
Content sampling error, p. 89
Error score, p. 87
Error variance, p. 90

Internal-consistency reliability, p. 93
Inter-rater differences, p. 90
Inter-rater reliability, p. 97
Kuder-Richardson formula 20, p. 95
Measurement error, p. 86
Obtained score, p. 87
Reliability, p. 86

Reliability coefficient, p. 90
Spearman-Brown formula, p. 94
Split-half reliability, p. 93
Standard error of measurement, p. 106
Test-retest reliability, p. 92
Time sampling error, p. 89
True score, p. 87
True score variance, p. 90

RECOMMENDED READINGS

American Educational Research Association, American Psychological Association, & National Council on Measurement in Education (1999). *Standards for educational and psychological testing.* Washington, DC: AERA. Chapter 5, Reliability and Errors of Measurement, is a great resource!

Feldt, L. S., & Brennan, R. L. (1989). Reliability. In R. L. Linn (Ed.), *Educational measurement* (3rd ed., pp. 105–146). Upper Saddle River, NJ: Merrill/Prentice Hall. A little technical at times, but a great resource for students wanting to learn more about reliability.

Ghiselli, E. E., Campbell, J. P., Zedeck, S. (1981). *Measurement theory for the behavioral sciences.* San Francisco, CA: W. H. Freeman. Chapters 8 and 9 provide outstanding discussions of reliability. A classic!

Nunnally, J. C., & Bernstein, I. H. (1994). *Psychometric theory* (3rd ed.). New York: McGraw-Hill. Chapter 6, The Theory of Measurement Error, and Chapter 7, The Assessment of Reliability are outstanding chapters. Another classic!

Subkoviak, M. J. (1984). Estimating the reliability of mastery–nonmastery classifications. In R. A. Berk (Ed.), *A guide to criterion-referenced test construction* (pp. 267–291). Baltimore: Johns Hopkins University Press. An excellent discussion of techniques for estimating the consistency of classification with mastery tests.

PRACTICE ITEMS

1. Consider these data for a five-item test that was administered to six students. Each item could receive a score of either 1 or 0. Calculate KR-20 using the following formula:

$$\text{KR-20} = k/k - 1 \times \left(\frac{\text{SD}^2 - \sum p_i \times q_i}{\text{SD}^2} \right)$$

where k = number of items
    SD^2 = variance of total test scores
    p_i = proportion of correct responses on item
    q_i = proportion of incorrect responses on item

	Item 1	Item 2	Item 3	Item 4	Item 5	Total Score
Student 1	0	1	1	0	1	
Student 2	1	1	1	1	1	
Student 3	1	0	1	0	0	
Student 4	0	0	0	1	0	
Student 5	1	1	1	1	1	
Student 6	1	1	0	1	0	
p_i						SD^2
q_i						
$p_i \times q_i$						

Note: When calculating SD^2, use n in the denominator.

2. Consider these data for a five-item test that was administered to six students. Each item could receive a score ranging from 1 to 5. Calculate coefficient alpha using the following formula:

$$\text{Coefficient alpha} = \left(\frac{k}{k-1} \right) \left(1 - \frac{\sum \text{SD}_i^2}{\text{SD}^2} \right)$$

where k = number of items
    SD_i^2 = variance of individual items
    SD^2 = variance of total test scores

	Item 1	Item 2	Item 3	Item 4	Item 5	Total Score
Student 1	4	5	4	5	5	
Student 2	3	3	2	3	2	
Student 3	2	3	1	2	1	
Student 4	4	4	5	5	4	
Student 5	2	3	2	2	3	
Student 6	1	2	2	1	3	
SD_i^2						$\text{SD}^2 =$

Note: When calculating SD_i^2 and SD^2, use n in the denominator.

5 Validity for Teachers

Validity refers to the degree to which evidence and theory support the interpretations of test scores entailed by proposed uses of the test. Validity is, therefore, the most fundamental consideration in developing and evaluating tests.

—AERA et al., 1999, p. 9

CHAPTER HIGHLIGHTS

Threats to Validity

Reliability and Validity

"Types of Validity" versus
   "Types of Validity Evidence"

Types of Validity Evidence

Validity: Practical Strategies for Teachers

LEARNING OBJECTIVES

After reading and studying this chapter, students should be able to:

1. Define validity and explain its importance in the context of educational assessment.
2. Describe the major threats to validity.
3. Explain the relationship between reliability and validity.
4. Trace the development of the contemporary conceptualization of validity.
5. Describe the five categories of validity evidence specified in the 1999 *Standards.*
6. For each category of validity evidence, give an example to illustrate the type of information provided.
7. Explain how validity coefficients are interpreted.
8. Define the standard error of estimate and explain its interpretation.
9. Explain how validity evidence is integrated to develop a sound validity argument.
10. Apply validity analyses to classroom assessments.

In the previous chapter we introduced you to the concept of the reliability of measurement. In this context, reliability refers to accuracy and consistency in test scores. Now we turn our attention to validity, another fundamental psychometric property. Messick (1989) defined

Validity **refers to the appropriateness or accuracy of the interpretations of test scores.**

validity as "an integrated evaluative judgment of the degree to which empirical evidence and theoretical rationales support the adequacy and appropriateness of inferences and actions based on test scores or other modes of assessment" (p. 13). Similarly, the *Standards for Educational and Psychological Testing* (AERA et al., 1999) defined validity as "the degree to which evidence and theory support the interpretations of test scores entailed by proposed uses of the tests" (p. 9). Do not let the technical tone of these definitions throw you. In simpler terms, both of these influential sources indicate that **validity** refers to the appropriateness or accuracy of the interpretations of test scores. If test scores are interpreted as reflecting intelligence, do they actually reflect intellectual ability? If test scores are used (i.e., interpreted) to predict success in college, can they accurately predict who will succeed in college? Naturally the validity of the interpretations of test scores is directly tied to the usefulness of the interpretations. Valid interpretations help us to make better decisions; invalid interpretations do not!

Although it is often done as a matter of convenience, it is not technically correct to refer to the validity of a test. Validity is a characteristic of the interpretations given to test scores. It is not technically correct to ask the question "Is the *Wechsler Intelligence Scale for Children— Fourth Edition* (WISC-IV) a valid test?" It is preferable to ask the question "Is the interpretation of performance on the WISC-IV as reflecting intelligence valid?" Validity must always have a context and that context is interpretation. What does performance on this test mean?

When test scores are interpreted in multiple ways, each interpretation needs to be evaluated.

The answer to this question is the interpretation given to performance and it is this interpretation that possesses the construct of validity, not the test itself. Additionally, when test scores are interpreted in multiple ways, each interpretation needs to be validated. For example, an achievement test can be used to evaluate a student's performance in academic classes, to assign the student to an appropriate instructional program, to diagnose a learning disability, or to predict success in college. Each of these uses involves different interpretations and the validity of each interpretation needs to be evaluated (AERA et al., 1999). To establish or determine validity is a major responsibility of the test authors, test publisher, researchers, and even test user.

Threats to Validity

Messick (1994) and others have identified the two major threats to validity as **construct underrepresentation** and **construct-irrelevant variance.** To translate this into everyday language, validity is threatened when a test measures either less (construct underrepresentation) or more (construct-irrelevant variance) than the construct it is

Validity is threatened when a test measures either less or more than the construct it is designed to measure.

supposed to measure (AERA et al., 1999). Construct underrepresentation occurs when a test does not measure important aspects of the specified construct. Consider a test designed to be a comprehensive measure of the mathematics skills covered in a 3rd-grade curriculum and convey information regarding mastery of each skill. If the test contained only division problems, it would not be an adequate representation of the broad array of math skills typically covered in a 3rd-grade curriculum (although, a score on such a test may predict performance on a more comprehensive measure). Division is an important aspect of the math curriculum, but not the only important aspect. To address this problem the content of the test would need to be expanded to reflect all of the skills typically taught in a 3rd-grade math curriculum. Construct-irrelevant variance is present when the test measures characteristics, content, or skills that are unrelated to the test construct. For example, if our 3rd-grade math test has extensive and complex written instructions, it is possible that in addition to math skills, reading comprehension skills are being measured. If the test were intended to measure only math skills, the inclusion of reading comprehension would reflect construct-irrelevant variance. To address this problem, one might design the test to minimize written instructions and to ensure that the reading level is low. As you might imagine, most tests leave out some aspects that some users might view as important, and include some aspects that some users view as irrelevant (AERA et al., 1999).

In addition to characteristics of the test itself, factors external to the test can impact the validity of the interpretation of results. Linn and Gronlund (2000) identify numerous factors external to the test that can influence validity. They highlight the following factors:

- *Instructional procedures:* With educational tests, in addition to the content of the test influencing validity, the way the material is presented can influence validity. For example, consider a test of critical thinking skills. If the students were coached and given solutions to the particular problems included on a test, validity would be compromised. This is a potential problem when teachers "teach the test."
- *Test administration and scoring procedures:* Deviations from standard administrative and scoring procedures can undermine validity. In terms of administration, failure to provide the appropriate instructions or follow strict time limits can lower validity. In terms of scoring, unreliable or biased scoring can lower validity.
- *Student characteristics:* Any personal factors that restrict or alter the examinees' responses in the testing situation can undermine validity. For example, if an examinee experiences high levels of test anxiety or is not motivated to put forth a reasonable effort, the results may be distorted.

external factors

Additionally, the validity of norm-referenced interpretations of performance on a test is influenced by the appropriateness of the reference group (AERA et al., 1999). As these examples illustrate, a multitude of factors can influence the validity of assessment-based interpretations. Due to the cumulative influence of these factors, validity is not an all-or-none concept. Rather, it exists on a continuum and we usually refer to degrees of validity or to the relative validity of the interpretation(s) given to a particular measurement.

Validity is not an all-or-none concept, but exists on a continuum.

Reliability and Validity

In the preceding chapter we addressed the issue of the reliability of measurement. Reliability refers to the stability or consistency of test scores and reflects the amount of random measurement error present. Reliability is a necessary but insufficient condition for validity. A test that does not produce reliable scores cannot produce valid interpretations. However, no

Reliability is a necessary but insufficient condition for validity.

matter how reliable measurement is, it is not a guarantee of validity. From our discussion of reliability you will remember that obtained score variance is composed of two components: true score variance and error variance. Only true score variance is reliable, and only true score variance can be systematically related to any construct the test is designed to measure. If reliability is equal to zero, then the true score variance component must also be equal to zero, leaving our obtained score to be composed only of error, that is, random variations in responses. Thus, without reliability there can be no validity.

Although low reliability limits validity, high reliability does not ensure validity. It is entirely possible that a test can produce reliable scores but inferences based on the test scores can be completely invalid. Consider the following rather silly example involving head circumference. If we use some care we can measure the circumference of our students' heads in a reliable and consistent manner. In other words, the measurement is reliable. However, if we considered head circumference to be an index of intelligence, our inferences would not be valid. The measurement of head circumference is still reliable, but when interpreted as a measure of intelligence it would result in invalid inferences.

A more relevant example can be seen in the various Wechsler intelligence scales. These scales have been shown to produce highly reliable scores on a Verbal Scale and a Performance Scale. There is also a rather substantial body of research demonstrating these scores are interpreted appropriately as reflecting types of intelligence. However, some psychologists have drawn the inference that score differences between the Verbal Scale and the Performance Scale indicate some fundamental information about personality and even forms of psychopathology. For example, one author argued that a person who, on the Wechsler scales, scores higher on the Verbal Scale relative to the Performance Scale is highly likely to have an obsessive-compulsive personality disorder! There is no evidence or research to support such an interpretation and, in fact, a large percentage of the population of the United States score higher on the Verbal Scale relative to the Performance Scale on each of the various Wechsler scales. Thus, while the scores are themselves highly reliable and *some* interpretations are highly valid (the Wechsler scales measure intelligence), other interpretations wholly lack validity despite the presence of high reliability.

"Types of Validity" versus "Types of Validity Evidence"

We have already introduced you to the influential *Standards for Educational and Psychological Testing* (AERA et al., 1999). This is actually the latest in a series of documents providing guidelines for the development and use of tests. At this point we are going to trace the evolution of the concept of validity briefly by highlighting how it has been defined and described in this series of documents. In the early versions (i.e., APA, 1954, 1966; APA et al., 1974, 1985) validity was divided into three distinct types. As described by Messick (1989), these are:

- *Content validity:* **Content validity** involves how adequately the test samples the content area of the identified construct. In other words, is the content of the test relevant and representative of the content domain? We speak of it being representative because every possible question that could be asked cannot as a practical matter be asked, so questions are chosen to sample or represent the full domain of questions. Content validity is typically based on professional judgments about the appropriateness of the test content.

- *Criterion-related validity:* **Criterion-related validity** involves examining the relationships between the test and external variables that are thought to be direct measures of the construct. Studies of criterion-related validity empirically examine the relationships between test scores and criterion scores using correlation or regression analyses.
- *Construct validity:* **Construct validity** involves an integration of evidence that relates to the meaning or interpretation of test scores. This evidence can be collected using a wide variety of research strategies and designs.

This classification terminology has been widely accepted by researchers, authors, teachers, and students and is often referred to as the traditional nomenclature (AERA et al., 1999). However, in the 1970s and 1980s measurement professionals began moving toward a conceptualization of validity as a **unitary concept.** That is, whereas we previously had talked about different types of validity (i.e., content, criterion-related, and construct validity), these "types" really represent only different ways of collecting evidence to support validity. To emphasize the view of validity as a unitary concept and get away from the perception of distinct types of validity, the 1985 *Standards for Educational and Psychological Testing* (APA et al., 1985) referred to "types of validity *evidence*" in place of "types of validity." Instead of content validity, criterion-related validity, and construct validity, the 1985 *Standards* referred to content-related evidence of validity, criterion-related evidence of validity, and construct-related evidence of validity.

Validity is a *unitary concept.*

This brings us to the current *Standards for Educational and Psychological Testing* (AERA et al., 1999). According to the 1999 *Standards:*

> Validity is a unitary concept. It is the degree to which all of the accumulated evidence supports the intended interpretation of test scores for the proposed purposes. (p. 11)

The 1999 document is conceptually similar to the 1985 document (i.e., "types of validity evidence" versus "types of validity"), but the terminology has expanded and changed somewhat. The change in terminology is not simply cosmetic, but is substantive and intended to promote a new way of conceptualizing validity, a view that has been growing in the profession for over two decades (Reynolds, 2002). The 1999 *Standards* identifies the following five categories of evidence that are related to the validity of test score interpretations:

- *Evidence based on test content:* This category includes evidence derived from an analysis of the test content, which includes the type of questions or tasks included in the test and administration and scoring guidelines.
- *Evidence based on relations to other variables:* This category includes evidence based on an examination of the relationships between test performance and external variables or criteria.

- *Evidence based on internal structure:* This category includes evidence regarding relationships among test items and components.
- *Evidence based on response processes:* This category includes evidence derived from an analysis of the processes engaged in by the examinee or examiner.
- *Evidence based on consequences of testing:* This category includes evidence based on an examination of the intended and unintended consequences of testing.

Sources of validity evidence differ in their importance according to factors such as the construct being measured, the intended use of the test scores, and the population being assessed.

These sources of evidence will differ in their importance or relevance according to factors such as the construct being measured, the intended use of the test scores, and the population being assessed. Those using tests should carefully weight the evidence of validity and make judgments about how appropriate a test is for each application and setting. Table 5.1 provides a brief summary of the different classification schemes that have been promulgated over the past four decades in the *Standards*.

At this point you might be asking, "Why are the authors wasting my time with a discussion of the history of technical jargon?" There are at least two important reasons. First, it is likely that in your readings and studies you will come across references to various "types of validity." Many older test and measurement textbooks refer to content, criterion, and construct validity, and some newer texts still use that or a similar nomenclature. We hope that when you come across different terminology you will not be confused, but instead will understand its meaning and origin. Second, the *Standards* are widely accepted and serve as professional guidelines for the development and evaluation of tests. For legal and ethical reasons test developers and publishers generally want to adhere to these guidelines. As a result, we expect test publishers will adopt the new nomenclature in the next few years. Currently test manuals and other test-related documents are adopting this new nomenclature (e.g., Reynolds, 2002). However, older tests typically have supporting literature that uses the older terminology, and you need to understand its origin and meaning. When reviewing test manuals and assessing the psychometric properties of a test, you need to be aware of the older as well as the newer terminology.

TABLE 5.1   Tracing Historical Trends in the Concept of Validity

1974 *Standards*	1985 *Standards*	1999 *Standards*
Content validity	Content-related validity	Validity evidence based on test content
Criterion validity	Criterion-related validity	Validity evidence based on relations to other variables
Construct validity	Construct-related validity	Validity (as a unitary construct)
		Validity evidence based on internal structure
		Validity evidence based on response processes
		Validity evidence based on consequences of testing

Types of Validity Evidence

At this point we will address each of the categories of validity evidence individually. As we do this we will attempt to highlight how the current nomenclature relates to the traditional nomenclature. Along these lines, it will hopefully become clear that construct validity as originally conceptualized is a comprehensive category that essentially corresponds with the contemporary conceptualization of validity as a unitary concept. As a result, construct validity actually encompasses content and criterion-related validity.

Evidence Based on Test Content

Valuable validity evidence can be gained by examining the relationship between the content of the test and the construct it is designed to measure.

The *Standards* (AERA et al., 1999) note that valuable validity evidence can be gained by examining the relationship between the content of the test and the construct or domain the test is designed to measure. In this context, test content includes the "themes, wording, and format of the items, tasks, or questions on a test, as well as the guidelines . . . regarding administration and scoring" (p. 11). Other writers provide similar descriptions. For example, Reynolds (1998b) notes that validity evidence based on test content focuses on how well the test items sample the behaviors or subject matter the test is designed to measure. In a similar vein, Anastasi and Urbina (1997) note that validity evidence based on test content involves the examination of the content of the test to determine whether it provides a representative sample of the domain being measured. Popham (2000) succinctly frames it as "Does the test cover the content it's supposed to cover?" (p. 96). In the past, this type of validity evidence was primarily subsumed under the label "content validity."

Test developers routinely begin considering the appropriateness of the content of the test at the earliest stages of development. Identifying what we want to measure is the first order of business, because we cannot measure anything very well that we have not first clearly defined. Therefore, the process of developing a test should begin with a clear delineation of the construct or content domain to be measured. Once the construct or content domain has been clearly defined, the next step is to develop a table of specifications. This **table of specifications** is essentially a blueprint that guides the development of the test. It delineates the topics and objectives to be covered and the relative importance of each topic and objective. Finally, working from this table of specifications the test developers write the actual test items. These steps in test development are covered in detail later in this text. Whereas teachers usually develop classroom tests with little outside assistance, professional test developers often bring in external consultants who are considered experts in the content area(s) covered by the test. For example, if the goal is to develop an achievement test covering American history, the test developers will likely recruit experienced teachers of American history for assistance developing a table of specifications and writing test items. If care is taken with these procedures, the foundation is established for a correspondence between the content of the test and the construct it is designed to measure. Test developers may include a detailed description of their procedures for writing items as validity evidence, including the number, qualifications, and credentials of their expert consultants.

A *table of specifications* is essentially a blueprint that guides the development of the test.

Item relevance and *content coverage* are two important factors to be considered when evaluating the correspondence between the test content and its construct.

After the test is written, it is common for test developers to continue collecting validity evidence based on content. This typically involves having expert judges systematically review the test and evaluate the correspondence between the test content and its construct or domain. These experts can be the same ones who helped during the early phase of test construction or a new, independent group of experts. During this phase, the experts typically address two major issues, item relevance and content coverage. To assess **item relevance,** the experts examine each individual test item and determine whether it reflects essential content in the specified domain. To assess **content coverage,** the experts look at the overall test and rate the degree to which the items cover the specified domain. To understand the difference between these two issues, consider these examples. For a classroom test of early American history, a question about the American Revolution would clearly be deemed a relevant item whereas a question about algebraic equations would be judged to be irrelevant. This distinction deals with the relevance of the items to the content domain. In contrast, if you examined the total test and determined that all of the questions dealt with the American Revolution and no other aspects of American history were covered, you would conclude that the test had poor content coverage. That is, because early American history has many important events and topics in addition to the American Revolution that are not covered in the test, the test does not reflect a comprehensive and representative sample of the specified domain. The concepts of item relevance and content coverage are illustrated in Figures 5.1 and 5.2.

As you can see, the collection of content-based validity evidence is typically qualitative in nature. However, although test publishers might rely on traditional qualitative approaches (e.g., the judgment of expert judges to help develop the tests and subsequently to evaluate the completed test), they can take steps to report their results in a more quantitative manner. For example, they can report the number and qualifications of the experts, the

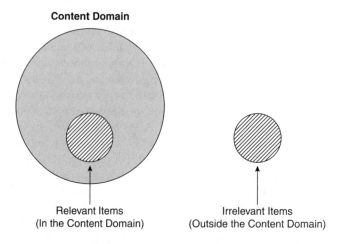

FIGURE 5.1   Illustration of Item Relevance

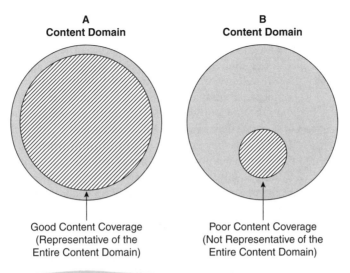

FIGURE 5.2   Illustration of Content Coverage

number of chances the experts had to review and comment on the assessment, and their degree of agreement on content-related issues. Taking these efforts a step further, Lawshe (1975) developed a quantitative index that reflects the degree of agreement among the experts making content-related judgments. Newer approaches are being developed that use a fairly sophisticated technique known as multidimensional scaling analysis (Sireci, 1998).

As we suggested previously, different types of validity evidence are most relevant, appropriate, or important for different types of tests. For example, content-based validity evidence is often seen as the preferred approach for establishing the validity of academic achievement tests. This applies to both teacher-made classroom tests and professionally developed achievement tests. Another situation in which content-based evidence is of primary importance is with tests used in the selection and classification of employees. For example, employment tests may be designed to sample the knowledge and skills necessary to succeed at a job. In this context, content-based evidence can be used to demonstrate consistency between the content of the test and the requirements of the job. The key factor that makes content-based validity evidence of paramount importance with both achievement tests and employment tests is that they are designed to provide a representative sample of the knowledge, behavior, or skill domain being measured. In contrast, content-based evidence of validity is usually less relevant for personality and aptitude tests (Anastasi & Urbina, 1997).

> **Content-based validity evidence is often the preferred approach for establishing the validity of achievement tests, including teacher-made classroom tests.**

> *Face validity* **is technically not a form of validity, but refers to a test "appearing" to measure what it is designed to measure.**

Face Validity.   Before leaving our discussion of content-based validity evidence, we need to highlight the distinction between it and face validity. **Face validity** is technically not a form of validity at all, but instead refers to a test "appearing" to measure what it is designed to measure. That is, does the test appear valid to untrained individuals who take, administer, or examine the test? Face validity really has nothing to do with what a test actually measures, just what it *appears to measure.* For example, does a test of achievement look like the general public expects an achievement test to look like? Does a test of intelligence look like the general public expects an intelligence test to look like? Naturally, the face validity of a test is closely tied to the content of a test. In terms of face validity, when untrained individuals inspect a test they are typically looking to see whether the items on the test are what they expect. For example, are the items on an achievement test of the type they expect to find on an achievement test? Are the items on an intelligence test of the type they expect to find on an intelligence test? Whereas content-based evidence of validity is acquired through a systematic and technical analysis of the test content, face validity involves only the superficial appearance of a test. A test can appear "face valid" to the general public, but not hold up under the systematic scrutiny involved in a technical analysis of the test content.

This is not to suggest that face validity is an undesirable or even irrelevant characteristic. A test that has good face validity is likely to be better received by the general public. If a test appears to measure what it is designed to measure, examinees are more likely to be cooperative and invested in the testing process, and the public is more likely to view the results as meaningful (Anastasi & Urbina, 1997). Research suggests that good face validity can increase student motivation, which in turn can increase test performance (Chan, Schmitt, DeShon, Clause, & Delbridge, 1997). If a test has poor face validity those using the test may have a flippant or negative attitude toward the test and as a result put little effort into completing it. If this happens, the actual validity of the test can suffer. The general public is not likely to view a test with poor face validity as meaningful, even if there is technical support for the validity of the test.

There are times, however, when face validity is undesirable. These occur primarily in forensic settings in which detection of malingering may be emphasized. Malingering is a situation in which an examinee intentionally feigns symptoms of a mental or physical disorder in order to gain some external incentive (e.g., receiving a financial reward; avoiding punishment). In these situations face validity is not desirable because it may help the examinee fake pathological responses.

Evidence Based on Relations to Other Variables

Important validity evidence can also be secured by examining the relationships between test scores and other variables (AERA et al., 1999). In describing this type of validity evidence, the *Standards* recognize two related, but fairly distinct applications of this approach. One involves the examination of test-criterion evidence and the other convergent and discriminant evidence. For clarity, we will address these two applications separately.

Test-Criterion Evidence.   Many tests are designed to predict performance on some variable that is typically referred to as a **criterion.** The *Standards* (AERA et al., 1999) define a criterion as "a measure of some attribute or outcome that is of primary interest" (p. 14). The criterion can be academic performance as reflected by the grade point average (GPA), job performance as measured by a supervisor's ratings, or anything else that is of importance to the user of the test. Historically, this type of validity evidence has been referred to as "predictive validity," "criterion validity," or "criterion-related validity."

There are two different types of validity studies typically used to collect *test-criterion evidence: predictive studies* and *concurrent studies.*

There are two different types of validity studies typically used to collect **test-criterion evidence: predictive studies** and **concurrent studies.** In a predictive study the test is administered, there is an intervening time interval, and then the criterion is measured. In a concurrent study the test is administered and the criterion is measured at about the same time.

To illustrate these two approaches we will consider the Scholastic Achievement Test (SAT). The SAT is designed to predict how well high school students will perform in college. To complete a predictive study, one might administer the SAT to high school students, wait until the students have completed their freshman year of college, and then examine the relationship between the predictor (i.e., SAT scores) and the criterion (i.e., freshman GPA). Researchers often use a correlation coefficient to examine the relationship between a predictor and a criterion, and in this context the correlation coefficient is referred to as a **validity coefficient.** To complete a concurrent study of the relationship between the SAT and college performance, the researcher might administer the SAT to a group of students completing their freshman year and then simply correlate their SAT scores with their GPAs. In predictive studies there is a time interval between the predictor test and the criterion; in a concurrent study there is no time interval. Figure 5.3 illustrates the temporal relationship between administering the test and measuring the criterion in predictive and concurrent studies.

A natural question is "Which type of study, predictive or concurrent, is best?" As you might expect (or fear), there is not a simple answer to that question. Very often in education and other settings we are interested in making predictions about future performance. Consider our example of the SAT; the question is which students will do well in college and which will not. Inherent in this question is the passage of time. You want to administer a test *before* students graduate from high school that will help predict the likelihood of their success in

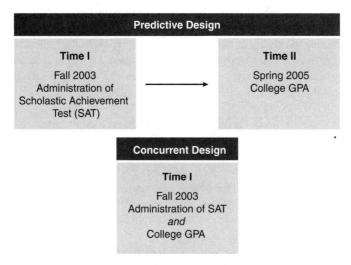

FIGURE 5.3   Illustration of Predictive and Concurrent Studies

college. In situations such as this, predictive studies maintain the temporal relationship and other potentially important characteristics of the real-life situation (AERA et al., 1999).

Because a concurrent study does not retain the temporal relationship or other characteristics of the real-life situation, a predictive study is preferable when prediction is the ultimate goal of assessment. However, predictive studies take considerable time to complete and can be extremely expensive. As a result, although predictive studies might be preferable from a technical perspective, for practical reasons test developers and researchers might adopt a concurrent strategy to save time and/or money. In some situations this is less than optimal and you should be cautious when evaluating the results. However, in certain situations concurrent studies are the preferred approach. Concurrent studies clearly are appropriate when the goal of the test is to determine current status of the examinee as opposed to predicting future outcome (Anastasi & Urbina, 1997). For example, a concurrent approach to validation would be indicated for a test designed to diagnose the presence of psychopathology in elementary school students. Here we are most concerned that the test give us an accurate assessment of the child's conditions at the time of testing, not at some time in the future. The question here is not "Who will develop the disorder?" but "Who has the disorder?" In these situations, the test being validated is often a replacement for a more time-consuming or expensive procedure. For example, a relatively brief screening test might be evaluated to determine whether it can serve as an adequate replacement for a more extensive psychological assessment process. However, if we were interested in selecting students at high risk of developing a disorder in the future, say, for participation in a prevention program, a prediction study would be in order. We would need to address how well or accurately our test predicts who will develop the disorder in question.

Selecting a Criterion.   In both predictive and concurrent studies, it is important that the criterion itself be reliable and valid. As noted earlier, reliability is a prerequisite for validity. If a measure is not reliable, whether it is a predictor test or a criterion measure, it cannot be valid. At the same time, reliability does not ensure validity. Therefore, we need to select criterion measures that are also valid. In our example of using the SAT to predict freshman GPA, we consider our criterion, GPA, to be a valid measure of success in college. In a concurrent study examining the ability of a test to diagnose psychopathology, the criterion might be the diagnosis provided by an extensive clinical assessment involving a combination of clinical interviews, behavioral observations, and psychometric testing. Optimally the criterion should be viewed as the "gold standard," the best existing measure of the construct of interest.

Criterion Contamination.   It is important that the predictor and criterion scores be independently obtained. That is, scores on the predictor should not in any way influence criterion scores. If predictor scores do influence criterion scores, the criterion is said to be contaminated. Consider a situation in which students are selected for a college program based on performance on an aptitude test. If the college instructors are aware of the students' performance on the aptitude test this might influence their evaluation of the students' performance in their class. Students with high aptitude test scores might be given preferential treatment or graded in a more lenient manner. In this situation knowledge of performance on the predictor is influencing performance on the criterion. **Criterion contamination** has occurred and any resulting validity coefficients will be artificially inflated. That is, the validity coefficients between the predictor test and the criterion will be larger than they would be had the criterion not been contaminated. The coefficients will suggest the validity is greater than it actually is. To avoid this undesirable situation, test developers must ensure that no individual who evaluates criterion performance has knowledge of the examinees' predictor scores.

Interpreting Validity Coefficients.   Predictive and concurrent validity studies examine the relationship between a test and a criterion and the results are often reported in terms of a validity coefficient. At this point it is reasonable to ask, "How large should validity coefficients be?" For example, should we expect validity coefficients greater than 0.80? Although there is no simple answer to this question, validity coefficients should be large enough to indicate that information from the test will help predict how individuals will perform on the criterion measure (e.g., Cronbach & Gleser, 1965). Returning to our example of the SAT, the question is whether the relationship between the SAT and the freshman GPA is sufficiently strong so that information about SAT performance helps predict who will succeed in college. If a test provides information that helps predict criterion performance *better* than any other existing predictor, the test may be useful even if its validity coefficients are relatively small. As a result, testing experts avoid specifying a minimum coefficient size that is acceptable for validity coefficients.

If a test provides information that helps predict criterion performance better than any other existing predictor, the test may be useful even if its validity coefficients are relatively small.

Although we cannot set a minimum size for acceptable validity coefficients, certain techniques are available that help us evaluate the usefulness of test scores for prediction purposes. In Chapter 2 we introduced **linear regression,** a mathematical procedure that allows you to predict values on one variable given information on another variable. In the context of validity analysis, linear regression allows you to predict criterion performance based on predictor test scores. When using linear regression, a statistic called the **standard error of estimate** is used to describe the amount of prediction error due to the imperfect validity of the test. The standard error of estimate is the standard deviation of prediction errors around the predicted score. The formula for the standard error of estimate is quite similar to that for the SEM introduced in the last chapter. We will not go into great detail about of the use of linear regression and the standard error of estimate, but Special Interest Topic 5.1 provides a very user-friendly discussion of linear regression.

The *standard error of estimate* is used to describe the amount of prediction error due to the imperfect validity of the test.

When tests are used for making decisions such as in student or personnel selection, factors other than the correlation between the test and criterion are important to consider. For example, factors such as the proportion of applicants needed to fill positions (i.e., **selection ratio**) and the proportion of applicants who can be successful on the criterion (i.e., **base rate**) can impact the usefulness of test scores. As an example of how the selection ratio can influence selection decisions, consider an extreme situation in which you have more positions to fill than you have applicants. Here you do not have the luxury of being selective and have to accept all the applicants. In this unfortunate situation no test is useful, no matter how strong a relationship there is between it and the criterion. However, if you have only a few positions to fill and many applicants, even a test with a moderate correlation with the criterion may be useful. As an example of how the base rate can impact selection decisions, consider a situation in which practically every applicant can be successful (i.e., a

SPECIAL INTEREST TOPIC   **5.1**
Regression, Prediction, and Your First Algebra Class

One of the major purposes of various aptitude measures such as IQ tests is to make predictions about performance on some other variable such as reading achievement test scores, success in a job training program, or even college grade point average. In order to make predictions from a score on one test to a score on some other measure, the mathematical relationship between the two must be determined. Most often we assume the relationship to be linear and direct with test scores such as intelligence and achievement. When this is the case, a simple equation is derived that represents the relationship between two test scores that we will call X and Y.

If our research shows that X and Y are indeed related—that is, for any change in the value of X there is a systematic (not random) change in Y—our equation will allow us to estimate this change or to predict the value of Y if we know the value of X. Retaining X and Y as we have used them so far, the general form of our equation would be:

$$Y = aX + b$$

This equation goes by several names. Statisticians are most likely to refer to it as a regression equation. Practitioners of psychology who use the equation to make predictions may refer to it as a prediction equation. However, somewhere around 8th or 9th grade, in your first algebra class, you were introduced to this expression and told it was the equation of a straight line. What algebra teachers typically do not explain at this level is that they are actually teaching you regression!

Let's look at an example of how our equation works. For this example, we will let X represent some individual's score on an intelligence test and Y the person's score on an achievement test a year in the future. To determine our actual equation, we would have had to test a large number of students on the IQ test, waited a year, and then tested the same students on an achievement test. We then calculate the relationship between the two sets of scores. One reasonable outcome would yield an equation such as this one:

$$Y = 0.5X + 10$$

In determining the relationship between X and Y, we calculated the value of a to be 0.5 and the value of b to be 10. In your early algebra class, a was referred to as the *slope* of your line and b as the Y-intercept (the starting point of your line on the Y-axis when $X = 0$). We have graphed this equation for you in Figure 5.1. When $X = 0$, Y is equal to 10 ($Y = .5(0) + 10$), so our line starts on the Y-axis at a value of 10. Because our slope is 0.5, for each increase in X, the increase in Y will be half, or 0.5 time, as much. We can use our equation or our prediction line to estimate or predict the value of Y for any value of X, just as you did in that early algebra class. Nothing has really changed except the names.

Instead of slope, we typically refer to a as a regression coefficient or a beta weight. Instead of the Y-intercept, we typically refer to b from our equation as a constant, because it is always being added to aX in the same amount on every occasion.

If we look at Figure 5.4, we can see that for a score of 10 on our intelligence test, a score of 15 is predicted on the achievement test. A score of 30 on our intelligence test, a 20-point increase, predicts an achievement test score of 25, an increase on Y equal to half the increase in X. These values are the same whether we use our prediction line or our equation—they are simply differing ways of showing the relationship between X and Y.

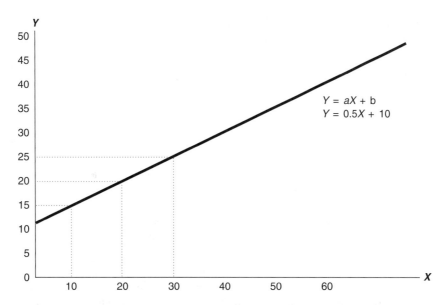

FIGURE 5.4   Example of a Graph of the Equation of a Straight Line, also Known as a Regression Line or Prediction Line

Note: $Y = aX + b$ when $a = 0.5$ and $b = 10$. For example, if X is 30, then $Y = (0.5)30 + 10 = 25$.

We are predicting Y from X, and our prediction is never perfect when we are using test scores. For any one person, we will typically be off somewhat in predicting future test scores. Our prediction actually is telling us the mean or average score on Y of all the students in the research study at each score on X. For example, the mean achievement score of all of our students who had a score of 40 on the intelligence test was 30. We know that not all of the students who earned a 40 on the intelligence test will score 30 on the achievement test. We use the mean score on Y of all our students who scored 40 on the intelligence measure as our predicted value for all students who score 40 on X nevertheless. The mean is used because it results in the smallest amount of error in all our predictions. In actual practice, we would also be highly interested in just how much error existed in our predictions, and this degree of error would be calculated and reported. Once we determine the average amount of error in our predictions, we make statements about how confident we are in predicting Y based on X. For example, if the average amount of error (called the standard error of estimate) in our prediction were 2 points, we might say that based on his score of 40 on the IQ measure, we are 68% confident John's achievement test score a year later will be between 38 and 42 and 95% confident that it will fall within the range of scores from 36 to 44.

very easy task). Because almost any applicant selected will be successful, no test is likely to be useful regardless of how strong a relationship there is between it and the criterion. However, if you have a difficult task and few applicants can be successful, even a test with a moderate correlation with the criterion may be useful. To take into consideration these factors, decision-theory models of utility have been developed (Messick, 1989). In brief,

Decision-theory models **help the test user determine how much information a predictor test can contribute when making classification decisions.**

decision-theory models help the test user determine how much information a predictor test can contribute when making classification decisions. We will not go into detail about decision theory, but interested students are referred to Anastasi and Urbina (1997) for a readable discussion of decision-theory models.

Validity Generalization. An important consideration in the interpretation of predictive and concurrent studies is the degree to which they can be generalized to new situations, that is, to circumstances similar to but not the same as those under which the validity studies were conducted. When a test is used for prediction in new settings, research has shown that validity coefficients can vary considerably. For example, a validation study may be conducted using a national sample, but different results may be obtained when the study is repeated using a restricted sample such as a local school district. Originally these results were interpreted as suggesting that test users were not able to rely on existing validation studies and needed to conduct their own local validation studies. However, subsequent research using a new statistical procedure known as *meta-analysis* indicated that much of the variability previously observed in validity coefficients was actually due to statistical artifacts (e.g., sampling error). When these statistical artifacts were taken into consideration the remaining variability was often negligible, suggesting that validity coefficients can be generalized more than previously thought (AERA et al., 1999). Currently, in many situations local validation studies are not seen as necessary. For example, if there is abundant meta-analytic research that produces consistent results, local validity studies will likely not add much useful information. However, if there is little existing research or the results are inconsistent, then local validity studies may be particularly useful (AERA et al., 1999).

Convergent and Discriminant Evidence. Convergent and discriminant evidence of validity have traditionally been incorporated under the category of construct validity. **Convergent evidence** of validity is obtained when you correlate a test with existing tests that measure similar constructs. For example, if you are developing a new intelligence test you might elect to correlate scores on your new test with scores on the *Wechsler Intelligence Scale for Children—Fourth Edition* (WISC-IV; Wechsler, 2003). Because the WISC-IV is a well-respected test of intelligence with considerable validity evidence, a strong correlation between the WISC-IV and your new intelligence test would provide evidence that your test is actually measuring the construct of intelligence.

Convergent evidence **of validity involves correlating a test with existing tests that measure similar constructs.**

Discriminant evidence of validity is obtained when you correlate a test with existing tests that measure dissimilar constructs. For example, if you were validating a test designed to measure anxiety, you might correlate your anxiety scores with a measure of sensation seeking. Because anxious individuals do not typically engage in sensation-seeking behaviors, you would expect a negative correlation between the measures. If your analyses produce the expected negative correlations, this would support your hypothesis.

Discriminant evidence **of validity involves correlating a test with existing tests that measure dissimilar constructs.**

There is a related, relatively sophisticated validation technique referred to as the **multitrait-multimethod matrix** (Campbell & Fiske,

1959). This approach requires that you examine two or more traits (e.g., anxiety and sensation seeking) using two or more measurement methods (e.g., self-report and teacher rating). The researcher then examines the resulting correlation matrix, comparing the actual relationships with *a priori* (i.e., preexisting) predictions about the relationships. In addition to revealing information about convergent and discriminant relationships, this technique provides information about the influence of common **method variance.** When two measures show an unexpected correlation due to similarity in their method of measurement, we refer to this as method variance. Thus, the multitrait-multimethod matrix allows one to determine what the test correlates with, what it does not correlate with, and how the method of measurement influences these relationships. This approach has considerable technical and theoretical appeal, yet difficulty with implementation and interpretation has limited its application to date.

Contrasted Groups Studies. Validity evidence can also be garnered by examining different groups, which are expected, based on theory, to differ on the construct the test is designed to measure. This is referred to as a **contrasted group study.** For example, if you are attempting to validate a new measure of intelligence, you might form two groups, individuals with mental retardation and normal control participants. In this type of study, the diagnoses or group assignment would have been made using assessment procedures that do not involve the test under consideration. Each group would then be administered the new test, and its validity as a measure of intelligence would be supported if the predefined groups differed in performance in the predicted manner. Although the preceding example is rather simplistic, it illustrates a general approach that has numerous applications. For example, many constructs in psychology and education have a developmental component. That is, you expect younger participants to perform differently than older participants. Tests designed to measure these constructs can be examined to determine whether they demonstrate the expected developmental changes by looking at the performance of groups reflecting different ages and/or education. In the past, this type of validity evidence has typically been classified as construct validity.

Evidence Based on Internal Structure

By examining the internal structure of a test (or battery of tests) one can determine whether the relationships between test items (or, in the case of test batteries, component tests) are consistent with the construct the test is designed to measure (AERA et al., 1999). For example, one test might be designed to measure a construct that is hypothesized to involve a single dimension, whereas another test might measure a construct thought to involve multiple dimensions. By examining the internal structure of the test we can determine whether its actual structure is consistent with the hypothesized structure of the construct it measures. **Factor analysis** is a sophisticated statistical procedure used to determine the number of conceptually distinct factors or dimensions underlying a test or battery of tests. Because factor analysis is a fairly complicated technique, we will not go into detail about its calculation. However, factor analysis plays a prominent role in test validation and you need to be aware of its use. In summary, test publishers and researchers use factor analysis either to confirm or to refute the proposition that the internal structure of the tests is consistent with that of the construct.

By examining the internal structure of the test we can determine whether its actual structure is consistent with the hypothesized structure of the construct it measures.

Factor analysis is not the only approach researchers use to examine the internal structure of a test. Any technique that allows researchers to examine the relationships between test components can be used in this context. For example, if the items on a test are assumed to reflect a continuum from very easy to very difficult, empirical evidence of a pattern of increasing difficulty can be used as validity evidence. If a test is thought to measure a one-dimensional construct, a measure of item homogeneity might be useful (AERA et al., 1999). The essential feature of this type of validity evidence is that researchers empirically examine the internal structure of the test and compare it to the structure of the construct of interest. This type of validity evidence has traditionally been incorporated under the category of construct validity and is most relevant with tests measuring theoretical constructs such as intelligence or personality.

Evidence Based on Response Processes

Validity evidence based on the response processes invoked by a test involves an analysis of the fit between the performance and actions the examinees actually engage in and the construct being assessed. Although this type of validity evidence has not received as much attention as the approaches previously discussed, it has considerable potential and in terms of the traditional nomenclature it would likely be classified under construct validity. For example, consider a test designed to measure mathematical reasoning ability. In this situation it would be important to investigate the examinees' response processes to verify that they are actually engaging in analysis and reasoning as opposed to applying rote mathematical algorithms (AERA et al., 1999). There are numerous ways of collecting this type of validity evidence, including interviewing examinees about their response processes and strategies, recording behavioral indicators such as response times and eye movements, or even analyzing the types of errors committed (AERA et al., 1999; Messick, 1989).

The *Standards* (AERA et al., 1999) note that studies of response processes are not restricted to individuals taking the test, but may also examine the assessment professionals who administer or grade the tests. When testing personnel record or evaluate the performance of examinees, it is important to make sure that their processes or actions are in line with the construct being measured. For example, many tests provide specific criteria or rubrics that are intended to guide the scoring process. The *Wechsler Individual Achievement Test—Second Edition* (WIAT-II; The Psychological Corporation, 2002) has a section to assess written expression that requires the examinee to write an essay. To facilitate grading, the authors include an analytic scoring rubric that has four evaluative categories: mechanics (e.g., spelling, punctuation), organization (e.g., structure, sequencing, use of introductory/concluding sentences, etc.), theme development (use of supporting statements, evidence), and vocabulary (e.g., specific and varied words, unusual expressions). In validating this assessment it would be helpful to evaluate the behaviors of individuals scoring the test to verify that the criteria are being carefully applied and that irrelevant factors are not influencing the scoring process.

Evidence Based on Consequences of Testing

Recently, researchers have started examining the consequences of test use, both intended and unintended, as an aspect of validity. In many situations the use of tests is largely based on the assumption that their use will result in some specific benefit (AERA et al., 1999). For

Researchers have started examining the consequences of test use, both intended and unintended, as an aspect of validity.

example, if a test is used to identify qualified applicants for employment, it is assumed that the use of the test will result in better hiring decisions (e.g., lower training costs, lower turnover). If a test is used to help select students for admission to a college program, it is assumed that the use of the test will result in better admissions decisions (e.g., greater student success and higher retention). This line of validity evidence simply asks the question, "Are these benefits being achieved?" This type of validity evidence, often referred to as consequential validity evidence, is most applicable to tests designed for selection and promotion.

Some authors have advocated a broader conception of validity, one that incorporates social issues and values. For example, Messick (1989) in his influential chapter suggested that the conception of validity should be expanded so that it "formally brings consideration of value implications and social consequences into the validity framework" (p. 20). Other testing experts have criticized this position. For example, Popham (2000) suggests that incorporating social consequences into the definition of validity would detract from the clarity of the concept. Popham argues that validity is clearly defined as the "accuracy of score-based inferences" (p. 111), and that the inclusion of social and value issues unnecessarily complicates the concept. The *Standards* (AERA et al., 1999) appear to avoid this broader conceptualization of validity. The *Standards* distinguish between consequential evidence that is directly tied to the concept of validity and evidence that is related to social policy. This is an important but potentially difficult distinction to make. Consider a situation in which research suggests that the use of a test results in different job selection rates for different groups. If the test measures only the skills and abilities related to job performance, evidence of differential selection rates does not detract from the validity of the test. This information might be useful in guiding social and policy decisions, but it is not technically an aspect of validity. If, however, the test measures factors unrelated to job performance, the evidence is relevant to validity. In this case, it may suggest a problem with the validity of the test such as the inclusion of construct-irrelevant factors.

Another component to this process is to consider the consequences of not using tests. Even though the consequences of testing may produce some adverse effects, these must be contrasted with the positive and negative effects of alternatives to using psychological tests. If more subjective approaches to decision making are employed, for example, the likelihood of cultural, ethnic, and gender biases in the decision-making process will likely increase.

Integrating Evidence of Validity

The *Standards* (AERA et al., 1999) state:

> Validation can be viewed as developing a scientifically sound validity argument to support the intended interpretation of test scores and their relevance to the proposed use. (p. 9)

The development of a *validity argument* typically involves the integration of numerous lines of evidence into a coherent commentary.

The development of this **validity argument** typically involves the integration of numerous lines of evidence into a coherent commentary. The development of a validity argument is an ongoing process; it takes into consideration existing research and incorporates new scientific findings. As we have noted, different types of validity evidence are most applicable to different type of tests. Here is a brief review of some of the prominent applications of different types of validity evidence.

- **Evidence based on test content:** This type of validity evidence is most often reported with academic achievement tests and tests used in the selection of employees.
- **Evidence based on relations to other variables:** Test-criterion validity evidence is most applicable when tests are used to predict performance on an external criterion. Convergent and discriminant validity evidence can be useful with a wide variety of tests, including intelligence tests, achievement tests, personality tests, and so on.
- **Evidence based on internal structure:** This type of validity can be useful with a wide variety of tests, but has traditionally been applied with tests measuring theoretical constructs such as personality or intelligence.
- **Evidence based on response processes:** This category of evidence can be useful with practically any test that requires examinees to engage in any cognitive or behavioral activity.
- **Evidence based on consequences of testing:** This type of validity evidence is most applicable to tests designed for selection and promotion, but can be useful with a wide range of tests.

You might have noticed that most types of validity evidence have applications to a broad variety of tests, and this is the way it should be. The integration of multiple lines of research or types of evidence results in a more compelling validity argument. It is also important to remember that every interpretation or intended use of a test must be validated. As we noted earlier, if a test is used for different applications, each use or application must be validated. In these situations it is imperative that different types of validity evidence be provided. Table 5.2 provides a summary of the major applications of different types of validity evidence.

TABLE 5.2   Sources of Validity Evidence

Source	Example	Major Applications
Evidence based on test content	Analysis of item relevance and content coverage	Achievement tests and tests used in the selection of employees
Evidence based on relations to other variables	Test-criterion; convergent and discriminant evidence; contrasted groups studies	Wide variety of tests
Evidence based on internal structure	Factor analysis, analysis of test homogeneity	Wide variety of tests, but particularly useful with tests of constructs such as personality or intelligence
Evidence based on response processes	Analysis of the processes engaged in by the examinee or examiner	Any test that requires examinees to engage in a cognitive or behavioral activity
Evidence based on consequences of testing structure	Analysis of the intended and unintended consequences of testing	Most applicable to tests designed for selection and promotion, but useful on a wide range of tests

Validity: Practical Strategies for Teachers

Although teachers typically do not have the time or resources to conduct large-scale validity studies, they can use some practical and sound procedures to evaluate the validity of the results of classroom assessments.

Validity refers to the appropriateness or accuracy of the interpretation of assessment results. The results of classroom assessments are used in many different ways in today's schools, and teachers need to consider the validity of all of these applications. One of the most prominent uses of classroom assessment results is the summative evaluation of student knowledge and skills in a specified content area (e.g., evaluating mastery and assigning grades). In this context, Nitko (2001) developed a set of guidelines for evaluating and improving the validity of the results of classroom assessments. These guidelines include the following.

Examination of Test Content. The evaluation of the validity of the results of classroom assessments often begins with an analysis of the test content. As we discussed earlier in this chapter, this typically involves an examination of item relevance and content coverage. Analysis of item relevance involves examining the individual test items and determining whether they reflect essential elements of the content domain. Content coverage involves examining the overall test and determining the degree to which the items cover the specified domain (refer back to Figure 5.1). The question here is "Does validity evidence based on the content of the test support the intended interpretations of test results?" In other words, is this test covering the content it is supposed to cover?

Examination of Student Response Processes. This guideline requires consideration of the validity evidence that examines the cognitive and behavioral processes engaged in by the students. In other words, do the assessments require the students to engage in the types of cognitive processes and behavioral activities that are specified in the learning objectives? For example, if your learning objectives involve problem solving, does the assessment require the students to engage in problem solving? In a later chapter we will describe how the use of a taxonomy of student abilities can help you develop tests that cover a broad range of abilities and skills.

Examination of Relations to Other Assessments. This guideline encourages you to examine the relationship between a given assessment and other sources of information about the students. That is, are the results of the assessment in question consistent with other sources of information (e.g., other tests; class projects; teacher's observation)? If the results are consistent, the validity of the assessment is supported. If they are inconsistent, then the validity of the assessment results may be questionable. If you have access to a computer and spreadsheet it is easy to calculate the correlation between scores on multiple assessments and examine them for evidence of consistency (e.g., moderate to high positive correlations among the different assessments).

Examination of Reliability. This guideline encourages you to consider evidence regarding the reliability of assessment results. As we noted earlier the reliability of test scores sets an upper limit on the validity of their interpretation. Although reliability does not assure validity, you cannot have valid score interpretations if those scores are not reliable. As a result, efforts to increase the reliability of assessment results can enhance validity.

Examination of Test Fairness.   This guideline suggests that teachers should examine their classroom assessments to ensure that they are fair to all students. For example, tests and other assessments should be fair to students from diverse ethnic and cultural backgrounds.

Examination of Practical Features.   This guideline encourages you to examine your classroom assessments to ensure that they are practical and efficient. This involves a consideration of the amount of time required to develop, administer, and score the assessment. Although assessment plays an extremely important role in today's schools, their development and use should not consume an inordinate amount of time.

Examination of the Overall Assessment Strategy.   Nitko (2001) notes that even when you follow all of the previous guidelines, perfect validity will always elude you. To counter this, he recommends that teachers employ a multiple-assessment strategy that incorporates the results of numerous assessments to measure student achievement.

We feel Nitko's (2001) guidelines provide a good basis for evaluating and improving the validity of classroom assessments. Although teachers typically do not have the time or resources to conduct large-scale validity studies, these guidelines provide some practical and sound advice for evaluating the validity of the results of classroom assessments.

Summary

In this chapter we introduced the concept of validity. In the context of educational and psychological tests and measurement, validity refers to the degree to which theoretical and empirical evidence supports the meaning and interpretation of test scores. In essence the validity question is "Are the intended interpretations of test scores appropriate and accurate?" Numerous factors can limit the validity of interpretations. The two major internal threats to validity are construct underrepresentation (i.e., the test is not a comprehensive measure of the construct it is supposed to measure) and construct-irrelevant variance (i.e., the test measures content or skills unrelated to the construct). Other factors that may reduce validity include variations in instructional procedures, test administration/scoring procedures, and student characteristics. There is also a close relationship between validity and reliability. For a test to be valid it must be reliable, but at the same time reliability does not ensure validity. Put another way, reliability is a necessary but insufficient condition for validity.

As a psychometric concept validity has evolved and changed over the last half a century. Until the 1970s validity was generally divided into three distinct types: content validity, criterion-related validity, and construct validity. This terminology was widely accepted and is still often referred to as the traditional nomenclature. However, in the 1970s and 1980s measurement professionals started conceptualizing validity as a unitary construct. That is, although there are different ways of collecting validity evidence, there are not distinct types of validity. To get away from the perception of distinct types of validity, today we refer to different types of validity evidence. The most current typology includes the following five categories:

- *Evidence based on test content:* This category consists of evidence derived from a detailed analysis of the test content, which includes the type of questions or tasks included in the test and guidelines for administration and scoring. Collecting content-based validity evidence is often based on the evaluation of expert judges about the correspondence between the test's content and its construct. The key issues addressed by these expert judges are to determine whether the test items assess relevant content (i.e., item relevance) and the degree to which the construct is assessed in a comprehensive manner (i.e., content coverage).
- *Evidence based on relations to other variables:* This category includes evidence based on an examination of the relationships between test performance and external variables or criteria. This category can actually be divided into two subcategories of validity evidence: test-criterion evidence and convergent and discriminant evidence. Test-criterion evidence is typically of interest when a test is designed to predict performance on a criterion such as job performance or success in college. Two types of studies are often used to collect test-criterion evidence: predictive and concurrent studies. They differ in the timing of test administration and criterion measurement. In a predictive study the test is administered and there is an interval of time before the criterion is measured. In concurrent studies the test is administered and the criterion is measured at approximately the same time. The collection of convergent and discriminant evidence involves examining the relationship between a test and other tests that measure similar constructs (convergent evidence) or dissimilar constructs (discriminant evidence). If the test scores demonstrate the expected relationships with these existing measures, this can be used as evidence of validity.
- *Evidence based on internal structure:* This category of evidence involves the examination of the relationships among test items and components. By examining the internal structure of the test we can determine whether the structure of the test is consistent with the hypothesized structure of the construct it measures.
- *Evidence based on response processes:* This category of evidence involves an analysis of the processes engaged in by the examinee or examiner. For example, if the test is designed to measure mathematical reasoning, it is helpful to verify that the examinees are actually engaging in mathematical reasoning and analysis as opposed to performing rote calculations.
- *Evidence based on consequences of testing:* This category of evidence is based on an examination of the intended and unintended consequences of testing. Because the use of tests is often based on the belief that some benefit will result, it is reasonable to confirm that these benefits are being achieved. This type of validity evidence has gained considerable attention in recent years and there is continuing debate regarding the scope of this evidence. Some authors feel that social consequences and values should be incorporated into the conceptualization of validity, whereas others feel such a broadening would detract from the clarity of the concept.

Different lines of validity evidence are integrated into a cohesive validity argument that supports the use of the test for different applications. The development of this validity argument is a dynamic process that integrates existing research and incorporates new scientific findings. Validation is the shared responsibility of the test authors, test publishers, researchers, and even test users. Test authors and publishers are expected to provide preliminary evidence of the validity of the proposed interpretations of test scores whereas researchers often pursue independent validity studies. Ultimately, those using tests are expected to weigh the validity evidence and make their own judgments about the appropriateness of the test in their own situations and settings, placing the practitioners or consumers of psychological tests in the final, most responsible role in this process.

KEY TERMS AND CONCEPTS

Base rate, p. 129
Concurrent studies, p. 127
Construct-irrelevant variance, p. 118
Construct underrepresentation, p. 118
Construct validity, p. 121
Content coverage, p. 124
Content validity, p. 120
Contrasted group study, p. 133
Convergent evidence, p. 132
Criterion, p. 126
Criterion contamination, p. 128
Criterion-related validity, p. 121
Decision-theory models, p. 132

Discriminant evidence, p. 132
Evidence based on consequences of testing, p. 122
Evidence based on internal structure, p. 122
Evidence based on relations to other variables, p. 121
Evidence based on response processes, p. 122
Evidence based on test content, p. 121
Face validity, p. 125
Factor analysis, p. 133
Item relevance, p. 124

Linear regression, p. 129
Method variance, p. 133
Multitrait-multimethod matrix, p. 132
Predictive studies, p. 127
Selection ratio, p. 129
Standard error of estimate, p. 129
Table of specifications, p. 123
Test-criterion evidence, p. 127
Validity, p. 118
Validity as a unitary concept, p. 121
Validity construct, p. 121
Validity argument, p. 135
Validity coefficient, p. 127

RECOMMENDED READINGS

American Educational Research Association, American Psychological Association, & National Council on Measurement in Education (1999). *Standards for educational and psychological testing.* Washington, DC: American Educational Research Association. Chapter 1 is a must read for those wanting to gain a thorough understanding of validity.

Cronbach, L. J., & Gleser, G. C. (1965). *Psychological tests and personnel decisions* (2nd ed.). Champaign: University of Illinois Press. A classic, particularly with regard to validity evidence based on relations to external variables!

Gorsuch, R. L. (1983). *Factor analysis* (2nd ed.). Hillsdale, NJ: Erlbaum. A classic for those really interested in understanding factor analysis.

Messick, S. (1989). Validity. In R. L. Linn (Ed.), *Educational measurement* (3rd ed., pp. 13–103). Upper Saddle River, NJ: Merrill/Prentice Hall. A little technical at times, but a very influential chapter.

Sireci, S. G. (1998). Gathering and analyzing content validity data. *Educational Assessment,* 5, 299–321. This article provides a good review of approaches to collecting validity evidence based on test content, including some of the newer quantitative approaches.

Tabachnick, B. G., & Fidel, L. S. (1996). *Using multivariate statistics* (3rd ed.). New York: HarperCollins. A great chapter on factor analysis that is less technical than Gorsuch (1993).

Item Analysis for Teachers

The better the items, the better the test.

CHAPTER HIGHLIGHTS

Item Difficulty Index (or Item Difficulty Level)

Item Discrimination

Distracter Analysis

Item Analysis: Practical Strategies for Teachers

Using Item Analysis to Improve Items

Item Analysis of Performance Assessments

Qualitative Item Analysis

Using Item Analysis to Improve Classroom
Instruction

LEARNING OBJECTIVES

After reading and studying this chapter, students should be able to:

1. Discuss the relationship between the reliability and validity of test scores and the quality of the items on a test.

2. Describe the importance of the item difficulty index and demonstrate its calculation and interpretation.

3. Describe how special assessment situations may impact the interpretation of the item difficulty index.

4. Describe the importance of the item discrimination and demonstrate its calculation and interpretation.

5. Describe the relationship between item difficulty and discrimination.

6. Describe how item-total correlations can be used to examine item discrimination.

7. Describe how the calculation of item discrimination can be modified for mastery tests.

8. Describe the importance of distracter analysis and demonstrate its calculation and interpretation.

9. Describe how the selection of distracters influences item difficulty and discrimination.

10. Apply practical strategies for item analysis to classroom tests.

11. Show how item analysis statistics can be used to improve test items.

12. Describe how item analysis procedures can be applied to performance assessments.

13. Describe qualitative approaches to improving test items.

14. Describe how information from item analyses can be used to improve classroom instruction.

A number of quantitative procedures are useful in assessing the quality and measurement characteristics of the individual items that make up tests. Collectively these procedures are referred to as item analysis statistics or procedures. Unlike reliability and validity analyses that evaluate the measurement characteristics of a test as a whole, **item analysis** procedures examine individual items separately, not the overall test. Item analysis statistics are useful in helping test developers, including both professional psychometricians and classroom teachers, decide which items to keep on a test, which to modify, and which to eliminate. In addition to helping test developers improve tests by improving the individual items, they can also provide valuable information regarding the effectiveness of instruction or training.

The reliability of test scores and the validity of the interpretation of test scores are dependent on the quality of the items on the test. If you can improve the quality of the individual items, you will improve the overall quality of your test. When discussing reliability we noted that one of the easiest ways to increase the reliability of test scores is to increase the number of items that go into making up the test score. This statement is generally true and is based on the assumption that when you lengthen a test you add items of the same quality as the existing items. If you use item analysis to delete poor items and improve other items, it is possible to end up with a test that is shorter than the original test and that also produces scores that are more reliable and result in more valid interpretations.

> The reliability and validity of test scores are dependent on the quality of the items on the test. If you can improve the quality of the individual items, you will improve the overall quality of your test.

Although quantitative procedures for evaluating the quality of test items will be the focus of the chapter, some qualitative procedures may prove useful when evaluating the quality of test items. These qualitative procedures typically involve an evaluation of validity evidence based on the content of the test and an examination of individual items to ensure that they are technically accurate and clearly stated. Although these qualitative procedures have not received as much attention as their quantitative counterparts, it is often beneficial to use a combination of quantitative and qualitative procedures.

We will begin our discussion by describing the major quantitative item analysis procedures. First, however, it should be noted that different types of items and different types of tests require different types of item analysis procedures. Items that are scored dichotomously (i.e., either right or wrong) are handled differently than items that are scored on a continuum (e.g., an essay that can receive scores ranging from 0 to 10). Tests that are designed to maximize the variability of scores (e.g., norm-referenced) are handled differently than mastery tests (i.e., scored pass or fail). As we discuss various item analysis procedures, we will specify which types of procedures are appropriate for which types of items and tests.

Item Difficulty Index (or Item Difficulty Level)

When evaluating items on ability tests, an important consideration is the difficulty level of the items. **Item difficulty** is defined as the percentage or proportion of test takers who cor-

Item difficulty **is defined as the percentage or proportion of test takers who correctly answer the item.**

rectly answer the item. The item difficulty level or index is abbreviated as p and calculated with the following formula:

$$p = \frac{\text{Number of Examinees Correctly Answering the Item}}{\text{Number of Examinees}}$$

For example, in a class of 30 students, if 20 students get the answer correct and 10 are incorrect, the item difficulty index is 0.67. The calculations are illustrated here.

$$p = \frac{20}{30} = 0.67$$

In the same class, if 10 students get the answer correct and 20 are incorrect, the item difficulty index is 0.33. The item difficulty index can range from 0.0 to 1.0 with easier items having larger decimal values and difficult items having lower decimal values. An item that is answered correctly by all students receives an item difficulty of 1.0 whereas an item that is answered incorrectly by all students receives an item difficulty of 0.0. Items with p values of either 1.0 or 0.0 provide no information about individual differences and are of no value from a measurement perspective. Some test developers will include one or two items with p values of 1.0 at the beginning of a test to instill a sense of confidence in test takers. This is a defensible practice from a motivational perspective, but from a technical perspective these items do not contribute to the measurement characteristics of the test. Another factor that should be considered about the inclusion of very easy or very difficult items is the issue of time efficiency. The time students spend answering ineffective items is largely wasted and could be better spent on items that enhance the measurement characteristics of the test.

For maximizing variability and reliability, the **optimal item difficulty level** is 0.50, indicating that 50% of the test takers answered the item correctly and 50% answered the item incorrectly. Based on this statement, you might conclude that it is desirable for all test items to have a difficulty level of 0.50, but this is not necessarily true for several reasons. One reason is that items on a test are often correlated with each other, which means the measurement process may be confounded if all the items have p values of 0.50. As a result, it is often desirable to select some items with p values below 0.50 and some with values greater than 0.50, but with a mean of 0.50. Aiken (2000) recommends that there should be approximately a 0.20 range of these p values around the optimal value. For example, a test developer might select items with difficulty levels ranging from 0.40 to 0.60, with a mean of 0.50.

For maximizing variability among test takers, the *optimal item difficulty level* **is 0.50, indicating that 50% of the test takers answered the item correctly and 50% answered the item incorrectly.**

Although a mean *p* **of 0.50 is optimal for maximizing variability and reliability, different levels are desirable in many different testing applications.**

Another reason why 0.50 is not the optimal difficulty level for every testing situation involves the influence of guessing. On constructed-response items (e.g., essay and short-answer items) for which guessing is not a major concern, 0.50 is typically considered the optimal difficulty level. However, with selected-response items (e.g., multiple choice and true–false items) for which test takers

TABLE 6.1 Optimal *p* Values for Items with Varying Numbers of Choices

Number of Choices	Optimal Mean *p* Value
2 (e.g., true–false)	0.85
3	0.77
4	0.74
5	0.69
Constructed response (e.g., essay)	0.50

Source: Based on Lord (1952).

might answer the item correctly simply by guessing, the optimal difficulty level varies. To take into consideration the effects of guessing, the optimal item difficulty level is set higher than for constructed-response items. For example, for multiple-choice items with four options the average *p* should be approximately 0.74 (Lord, 1952). That is, the test developer might select items with difficulty levels ranging from 0.64 to 0.84 with a mean of approximately 0.74. Table 6.1 provides information on the optimal mean *p* value for selected-response items with varying numbers of alternatives or choices.

Special Assessment Situations and Item Difficulty

Our discussion of item difficulty so far is most applicable to norm-referenced tests. For criterion-referenced tests, particularly mastery tests, item difficulty is evaluated differently. On mastery tests the test taker typically either passes or fails and there is the expectation that most test takers will eventually be successful. As a result, on mastery tests it is common for items to have average *p* values as high as 0.90. Other tests that are designed for special assessment purposes may vary in terms of what represents desirable item difficulty levels. For example, if a test were developed to help employers select the upper 25% of job applicants, it would be desirable to have items with *p* values that average around 0.25. If it is desirable for a test to be able to distinguish between the highest-performing examinees (e.g., in testing gifted and talented students), it may also be desirable to include at least some very difficult items. In summary, although a mean *p* of 0.50 is optimal for maximizing variability among test takers, different difficulty levels are desirable in many testing applications (see Special Interest Topic 6.1 for another example). Later in this chapter we will provide some examples of how test developers use information about item difficulty and other item analysis statistics to select items to retain, revise, or delete from future administrations of the test. First, we will discuss another popular item analysis procedure—the item discrimination index.

Item Discrimination

Item discrimination refers to how well an item can discriminate or differentiate among test takers who differ on the construct being measured by the test. For example, if a test is de-

Item Difficulty Indexes and Power Tests

As a rule of thumb and for psychometric reasons explained in this chapter, we have noted that item difficulty indexes of 0.50 are desirable in many circumstances on standardized tests. However, it is also common to include some very easy items so all or most examinees get some questions correct, as well as some very hard items, so the test has enough ceiling. With a power test, such as an IQ test, that covers a wide age range and whose underlying construct is developmental, item selection becomes much more complex. Items that work very well at some ages may be far too easy, too hard, or just developmentally inappropriate at other ages. If a test covers the age range of say 3 years up to 20 years, and the items all have a difficulty level of 0.50, you could be left with a situation in which the 3-, 4-, 5-, and even 6-year-olds typically pass no items and perhaps the oldest individuals nearly always get every item correct. This would lead to very low reliability estimates at the upper and lower ages and just poor measurement of the constructs generally, except near the middle of the intended age range. For such power tests covering a wide age span, item statistics such as the difficulty index and the discrimination index are examined at each age level and plotted across all age levels. In this way, items can be chosen that are effective in measuring the relevant construct at different ages. When the item difficulty indexes for such a test are examined across the entire age range, some will approach 0.0 and some will approach 1.00. However, within the age levels, for example, for 6-year-olds, many items will be close to 0.50. This affords better discrimination and gives each examinee a range of items on which they can express their ability on the underlying trait.

Item discrimination **refers to how well an item can accurately discriminate between test takers who differ on the construct being measured.**

signed to measure reading comprehension, item discrimination reflects an item's ability to distinguish between individuals with good reading comprehension skills and those with poor reading skills. Unlike item difficulty level about which there is agreement on how to calculate the statistic, over fifty different indexes of item discrimination have been developed over the years (Anastasi & Urbina, 1997). Fortunately, most of these indexes produce similar results (Engelhart, 1965; Oosterhof, 1976).

Discrimination Index

Probably the most popular method of calculating an index of item discrimination is based on the difference in performance between two groups. Although there are different ways of selecting the two groups, they are typically defined in terms of total test performance. One common approach is to select the top and bottom 27% of test takers in terms of their overall performance on the test, and exclude the middle 46% (Kelley, 1939). Some assessment experts have suggested using the top and bottom 25%, some the top and bottom 33%, and some the top and bottom halves. In practice, all of these are probably acceptable (later in this chapter we will show you a more practical approach that saves both time and effort). The

Probably the most popular method of calculating an index of item discrimination is based on the difference between those who score well on the overall test and those who score poorly.

difficulty of the item is computed for each group separately, and these are labeled p_T and p_B (*T* for top, *B* for bottom). The difference between p_T and p_B is the discrimination index, designated as *D,* and is calculated with the following formula (e.g., Johnson, 1951):

$$D = p_T - p_B$$

where D = discrimination index

            p_T = proportion of examinees in the top group getting the item correct

            p_B = proportion of examinees in the bottom group getting the item correct

To illustrate the logic behind this index, consider a classroom test designed to measure academic achievement in some specified area. If the item is discriminating between students who know the material and those who do not, then students who are more knowledgeable (i.e., students in the top group) should get the item correct more often than students who are less knowledgeable (i.e., students in the bottom group). For example, if $p_T = 0.80$ (indicating 80% of the students in the top group answered the item correctly) and $p_B = 0.30$ (indicating 30% of the students in the bottom group answered the item correctly), then:

$$D = 0.80 - 0.30 = 0.50$$

Hopkins (1998) provided guidelines for evaluating items in terms of their *D* values (see Table 6.2). According to these guidelines, *D* values of 0.40 and above are considered excellent, between 0.30 and 0.39 are good, between 0.11 and 0.29 are fair, and between 0.00 and 0.10 are poor. Items with negative *D* values are likely miskeyed or there are other serious problems. Other testing assessment experts have provided different guidelines, some more rigorous and some more lenient.

As a general rule, we recommend that items with *D* values over 0.30 are acceptable, and items with *D* values below 0.30 should be carefully reviewed and possibly revised or deleted.

As a general rule, we suggest that items with *D* values over 0.30 are acceptable (the larger the better), and items with *D* values below 0.30 should be carefully reviewed and possibly revised or deleted. However, this is only a general rule and there are exceptions. For example, most indexes of item discrimination, including the item dis-

TABLE 6.2   Guidelines for Evaluating *D* Values

Difficulty	
0.40 and larger	Excellent
0.30–0.39	Good
0.11–0.29	Fair
0.00–0.10	Poor
Negative values	Miskeyed or other major flaw

Source: Based on Hopkins (1998).

TABLE 6.3   Maximum *D* Values at Different Difficulty Levels

Item Difficulty Index (*p*)	Maximum *D* Value
1.0	0
0.90	0.20
0.80	0.40
0.70	0.60
0.60	0.70
0.50	1.0
0.40	0.70
0.30	0.60
0.20	0.40
0.10	0.20
0.00	0

crimination index (*D*), are biased in favor of items with intermediate difficulty levels. That is, the maximum *D* value of an item is related to its *p* value (see Table 6.3). Items that all test takers either pass or fail (i.e., *p* values of either 0.0 or 1.0) cannot provide any information about individual differences and their *D* values will always be zero. If half of the test takers correctly answered an item and half failed (i.e., *p* value of 0.50), then it is possible for the item's *D* value to be 1.0. This does not mean that all items with *p* values of 0.50 will have *D* values of 1.0, but just that the item can conceivably have a *D* value of 1.0. As a result of this relationship between *p* and *D*, items that have excellent discrimination power (i.e., *D* values of 0.40 and above) will necessarily have *p* values between 0.20 and 0.80. In testing situations in which it is desirable to have either very easy or very difficult items, *D* values can be expected to be lower than those normally desired. Additionally, items that measure abilities or objectives that are not emphasized throughout the test may have poor discrimination due to their unique focus. In this situation, if the item measures an important ability or learning objective and is free of technical defects, it should be retained (e.g., Linn & Gronlund, 2000).

In summary, although low *D* values often indicate problems, the guidelines provided in Table 6.2 should be applied in a flexible, considered manner. Our discussion of the calculation of item difficulty and discrimination indexes has used examples with items that are dichotomously scored (i.e., correct/incorrect, 1 or 0). Special Interest Topic 6.2 provides a discussion of the application of these statistics with constructed-response items that are not scored in a dichotomous manner.

Another approach to examining item discrimination is to correlate performance on the item with the total test score.

Item-Total Correlation Coefficients

Another approach to examining item discrimination is to correlate performance on the items (scored as either 0 or 1) with the total test score. This is referred to as an **item-total correlation**. The total test

SPECIAL INTEREST TOPIC **6.2**

Item Analysis for Constructed-Response Items

Our discussion and examples of the calculation of the item difficulty index and discrimination index used examples that were dichotomously scored (i.e., scored right or wrong: 0 or 1). Although this procedures works fine with selected-response items (e.g., true–false, multiple-choice), you need a slightly different approach with constructed-response items that are scored in a more continuous manner (e.g., an essay item that can receive scores between 1 and 5 depending on quality). To calculate the item difficulty index for a continuously scored constructed-response item, use the following formula (Nitko, 2001):

$$p = \frac{\text{Average Score on the Item}}{\text{Range of Possible Scores}}$$

The range of possible scores is calculated as the maximum possible score on the item minus the minimum possible score on the item. For example, if an item has an average score of 2.7 and is scored on a 1 to 5 scale, the calculation would be:

$$p = \frac{2.7}{5 - 1} = \frac{2.7}{4} = 0.675$$

Therefore, this item has an item difficulty index of 0.675. This value can be interpreted the same as the dichotomously scored items we discussed.

To calculate the item discrimination index for a continuously scored constructed-response item, you use the following formula (Nitko, 2001):

$$D = \frac{\text{Average Score for the Top Group } - \text{ Average Score for the Bottom Group}}{\text{Range of Possible Scores}}$$

For example, if the average score for the top group is 4.3, the average score for the bottom group is 1.7, and the item is scored on a 1 to 5 scale, the calculation would be:

$$D = \frac{4.3 - 1.7}{5 - 1} = \frac{2.6}{4} = 0.65$$

Therefore, this item has an item discrimination index of 0.65. Again, this value can be interpreted the same as the dichotomously scored items we discussed.

---

score is usually the total number of items answered correctly (unadjusted) or the total number of items answered correctly omitting the item being examined (adjusted). Either way, the item-total correlation is usually calculated using the **point-biserial correlation**. As you remember from our discussion of basic statistics the point-biserial is used when one variable is a dichotomous nominal score and the other variable is measured on an interval or ratio scale. Here the dichotomous variable is the score on a single item (e.g., right or wrong) and the variable measured on an interval scale is the total test score. A large item-total correlation is taken as evidence that an item is measuring the same construct as the overall test measures and that the item discriminates between individuals high on that construct and those low on the construct. An item-total correlation calculated on the adjusted total will be lower than that computed on the adjusted total and is preferred because the item being examined does not "contaminate" or inflate the correlation. The results of an item-total correlation will be similar to those of an item discrimination index and can be interpreted in a similar manner (Hopkins, 1998). As teachers gain more access to computer test scoring programs, the item-total correlation will become increasingly easy to compute and will likely become the dominant approach for examining item discrimination.

Item Discrimination on Mastery Tests

Several different approaches have been suggested for determining *item discrimination on mastery tests.*

As we noted previously, the item difficulty indexes on mastery tests tend to be higher (indicating easier items) than on tests designed primarily to produce norm-referenced scores. This is because with mastery testing it is usually assumed that most examinees will be successful. As a result, on mastery tests it is common for items to have average p values as high as 0.90 and the standard approach to interpreting item difficulty levels needs to be modified to accommodate this tendency.

The interpretation of indexes of discrimination is also complicated on mastery tests. Because it is common to obtain high p values for both high- and low-scoring examinees, it is normal for traditional item discrimination indexes to underestimate an item's true measurement characteristics. Several different approaches have been suggested for determining **item discrimination on mastery tests** (e.g., Aiken, 2000; Popham, 2000). One common approach involves administering the test to two groups of students: one group that has received instruction and one that has not received instruction. The formula is:

$$D = p_{\text{instruction}} - p_{\text{no instruction}}$$

where $p_{\text{instruction}}$ = proportion of instructed students getting the answer correct
$p_{\text{no instruction}}$ = proportion of students without instruction getting the answer correct

This approach is technically adequate, with the primary limitation being potential difficulty obtaining access to an adequate group that has not received instruction or training on the relevant material. If one does have access to an adequate sample, this is a promising approach.

Another popular approach involves administering the test to the same sample twice, once before instruction and once after instruction. The formula is:

$$D = p_{\text{posttest}} - p_{\text{pretest}}$$

where p_{posttest} = proportion of examinees getting the answer correct on posttest
p_{pretest} = proportion of examinees getting the answer correct on pretest

Some drawbacks are associated with this approach. First, it requires that the test developers write the test, administer it as a pretest, wait while instruction is provided, administer it as a posttest, and then calculate the discrimination index. This can take an extended period of time in some situations, and test developers often want feedback in a timely manner. A second limitation is the possibility of carryover effects from the pre- to the posttest. For example, examinees might remember items or concepts emphasized on the pretest, and this carryover effect can influence how they respond to instruction, study, and subsequently prepare for the posttest.

Aiken (2000) proposed another approach for calculating discrimination for mastery tests. Instead of using the top and bottom 27% of students (or the top and bottom 50%), he recommends using item difficulty values based on the test takers who reached the mastery cut score (i.e., mastery group) and those who did not reach mastery (i.e., nonmastery group). The formula is:

$$D = p_{mastery} - p_{nonmastery}$$

where
$$p_{mastery} = \text{proportion of mastery examinees getting the answer correct}$$
$$p_{nonmastery} = \text{proportion of nonmastery examinees getting the answer correct}$$

The advantage of this approach is that it can be calculated based on the data from one test administration with one sample. A potential problem is that because it is common for the majority of examinees to reach mastery, the p value of the nonmastery group might be based on a small number of examinees. As a result the statistics might not be stable and lead to erroneous conclusions.

Item Analysis of Speed Tests

Based on our discussion up to this point it should be clear that there are situations in which the interpretation of indexes of item difficulty and discrimination are complicated. One situation in which the interpretation of item analysis results is complicated is with speed tests, whereby performance depends primarily on the speed of performance. Items on speed tests are often fairly easy and could be completed by most test takers if there were no time limits. However, there are strict time limits, and these limits are selected so that no test taker will be able to complete all of the items. The key factor is how many items the test taker is able to complete in the allotted time. On power tests everyone is given sufficient time to attempt all the items, but the items vary in difficulty with some being so difficult that no test takers will answer them all correctly. In many situations tests incorporate a combination of speed and power, so the speed–power distinction is actually one of degree.

On speed tests, measures of item difficulty and discrimination will largely reflect the position of the item in the test rather than the actual difficulty of the item or its discriminative ability.

On speed tests, measures of item difficulty and discrimination will largely reflect the location of the item in the test rather than the item's actual difficulty level or ability to discriminate. Items appearing late on a speed test will be passed by fewer individuals than items that appear earlier simply because the strict time limits prevent students from being able to attempt them. The items appearing later on the test are probably not actually more difficult than the earlier items, but their item difficulty index will suggest that they are more difficult. Similar complications arise when interpreting indexes of discrimination with speed tests. Because the individuals completing the later items also tend to be the most capable test takers, indexes of discrimination may exaggerate the discriminating ability of these items. Although different procedures have been developed to take into consideration these and related factors, they all have limitations and none have received widespread acceptance (e.g., Aiken, 2000; Anastasi & Urbina, 1997). Our recommendation is that you should be aware of these issues and take them into consideration when interpreting the item analyses of highly speeded tests.

Distracter Analysis

The final quantitative item analysis procedure we will discuss in this chapter involves the analysis of individual distracters. On multiple-choice items, the incorrect alternatives are referred to as distracters because they serve to "distract" examinees who do not actually know the correct response. Some test developers routinely examine the performance of distracters for all multiple-choice items, whereas others reserve **distracter analysis** for items with p or D values that suggest problems. If you are a professional test developer you can probably justify the time required to examine each distracter for each item, but for busy teachers it is reasonable to reserve distracter analysis procedures for items that need further scrutiny based on their p or D values.

Distracter analysis **allows you to examine how many students in the top and bottom groups selected each option on a multiple-choice item.**

We expect distracters to be selected by more examinees in the bottom group than examinees in the top group.

Distracter analysis allows you to examine how many examinees in the top and bottom groups selected each option on a multiple-choice item. The key is to examine each distracter and ask two questions. First, did the distracter distract some examinees? If no examinees selected the distracter it is not doing its job. An effective distracter must be selected by some examinees. If a distracter is so obviously incorrect that no examinees select it, it is ineffective and needs to be revised or replaced. The second question involves discrimination. Did the distracter attract more examinees in the bottom group than in the top group? Effective distracters should. When looking at the correct response we expect more examinees in the top group to select it than examinees in the bottom group (i.e., it demonstrates positive discrimination). With distracters we expect the opposite. We expect more examinees in the bottom group to select a distracter than examinees in the top group. That is, distracters should demonstrate *negative* discrimination!

Consider the following example:

Item 1	Options			
	A*	*B*	*C*	*D*
Number in top group	22	3	2	3
Number in bottom group	9	7	8	6

*Correct answer

This item has a $p = 0.52$ (moderate difficulty) and a $D = 0.43$ (excellent discrimination). Based on these values, this item would probably not require further examination. However, this can serve as an example of what might be expected with a "good" item. As reflected in the D value, more examinees in the top group than the bottom group selected the correct answer (i.e., option A). By examining the distracters (i.e., options B, C, and D), you see that they were all selected by some examinees, which means they are serving their purpose (i.e., distracting examinees who do not know the correct response). Additionally, all three distracters were selected more by members of the bottom group than the top group. This is the desired outcome! While we want more high-scoring examinees to select the correct answer than low-scoring examinees (i.e., positive discrimination), we want more low-scoring examinees to select distracters than high-scoring examinees (i.e., negative discrimination). In summary, this is a good item and all of the distracters are performing well.

Now we will look at an example that illustrates some problems.

	Options			
Item 1	*A**	*B*	*C*	*D*
Number in top group	17	9	0	4
Number in bottom group	13	6	0	11

*Correct answer

This item has a $p = 0.50$ (moderate difficulty) and a $D = 0.14$ (fair discrimination but further scrutiny suggested). Based on these values, this item needs closer examination and possible revision. By examining option B you will notice that more examinees in the top group than in the bottom group selected this distracter. This is not a desirable situation because it indicates that more top-performing examinees selected this distracter than poor-performing examinees. Option B needs to be examined to determine why it is attracting top examinees. It is possible that the wording is ambiguous or that the option is similar in some way to the correct answer. By examining option C you note that no one selected this distracter. It attracted no examinees, was obviously not the correct answer, and needs to be replaced. To be effective, a distracter must distract some examinees. Finally, option D performed well. More poor-performing examinees selected this option than top-performing examinees (i.e., 11 versus 4). It is likely that if the test developer revises options B and C this will be a more effective item.

How Distracters Influence Item Difficulty and Discrimination

Before leaving our discussion of distracters, we want to highlight how the selection of distracters impacts both item difficulty and discrimination. Consider the following item:

1. In what year did Albert Einstein first publish his full general theory of relativity?
    a. 1910
    b. 1912
    c. 1914
    d. 1916
    e. 1918

Unless you are very familiar with Einstein's work, this is probably a fairly difficult question. Now consider this revision:

1. In what year did Albert Einstein first publish his full general theory of relativity?
   a. 1655
   b. 1762
   c. 1832
   d. 1916
   e. 2001

The selection of distracters can significantly impact the difficulty of the item and consequently the ability of the item to discriminate.

This is the same question but with different distracters. This revised item would likely be a much easier item in a typical high school science class. The point is that the selection of distracters can significantly impact the difficulty of the item and consequently the ability of the item to discriminate.

Item Analysis: Practical Strategies for Teachers

Teachers typically have a number of practical options for calculating item analysis statistics for their classroom tests.

Teachers typically have a number of practical options for calculating item analysis statistics for their classroom tests. Many teachers will have access to computer scoring programs that calculate the various item analysis statistics we have described. Numerous commercial companies sell scanners and scoring software that can scan answer sheets and produce item analysis statistics and related printouts (see Table 6.4 for two examples). If you do not have access to computer scoring at your school, Website Reactions has an excellent Internet site that allows you to compute common item analysis statistics online (www.surveyreaction.com/itemanalysis.asp).

If you do not have access to a computer or simply prefer to perform the calculations by hand, several authors have suggested some abbreviated procedures that make the calculation

TABLE 6.4   Two Examples of Test Scoring and Item Analysis Programs

Assessment Systems Corporation
One of its products, ITEMAN, can score and analyze a number of item formats, including multiple-choice and true–false items. This product will compute common item analysis and test statistics (e.g., mean, variance, standard deviation, KR-20). Its Internet site is www.assess.com/Software/sItemTest.htm.

Principia Products
One of its products, Remark Office OMR, will grade tests and produce statistics and graphs reflecting common item analysis and test statistics. Its Internet site is www.principiaproducts.com/office/index.html.

of common item analysis statistics fairly easy (e.g., Educational Testing Service, 1973; Linn & Gronlund, 2000). Although there are some subtle differences between these procedures, they generally involve the following steps:

1. Once the tests are graded, arrange them according to score (i.e., lowest score to highest score).
2. Take the 10 papers with the highest scores and the 10 papers with the lowest scores. Set these into two piles, one with the 10 highest scores (i.e., top group) and one with the lowest scores (i.e., bottom group). Set aside the remaining papers; they will not be used in these analyses.
3. For each item, determine how many of the students in the top group correctly answered it and how many in the bottom group correctly answered it. With this information you can calculate the overall item difficulty index (i.e., p) and separate item difficulty indexes for the top group (p_T) and bottom group (p_B). For example, if 8 students in the top group answered the item correctly and 3 in the bottom group answered the item correctly, add these together ($8 + 3 = 11$) and divide by 20 to compute the item difficulty index: $p = 11/20 = 0.55$. Although this item difficulty index is based on only the highest and lowest scores, it is usually adequate for use with classroom tests. You can then calculate p_T and p_B. In this case: $p_T = 8/10 = 0.80$ and $p_B = 3/10 = 0.30$.
4. You now have the data needed to calculate the discrimination index for the items. Using the data for our example: $D = p_T - p_B = 0.80 - 0.30 = 0.50$.

Using these simple procedures you see that for this item $p = .55$ (moderate difficulty) and $D = 0.50$ (excellent discrimination). If your items are multiple choice you can also use these same groups to perform distracter analysis.

Continuing with our example, consider the following results:

	Options			
	A	B$_*$	C	D
Top group (top 10)	0	8	1	1
Bottom group (bottom 10)	2	3	3	2

*Correct answer

As reflected in the item D value (i.e., 0.50), more students in the top group than bottom group selected the correct answer (i.e., option B). By examining the distracters (i.e., options A, C, and D), you see that they each were selected by some students (i.e., they are all distracting as hoped for) and they were all selected by more students in the bottom group than the top group (i.e., demonstrating negative discrimination). In summary, this item is functioning well!

Using Item Analysis to Improve Items

At this point we will provide a few examples and illustrate a step-by-step procedure for evaluating the quality of test items. Other authors have provided similar guidelines (e.g., Kubiszyn & Borich, 2000) that pose essentially the same questions.

Consider this information:

Example 1

$p = 0.63$ $D = 0.40$	Options			
	A	B*	C	D
Number in top group	2	25	2	1
Number in bottom group	6	13	6	5

*Correct answer

To illustrate our step-by-step procedure for evaluating the quality of test items, consider this series of questions and how it applies to the first example.

1. *Is the item difficulty level appropriate for the testing application?* A p of 0.63 is appropriate for a multiple-choice item on a norm-referenced test. Remember, the optimal mean p value for a multiple-choice item with four choices is 0.74.
2. *Does the item discriminate adequately?* With a D of 0.40 this item does an excellent job of discriminating between examinees who performed well on the test and those doing poorly.
3. *Are the distracters performing adequately?* Because the answers to the previous two questions were positive, we might actually skip this question. However, because we have the data available we can easily examine the result. All three distracters (i.e., A, C, and D) attracted some examinees and all three were selected more frequently by members of the bottom group than the top group. This is the desired outcome.
4. *Overall evaluation?* In summary, this is a good item and no revision is necessary.

Now we will consider an item that is problematic. Examine these data:

Example 2

$p = 0.20$ $D = -0.13$	Options			
	A	B	C*	D
Number in top group	20	4	4	2
Number in bottom group	11	6	8	5

*Correct answer

1. *Is the item difficulty level appropriate for the testing application?* A p of 0.20 suggests that this item is too difficult for most applications. Unless there is some reason for including items that are this difficult, this is cause for concern.

2. *Does the item discriminate adequately?* A D of –0.13 suggests major problems with this item. It may be miskeyed or some other major flaw is present.

3. *Are the distracters performing adequately?* Option A, a distracter, attracted most of the examinees in the top group and a large number of examinees in the bottom group. The other three options, including the one keyed as correct, were negative discriminators (i.e., selected more by examinees in the bottom group than the top group).

4. *Overall evaluation?* There is a major problem with this item! Because five times as many examinees in the top group selected option A than option C, which is keyed as correct, we need to verify that option C actually is the correct response. If the item is miskeyed and option A is the correct response, this would likely be an acceptable item ($p = 0.52$, $D = 0.30$) and could be retained. If the item was not miskeyed, there is some other major flaw and the item should be deleted.

Now consider this example:

Example 3

	Options			
p = 0.43 D = 0.20	A	B	C	D*
Number in top group	9	2	3	16
Number in bottom group	4	7	9	10

*Correct answer

1. *Is the item difficulty level appropriate for the testing application?* A p of 0.43 suggests that this item is moderately difficult.

2. *Does the item discriminate adequately?* A D of 0.20 indicates this item is only a fair discriminator.

3. *Are the distracters performing adequately?* Options B and C performed admirably with more examinees in the bottom group selecting them than examinees in the top group. Option A is another story! Over twice as many examinees in the top group selected it than examinees in the bottom group. In other words, this distracter is attracting a fairly large number of the top-performing examinees. It is likely that this distracter either is not clearly stated or resembles the correct answer in some manner. Either way, it is not effective and should be revised.

4. *Overall evaluation?* In its current state, this item is marginal and can stand revision. It can probably be improved considerably by carefully examining option A and revising this distracter. If the test author is able to replace option A with a distracter as effective as B or C, this would likely be a fairly good item.

We will look at one more example:

Example 4

p = 0.23	Options			
D = 0.27	A	B	C*	D
Number in top group	6	7	11	6
Number in bottom group	9	10	3	8

*Correct answer

1. *Is the item difficulty level appropriate for the testing application?* A p of 0.23 suggests that this item is more difficult than usually desired.
2. *Does the item discriminate adequately?* A D of 0.27 indicates this item is only a fair discriminator.
3. *Are the distracters performing adequately?* All of the distracters (i.e., options A, B, and D) were selected by some examinees, which means that they are serving their purpose. Additionally, all of the distracters were selected more by the bottom group than the top group (i.e., negative discrimination), the desired outcome.
4. *Overall evaluation?* This item is more difficult than typically desired and demonstrates only marginal discrimination. However, its distracters are all performing properly. If this item is measuring an important concept or learning objective, it might be desirable to leave it in the test. It might be improved by manipulating the distracters to make the item less difficult.

Item Analysis of Performance Assessments

In Chapter 1 we introduced you to performance assessments, noting that they have become very popular in educational settings in recent years. Performance assessments require test takers to complete a process or produce a product in a setting that closely resembles real-life situations (AERA et al., 1999). Traditional item analysis statistics have not been applied to performance assessments as routinely as they have to more traditional paper-and-pencil tests. One factor limiting the application of item analysis statistics is that performance assessments often involve a fairly small number of tasks (and sometimes only one task). However, Linn and Gronlund (2000) suggest that if the assessment involves several tasks, item analysis procedures can be adopted for performance assessments. For example, if a performance assessment involves five individual tasks that receive scores from 0 (no response) to 5 (exemplary response), the total scores would theoretically range from a low of 0 to a high of 25. Using the practical strategy of comparing performance between the top 10 high-scoring students with that of the low-scoring students, one can examine each task to determine whether the task discriminates between the two groups.

Traditional item analysis statistics have not been routinely applied to performance assessments, but in many situations these procedures could be adopted for performance assessments.

Consider this example:

Performance Assessment Task 1

	Scores						
Group	*0*	*1*	*2*	*3*	*4*	*5*	*Mean Score*
Top group (top 10)	0	0	0	1	4	5	4.4
Bottom group (bottom 10)	1	3	5	1	0	0	1.6

On this task the mean score of the top-performing students was 4.4 while the mean score of the low-performing students was 1.6. This relatively large difference between the mean scores suggests that the item is discriminating between the two groups.

Now examine the following example:

Performance Assessment Task 2

	Scores						
Group	*0*	*1*	*2*	*3*	*4*	*5*	*Mean Score*
Top group (top 10)	0	2	3	3	1	1	2.6
Bottom group (bottom 10)	0	2	4	3	1	0	2.3

On this task the mean score of the top-performing students was 2.6 while the mean score of the low-performing students was 2.3. A difference this small suggests that the item is not discriminating between the two groups. Linn and Gronlund (2000) suggest that two possible reasons for these results should be considered. First, it is possible that this item is not discriminating because the performance measured by this task is ambiguous. If this is the case, the task should be revised or discarded. Second, it is possible that this item is measuring skills and abilities that differ significantly from those measured by the other four tasks in the assessment. If this is the case, it is not necessarily a poor item that needs to be revised or discarded.

Qualitative Item Analysis

In addition to quantitative item analysis procedures, test developers can also use *qualitative item analysis* **procedures to improve their tests.**

In addition to the quantitative item analysis procedures described to this point, test developers can also use **qualitative item analysis** procedures to improve their tests. Along these lines, Popham (2000) provides some useful suggestions. He recommends that after writing the test the developer set the test aside for a few days to gain some distance from it. We can tell you from our own experience this is good advice. Even though you carefully proof a test immediately after writing it, a review a few days later will often reveal a number of errors. This delayed review often catches both clerical errors (e.g., spelling or grammar) and less obvious errors that might make an item unclear or inaccurate. After a "cooling-off" period we are often amazed that an "obvious" error evaded detection earlier. Somehow the introduction of a period of time provides distance that seems to make errors more easily detected. The time you spend proofing a test is well spent and can help you avoid problems once the test is administered and scored.

Popham (2000) also recommends that you have a colleague review the test. Ideally this should be a colleague familiar with the content of the test. For example, a history teacher might have another history teacher review the test. In addition to checking for clerical errors, clarity, and accuracy, the reviewer should determine whether the test is covering the material that it is designed to cover. This is akin to collecting validity evidence based on the content of the test. For example, on a classroom achievement test you are trying to determine whether the items cover the material that the test is supposed to cover. Finally, Popham recommends that you have the examinees provide feedback on the test. For example, after completing the test you might have the examinees complete a brief questionnaire asking whether the directions were clear and if any of the questions were confusing.

Ideally a test developer should use both quantitative and qualitative approaches to improve tests. We regularly provide a delayed review of our own tests and use colleagues as reviewers whenever possible. After administering a test and obtaining the quantitative item analyses, we typically question students about problematic items, particularly items for which the basis of the problem is not obvious. Often a combination of quantitative and qualitative procedures will result in the optimal enhancement of your tests.

We recommend the use of both quantitative and qualitative approaches to improve the quality of test items.

Popham (2000) notes that historically quantitative item analysis procedures have been applied primarily to tests using norm-referenced score interpretations and qualitative procedures have been used primarily with tests using criterion-referenced interpretations. This tendency can be attributed partly to some of the technical problems we described earlier about using item analysis statistics with mastery tests. Nevertheless, we recommend the use of both quantitative and qualitative approaches with both types of score interpretations. When improving tests, we believe the more information the better.

Having spent the time to develop and analyze test items, you might find it useful to develop a test bank to catalog your items. Special Interest Topic 6.3 provides information on this process.

Using Item Analysis to Improve Classroom Instruction

In describing the benefits of item analysis procedures, we indicated that they can provide information about the quality of the items and also the effectiveness of classroom instruction. We have spent considerable time describing how item analysis procedures can be used to evaluate the quality of test items and will now briefly address how they can help improve classroom instruction. For example, by examining p values teachers can learn which items are difficult for a group of students and which are easy. This provides valuable information

SPECIAL INTEREST TOPIC   **6.3**

Developing Item Banks

Many teachers at all grade levels find it helpful to develop a test bank to catalog and archive their test items. This allows them to easily write new tests using test items that they have used previously and have some basic measurement information on. Several sources have provided guidelines for developing item banks (e.g., Linn & Gronlund, 2000; Ward & Murray-Ward, 1994). Consider the following example.

Course: Tests and Measurement   **Chapter:** 2—Basic Math of Measurement

Learning Objective: Describe the measures of variability and their appropriate use.

If the standard deviation of a set of test scores is equal to 9, the variance is equal to:

 a. 3
 b. 18
 c. 36
 d. 81*

Administration date: February 7, 2002

$p = 0.58$ $D = 0.43$	Options			
	A	B	C	D*
Number in top group	4	2	0	24
Number in bottom group	9	7	3	11

*Correct answer

Administration date: September 3, 2003

$p = 0.68$ $D = 0.37$	Options			
	A	B	C	D*
Number in top group	1	2	1	26
Number in bottom group	8	5	2	15

*Correct answer

This indicates that this item has been administered on two different occasions. By including information from multiple administrations, you will have a better idea of how the item is likely to perform on a future test. If you are familiar with computer databases (e.g., Microsoft Access), you can set up a database that will allow you to access items with specific characteristics quickly and efficiently. Professionally developed item bank programs are also available. For example, the Assessment Systems Corporation's FastTEST product will help you create and maintain item banks, as well as construct tests (see www.assess.com).

about which learning objectives have been achieved and which need further elaboration and review. Sometimes as teachers we believe that our students have grasped a concept only to discover on a test that items measuring understanding of that concept were missed by a large number of them. When this happens it is important to go back and carefully review the material, possibly trying a different instructional approach to convey the information. At another level of analysis, information about which distracters are being selected by students can help teachers pinpoint common misconceptions and thereby correct them. In these ways, item analysis can result not only in better tests but also in better teaching.

Item analysis can result not only in better tests but also in better teaching.

Summary

In this chapter we descried several procedures that can be used to assess the quality of the individual items making up a test. These include the following.

- *Item difficulty level:* The item difficulty level or index is defined as the percentage or proportion of examinees correctly answering the item. The item difficulty index (i.e., p) ranges from 0.0 to 1.0 with easier items having larger decimal values and difficult items having smaller values. For maximizing variability among examinees, the optimal item difficulty level is 0.50, indicating that half of the examinees answered the item correctly and half answered it incorrectly. Although 0.50 is optimal for maximizing variability, in many situations other values are preferred.
- *Item discrimination:* Item discrimination refers to the extent to which an item accurately discriminates between examinees who vary on the test's construct. For example, on an achievement test the question is whether the item can distinguish between examinees who are high achievers and those who are poor achievers. Although a number of different approaches have been developed for assessing item discrimination, we focused our discussion on the popular item discrimination index (i.e., D). We provided guidelines for evaluating item discrimination indexes, and as a general rule items with D values over 0.30 are acceptable, and items with D values below 0.30 should be reviewed. However, this is only a general rule and we discussed a number of situations in which smaller D values might be acceptable.
- *Distracter analysis:* The final quantitative item analysis procedure we described was distracter analysis. In essence distracter analysis allows the test developer to evaluate the distracters on multiple-choice items (i.e., incorrect alternatives) and determine whether they are functioning properly. This involves two primary questions. First: Did the distracter distract some examinees? If a distracter is so obviously wrong that no examinees selected it, it is useless and deserves attention. The second question involves discrimination. Did the distracter attract more examinees in the bottom group than in the top group? Distracter analysis allows you to answer these two questions.

After introducing these different item analysis statistics, we described some practical strategies teachers can use to examine the measurement characteristics of the items on their classroom assessments. We also introduced a series of steps that teachers can engage in to use the information provided by item analysis procedures to improve the quality of the items they use in their assessments.

In addition to quantitative item analysis procedures, test developers can also use qualitative approaches to improve their tests. Popham (2000) suggested that the test developer carefully proof the test after setting it aside for a few days. This break often allows the test author to gain some distance from the test and provide a more thorough review of it. He also recommends getting a trusted colleague to review the test. Finally, he recommends that the test developer solicit feedback from the examinees regarding the clarity of the directions and the identification of ambiguous items. Test developers are probably best served by using a combination of quantitative and qualitative item analysis procedures. In addition to helping improve tests, in the classroom the information obtained with item analysis procedures can help the teacher identify common misconceptions and material that needs further instruction.

KEY TERMS AND CONCEPTS

Distracter analysis, p. 151
Item analysis, p. 142
Item analysis of performance
   assessments, p. 157
Item analysis of speed tests, p. 150

Item difficulty, p. 142
Item discrimination, p. 144
Item discrimination on mastery
   tests, p. 149
Item-total correlation, p. 147

Optimal item difficulty level,
   p. 143
Point-biserial correlation,
   p. 148
Qualitative item analysis, p. 158

RECOMMENDED READINGS

Anastasi, A., & Urbina, S. (1997). *Psychological testing* (7th ed.). Upper Saddle River, NJ: Prentice Hall. Chapter 7, Item Analysis, presents a readable but comprehensive discussion of item analysis that is slightly more technical than that provided in this text.

Johnson, A. P. (1951). Notes on a suggested index of item validity: The U-L index. *Journal of Educational Measurement, 42,* 499–504. This is a seminal article in the history of item analysis.

Kelley, T. L. (1939). The selection of upper and lower groups for the validation of test items. *Journal of Educational Psychology, 30,* 17–24. A real classic!

Nitko, A. J., & Hsu, T-C. (1984). A comprehensive microcomputer system for classroom testing. *Journal of Educational Measurement, 21,* 377–390. Describes a set of computer programs that archives student data, performs common item analyses, and banks the test question to facilitate test development.

7 The Initial Steps in Developing a Classroom Test

Deciding What to Test and How to Test It

The Standards for Educational and Psychological Testing *(1999) indicate that the initial steps in developing a test are to specify the purpose and scope of the test and develop test specifications. In the development of classroom achievement tests, this process begins with the specification of educational objectives and development of a table of specifications.*

CHAPTER HIGHLIGHTS

Characteristics of Educational Objectives

Taxonomy of Educational Objectives

Behavioral versus Nonbehavioral Educational Objectives

Writing Educational Objectives

Developing a Table of Specifications (or Test Blueprint)

Implementing the Table of Specifications and Developing an Assessment

Preparing Your Students and Administering the Assessment

LEARNING OBJECTIVES

After reading and studying this chapter, students should be able to:

1. Describe the importance of educational objectives in terms of both instruction and assessment.
2. Describe three prominent characteristics of educational objectives.
3. Describe and give examples of how educational objectives can differ in terms of scope.
4. Describe and give examples of the three domains covered by educational objectives.
5. Describe Bloom's taxonomy of cognitive objectives. Explain and give examples of each category.
6. Describe and give examples of behavioral and nonbehavioral educational objectives.

7. Illustrate a thorough understanding of the principles for writing effective educational objectives by writing objectives for a specified content area.

8. Explain the importance of developing a table of specifications before beginning to write an assessment.

9. Illustrate a thorough understanding of the principles for developing a table of specifications by developing one for a specified content area.

10. Describe norm-referenced and criterion-referenced score interpretations and their application in classroom assessments.

11. Compare and contrast the strengths and weaknesses of selected-response and constructed-response items.

12. Discuss major considerations involved with assembling an assessment.

13. Discuss major considerations involved with preparing your students and administering an assessment.

14. Be able to apply strategies for reducing test anxiety.

15. Be able to apply strategies for reducing the likelihood of cheating.

As noted in Chapter 1, classroom testing has important implications and its effects are felt immediately by students and teachers alike. It has been estimated that assessment activities consume as much as 30% of the available instructional time (Stiggins & Conklin, 1992). Because testing activities are such important parts of the educational process, all teachers who develop and use tests should work diligently to ensure their assessment procedures are adequate and efficient. In this chapter we will start discussing the development of classroom achievement tests. The initial steps in developing a classroom achievement test are to specify the educational objectives, develop a table of specifications, and select the type of items you will include in your assessment. These activities provide the foundation for all classroom tests and many professionally designed tests of educational achievement.

The identification and statement of educational objectives is an important first step in developing tests. **Educational objectives** are simply educational goals; that is, what you hope the students will learn or accomplish. Educational objectives are also referred to as instructional or learning objectives. The teaching of any lesson, unit, or course has one or more educational objectives. These objectives are sometimes clearly stated and sometimes (all too often) implicit. Even when the objectives are implicit they can usually be inferred by carefully examining the materials used in instruction, the topics covered, and the instructional processes employed. A good classroom test can be written from clearly stated objectives much more easily than can one from vague or poorly developed objectives. Clearly stated objectives help you make sure that the test measures what has been taught in class and greatly facilitate the test development process. Establishing explicit, clearly stated educational objectives also has the added benefit of enhancing the quality of teaching. If you know what your educational goals are, you are much more likely to reach them. The educational reform movement of the 1990s focused considerable attention on the development and statement of content standards. It is likely that your

> **The identification and statement of *educational objectives* is an important first step in developing tests.**

state or school district has developed fairly explicit curriculum guidelines that dictate to some degree the educational objectives you have for your students.

Characteristics of Educational Objectives

This textbook is not devoted to curriculum development or the construction of educational objectives to organize curriculum by content or sequence. However, any reasonable school assessment procedure should be closely tied to the curriculum and its objectives. Classroom tests should reflect what was taught in class, and tests should emphasize what was emphasized in class. As a result, any discussion of the development of classroom tests should touch on educational objectives. It is probably best to begin by describing some of the characteristics of educational objectives. Probably the three most prominent characteristics of educational objectives involve their **scope** (i.e., how specific or broad the objective is), **domain** (i.e., cognitive, affective, or psychomotor domain), and **format** (i.e., behavioral versus nonbehavioral). We will start by discussing how objectives can differ in terms of scope.

Any reasonable school assessment procedure should be closely tied to the curriculum and its objectives.

Scope

Scope refers to how broad or narrow an objective is. An example of a broad objective is:

> The student will be able to analyze and discuss the effects of the Civil War on twentieth-century American politics.

An example of a narrow or specific objective is:

> The student will be able to list the states that seceded from the Union during the Civil War.

Clearly different kinds of student responses would be expected for tests questions developed from such different objectives. Objectives with a broad scope are often broken down into objectives with a more narrow scope. The broad objective above might have been appended to the following objectives:

1. The student will be able to analyze and discuss the effects of the Civil War on twentieth-century American politics.
    1a. The student will be able to discuss the political effects of post–Civil War occupation by federal troops on Southern state politics.
    1b. The student will be able to trace the rise and fall of African Americans' political power during and after Reconstruction.
    1c. The student will be able to discuss the long-term effects of the economic depression in the South after the Civil War.
    1d. The student will be able to list three major effects of the Civil War on twentieth-century U.S. politics.

Although these four specific objectives all might help the student attain the broad objective, they do not exhaust all of the potential objectives that could support the broad objective. In fact a whole course might be needed to completely master the broad objective.

If you use only very specific educational objectives, you may end up with a large number of disjointed items that emphasize rote memory and other low-level cognitive abilities.

It is probably best to strike a balance between broad objectives and narrow objectives.

On the other hand, if you use only broad educational objectives, you may not have the specific information needed to help you develop tests with good measurement characteristics. Although you can find test development experts who promote the use of narrow objectives and other experts who promote broad objectives, in practice it is probably best to strike a balance between the two extremes. This can best be accomplished using two approaches. First, you can write objectives that are at an intermediate level of specificity. Here the goal is to write objectives that provide the specificity necessary to guide test development but are not so narrow as to limit assessment to low-level abilities. The second approach is to use a combination of broad and specific objectives as demonstrated earlier. That is, write broad objectives that are broken down into more specific objectives. Either of these approaches can help you develop well-organized tests with good measurement characteristics.

Taxonomy of Educational Objectives

In addition to the scope of educational objectives, they also differ in the domain or the type of ability/characteristic being measured. The domains typically addressed by educational objectives involve cognitive, affective, or psychomotor abilities or characteristics. These three domains are usually presented as hierarchies that involve different levels that reflect varying degrees of complexity. We will start by discussing the cognitive domain.

Cognitive Domain　＊ Primary importance

The objectives presented in the previous section are referred to as **cognitive objectives** because they deal with activities such as memorizing, interpreting, analyzing, and so on. Remember these two objectives? – comprehend

1. The student will be able to analyze and discuss the effects of the Civil War on twentieth-century American politics.
2. The student will be able to list the states that seceded from the Union during the Civil War.

When we first discussed these two objectives we emphasized how they differed in scope. The first objective is broad and could be the basis for a whole course of study. The second one is narrow and specific. In addition to scope they also differ considerably in the complexity of the cognitive processes involved. The first one requires "analysis and discussion" whereas the second requires only "listing." If a student can memorize the states that seceded from the Union, he or she can be successful on the second objective, but memorization of

***Bloom's taxonomy* provides a useful way of describing the complexity of an objective by classifying it into one of six hierarchical categories.**

facts would not be sufficient for the first objective. Analysis and discussion require more complex cognitive processes than rote memorization. A taxonomy of cognitive objectives developed by Bloom, Englehart, Furst, Hill, and Krathwohl (1956) is commonly referred to as **Bloom's taxonomy.** This taxonomy provides a useful way of describing the complexity of an objective by classifying it into one of six hierarchical categories ranging from the most simple to the most complex. Table 7.1 provides a summary of Bloom's taxonomy. The categories include the following:

Knowledge. The simplest level of the taxonomy is **knowledge.** Objectives at the knowledge level involve learning or memorizing specific facts, terms, names, dates, and so forth. Examples of educational objectives in the knowledge category include:

- The student will be able to name each state capital.
- The student will be able to list U.S. presidents in the order they served.

Comprehension. Objectives at the **comprehension** level require understanding, not simply rote memorization. Objectives at this level often use verbs such as *interpret, translate, explain,* and *summarize.* Examples of educational objectives at the comprehension level include:

- The student will be able to describe the use of each symbol on a U.S. Geographical Survey map.
- The student will be able to explain how interest rates affect unemployment.

TABLE 7.1 Bloom's Taxonomy of Educational Objectives

Level	Description	Example
Knowledge	Rote memory, learning facts	Name each state capital.
Comprehension	Summarize, interpret, or explain material	Summarize the use of every symbol on a geographical survey map.
Application	Use general rules and principles to solve new problems	Write directions for traveling by numbered road from any city on a map to any other city.
Analysis	Reduction of concepts into parts and show the relationship of parts to the whole	Describe maps in terms of function and form.
Synthesis	Creation of new ideas or results from existing concepts	Construct a map of a hypothetical country with given characteristics.
Evaluation	Judgment of value or worth	The student will evaluate the usefulness of a map to enable him or her to travel from one place to another.

Source: Based on Bloom et al. (1956).

· apply knowledge to solve new problem

Application.   Objectives at the **application** level involve the use of general rules, principles, or abstract concepts to solve a problem not previously encountered. Examples of objectives at the application level include:

- The student will be able to write directions for traveling by numbered roads from any city on a map to any other city.
- The student will be able to apply multiplication and division of double digits in applied math problems.

Analysis.   ↦ *breakdown complex parts*   Objectives at the **analysis** level require the student to reduce or break down a complex concept into its basic parts or elements in a manner that illustrates the relationship of parts to whole. Examples of educational objectives at this level include:

- The student will describe maps in terms of function and form.
- The student will distinguish the different approaches to establishing validity and illustrate their relationship to each other.

Synthesis.   Objectives at the **synthesis** level require the student to blend existing elements in such a way that they form new structures or patterns. Examples of objectives at the synthesis level include:

- The student will construct a map of a hypothetical country with given characteristics.
- The student will propose a viable plan for establishing the validity of an assessment instrument following the guidelines presented in the *Standards for Educational and Psychological Testing* (1999).

Evaluation.   ↦ *decide how important information is*   Objectives at the **evaluation** level require the student to make evaluative judgments regarding the quality, value, or worth of something for a stated purpose. Examples of objectives at the evaluation level include:

- The student will evaluate the usefulness of a map to enable him or her to travel from one place to another.
- The student will judge the quality of validity evidence for a specified assessment instrument.

Although it is somewhat dated, we agree with others (e.g., Hopkins, 1998) who feel that Bloom's taxonomy is helpful because it presents a framework that helps remind teachers to include items reflecting more complex educational objectives in their tests. Popham (1999) suggests that teachers tend to focus almost exclusively on objectives at the knowledge level. He goes as far as to suggest that in practice one can actually simplify the taxonomy by having just two levels: knowledge and anything higher than knowledge. We will not go quite that far, but we do agree that instruction and assessment are often limited to rote memorization, and higher-level educational objectives should be emphasized.

Instruction and assessment are too often limited to rote memorization, and higher-level objectives should be emphasized.

This is not to imply that lower-level objectives are trivial and should be ignored. For each objective in your curriculum you must decide at what level you expect students to perform. In a brief introduction to a topic it may be sufficient to expect only knowledge and comprehension of major concepts. In a more detailed study of a topic, higher, more complex levels of mastery will typically be required. However, it is often not possible to master high-level objectives without first having mastered lower-level objectives. Although we strongly encourage the development of higher-level objectives, it is not realistic to require high-level mastery of everything. Education is a pragmatic process of choosing what is most important to emphasize in a limited amount of instructional time. Our culture helps us make some of these choices, as do legislative bodies, school boards, administrators, and even occasionally parents and students. In some school districts the cognitive objectives are provided in great detail; in others they are practically nonexistent. As noted earlier, the current trend is for federal and state lawmakers to exert more and more control over curriculum content.

Affective Domain

Most people think of cognitive objectives when they think of a student's educational experiences. However, two other domains of objectives appear in the school curriculum: affective and psychomotor objectives. The affective domain involves characteristics such as values, attitudes, interests, and behavioral actions. As a result, **affective objectives** involve the attitudes and actions of students in relation to a school subject. For example:

– interested, bored, active

> The student will demonstrate interest in earth science by conducting a science fair project in some area of earth science.

As a general rule, affective objectives are emphasized more in elementary school curricula than secondary curricula. A taxonomy of affective objectives developed by Krathwohl, Bloom, and Masia (1964) is presented in Table 7.2. This taxonomy involves levels of

TABLE 7.2   Krathwohl's Taxonomy of Affective Objectives

Level	Description	Sublevels
Receiving (attending)	Being aware of and willing to attend to something (e.g., instruction)	Awareness, willingness to attend, and selective attention
Responding	Actively participating in an activity or process	Acquiescence, willingness, and satisfaction
Valuing	Assigning value or worth to an activity or idea	Acceptance, preference, and commitment
Organization	Ideas and values become internalized and organized into one's personal system of values and beliefs	Conceptualization and organization
Characterization by a value or value complex	Individual values are exemplified in a characteristic set of behaviors and actions	Generalized set and characterization

Source: Based on Krathwohl et al. (1964).

increasing sophistication, with each level building on preceding levels. It depicts a process whereby new ideas, values, and beliefs are gradually accepted and internalized as one's own.

Krathwohl's taxonomy of affective objectives has never approached the popularity of Bloom's taxonomy of cognitive objectives probably because the affective domain has been more difficult to define and is also a more controversial area of education. In schools, affective objectives are almost always adjuncts to cognitive objectives. For example, we want our students to learn about science and as a result to appreciate or enjoy it. Classroom tests predominantly focus on cognitive objectives, but affective objectives are found in school curricula, either explicitly or implicitly. Because affective objectives appear in the school curriculum, their specification enhances the chance of them being achieved.

Psychomotor Domain — ex: writing

The third class of objectives deals with physical activity and is referred to as **psychomotor objectives.** Behavioral objectives typically occur in physical education, dance, speech, theater, laboratory (e.g., biology or computer science), or career–technical classes such as woodworking, electronics, automotive, or metalwork. For example, in physical education there are countless psychomotor activities such as rolling a bowling ball a certain way or hitting tennis balls with a certain motion. Biology classes also have many psychomotor activities, including focusing a microscope, staining cells, and dissection. Computer science courses require skill in using a computer keyboard and assembling computer hardware. Taxonomies of psychomotor objectives have been developed and Harrow's (1972) model is illustrated in Table 7.3. Psychomotor objectives are typically tied to cognitive objectives

TABLE 7.3   Harrow's Taxonomy of Psychomotor Objectives

Level	Description	Sublevels
Reflex movements	Involuntary actions	Segmental, intersegmental, and suprasegmental reflexes
Basic-fundamental movements	Inherent movement patterns that are a combination of reflex movements and serve as the basis for more complex movements	Locomotor, nonlocomotor, and manipulative movements
Perceptual abilities	Involves interpretation of sensory input that in turn guides movement	Kinesthetic, visual, auditory, and tactile discrimination, coordinated abilities
Physical abilities	Functional physical characteristics that serve as the basis for skilled movements	Endurance, strength, flexibility, and agility
Skilled movements	Complex movements that are the result of learning and based on inherent movement patterns (see level 2)	Simple, compound, and complex adaptive skills
Nondiscursive communication	Nonverbal communication ranging from facial expressions to expressive dance	Expressive and interpretive movements

Source: Based on Harrow (1972).

because almost every physical activity involves cognitive processes. As a result, like affective objectives, psychomotor objectives typically are adjuncts to cognitive objectives. Nevertheless, they do appear in the school curriculum and their specification may enhance instruction and assessment.

Behavioral versus Nonbehavioral Educational Objectives

Educational objectives are often classified as either *behavioral* or *nonbehavioral*.

Educational objectives are often classified as either behavioral or nonbehavioral. To illustrate this distinction, consider the following examples:

> *Behavioral:* The student will be able to list the reasons cited in the curriculum guide for the United States' entry into World War I with 80% accuracy.

> *Nonbehavioral:* The student will be able to analyze the reasons for the United States' entry into World War I.

These two objectives differ in the activity to be performed. The behavioral objective requires that the student list the reasons; the nonbehavioral objective requires that the student analyze the reasons. **Behavioral objectives** specify activities that are observable and measurable whereas **nonbehavioral objectives** specify activities that are unobservable and not directly measurable. Behavioral objectives can be immediately and directly observed and measured by the teacher. Nonbehavioral activities must be inferred. Behavioral activities include *arrange, build, create, define, develop, identify, list, recite,* and *relate.* Nonbehavioral activities include *analyze, examine, judge, know,* and *understand.* Although it is possible to write either behavioral or nonbehavioral objectives at all levels of the cognitive taxonomy, teachers often find it easier to write behavioral objectives for the lower levels (e.g., knowledge, comprehension, and application) and to write nonbehavioral objectives for the higher levels (e.g., analysis, synthesis, and evaluation).

It is also common for behavioral objectives to specify an outcome criterion. For example, in the previous example, the criterion is listing "the reasons cited in the curriculum guide . . . with 80% accuracy." As illustrated, behavioral objectives often state outcome criteria as a percentage correct that represents mastery. Here is another example:

> The student will be able to diagram correctly 80% of sentences presented from a standard list.

Although behavioral objectives frequently specify an outcome criterion, it is often difficult to determine what represents mastery. Does 80% accuracy reflect mastery, or should you require 90% or even 100%? Occasionally the nature of the material and the results of not reaching 100% mastery will dictate a criterion. For example, most of the students who demonstrate 80% mastery on a test measuring knowledge of the safe use of power tools in an industrial arts class may be accident free, yet a 5% accident rate may be completely intolerable. In this situation the criterion for mastery may need to be raised to 100% to achieve an acceptable accident rate (e.g., < 1%). When training pilots to fly fighter jets, the Air Force may likewise require 100% mastery of all ground flight objectives because a single mistake may result in death and the loss of expensive equipment.

The use of behavioral objectives received widespread acceptance in the 1960s and 1970s because they helped teachers clearly specify their objectives. However, a disadvantage of behavioral objectives is that if carried to an extreme they can be too specific and too numerous, and as a result no longer facilitate instruction or assessment. The ideal situation is to have objectives that are broad enough to help you organize your instruction and assessment procedures, but that also specify clearly measurable activities.

Writing Educational Objectives

So far we have defined educational objectives and described some of their major characteristics. Consistent with our goal of limiting our discussion to the information teachers really need to know to develop, use, and interpret tests effectively, we have kept our discussion relatively brief. Because the specification of educational objectives plays an important role in the development of classroom tests, we will provide a few general suggestions for writing useful objectives. These include the following:

Your educational objectives should cover a broad spectrum of abilities.

1. Write objectives that cover a broad spectrum of abilities. As we have suggested repeatedly, it is desirable to specify objectives that cover a broad range of abilities. Go beyond rote memorization and specify higher-level cognitive abilities.

2. When feasible, identify behaviors that are observable and directly measurable. Ideally, objectives should specify behaviors that are observable and measurable. One way to determine whether this criterion is achieved is to ask whether different people independently observing the student would agree regarding the achievement of the objective. As we noted, this is usually best accomplished by using action verbs such as *arrange, build, create, define, develop, identify, list,* and *recite.* Objectives requiring the student to *analyze, examine, judge, know,* and *understand* are not as easily observed and measured and often must be inferred. Nevertheless, it may be necessary to specify behaviors that are not directly observable in order to assess some of the more complex cognitive abilities (e.g., analysis, synthesis, and evaluation). As a general rule, when possible specify observable and measurable behaviors, but when necessary use nonbehavioral objectives to describe higher-level abilities or behaviors.

3. State special conditions. If the target activity is to be demonstrated under specific conditions, these conditions should be clearly stated. Consider this example:

giving map as special condition

Given a map of the United States, the student will be able to correctly identify each state and name its capital.

In this example, a map of the United States is identified as material necessary for achieving the objective. Kubiszyn and Borich (2000) list specific times, settings, equipment, and resources as conditions that should be included in an objective when they are relevant.

TABLE 7.4   Learning Objectives for Chapter 2, The Basic Math of Measurement

After reading and studying Chapter 2, the student should be able to:

1. Define measurement.
2. Describe the different scales of measurement and give examples.
3. Describe the measures of central tendency and their appropriate use.
4. Describe the measures of variability and their appropriate use.
5. Explain the meaning of correlation coefficients and how they are used.
6. Explain how scatterplots are used to describe the relationships between two variables.
7. Describe how linear regression is used to predict performance.
8. Describe major types of correlation coefficients.
9. Distinguish between correlation and causation.

4. When appropriate, specify an outcome criterion. As we discussed earlier, it is sometimes beneficial to specify an outcome criterion. That is the level of performance viewed as indicating that the student has achieved the objective. This is most applicable when using behavioral objectives.

The development of educational objectives is not an area in which there is complete agreement among testing experts. Although every test development expert we know of believes educational objectives need to be specified, different writers support slightly different approaches. Some recommend writing content-free objectives whereas others recommend content-centered objectives. Some writers recommend the use of behavioral objectives whereas others see this approach as too restrictive. Our guidelines are simply suggestions that you can use in a flexible manner to meet your specific needs. We believe it is very important for teachers to develop and specify educational objectives, but the exact format they adopt is less important. In Table 7.4 we restate the learning objectives provided in Chapter 2 of this text. We do this because we will be using this chapter and its associated objectives in the next section to demonstrate the development of a table of specifications for a test.

Developing a Table of Specifications (or Test Blueprint)

The *table of specifications* is used to ensure congruence between classroom instruction and test content.

You might be asking why we have spent so much time discussing educational objectives. The reason is that the development of a classroom test should be closely tied to the class curriculum and educational objectives. As we noted earlier classroom tests should measure what was taught. Classroom tests should emphasize what was emphasized in class. The method of ensuring congruence between classroom instruction and test content is the development and application of a **table of specifications,** also referred to as a **test blueprint.** An example is given in Table 7.5 for

TABLE 7.5 Table of Specifications for Test on Chapter 2 Based on Content Areas (Number of Items)

	Level of Objective						
Content Area	Knowledge	Comprehension	Application	Analysis	Synthesis	Evaluation	Total
Scales of measurement	2	2		2			6
Measures of central tendency	3	3					6
Measures of variability	3	3	3				9
Correlation and regression	2	3		2	2		9

Chapter 2 of this text. The column on the left, labeled Content Area, lists the major content areas to be covered in the test. These content areas are derived by carefully reviewing the educational objectives and selecting major content areas to be included in the test. Across the top of the two-way table we list the levels of Bloom's cognitive taxonomy. The inclusion of this section encourages us to consider the complexity of the cognitive processes we want to measure. As noted earlier, there is a tendency for teachers to rely heavily on lower-level processes (e.g., rote memory) and to underemphasize higher-level cognitive processes. By incorporating these categories in our table of specifications, we are reminded to incorporate a wider range of cognitive processes into our tests.

The numbers in the body of the table reflect the number of items to be devoted to assessing each content area at each cognitive taxonomic level. Table 7.4 depicts specifications for a 30-item test. If you examine the first content area in Table 7.4 (i.e., scales of measurement) you see three *knowledge*-level items, three *comprehension*-level items, and two *analysis*-level items will be devoted to assessing this content area. The next content area (i.e., measures of central tendency) will be assessed by three *knowledge*-level items and three *comprehension*-level items. The number of items dedicated to assessing each objective should reflect the importance of the objective in the curriculum and how much instructional time was devoted to it. In our table of specifications we determined the number of items dedicated to each content area/objective by examining how much material was devoted to each topic in the text and how much time we typically spend on each topic in class lectures.

Some testing experts recommend using percentages instead of the number of items when developing a table of specifications. This approach is illustrated in Table 7.6. For example, you might determine that approximately 20% of your instruction involved the different scales of measurement. You would like to reflect this weighting in your test so you devote 20% of the test to this content area. If you are developing a 30-item test this means you will write 6 items to assess objectives related to scales of measurement (.20 × 30 = 6). If you are developing a 40-item test, this means you will write 8 items to assess objectives related to scales of measurement (.20 × 40 = 8). An advantage of using percentages rather

TABLE 7.6 Table of Specifications for Test on Chapter 2 Based on Content Areas (Percentages)

Content Areas	Level of Objective						
	Knowledge	*Comprehension*	*Application*	*Analysis*	*Synthesis*	*Evaluation*	*Total*
Scales of measurement	6.7%	6.7%		6.7%			20%
Measures of central tendency	10%	10%					20%
Measures of variability	10%	10%	10%				30%
Correlation and regression	6.7%	10%		6.7%	6.7%		30%

than number of items is that you do not have to determine beforehand how many items you will have on a test. Nevertheless, the decision to use percentages or numbers of items is probably best left to the individual teacher because either approach can result in useful specification tables.

Each test a teacher constructs should be based on a table of specifications. It may be relatively informal when constructing a brief quiz, or as fully developed as in Table 7.4 when constructing a major examination. A table of specifications helps teachers review the curriculum content and minimizes the chance of overlooking important concepts or including irrelevant concepts. A table of specifications also encourages the teacher to use items of varying complexity. For students the table can serve as a basis for study and review. There will be few student or parental complaints of "unfair" testing if students are aware of the elements of the table of specifications prior to the test. Although we have concentrated on achievement tests and cognitive objectives in this section, tables of specifications can be developed for affective and psychomotor tasks in a similar manner, substituting the taxonomy being used in those domains for the cognitive taxonomy.

Implementing the Table of Specifications and Developing an Assessment

So far in this chapter we have focused on what we want students to learn and what content we want our tests to cover. This has involved a discussion of educational objectives and the development of a table of specifications or test blueprint. Before we actually start writing the test, however, we still have several more important decisions to make. One important decision involves how to interpret test scores (norm-referenced and criterion-referenced approaches to score interpretation were introduced in Chapter 3). Another important decision involves selecting the types of items to include in the assessment. We will now briefly review information about norm-referenced and criterion-referenced assessment and frame it in terms of the development of classroom tests.

Norm-Referenced versus Criterion-Referenced Score Interpretations

Remember our earlier discussion of norm-referenced and criterion-referenced score interpretations. In review, with norm-referenced assessment a student's performance is interpreted in relation to the performance of other students. Norm-referenced interpretation is *relative* because it involves the performance of the student relative to other students. Percentile ranks and standard scores are common **norm-referenced scores** that are used in schools today. In contrast, criterion-referenced interpretation compares a student's performance to an absolute standard or criterion, not to the performance of other students. Criterion-referenced interpretation is *absolute* because it reflects the degree to which the student has mastered the content or domain the test represents. **Criterion-referenced scores** include percent correct and mastery/nonmastery scores. If the results indicate that the student scored at the 80th percentile, meaning he or she scored better than 80% of the students in the norm group, the interpretation is norm-referenced. If the results indicate that the student correctly answered 80% of the test items, the interpretation is criterion-referenced.

Norm-referenced score interpretations compare a student's performance with that of other students.

Criterion-referenced score interpretations compare a student's performance to an absolute standard or criterion.

Although it is common for people to refer to norm-referenced or criterion-referenced tests, this is somewhat misleading. Classification as norm-referenced or criterion-referenced actually refers to the interpretation of test results. A test can actually be interpreted in both a norm-referenced or a criterion-referenced manner. For example, a student's performance on a test might indicate that 80% of the test items were correctly answered (criterion-referenced interpretation), scoring at the 90 percentile (norm-referenced interpretation). The decision to use a norm-referenced or a criterion-referenced approach should be based on how the results will be used. If you need to determine a student's standing relative to a specified norm group, a norm-referenced interpretation is indicated. If you need to determine what the student knows or what tasks they can perform, a criterion-referenced interpretation is indicated.

Norm-referenced achievement assessment typically assesses broader content areas of achievement (e.g., social studies) whereas criterion-referenced assessment typically assesses more narrowly defined areas (e.g., a specific chapter or unit of instruction). Typically, classroom tests are used to assess students' knowledge in fairly specific areas and/or determine what tasks they can and cannot execute successfully. We are usually not interested in how a student compares with others, but with the student's level of mastery of the educational objectives. As a result, criterion-referenced interpretations are typically most useful in the classroom.

Selecting Which Types of Items to Use

Another important decision involves the types of items or tasks to include in your test. Different authors use different classification systems or schemes when categorizing test items. Historically a popular approach has been to classify test items as either "objective" or "subjective." This distinction usually referred to how the items were scored (i.e., in either an objective or a subjective manner). For example, there should be no disagreement between different individuals grading multiple-choice items. The items should be easily scored "correct" or "incorrect" according to the scoring criteria. The same goes for true–false and matching items. They can all be scored in an objective manner and are classified as objective: Everyone agrees on which answers are keyed as correct and incorrect. In contrast, essay items are considered subjective because grading them involves subjective judgment on the part of the individual grading the test. It is not too surprising that two graders might assign different grades to the same essay item. Another example could be a student's responses on an oral examination. Here there also might be considerable subjectivity in scoring and two individuals might score the responses differently. As a result, essay and other test items involving more subjective scoring are classified as subjective.

Although the objective–subjective distinction is generally useful, there is some ambiguity. For example, are short-answer items objective or subjective? Many authors refer to them as objective items, but as you will see in a later chapter scoring short-answer items often involves considerable subjectivity. A more direct approach is to classify items as either selected-response or constructed-response items. With this approach, if an item requires a student to select a response from available alternatives it is classified as a **selected-response item**. Multiple-choice, true–false, and matching items are all selected-response items. If an item requires students to create or construct a response, it is classified as a **constructed-response item**. Constructed-response items include fill-in-the-blank, short-answer, and essay items. In a broader sense, constructed-response assessments also include performance assessments and portfolios. The selected-response–constructed-response classification system is the one we will use in this textbook. In subsequent chapters we will delve into greater detail into the development of these different types of items. For now, we will just provide a brief overview of some of the major characteristics of selected-response and constructed-response items.

On *selected-response items* the students select the appropriate response from options that are provided.

As we indicated, on selected-response items students select the appropriate response from options that are provided. On a true–false item the student simply selects *true* or *false* to answer the item. On multiple-choice items the student selects the best response from a list of alternatives. On matching items the student matches premises (typically listed on the left) with the appropriate responses (typically listed on the right). The key factor is that all selected-response items provide the answer; the student simply selects the appropriate one. Although there are considerable differences among these selected-response item formats, we can make some general statements about their strengths and limitations (see Table 7.7). Strengths include:

- Students can generally respond to a relatively large number of selected-response items in a limited amount of time. This means you can include more items in your test. Because tests are essentially samples of the content domain, and large samples are better than small samples, the inclusion of a large number of items tends to enhance the measurement characteristics of the test.
- Selected-response items can be scored in an efficient, objective, and reliable manner. A computer can often score selected-response items. As a result, scoring takes less time and there are fewer grading errors. This can produce tests with desirable measurement characteristics.

TABLE 7.7   **Strengths and Weaknesses of Selected-Response Items**

Strengths of Selected-Response Items
1. You can typically include a relatively large number of selected-response items in your test. This facilitates adequate sampling of the content domain.
2. They can be scored in an efficient, objective, and reliable manner.
3. They are particularly good for measuring lower-level objectives.
4. They can reduce the influence of certain construct-irrelevant factors.

Weaknesses of Selected-Response Items
1. They are relatively difficult to write.
2. They are not able to assess all educational objectives (e.g., writing ability).
3. They are subject to random guessing.

- Selected-response items are particularly good for measuring lower-level cognitive objectives (e.g., knowledge, comprehension, and application).
- Selected-response items decrease the influence of certain construct-irrelevant factors that can impact test scores (e.g., the influence of writing ability on a test measuring scientific knowledge).

Naturally, there are limitations associated with the use of selected-response items. These include:

- Selected-response items are challenging to write. Relative to constructed-response items, they typically take more effort and time to write. This is not to say that writing constructed-response items is an easy task, just that the development of effective selected-response items is usually more difficult and time consuming.
- Although selected-response items are particularly well suited for assessing lower-level cognitive objectives, they are not as well suited for assessing higher-level objectives (i.e., analysis, synthesis, and evaluation). This is especially true for true–false and matching items that are often limited to the assessment of lower-level educational objectives. Multiple-choice items can be written to assess higher-level objectives, but this often takes a little more effort and creativity.
- Selected-response items are subject to blind guessing.

On *constructed-response items* the students actually create or construct an appropriate response.

Constructed-response items include short-answer items, essays, performance assessments, and portfolios. Most people are familiar with short-answer items and essays. Short-answer items require the student to supply a word, phrase, or number in response to a direct question. Short-answer items may also take the form of an incomplete sentence that the student completes (i.e., fill in the blank). Essay items pose a question or problem for the student to respond to in a written format. Essay items can typically be classified as either restricted-response or extended-response. As the name suggests, restricted-response essays are highly structured and place restrictions on the nature and scope of the students' responses. In contrast, extended-response essays are less structured and provide more freedom to students in how they respond. Although we have mentioned performance assessments a number of times in this text to this point, you may not be very familiar with them. Previously, we noted that **performance assessments** require students to complete a process or produce a product in a context that closely resembles real-life situations. **Portfolios,** a form of performance assessment, involve the systematic collection of student work products over a specified period of time according to a specific set of guidelines (AERA et al., 1999). Constructed-response assessments have their own associated strengths and weaknesses (see Table 7.8). Their strengths include:

- Compared to selected-response items, some constructed-response assessments (e.g., short answer and essays) may be easier to write or develop. Not easy, but *easier*!
- Constructed-response items are well suited for assessing higher-order cognitive abilities and complex task performance, and some tasks simply require a constructed-response format (e.g., composing a letter, demonstrating problem-solving skills). As a result they expand the range of learning objectives that can be assessed.
- Constructed-response items eliminate blind guessing.

Their weaknesses include:

- Constructed-response items take more time for students to complete. You cannot include as many constructed-response items or tasks on a test as you can selected-response items. As a result, you are not able to sample the content domain as thoroughly.
- Constructed-response items are difficult to score. In addition to scoring being more difficult and time consuming compared to selected-response items, scoring is more subjective and less reliable.
- Although constructed-response items eliminate blind guessing, they are vulnerable to "bluffing." That is, students who do not actually know the correct response might feign a response that superficially resembles a correct response.
- Constructed-response items are vulnerable to the influence of extraneous or construct-irrelevant factors that can impact test scores (e.g., the influence of writing ability on a test measuring scientific knowledge).

TABLE 7.8   Strengths and Weaknesses of Constructed-Response Items

Strengths of Constructed-Response Items
1. Compared to selected-response items, they are often easier to write.
2. They are well suited for assessing higher-order cognitive abilities and complex task performance.
3. They eliminate random guessing.

Weaknesses of Constructed-Response Items
1. Because they typically take more time than selected-response items for the students to complete, you cannot include as many items in a test. As a result, you are not as able to sample the content domain as thoroughly.
2. They are more difficult to score in a reliable manner.
3. They are vulnerable to feigning.
4. They are vulnerable to the influence of construct-irrelevant factors.

As you see, selected-response and constructed-response assessments have specific strengths and weaknesses, which deserve careful consideration when selecting an assessment format. However, typically the key factor in selecting an assessment or item format involves identifying the format that most directly measures the behaviors specified by the educational objectives. That is, you want to select the item format or task that will be the most pure, direct measure of the objective you are trying to measure. For example, if you want to assess students' ability to demonstrate their writing abilities, an essay is the natural choice. If you want to assess students' ability to engage in oral debate, a performance assessment would be the logical choice. Although the nature of some objectives dictates the use of constructed-response items (e.g., writing skills), some objectives can be measured equally well using either selected-response or constructed-response items. If after careful consideration you determine that both formats are appropriate, we generally recommend the use of selected-response items because they allow broader sampling of the content domain and more objective and reliable scoring procedures. Both of these factors enhance the measurement characteristics of your test. We will be discussing these assessment formats in the next three chapters, and this discussion will help you determine which format is most appropriate for your tests. We believe that ideally educational assessments should contain a variety of assessment procedures (e.g., multiple-choice, short answer, and performance assessments) that are specifically tailored to measure the educational objectives of interest.

> **You want to select an item format or task that provides the most pure, direct measure of the objective you are trying to assess.**

Putting the Assessment Together

We will now provide some suggestions for organizing and assembling your classroom assessment. Many of these suggestions will be addressed in more detail in the context of the different item formats, but their introduction here will hopefully help you begin to consider some of the main issues. Some of these suggestions might seem obvious, but sometimes the obvious is overlooked! Table 7.9 summarizes these suggestions.

Follow Your Table of Specifications.   We hopefully conveyed the importance of explicitly stating your educational objectives and developing a thorough table of specifications for

---

TABLE 7.9   Practical Suggestions for Assembling an Assessment

1. Adhere to your table of specifications.
2. Provide clear instructions.
3. State items clearly.
4. Develop items that can be scored in a decisive manner.
5. Avoid inadvertent cues to the correct answers.
6. Arrange items in a manner that facilitates student performance and scoring.
7. Include items that contribute to the reliability and validity of your assessment results.
8. When determining how many items to include in an assessment, consider factors such as the age of the students, the types of items employed, and the type and purpose of the test.

your test. Once you have invested the time and energy in that process, we encourage you to follow through and use it as a guide or blueprint for developing your test. Remember that your table of specifications is a tool that helps ensure congruence between your classroom instruction and the content of your test.

Provide Clear Directions. It is common for teachers to take for granted that students understand how to respond to different item formats. This may not be the case! When creating a test always include thorough directions that clearly specify how the student should respond to each item format. Just to be safe, assume that the students have never seen a test like it before and provide directions in sufficient detail to ensure they know what is expected of them.

State the Question, Problem, or Task in as Clear and Straightforward a Manner as Possible. You want students who have mastered the learning objective to get the item correct and students who have not mastered the objective to get it wrong. If students have mastered the learning objective, you do not want ambiguous wording, complex syntax, or an overly difficult vocabulary to cause them to miss the question.

Develop Items and Tasks That Can Be Scored in a Decisive Manner. Ask yourself whether the items have clear answers that virtually every expert would agree with. In terms of essays and performance assessments, the question may be if experts would agree about the quality of performance on the task. The grading process can be challenging even when your items have clearly "correct" answers. When there is ambiguity regarding what represents a definitive answer or response, scoring can become much more difficult.

Avoid Inadvertent Cues to the Correct Answers. It is easy for unintended cues to the correct response to become embedded in a test. These cues have the negative effect of allowing students who have not mastered the material to correctly answer the item. This confounds intelligence (i.e., figuring out the correct answer based on detected cues) with achievement (i.e., having learned the material). To paraphrase Gronlund (1998), only the students who have mastered an objective should get the item right, and those who have not mastered it, no matter how intelligent they are, should not get it correct.

Items should be arranged in a systematic manner that facilitates student performance.

Arrange the Items in an Assessment in a Systematic Manner. You should arrange the items in your assessment in a manner that promotes the optimal performance of your students. If your test contains multiple item formats, the items should be arranged in sections according to the type of item. That is, place all the multiple-choice items together, all the short-answer items together, and so on. This allows the students to maintain the same mental set throughout the section. It has the added benefit of making it easier for you to score the items. After arranging the items by format, you should arrange the items in each section (e.g., multiple-choice items) according to their level of difficulty. That is, start with the easy items and move progressively to the more difficult items. This arrangement tends to reduce anxiety, enhances motivation, and allows students to progress quickly through the easier items and devote the remaining time to the more difficult items.

Some assessment experts suggest that you arrange the items in the order that the material was presented in your class instruction. This is thought to help students retrieve the information more easily. If you adopt this approach, however, it is recommended that you encourage students to skip the most difficult items and return to them as time permits. A logical variation on this approach is to arrange the items from the easiest to the most difficult within each specific content area (e.g., Nitko, 2001). For example, on a multiple-choice section covering reliability, validity, and item analysis, you would arrange all of the items related to reliability in order of difficulty, followed by the items on validity in order of difficulty, and finally the items on item analysis in order of difficulty.

Include Test Items and Tasks That Will Result in an Assessment That Produces Reliable and Valid Test Results.   In the first section of this text we discussed the important properties of reliability and validity. No matter which format you select for your test, you should not lose sight of the importance of developing tests that produce reliable and valid results. To make better educational decisions, you need high-quality information.

How Many Items Should You Include?   As is often the case, there is no simple answer to this question. The optimal number of items to include in an assessment is determined by factors such as the age of the students, the types of items, the breadth of the material or topics being assessed (i.e., scope of the test), and the type of test. Let's consider several of these factors separately:

Age of Students.   For students in elementary school it is probably best to limit regular classroom exams to approximately 30 minutes in order to maximize effort, concentration, and motivation. With older students you can increase this period considerably, but it is probably desirable to limit assessments to approximately one hour in order to maximize performance and accommodate class schedules. Naturally these are just flexible guidelines. For example, when administering six-week or semester exams, more time may be necessary to adequately assess the learning objectives. Additionally, you will likely need help with the administration of standardized assessments that take significantly more time than the standard classroom exam.

Types of Items.   Obviously, students can complete more true–false items than they can essay items in a given period of time. Gronlund (2003) estimates that high school students should be able to complete approximately one multiple-choice item, three true–false items, or three fill-in-the-blank items in one minute if the items are assessing objectives at the knowledge level. Naturally, with younger students or more complex objectives, more time will be needed. When you move to restricted-response essays or performance assessments, significantly more time will be needed, and when you include extended-response tasks the time demands increase even more. As we have already alluded to, the inclusion of more "time-efficient" items will enhance the sampling of the content domain.

Type and Purpose of the Test.   Maximum performance tests can typically be categorized as either *speed* or *power* tests. Pure **speed tests** generally contain items that are relatively easy but have strict time limits that prevent examinees from successfully completing all the items. On pure **power tests**, the speed of performance is not an issue. Everyone is given enough time to attempt all the items, but the items are ordered according to difficulty, with some items being so difficult that no examinee is expected to answer them all. The distinction between speed and power tests is one of degree rather than being absolute. Most often a test is not a *pure* speed test or a *pure* power test, but incorporates some combination of the two approaches. The decision to use a speed test, a power test, or some combination of the two will influence the number and type of items you include on your test.

Scope of the Test.   In addition to the speed versus power test distinction, the scope of the test will influence how many items you include in an assessment. For a weekly exam designed to assess progress in a relatively narrow range of skills and knowledge, a brief test will likely be sufficient. However, for a six-week or semester assessment covering a broader range of skills and knowledge, a more comprehensive (i.e., longer) assessment is typically indicated.

When estimating the time needed to complete the test you should also take into consideration test-related activities such as handing out the test, giving directions, and collecting the tests. Most professional test developers design power tests that approximately 95% of their samples will complete in the allotted time. This is probably a good rule of thumb for classroom tests. This can be calculated in the classroom by dividing the number of students completing the entire test by the total number of subjects.

Preparing Your Students and Administering the Assessment

In this final section of the chapter we will provide some suggestions on how you can best prepare your students for and then administer an assessment. Obviously, it would be regretful to develop an exemplary assessment and then have its results compromised by poor preparation or inappropriate administration procedures. Your goal should be to promote conditions that allow students to perform their best. Before administering an assessment, you should take appropriate steps to prepare the students. This can include announcing in advance when the test will be administered, describing what content and skills will be covered, the basic parameters of the test (e.g., one-hour test including short-answer and restricted-response essay items), how it will be scored, and how the results will be used (e.g., Linn & Gronlund, 2000). It is also beneficial to give the students examples of the types of items that will be included on the test and provide general instruction in basic test-taking skills. You also want to do your best to minimize excessive test anxiety because it can be a source of construct-irrelevant variance that undermines the validity of your interpretations. Although stressing the importance of an upcoming assessment can help motivate students, there is a point at which it is no longer motivating and becomes counterproductive. Special Interest Topic 7.1 provides some suggestions for helping students manage their anxiety.

> **Before administering an assessment, you should take appropriate steps to prepare the students.**

SPECIAL INTEREST TOPIC **7.1**

Suggestions for Reducing Test Anxiety

Research suggests that there is a curvilinear relationship between anxiety and performance. That is, at relatively low levels anxiety may have a motivating effect. It can motivate students to study in a conscientious manner and put forth their best effort. However, when anxiety exceeds a certain point it becomes detrimental to performance. It will enhance the validity of your interpretations if you can reduce the influence of debilitating test anxiety. Remember, in most classroom situations you are striving to measure student achievement, not the impact of excessive anxiety. In this situation test anxiety is a source of *construct-irrelevant variance*. If you reduce anxiety, you reduce construct-irrelevant variance and increase the validity of your interpretations. Researchers have provided suggestions for helping students control test anxiety (e.g., Hembree, 1988; Linn & Gronlund, 2000; Mealey & Host, 1992; Nitko, 2001; Tippets & Benson, 1989). These suggestions include the following:

- Students with test anxiety may benefit from relaxation training. In many schools students with debilitating test anxiety may be referred to a school counselor or school psychologist who can teach them some fairly simple relaxation techniques.
- Although it is good practice to minimize environmental distractions for all students, this is even more important for highly anxious students. Highly anxious students tend to be more easily distracted by auditory and visual stimuli than their less anxious peers.
- Do not make the test a do-or-die situation. Although it is reasonable to emphasize the importance of an assessment, it is not beneficial to tell your students that this will be the most difficult test they have ever taken or that their future is dependent on their performance on the test.
- Provide a review of the material to be covered on the test before the testing date. This is a good instructional strategy that can facilitate the integration of material, students will appreciate the review, and anxiety will be reduced.
- Arrange the items on your test from easy to difficult. Have you ever taken a test in which the first item was extremely difficult or covered some obscure topic you had never heard of? If so, you probably experienced a sudden drop in confidence, even if you initially felt well prepared to take the test. To avoid this, many instructors will intentionally start the test with a particularly easy item. It might not do much from a technical perspective (e.g., item difficulty or discrimination), but it can have a positive influence on student motivation and morale.
- It is beneficial to have multiple assessments over the course of a grading period rather than basing everything on one or two assessments. When there are only a limited number of assessments, the stakes may seem so high that student anxiety is increased unnecessarily.
- Prepare all of your students for the test by teaching appropriate test-taking strategies. A novel or unfamiliar test format provokes anxiety in many students, and this tendency is magnified in students prone to test anxiety.
- When the students are seated and ready to begin the test, avoid unnecessary discussion before letting them begin. The students are typically a little "on edge" and anxious to get started. If the teacher starts rambling about irrelevant topics, this tends to increase student anxiety.

The scheduling of an assessment is also a decision that deserves careful consideration. You should try to schedule the test at a time when the students will not be distracted by other events. For example, scheduling a test the last day before a big holiday is probably not optimal. In this situation the students are likely to be more focused on the upcoming holiday

Take steps to ensure that the testing environment is conducive to optimal student performance.

than on the test. The same goes with major events at the school. Scheduling tests the day of the big homecoming game or the senior prom is probably not desirable. Teachers should make every effort to ensure that the physical environment is conducive to optimal student performance. You should take steps to ensure that the room is comfortable (e.g., temperature, proper ventilation), that there is proper lighting, and that extraneous noise is minimized. Additionally, you should make efforts to avoid any unexpected interruptions (e.g., ask whether a firedrill is scheduled, place a "Test in Progress" sign on the door).

Once the students have started the test, be careful about providing help to students. Students can be fairly crafty when it comes to coaxing information from teachers during a test. They may come asking for clarification while actually "fishing" for hints or clues to the answer. As a teacher you do not want to discourage students from clarifying the meaning of ambiguous items, but you also do not want to inadvertently provide hints to the answer of clearly stated items. Our suggestion is to carefully consider the student's question and determine whether the item is actually ambiguous. If it is, make a brief clarifying comment to the whole class. If the item is clear and the student is simply fishing for a clue to the answer, simply instruct the student to return to his or her seat and carefully read and consider the meaning of the item. Finally, take reasonable steps to **discourage cheating.** Cheating is another source of construct-irrelevant variance that can undermine the validity of your score interpretations. Special Interest Topic 7.2 provides some strategies for preventing cheating on classroom tests.

Summary

In this chapter we addressed the initial steps a teacher should follow in developing classroom achievement tests. We noted that the first step is to specify the educational objectives or goals you have for your students. It is important to do this because these objectives will serve as the basis for your test. In writing educational objectives, we noted that there are several factors to consider, including the following:

- *Scope:* Educational objectives can be written on a continuum from very specific to very broad. We noted that there are limitations associated with objectives at either end of this continuum and suggested strategies to help you minimize these limitations.
- *Domain:* Educational objectives also differ in the type of ability or characteristic being measured. Educational objectives typically involve cognitive, affective, or psychomotor abilities. While all three of these domains are important in school settings, the cognitive domain is of primary importance. We presented Bloom's taxonomy of cognitive objectives, which presents six hierarchical categories including knowledge, comprehension, application, analysis, synthesis, and evaluation.
- *Format:* Educational objectives are often classified as behavioral or nonbehavioral. Although behavioral objectives have advantages, if the behavioral format is taken to the extreme it also has limitations. We noted that it is optimal to have objectives that are broad enough to help you organize your instruction and testing procedures, but that also state measurable activities.

SPECIAL INTEREST TOPIC **7.2**

Strategies for Preventing Cheating

Cheating on tests is as old as assessment! In ancient China, examinees were searched before taking civil service exams, and the actual exams were administered in individual cubicles to prevent cheating. The punishment for cheating was death (Hopkins, 1998)! We do not punish cheaters as severely today, but cheating continues to be a problem in schools. Like test anxiety, cheating is another source of construct-irrelevant variance that undermines the validity of test interpretations. If you can reduce cheating you will enhance the validity of your interpretations. Many authors have provided suggestions for preventing cheating (e.g., Hopkins, 1998; Linn & Gronlund, 2000; Popham, 2000). These include the following:

- Keep the assessment materials secure. Tests and other assessments have a way of getting into the hands of students. To avoid this, do not leave the assessments in open view in unlocked offices, make sure that the person copying the tests knows to keep them secure, and number the tests so you will know if one is missing. Verify the number of tests when distributing them to students and when picking them up from students.
- Possibly the most commonsense recommendation is to provide appropriate supervision of students during examinations. This is not to suggest that you hover over students (this can cause unnecessary anxiety), but simply that you provide an appropriate level of supervision. This can involve either observing from a position that provides an unobstructed view of the entire room or occasionally strolling around the room. Possibly the most important factor is to be attentive and visible; this will probably go a long way toward reducing the likelihood of cheating.
- Have the students clear their desks before distributing the tests.
- When distributing the tests, it is advisable to individually hand each student a test. This will help you avoid accidentally distributing more tests than there are students (an accident that can result in a test falling into the wrong hands).
- If students are allowed to use scratch paper, you should require that they turn this in with the test.
- When possible, use alternative seating with an empty row of seats between students.
- Create two forms of the test. This can be accomplished by simply changing the order of test items slightly so that the items are not in exactly the same order. Give students sitting next to each other alternate forms.

In concluding our discussion of educational objectives, we provided some general suggestions to help you write objectives. These suggestions included (1) write objectives that cover a broad spectrum of abilities; (2) when feasible, identify behaviors that are observable and directly measurable; (3) state any special conditions; and (4) when appropriate, specify an outcome criterion.

The next step in developing a classroom test is to develop a table of specifications, which is essentially a blueprint for the test that helps you organize the educational objectives and make sure that the test content matches the curriculum content. A table of specifications also helps you include items of varying degrees of complexity. Before actually proceeding with writing your test, you have some other important decisions to make. One decision is whether to use a norm-referenced or criterion-referenced interpretation of performance. We noted that in most situations criterion-referenced assessment is most useful in the classroom. Another decision deals with the use of selected-response and constructed-response items. Although we will be devoting the next three chapters to detailed discussions of these items, we provided an overview of some of the advantages and limitations of both item formats.

We closed this chapter by providing some practical suggestions for assembling your test, preparing your students for the assessment, and administering it. When assembling your test, we recommend (1) adhering to your table of specifications, (2) providing clear instructions, (3) stating questions clearly, (4) developing items that can be scored in a decisive manner, (5) avoiding cues to the correct answers, (6) arranging items in a systematic manner, and (7) including items that will contribute to the reliability and validity of your assessment results. We also discussed some factors to consider when determining how many items to include in an assessment. These factors included the age of your students, the types of items you are using, and the type of test you are developing.

In terms of preparing students for and administering an assessment, we described a number of things teachers can do to enhance student performance and increase the reliability and validity of assessment results. These include (1) preparing your students for the assessment, (2) scheduling the assessment at an appropriate time, (3) ensuring that the testing conditions are adequate (e.g., comfortable, proper lighting, quiet), (4) avoiding answering questions that might "give away" the answers, and (5) taking reasonable steps to discourage cheating.

KEY TERMS AND CONCEPTS

Affective objectives, p. 169
Analysis, p. 168
Application, p. 168
Behavioral objectives, p. 171
Bloom's taxonomy, p. 167
Cognitive objectives, p. 166
Comprehension, p. 167
Constructed-response items, p. 177
Criterion-referenced scores, p. 176
Discouraging cheating, p. 185

Domain, p. 165
Educational objectives, p. 164
Evaluation, p. 168
Format, p. 165
Knowledge, p. 167
Nonbehavioral objectives, p. 171
Norm-referenced scores, p. 176
Performance assessments, p. 179
Portfolios, p. 179
Power tests, p. 183

Psychomotor objectives, p. 170
Reducing test anxiety, p. 184
Scope, p. 165
Selected-response items, p. 177
Speed tests, p. 183
Synthesis, p. 168
Table of specifications, p. 173
Test blueprint, p. 173

RECOMMENDED READINGS

Gronlund, N. E. (2000). *How to write and use instructional objectives* (6th ed.). Upper Saddle River, NJ: Merrill/Prentice Hall. This is an excellent example of a text that focuses on the development of educational objectives.

Lorin, W. (2003). Benjamin S. Bloom: His life, his works, and his legacy. In B. Zimmerman (Ed.), *Educational psychology: A century of contributions* (pp. 367–389). Mahwah, NJ: Erlbaum. This chapter provides a biographical sketch of Dr. Bloom and reviews his influence in educational psychology.

8

The Development and Use of Selected-Response Items

Some educators embrace selected-response items because they can contribute to the development of psychometrically sound tests. Other educators reject them because they believe they cannot adequately measure the really important knowledge and skills they want students to acquire.

CHAPTER HIGHLIGHTS

Multiple-Choice Items
True–False Items
Matching Items

LEARNING OBJECTIVES

After reading and studying this chapter, students should be able to:

1. Describe the major types of selected-response items and their characteristics.
2. Describe the components and types of multiple-choice items and give examples.
3. Describe the principles involved with developing effective multiple-choice items.
4. Develop effective multiple-choice items for a given content area.
5. Discuss the strengths and weaknesses of multiple-choice items.
6. Describe the principles involved with developing effective true–false items.
7. Develop effective true–false items for a given content area.
8. Discuss the strengths and weaknesses of true–false items.
9. Describe the principles involved with developing effective matching items.
10. Develop effective matching items for a given content area.
11. Discuss the strengths and weaknesses of matching items.
12. Be able to apply and interpret a correction for guessing.

In the last chapter we addressed the development of educational objectives and provided some general suggestions for developing, assembling, and administering your assessments. In the next three chapters we will discuss the development of specific types of test items. In this chapter we will focus on the development of selected-response items. As we noted in the last chapter, if an item requires a student to select a response from available alternatives, it is classified as a **selected-response item.** Multiple-choice, true–false, and matching items are all selected-response items. If an item requires a student to create or construct a response, it is classified as a **constructed-response item.** Essay and short-answer items are constructed-response

If an item requires a student to select a response from available alternatives, it is classified as a *selected-response item*. If it requires a student to create or construct a response, it is classified as a *constructed-response item*.

items, but this category also includes other complex activities such as making a class presentation, composing a poem, or painting a picture.

In this chapter we will address selected-response items in detail. We will discuss their strengths and weaknesses and provide suggestions for developing effective items. In the next chapter we will address essay and short-answer items. In Chapter 10 we will address performance assessments and portfolios—types of constructed-response assessments that have gained increased popularity in recent years. In these chapters we will focus on items used to assess student achievement (as opposed to interests, personality characteristics, etc.).

Multiple-Choice Items

Multiple-choice items are by far the most popular selected-response items.

Multiple-choice items are by far the most popular of the selected-response items. They have gained this degree of popularity because they can be used in a variety of content areas and can assess both simple and complex learning outcomes. Multiple-choice items take the general form of a question or an incomplete statement with a set of possible answers, one of which is correct. The part of the item that is either a question or an incomplete statement is referred to as the **stem.** The possible answers are referred to as **alternatives.** The correct alternative is simply called the answer and the incorrect alternatives are referred to as **distracters** (i.e., they serve to "distract" students who do not actually know the correct response).

Multiple-choice items can be written as a direct question or an incomplete sentence.

Multiple-choice items can be written so the stem is in the form of a direct question or an incomplete sentence. Most writers prefer the **direct-question format** because they feel it presents the problem in the clearest manner. The advantage of the **incomplete-sentence format** is that it may present the problem in a more concise manner. If the question is formatted as an incomplete statement, it is suggested that the omission occur near the end of the stem. Our recommendation is to use the direct-question format unless the problem can be stated more concisely using the incomplete-sentence format without any loss of clarity. Examine these examples of the two formats.

Example 1   Direct-Question Format

1. Which river is the largest in the United States of America?
   A. Mississippi <
   B. Missouri
   C. Ohio
   D. Rio Grande

Example 2   Incomplete-Sentence Format

2. The largest river in the United States of America is the _____
   A. Mississippi. <
   B. Missouri.
   C. Ohio.
   D. Rio Grande.

Another distinction is made between multiple-choice items that have what is known as the **correct-answer** versus the **best-answer format**. Examples 1 and 2 are correct-answer items. The Mississippi is the largest river in the United States of America and the other answers are incorrect. However, multiple-choice items can be written for situations having more than one correct answer. The objective is to identify the "best answer."

Example 3   Best-Answer Format

1. Which variable is generally thought to be the most important when buying a house?
   - **A.** cost
   - **B.** builder
   - **C.** design
   - **D.** location <

In Example 3 all the variables listed are important to consider when buying a house, but as almost any realtor will tell you, location is the most important. Most test developers prefer the best-answer format for two reasons. First, in some situations it is difficult to write an answer that everyone will agree is correct. The best-answer format allows you to frame it as an answer that most experts will agree with. Second, the best-answer format often requires the student to make more subtle distinctions among the alternatives, which results in more demanding items that measure more complex educational objectives.

Guidelines for Developing Multiple-Choice Items

Use a Printed Format That Makes the Item as Clear as Possible.   While there is not a universally accepted format for multiple-choice items, here are a few recommendations regarding physical layout that can enhance clarity.

- Provide brief but clear directions. Directions should include how the selected alternative should be marked.
- The item stem should be numbered for easy identification, while the alternatives are indented and identified with letters.
- Either capital or lowercase letters followed by a period or parenthesis can be used for the alternatives. If a scoring sheet is used, make the alternative letters on the scoring sheet and the test as similar as possible.
- There is no need to capitalize the beginning of alternatives unless they begin with a proper name.
- When the item stem is a complete sentence, there should not be a period at the end of the alternatives (see Example 4).
- When the stem is in the form of an incomplete statement with the missing phrase at the end on the sentence, alternatives should end with a period (see Example 5).
- Keep the alternatives in a vertical list instead of placing them side by side because it is easier for students to scan a vertical list quickly.
- Use correct grammar and formal language structure in writing items.
- All items should be written so that the entire question appears on one page.

The following use formats that promote clarity, illustrating many of these suggestions.

Example 4

Directions: Read each question carefully and select the best answer. Circle the letter of the answer you have selected.

1. Which type of validity study involves a substantial time interval between when the test is administered and when the criterion is measured?
    A. delayed study
    B. content study
    C. factorial study
    D. predictive study <

Example 5

2. The type of validity study that involves a substantial time interval between when the test is administered and when the criterion is measured is a _____
    A. delayed study.
    B. content study.
    C. factorial study.
    D. predictive study. <

Have the Item Stem Contain All the Information Necessary to Understand the Problem or Question.   When writing multiple-choice items, the problem or question should be fully developed in the item stem. Poorly developed multiple-choice items often contain an inadequate stem that leaves the test taker unclear about the central problem or question. Compare the stems in the following two examples.

Example 6   Poor Item—Inadequate Stem

1. Absolute zero point.
    A. interval scale
    B. nominal scale
    C. ordinal scale
    D. ratio scale <

Example 7   Better Item—Adequate Stem

1. Which scale of measurement incorporates a true or absolute zero point?
    A. interval scale
    B. nominal scale
    C. ordinal scale
    D. ratio scale <

Your students are not mind readers, and item stems that are not fully developed can result in misinterpretations by students. One way to determine whether the stem is adequate is to read the stem without examining the alternatives. If the stem is adequate, a knowledgeable individual should be able to answer the question with relative ease. In Examples 6 and 7, the first item fails this test whereas the second item passes. This test is equally applicable if the question is framed as a question or as an incomplete statement.

While we encourage you to develop the problem fully in the item stem, it is usually not beneficial to include irrelevant material in the stem. Consider this example.

Example 8   Poor Item—Unnecessary Content

1. There are several different scales of measurement used in educational settings. Which scale of measurement incorporates a true or absolute zero point?

    A. interval scale
    B. nominal scale
    C. ordinal scale
    D. ratio scale <

In Example 8 the addition of the sentence "There are several different scales of measurement used in educational settings" does not serve to add clarity. It simply takes more time to read.

Provide between Three and Five Alternatives.   Although there is no "correct" number of alternatives, it is recommended that you use between three and five. Four are most commonly used, but some test developers suggest using five to reduce the chance of correctly guessing the answer. For example, the chance of correctly guessing the answer with three alternatives is 1 in 3 (i.e., 33%); with four alternatives is 1 in 4 (i.e., 25%); and with five is 1 in 5 (i.e., 20%). The use of five alternatives is probably the upper limit. Many computer scoring programs accommodate only five alternatives, and it can be difficult to develop plausible distracters (the addition of distracters that are clearly wrong and not selected by any students does not reduce the chance of correctly guessing the answer). In some situations three alternatives may be sufficient. It takes students less time to read and answer items with three alternatives instead of four (or five), and it is easier to write two good distracters than three (or four). Certain research even suggests that items with three alternatives can be as effective as items with four or five alternatives (e.g., Costin, 1970; Grier, 1975; Sidick, Barrett, & Doverspike, 1994).

Keep the Alternatives Brief and Arrange Them in an Order That Promotes Efficient Scanning.   As we noted, the item stem should contain as much of the content as possible and should not contain irrelevant material. A correlate of this is that the alternatives should be as brief as possible. This brevity makes it easier for the students to scan the alternatives looking for the correct answer. Consider Examples 9 and 10. While they both measure the same content, the first one contains an inadequate stem and lengthy alternatives whereas the second one has an adequate stem and brief alternatives.

Example 9   Poor Item—Inadequate Stem and Lengthy Alternatives

1. Andrew Jackson _____

    A. was born in Virginia.
    B. did not fight in the American Revolution due to a childhood illness.
    C. was the 7th president of the United States. <
    D. served three terms as president of the United States.

Example 10   Better Item—Adequate Stem and Brief Alternatives

2. Who was the 7th president of the United States of America?

    A. Andrew Jackson <
    B. James Monroe
    C. John Adams
    D. Martin Van Buren

When applicable, alternatives should be arranged in a logical order to promote efficient scanning. For example, numbers should be placed in ascending order, dates ordered in temporal sequence, and nouns and names alphabetized. See Examples 11 and 12.

Example 11   Poor Item—Illogical Arrangement of Alternatives

1. What year did the Spanish-American War occur?
   - **A.** 1912
   - **B.** 1890
   - **C.** 1908
   - **D.** 1898 <
   - **E.** 1902

Example 12   Better Item—Logical Arrangement of Alternatives

2. What year did the Spanish-American War occur?
   - **A.** 1890
   - **B.** 1898 <
   - **C.** 1902
   - **D.** 1908
   - **E.** 1912

Avoid Negatively Stated Stems in Most Situations.   As a general rule you should avoid using negatively stated stems. Limit the use of terms such as *except, least, never,* and *not.* Students might overlook these terms and miss the question even if they have mastered the learning objective being measured. Unless you intend to measure the student's ability to attend to the details of the item, this is not a desired outcome and undermines the validity of the test's results. In most situations this can be avoided by rephrasing the stem.

Occasionally it may be necessary or desirable to state stems in the negative. For example, in some situations it is important for students to know what not to do (e.g., what should you *not* do if you smell gas?) or identify an alternative that differs in some way from the other alternatives. In these situations you should highlight the negative terms by capitalizing, underlining, or printing them in bold type. Examine Examples 13 and 14.

Example 13   Poor Item—Negatively Stated Stem

1. Which state does not have a coastline on the Gulf of Mexico?
   - **A.** Alabama
   - **B.** Florida
   - **C.** Tennessee <
   - **D.** Texas

Example 14   Better Item—Negative Term Highlighted

2. Which state does **NOT** have a coastline on the Gulf of Mexico?
   - **A.** Alabama
   - **B.** Florida
   - **C.** Tennessee <
   - **D.** Texas

Double negatives should always be avoided. Logicians know that a double negative indicates a positive, but students should not have to decipher this logic problem.

Make Sure Only One Alternative Is Correct or Represents the Best Answer. Carefully review your alternatives to ensure there is only one correct or best answer. Commonly teachers are confronted by students who feel they can defend one of the distracters as a correct answer. It is not possible to avoid this situation completely, but you can minimize it by carefully evaluating the distracters. We recommend setting the test aside for a period of time and returning to it later for proofing. Fatigue and tight deadlines can allow undetected errors.

Occasionally it might be appropriate to include more than one correct alternative in a multiple-choice item and require the students to identify all of the correct alternatives. It is usually best to format these questions as a series of true–false items, an arrangement referred to as a cluster-type or **multiple true–false item**. See Examples 15 and 16.

Example 15   Poor Item—Multiple-Choice Item with Multiple Correct Alternatives

1. Which states have a coastline on the Gulf of Mexico?

    A. Alabama <
    B. Florida <
    C. Tennessee
    D. Texas <

Example 16   Better Item—Multiple True-False Item

2. Which of the following states have a coastline on the Gulf of Mexico? Circle the T if the state has a Gulf coastline, the F if the state does not have a Gulf coastline.

Alabama	**T**	F
Florida	**T**	F
Tennessee	T	**F**
Texas	**T**	F

Avoid Cues That Inadvertently Identify the Correct Answer. Item stems should not contain information that gives away the answer. A **cue** is something in the stem that provides a clue to the answer that is not based on knowledge. It often involves an association between the words in the stem and the correct alternative. See Examples 17 and 18.

Example 17   Poor Item—Stem Contains a Cue to the Correct Answer

1. Which type of validity study examines the ability of test scores to predict a criterion?

    A. interval study
    B. content study
    C. factorial study
    D. predictive study <

Example 18   Better Item—Cues Avoided

2. Which type of validity study involves a substantial time interval between when the test is administered and when the criterion is measured?

    A. interval study
    B. content study
    C. factorial study
    D. predictive study <

In Example 17, the use of *predict* in the stem and *predictive* in the correct alternative provides a cue to the correct answer. This is corrected in Example 18. Additionally, in the second example there is an intentional verbal association between the stem and the first distracter (i.e., *interval*). This association makes the first distracter more attractive, particularly to students relying on cues, who do not know the correct answer.

In addition to the stem containing cues to the correct answer, the alternatives can themselves contain cues. One way to avoid this is to ensure that all alternatives are approximately equal in length and complexity. In an attempt to be precise, teachers may make the correct answer longer or more complex than the distracters. This can serve as another type of cue for students. Although in some cases it might be possible to both maintain precision and shorten the correct alternative, it is usually easier to lengthen the distracters (though this does make scanning the alternatives more difficult for students). Compare Examples 19 and 20.

Example 19   Poor Item—Unequal Length and Complexity of Alternatives

1. Ecology is the study of _____

    A. genetics.
    B. organisms and their relationship to the environment. <
    C. internal balances.
    D. evolution.

Example 20   Better Item—Alternatives Similar in Length and Complexity

2. Ecology is the study of _____

    A. the genetic and molecular basis of organisms.
    B. organisms and their relationship to the environment. <
    C. how organisms maintain their delicate internal balance.
    D. how organisms have slowly evolved over the last million years.

When dealing with numerical alternatives, the visual characteristics of the choices can also serve as a cue. Examine the following examples.

Example 21   Poor Item—Alternative Contains
a Visual Cue to the Correct Answer

1. The correlation between two measures is 0.90. What is the coefficient of determination?

    A. 0.1
    B. 0.3
    C. 0.81 <
    D. 0.9

Example 22   Better Item—Cues Avoided

2. The correlation between two measures is 0.90. What is the coefficient of determination?

    A. .10
    B. .30
    C. .81 <
    D. .99

In Example 21, the third option (i.e., C) is the only alternative that, like the number in the stem, has two decimal places. The visual characteristics of this alternative may attract the student to it independent of the knowledge required to answer it. In Example 22, each alternative has an equal number of decimal places and is equally visually attractive.

Make Sure All Alternatives Are Grammatically Correct Relative to the Stem. Grammatical cues that may help the uninformed student select the correct answer are usually the result of inadequate proofreading. Examine the following examples.

Example 23   Poor Item—Grammatical Cue Present

1. Which individuals are credited with making the first successful flights in a heavier-than-air aircraft that was both powered and controlled?
   - **A.** Octave Chanute
   - **B.** Otto Lilienthal
   - **C.** Samuel Langley
   - **D.** Wilbur and Orville Wright <

Example 24   Better Item—Grammatical Cue Avoided

2. Which individuals are credited with making the first successful flights in a heavier-than-air aircraft that was both powered and controlled?
   - **A.** Octave Chanute and Sir George Cayley
   - **B.** Otto Lilienthal and Francis Herbert Wenham
   - **C.** Samuel Langley and Alphonse Penaud
   - **D.** Wilbur and Orville Wright <

In Example 23 the phrase "individuals are" in the stem indicates a plural answer. However, only the fourth alternative (i.e., D) meets this requirement. This is corrected in Example 24 by ensuring that each alternative reflects a plural answer.

Another common error is inattention to the articles *a* and *an*. See the following.

Example 25   Poor Item—Grammatical Cue Present

1. A coherent and unifying explanation for a class of phenomena is a _____
   - **A.** analysis.
   - **B.** experiment.
   - **C.** observation.
   - **D.** theory. <

Example 26   Better Item—Grammatical Cue Avoided

2. A coherent and unifying explanation for a class of phenomena is a _____
   - **A.** conjecture.
   - **B.** hypothesis.
   - **C.** prediction.
   - **D.** theory. <

Example 27   Better Item—Grammatical Cue Avoided

3. A coherent and unifying explanation for a class of phenomena is a(n) _____
   - **A.** experiment.
   - **B.** hypothesis.
   - **C.** observation.
   - **D.** theory. <

In Example 25, the use of the article *a* indicates an answer beginning with a consonant instead of a vowel. An observant student relying on cues will select the fourth alternative (i.e., D) because it is the only one that is grammatically correct. This is corrected in Example 26 by ensuring that all alternatives begin with consonants and in Example 27 by using *a(n)* to accommodate alternatives beginning with either consonants or vowels.

Make Sure No Item Reveals the Answer to Another Item.   One item should not contain information that will help a student answer another item. Also, a correct answer on one item should not be necessary for answering another item. This would give double weight to the first item.

Have All Distracters Appear Plausible.   Distracters should be designed to distract unknowledgeable students from the correct answer. Therefore, all distracters should appear plausible and should be based on common student errors. For example, what concepts, terms, events, techniques, or individuals are commonly confused? After you have administered the test once, analyze the distracters to determine which are effective and which are not. Replace or revise the ineffective distracters. There is little point in including a distracter that can be easily eliminated by uninformed students. This simply wastes time and space.

Use Alternative Positions in a Random Manner for the Correct Answer.   The correct answer should appear in each of the alternative positions approximately the same number of times. When there are four alternatives (e.g., A, B, C, and D), teachers tend to overuse the middle alternatives (i.e., B and C). Alert students are likely to detect this pattern and use it to answer questions of which they are unsure. Students have indicated that when faced with a question they cannot answer based on knowledge they simply select B or C. Additionally, you should ensure there is no detectable pattern in the placement of correct answers (e.g., A, C, B, D, A, etc.). If there is no logical ordering for the alternatives (see the earlier recommendation), they should be randomly arranged. Attempt random assignment when possible then once the test is complete, count the number of times the correct answer appears in each position. If any positions are over- or underrepresented, make adjustments to correct the imbalance.

Minimize the Use of "None of the Above" and Avoid Using "All of the Above."   There is some disagreement among test development experts regarding the use of "none of the above" and "all of the above" as alternatives. The alternative "none of the above" is criticized because it automatically forces the item into a correct-answer format. As noted earlier, the correct-answer form is often limited to lower-level educational objectives and easier items. Although there are times when "none of the above" is appropriate as an alternative, it should be used sparingly. Testing experts are more unified in their criticism of "all of the above" as an alternative. There are two primary concerns. First, students may read alternative A, see that it is correct, and mark it without ever reading alternatives B, C, and D. In this situation the response is incorrect because the students did not read all of the alternatives, not necessarily because they have not mastered the educational objective. Second, students may know that two of the alternatives are correct and therefore conclude that "all of the above" is correct. In this situation the response is correct but is based on incomplete knowledge. Our recommendation is to use "none of the above" sparingly and avoid using "all of the above."

Avoid Artificially Inflating the Reading Level.   Unless it is necessary to state the problem clearly and precisely, avoid obscure words and an overly difficult reading level. This does not mean to avoid scientific or technical terms necessary to state the problem, but simply to avoid the unnecessary use of complex incidental words.

Limit the Use of* Always *and* Never *in the Alternatives.   The use of *always* and *never* should generally be avoided because it is only in mathematics that their use is typically justified. Savvy students know this and will use this information to rule out distracters.

Avoid Using the Exact Phrasing from the Text.   Most measurement specialists suggest that you avoid using the exact wording used in a text. Exact phrasing may be appropriate if rote memorization is what you desire, but it is of limited value in terms of concept formation and the ability to generalize. Exact phrasing should be used sparingly.

Organize the Test in a Logical Manner.   The topics in a test should be organized in a logical manner rather than scattered randomly. However, the test does not have to exactly mirror the text or lectures. Strive for an organization that facilitates student performance.

Give Careful Consideration to the Number of Items on Your Test.   Determining the number of items to include on a test is a matter worthy of careful consideration. On one hand you want to include enough items to ensure adequate reliability and validity. Recall that one way to enhance the reliability of a score is to increase the number of items that go into making up the score. On the other hand there is usually a limited amount of class time allotted to testing. Occasionally teachers will include so many items on a test that students do not have enough time to make reasoned responses. A test with too many items essentially becomes a "speed test" and unfairly rewards students who respond quickly even if they know no more than students who were slower in responding.

Companies who publish tests estimate a completion time for each item. For example, an item may be considered a 30-second item, a 45-second item, or a 60-second item. Making similar estimates can be useful, but unless you are a professional test developer you will probably find it difficult to accurately estimate the time necessary to complete every item. As a general rule you should allot at least one minute for secondary school students to complete a multiple-choice item that measures a lower-level objective (e.g., Gronlund, 2003). Younger students or items assessing higher-level objectives typically require more time.

Be Flexible When Applying These Guidelines.   Apply these guidelines in a flexible manner. Although these suggestions apply in most cases, there are exceptions. The goal is to write items that measure your educational objectives and contribute to psychometrically sound tests. As you gain more experience writing items you may occasionally need to violate one of the guidelines to write the most efficient and effective item. This is clearly ap-

TABLE 8.1   Checklist for the Development of Multiple-Choice Items

1. Are the items clear and easy to read? _____

2. Does the item stem clearly state the problem or question? _____

3. Are there between three and five alternatives? _____

4. Are the alternatives brief and arranged in an order that promotes efficient scanning? _____

5. Have you avoided negatively stated stems? _____

6. Is there only one alternative that is correct or represents the best answer? _____

7. Have you checked for cues that accidentally identify the correct answer? _____

8. Are all alternatives grammatically correct relative to the stem? _____

9. Have you checked to make sure no item reveals the answer to another item? _____

10. Do all distracters appear plausible? _____

11. Did you use alternative positions in a random manner for the correct answer? _____

12. Did you minimize the use of "none of the above" and avoid using "all of the above"? _____

13. Is the reading level appropriate? _____

14. Did you limit the use of *always* and *never* in the alternatives? _____

15. Did you avoid using the exact phrasing from the text? _____

16. Is the test organized in a logical manner? _____

17. Can the test be completed in the allotted time period? _____

propriate, but if you find yourself doing it routinely, you are most likely being lazy or careless in your test preparation. Table 8.1 provides a summary of these guidelines.

Strengths and Weaknesses of Multiple-Choice Items

As we noted earlier the multiple-choice format is the most popular selected-response format. Major strengths of multiple-choice include the following.

Multiple-Choice Items Are Versatile.   Multiple-choice items can be used to access achievement in a wide range of content areas from history and geography to statistics and research design. They can be used to assess a variety of educational objectives ranging from the simple to the complex. One of the most frequent (but unfounded) criticisms of multiple-choice items is that they are limited to lower-level objectives. With creativity and effort multiple-choice items can be written that measure more complex objectives. Consider

Multiple-choice items can be used to assess a variety of educational objectives ranging from the simple to the complex.

the following example suggested by Green (1981) of an item designed to assess a complex learning objective.

Example 28   Item Assessing Complex Objectives

1. The correlation of SAT verbal and SAT math among all test takers is about 0.5. What is the correlation between SAT verbal and SAT math among applicants admitted to Harvard?

   A. greater than 0.50
   B. about 0.50
   C. less than 0.50
   D. there is no basis for a guess

To answer this item correctly, students must understand that the strength of a correlation is affected by the variability in the sample. More homogeneous samples (i.e., samples with less variability) generally result in lower correlations. The students then have to reason that because Harvard is an extremely selective university, the group of applicants admitted there would have more homogeneous SAT scores than the national standardization sample. That is, there will be less variance in SAT scores among Harvard students relative to the national sample. Because there is less variance in the Harvard group, the correlation will be less than the national sample (if this is unclear, review the section on correlation one more time). This illustrates that multiple-choice items can measure fairly complex learning objectives. Special Interest Topic 8.1 describes research that found that, contrary to claims by critics, multiple-choice items do not penalize creative or "deep thinking" students.

Multiple-Choice Items Can Be Scored in an Objective Manner.   Multiple-choice items are easy to score. Many schools even have computer-scoring systems that will score multiple-choice tests for you. By removing subjectivity in scoring, the reliability of your students' test scores is increased. Although creating a reliable test score does not ensure that your test scores are valid, scores cannot be valid without being reliable.

Multiple-Choice Items Are Not Unduly Subject to Guessing.   Although multiple-choice items are subject to guessing (like all selected-response items), they are not as subject to guessing as are true–false items. This aspect also enhances the reliability of these items. See Special Interest Topic 8.2 for information about a correction for guessing that can be applied to multiple-choice and true–false items.

Multiple-Choice Items Are Not Significantly Influenced by Response Sets.   A **response set** is a tendency for an individual to respond in a specific manner. For example, when unsure of the correct response on a true–false item, there is an "acquiescence set" whereby students are more likely to select *true* than *false* (Cronbach, 1950). Although students might have a tendency to select the middle alternatives when unsure of the answer, this

SPECIAL INTEREST TOPIC   **8.1**

Do Multiple-Choice Items Penalize Creative Students?

Critics of multiple-choice and other selected-response items have long asserted that these items measure only superficial knowledge and conventional thinking and actually penalize students who are creative, deep thinkers. In a recent study, Powers and Kaufman (2002) examined the relationship between performance on the Graduate Record Examination (GRE) General Test and selected personality traits, including creativity, quickness, and depth. In summary, their analyses revealed that there was no evidence that deeper-thinking students were penalized by the multiple-choice format. The correlation between GRE scores and Depth were as follows: Analytical = 0.06, Quantitative = 0.08, and Verbal = 0.15. The results in terms of creativity were more positive, with the correlation between GRE scores and Creativity as follows: Analytical = 0.24, Quantitative = 0.26, and Verbal = 0.29 (all $p < .001$). Similar results were obtained with regard to Quickness, with the correlation between GRE scores and Quickness as follows: Analytical = 0.21, Quantitative = 0.15, and Verbal = 0.26 (all $p < .001$). In summary, there is no evidence that individuals who are creative, deep thinking, and mentally quick are penalized by multiple-choice items. In fact, the research reveals modest positive correlations between the GRE scores and these personality traits. To be fair, there was one rather surprising finding, a slightly negative correlation between GRE scores and Conscientious (e.g., careful, avoids mistakes, completes work on time). The only hypothesis the authors proposed was that "conscientious" does not benefit students particularly well on timed tests, such as the GRE, that place a premium on quick performance.

tendency does not appear to significantly impact performance on multiple-choice tests (e.g., Hopkins, 1998).

Multiple-choice items are efficient at sampling the content domain.

Multiple-Choice Items Are an Efficient Way of Sampling the Content Domain.   Multiple-choice tests allow teachers to broadly sample the test's content domain in an efficient manner. That is, because students can respond to multiple-choice items in a fairly rapid manner, a sufficient number of items can be included to allow the teacher to adequately sample the content domain. Again, this enhances the reliability of the test.

Multiple-Choice Items Are Easy to Improve Using the Results of Item Analysis.   The careful use of difficulty and discrimination indexes and distracter analysis can help refine and enhance the quality of the items.

Multiple-Choice Items Provide Information about the Type of Errors That Students Are Making.   Teachers can gain diagnostic information about common student errors and misconceptions by examining the distracters that students commonly endorse. This information can be used to improve instruction in the future, and current students' knowledge base can be corrected in class review sessions.

SPECIAL INTEREST TOPIC   **8.2**

Correction for Guessing

Some testing experts support the use of a "correction for guessing" formula with true–false and multiple-choice items. Proponents of this practice use it because it discourages students from attempting to raise their scores through blind guessing. The most common formula for correcting for guessing is:

$$\text{Corrected Score} = \text{Right} - \text{Wrong}/(n - 1)$$

where
      right = number of items answered correctly
    wrong = number of items answered incorrectly
        n = number of alternatives or potential answers

For true–false items it is simply calculated as:

$$\text{Corrected Score} = \text{Right} - \text{Wrong}$$

For multiple-choice items with four alternatives it is calculated as:

$$\text{Corrected Score} = \text{Right} - \text{Wrong}/3$$

Consider this example: Susan correctly answered 80 multiple-choice items on a 100-item test (each item having 4 alternatives). She incorrectly answered 12 and omitted 8. Her uncorrected scores would be 80 (or 80% correct). Applying the formula to these data:

$$\text{Corrected Score} = 80 - 12/3$$
$$\text{Corrected Score} = 76$$

Susan's corrected score is 76 (or 76%). Note that the omitted items are not counted in the corrected score, only the items answered correctly and incorrectly. What the correction formula does is remove the number of items assumed to be the result of blind guessing.

Should you use a correction for guessing? This issue has been hotly debated among assessment professionals. The debate typically centers on the assumptions underlying the correction formula. For example, the formula is based on the questionable assumption that all guesses are random, and none are based on partial knowledge or understanding of the item content. Probably anyone who has ever taken a test knows that all guesses are not random and that sometimes students are able to rule out some alternatives using partial knowledge of the item content. As a result, many assessment experts don't recommend using a correction for guessing with teacher-made classroom tests. Some authors suggest that their use is defensible in situations in which students have insufficient time to answer all the items or in which guessing is contraindicated due to the nature of the test content (e.g., Linn & Gronlund, 2000). Nevertheless, on most classroom assessments a correction for guessing is not necessary. In fact, in most situations the relative ranking of students using corrected and uncorrected scores will be about the same (Nitko, 2001).

Two related issues need to be mentioned. First, if you are *not* using a correction for guessing, your students should be encouraged to attempt every item. If you are using a correction for guessing, your students should be informed of this, something along the lines of "Your score will be corrected for guessing, so it is not in your best interest to guess on items."

The second issue involves professionally developed standardized tests. When you are using a standardized test it is imperative to strictly follow the administration and scoring instructions. If the test manual instructs you to use a correction for guessing, you must apply it for the test's normative data to be usable. If the test manual instructs you simply to use the "number correct" when calculating scores, these instructions should be followed. In subsequent chapters we will describe the administration and use of professionally developed standardized tests.

Although multiple-choice items have many strengths to recommend their use, they do have limitations. These include the following.

Multiple-Choice Items Are Not Effective for Measuring All Educational Objectives. Although multiple-choice items can be written to measure both simple and complex objectives, they are not optimal for assessing all objectives. For example, some objectives simply cannot be measured using multiple-choice items (e.g., writing a poem, engaging in a debate, performing a laboratory experiment).

Multiple-choice items are not easy to write, and they are not effective for measuring all educational objectives.

Multiple-Choice Items Are Not Easy to Write. Although ease and objectivity of scoring are advantages of multiple-choice items, it does take time and effort to write effective items with plausible distracters.

In summary, multiple-choice items are by far the most popular selected-response format. They have many advantages and few weaknesses. As a result, they are often the preferred format for professionally developed tests. When skillfully developed, they can contribute to the construction of psychometrically sound classroom tests. Table 8.2 summarizes the strengths and weaknesses of multiple-choice items.

TABLE 8.2   Strengths and Weaknesses of Multiple-Choice Items

Strengths of Multiple-Choice Items
- Multiple-choice items are versatile.
- Multiple-choice items can be scored in an objective and reliable manner.
- Multiple-choice items are not overly subject to guessing.
- Multiple-choice items are not significantly influenced by response sets.
- Multiple-choice items are an efficient way of sampling the content domain.
- Multiple-choice items are easy to refine using the results of item analysis.
- Multiple-choice items provide diagnostic information.

Weaknesses of Multiple-Choice Items
- Multiple-choice items are not effective for measuring all educational objectives.
- Multiple-choice items are not easy to write.

True–False Items

True–false items **involve a statement or question that the student marks as true or false, agree or disagree, yes or no, and so on.**

The next selected-response format we will discuss is the true–false format. **True–false items** are very popular, second only to the multiple-choice format. We will actually use the term **true–false items** to refer to a broader class of items. Sometimes this category is referred to as binary-choice items, two-option items, or alternate-choice items. The common factor is that all these items involve a statement or question that the student marks as true or false, agree or disagree, correct or incorrect, yes or no, fact or opinion, and so on. Because the most common form is true–false, we will use this term generically to refer to all two-option items.

Here follow examples of true–false items. Example 29 takes the form of the traditional true–false format. Example 30 takes the form of the correct–incorrect format. We also provide examples of the type of directions needed with these questions.

Example 29   True–False Item with Directions
Directions: Carefully read each of the following statements. If the statement is *true,* **circle the T. If the statement is** *false,* **circle the F.**

1. T   **F**   In recent years, malaria has been eliminated worldwide.
2. **T**   F   The ozone layer protects us from harmful ultraviolet radiation.

Example 30   Correct–Incorrect Item with Directions
Directions: Carefully read each of the following sentences. If the sentence is grammatically *correct,* **circle C. If the sentence contains a grammatical error, circle I for** *incorrect.*

1. **C**   I   He set the book on the table.
2. C   **I**   She set on the couch.

Two variations of the true–false format are fairly common and deserve mention. The first is the multiple true–false format we briefly mentioned when discussing multiple-choice items. On traditional multiple-choice items the student must select one correct answer from the alternatives, whereas on *multiple true–false items* the student indicates whether each one of the alternatives is true or false. Frisbie (1992) provides an excellent discussion of the multiple true–false format. Example 31 is a multiple true–false item.

Example 31   Multiple True–False Item
1. Which of the following Apollo astronauts actually landed on the moon? Circle the T if the astronaut landed on the moon, the F if the astronaut did not land on the moon.

Edwin Aldrin	**T**	F
Frank Borman	T	**F**
Neil Armstrong	**T**	F
Pete Conrad	**T**	F
Thomas Patten	T	**F**
Walter Cunningham	T	**F**

In the second variation of the traditional true–false format, the student is required to correct false statements. This is typically referred to as **true–false with correction** format. With this format it is important to indicate clearly which part of the statement may be changed by underlining it (e.g., Linn & Gronlund, 2000). Consider Example 32.

> *Example 32   True–False Items with Correction of False Items*
> **Directions: Read each of the statements. If the statement is true, circle the T. If the statement is false, circle the F and change the word or words that are *underlined* to make the statement true. To make the correction, write the correct word or words in the blank space.**
>
> 1. T   **F**   _Apollo 7_   _Apollo 5_ was the first Apollo mission to conduct an orbit flight test of the Command and Service Module (CSM).
> 2. **T**   F   _____   _Apollo 8_ was the first Apollo mission to achieve lunar orbit.

Although this variation makes the true–false items more demanding and less susceptible to guessing, it also introduces some subjectivity in scoring, which may reduce reliability.

Guidelines for Developing True–False Items

Avoid Including More than One Idea in the Statement.   True–false items should address only one central idea or point. Consider the following examples.

> *Example 33   Poor Item—Statement Contains More Than One Idea*
> 1. T   F   The study of biology helps us understand living organisms and predict the weather.

> *Example 34   Better Item—Statement Contains Only One Idea*
> 2. **T**   F   The study of biology helps us understand living organisms.

> *Example 35   Better Item—Statement Contains Only One Idea*
> 3. T   **F**   The study of biology helps us predict the weather.

Example 33 contains two ideas, one that is correct and one that is false. Therefore it is partially true and partially false. This can cause confusion as to how students should respond. Examples 34 and 35 each address only one idea and are less likely to be misleading.

Avoid Specific Determiners and Qualifiers That Might Serve as Cues to the Answer.
Specific determiners such as *never, always, none,* and *all* occur more frequently in false statements and serve as cues to uninformed students that the statement is too broad to be true. Accordingly, moderately worded statements including *usually, sometimes,* and *frequently* are more likely to be true and these qualifiers also serve as cues to uninformed students. Although it would be difficult to avoid using qualifiers in true–false items, they can be used equally in true and false statements so their value as cues is diminished. Examine the following examples.

Example 36   Poor Item—Specific Determiners Serve as Cue

1. T   **F**   Longer tests always produce more reliable scores than shorter tests.

Example 37   Better Item—Cue Eliminated

2. T   **F**   Shorter tests usually produce more reliable scores than longer tests.

In Example 36 *always* may alert a student that the statement is too broad to be true. Example 37 contains the qualifier *usually,* but the statement is false so a student relying on cues would not benefit from it.

Ensure That True and False Statements Are of Approximately the Same Length.
There is a tendency to write true statements that are longer than false statements. To prevent statement length from serving as an unintentional cue, visually inspect your statements and ensure that there is no conspicuous difference between the length of true and false statements. It is usually easier to increase the length of false statements by including more qualifiers than it is to shorten true statements.

Avoid Negative Statements.   Avoid using statements that contain *no, none,* and *not.* The use of negative statements can make the statement more ambiguous, which is not desirable. The goal of a test item should be to determine whether the student has mastered a learning objective, not to see whether the student can decipher an ambiguous question.

Avoid Long and/or Complex Statements.   All statements should be presented as clearly and concisely as possible. As noted in the previous guideline, the goal is to make all statements clear and precise.

Include an Approximately Equal Number of True and False Statements.   As noted earlier when discussing response sets in the context of multiple-choice items, some students are more likely to select *true* when they are unsure of the correct response (i.e., acquiescence set). There are also students who have adopted a response set whereby they mark *false* when unsure of the answer. To prevent students from artificially inflating their scores with either of these response sets, include an approximately equal number of *true* and *false* items.

Avoid Including the Exact Wording from the Textbook.   As on multiple-choice items you should avoid the exact wording used in a text. Students will recognize this over time, and it tends to reward rote memorization rather than the development of a more thorough understanding of the content (Hopkins, 1998). Table 8.3 provides a summary of the guidelines for developing true–false items.

Strengths and Weaknesses of True–False Items

Testing experts provide mixed evaluations of true–false items. Some experts are advocates of true–false items whereas others are much more critical of this format. We tend to fall toward the more critical end of the continuum. Strengths of true–false items include the following.

TABLE 8.3　Checklist for the Development of True–False Items

1. Does each statement include only one idea?　　　_____
2. Have you avoided using specific determiners and qualifiers that could　　　_____
   serve as cues to the answer?
3. Are true and false statements of approximately the same length?　　　_____
4. Have you avoided negative statements?　　　_____
5. Have you avoided long and complex statements?　　　_____
6. Is there an approximately equal number of true and false statements?　　　_____
7. Have you avoided using the exact wording from the textbook?　　　_____

True–false items are effective at sampling the content domain and can be scored in a reliable manner.

True–False Items Can Be Scored in an Objective Manner. Like other selected-response items, true–false items can be scored easily, objectively, and reliably.

True–False Items Are Efficient. Students can respond quickly to true–false items, even quicker than they can to multiple-choice items. This allows the inclusion of more items on a test designed to be administered in a limited period of time.

Weaknesses of true–false items include the following.

True–False Items Are Not Particularly Useful except with the Simplest Educational Objectives. Many testing experts believe that true–false items are useful only for assessing low-level objectives such as knowledge and comprehension. Much of what we hope to teach our students cannot be divided into the clear dichotomies represented by true–false items and, as a result, is not well suited for this format. Additionally, many experts believe true–false items promote rote memorization (even if you avoid using the exact wording from the text or lecture).

True–false items are particularly vulnerable to guessing and are usually limited to measuring the simplest educational objectives.

True–False Items Are Very Vulnerable to Guessing. Because there are only two options on true–false items, students have a 50% chance of getting the answer correct simply by chance. Because unintended cues to the correct answer are often present, an observant but uninformed student can often get considerably more than 50% of these items correct. As a result, guessing can have a significant influence on test scores. Guessing also reduces the reliability of the individual items. To compensate, true–false tests often need many items in order to reduce the influence of guessing and demonstrate adequate reliability.

True–False Items Are Subject to Response Sets. True–false items are considerably more susceptible to the influence of response sets than are other selected-response items.

True–False Items Provide Little Diagnostic Information.   Teachers can often gain diagnostic information about common student errors and misconceptions by examining incorrect responses to other test items, but true–false items provide little diagnostic information.

True–False Items May Produce a Negative Suggestion Effect.   Some testing experts have expressed concern that exposing students to the false statements inherent in true–false items might promote learning false information (e.g., Hopkins, 1998).

Effective True–False Items Appear Easy to Write to the Casual Observer. This Is Not the Case!   Most individuals believe that true–false items are easy to write. Writing effective true–false items, like all effective test items, requires considerable thought and effort. Simply because they are brief does not mean they are easy to write.

In summary, true–false items are a popular selected-response format. They can be scored in an objective and reliable manner and students can answer many items in a short period of time. However, they have numerous weaknesses including being limited to the assessment of simple learning objectives and being vulnerable to guessing. Before using true–false items, we suggest that you weight their strengths and weaknesses and ensure that they are appropriate for assessing the specific learning objectives. Table 8.4 provides a summary of the strengths and weaknesses of true–false items.

Matching Items

The final selected-response format we will discuss are the matching items. **Matching items** usually contain two columns of words or phrases. One column contains words or phrases for which the student seeks a match. This column is traditionally placed on the left and the phrases are referred to as premises. The second column contains words that

---

TABLE 8.4   Strengths and Weaknesses of True–False Items

Strengths of True–False Items
- True–false items can be scored in an objective and reliable manner.
- True–false items are efficient.

Weaknesses of True–False Items
- True–false items are not particularly useful except with the simplest educational objectives.
- True–false items are vulnerable to guessing.
- True–false items are subject to response sets.
- True–false items provide little diagnostic information.
- True–false items may produce a negative suggestion effect.
- Effective true–false items are not easy to write.

Matching items **usually contain two columns of words or phrases. One column, typically located on the left, contains words or phrases for which the student seeks a match.** are available for selection. The items in this column are referred to as responses. The premises are numbered and the responses are identified with letters. Directions are provided that indicate the basis for matching the items in the two lists. Here is an example of a matching item.

Example 38   Matching Items
Directions: Column A lists major functions of the brain. Column B lists different brain structures. Indicate which structure primarily serves which function by placing the appropriate letter in the blank space to the left of the function. Each brain structure listed in Column B can be used once, more than once, or not at all.

Column A

  _b_   **1.** Helps initiate and control rapid movement of the arms and legs.

  _g_   **2.** Serves as a relay station connecting different parts of the brain.

  _e_   **3.** Is involved in the regulation of basic drives and emotions.

  _a_   **4.** Helps control slow, deliberate movements of the arms and legs.

  _c_   **5.** Connects the two hemispheres.

  _d_   **6.** Controls the release of certain hormones important in controlling the internal environment of the body.

Column B

a. basal ganglia

b. cerebellum

c. corpus callosum

d. hypothalamus

e. limbic system

f. medulla

g. thalamus

This item demonstrates an imperfect match because there are more responses than premises. Additionally, the instructions also indicate that each response may be used once, more than once, or not at all. These procedures help prevent students from matching items simply by elimination.

Guidelines for Developing Matching Items

Limit Matching Items to Homogeneous Material.   Possibly the most important guideline to remember when writing matching items is make sure the lists contain **homogeneous content.** By this we mean you should base the lists on a common theme. For example, in the previous example (Example 38) all of the premises specified functions served by brain structures, and all of the responses were brain structures. Other examples of homogeneous lists could be the achievements matched with famous individuals, historical events matched with dates, definitions matched with words, and so on. What should be avoided is including heterogeneous material in your lists. For example, consider Example 39.

Example 39   Poor Item—Heterogeneous Content
Directions: Match the items in Column A with the items in Column B. Each item in Column B can be used once, more than once, or not at all.

Column A

___*e*___ **1.** Most populous U.S. city.

___*b*___ **2.** Largest country in South America.

___*a*___ **3.** Largest river in the Western Hemisphere.

___*g*___ **4.** Canada's leading financial and manufacturing center.

___*c*___ **5.** Largest freshwater lake in the world.

___*f*___ **6.** Largest country in Central America.

Column B

a. Amazon

b. Brazil

c. Lake Superior

d. Mississippi

e. New York City

f. Nicaragua

Although this is an extreme example, it does illustrate how heterogeneous lists can undermine the usefulness of matching items. For example, premise 1 asks for the most populous U.S. city and the list of responses includes only two cities, only one of which is in the United States. Premise 2 asks for the largest country in South America and the list of responses includes only two countries, only one of which is in South America. In these questions students do not have to possess much information about U.S. cities or South America to answer them correctly. It would have been better to develop one matching list to focus on U.S. cities, one to focus on countries in the Western Hemisphere, one to focus on major bodies of water, and so forth.

Indicate the Basis for Matching Premises and Responses in the Directions.   Clearly state in the directions the basis for matching responses to premises. You may have noticed that in our example of a poor heterogeneous item (Example 39), the directions do not clearly specify the basis for matching. This was not the case with our earlier example involving brain functions and brain structures (Example 38). If you have difficulty specifying the basis for matching all the items in your lists, it is likely that your lists are too heterogeneous.

Review Items Carefully for Unintentional Cues.   Matching items are particularly susceptible to unintentional cues to the correct response. In Example 39, the use of *lake* in premise 5 and response c may serve as a cue to the correct answer. Carefully review matching lists to minimize such cues.

Include More Responses than Premises.   By including more responses than premises, you reduce the chance that an uninformed student can narrow down options and successfully match items by guessing.

Indicate That Responses May Be Used Once, More than Once, or Not at All.   By adding this statement to your directions and writing responses that are occasionally used more than once or not at all, you also reduce the impact of guessing.

Limit the Number of Items.   For several reasons it is desirable to keep the list of items fairly brief. It is easier for the person writing the test to ensure that the lists are homogeneous when the lists are brief. For the student taking the test, it is easier to read and respond to a shorter list of items. Although there is not universal agreement regarding the number of items to include in a matching list, a maximum of 10 appears reasonable with lists between 5 and 8 items generally recommended.

Ensure That the Responses Are Brief and Arrange Them in a Logical Order. Students should be able to read the longer premises and then scan the briefer responses in an efficient manner. To facilitate this process, keep the responses as brief as possible and arrange them in a logical order when appropriate (e.g., alphabetically, numerically).

Place All Items on the Same Page. Finally, keep the directions and all items on one page. It greatly reduces efficiency in responding if the students must turn the page looking for responses. Students also are more likely to transpose a letter or number if they have to look back and forth across two pages, leading to errors in measuring what the student has learned. Table 8.5 summarizes the guidelines for developing matching items.

Strengths and Weaknesses of Matching Items

Testing experts generally provide favorable evaluations of the matching format. Although this format does not have as many advantages as multiple-choice items, it has fewer limitations than the true–false format. Strengths of matching items include the following:

Matching items can be scored in a reliable manner, are efficient, and are relatively simple to write.

Matching Items Can Be Scored in an Objective Manner. Like other selected-response items, matching items can be scored easily, objectively, and reliably.

Matching Items Are Efficient. They take up little space and students can answer many items in a relatively brief period.

Matching Items Are Relatively Simple to Write. Matching items are relatively easy to write, but they still take time, planning, and effort. The secret to writing good matching items

TABLE 8.5   Checklist for the Development of Matching Items

1. Is the material homogeneous and appropriate for the matching format?	_____
2. Do the directions indicate the basis for matching premises and responses?	_____
3. Have unintentional cues to the correct answer been avoided?	_____
4. Are there more responses than premises?	_____
5. Do the directions indicate that responses may be used once, more than once, or not at all?	_____
6. Are the lists relatively short to facilitate scanning (e.g., < 10)?	_____
7. Are the responses brief and arranged in a logical order?	_____
8. Are all the items on the same page?	_____

is developing two homogeneous sets of items to be matched and avoiding cues to the correct answer. If they are not developed well, efficiency and usefulness are lost.

Weaknesses of matching items include the following:

Matching Items Have Limited Scope and Application in Assessing Student Learning.
With matching items, students are asked to match two things based on logical and usually simple associations. Although matching items measure this type of learning outcome fairly well, much of what we teach students involves greater understanding and higher-level skills.

Matching items are fairly limited in scope and may promote rote memorization.

Matching Items May Promote Rote Memorization.   Due to their focus on factual knowledge and simple associations, the use of matching items may encourage rote memorization.

Matching Items Are Vulnerable to Cues That Increase the Chance of Guessing.   Unless written with care, matching items are particularly susceptible to cues that accidentally suggest the correct answer.

It Is Often Difficult to Develop Homogeneous Lists of Relevant Material.   When developing matching items it is often difficult to generate homogeneous lists for matching. As a result, there are two common but unattractive outcomes; the lists may become heterogeneous, or information that is homogeneous but trivial may be included. Neither one of these outcomes is desirable because they both undermine the usefulness of the items.

In summary, matching items are a prevalent selected-response format. They can be scored in an objective manner, are relatively easy to write, and are efficient. They do have weaknesses, including being limited in the types of learning outcomes they can measure and potentially encouraging students to simply memorize facts and simple associations. You also need to be careful when writing matching items to avoid cues that inadvertently provide hints to the correct answer. Nevertheless, when dealing with information that has a common theme and that lends itself to this item format, they may be particularly useful. Table 8.6 provides a summary of the strengths and weaknesses of matching items.

TABLE 8.6   Strengths and Weaknesses of Matching Items

Strengths of Matching Items
- Matching items can be scored in an objective and reliable manner.
- Matching items are efficient.
- Matching items are relatively simple to write.

Weaknesses of Matching Items
- Matching items have limited scope and application in assessing student learning.
- Matching items may promote rote memorization.
- Matching items are vulnerable to cues that increase the chance of guessing.
- It is often difficult to develop homogeneous lists of meaningful material.

S P E C I A L   I N T E R E S T   T O P I C   **8.3**
What Research Says about "Changing Your Answer"

Have you ever heard that it is usually not in your best interest to change your answer on a multiple-choice test? Many students *and* educators believe that you are best served by sticking with your first impression. That is, don't change your answer. Surprisingly this is not consistent with the research! Pike (1979) reviewed the literature and came up with these conclusions:

- Examinees change their answers only on approximately 4% of the questions.
- When they do change their answer, more often than not it is in their best interest. Typically there are approximately two favorable changes (i.e., *incorrect* to *correct*) for every unfavorable one (i.e., *correct* to *incorrect*).
- These positive effects tend to decrease on more difficult items.
- High-scoring students are more likely to profit from changing their answers than are low-scoring students.

This does not mean that you should encourage your students to change their answers on a whim. However, if students feel a change is indicated based on careful thought and consideration, they should feel comfortable doing so. Research suggests that they are probably doing the right thing to enhance their score.

Summary

All test items can be classified as either selected-response items or constructed-response items. Selected-response items include multiple-choice, true–false, and matching items whereas constructed-response items include essay items, short-answer items, and performance assessments. We discussed each specific selected-response format, describing how to write effective items and their individual strengths and weaknesses.

- *Multiple-choice* items are the most popular selected-response format. They have numerous strengths including versatility, objective and reliable scoring, and efficient sampling of the content domain. The only weaknesses are that multiple-choice items are not effective for measuring all learning objectives (e.g., organization and presentation of material; writing ability; performance tasks) and they are not easy to develop. Testing experts generally support the use of multiple-choice items as they can contribute to the development of reliable and valid assessments.
- *True–False* items are another popular selected-response format. Although true–false items can be scored in an objective and reliable manner and students can answer many items in a short period of time, they have numerous weaknesses. For example, they are limited to the assessment of fairly simple learning objectives and are very vulnerable to guessing. Although true–false items have a place in educational assessment, before using them we recommend that you weight their strengths and weaknesses and ensure that they are the most appropriate item format for assessing the specific learning objectives.

■ *Matching items* were the last selected-response format we discussed. These items can be scored in an objective and reliable manner, can be completed in a fairly efficient manner, and are relatively easy to develop. Their major limitations include a rather limited scope and the possibility of promoting rote memorization of material by your students. Nevertheless, carefully developed matching items can effectively assess lower-level educational objectives.

In the next two chapters we will address constructed-response items, including essays, short-answer items, performance assessments, and portfolios. We stated earlier in the textbook that typically the deciding factor when selecting an assessment or item format involves identifying the format that most directly measures the behaviors specified by the educational objectives. The very nature of some objectives mandates the use of constructed-response items (e.g., writing a letter), but some objectives can be measured equally well using either selected-response or constructed-response items. If after thoughtful consideration you determine that both formats are equally well suited, we typically recommend the use of selected-response items because they allow broader sampling of the content domain and can be scored in a more reliable manner. However, we do not want you to think that we have a bias against constructed-response items. We believe that educational assessments should contain a variety of assessment procedures that are individually tailored to assess the educational objectives of interest.

KEY TERMS AND CONCEPTS

Alternatives, p. 189
Best-answer format, p. 190
Constructed-response items, p. 188
Correct-answer format, p. 190
Cue, p. 194
Direct-question format, p. 189
Distracters, p. 189

Homogeneous content, p. 209
Incomplete-sentence format, p. 189
Matching items, p. 208
Multiple-choice items, p. 189
Multiple true–false item, p. 194
Negative suggestion effect, p. 208
Response sets, p. 200

Selected-response items, p. 188
Stems, p. 189
True–false items, p. 204
True–false with correction,
    p. 205

SUGGESTED READINGS AND INTERNET SITES

Aiken, L. R. (1982). Writing multiple-choice items to measure higher-order educational objectives. *Educational & Psychological Measurement, 42,* 803–806. A respected author presents suggestions for writing multiple-choice items that assess higher-order learning objectives.

Beck, M. D. (1978). The effect of item response changes on scores on an elementary reading achievement test. *Journal of Educational Research, 71,* 153–156. This article is an example of the research that has examined the issue of students changing their responses on achievement tests. A good example!

Dewey, R. A. (2000, December 12). *Writing multiple choice items which require comprehension.* Retrieved November 29, 2004 from www.psywww.com/selfquiz/aboutq.htm. At this site the author provides some good suggestions for making multiple-choice distracters more attractive.

Ebel, R. L. (1970). The case for true–false items. *School Review,* 78, 373–389. Although many assessment experts are opposed to the use of true–false items for the reasons cited in the text, Ebel comes to their defense in this article.

Sidick, J. T., Barrett, G. V., and Doverspike, D. (1994). Three-alternative multiple-choice tests: An attractive option. *Personnel Psychology, 47,* 829–835. In this study the authors compare tests with three-choice items multiple-choice items with ones with five-choice items. The results suggest that both have similar measurement characteristics and that a case can be made supporting the use of three-choice items.

9 The Development and Use of Constructed-Response Items

In recent years there has been increased criticism of selected-response items and a call for relying more on constructed-response items. Proponents of constructed-response items claim that they provide a more "authentic" assessment of student abilities, one that more closely resembles the way these abilities are applied in the real world.

CHAPTER HIGHLIGHTS

Oral Testing: The Oral Essay as a
   Precursor of Constructed-Response Items
Essay Items

Short-Answer Items

A Final Note: Constructed-Response versus
   Selected-Response Items

LEARNING OBJECTIVES

After reading and studying this chapter, students should be able to:

1. Trace the history of constructed-response assessment.
2. Explain how essay items can differ in terms of purpose and level of complexity.
3. Compare and contrast restricted-response and extended-response essay items.
4. Describe the principles involved with developing effective essay items.
5. Develop effective essay items for a given content area.
6. Discuss the strengths and weaknesses of essay items.
7. Describe the principles involved with grading essays.
8. Demonstrate the ability to grade essays in a reliable and valid manner.
9. Describe the principles involved with developing effective short-answer items.
10. Develop effective short-answer items for a given content area.
11. Discuss the strengths and weaknesses of short-answer items.
12. Discuss prominent issues to be considered when considering whether to use selected-response or constructed-response items.

We have noted that most test items used in the classroom can be classified as either selected-response or constructed-response items. If an item requires a student to select a response from a list of alternatives, it is classified as a selected-response item. Examples of selected-response items include multiple-choice, true–false, and matching items. In contrast, if an item requires students to create or construct a response, it is classified as a constructed-response item. Essay and short-answer items are common examples of constructed-response items and will be the focus of this chapter. We will discuss their strengths and weaknesses and provide suggestions for developing effective items. In the next chapter we will address performance and portfolio assessments, which are types of constructed-response assessments that have gained increased popularity in recent years. In all of these chapters we will focus on the development of items to assess classroom achievement.

Oral Testing: The Oral Essay as a Precursor of Constructed-Response Items

We would like to begin our discussion of constructed-response items by briefly tracing their history. Written constructed-response items had their beginning in oral testing. **Oral testing** as a method of examination was a prominent aspect of Greek teachings as far back as the fourth century B.C. Subsequently oral testing was adopted by the Romans and continued when universities were established during the Dark Ages. Oral examinations have persisted in Western universities to the present, most commonly being found in various forms at the master's and doctoral degree level (e.g., a thesis or dissertation defense). The following procedure typifies an oral examination. Students are typically examined by a group of examiners, each of whom may ask one or more questions. General topics for questioning are agreed on beforehand and the student must respond immediately to questions. Often the examiners qualify or clarify questions when the student experiences difficulty. Although students may fail portions of the examination, complete failures are relatively rare. Except for their use in graduate programs, oral testing is not very common in public schools and universities. Even though students are still called on to answer questions in the classroom, extended responses are rarely required or desired by the teacher. We have a few colleagues at universities who require oral examinations for their courses, but they are the exceptions rather than the rule. Some professional licensing boards require applicants to sit for an oral examination in addition to meeting other requirements. In such instances, the oral examination is usually the final hurdle. For example, after obtaining a Ph.D. in a relevant area of psychology, one is required to obtain a license to practice or offer psychological services to the public. The state of Texas requires each applicant to pass two written examinations (both are multiple-choice, or selected-response, exams) prior to sitting for an hour oral examination with two examiners.

> Oral testing was a prominent aspect of Greek teaching as far back as the fourth century B.C.

The problems with oral testing are numerous and well documented. For fair evaluation each person taking a common examination should take the test under uniform conditions. These conditions include both testing procedures (e.g., time available) and the format, content, and scoring of questions. For example, although it is clearly possible to present the same questions in the same format to all students, this does not always occur. Unless the examiners specify the questions beforehand and write them down, it is difficult for oral examiners to present them in the same manner to all students or even to ask the same questions of all students. Scoring responses can also be problematic. Examiners usually do not record the responses verbatim (if at all), and they subjectively review and score the responses based on their memory. In oral examinations a premium is often placed on the student's facility with oral responding. For example, students are rarely given extended time to formulate a response, and hesitation is often taken as lack of knowledge. With this arrangement the achievement being measured may be achievement in the articulation of subject matter rather than knowledge of subject matter. If that is the expressed educational objective, as in rhetoric or debate, then the oral test is clearly appropriate. Otherwise it may not be a valid measure of the specified educational objectives. A final limitation of oral testing is one first recognized during the nineteenth-century industrialization process: inefficiency. The total testing time for a class is equal to the number of students times the number of minutes allotted to each student times the number of examiners. As you can see, the testing time adds up quickly. Teachers are very busy professionals and time is at a premium. All of these shortcomings of oral testing provide sufficient reason for its use to be quite restricted.

Essay Items

An *essay item* poses a question or problem for the student to respond to in a written format.

An **essay item** is a test item that poses a question or problem for the student to respond to in a written format. Being a constructed-response item, the student must respond by constructing a response, not by selecting among alternatives. Although essay items vary in the degree of structure they impose on the student's response, they generally provide considerable freedom to the student in composing a response. Good essay items challenge the student to organize, analyze, integrate, and synthesize information. At their best, essay items elicit novel and creative cognitive processes from students. At their worst they present an ambiguous task to students that is difficult, if not impossible, to score in a reliable manner.

Written essay items were used in Chinese civil service examinations as long as two thousand years ago, but they did not become popular in Western civilization until much later. In the nineteenth century, technical developments (e.g., increased availability of paper, development of lead pencils, now principally using graphite) made written examinations cheaper and more practical in both America and Europe. About the same time, Horace Mann, an influential nineteenth-century educator, argued about the evils of oral testing and the superiority of the written essay. This set the stage for the emergence of essay (and other constructed-response) tests. Although essay items have their own limitations, they have addressed some of the problems associated with oral testing. They afforded more uniformity in test content (i.e., students get the same questions presented in the same order), there was a written record of the student's response, and they were more efficient (i.e., they take less testing time).

Essay items can be classified according to their educational purpose or focus (i.e., evaluating content, style, or grammar), the complexity of the task presented (e.g., knowledge, comprehension, application, analysis, synthesis, and evaluation), and how much structure they provide (restricted or extended response). We will begin by discussing how essay items can vary according to their educational purpose.

Purposes of Essay Testing

Table 9.1 illustrates different purposes for which essay items are typically used when assessing student achievement. The major purposes are for assessing **content, style, and**

TABLE 9.1   Purposes of Essay Testing

	Content	Style	Grammar
Content	Assess cognitive objectives or knowledge of content *only*	Assess content and writing style	Assess content and grammar
Style		Assess writing ability and style *only*	Assess writing style and grammar
Grammar			Assess grammar only

Content—Style—Grammar
Assess content knowledge, writing style, and grammar

Essay items can be scored in terms of *content, style, and grammar.*

grammar (which we take to include writing mechanics such as spelling). In Table 9.1 the three purposes have been crossed to form a nine-element matrix. These elements represent different assessment goals. The composition of the elements in the diagonal is as follows:

- The content–content element represents testing solely for cognitive achievement. When scoring for this purpose, you attend only on the content of the response and ignore the student's achievement in writing style and in grammar. The purpose is to determine what the student knows or can produce. Here, all levels of the cognitive taxonomy can be measured. Essay testing in this context should not penalize a student deficient in skills unrelated to the content being assessed. For example, poor organization and misspellings are not counted against the student.
- The style–style element is the purpose often found in writing composition classes. The content of the essay is largely irrelevant. The student is told to pick a topic and write in a specified manner. All measurement is based on objectives related to organization, structure, phrasing, transition, and other components of the writing process. Here grammar is also unimportant.
- The grammar–grammar element is one in which the objective is to examine the student's ability to apply grammatical rules. This category typically involves all aspects of writing mechanics (e.g., spelling, punctuation, etc.). Content and style are unimportant and are not scored.

All the other elements (i.e., off-diagonal elements) combine two purposes. For example, the purpose of an essay item could involve the combination of content–style, content–grammar, or style–grammar. Although not represented in this matrix, an item may have a three-element purpose in which the student's essay is evaluated in terms of content, style, and grammar. This latter purpose is often encountered in take-home assignments such as reports, term papers, or final examinations. All of these different combinations may be considered essay examinations, and the topics of this chapter will apply in varying degrees to the elements in Table 9.1.

While theoretically essay items can be scored independently based on these three purposes, this is actually much more difficult than it appears. For example, research has shown that factors such as grammar, penmanship, and even the length of the answer influence the scores assigned, even when teachers are instructed to grade only on content and disregard style and grammar. We will come back to this and other scoring issues later in this chapter.

Essay Items at Different Levels of Complexity

Essay items can be written to measure objectives at all levels of the cognitive taxonomy.

Essay items can be written to measure objectives at all levels of the cognitive taxonomy. Some examples of items written at each level of the cognitive taxonomy follow.

Knowledge.   At the knowledge level, essay items are likely to include verbs such as *define, describe, identify, list,* and *state.* A knowledge level item follows:

Example 1   Knowledge Level Item
1. List the four scales of measurement and define each scale.

Comprehension.   Comprehension level essay items often include verbs such as *explain, paraphrase, summarize,* and *translate.* An example of a comprehension level question follows:

Example 2   Comprehension Level Item
1. Explain the use of the Spearman-Brown formula in calculating split-half reliability.

Knowledge and comprehension level objectives can also be assessed with selected-response items (e.g., multiple-choice), but there is a distinction. Selected-response items require only *recognition* of the correct answer, whereas essay items require *recall.* That is, with essay items students must remember the correct answer without having the benefit of having it in front them. There are instances when the recall/recognition distinction is important, and instances when it is not. When recall is important, essay items should be considered.

Application.   Application level essay items typically include verbs such as *apply, compute, develop, produce, solve,* and *use.* An example of an application level item follows:

Example 3   Application Level Item
1. For the objective listed below, develop a multiple-choice item and a true–false item.

    Objective: The student will be able to compute the reliability for a test that is doubled in length and had an initial reliability of 0.50.

Example 3 demonstrates the application of a general procedure, principle, or rule, in this case the production of an item from an educational objective. Application level essay items typically require the student to solve a problem with a specific method or approach.

Analysis.   Analysis level items are frequently encountered in essay tests. Verbs used at the analysis level include *analyze, break down, differentiate, illustrate, outline,* and *summarize.* Consider this example:

Example 4   Analysis Level Item
1. Summarize in a systematic, coherent manner the effects of the Industrial Revolution on educational testing.

In Example 4 the student is asked to analyze the material by identifying and describing the effects of the Industrial Revolution on educational testing. Many teachers simply use the verb *discuss* in this context (i.e., Discuss the effects . . .), and this may be acceptable if the students understand what is expected of them. Otherwise, it introduces ambiguity into the assessment process, something to be avoided.

Synthesis.   Essay items written at the synthesis level require students to create something new and original. Verbs often encountered at the synthesis level include *compose, create, develop,* and *design.* Here is an example of an essay item at the synthesis level:

Example 5   Synthesis Level Item
1. Create a new educational objective and corresponding essay item at the analysis level for the content area of your choice.

Evaluation.   The evaluation level of the cognitive taxonomy requires judgments concerning value and worth. Essay items written at this level often involve "choice" as in the next example.

Example 6   Evaluation Level Item
1. Specify what you view as the best type of item for assessing analysis level objectives and defend your choice. Be sure to stipulate the basis for your choice, highlighting the qualities that make this item type optimal and the reasons you selected it over the other item types.

Here students select the best item type, a subjective choice, and defends their selection. Words most often used in essay items at the evaluation level include *appraise, choose, criticize, debate, evaluate, judge,* and others involving a determination of worth.

   In place of a personal subjective choice, the criteria may be defined in terms of scientific, legal, social, or other external standards. Consider this example:

Example 7   Evaluation Level Item
1. Do you believe essay tests are biased against minorities? State your position and defend it using current legal, scientific, and social standards.

In Example 7 the students must choose a position and build a case for it based on their understanding of current mores and standards as well as psychometric expertise.

Restricted-Response versus Extended-Response Essays

So far we have discussed how essay items can be used for different purposes (i.e., content, style, and grammar) and to measure objectives at different levels of the cognitive complexity (e.g., knowledge, comprehension, application, analysis, synthesis, and evaluation). In addition to these distinctions, essay items are often classified as either restricted response or extended response. **Restricted-response items** are highly structured and clearly specify

Essay items can be written to elicit *restricted responses* or *extended responses.* the form and scope of a student's response. Restricted-response items typically require students to list, define, describe, or give reasons. These items may specify time or length limits for the response. Here are examples of restricted-response items.

Example 8   *Restricted-Response Items*

1. In the space provided, define homeostasis and describe its importance.
2. List the types of muscle tissue and state the function of each.

Extended-response items provide more latitude and flexibility in how the students can respond to the item. There is little or no limit on the form and scope of the response. When limitations are provided they are usually held to a minimum (e.g., page and time limits). Extended-response items often require students to compose, summarize, formulate, compare/interpret, interpret, and so forth. Examples of extended-response items include the following:

Example 9   *Extended-Response Items*

1. Summarize and write a critical evaluation of the research on global warming. Include a detailed analysis of the strengths and weaknesses of the empirical research, and provide an evaluative statement regarding your conclusions on the topic.
2. Compare and contrast asthma and emphysema in terms of physiological processes, treatment options, and prognosis.

Extended-response items provide less structure and this promotes greater creativity, integration, and organization of material.

As you might expect, restricted-response and extended-response essay items have their own strengths and limitations. Restricted-response essay items are particularly good for assessing objectives at the knowledge, comprehension, and application levels. They can be answered in a timely fashion by students, which allows you to include more items, and they are easier to score in a reliable manner than extended-response items. In contrast, extended-response items are particularly well suited for assessing higher-level cognitive objectives. However, they are difficult to score in a reliable manner and because they take considerable time for students to complete, you typically have to limit your test to relatively few items, which results in limited sampling of the content domain. Although restricted-response items have the advantage of more reliable and efficient scoring, along with better sampling of the content domain, certain learning objectives simply require the use of extended-response essay items. In these situations, it is important to write and score extended-response items as carefully as possible and take into consideration the limitations. To that end, we will start by giving you some general guidelines for writing good essay items.

Guidelines for Developing Essay Items

Write in a Clear, Straightforward Manner.   The most important criterion for a good essay item is that it clearly specifies the assessment task. The assessment task is simply what

It is important that essay items specify the assessment task in a clear and straightforward manner.

you want the student to do. We recommend that you provide enough information in your essay item that there is no doubt about what you expect. If you want the students to list reasons, specify that you want a list. If you want them to make an evaluative judgment, clearly state it. If you want a restricted response, specify that. If you want an extended response, make that clear. When appropriate, indicate the

point value of the item or how much time students should devote to it. On extended-response items, some experts recommend that you specify your grading criteria so the students will have a clear picture of what you expect (e.g., Gronlund, 1998). Also, avoid using unnecessarily difficult or technical language. The student should not have to guess your intentions from obtuse wording or technical jargon. We are not suggesting that your essay items be unnecessarily lengthy. In fact we recommend that they be as brief as possible, that is, as brief as possible and still clearly specify the assessment task. Consider the following examples, one of a poor essay item, the other of a better, more specific essay item.

Example 10   Poor Item—Unclear Assessment Task

1. Why did World War II begin?

Example 11   Better Item—Clear Assessment Task

2. Describe the course of events that led up to Britain and France's policy of appeasement toward Germany in 1938. In your response explain why Chamberlain and Daladier pursued this policy. Explain what event or events later convinced Britain and France to abandon their policy of appeasement? Answer in the space provided. (counts as 25% of the test grade)

Consider Carefully the Amount of Time Students Will Need to Respond to the Essay Items.   This is a practical recommendation that you pay attention to the amount of time the students will need to complete each essay item. For example, you might estimate that students need approximately 15 minutes to complete one item and 30 minutes for another. As a general rule, teachers tend to underestimate the time students need to respond to essay items. As teachers we may estimate only the time necessary to write the response whereas students actually need time to collect and organize their thoughts before even starting the writing process. As a rule of thumb, we recommend you construct a test you think is appropriate to the available time and reduce it in length by about 25%.

Do Not Allow Students to Select the Items to Which They Will Respond.   Some teachers provide a number of items and allow the students to select a specified number of items to respond to. For example, a test might include eight items and the students are required to select five items to respond to. As a general rule this practice is to be avoided. When students respond to different items, they are essentially taking different tests. When they take different tests, they cannot be evaluated on a comparative basis. In addition, when students respond only to the items they are best prepared for or knowledgeable about, you get a less representative sample of their knowledge (e.g., Gronlund, 1998). As you know, anything that results in less effective content sampling compromises the measurement properties of the test.

Use More Restricted-Response Items in Place of a Smaller Number of Extended-Response Items.   Restricted-response items have measurement characteristics that may make them preferable over extended-response items. First, they are easier to score in a reliable manner. Second, because students can respond to a larger number of items in a given amount of time, they can provide superior sampling of content domain. Although some educational objectives require the use of extended-response items, when you have a choice we recommend using multiple restricted-response items.

Limit the Use of Essay Items to Educational Objectives That Cannot Be Measured Using Selected-Response Items.   While essays are extremely popular among many teachers and have their strengths, they do have limitations that we have alluded to and will outline in the next section. For now, we just want to recommend that you restrict the use of essay items to the measurement of objectives that cannot be measured adequately using selected-response items. For example, if you want to assess the student's ability to organize and present material in a written format, an essay item would be a natural choice. These guidelines are summarized in Table 9.2.

Strengths and Weaknesses of Essay Items

So far we have alluded to some of the strengths and weaknesses of essay items, and this is probably an opportune time to discuss them more directly. First, we will address their strengths.

Essay Items Can Be Written to Assess Higher-Level Cognitive Skills.   In the last chapter we argued that multiple-choice items can be written to assess higher-level cognitive objectives. We still stand by that statement. Nevertheless, some educational objectives are most easily measured with essay items, and these tend to be higher-level objectives. Some objectives such as writing skills literally require the use of essay items. Essay items also have the advantage of requiring

Essay items can be written to assess higher-level cognitive skills and are ideal for measuring some objectives such as writing skills.

TABLE 9.2   Checklist for the Development of Essay Items

1. Are the items written in a clear, straightforward manner?   _____
2. Will the students be able to complete the test in the time available?   _____
3. Will all students respond to the same set of items?   _____
4. When appropriate, did you use more restricted-response items in place of   _____
   fewer extended-response items?
5. Did you limit the use of essay items to objectives that cannot be measured   _____
   with selected-response items?

recall, often denoting stronger mastery of the material than recognition as required with selected-response items.

It Generally Takes Less Time to Write Essay Items than Selected-Response Items.
Writing an essay test typically takes less time than preparing a test with selected-response items. Because most essay tests contain only a fraction of the number of items that an objective test might, you will usually have fewer items to write. It is also tempting to say that essay items are easier to write than objective items. While this is probably true, we don't want to mislead you into thinking that writing essay items is effortless. Writing good essay items requires considerable thought and effort. Essay items are probably easier to write than objective items, but that does not necessarily make them easy.

The Use of Essay Items Largely Eliminates Blind Guessing.
Because essay items require the student to produce a response as opposed to simply selecting one, students are not able to guess successfully the desired answer.

When Studying for Essay Tests, Students May Spend Less Time on Rote Memorization and More Time Analyzing and Synthesizing Information.
Many teachers believe that students study differently for essay tests than they do for selected-response tests, and some research supports this claim (e.g., Coffman, 1972; Hakstian, 1971). It is possible that students preparing for essay tests spend more time analyzing and synthesizing information rather than memorizing facts. Hopkins (1998) suggests that teachers may combine a few essay items with selected-response items to achieve this potential instructional benefit.

Now we will address the weaknesses.

It is difficult to score essay items in a reliable manner.

Reliable Scoring of Essay Items Is Difficult.
As we noted in our chapter on reliability, when scoring relies on subjective judgment, it is important to evaluate the degree of agreement when different individuals score the test. This is referred to as inter-scorer or inter-rater reliability. Studies of the inter-rater reliability of essay items have shown that there is often disagreement between raters. In addition to inconsistency between scores assigned by different raters (**inter-rater inconsistency**), there is also often inconsistency in the scores assigned by the same rater at different times (**intra-rater inconsistency**). When scoring essay items, a multitude of factors can contribute to this unreliability. These factors or effects include the following.

Content Indeterminancy Effects.   **Content indeterminancy effects** are the result of an inadequate or ambiguous understanding by the teacher of the response required by the essay item. When scoring an essay item the teacher should have a very clear idea of what constitutes a "good" response. Obviously if two teachers scoring an essay have different ideas about what the desired response is, they are not likely to agree on the score to be assigned. Even an individual teacher who has only a vague idea of what a good response is will likely have difficulty scoring essays in a consistent manner. This ambiguity or indeterminancy regarding what constitutes a good response leads to unreliable, inconsistent scoring.

Expectancy Effects. **Expectancy effects** occur when the teacher scoring the test allows irrelevant characteristics of the student to affect scoring. This is also referred to as the "halo effect." For example, if a teacher has a favorable overall impression of a student with a history of academic excellence, the teacher might be inclined to assign a higher score to the student's responses (e.g., Chase, 1979). In contrast, a teacher might tend to be more critical of a response by a student with a poor academic record who is viewed as difficult or apathetic. These effects are not typically intentional or even conscious, but they are often present nevertheless. Similar effects can also carry over from one item to the next within a test. That is, if you see that a student performed well on an earlier item, it might influence scoring on later items.

Handwriting, Grammar, and Spelling Effects. Research dating from the 1920s has shown that teachers are not able to score essay items solely on content even when they are instructed to disregard style and grammar factors (e.g., James, 1927; Sheppard, 1929). For example, good handwriting raises scores and poor handwriting, misspellings, incorrect punctuation, and poor grammar reduce scores even when content is the only criteria for evaluation. Even the length of the response impacts the score. Teachers tend to give higher scores to lengthy responses, even when the content is not superior to that of a shorter response (Hopkins, 1998), something students have long suspected!

Order Effects. **Order effects** are changes in scoring that emerge during the grading process. As a general rule, essays scored early in the grading process receive better grades than essays scored later (Coffman & Kurfman, 1968; Godshalk, Swineford, Coffman, & ETS, 1966). Research has also shown that the quality of preceding responses impacts the scores assigned. That is, essays tend to receive higher scores when they are preceded by poor-quality responses as opposed to when they are preceded by high-quality responses (Hales & Tokar, 1975; Hughes, Keeling, & Tuck 1980).

Fatigue Effects. The teacher's physical and cognitive abilities are likely to degrade if essay scoring continues for too long a period. The maximum period of time will probably vary according to the complexity of the responses, but reading essays for more than two hours without sufficient breaks will likely produce **fatigue effects.**

As you can see a number of factors can undermine reliability when scoring essay items. In earlier chapters we emphasized the importance of reliability, so this weakness should be given careful consideration when developing and scoring essay items. It should also be noted that reduced reliability undermines the validity of the interpretation of test performance.

Restricted Sampling of the Content Domain. Because essay items typically require a considerable amount of time to evaluate and to construct a response to, students are able to respond to only a few items in a testing period. This results in limited sampling of the content domain and potentially reduced reliability. This is particularly true of extended-response essay items but may also apply to restricted-response items.

Scoring Essay Items Is Time Consuming. In addition to it being difficult to score essay items in a reliable manner, it is a tedious, time-consuming process. Although selected-response items tend to take longer to develop, they can usually be scored easily, quickly, and reliably.

TABLE 9.3   Strengths and Weaknesses of Essay Items

Strengths of Essay Items
- Essay items are good for assessing some higher-level cognitive skills.
- Essay items are easier to write than objective items.
- Essay items eliminate blind guessing.
- Essay items may promote a higher level of learning.

Weaknesses of Essay Items
- Essay items are difficult to score in a reliable manner.
- The use of essay items may result in a limited sample of the content domain.
- Scoring essay items is a tedious and time-consuming process.
- Essay items are subject to bluffing.

Bluffing.   Although the use of essay items eliminates random guessing, bluffing is introduced. Bluffing occurs when a student does not possess the knowledge or skills to respond to the item, but tries to "bluff" or feign a response. Due to the subjective nature of essay scoring, student bluffing may result in them receiving partial or even full credit. Experience has shown that some students are extremely proficient at bluffing. For example, a student may be aware that teachers tend to give lengthy responses more credit and so simply reframe the initial question as a statement and then repeat the statement in slightly different ways. Table 9.3 provides a summary of the strengths and weaknesses of essay items.

Guidelines for Scoring Essay Items

To enhance the reliability of essay tests, you need to develop structured, unbiased scoring procedures.

It should be obvious from the preceding discussion that there are significant concerns regarding the reliability and validity of essay tests. To enhance the measurement characteristics of essay tests, you need to concentrate on developing structured, unbiased scoring procedures. Here are a few suggestions to help you score essay items in a consistent, reliable way.

Use Predetermined Scoring Criteria to Reduce Content Indeterminancy Effects.   Indeterminancy scoring effects are the result of an imperfect understanding of the response required by the essay item. When scoring an essay item the teacher should have a very clear idea of what constitutes a "good" response. Obviously if two teachers scoring an essay have different ideas about what the desired response is, they are not likely to agree on the score to be assigned. You can reduce content indeterminancy effects by clearly specifying the important elements of the desired response. A written guide that helps you score constructed-response items is typically referred to as a scoring **rubric.** For restricted-response essay items at the lower levels of the cognitive domain (knowledge, comprehension, application, and analysis), the criteria for scoring can often be specified by writing a sample answer or simply listing the major elements. However, for extended-response items and items at the higher levels of the cognitive domain, more complex rubrics are often required. For extended-response items, due to the freedom given to the student, it may not be possible to write a sample answer that takes into consideration all possible "good" responses. For items at the synthesis and evaluation levels, new or novel responses are expected. As a result the exact form and content of the response cannot be anticipated and a simple model response cannot be delineated.

Scoring rubrics are often classified as either analytic or holistic. Analytic scoring rubrics identify different aspects or dimensions of the response and the teacher scores each dimension separately. For example, an analytic scoring rubric might distinguish between content, writing style, and grammar/mechanics. With this scoring rubric the teacher will score each response in terms of these three categories. With **analytic rubrics** it is usually necessary to specify the value assigned to each characteristic. For example, for a 15-point essay item in a social science class wherein the content of the response is of primary concern, the teacher may designate 10 points for content, 3 points for writing style, and 2 points for grammar/mechanics. If content were of equal importance with writing style and grammar/mechanics, the teacher could assign 5 points for each category. In many situations two or three categories are sufficient whereas in other cases more elaborate schemes are necessary. An advantage of analytic scoring rubrics is that they provide specific feedback to students regarding the adequacy of their responses in different areas. This helps students know which aspects of their responses were adequate and which aspects need improvement. The major drawback of analytic rubrics is that their use can be fairly time consuming, particularly when the rubric specifies many dimensions to be graded individually.

With a **holistic rubric,** the teacher assigns a single score based on the overall quality of the student's response. Holistic rubrics are often less detailed than analytic rubrics. They are easier to develop and scoring usually proceeds faster. Their primary disadvantage is that they do not provide specific feedback to students about the strengths and weaknesses of their responses.

Some testing experts suggest that, instead of using holistic rubrics to assign a numerical or point score, you use an ordinal or ranking approach. With this approach, instead of assigning a point value to each response, you read and evaluate the responses and sort them into categories reflecting different qualitative levels. Many teachers use five categories to correspond to letter grades (i.e., A, B, C, D, and F). When using this approach Gronlund (1998) recommends that teachers read each item twice. You initially read through the essay items and sort them into the designated categories. Subsequently you read the items in each category as a group checking for consistency. If any items appear to be either superior or inferior to the other items in that category, you make the necessary adjustment.

To illustrate the differences between holistic and analytic scoring rubrics, consider this essay question:

Example 12   Sample Essay Item
1. Describe and then compare and contrast Thurstone's model of intelligence with that presented by Gardner. Give examples of the ways they are similar and the ways they differ.

Table 9.4 presents a holistic scoring rubric that might be used when scoring this item. Table 9.5 presents an analytic scoring rubric that might be used when scoring this item. Our

TABLE 9.4 Holistic Scoring Rubric (5-Point Scale)

Essay Item: Compare and contrast Thurstone's model of intelligence with that presented by Gardner. Give examples of the ways they are similar and the ways they differ.

Classification	Description	Rating
Excellent	The student demonstrated a thorough understanding of both models of intelligence and could accurately describe in detail similarities and differences and give examples. This is an exemplary response.	5
Good	The student demonstrated a good understanding of the models and could describe similarities and differences and give examples.	4
Average	The student demonstrated an adequate understanding of the models and could describe some similarities and differences. Depth of understanding was limited and there were gaps in knowledge.	3
Marginal	The student showed limited understanding of the models and could provide no more than vague references to similarities and differences. Some information was clearly inaccurate. Examples were either vague, irrelevant, or not applicable.	2
Poor	The student showed very little understanding of the models and was not able to describe any similarities or differences.	1
Very poor	The student showed no understanding of the models.	0

TABLE 9.5 Analytic Scoring Rubric (15-Point Item)

Essay Item: Compare and contrast Thurstone's model of intelligence with that presented by Gardner. Give examples of the ways they are similar and the ways they differ.

Area	Poor (0 points)	Average (1 point)	Above Average (2 points)	Excellent (3 Points)
The student demonstrated an understanding of Thurstone's model.	_____	_____	_____	_____
The student demonstrated an understanding of Gardner's model.	_____	_____	_____	_____
The student was able to compare and contrast the models.	_____	_____	_____	_____
The student was able to present relevant and clear examples high-lighting similarities and differences.	_____	_____	_____	_____
The response was clear, well organized, and showed a thorough understanding of the material.	_____	_____	_____	_____

Total Number of Points Awarded _____

final comment regarding scoring rubrics is that to be effective they should be used in a consistent manner. Keep the rubric in front of you while you are scoring and apply it in a fair, evenhanded manner.

Avoid Expectancy Effects. As you remember, expectancy effects occur when the teacher allows irrelevant characteristics of the student to affect scoring (also referred to as the "halo effect"). The obvious approach to minimizing expectancy effects is to score essay items in a way that the test taker's identity is not known. If you use test booklets fold back the cover so that the student's name is hidden. If you use standard paper we suggest that students write their names on the back of essay sheets and that only one side of the sheet be used. The goal is simply to keep you from being aware of the identity of the student whose paper you are currently scoring. To prevent the student's performance on one item from influencing scores on subsequent items, we recommend that you start each essay item on a separate page. This way, exceptionally good or poor performance on a previous item will not inadvertently influence your scoring of an item.

Consider Writing Effects (e.g., Handwriting, Grammar, and Spelling). If one could adhere strictly to the guidelines established in the scoring rubrics, writing effects would not influence scoring unless they were considered essential. However, as we noted, even when writing abilities are not considered essential they tend to impact the scoring of an item. These effects are difficult to avoid other than to warn students early in their academic careers that these effects exist and suggest that they develop good writing abilities. For those with poor cursive writing, a block letter printing style might be preferred. Because personal computers are readily available in schools today, you might allow students to complete essays using word processors and then print their tests. You should encourage students to apply grammatical construction rules and to phrase sentences in a straightforward manner that avoids awkward phrasing. To minimize spelling errors you might elect to provide dictionaries to all students because this will mirror more closely the writing situation in real life and answer critics who say essay tests should not be spelling tests. The use of word processors with spelling and grammar checkers might also help reduce these effects.

Minimize Order Effects. To minimize order effects, it is best to score the same question for all students before proceeding to the next item. The tests should then be reordered in a random manner before moving on to scoring the next item. For example, score item 1 for all students; reorder the tests in a random fashion; then score essay item 2 and so forth.

Avoid Fatigue. The difficult task of grading essays is best approached as a series of one- or two-hour sessions with adequate breaks between them. Although school schedules often require that papers be scored in short periods of time, you should take into consideration the effects of fatigue on scoring and try to arrange a schedule for grading that permits frequent rest periods.

Score Essays More than Once. Whenever possible it is desirable to score essays items at least two times. This can be accomplished either by you scoring the items twice or having a colleague score them after you have scored them. When the two scores or ratings are

TABLE 9.6   Guidelines for Scoring Essay Items

1. Develop a scoring rubric for each item that clearly specifies the scoring criteria.
2. Take steps to avoid knowing whose paper you are scoring.
3. Avoid allowing writing effects to influence scoring if they are not considered essential.
4. Score the same question for all students before proceeding to the next item.
5. Score the essays in one- or two-hour periods with adequate rest breaks.
6. Score each essay more than one time (or have a colleague score them once after you have scored them).

consistent you can be fairly confident in the score. If the two ratings are significantly different you should average the two scores. Table 9.6 summarizes our suggestions for scoring essay items. Special Interest Topic 9.1 presents a brief discussion of automated essay scoring systems that are being used in several settings.

Short-Answer Items

Short-answer items are items that require the student to supply a word, phrase, number, or symbol.

Short-answer items are the final type of constructed-response item we will discuss in this chapter. **Short-answer items** require the student to supply a word, phrase, number, or symbol in response to a direct question. Short-answer items can also be written in an **incomplete-sentence format** instead of a **direct-question format** (this format is sometimes referred to as a completion item). Here are examples of both formats.

Example 13   Direct-Question Format
1. What is the membrane surrounding the nucleus called? _____
2. What is the coefficient of determination if the correlation coefficient is 0.60? _____

Example 14   Incomplete-Sentence Format
1. The membrane surrounding the nucleus is called the _____.
2. For a correlation coefficient of 0.60, the coefficient of determination is _____.

Relative to essay items, short-answer items place stricter limits on the nature and length of the response. Practically speaking, short-answer items can be viewed as a type of restricted-response essay item. As we noted, restricted-response essay items provide more structure and limit the form and scope of a student's response relative to an extended-response essay item. Short-answer items take this a step further, providing even more structure and limits on the student's response.

SPECIAL INTEREST TOPIC　**9.1**

Automated Essay Scoring Systems

Myford and Cline (2002) note that even though essays are respected and desirable assessment techniques, their application in large-scale standardized assessment programs has been limited because scoring them with human raters is usually expensive and time consuming. For example, they note that when using human raters, students may take a standardized essay test at the end of an academic year and not receive the score reports until the following year. The advent of automated essay-scoring systems holds promise for helping resolve these problems. By using an automated scoring system, testing companies can greatly reduce expense and the turnaround time. As a result, educators and students can receive feedback in a fraction of the time. Although such systems have been around since at least the 1960s, they have become more readily available in recent years. Myford and Cline (2002) note that these automated systems generally evaluate essays on the basis of either content (i.e., subject matter) or style (i.e., linguistic style). Contemporary essay scoring systems also provide constructive feedback to students in addition to an overall score. For example, a report might indicate that the student is relying too much on simple sentences or a limited vocabulary (Manzo, 2003).

In addition to being more cost- and time-efficient, these automated scoring systems have the potential for increasing the reliability of essay scores and the validity of their interpretation. For example, the correlation between grades assigned by a human and an automated scoring program is essentially the same as that between two human graders. However, in contrast to humans, computers never have a bad day, are never tired or distracted, and assign the same grade to the same essay every time (Viadero & Drummond, 1998).

In addition to expediting scoring of large-scale assessment, these automated essay scoring programs have recently found application in the classroom. Manzo (2003) gave the example of a middle school language arts teacher who regularly assigns essay assignments. She has more than 180 students and in the past would spend up to 60 hours grading a single assignment. She is currently using an automated online scoring system that facilitates her grading. She has the program initially score the essays, then she reviews the program's evaluation and adds her own comments. In other words, she is not relying exclusively on the automated scoring system, but using it to supplement and enhance her personal grading. She indicates that the students can receive almost instantaneous feedback on their essays and typically allows the students to revise their daily assignments as many times as they desire, which has an added instructional benefit.

These programs are receiving more and more acceptance in both classrooms and large-scale standardized assessment programs. Here are examples of some popular programs and Web sites at which you can access information about them:

- e-rater, www.ets.org/research/erater.htm+1
- Intelligent Essay Assessor, www.knowledgetechnologies.com
- IntelliMetric, www.intellimetric.com
- Bayesian Essay Scoring System, http://ericae.net/betsy

Guidelines for Developing Short-Answer Items

Structure the Item So That the Response Is as Short as Possible.   As the name implies, you should write short answer-items so that they require a short answer. This makes scoring easier, less time consuming, and more reliable.

Make Sure There Is Only **One** *Correct Response.*   In addition to brevity, it is important that there only be one correct response. This is more difficult than you might imagine. When writing a short-answer item, ask yourself if the student can interpret it in more than one way. Consider this example:

John Adams was born in _____.

The correct response could be "Massachusetts." Or it could be "Braintree" (now Quincy) or even the "United States of America." It could also be "1735" or even "the eighteenth century." All of these would be correct! This highlights the need for specificity when writing short-answer items. A much better item would be:

John Adams was born in what city and state? _____

Use the Direct-Question Format in Preference to the Incomplete-Sentence Format. There is usually less chance of student confusion when the item is presented in the direct-question format. This is particularly true when writing tests for young students, but even secondary students may find direct questions more understandable than incomplete sentences. Most experts recommend using only the incomplete-sentence format when it results in a briefer item without any loss in clarity.

Have Only One Blank Space when Using the Incomplete-Sentence Format, Preferably Near the End of the Sentence.   As we noted, unless incomplete-sentence items are carefully written, they may be confusing or unclear to students. Generally the more blank spaces an item contains, the less clear the task becomes. Therefore, we recommend that you usually limit each incomplete sentence to one blank space. We also recommend that the blank space be located near the end of the sentence. This arrangement tends to provide more clarity than if the blank appears early in the sentence.

Avoid Unintentional Cues to the Answer.   As with selected-response items, you should avoid including any inadvertent clues that might alert an uninformed student of the correct response. For example, provide blanks of the same length for all short-answer items (both direct questions and incomplete sentences). This way you avoid giving cues about the relative length of different answers. Also be careful about grammatical cues. The use of the article *a* indicates an answer beginning with a consonant instead of a vowel. An observant student relying on cues will detect this and it may help him or her narrow down potential responses. This can be corrected by using *a(n)* to accommodate answers that begin with either consonants or vowels.

Make Sure the Blanks Provide Adequate Space for the Student's Response.   A previous guideline noted that all blanks should be the same length to avoid unintentional cues to the correct answer. You should also make sure that each blank provides adequate space for the student to write the response. As a result, you should determine how much space is necessary for providing the longest response in a series of short-answer items, and use that length for all other items.

Indicate the Degree of Precision Expected in Questions Requiring Quantitative Answers. For example, if you want your answer stated in inches, specify that. If you want all fractions reduced to their lowest terms or all numerical answers rounded to the second decimal point, specify these expectations.

Avoid Lifting Sentences Directly Out of the Textbook and Converting Them into Short-Answer Items. Sentences taken directly from textbooks often produce ambiguous short-answer items. Sentences typically need to be understood in the context of surrounding material, and when separated from that context their meaning often becomes unclear. Additionally, if you copy sentences directly from the text, some students may rely on simple word associations to answer the items. This may promote rote memorization rather than developing a thorough understanding of the material (Hopkins, 1998).

Create a Scoring Rubric and Consistently Apply It. As with essay items, it is important to create and consistently use a scoring rubric when scoring short-answer items. When creating this rubric, take into consideration any answers besides the preferred or "best" response that will receive full or partial credit. For example, remember this item?

John Adams was born in what city and state? _____

How would you score it if the student responded only "Braintree" or only "Massachusetts"? This should be specified in the scoring rubric.

These guidelines are summarized in Table 9.7.

TABLE 9.7   Checklist for the Development of Short-Answer Items

1. Does the item require a short response?	_____
2. Is there only one correct response?	_____
3. Did you use an incomplete sentence only when there was no loss of clarity relative to a direct question?	_____
4. Do incomplete sentences contain only one blank?	_____
5. Are blanks in incomplete sentence near the end of the sentence?	_____
6. Have you carefully checked for unintentional cues to the answer?	_____
7. Do the blanks provide adequate space for the answers?	_____
8. Did you indicate the degree of precision required for quantitative answers?	_____
9. Did you avoid lifting sentences directly from the textbook?	_____
10. Have you created a scoring rubric for each item?	_____

Strengths and Weaknesses of Short-Answer Items

Like all item types, short-answer items have their own strengths and weaknesses. First, we will address their strengths.

When recall is important, when dealing with quantitative problems, and when interpreting graphic material, short-answer items can be extremely effective.

Short-Answer Items Require Recall, Not Just Recognition. Whereas selected-response items require only recognition of the correct answer, short-answer items require recall. That is, with these items students must remember the correct answer without having it provided for them. There are instances when the recall/recognition distinction is important, and when recall is important, short-answer items can be useful. Also, because short-answer items require recall, blind guessing is reduced.

Short-Answer Items Are Particularly Well Suited for Quantitative Problems and Problems Requiring the Interpretation of Graphic Material. When the problem involves mathematical computations or the interpretation of graphic material such as charts, diagrams, or illustrations, the short-answer format can be particularly useful (e.g., Hopkins, 1998).

Because Students Can Answer More Short-Answer Items than Essay Items, They May Allow Better Content Sampling. Because students can usually answer short-answer items fairly quickly, you can include more short-answer items than essay items on a test. This can result in more representative sampling of the content domain and enhanced reliability.

Short-Answer Items Are Relatively Easy to Write. We are always cautious when we say an item type is easy to write, so we say it is relatively easy to write. Compared to multiple-choice items, short-answer items are easier to write. Even though they are relatively easy to write, they still need to be developed with care following the guidelines provided.

Now we will address the weaknesses of short-answer items.

Scoring Short-Answer Items in a Reliable Manner Is Difficult. Some authors classify short-answer items as objective items, which suggests they can be scored in an objective manner. Actually there is considerable subjective judgment involved in scoring short-answer items. For example, how will you score misspellings and responses that are only partially legible? What if the misspelling is so extreme it is difficult to determine what the student is actually attempting to spell? Also, no matter how carefully you write short-answer items, inevitably a student will provide a response that is not what was desired or expected, but can still be construed as at least partially correct. Although scoring well-written short answer items in a reliable manner is easier than scoring extended-response essay items, there is still a significant degree of subjectivity involved and it can be a lengthy and tiresome process.

With the Exception of Quantitative Problems and the Interpretation of Graphic Material, Short-Answer Items Are Often Limited to Assessing Fairly Simple Educational Objectives. If you rely extensively on short-answer items, it may encourage students to emphasize rote memorization when studying rather than developing a more thorough under-

TABLE 9.8 Strengths and Weaknesses of Short-Answer Items

Strengths of Short-Answer Items
- Short-answer items require recall, not just recognition.
- Short-answer items are well suited for assessing quantitative problems and problems requiring the interpretation of graphic material.
- Because students can answer more short-answer items than essay items, they may allow better content sampling.
- Short-answer items are relatively easy to write.

Weaknesses of Short-Answer Items
- Short-answer items are difficult to score in a reliable manner.
- With the exception of quantitative problems and the interpretation of graphic material, short-answer items are often limited to assessing fairly simple educational objectives.

standing of the material. This can be countered by not relying exclusively on short-answer items and incorporating other item types that demand higher-level cognitive processes.

As a result of these limitations, we generally recommend that the use of short-answer items be limited to those situations for which they are uniquely effective. When recall is important, when dealing with quantitative problems, and when interpreting graphic material, short-answer items can be extremely effective. However, if the educational objective can be assessed equally well with a selected-response item, it is preferable to use the selected-response format due to potentially enhanced reliability and validity. These strengths and weaknesses are summarized in Table 9.8.

A Final Note: Constructed-Response versus Selected-Response Items

Throughout much of the twentieth century, critics of essay items emphasized their weaknesses (primarily unreliable scoring and reduced content sampling) and promoted the use of selected-response items. In recent years there has been increased criticism of selected-response items and a call for relying more on essays and other constructed-response items. Proponents of constructed-response tests, particularly essay items (and performance assessments, discussed in the next chapter), generally claim they provide a more "authentic" assessment of student abilities, one that more closely resembles the way abilities and knowledge are demonstrated or applied in the real world. Arguments on both sides are pervasive and often passionate. We take the position that both formats have an important role to play in educational assessment. As we have repeated numerous times, to adequately assess the complex array of knowledge and skills emphasized in today's schools, teachers need to take advantage of the full range of assessment procedures available. Due to the tendency for selected-response items to provide reliable and valid measurement, we promote their use when they can adequately assess the educational objectives. However, it is important to recognize

To adequately assess the complex array of knowledge and skills emphasized in today's schools, teachers need to take advantage of the full range of assessment procedures available.

that there are educational objectives that cannot be adequately assessed using selected-response items. In these situations you should use constructed-response items. By being aware of the weaknesses of constructed-response items and using the guidelines for developing and scoring them outlined in this chapter you will be able to write items that produce results you can have considerable confidence in. Remember that the best practice is to select items that provide the most valid and reliable information about your students' knowledge and skills.

Summary

In this chapter we focused on the development and use of constructed-response items. Essay items have a long history, dating back to China over two thousand years ago. An essay item poses a question or problem that the student responds to in a written format. Although essay items vary in terms of the limits they place on student responses, most essay items give students considerable freedom in developing their responses. Essay tests gained popularity in the United States in the nineteenth century largely due to problems associated with oral testing. Even though written essay tests addressed some of the problems associated with oral testing, essays have their own associated problems. The most prominent weaknesses of essay items involve difficulty scoring in a reliable manner and limited content sampling. Both of these issues can result in reduced reliability and validity. On the positive side, essay items are well suited for measuring many complex educational objectives and are relatively easy to write. We provided numerous suggestions for writing and scoring essay items, but encouraged teachers to limit the use of essay items to the measurement of educational objectives that are not easily assessed using selected-response items.

The second type of constructed-response item addressed in this chapter was short-answer items. Like essay items, students respond to short-answer items by providing a written response. However, instead of having a large degree of freedom in drafting their response, on short-answer items the student is usually required to limit the response to a single word, a brief phrase, or a symbol/number. Similar to essay items, short-answer items are somewhat difficult to score in a reliable manner. On the positive side, short-answer items are well suited for measuring certain educational objectives (e.g., math computations) and are relatively easy to write. We provided several suggestions for writing short-answer items, but nevertheless encouraged teachers to limit their use to those situations for which they are uniquely qualified. As with essay items, short-answer items have distinct strengths, but should be used in a judicious manner.

We ended this chapter by highlighting the classic debate between proponents of selected-response and constructed-response formats. We believe both have a role to play in educational assessment and that by knowing the strengths and limitations of both formats one will be better prepared to develop and use tests in educational settings. In the next chapter we will turn your attention to performance assessments and portfolios. These are special types of constructed-response items (or tasks) that have been around for many years, but have gained increasing popularity in schools in recent years.

KEY TERMS AND CONCEPTS

RECOMMENDED READINGS

Fleming, K., Ross, M., Tollefson, N., & Green, S. (1998). Teacher's choices of test-item formats for classes with diverse achievement levels. *Journal of Educational Research, 91,* 222–228. This interesting article reports that teachers tend to prefer using essay items with high-achieving classes and more recognition items with mixed-ability or low-achieving classes.

Gellman, E., & Berkowitz, M. (1993). Test-item type: What students prefer and why. *College Student Journal, 27,* 17–26. This article reports that the most popular item types among students are essays and multiple-choice items. Females overwhelmingly prefer essay items whereas males show a slight preference for multiple-choice items.

Gulliksen, H. (1986). Perspective on educational measurement. *Applied Psychological Measurement, 10,* 109–132. This paper presents recommendations regarding the development of educational tests, including the development and grading of essay items.

10 Performance Assessments and Portfolios

Performance assessment is claimed to be useful for evaluating programs, improving instruction, comparing districts, and evaluating university and job applicants. Tomorrow's news will probably report it lowers cholesterol.

—Linn & Baker, 1992, p. 1

CHAPTER HIGHLIGHTS

What Are Performance Assessments?

**Guidelines for Developing
  Effective Performance Assessments**

**Strengths and Weaknesses
  of Performance Assessments**

Portfolios

LEARNING OBJECTIVES

After reading and studying this chapter, students should be able to:

1. Define and give examples of performance assessments.

2. Explain why performance assessments have become popular in schools in recent years.

3. Describe differences in the ways educators define performance assessments and identify some characteristics common to most definitions.

4. Describe the principles involved with developing effective performance assessments.

5. Develop effective performance assessments for a given content area.

6. Discuss the strengths and weaknesses of performance assessments.

7. Describe the principles involved with developing effective portfolio assessments.

8. Develop effective portfolios for a given content area.

9. Discuss the strengths and weaknesses of portfolios.

In Chapter 1, we noted that one of the current trends in educational assessment is the rising popularity of performance assessments and portfolios. Performance assessments and portfolios are not new creations. In fact as far back as written records have been found there is evidence that students were evaluated with what are currently referred to as performance as-

As far back as written records have been found, there is evidence that students were evaluated with what is currently referred to as performance assessments.

sessments. However, interest in and the use of performance assessments and portfolios in schools has increased considerably in the last decade. Although traditional paper-and-pencil assessments, particularly multiple-choice and other selected-response formats (e.g., true–false, matching), have always had their critics, their opposition has become much more vocal in recent years. Opponents of traditional paper-and-pencil assessments complain that they emphasize rote memorization and other low-level cognitive skills and largely neglect higher-order conceptual and problem-solving skills. To make the situation worse, critics claim that reliance on paper-and-pencil assessments may have negative effects on what teachers teach and what students learn. They note that in the era of high-stakes assessment teachers often feel compelled to teach to the test. As a result, if high-stake tests measure only low-level skills, teachers may teach only low-level skills.

To address these shortcomings, many educational assessment experts have promoted the use of performance assessments and portfolios. The *Standards* (AERA et al., 1999) note

Performance assessments **require students to complete a process or produce a product in a context that closely resembles real-life situations (AERA et al., 1999).**

that **performance assessments** require test takers to complete a process or produce a product in a context that closely resembles real-life situations. For example, a medical student might be required to interview a mock patient, select medical tests and other assessment procedures, arrive at a diagnosis, and develop a treatment plan. Portfolios, a specific form of performance assessment, involve the systematic collection of a student's work products over a specified period of time according to a specific set of guidelines. Artists, architects, writers, and others have used portfolios to represent their work for many years, and in the last decade portfolios have become increasingly popular in the assessment of students.

What Are Performance Assessments?

We just gave you the definition of performance assessments provided by the *Standards* (AERA et al., 1999). The Joint Committee on Standards for Educational Evaluation (2003) provides a slightly different definition. It defines a performance assessment as:

> A formal assessment method in which a student's skills in carrying out an activity and producing a product is observed and judged (e.g., construction of a woodworking project; completion of an essay in English, research report in history, or lab in science). (p. 230)

Notice that whereas the *Standards'* definition of performance assessments requires test takers to complete a task in a context or setting that closely resembles real-life situations, the definition provided by the Joint Committee on Standards for Educational Evaluation does not. This may alert you to the fact that not everyone agrees as to what qualifies as a performance assessment. Commenting on this, Popham (1999) observed that the distinction between performance assessments and more traditional assessments is not always clear. For example, some educators consider practically any constructed-response assessment a performance assessment. To them a short-answer or essay test is a type of performance assessment. Other educators and assessment professionals set more rigorous standards for what qualifies as a performance assessment. They hold that genuine performance assessments differ from more traditional paper-and-pencil assessments in a number of important ways, such as the following.

Performance assessments more closely reflect real-life settings and applications than traditional paper-and-pencil assessments.

Performance Assessments More Closely Reflect Real-Life Settings and Applications than Traditional Paper-and-Pencil Assessments. Possibly the most prominent factor distinguishing between performance and more traditional assessments is the degree to which the assessment mirrors an important real-life situation. For example, a paper-and-pencil assessment could contain multiple-choice, short-answer, and essay items about how to diagnose and repair an automobile engine, but a performance assessment would require that the student actually repair a defective engine. Naturally, performance assessments do differ in terms of how closely they mirror real-life activities. To capture these differences, some authors use different labels to reflect how closely the assessment mirrors the real-life situation. These include the following:

Actual Performance Assessment. An **actual performance assessment** takes place in the actual setting in which the real-life activity occurs or in a simulation that re-creates the actual setting. An example of an actual performance assessment that most people have experienced is the driving portion of a driver's licensing examination. Most states have a two-part assessment process for acquiring a driver's license. The first part is a written exam that is designed to determine whether the applicant has acquired the basic knowledge necessary to successfully and safely operate a motor vehicle (e.g., state motoring laws and standards). The second part, the actual driving examination, is designed to determine whether the applicant can actually drive an automobile in a safe and lawful manner. Typically the driving portion of the examination is completed on the same public roads on which the applicant will drive once licensed.

Analogue Performance Assessments. In many situations it is not possible to assess people in real-life conditions because of the potential consequences of failure, and so **analogue performance assessments** are performed. For example, nuclear power plant operators must be recertified every few months, and the recertification process requires an assessment of their operation of a nuclear power plant control system. Because mistakes in the real system could be catastrophic, a simulator that is a re-creation of the control room is used to generate problems for the operator to respond to and correct. Similarly, airline pilots attempting to qualify on a new model aircraft are assessed in simulators that act like actual aircraft, incorporating complex hydraulic systems that move the simulator cabin to simulate flight.

Artificial Performance Assessment. **Artificial performance assessment** is considerably less realistic than the previous categories and typically involves merely establishing conditions that the test taker must consider when performing a task. This type of assessment is common in the schools. Here a student may be asked to create the testing environment mentally and solve the problem posed. For example, a student may be asked to step through the process of creating a menu of meals for the week and purchasing food at a supermarket with a limited budget and specific food requirements. This type of assessment assumes that the student is familiar with the real-life setting and the elements of the problem. Clearly, the assumption is made that a student who can solve the artificial problem can also solve an actual performance problem of the same sort. That assumption is rarely tested and is problematic in many instances.

Performance Assessments Involve Multiple Assessment Criteria.   This distinction requires that a student's performance must be evaluated on multiple criteria (Popham, 1999, 2000). Popham gives the example of a student's ability to speak in a foreign language being evaluated in terms of accent, syntax, and vocabulary. Instead of focusing on just one aspect of the student's performance, multiple criteria are evaluated.

Performance Assessments Involve Subjective Evaluation of Student Performance.
Whereas many traditional assessments can be scored in an objective manner, genuine performance assessments involve the subjective evaluation of the student's performance (Popham, 1999, 2000).

A natural question is "Which approach to defining performance assessment is correct?" On one hand you have those with a very broad definition of performance assessments, which includes essentially any assessment that involves the construction of a response; on the other hand are those that set more rigorous standards for what qualifies as a performance assessment. This is one of those situations in which there is really no right and wrong position. Just be aware that different people assign different meanings to the term *performance assessment.*

Some educators refer to performance assessments as *authentic assessments* or *alternative assessments*.

To complicate the situation even more, not everyone uses the term *performance assessment* to describe these procedures. Some educators use the term **authentic assessment** to refer to essentially the same procedures we refer to as performance assessment. They generally prefer the term *authentic assessment* because it implies that the assessment more closely mirrors real-life situations. Personally, we find this title a little pompous because it seems to imply that more traditional assessments are "not authentic." Some educators use the term **alternative assessments** to signify that they are an "alternative" to traditional paper-and-pencil assessments. Some authors argue that there are substantive differences between authentic, alternative, and performance assessments and that the terms should not be used interchangeably (e.g., Nitko, 2001). However, from our experience, educators usually do use these terms interchangeably. We have elected to use the term *performance assessment* in this text because we feel it is the most descriptive title and has received the most widespread use and acceptance.

Now that we have provided some background information, it may be useful to illustrate some of the many applications of performance assessments in today's schools. As most educators recognize, many learning objectives simply cannot be measured using standard paper-and-pencil tasks, and these are situations in which performance assessments excel. Consider the following examples:

- *Laboratory classes:* Students may be asked to demonstrate problem-solving skills, conduct an experiment, use a microscope, dissect an animal, evaluate chemical compositions, estimate the velocity of objects, produce a diorama, or write a lab report.

- *Mathematics classes:* Students may be required to demonstrate quantitative problem-solving skills with problems constructed around real-life problems in areas such as engineering, architecture, landscaping, political polling, business finance, economics, or family budgeting. See Special Interest Topic 10.1 for an example of a performance assessment in mathematics.
- *English, foreign-language, debate classes:* In classes that emphasize communication skills, performance assessments typically play an important role. For example, students may be required to give a speech; speak in a foreign language; engage in an oral debate; recite a poem; or write a poem, essay, or position paper.
- *Social studies classes:* Students may be required to demonstrate the use of maps and globes, debate opposing political positions, make oral presentations, produce dioramas, demonstrate problem-solving skills, or write theme papers.
- *Art classes:* Students typically engage in a variety of art projects that result in work products.
- *Music classes:* Students engage in performances ranging from solo recitals to group productions.
- *Physical education classes:* Students perform a wide variety of psychomotor activities such as hitting a tennis or golf ball, demonstrating different swimming strokes, executing a dive, playing a position in team sports, and individual training activities.

Performance assessments may be the primary approach to assessment in classes such as art, music, physical education, theater, and shop.

Even in classes in which traditional paper-and-pencil assessments are commonly used, performance assessments can be useful adjuncts.

This is only a partial list of the many applications for performance assessments in schools. Consider shop classes, theater classes, home economics classes, typing/keyboarding classes, and computer classes. Even in classes in which traditional paper-and-pencil assessments are commonly used, performance assessments can be useful adjuncts to the more traditional assessments. For example, in college tests and measurement classes it is beneficial to have students select a test construct, develop a test to measure that construct, administer the test to a sample of subjects, and complete preliminary analyses on the resulting data. Like many performance assessments, this activity demands considerable time and effort. However, it measures skills that are not typically assessed when relying on traditional paper-and-pencil assessments.

We just noted that performance assessments can be very time consuming, and this applies to both the teacher and the students. Performance assessments take considerable time for teachers to construct, for students to complete, and for teachers to score. However, not all performance assessments make the same demands on students and teachers. It is common to distinguish between **extended-response performance assessments** and **restricted-response performance assessments.** Extended-response performance tasks typically are broad in scope, measure multiple learning objectives, and are designed to closely mirror real-life situations. In contrast, restricted-response performance tasks typically measure a specific learning objective and relative to extended-response assessments are easier to administer and score. However, restricted-response tasks are less likely to mirror real-life situations.

Example of a Performance Assessment in Mathematics

The issues involved in assessing mathematics problem solving are similar to those in all performance assessments, so we will use this topic to highlight them. Almost all states have incorporated so-called higher-order thinking skills in their curricula and assessments. In mathematics this is commonly focused on problem solving. Common arithmetic and mathematics performance assessments in standardized tests that are developed by mathematicians and mathematics educators focus on common problem situations and types. For example, algebra problems may be developed around landscape architectural requirements for bedding perimeters or areas, as well as driving times and distance problems. Students are asked in a series of questions to represent the problem, develop solutions, select a solution, solve the problem, and write a verbal description of the solution.

Each part of a mathematics problem such as that just mentioned will be evaluated separately. In some assessments each part is awarded points to be cumulated for the problem. How these points are set is usually a judgment call, and there is little research on this process. Correlational analysis with other indicators of mental processing, factor analysis, and item response theory can all provide help in deciding how to weight parts of a test, but these are advanced statistical procedures. As with essay testing, however, each part of a mathematics problem of this kind will be addressed in a scoring rubric. Typically the rubric provides a set of examples illustrating performances at different score levels. For example, a 0 to 4 system for a solution generation element would have examples of each level from 1 to 4. Typically a 0 is reserved for no response, a 1-point response reflects a poorly developed response that is incorrect, a 2-point response reflects a single correct but simple solution, whereas 3 and 4 are reserved for multiple correct and increasingly well-developed solutions. An example of a performance assessment in mathematics follows. The assessment is similar to those used in various state and national assessments. Note that some parts require responses that are simply multiple-choice, whereas others require construction of a response along with the procedures the student used to produce the answer. The process or procedures employed are evaluated as well as the answer. One of the reasons for examining the student's construction process is that students sometimes can get the correct answer without knowing the procedure (they may conduct various arithmetic operations and produce a response that corresponds to an option on a multiple-choice item).

1. Why did the number of border bricks increase as gray paving blocks were added?

    _____

    _____

    _____

2. Complete the table below. Decide how many paving stones and border bricks the 5th patio design would have.

Patio Design	Number of Paving Stones	Number of Border Bricks
1	1	8
2	(4)	(12)
3	(9)	(16)
4	(16)	(20)
5	(25)	(24)

(continued)

SPECIAL INTEREST TOPIC   **10.1**   **Continued**

CONSTRUCTED-RESPONSE MATHEMATICS ITEM, GRADE 6–8 ALGEBRA CONCEPTS

Directions: All of the questions are about the same problem shown below. Read the problem and then answer each question in the boxes given with each question.

Sue is a landscaper who builds patios with gray paving stones and white bricks that make the border. The number of paving stones and bricks depends on the size of the patio as shown below:

Patio Design 1

Patio Design 2

Patio Design 3

Patio Design 4

---

3. From the pattern in the table on p. 243, write a statement about how many more border bricks will be needed as the patio design goes from 5 to 6.

_____

_____

_____

4. The number of the patio design is the same as the number of rows of paving stones in the design. As a new row is added, how many border bricks are added? ANSWER _____

5. Notice that if you multiply the value 1 for Patio Design 1 by 4 and add 4, you get the number of border bricks, 8. Does the same thing work for Patio Design 2? ANSWER _____

Now write a math statement about the number of the patio design and the number of border bricks: You can use P for patio design and N for the number of border bricks. Thus, your statement should start, $N = \ldots$

_____

_____

_____

Guidelines for Developing
Effective Performance Assessments

Due to the great diversity in the types of objectives measured by performance assessments, it is somewhat difficult to develop specific guidelines for developing effective performance assessments. However, most experts tend to agree on some general guidelines for this process (e.g., Gronlund, 1998; Linn & Gronlund, 2000; Nitko, 2001; Popham, 1999, 2000; Stiggins, 2001). These can be classified as suggestions for selecting appropriate performance tasks, developing clear instructions for students, developing procedures for evaluating students' performance, and implementing procedures to minimize rating errors. In summarizing these guidelines, the logical place to start is with the selection of a performance task.

Selecting Appropriate Performance Tasks

The first major task in developing a performance assessment is to select an appropriate performance task.

A performance task is an assessment activity that requires a student to produce a written or spoken response, to engage in an activity, or to create a product (Nitko, 2001). Here are some factors that should be considered.

Select Performance Tasks That Provide the Most Direct Assessment of the Educational Objectives You Want to Measure. One principle we have touched on several times is that you should select assessment techniques that provide the most direct measurement of the educational objective of interest. This applies when selecting what type of assessment to use (e.g., selected-response, constructed-response, or performance assessment) and also when selecting the specific task that you will employ. To this end, carefully examine the educational objectives you are targeting and select performance tasks that capture the essential features of those objectives.

Select Performance Tasks That Maximize Your Ability to Generalize the Results of the Assessment.   One of the most important considerations when selecting a performance task is to choose one that will allow you to generalize the results to comparable tasks. In other words, if a student can perform well on the selected task, there should be a high probability that he or she can perform well on other tasks that involve similar skills and knowledge.

Select Performance Tasks That Reflect Essential Skills.   As a general rule, performance assessments should be used only for assessing the most important or essential skills. Because performance assessments require considerable time and energy to complete (for both teachers and students), to promote efficiency use them only for assessing the really important skills that you want to ensure your students have mastered.

Select Performance Tasks That Encompass More than One Learning Objective.   Because performance assessments often require such extensive time and energy commitments, it is highly desirable to select tasks that allow the assessment of multiple important educational objectives. Although this may not always be possible, when it is it enhances the efficiency of the assessment process.

Select Performance Tasks That Focus Your Evaluation on the Processes and/or Products You Are Most Interested In.   Before selecting a performance task you should determine whether you are primarily interested in assessing the process the students engage in, the product they produce, or some combination of the two. Sometimes the answer to this question is obvious; sometimes it is less clear. Some performance tasks do not result in a product and in this situation it is obvious that you will focus on the process. For example, assessment of musical performances, speeches, debates, and dance routines require evaluation of the process in real time. In contrast, when evaluating a student-developed diorama, poem, or sculpture, the process is often less important than the end product. Assessment experts (e.g., Nitko, 2001) recommend that you focus on the process when:

- No product is produced.
- A specific sequence of steps or procedures is taught.
- The specific steps or procedures are essential to success.
- The process is clearly observable.
- Analysis of the process can provide constructive feedback.
- You have the time to devote to observing the students perform the task.

Focus on products is recommended when:

- An equally good product can be produced using different procedures.
- The process in not directly observable.
- The quality of the product can be objectively judged.

As we noted, it is possible and often desirable to evaluate both process and product. Additionally, the emphasis on process or product may change at different stages of instruction. Gronlund (1998) suggests that process is often more important early in the learning process, but after the procedural steps have been mastered, the product assumes primary importance. For example, in painting the teacher's focus may be on procedure and technique in the early stages of instruction and then shift to the quality of the finished painting in later stages of instruction. When the process has been adequately mastered, it may be preferable to focus your evaluation on the product because it can usually be evaluated in a more objective manner, at a time convenient to the teacher, and if necessary the scoring can be verified.

Select Performance Tasks That Provide the Desired Degree of Realism.   This involves considering how closely your task needs to mirror real-life applications. This is along the lines of the distinction between actual, analogue, and artificial performance assessments. This distinction can be conceptualized as a continuum, with actual performance tasks being the most realistic and artificial performance tasks the least realistic. Although it may not be possible to conduct actual or even analogue performance assessments in the classroom, considerable variability in the degree of realism can be found in artificial performance assessments. Gronlund (1998) identifies four factors to consider when determining how realistic your performance assessment should be:

- *The nature of the educational objective being measured:* Does the objective require a high, medium, or low level of realism?
- *The sequential nature of instruction:* Often in instruction the mastery of skills that do not require a high level of realism to assess can and should precede the mastery of skills that demand a high level of realism in assessment. For example, in teaching the use of power tools in a shop class it would be responsible to teach fundamental safety rules (which may be measured using paper-and-pencil assessments) before proceeding to hands-on tasks involving the actual use of power tools.
- *Practical constraints:* Consider factors such as time requirements, expenses, mandatory equipment, and so forth. As a general rule, the more realistic the task, the greater the demands in terms of time and equipment.
- *The nature of the task:* Some tasks by their very nature preclude actual performance assessment. Remember our example regarding the recertification of nuclear power plant operators. In this context, mistakes in the real system could be disastrous, so a simulator that re-creates the control room is used for assessment purposes.

Select Performance Tasks That Measure Skills That Are "Teachable."   That is, make sure your performance assessment is measuring a skill that is acquired through direct instruction and not one that reflects innate ability. Ask yourself, "Can the students become more proficient on this task as a result of instruction?" Popham (1999) notes that when evaluation criteria focus on "teachable skills" it strengthens the relationship between instruction and assessment, making both more meaningful.

Select Performance Tasks That Are Fair to All Students.   Choose tasks that are fair to all students regardless of gender, ethnicity, or socioeconomic status.

Select Performance Tasks That Can Be Assessed Given the Time and Resources Available.   Consider the practicality of a performance task. For example, can the assessment realistically be completed when considering the expense, time, space, and equipment required? Consider factors such as class size; what might be practical in a small class of 10 students might not be practical in a class of 30 students. From our experience it is common for teachers to underestimate the time students require to complete a project or activity. This is because the teacher is an expert on the task and can see the direct, easy means to completion. In contrast students can be expected to flounder to some degree. Not allowing sufficient time to complete the tasks can result in student failure and a sense that the assessment was not fair. To some extent experience is needed to determine reasonable times and deadlines for completion. New teachers may find it useful to consult with more experienced colleagues for guidance in this area.

Select Performance Tasks That Can Be Scored in a Reliable Manner.   Choose performance tasks that will elicit student responses that can be measured in an objective, accurate, and reliable manner.

Select Performance Tasks That Reflect Educational Objectives That Cannot Be Measured Using More Traditional Measures.   As you will learn when we describe the strengths and weaknesses of performance assessments, there are some significant limitations associated with the use of these assessments. As a result, most assessment experts recommend that you reserve their use to measuring educational objectives that simply cannot be assessed using more traditional paper-and-pencil assessments. However, if you are a strong supporter of performance assessments do not be dismayed; as we have indicated, many educational objectives require the use of performance assessments.

Table 10.1 provides a summary of guidelines for selecting performance tasks.

TABLE 10.1   Guidelines for Selecting Performance Tasks

1. Select performance tasks that provide the most direct assessment of the educational objectives you want to measure.
2. Select performance tasks that maximize your ability to generalize the results of the assessment.
3. Select performance tasks that reflect essential skills.
4. Select performance tasks that encompass more than one learning objective.
5. Select performance tasks that focus your evaluation on the processes and/or products you are most interested in.
6. Select performance tasks that provide the desired degree of realism.
7. Select performance tasks that measure skills that are "teachable."
8. Select performance tasks that are fair to all students.
9. Select performance tasks that can be assessed given the time and resources available.
10. Select performance tasks that can be scored in a reliable manner.
11. Select performance tasks that reflect educational objectives that cannot be measured using more traditional measures.

Developing Instructions

Because performance tasks often require fairly complex student responses, it is important that your instruction precisely specify the types of responses you are expecting. Because originality and creativity are seen as desirable educational outcomes, performance tasks often give students considerable freedom in how they approach the task. However, this does not mean it is appropriate for teachers to provide vague or ambiguous instructions. Few things in the classroom will create more negativity among students than confusing instructions that they feel result in a poor evaluation. It is the teacher's responsibility to write instructions clearly and precisely so that students do not need to "read the teacher's mind" (this applies to all assessments, not only performance assessments). Possibly the best way to avoid problems in this area is to have someone else (e.g., an experienced colleague) read and interpret the instructions before you administer the assessment to your students. Accordingly, it may be beneficial to try out the performance activity with one or two students before administering it to your whole class to ensure that the instructions are thorough and understandable. Your instructions should clearly specify the types of responses you are expecting and the criteria you will use when evaluating students' performance. Here is a list of questions that assessment professionals recommend you consider when evaluating the quality of your instructions (e.g., Nitko, 2001):

The second major task in developing performance assessments is to develop instructions that clearly specify what students are expected to do.

- Do your instructions match the educational level of your students?
- Do your instructions contain unnecessary jargon and overly technical language?
- Do your instructions clearly specify the purpose or goal of the task?
- Do your instructions clearly specify the type of response you expect?
- Do your instructions specify all the important parameters of the performance task (e.g., time limits, the use of equipment or materials)?
- Do your instructions clearly specify the criteria you will use when evaluating the student responses?
- Will students from diverse cultural and ethnic backgrounds interpret the instructions in an accurate manner?

Table 10.2 provides a summary of these guidelines for developing instructions for your performance assessments.

Developing Procedures for Evaluating Responses

The third major step in developing performance assessments is to develop procedures for evaluating the students' responses.

Whether you are evaluating process, product, or a combination of the two, it is imperative that you develop systematic, objective, and reliable procedures for evaluating student responses. Performance assessments are essentially constructed-response assessments, and as such share many of the scoring problems associated with essays we discussed in Chapter 9. The scoring procedures applied to performance assessments are often referred to as **scoring rubrics,** which we initially introduced when discussing essay items in

TABLE 10.2   Guidelines for Developing Instructions for Performance Assessments

1. Make sure that your instructions clearly specify the types of responses you are expecting.
2. Make sure that your instructions specify any important parameters of the performance task (e.g., time limits, the use of equipment or materials).
3. Make sure that your instructions clearly specify the criteria you will use when evaluating the students' responses.
4. Have a colleague read and interpret the instructions before you administer the assessment to your students.
5. Try out the performance activity with one or a limited number of students before administering it to your whole class to ensure that the instructions are thorough and understandable.
6. Write instructions that students from diverse cultural and ethnic backgrounds will interpret in an accurate manner.

the preceding chapter. A rubric is simply a written guide that helps you score constructed-response assessments. In discussing the development of scoring rubrics for performance assessments, Popham (1999) identified three essential tasks that need to be completed:

Select Important Criteria That Will Be Considered When Evaluating Student Responses.   Start by selecting the criteria or response characteristics that you will employ when judging the quality of a student's response. We recommend that you give careful consideration to the selection of these characteristics because this is probably the most important step in developing good scoring procedures. Limit it to three or four of the most important response characteristics to keep the evaluation process from becoming unmanageable. The criteria you are considering when judging the quality of a student's response should be described in a precise manner so there is no confusion about what the rating refers to. It is also highly desirable to select criteria that can be directly observed and judged. Characteristics such as interest, attitude, and effort are not directly observable and do not make good bases for evaluation.

Specify Explicit Standards That Describe Different Levels of Performance.   For each criterion you want to evaluate, you should develop clearly stated standards that distinguish among levels of performance. In other words, your standards should spell out what a student's response must encompass or look like to be regarded as excellent, average, or inferior. It is often helpful to provide behavioral descriptions and/or specimens or examples to illustrate the different levels of performance.

Determine What Type of Scoring Procedure You Will Use.   Scoring rubrics can be classified as either holistic or analytic. With **analytic scoring rubrics** the teacher awards credit on a criterion-by-criterion basis whereas with **holistic rubrics** the teacher assigns a single score reflecting the overall quality of the student's response. Analytic scoring rubrics have the advantage of providing specific feedback to students regarding the strengths and weaknesses of their response. This informs students which aspects of their responses were adequate and which need improvement. The major limitation of analytic rubrics is that they can take considerable time to complete. Holistic rubrics are often less detailed than analytic rubrics and as a result are easier to develop and complete. Their major disadvantage is that they do not provide specific feedback to students about the strengths and weaknesses of their responses. Tables 9.2 and 9.3 in Chapter 9 provide examples of holistic and analytic scoring rubrics.

Linn and Gronlund (2000) identify rating scales and checklists as popular alternatives to the traditional scoring rubrics. Noting that the distinction between rating scales and traditional rubrics is often subtle, they find that **rating scales** typically use quality judgments (e.g., outstanding, good, average, marginal, poor) to indicate performance on each criterion as opposed to the more elaborate descriptive standards common on scoring rubrics. In place of quality judgments, some rating scales indicate frequency judgments (e.g., always, often, sometimes, seldom, never). Table 10.3 provides an example of a rating scale using verbal descriptions.

A number of different types of rating scales are commonly used in scoring performance assessments. On some rating scales the verbal descriptions are replaced with numbers to facilitate scoring. Table 10.4 provides an example of a numerical rating scale. Another variation, referred to as a graphic rating scale, uses a horizontal line with ratings positioned along the lines. Table 10.5 provides an example of a graphic rating scale. A final popular type of rating scale combines the graphic format with brief descriptive phrases as anchor points. This is typically referred to as a descriptive graphic scale. Linn and Gronlund (2000) suggest that this type of rating scale has a number of advantages that support its use with performance assessments. It communicates more information to the students regarding their performance and it helps teachers rate their students' performance with greater objectivity and accuracy. Table 10.6 provides an example of a descriptive graphic rating scale. When developing rating scales it is usually desirable to have between three and seven rating points. For example, at a minimum you would want your rating scale to include ratings of *poor, average,* and *excellent.* Most experts suggest that including more than seven positions is not useful because raters usually cannot make finer discriminations than this.

Checklists are another popular procedure used to score performance assessments. Checklists are similar to rating scales, but whereas rating scales note the quality of performance or the frequency of a behavior, checklists require a simple yes/no judgment. Table 10.7 provides an example of a checklist that might be used with preschool children.

(text continues on p. 254)

TABLE 10.3   Example of a Rating Scale Using Verbal Descriptions

Directions: Indicate the student's ability to successfully perform the specified activity by circling the appropriate descriptor.

1. Rate the student's ability to serve the ball.

| Poor | Marginal | Average | Good | Excellent |

2. Rate the student's ability to strike the tennis ball using the forehand stroke.

| Poor | Marginal | Average | Good | Excellent |

3. Rate the student's ability to strike the tennis ball using the backhand stroke.

| Poor | Marginal | Average | Good | Excellent |

TABLE 10.4   Example of a Numerical Rating Scale

Directions: Indicate the student's ability to successfully perform the specified activity by circling the appropriate number. On this scale, the numbers represent the following evaluations: 1 = Poor, 2 = Marginal, 3 = Average, 4 = Good, and 5 = Excellent.

1. Rate the student's ability to serve the ball.

    1   2   3   4   5

2. Rate the student's ability to strike the tennis ball using the forehand stroke.

    1   2   3   4   5

3. Rate the student's ability to strike the tennis ball using the backhand stroke.

    1   2   3   4   5

TABLE 10.5   Example of a Graphic Rating Scale

Directions: Indicate the student's ability to successfully perform the specified activity by marking an X anywhere along the horizontal line below each item.

1. Rate the student's ability to serve the ball.

Poor	Average	Excellent

2. Rate the student's ability to strike the tennis ball using the forehand stroke.

Poor	Average	Excellent

3. Rate the student's ability to strike the tennis ball using the backhand stroke.

Poor	Average	Excellent

TABLE 10.6   Example of a Descriptive Graphic Rating Scale

Directions: Indicate the student's ability to successfully perform the specified activity by marking an X anywhere along the horizontal line below each item.

1. Rate the student's ability to serve the ball.

Form is poor and accuracy is poor	Form and accuracy usually within the average range	Form and accuracy are consistently superior

2. Rate the student's ability to strike the tennis ball using the forehand stroke.

Form is poor and accuracy is poor	Form and accuracy usually within the average range	Form and accuracy are consistently superior

3. Rate the student's ability to strike the tennis ball using the backhand stroke.

Form and accuracy are typically poor	Form and accuracy usually within the average range	Form and accuracy are consistently superior

TABLE 10.7 Example of a Checklist Used with Preschool Children

Directions: Circle Yes or No to indicate whether each skill has been demonstrated.

Self-Help Skills

Yes	No	Attempts to wash face and hands
Yes	No	Helps put toys away
Yes	No	Drinks from a standard cup
Yes	No	Eats using utensils
Yes	No	Attempts to use the toilet
Yes	No	Attempts to dress self

Language Development

Yes	No	Follows simple directions
Yes	No	Verbalizes needs and feelings
Yes	No	Speech can be understood most of the time
Yes	No	Speaks in sentences of three or more words

Basic Skills Development

Yes	No	Can count to ten
Yes	No	Recognizes numbers to 10

Can name the following shapes:

Yes	No	Circle
Yes	No	Square
Yes	No	Triangle
Yes	No	Star

Can identify the following colors:

Yes	No	Red
Yes	No	Blue
Yes	No	Green

Understands the following concepts:

Yes	No	Up and down
Yes	No	Big and little
Yes	No	Open and closed
Yes	No	On and off
Yes	No	In and out

Social Development

Yes	No	Plays independently
Yes	No	Plays parallel to other students
Yes	No	Plays cooperatively with other students
Yes	No	Participates in group activities

Linn and Gronlund (2000) suggest that checklists are most useful in primary education because a majority of assessment is based on observation rather than formal testing. Checklists are also particularly useful for skills that can be divided into a series of behaviors.

Although there is overlap between traditional scoring rubrics such as those used for scoring essays, rating scales, and checklists, there are differences that may make one preferable for your performance assessment. Consider which format is most likely to produce the most reliable and valid results and which will provide the most useful feedback to the students.

Implementing Procedures to Minimize Errors in Rating

The final major step in developing performance assessments is to implement procedures to minimize errors in rating.

When discussing the scoring of essay items in the preceding chapter, we noted that a multitude of factors could introduce error into the scoring process. Similar factors need to be considered when scoring performance assessments. Common sources of error when teachers rate the performance of students include the following.

- *Halo effect:* We introduced you to the concept of expectancy effects when discussing the scoring of essay items, noting that these effects come into play when the teacher scoring the test allows irrelevant characteristics of the student to influence scoring. In the context of ratings this phenomenon is often referred to as the halo effect. The **halo effect** is the tendency for raters to be influenced by a single positive or negative trait, unrelated to the trait or skill being assessed, that affects their rating of the student's other characteristics. In other words, if students impressed a teacher with their punctuality and good manners, the teacher might tend to rate them more favorably when scoring performance assessments. Obviously this is to be avoided because it undermines the validity of the results.

- *Leniency, severity, and central tendency errors:* **Leniency errors** occur because some teachers tend to give all students good ratings whereas **severity errors** occur because some teachers tend to give all students poor ratings. **Central tendency errors** occur because some teachers tend to give all students scores in the middle range (e.g., indicating average performance). Leniency, severity, and central tendency errors all reduce the range of scores and make scores less reliable.

- *Personal biases:* **Personal biases** may corrupt ratings if teachers have a tendency to let stereotypes influence their ratings of students' performance.

- *Logical errors:* **Logical error** occurs when a teacher assumes that two characteristics are related and tends to give similar ratings based on this assumption (Nitko, 2001). An example of a logical error would be teachers assuming that all students with high aptitude scores should do well in all academic areas, and letting this belief influence their ratings.

- *Order effects:* **Order effects** are changes in scoring that emerge during the grading process. These effects are often referred to as rater drift or **reliability decay.** Nitko (2001) notes that when teachers start using a scoring rubric they often adhere to it closely and apply it consistently, but over time there is a tendency for them to adhere to it less closely, and as a result the reliability of their ratings decreases or decays.

Obviously these sources of errors can undermine the reliability of scores and the validity of their interpretations. Therefore, it is important for teachers to take steps to minimize the influence of these factors that threaten the accuracy of ratings. Here are some suggestions for improving the reliability and accuracy of teacher ratings that are based on our own experiences and the recommendations of other authors (e.g., Linn & Gronlund, 2000; Nitko, 2001; Popham, 1999, 2000):

Before Administering the Assessment, Have One or More Trusted Colleagues Evaluate Your Scoring Rubric. If you have other teachers who are familiar with the performance area review and critique your scoring rubric, they may be able to identify any limitations before you start the assessment.

When Possible, Rate Performances without Knowing the Student's Identity. This corresponds with the recommendation we made with regard to grading essay items. Anonymous scoring reduces the chance that ratings will be influenced by halo effects, personal biases, or logical errors.

Rate the Performance of Every Student on One Task before Proceeding to the Next Task. It is easier to apply the scoring criteria uniformly when you score one task for every student before proceeding to the next task. That is, score task number one for every student before proceeding to the second task. Whenever possible, you should also randomly reorder the students or their projects before moving on to the next task. This will help minimize order effects.

Be Sensitive to the Presence of Leniency, Severity, or Central Tendency Errors. As you are rating the tasks keep a tally of how often you use each point on the rating scale. If it becomes apparent that there is little variability in your ratings (all very high, all very low, or all in the middle), you may need to modify your rating practice to more accurately reflect differences in your students' performance.

Conduct a Preliminary Reliability Analysis to Determine Whether Your Ratings Have Acceptable Reliability. For example, rescore a subset of the assessments, or even the entire set, to determine consistency in ratings. Special Interest Topic 10.2 provides a discussion of reliability issues in performance assessments and illustrates some approaches to estimating the reliability of ratings.

Have More than One Teacher Rate Each Student's Performance. The combined ratings of several teachers will typically yield more reliable scores than the ratings of only one teacher. This is particularly important when the results of an assessment will have significant consequences for the students.

Table 10.8 provides a summary of these guidelines for developing and implementing procedures for scoring your performance assessments. Special Interest Topic 10.3 presents a discussion of the problems some states have experienced incorporating performance assessments into their high-stakes assessment programs.

(text continues on p. 258)

SPECIAL INTEREST TOPIC 10.2
Reliability Issues in Performance Assessments

Reliable scoring of performance assessments is hard to achieve. When estimating the reliability of performance assessments used in standardized assessment programs, multiple readers (also termed raters) are typically given the same student response to read and score. Because it is cost prohibitive for readers to read and score all responses in high-stakes testing, the responses are typically assigned randomly to pairs of readers. For each response the scores given by the two readers are compared. If they are identical the essay is given the common score. If they differ meaningfully, such as one score represents a passing performance and the other failing, a procedure to decide on the score given is invoked. Sometimes this involves a third reader, or if the scores are close an average score is given. For tasks with multiple parts the same two readers evaluate the entire problem. It is important to note that reliability of the parts will be much lower than reliability of the entire problem. Summing the scores of the various parts of the problem will produce a more reliable score than that for any one part, so it is important to decide at what level score reliability is to be assessed. It will be much more costly to require high reliability for scoring each part than for the entire problem.

Prior to reading the responses the readers must be given training. This training usually includes review of the rubrics, practice with samples of responses, and repeated scoring until the readers reach some criterion performance themselves. Readers may be required to agree with a predetermined score value. For example, readers may be expected to reach a criterion agreement of 70% or 80% with the predetermined score value over a set of responses. This agreement means that a reader achieves 70% agreement with the assigned score (the assigned scores were established by experts). Statistically, this agreement itself is dependent on the number of responses a reader is given. That is, if a reader scores 10 responses and obtains an exact match in scoring 7 of them, the reader may have achieved the required reliability for scoring. However, from a purely statistical perspective they may have a percent agreement as low as 0.41. This is based on statistical probability for a percentage. It is calculated from the equation for the standard deviation of a percent:

$$S_{proportion} = \sqrt{\frac{0.70 \times 0.30}{10}} = .145$$

From the distribution of normal scores, plus or minus 1.96 standard deviations will capture 95% of the values of the percent a reader would obtain over repeated scoring of 10 responses. This is about 2 standard deviations, so that subtracting 2×0.145 from 0.70 leaves a percent as low as 0.41. Clearly, 10 responses is a poor sample to decide whether a reader has a true percent agreement score of 0.70. If the number of essays is increased to 100, the standard error becomes 0.046, and the lower bound of the interval around 0.70 becomes 0.70 minus 2×0.046, or about 0.60. Reading 100 responses is very time consuming and costly, increasing the cost of the entire process greatly. If we want a true minimal agreement value of 0.70, using this process, we would require the actual agreement for readers to be well above 0.80 for 100 responses, and above 0.95 for only 10. Unfortunately, it is not generally reported for high-stakes testing how many responses are scored to achieve the state-mandated level of reliability. Most of these assessments prescribe the minimal level of agreement, but in some cases the agreement is between readers, not necessarily with an expert. This produces yet another source of unreliability, the degree of *inter-rater agreement*. The more common approach to inter-rater agreement is to construct the percent agreement across a set of responses and then correct it for the chance agreement that could occur even if there were no real agreement. That is, suppose that for practical purposes in a 0-4 system, the score of 0 represents a blank sheet—that is, the student did not respond. These are easily separated from the rest of the responses but have no real contribution to meaningful agreement so they are not considered. This leaves a 1–4 range for scoring. It is easy to show that if scores were distributed equally across the range, a random pairing of scores would produce 25% agreement. If the score distribution for the population of students is actually normally distributed, centered at 2.5, for example, the chance agreement is quite a bit greater, as high as almost 80%, depending on the assumptions about the performance underlying the testing and scoring. In any case, the apparent agreement among raters must be accounted for. One solution is to calculate Cohen's kappa, an agreement measure that subtracts the chance agreement from the observed agreement.

$$\text{Cohen's kappa} = (p_{\text{agreement}} - p_{\text{chance agreement}}) / (1 - p_{\text{chance agreement}})$$

The calculations illustrated next are for hypothetical data for two raters. Note that we would need a much higher observed agreement to ensure a minimal 70% agreement beyond chance. Because the classical estimate of reliability is always based on excluding error such as chance, Cohen's kappa is theoretically closer to the commonly agreed-on concept of reliability. Unfortunately, there is little evidence that high-stakes assessments employ this method. Again, the cost of ensuring this level of true agreement becomes quite high.

Computation of Cohen's Kappa for Two Raters

		Rater 2 Scores				
		1	2	3	4	Percent
Rater 1 Scores	1	2	1	0	0	30%
	2	0	3	0	0	30%
	3	0	1	1	0	20%
	4	0	1	0	1	20%
	Percent	20%	60%	10%	10%	100%

Calculation of Cohen's kappa

$$\text{Kappa} = (p_{\text{agreement}} - p_{\text{chance agreement}}) / (1 - p_{\text{chance agreement}})$$

$$p_{\text{agreement}} = 70\%$$

$$p_{\text{chance agreement}} = (30\% \times 20\%) + (30\% \times 60\%) + (20\% \times 10\%) + (20\% \times 10\%)$$

$$= 6\% + 18\% + 2\% + 2\%$$

$$= 28\%$$

Cohen's kappa $= (70\% - 28\%) / (1 - 28\%)$

$$= 0.42 / 0.72$$

$$= 0.583$$

(continued)

SPECIAL INTEREST TOPIC   **10.2**   **Continued**

Notice that this value does not depend on the number of essays scored. As with all statistical methods, the standard deviation of this value, however, depends on the number of scores. The standard error of kappa is equal to

Se = 0.3945

A number of Web sites produce this computation. Simply search with the term *Cohen's kappa* using an Internet search engine to find one of these sites. For example, a site at Vassar University produced the computations just used (Lowry, 2003).

For 20 essays, doubling the number of cases in the table, the estimate remains the same, but the standard error is reduced to 0.2789. For 80 responses, multiplying the numbers in the table by 8, the standard error is 0.1395. Thus, even with 80 responses, given a 70% observed agreement among two raters, the actual Cohen's kappa chance corrected agreement is as low as 0.42 (approximately $0.70 - 1.96 \times 0.1395$).

TABLE 10.8   Guidelines for Developing and Implementing Scoring Procedures

1. Ensure that the criteria you are evaluating are clearly specified and directly observable.
2. Ensure that the standards clearly distinguish among levels of performance.
3. Select the type of scoring procedure that is most appropriate.
4. Have one or more trusted colleagues evaluate your scoring rubric.
5. When possible, rate performances without knowing the student's identity.
6. Rate the performance of every student on one task before proceeding to the next task.
7. Be sensitive to the presence of leniency, severity, or central tendency errors.
8. Conduct a preliminary reliability analysis to determine whether your ratings have acceptable reliability.
9. Have more than one teacher rate each student's performance.

Strengths and Weaknesses of Performance Assessments

Much has been written about the strengths and weaknesses of performance assessments, and this is good time to examine them in more detail. First, we will address their strengths.

Performance Assessments Can Measure Abilities That Are Not Assessable Using Other Assessments.   Possibly the greatest strength of performance assessments is that they can measure abilities that simply cannot be measured with other types of assessments. If you want to measure abilities such as a student's ability to engage in an oral debate, paint a picture, tune an engine, or use a microscope, performance assessments fit the bill.

Performance assessments can measure learning outcomes that are not assessable using other assessments.

Performance Assessments in High-Stakes Testing

Several states have experimented with performance assessments in different subject areas. For example, in Vermont teachers were required to cumulate a portfolio of each of their students' school products over the school year, which were to be evaluated and scored. Koretz, Stecher, and Deibert (1993) found the reliability of this procedure to be quite low, about 0.3, and this low consistency led ultimately to the state's revision of its assessment practices in 1996 toward standardized assessments in more traditional formats. The state Web site indicates that portfolios are still required in combination with various traditional standardized tests to assess state standards for achievement. Although references appear to both state-level and district-level portfolios, the emphasis seems clearly to be on traditional testing. Some resources provided by the state Web site (www.vermont institutes.org/assessment/index.htm) reiterate the limitations of portfolio reliability discussed here, as well as comment on the sampling problem in selecting pieces of student's work. That is, unless all student work is included in a body of products for a student, the selection of the pieces to be included contributes to both the unreliability in scoring and the invalidity of content and construct validity of the score.

The state of Kentucky also experimented with portfolios in its assessment of students. As reported by the National Center for Research in Vocational Education (NCRVE) at the University of California—Berkeley (http://ncrve.berkeley.edu/abstracts/MDS-1206/MDS-1206-kentuck.html):

> Under the far-reaching Kentucky Education Reform Act (KERA) of 1990, extensive procedures for measuring the achievement of Kentucky students were created under a system called Kentucky Instructional Results Information System (KIRIS). . . . Individual teachers at schools rewarded with incentive funds were allowed to vote on how the funds would be spent, and KIRIS provided a list of schools in need of assistance and state intervention. By tying incentives and state intervention to a new system of assessment, KIRIS proved quite controversial. In addition, KIRIS assessments were based primarily on portfolios, performance-based exams, and writing samples completed during class. While arguably, these are more authentic measures of student achievement, Kentucky found that these kinds of assessments were nonetheless harder to implement because of problems related to scoring reliability and comparability across schools. . . . In April of 1998, the Kentucky legislature replaced KIRIS with a new assessment program.

The new system was implemented in 1999 and consisted of multiple-choice tests (www.kde.state .ky.us/KDE/Instructional+Resources/Curriculum+Documents+and+Resources/Core+Content+for+ Assessment.htm).

This experience parallels those in other states that have tried prematurely to include portfolios, extended performance assessments, and related activities into high-stakes tests. Although the intent of these assessments has consistently been to more closely mirror real-world experiences students might be expected to encounter, the results to date have been uniformly problematic, due to unreliability of scoring, extremely high costs, and not the least, the suspicion of the public and legislators that the scores associated with the performances can be somehow subverted politically. Of course that suspicion ignores the conclusion that current traditional statewide and national test scores can also be subverted through manipulation of item selection, definition of *passing* or *acceptable performance,* and other behind-the-scenes actions that have been associated with testing for well over one hundred years (Madaus & Kellaghan, 1993).

The Use of Performance Assessments Is Consistent with Modern Learning Theory.
Modern learning theory holds that for optimal learning to occur students need to integrate
new information with existing knowledge and be actively engaged in complex tasks that
mirror real-life applications. Many assessment experts agree that performance assessments
are consistent with the principles supported by modern learning theory.

The Use of Performance Assessments May Result in Better Instruction.   Because
teachers may be motivated to teach to the test, the use of performance assessments may
help broaden instruction to cover more complex educational objectives that parallel real-
life applications.

**Performance assessments may
make learning more meaningful
and help motivate students.**

*Performance Assessments May Make Learning More Meaning-
ful and Help Motivate Students.*   Performance assessments are inherently attractive to teachers and students. To many students testing
them under conditions that are similar to those they will encounter in
the real world is more meaningful than testing them with paper-and-pencil tests. As a result,
students might be more motivated to be actively engaged in the assessment process.

Performance Assessments Allow You to Assess Process as Well as Products.   Performance assessments give teachers the opportunity to evaluate the ways students solve problems and perform tasks, as well as the products they produce.

The Use of Performance Assessments Broadens Your Approach to Assessment.
Throughout this text we have emphasized the advantages of using multiple approaches when
assessing student achievement. We concur with these comments from the U.S. Department
of Education (1997):

> A single measure or approach is unlikely to adequately measure the knowledge, skills, and
> complex procedures covered by rigorous content standards. Multiple measures and ap-
> proaches can be used to capitalize on the strengths of each measurement technique, enhanc-
> ing the utility of the assessment system and strengthening the validity of decisions based on
> assessment results. (p. 9)

Although performance assessments have a number of strengths that support their use,
there are some disadvantages. We will now summarize these disadvantages.

**Performance assessments are
time consuming and difficult to
score in a reliable manner.**

*Scoring Performance Assessments in a Reliable Manner Is Dif-
ficult.*   Probably the most common criticism of performance assessments is that due to the inherent subjectivity in scoring they
often result in unreliable scores both across raters and across time.
That is, the same rater is likely to assign different scores if he or she
scores the same performance at different times, and two different raters are likely to assign
different scores to the same performance. The best way to minimize this tendency is to follow the guidelines for developing and implementing scoring procedures we described previously (see Table 10.8).

Performance Assessments Typically Provide Limited Sampling of the Content Domain, and It Is Difficult to Make Generalizations about the Skills and Knowledge the Students Possess. Because students typically are able to respond to only a limited number of performance tasks, there is limited sampling of the content domain. Research has shown that performance on one task does not allow teachers to predict with much accuracy how students will perform on other tasks that measure similar skills and abilities (e.g., Shavelson, Baxter, & Gao, 1993). For example, if students do well on one performance task, you cannot be sure that they have actually mastered the skills and knowledge encompassed by the task, or were simply lucky on this one task. Likewise, if students perform poorly on one performance task, you cannot be sure that their performance reflects inadequate skills and knowledge, because it is possible that a misunderstanding of the task requirements undermined their performance. Because students typically complete a limited number of tasks, your ability to generalize with much confidence is limited. The solution to this limitation is to have students complete multiple performance tasks in order to provide adequate domain sampling. Regretfully, due to their time-consuming nature, this is not always possible.

Performance Assessments Are Time Consuming and Difficult to Construct, Administer, and Score. Performance assessments are not quick and easy! It takes considerable time to develop good performance tasks and scoring procedures, to allow students time to complete the task, and for you to adequately evaluate their performance. Regretfully, there are no shortcuts to make them quick and easy. As Stiggins (2001) noted:

> Performance assessment is complex. It requires users to prepare and conduct their assessments in a thoughtful and rigorous manner. Those unwilling to invest the necessary time and energy will place their students directly in harm's way. (p. 186)

There Are Practical Limitations That May Restrict the Use of Performance Assessments. In addition to high time demands, other practical limitations might restrict the use of performance assessments. These can include factors such as space requirements and special and potentially expensive equipment and materials necessary to simulate a real-life setting.

In summary, performance assessments have numerous strengths and they represent an important assessment option available to teachers. At the same time they have some significant limitations that should be taken into consideration. Although some educational professionals are so enamored with performance assessments that they appear blind to their limitations, most recognize these limitations and recommend that these assessments be used in an appropriately cautious manner. We recommend that you limit the use of performance assessments to the measurement of educational objectives that cannot be adequately measured using techniques that afford more objective and reliable scoring. When you do use performance assessments, be cognizant of their limitations and follow the guidelines we have provided to enhance the reliability of their scores and the validity of your inferences. Table 10.9 provides a summary of the strengths and weaknesses of performance assessments.

We recommend that you limit the use of performance assessments to the measurement of educational objectives that cannot be adequately measured using techniques that afford more objective and reliable scoring.

TABLE 10.9   Strengths and Weaknesses of Performance Assessments

Strengths of Performance Assessments
- Performance assessments can measure abilities that are not assessable using other assessments.
- The use of performance assessments is consistent with modern learning theory.
- The use of performance assessments may result in better instruction.
- Performance assessments may make learning more meaningful and help motivate students.
- Performance assessments allow you to assess process as well as products.
- The use of performance assessments broadens your approach to assessment.

Weaknesses of Performance Assessments
- Performance assessments are notorious for producing unreliable scores.
- With performance assessments it is difficult to make generalizations about the skills and knowledge the students possess.
- Performance assessments are time consuming and difficult to construct, administer, and score.
- There are practical limitations that may restrict the use of performance assessments.

Portfolios

Portfolios **are a specific type of performance assessment that involves the systematic collection of a student's work products over a specified period of time according to a specific set of guidelines (AERA et al., 1999).**

Portfolios are a specific type of performance assessment that involves the systematic collection of a student's work products over a specified period of time according to a specific set of guidelines (AERA et al., 1999). As we noted earlier, artists, photographers, writers, and others have long used portfolios to represent their work, and in the last decade portfolios have become increasingly popular in the classroom. As typically applied in schools today, portfolios may best be conceptualized as a systematic way of collecting, organizing, and evaluating examples of students' work products. As such, portfolios can conceivably serve as the basis for evaluating students' achievements and providing feedback to the students and their parents.

Guidelines for Developing Portfolio Assessments

Like all performance assessments, there is such diversity in portfolios that it is somewhat difficult to specify specific guidelines for their development. However, also like performance assessments, there are some general guidelines that most assessment professionals accept (AERA et al., 1999; Gronlund, 1998; Linn & Gronlund, 2000; Nitko, 2001; Popham, 1999, 2000). These are summarized next.

Decide on the Purpose of the Portfolio. The first step in developing a portfolio is to determine the purpose or use of the portfolio. This is of foremost importance because it will largely determine the content of your students' portfolios. For example, you will need to decide whether the portfolio will be used purely to enhance learning, as the basis for grades (i.e., a scorable portfolio), or some combination of the two. If the purpose is only to enhance learning, there is little need to ensure comparability among the entries in the portfolios. Students can be given considerable freedom to include entries at their discretion. However, if the portfolio is going to be used for summative evaluation and the assignment of grades, then it is important to have standardized content across portfolios. This is necessary to promote a degree of comparability when evaluating the portfolios.

Decide on What Type of Items Will Be Placed in the Portfolio. It is also important to determine whether the portfolios will showcase the students' "best work," representative products, or indicators of progress or growth. **Best work portfolios** contain what the students select as their exemplary work, **representative portfolios** contain a broad representative sample of the students' work (including both exemplary and below-average examples), and **growth or learning-progress portfolios** include selections that illustrate the students' progress over the academic period. A fourth type of portfolio referred to as **evaluation portfolios** is designed to help teachers determine whether the students have met established standards of performance. As such, they should contain products that demonstrate the achievement of specified standards.

Decide Who Will Select the Items to Include in the Portfolio. The teacher must decide who will be responsible for selecting the items to include in the portfolio: the teacher, the student, or both. When selecting items the guiding principle should be to choose items that will allow the teacher or other raters to make valid inferences about the students' skills and knowledge. To promote student involvement in the process, most professionals recommend that teachers and students collaborate when selecting items to be included in the portfolio. However, certain times it may be necessary for the teacher to exert considerable control of the selection of work products. For example, when it is important for scoring purposes to ensure standardization of content, the teacher needs to closely supervise the selection of work products.

Establish Procedures for Evaluating or Scoring the Portfolio. Student portfolios are typically scored using scoring rubrics similar to those discussed in the context of scoring essays and performance assessments. As described earlier, scoring rubrics should:

- Specify the evaluation criteria to be considered when evaluating the students' work products,
- Provide explicit standards that describe different levels of performance on each criterion, and
- Indicate whether the criteria will be evaluated in a holistic or analytical manner.

Promote Student Involvement in the Process. Actively involving students in the assessment process is a goal of all performance assessments, and portfolio assessments provide particularly good opportunities to solicit student involvement. As we suggested, students should be involved to the greatest extent possible in selecting what items are included in their portfolios. Accordingly, they should be involved in maintaining the portfolio and evaluating the quality of the products it contains. Along these lines, it is highly desirable for teachers to

TABLE 10.10   Guidelines for Developing Portfolio Assessments

1. Decide on the purpose of the portfolio
    a. Enhance learning, assign grades, or some combination
    b. Best work, representative products, growth or learning progress, or
       evaluation
2. Decide who will select the items to include in the portfolio
    a. Teacher
    b. Student
    c. Teachert and student in collaboration
3. Establish procedures for evaluating or scoring the portfolio
    a. Specify the evaluation criteria
    b. Provide specific standards
    c. Decide on a holistic or analytic approach
4. Promote student involvement in the process

schedule regular student–teacher meetings to review the portfolio content and compare their evaluations with those of the students. This enhances the students' self-assessment skills, helps them identify individual strengths and weaknesses, and increases their personal involvement in the learning process (e.g., Gronlund, 1998).

Table 10.10 provides a summary of the guidelines for developing portfolios.

Strengths and Weaknesses of Portfolio Assessments

Like all assessment techniques, portfolios have their own set of strengths and weaknesses (Gronlund, 1998; Kubiszyn & Borich, 2003; Linn & Gronlund, 2000; Nitko, 2001; Popham 1999, 2000). Specific strengths of portfolios include the following.

Portfolios are particularly good at reflecting student achievement and growth over time.

Portfolios Are Particularly Good at Reflecting Student Achievement and Growth over Time.   Possibly the greatest strength of portfolios is that they are exemplary at illustrating a student's progress over an extended period of time. As a result, they can greatly facilitate communication with students and parents by providing actual examples of the student's work.

Portfolios May Help Motivate Students and Get Them More Involved in the Learning Process.   Because students typically help select items, maintain the portfolio, and evaluate their progress, they may be more motivated to become actively involved in the learning and assessment process.

Portfolios May Enhance Students' Ability to Evaluate Their Own Performances and Products.   Because students are typically asked to evaluate their own progress, it is expected that they will demonstrate enhanced self-assessment skills.

When used correctly portfolios can strengthen the relationship between instruction and assessment.

When Used Correctly Portfolios Can Strengthen the Relationship between Instruction and Assessment.   Because portfolios often incorporate products closely linked to classroom instruction, they can help strengthen the relationship between instruction and assessment.

Portfolios Can Enhance Teachers' Communication with Both Students and Parents. Providing regular student–teacher and parent–teacher conferences to review the contents of portfolios is an excellent way to enhance communication.

Now we will briefly review the weaknesses of portfolio assessments.

Scoring portfolios in a reliable manner is difficult.

Scoring Portfolios in a Reliable Manner Is Difficult.   Scoring portfolios reliably is a very challenging task. In addition to the error introduced by the subjective judgment of raters and difficulty establishing specific scoring criteria, inadequate standardization of portfolio content often results in limited comparability across students. As a result, reliability can be dismally low. For example, Nitko (2001) notes that the reliability of portfolio results is typically in the 0.40 to 0.60 range. If you think back on what you learned about interpreting reliability coefficients in Chapter 4, you will recall that this indicates that as much as 60% of the variability in portfolio scores is the result of measurement error. This should give all educators a reason to be cautious when using the results of portfolio assessments in assigning grades or making high-stakes decisions.

Conducting Portfolio Assessments Properly Is a Time-Consuming and Demanding Process.   Most educators agree that for portfolios to be an effective assessment technique teachers need to be committed to the process and willing to invest the time and energy necessary to make them work.

In summary, portfolios have significant strengths and weaknesses. On the positive side they provide a broad framework for examining a student's progress, encourage student participation in the assessment process, enhance communication, and strengthen the relationship between instruction and assessment. Clearly, these are laudable features. On the down side they demand considerable time and energy and have questionable reliability. Consider the comments of Hopkins (1998):

> The use of portfolios has great potential for enriching education and student assessment but should not be viewed as an alternative to traditional tests and examinations. Students still need to demonstrate proficiency on uniform tasks designed to be a representative sample of the objectives of a course of study. One may have wonderful tasks in a science portfolio (collections of rocks, leaves, insects, experiments) but have great gaps in understanding about major laws of physics, genetics, and so on. (p. 311)

We largely concur with Dr. Hopkins. Portfolios (and other performance assessments) hold great potential for enriching educational assessment practices. They have considerable strengths and when used in a judicious manner will enhance the assessment of students. At

TABLE 10.11   Strengths and Weaknesses of Portfolio Assessments

Strengths of Portfolio Assessments
1. Portfolios are particularly good at reflecting student achievement and growth over time.
2. Portfolios may help motivate students and get them more involved in the learning process.
3. Portfolios may enhance students' ability to evaluate their own performances and products.
4. When used correctly portfolios can strengthen the relationship between instruction and assessment.
5. Portfolios can enhance teachers' communication with both students and parents.

Weaknesses of Portfolio Assessments
1. Scoring portfolios in a reliable manner is difficult.
2. Conducting portfolio assessments properly is a time-consuming and demanding process.

the same time we encourage teachers to be aware of the specific strengths and weaknesses of *all* assessment techniques and to factor these in when developing their own procedures for assessing student achievement. No approach to assessment—whether it is selected-response items, constructed-response items, performance assessments, or portfolios—should be viewed as *the only way* to assess student achievement. As we have repeatedly stated, no single assessment approach can adequately assess all of the complex skills and knowledge taught in today's schools. By using multiple approaches to assessment, one can capitalize on the strengths of the different approaches in order to elicit the most useful, reliable, and accurate information possible. Table 10.11 provides a summary of the strengths and weaknesses of portfolio assessments.

Summary

In this chapter we focused on performance assessments and portfolios. These special types of constructed-response tasks have been around for many years, but have gained increasing popularity in schools in recent years. To many educators performance assessments are seen as a positive alternative to traditional paper-and-pencil tests. Critics of traditional paper-and-pencil tests complain that they emphasize rote memory and other low-level learning objectives. In contrast they praise performance assessments, which they see as measuring higher-level outcomes that mirror real-life situations.

Performance assessments require students to complete a process or produce a product in a setting that resembles real-life situations (AERA et al., 1999). Performance assessments can be used to measure a broad range of educational objectives, ranging from those emphasizing communication skills (e.g., giving a speech, writing a term paper), to art (e.g., painting, sculpture), to physical education (e.g., tennis, diving, golf). Due to this diversity, it is difficult to develop specific guidelines, but some general suggestions can facilitate the development of performance assessments. These can be categorized as guidelines for selecting performance tasks, developing clear instructions, developing procedures for evaluating students' performance, and implementing procedures for minimizing rating errors. These are listed next.

Selecting Appropriate Performance Tasks
- Select tasks that provide the most direct measure of the educational objective.
- Select tasks that maximize your ability to generalize.
- Select tasks that reflect essential skills.
- Select tasks that encompass more than one educational objective.
- Select tasks that focus evaluation on the processes and/or products you interested in.
- Select tasks that provide the desired degree of realism.
- Select tasks that measure skills that are "teachable."
- Select tasks that are fair.
- Select tasks that can be assessed given the time and resources available.
- Select tasks that can be scored in a reliable manner.
- Select tasks that reflect objectives that cannot be measured using traditional assessments.

Developing Instructions That Clearly Specifies
What the Student Is Expected to Do
- Instructions should match the educational level of the students.
- Instructions should avoid jargon or unnecessary technical language.
- Instructions should specify the purpose or goal of the task.
- Instructions should specify the type of response you expect.
- Instructions should specify all the important parameters of the task (e.g., time limits).
- Instructions should specify the criteria used to evaluate the student's responses.
- Instructions should be clear to students from different backgrounds.

Developing Procedures to Evaluate
the Students' Responses
- Select important criteria that will be considered when evaluating student responses.
- Specify explicit standards that illustrate different levels of performance on each criteria.
- Determine what type of scoring procedure you will use (e.g., rating scale, checklist).

Implementing Procedures to Minimize Errors in Rating
- Have trusted colleagues evaluate your scoring rubric.
- Rate performances without knowing the student's identity.
- Rate the performance of every student on one task before proceeding to the next task.
- Be sensitive to the presence of leniency, severity, or central tendency errors.
- Conduct a preliminary reliability analysis.
- Have more than one teacher rate each student's performance.

As with all types of assessments procedures, performance assessments have strengths and weaknesses. Strengths of performance assessments include:

- They can measure abilities not assessable using other assessments.
- They are consistent with modern learning theory.
- They may result in better instruction.
- They may make learning more meaningful and help motivate students.

- They allow you to assess process as well as products.
- They can broaden your approach to assessment.

Their weaknesses include:

- They are difficult to score in a reliable manner.
- They provide limited sampling of the content domain, and it is often difficult to make generalizations about the knowledge and skills the students possess.
- They are time consuming and require considerable effort.

Portfolios are a specific type of performance assessment that involves the systematic collection of a student's work products over a period of time according to a specific set of guidelines (AERA et al., 1999). Guidelines for developing and using portfolios include:

- Specify the purpose of the portfolio (e.g., enhance learning, grading, both?).
- Decide on what type of items will be placed in the portfolio.
- Specify who will select the items to include in the portfolio.
- Establish procedures for evaluating the portfolios.
- Promote student involvement in the process.

Strengths of portfolios include:

- Portfolios are good at reflecting student achievement and growth over time.
- Portfolios may help motivate students and get them more involved in the learning process.
- Portfolios may enhance students' ability to evaluate their own performances and products.
- When used correctly portfolios can strengthen the relationship between instruction and assessment.
- Portfolios can enhance teachers' communication with both students and parents.

Weaknesses of portfolios include:

- Scoring portfolios in a reliable manner is difficult.
- Conducting portfolio assessments properly is a time-consuming and demanding process.

We concluded this chapter by noting that performance assessments have considerable strengths and when used in a prudent manner they can enhance the assessment of students. As a general rule, we recommend that you limit the use of performance assessments to the measurement of educational objectives that cannot be adequately measured using techniques that afford more objective and reliable scoring. At the same time we noted that there are many such objectives. We stressed that no single approach to assessment should be viewed as the one and only way to assess student achievement. As stated before, no single assessment approach can adequately assess all of the complex skills and knowledge taught in today's schools. By using multiple approaches to assessment, one can take advantage of the strengths of the different approaches and obtain the most useful, reliable, and accurate information possible.

KEY TERMS AND CONCEPTS

Actual performance assessment,
    p. 240
Alternative assessments, p. 241
Analogue performance assessment,
    p. 240
Analytic scoring rubrics, p. 250
Artificial performance assessment,
    p. 240
Authentic assessment, p. 241
Best work portfolios, p. 263
Central tendency errors,
    p. 254

Checklists, p. 251
Evaluation of products and
    processes, p. 260
Evaluation portfolios, p. 263
Extended-response performance
    assessment, p. 242
Growth or learning-progress
    portfolios, p. 263
Halo effect, p. 254
Holistic rubrics, p. 250
Leniency errors, p. 254
Logical error, p. 254

Order effects, p. 254
Performance assessments, p. 239
Personal biases, p. 254
Portfolios, p. 262
Rating scales, p. 251
Reliability decay, p. 254
Representative portfolios,
    p. 263
Restricted-response performance
    assessment, p. 242
Scoring rubrics, p. 249
Severity error, p. 254

RECOMMENDED READINGS

Feldt, L. (1997). Can validity rise when reliability declines? *Applied Measurement in Education, 10,* 377–387. This extremely interesting paper argues that at least in theory performance tests of achievement can be more valid than constructed-response tests even though the performance assessments have lower reliability. He notes that now the challenge is to find empirical examples of this theoretical possibility.

Rosenquist, A., Shavelson, R., & Ruiz-Primo, M. (2000). On the "exchangeability" of hands-on and computer-simulated science performance assessments (CSE Technical Report 531). Stanford University, CA: CRESST. Previous research has shown inconsistencies between scores on hands-on and computer-simulated performance assessments. This paper examines the sources of these inconsistencies.

INTERNET SITE OF INTEREST

www.cresst.org
    The Web site for the National Center for Research on Evaluation Standards and Student Testing (CRESST) provides a plethora of informational resources on performance assessment and portfolios. For example, you can access previous newsletters and reports.

11 Assigning Grades on the Basis of Classroom Assessments

I love teaching, but I find assigning grades at the end of a semester to be a very difficult and unpleasant process!

C H A P T E R   H I G H L I G H T S

Feedback and Evaluation

Reporting Student Progress:
  Which Symbols to Use?

The Basis for Assigning Grades

Frame of Reference

Combining Grades into a Composite

Informing Students of Grading System

Parent Conferences

L E A R N I N G   O B J E C T I V E S

After reading and studying this chapter, students should be able to:

1. Define formative and summative evaluation and explain the roles they play in teaching.
2. Describe the advantages and disadvantages of assigning grades or marks.
3. Explain what is meant by formal and informal evaluation, and the advantage of formal evaluation.
4. Describe the use of formative evaluation in summative evaluation, including when it is desirable and when it is not desirable.
5. Describe the common symbols used for reporting student progress.
6. Explain why assessment experts recommend against mixing achievement and nonachievement factors when assigning grades.
7. Compare and contrast the strengths and weaknesses of norm-referenced and criterion-referenced grading procedures.
8. Explain why assessment experts recommend against using achievement relative to aptitude, improvement, or effort as a frame of reference for assigning grades.
9. Explain and demonstrate the appropriate procedures for combining grades into a composite.
10. Explain the importance of providing students and parents information on your grading system.
11. Explain some considerations when holding conferences with parents.

The process of teaching is a dialogue between the teacher and the student. One important aspect of this dialogue, both oral and written, is the evaluation of student performance. This evaluative process includes the testing procedures described in the last four chapters. Additionally, in most schools it is mandatory for student evaluations to include the assignment of grades or marks. In this context, **marks** are typically defined as cumulative grades that reflect students' academic progress during a specific period of instruction. In this chapter we will be using the term **score** to reflect performance on a single assessment procedure (e.g., test or homework assignment), and **grades** and *marks* interchangeably to denote a cumulative evaluation of student performance (e.g., cumulative semester grade). In actual practice, people will often use *score, grade,* and *mark* synonymously.

Marks **are cumulative grades that reflect student progress during a specific period of instruction.**

Our discussion will address a variety of issues associated with the process of assigning grades or marks. First we will discuss some of the ways tests and other assessment procedures are used in schools. This includes providing feedback to students and making evaluative judgments regarding their progress and achievement. In this context we also discuss the advantages and disadvantages of assigning grades. Next we discuss some of the more practical aspects of assigning grades. For example, "What factors should be considered when assigning grades?" and "What frame of reference should be used when assigning grades?" We then turn to a slightly technical, but hopefully practical, discussion of how to combine scores into a composite or cumulative grade. Finally, we present some suggestions on presenting information about grades to students and parents.

Feedback and Evaluation

We have noted that tests and other assessment procedures are used in many ways in school settings. For example, tests can be used to provide feedback to students about their progress, to evaluate their achievement, and to assign grades. Often, testing applications can be classified as either formative or summative. **Formative evaluation** involves evaluative activities that are aimed at providing feedback to students. In this context, feedback implies the communication of information concerning a student's performance or achievement that is intended to have a corrective effect. Formative evaluation is typically communicated directly to the students and is designed to direct, guide, and modify their behavior. To be useful it should indicate to the students what is being done well and what needs improvement. By providing feedback in a timely manner, formative evaluation can help divide the learning experience into manageable components and provide structure to the instructional process. Because tests can provide explicit feedback about what one has learned and what yet needs to be mastered, they make a significant contribution to the learning process. The students are made aware of any gaps in their knowledge and learn which study strategies are effective and which are not. In addition to guiding learning, tests may enhance or promote student motivation. Receiving a "good" score on a weekly test

Formative evaluation **involves evaluative activities aimed at providing feedback to students.** *Summative evaluation* **involves the determination of the worth, value, or quality of an outcome.**

may provide positive reinforcement to students, and avoiding "poor" scores can motivate students to increase their study activities.

Summative evaluation involves the determination of the worth, value, or quality of an outcome. In the classroom summative evaluation typically involves the formal evaluation of performance or progress in a course, often in the form of a numerical or letter grade or mark. Summative evaluation is often directed to others beside the student, such as parents and administrators. Grades are generally regarded in our society as formal recognition of a specific level of mastery. Significant benefits of grades include:

Grades **are generally regarded in our society as formal recognition of a specific level of mastery.**

- Although there is variation in the way grades are reported (e.g., letter grades, numerical grades), most people are reasonably familiar with their interpretation. Grades provide a practical system for communicating information about student performance.
- Ideally, summative evaluations provide a fair, unbiased system of comparing students that minimizes irrelevant criteria such as socioeconomic status, gender, race, and so on. This goal is worthy even if attainment is less than perfect. If you were to compare the students who entered European or American universities a century ago with those of today, you would find that privilege, wealth, gender, and race count much less today than at that time. This is due in large part to the establishment of testing and grading systems that have attempted to minimize these variables. This is not to suggest that the use of tests has completely eliminated bias, but that they reflect a more objective approach to evaluation that may help reduce the influence of irrelevant factors.

Naturally, summative evaluations also have significant limitations, including:

Although grades have their advantages, they are only brief summary statements that fail to convey rich details about a student's achievement.

- Grades are only brief summary statements that fail to convey a great deal of the information carefully collected by teachers. For example, a grade of a B only hints at a general level of mastery and tells little or nothing about specific strengths and weaknesses.
- Although most people are familiar with grades and their general meaning, there is considerable variability in the meaning of grades across teachers, departments, and schools. For example, an A in one class might reflect a higher degree of achievement or mastery than is required to receive an A in another class. Some teachers and schools are more rigorous and have higher standards than others. Most students in college have been urged by friends to take a course being offered by a specific professor because he or she is a more lenient grader than other professors. As a result, it is difficult to generalize about the absolute meaning of a specific grade.
- Although grades are only a brief summary of performance, competition for high grades may become more important than mastery of content. That is, grades become the goal in and of themselves and actual achievement becomes secondary. As a correlate of this, students sometimes have difficulty separating their worth as individuals from their achievement in school. Particularly in an academically oriented home in which achievement is highly valued, students may misinterpret grades as an assess-

ment of self-worth. To ameliorate this tendency, teachers and parents should be careful to differentiate academic performance from personal value and worth.

As you can see from this brief discussion, grades have both significant benefits and limitations. Nevertheless, they are an engrained aspect of most educational systems and are more than likely going to be with us for the foreseeable future. As a result, it behooves us to understand how to assign grades in a responsible manner that capitalizes on their strengths and minimizes their limitations. Special Interest Topic 11.1 provides a brief history of grading policies in universities and public schools.

SPECIAL INTEREST TOPIC **11.1**

A Brief History of Grading

Brookhart (2004) provides a discussion of the history of grading in the United States. Here are a few of the key developments she notes in this time line.

- **Pre 1800:** Grading procedures were first developed in universities. Brookhart's research suggests that the first categorical grading scale was used at Yale in 1785 and classified students as *Optimi* (i.e., best), *Second Optimi* (i.e., second best), *Inferiores* (i.e., lesser), and *Pejores* (i.e., worse). In 1813 Yale adopted a numerical scale by which students were assigned grades between 1 and 4 with decimals used to reflect intermediary levels. Some universities developed scales with more categories (e.g., 20) whereas others tried simple pass–fail grading.
- **1800s:** The common school movement of the 1800s saw the development of public schools designed to provide instruction to the nation's children. Initially these early schools adopted grading scales similar to those in use at universities. About 1840 schools started the practice of distributing report cards. Teachers at the time complained that assessment and grading were too burdensome and parents complained the information was difficult to interpret. These complaints are still with us today!
- **1900s:** Percentage grading was common in secondary schools and universities at the beginning of the twentieth century. By 1910, however, educators began to question the reliability and accuracy of using a scale with 100 different categories or scale points. By the 1920s the use of letter grades (A, B, C, D, and F) was becoming the most common practice. During the remainder of the 1900s, a number of grading issues came to the forefront. For example, educators became increasingly aware that nonachievement factors (e.g., student attitudes and behaviors and teacher biases) were influencing the assignment of grades and recognized that this was not a desirable situation. Additionally there was a debate regarding the merits of norm-referenced versus criterion-referenced grading systems. Finally, efforts were made to expand the purpose of grades so they not only served to document the students' level of academic achievement but also served to enhance the learning of students. As you might expect, these are all issues that educators continue to struggle with to this day also.

In some aspects we have come a long way in refining the ways we evaluate the performance of our students. At the same time, we are still struggling with many of the same issues we struggled with a hundred years ago.

Formal and Informal Evaluation

Summative evaluation, by its very nature, is typically formal and documented in writing. Formative evaluation, however, is often informal. Teachers are constantly evaluating student performance throughout the school day. **Informal evaluation** is not planned beforehand and is not standardized. Often the feedback takes the form of a comment such as "that is outstanding," or "that is not quite right, try again." Although it is usually presented is a non-threatening manner, public evaluation can be embarrassing or humiliating when thoughtlessly conducted by the teacher. This can result in students developing negative attitudes toward both teachers and school. These negative attitudes can be very difficult to change and these regrettable situations should be avoided. Another potential problem with informal evaluations is that they may not be applied in a consistent manner. For example, some students may receive more consistent feedback than others, which may give them an advantage on upcoming tests and assignments. Additionally, informal evaluations are rarely recorded or documented. Although some teachers do develop daily summative ratings based on their general impression of the students' performance, this is not standard practice and represents the exception rather than the rule.

> **Whereas summative evaluation is typically formal and documented in writing, formative evaluation is often informal.**

Whereas formative evaluation is often informal, a formal approach is superior because it is more likely to be applied consistently and result in a written record. In fact the development of processes of **formal evaluation** was largely in response to the unreliability and invalidity of informal evaluations. Probably every teacher has perceived a student to be doing well in class until an examination brings to light gross deficiencies in the student's knowledge or skills. In contrast, most of us have known students who appear disengaged or otherwise doing poorly in class until an assessment allows them to demonstrate mastery of the relevant knowledge and skills. Most teachers report to students their progress by assigning scores to tests and other assignments. These scores are formal evaluations, but they are of limited utility as feedback unless greater detail is provided regarding specific student strengths and weaknesses. As a result, a formal approach to formative evaluation should always include comments reflecting which learning objectives have been mastered and which have not. It can be very frustrating for students to receive a score of 75 on a writing homework assignment without any indication of how they can improve their performance. Accordingly, a midterm examination will provide little useful feedback unless the teacher provides a thorough review of the test. A score of 75 tells the student practically nothing of the areas in which he or she is deficient or how to perform better in the future.

The Use of Formative Evaluation in Summative Evaluation

> **Formative evaluations are often incorporated into a summative evaluation. This procedure is reasonable if the material is topical and questionable if the content is sequential.**

Formative evaluations are often incorporated into a summative evaluation. For example, teachers will often have a number of small assignments and tests that are primarily designed to evaluate student progress and provide feedback to students, with the scores on these assignments contributing to the final course grade. This procedure is reasonable if the material is topical and questionable if the content is sequential. Sequential content is material that must be learned in a particular order, such as mathematics. For example, students learn addition and subtraction of single digits before progressing to double digits. Topical content, on the other hand, can often be learned equally well in various orders. Literature typically can be taught in many different ways because the various topics can be ordered to fit many different teaching strategies. For example, in literature a topic can be taught chronologically, such as with the typical survey of English literature, or topically, such as with a course organized around the type of writing: essay, poem, short story, and novel. In this last example, content within each category might itself be organized in a topical or sequential manner.

The cumulative grade or mark in a course is typically considered a judgment of the mastery of content or overall achievement. If certain objectives are necessary to master later ones, it makes little sense in grading the early objectives as part of the final grade because they must have been attained in order to progress to the later objectives. For example, in studying algebra one must master the solution of single-variable equations before progressing to the solution of two-variable equations. Suppose a student receives a score of 70 on a test involving single-variable equations and a 100 on a later test involving two-variable equations. Should the 70 and 100 be averaged? If so, the resulting grade reflects the average mastery of objectives at selected times in the school year, not final mastery of objectives. Should only the latest score be used? If so, what of the student who got a 100 on the first test and a 70 on the second test? These grades indicate a high degree of mastery of the earlier objectives and less mastery of later objectives. What should be done? Our answer is that for sequential content, summative evaluation should be based *primarily* on performance at the conclusion of instruction. At that point the student will demonstrate which objectives have been mastered and which have not. Earlier evaluations indicate only the level of performance at the time of measurement and penalize students who take longer to master the objectives but who eventually master them within the time allowed for mastery. This is not to minimize the importance or utility of employing formative evaluation with sequential material, only that formative evaluation may be difficult to meaningfully incorporate into summative evaluation. With sequential material, use formative evaluations to provide feedback, but when assigning grades emphasize the students' achievement at the conclusion of instruction.

Topical content, material that is related but with objectives that need not be mastered in any particular order, can be evaluated more easily in different sections. Here formative evaluations can easily serve as part of the summative evaluation. There is little need or reason to repetitively test the objectives in each subsequent evaluation. Mixed content, in which some objectives are sequential and others topical, should be evaluated by a combination of the two approaches. Later in this chapter we will show you how you can "weight" different assessments and assignments to meet your specific needs.

Reporting Student Progress: Which Symbols to Use?

Letter grades **are the most popular method of reporting student progress and are used in the majority of schools.**

The decision about how to report student achievement is often decided for teachers by administrators at the state or district level. **Letter grades** (i.e., A, B, C, D, F) are the most popular method of reporting student progress and are used in the majority of schools and universities today. Although there might be some variation in the meaning attached to them, letter grades are typically interpreted as:

A = excellent or superior achievement
B = above-average achievement
C = average achievement
D = below-average or marginal achievement
F = failing or poor performance

Students and parents generally understand letter grades, and the evaluative judgment represented by the grade is probably more widely accepted than any other system available. However, as we alluded to in the previous section, letter grades do have limitations. One significant limitation of letter grades is that they are only a summary statement and convey relatively little useful information beyond the general or aggregate level of achievement. Although teachers typically have considerable qualitative information about their students' specific strengths and weaknesses, much of this information is lost when it is distilled down to a letter grade. In some schools teachers are allowed to use pluses and minuses with letter grades (e.g., A– or C+). This approach provides more categories for classification, but still falls short of conveying rich qualitative information about student achievement. Special Interest Topic 11.2 provides information on how some schools are experimenting with deleting "Ds" from their grading scheme.

Naturally, other grading systems are available, including the following.

Numerical Grades. **Numerical grades** are similar to letter grades in that they attempt to succinctly represent student performance, here with a number instead of a letter. Numerical grades may provide more precision than letter grades. For example, the excellent performance represented by a grade of A may be further divided into numerical grades ranging from the elusive and coveted 100 to a grade of 90. Nevertheless, numerical grades still only summarize student performance and fail to capture much rich detail.

Verbal Descriptors. Another approach is to replace letter grades with **verbal descriptors** such as *excellent, above average, satisfactory,* or *needs improvement.* Although the number of categories varies, this approach simply replaces traditional letter grades with verbal descriptors in an attempt to avoid any ambiguity regarding the meaning of the mark.

Pass–Fail. **Pass–fail grades** and other two-category grading systems have been used for many years. For example, some high schools and universities offer credit/no-credit grading for selected courses (usually electives). A variant is mastery grading, which is well suited for situations that emphasize a mastery learning approach in which all or most students are expected to master the learning objectives and given the time necessary to do so. In situations in which the learning objectives are clearly specified, a two-category grading system may be appropriate, but otherwise it may convey even less information than traditional letter/numerical grades or verbal descriptors.

SPECIAL INTEREST TOPIC **11.2**

Schools No Longer Assigning Ds?

Hoff (2003) reports that some California high schools are considering deleting the letter D from their grading systems. He notes that at one high school the English department has experimented with deleting Ds with some success. The rationale behind the decision is that students who are making Ds are not mastering the material at the level expected by the schools. This became apparent when schools noticed that the students making Ds in English were, with very few exceptions, failing the state-mandated exit examination. This caused them to question whether it is appropriate to give students a passing grade if it is almost assured that they will not pass the standardized assessment required for them to progress to the next grade or graduate. Schools also hoped that this policy would motivate some students to try a little harder and elevate their grades to Cs. There is some evidence that this is happening. For example, after one English department did away with Ds, approximately one-third of the students who had made Ds the preceding quarter raised their averages to a C level, while about two-thirds received Fs. The policy has generally been well received by educators and is likely to be adopted by other departments and schools.

Supplemental Systems.   Many teachers and/or schools have adopted various approaches to replace or supplement the more traditional marking systems. For example, some teachers use a checklist of specific learning objectives to provide additional information about their students' strengths and weaknesses. Other teachers use letters, phone conversations, or individual conferences with parents to convey more specific information about their students' individual academic strengths and weaknesses. Naturally, all of these approaches can be used to supplement the more traditional grading/marking systems.

The Basis for Assigning Grades

Another essential question in assigning grades involves a decision regarding the **basis for grades.** By this we mean "Are grades assigned purely on the basis of academic achievement, or are other student characteristics taken into consideration?" For example, when assigning grades should one take into consideration factors such as a student's attitudes, behavior, class participation, punctuality, work/study habits, and so forth? As a general rule these nonachievement factors receive more consideration in elementary school, whereas in the secondary grades the focus narrows to achievement (Hopkins, 1998). While recognizing the importance of these nonachievement factors, most assessment experts recommend that actual academic achievement be the sole basis for assigning achievement grades. If desired, teachers should assign separate ratings for these nonachievement factors (e.g., excellent, satisfactory, and unsatisfactory). The key is that these factors should be rated separately and independently from achievement grades. This keeps academic grades as relatively pure marks of achievement that are not contaminated by nonachievement factors. When educators mix achievement and nonachievement factors, the meaning of the grades is blurred.

When educators mix achievement and nonachievement factors, the meaning of grades is blurred.

TABLE 11.1   Report Form Reflecting Achievement and Nonachievement Factors

Student Achievement: The following grades reflect the student's achievement in each academic area.

Grades: A = Excellent
B = Above Average
C = Average
D = Below Average
F = Failing

Subject	Grade
Reading	_____
Writing	_____
English	_____
Math	_____
Social studies	_____
Science	_____

Student Behavior: The following scores reflect the student's behavior at school.

Rating Scale: E = Excellent
S = Satisfactory
N = Needs Improvement
U = Unsatisfactory

Student's effort	E	S	N	U
Follows directions	E	S	N	U
Acts responsibly	E	S	N	U
Completes and returns work	E	S	N	U
Interacts well with peers	E	S	N	U
Interacts well with adults	E	S	N	U
Overall Classroom Behavior	**E**	**S**	**N**	**U**

Table 11.1 provides an example of an elementary school report intended to separate achievement from other factors. Special Interest Topic 11.3 addresses the issue of lowering grades as a means of classroom discipline.

Frame of Reference

Once you have decided what to base your grades on (hopefully academic achievement), you need to decide on the **frame of reference** you will use. In the following sections we will discuss the most common frames of references.

Norm-Referenced Grading (Relative Grading)

Norm-referenced or relative grading involves comparing each student's performance to that of a specific reference group.

The first frame of reference we will discuss is referred to as **norm-referenced grading** or **relative grading** and involves comparing each student's performance to that of a specific reference group (comparable to the norm-referenced approach to score interpretation discussed in Chapter 3). This approach to assigning grades is also re-

SPECIAL INTEREST TOPIC **11.3**

Grading and Punishment?

Nitko (2001) distinguishes between "failing work" and "failure to try." Failing work is work of such poor quality that it should receive a failing grade (i.e., F) based on its merits. Failure to try is when the student, for some reason, simply does not do the work. Should students who fail to try receive a failing grade? What about students who habitually turn in their assignments late? Should they be punished by lowering their grades? What about students who are caught cheating? Should they be given a zero? These are difficult questions that don't have simple answers.

Nitko (2001) contends that it is invalid to assign a grade of F for both failing work and failure to try because they do not represent the same construct. The F for failing work represents unacceptable achievement or performance. In contrast, failing to try could be due to a host of factors such as forgetting the assignment, misunderstanding the assignment, or simply defiant behavior. The key factor is that failing to try does not necessarily reflect unacceptable achievement or performance. Likewise, Nitko contends that it is invalid to lower grades as punishment for turning in assignments late. This confounds achievement with discipline.

Along the same lines, Stiggins (2001) recommends that students caught cheating should not be given a zero because this does not represent their true level of achievement. In essence, these authors are arguing that from a measurement perspective you should separate the grade from the punishment or penalty. Nitko (2001) notes that these are difficult issues, but they are classroom management or discipline issues rather than measurement issues. As an example of a suggested solution, Stiggins (2001) recommends that instead of assigning a zero to students caught cheating, it is preferable to administer another test to the student and use this grade. This way, punishment is addressed as a separate issue that the teacher can handle in a number of ways (e.g., detention or in-school suspension). Teachers face these issues on a regular basis, and you should consider them carefully before you are faced with them in the classroom.

ferred to as "grading on the curve." Although the reference group varies, it is often the students in a single classroom. For example, a teacher might specify the following criteria for assigning marks:

Mark	Percentage of Students Receiving Mark
A	10%
B	20%
C	40%
D	20%
F	10%

With this arrangement, in a class of 20 students, the 2 students receiving the highest grades will receive As, the next 4 students will receive Bs, the next 8 students will receive Cs, the next 4 students will receive Ds, and the 2 students with the lowest scores will receive Fs. An advantage of this type of grading system is that it is straightforward and clearly specifies what grades students will receive. A second advantage is that it helps prevent *grade inflation,* which occurs when teachers are too lenient in their grading and a large proportion of their students receive unwarranted high marks.

This approach to assigning grades does have limitations. Possibly the most prominent limitation is that there can be considerable variability among reference groups. If the reference group is a single classroom, some classes will be relatively high achieving and some relatively low achieving. If a student is fortunate enough to be in a low-achieving class, he or she will stand a much better chance of receiving a high grade than if he or she is in a high-achieving class. But consider the unlucky "average" student who is assigned to a very high-achieving class. Although this student's performance might have been sufficient to earn a respectable mark in an average classroom, relative to the high-achieving students the student might receive a poor grade. Additionally, if the teacher strictly follows the guidelines, a certain percentage of students will receive poor grades by default. To overcome this, some teachers maintain records over several years in order to establish more substantive reference data. In this manner a teacher can reduce the influence of variability in class achievement. The use of large reference groups containing data from many classes accumulated over time is the one of the best approaches to help minimize this limitation.

Gronlund (1998) provides another approach to reducing the effect of variability in class achievement. He recommends using ranges of percentages instead of precise percentages. For example:

Mark	Percentage of Students Receiving Mark
A	10–20%
B	20–30%
C	40–50%
D	10–20%
F	0–10%

This approach gives the teacher some flexibility in assigning grades. For example, in a gifted and talented class one would expect more As and Bs, and few Ds or Fs. The use of percent ranges provides some needed flexibility.

Another limitation of the norm-referenced approach is that the percentage of students being assigned specific grades is often arbitrarily assigned. In our example we used 20% for Bs and 40% for Cs; however, it would be just as defensible to use 15% for Bs and 50% for Cs. Often these percentages are set by the district or school administrators, and one criteria is not intrinsically better than another. A final limitation is that with relative grading, grades are not specifically linked to an absolute level of achievement. At least in theory it would be possible for students in a very low-achieving group to receive relatively high marks without actually mastering the learning objectives. Accordingly, in a high-achieving class some students may fail even when they have mastered much of the material. Obviously neither of these outcomes is desirable!

Criterion-Referenced Grading (Absolute Grading)

Criterion-referenced grading or **absolute grading** involves comparing a student's performance to a specified level of performance. Although modern usage of the phrase "criterion-

Criterion-referenced or *absolute grading* **involves comparing a student's performance to a specified level of performance.**

referenced" is often associated with dichotomous conditions (e.g., pass or fail; mastery or nonmastery), this approach can also reflect a continuum of achievement. One of the most common criterion-referenced grading systems is the traditional percentage-based system. In it grades are based on percentages, usually interval bands based on a combination of grades from tests and other assignments. For example:

Mark	Percentage Required for Mark
A	90–100%
B	80–89%
C	70–79%
D	60–69%
F	< 60%

Many schools list such bands as formal criteria even though they are often modified in actual practice. An advantage of this grading approach is that the marks directly describe the performance of students without reference to other students. As a result, there is no limit on the number of students that receive any specific grade. For example, in a high-achieving class all students could conceivably receive As. Although such an extreme outcome is not likely in most schools, the issue is that there is no predetermined percentage of students that must receive each grade. Another advantage is that this system, like the norm-referenced approach, is fairly straightforward and easy to apply.

The major limitation of criterion-referenced or absolute grading is that there is considerable variability in the level of difficulty among tests and other academic assignments assigned by teachers. Some teachers create tests that are extremely difficult and others write relatively easy tests. Some teachers are consistently more rigorous in their grading than others. As a result, a rigorous teacher might have a class average of only 60% or 70%, whereas a more lenient teacher might have a class average of 80% or 90%. This inherent variability in difficulty level across courses makes it difficult to interpret or compare the meaning of scores based on an absolute standard in a consistent manner.

Achievement in Relation to Improvement or Effort

Some teachers feel students should be graded based on the amount of progress they demonstrate during the course of instruction. For example, if students with very poor skills at the beginning of instruction achieve a moderate level of achievement, they should receive a better grade than high-achieving students who have demonstrated only small gains. There are numerous problems with this approach. Examine the data listed in Table 11.2. If one takes the position that effort as measured by improvement should be the basis for grades, Joe's improvement, in number and percentage of words gained, is much greater than Mary's improvement. In contrast if the teacher bases grades on achievement, Joe's performance is far short of Mary's and she would receive the higher grade. To reward Joe more highly than Mary can be a risky procedure. What if Joe, knowing the basis for grading, deliberately scored low on the initial test in order to ensure a large gain? Should such actions be rewarded?

TABLE 11.2   Examples of Grading Based on Effort versus Achievement

	Joe	Mary
Score on spelling pretest	17	62
Score on spelling posttest	43	80
Gain	26	22
Percentage gain	153%	35%
Grade based on effort	A	C
Grade based on achievement	C	A

There are other problems associated with basing grades on effort or improvement. For example, the measurement of improvement or change is plagued with numerous technical problems (Cronbach & Furby, 1970). Additionally, you have the mixing of achievement with another factor, in this instance effort or improvement. As we suggested before, if you want to recognize effort or improvement, it is more defensible to assign separate scores to these factors. Achievement grades should reflect achievement and not be contaminated by other factors. Finally, although this approach is typically intended to motivate poor students, it can have a negative effect on better students. Based on these problems, our recommendation is not to reward effort/improvement over achievement except in special situations. One situation in which the reward of effort may be justified is in the evaluation of students with severe disabilities for whom grades may appropriately be used to reinforce effort.

If you want to recognize effort or improvement, it is best to assign separate scores to these factors.

Achievement Relative to Ability

Although some teachers have tried to base grades on effort/improvement, others have attempted to base grades on achievement relative to ability or aptitude. In this context, ability or aptitude is usually based on performance on an intelligence test. For example, a student with average intelligence who scores above average on tests of achievement is considered an overachiever and receives good grades. Accordingly, an underachiever is a student whose achievement is considered low in relation to his or her level of intelligence. Like attempts to base grades on effort/improvement, there are numerous problems associated with this approach, including (1) technical problems (e.g., unreliable comparisons), (2) inconsistency in the way IQ is measured, and (3) teachers are not typically given the advanced training necessary to interpret intelligence or aptitude tests. These problems all argue against basing grades on a comparison of achievement and aptitude.

Recommendation

Although we recommend against using achievement relative to aptitude, effort, or improvement as a frame of reference for assigning grades, we believe both absolute and relative grad-

Both norm-referenced (i.e., relative) and criterion-referenced (i.e., absolute) grading systems can be used successfully.

ing systems can be used successfully. They both have advantages and limitations, but when used conscientiously either approach can be effective. It is even possible for teachers to use a combination of absolute and relative grading systems in secondary schools and universities. For example, Hopkins (1998) recommends that high schools and colleges report a conventional absolute grade and also the students' relative standing in their graduating class (e.g., percentile rank). This would serve to reduce the differences in grading across schools. For example, a student might have a grade point average (GPA) of 3.0 but a percentile rank of 20. Although the GPA is adequate, the percentile rank of 20 (i.e., indicating the student scored better than only 20% of the other students) suggests that this school gives a high percentage of high grades.

Combining Grades into a Composite

When it is time to assign grades at the end of a six-week period, semester, or some other grading period, teachers typically combine results from a variety of assessments. This can include tests, homework assignments, performance assessments, and the like. The decision of how to weight these assessments is usually left to the teacher and reflects his or her determination of what should be emphasized and to what degree (see Special Interest Topic 11.4). For example, if a teacher believes the primary determiner of a course grade should be performance on tests, he or she would weight test performance heavily and place less emphasis on homework and term papers. Another teacher, with a different grading philosophy, might decide to emphasize homework and papers and place less emphasis on test performance. Whatever your grading philosophy, you need a system for effectively and efficiently combining scores from a variety of assessment procedures into a *composite score*. On initial examination this might appear to be a fairly simple procedure, but it is often more complicated than it appears.

The decision of how to weight assessments when calculating grades is usually left to the teachers and reflects their determination of what should be emphasized and to what degree.

Consider the following data illustrating a simple situation. Here we have two assessment procedures, a test and a homework assignment. For our initial example we will assume the teacher wants to weight them equally. The test has a maximum score of 100 whereas the homework assignment has a maximum value of 50.

Assessment	Range	Johnny	Sally
Achievement test	(40–100)	100	40
Homework	(20–50)	20	50
Composite		120	90

Johnny had a perfect score on the test but the lowest grade on the homework assignment. Sally had the opposite results, a perfect score on the homework assignment and the lowest score on the test. If the summed scores were actually reflecting equal weighting as the

SPECIAL INTEREST TOPIC   **11.4**

Some Thoughts on Weighting Assessment Procedures

The decision regarding how to weight different assessment procedures is a personal decision based on a number of factors. Some teachers emphasize homework, some tests, some term papers, and some performance assessments. No specific practice is clearly right or wrong, but an understanding of psychometric principles may offer some guidance. First, as we have stated numerous times, it is desirable to provide multiple assessment opportunities. Instead of relying on only a midterm and a final, it is best to provide numerous assessment opportunities spread over the grading period. Second, when possible it is desirable to incorporate different types of assessment procedures. Instead of relying exclusively on any one type of assessment, when feasible try to incorporate a variety. Finally, when determining weights, consider the psychometric properties of the different assessment procedures. For example, we often weight the assessments that produce the most reliable scores and valid interpretations more heavily than those with less sound psychometric properties. Table 11.2 provides one of our weighting procedures for an introductory psychology course in tests and measurement. All of the tests are composed of multiple-choice and short-answer items and make up 90% of the final grade. We include a term paper, but we are aware that its scores are less reliable and valid so we count it for only 10% of the total grade.

Naturally this approach emphasizing more objective tests is not appropriate for all classes. For example, it is difficult to assess performance in a graduate level course on professional ethics and issues using assessments that emphasize multiple-choice and short-answer. In this course we use a combination of tests composed of multiple-choice items, short-answer items, and restricted-response essays along with class presentations and position papers. The midterm and final examination receive a weighting of approximately 60% of the final grade, with the remaining 40% accounted for by more subjective procedures. In contrast, in an introductory psychology course, which typically has about 100 students in every section, we would likely use all multiple-choice tests. We would not be opposed to requiring a term paper or including some short-answer or restricted-response items on the tests, but due to the extensive time required to grade these procedures we rely on the objectively scored tests (which are scored in the computer center). We do provide multiple assessment opportunities in this course (four semester tests and a comprehensive final).

In addition to reliability/validity issues and time considerations, you may want to consider other factors. For example, because students may receive assistance from parents (or others) on homework assignments, their performance might not be based solely on their own abilities. This is also complicated by variability in the amount of assistance students receive. Some students may get considerable support/assistance from parents while others receive little or none. The same principle applies to time commitment. An adolescent with few extracurricular activities will have more time to complete homework assignments than one who is required to maintain a part-time job (or is involved in athletics, band, theater, etc.). If you provide no weight to homework assignments it removes any incentive to complete the work, whereas basing a large proportion of the grade on homework will penalize students who receive little assistance from parents or who are involved in many outside activities. Our best advice is to take these factors into consideration and adopt a balanced approach. Good luck!

teacher expects, the composite scores would be equal. Obviously they are not. Johnny's score (i.e., 120) is considerably higher than Sally's score (i.e., 90). The problem is that achievement test scores have more variability, and as a result they have an inordinate influence on the composite score.

To correct this problem you need to equate the scores by taking into consideration the differences in variability. Although different methods have been proposed for equating the scores, this can be accomplished in a fairly accurate and efficient manner by simply correcting for differences in the range of scores (it is technically preferable to use a more precise measure of variability than the range, but for classroom applications the range is usually sufficient). In our example, the test scores had a range of 60 while the homework scores had a range of 30. By multiplying the homework scores by 2 (i.e., our equating factor) we can equate the ranges of the scores and give them equal weight in the composite score. Consider the following illustration.

Student	Test Score	Equating Factor	Corrected Score	Homework Score	Equating Factor	Corrected Score	Composite Score
Johnny	100	× 1	**100**	20	× 2	**40**	140
Sally	40	× 1	**40**	50	× 2	**100**	140

Note that this correction resulted in the assignments being weighted equally; both students received the same composite score. If in this situation the teacher wanted to calculate a percentage-based composite score, he or she would simply divide the obtained composite score by the maximum composite score (in this case 200) and multiplying by 100. This would result in percentage-based scores of 70% for both Johnny and Sally.

In the previous example we assumed the teacher wanted the test and homework scores to be equally weighted. Now we will assume that the teacher wants the test score to count three times as much as the homework score. In this situation we would add another multiplier to weight the test score as desired.

Student	Test Score	Equating Factor	Desired Weight	Corrected Score	Homework Score	Equating Factor	Corrected Score	Composite Score
Johnny	100	× 1	× 3	**300**	20	× 2	**40**	340
Sally	40	× 1	× 3	**120**	50	× 2	**100**	220

With this weighting, Johnny's composite score (i.e., 340) is considerably higher than Sally's composite score (i.e., 220) because the teacher has chosen to place more emphasis on the test score relative to the homework assignments. If the teacher wanted to calculate a percentage-based composite score, he or she would divide the obtained composite score by the maximum composite score (in this case 400) and multiply by 100. This would result in percentage-based scores of 85% for Johnny and 55% for Sally.

A Short Cut.   Although the preceding approach is preferred from a technical perspective, it can be a little unwieldy and time consuming. Being sensitive to the many demands on a teacher's time, we will now describe a simpler and technically adequate approach that may be employed (e.g., Kubiszyn & Borich, 2000). With this approach, each component grade is converted to a percentage score by dividing the number of points awarded by the total potential number of points. Using data from the previous examples with an achievement test with a maximum score of 100 and a homework assignment with a maximum score of 50, we have the following results:

Assessment	Maximum	Johnny	Sally
Achievement test	(100)	$100/100 \times 100 = 100\%$	$40/100 \times 100 = 40\%$
Homework	(50)	$20/50 \times 100 = 40\%$	$50/50 \times 100 = 100\%$

This procedure equated the scores by converting them both to a 100-point scale (based on the assumption that the converted scores are comparable in variance). If one were then to combine these equated scores with equal weighting, you would get the following results:

	Achievement Test	Homework	Composite
Johnny	100%	40%	$140/2 = 70\%$
Sally	40%	100%	$140/2 = 70\%$

If one wanted to use different weights for the assessments, you would simply multiply each equated score by a percentage that represents the desired weighting of each assessment. For example, if you wanted the test score to count three times as much as the homework assignment, you would multiply the equated test score by 0.75 (i.e., 75%) and the equated homework score by 0.25 (i.e., 25%). Note that the weights (i.e., 75% and 25%) equal 100%. You would get the following results:

	Achievement Test	Homework	Composite
Johnny	$100 \times .75 = 75$	$40 \times .25 = 10$	$75 + 10 = 85\%$
Sally	$40 \times .75 = 30$	$100 \times .25 = 25$	$30 + 25 = 55\%$

As computers become increasingly available, more teachers will have access to computerized or electronic grade books. These grade books can greatly simplify the process of recording scores and computing grades.

Table 11.3 provides an expanded example of how this procedure can be used to calculate grades. As computers become increasingly available, more teachers will have access to computerized or electronic grade books. These grade books can greatly simplify the process of recording scores and computing grades. Table 11.4 provides some information on a few of the computerized grade books that are available commercially to help teachers record scores and calculate grades. Many textbook publishers and other educational suppliers provide similar grade book software to schools and teachers. These

TABLE 11.3   Example of Weighting Different Assessment Procedures

For this example, we will use the following weights:

Assessment Procedure	Value
Test 1	20%
Test 2	20%
Test 3	20%
Term paper	10%
Final examination	30%
Total	100%

The scores reported for each assessment procedure will be percent correct. As noted, a relatively easy way to equate your scores on different procedures is to report them as percent correct (computed as the number of points obtained by the student divided by the maximum number of points). We use the scores of three students in this illustration.

Assessment Procedure	Julie	Tommy	Stacey
Test 1	95 × .20 = 19	75 × .20 = 15	65 × .20 = 13
Test 2	97 × .20 = 19.4	80 × .20 = 16	55 × .20 = 11
Test 3	93 × .20 = 18.6	77 × .20 = 15.4	67 × .20 = 13.4
Term paper	92 × .10 = 9.2	85 × .10 = 8.5	72 × .10 = 7.2
Final examination	94 × .30 = 28.2	80 × .30 = 24	70 × .30 = 21
Total	94.4	78.9	65.6

As illustrated here, Julie's composite score is 94.4, Tommy's is 78.9, and Stacey's is 65.6. Using these fairly simple procedures, a teacher can weight any number of different assessment procedures in any desired manner.

TABLE 11.4   Commercially Available Grade Book Programs

As we indicated, there are a number of commercially available grade book programs. There are programs for both Mac and PC users and many of these programs reside completely on your computer. A new trend is Web-based applications that in addition to recording scores and calculating grades allow students and parents to check on their progress. Clearly with technological advances these programs will become more sophisticated and more widely available. Here are just a few of the many grade book programs available and their Web addresses:

- ClassAction Gradebook   www.classactiongradebook.com
- Jackson GradeQuick   www.jacksoncorp.com
- MyGrade Book   www.mygradebook.com
- ThinkWare Educator   www.thinkware.com

commercial grade books can greatly simplify the process of recording scores and computing grades.

Informing Students of Grading System

Students clearly have a right to know the procedures that will be used to determine their grades. This information should be given to the students early in a course and well before any assessment procedures are administered that are included in the grading process. A common question is "How old should students be before they can benefit from this information?" We believe any students who are old enough to be administered a test or given an assignment are also old enough to know how their grades will be determined. Parents should also be informed in a note or in person during conferences or visits what is expected of their children and how they will be graded. For students in upper elementary grades and beyond, an easy way to inform them of grading requirements is a handout such as shown in Table 11.5. This system is similar to those used by one of the authors in his classes.

Any students who are old enough to be administered a test are also old enough to know how their grades will be determined.

Parent Conferences

Most school systems try to promote parent–teacher communication, often in the form of parent conferences. Typically conferences serve to inform parents of all aspects of their child's progress, so preparation for a parent conference should result in a file folder containing a record of the child's performance in all areas. This may include information on social and behavioral development as well as academic progress. Conferences should be conducted as confidential, professional sessions. The teacher should focus on the individual student and avoid discussions of other students, teachers, or administrators. The teacher should present samples of students' work and other evidence of their performance as the

TABLE 11.5   Example of Grading Requirements Presented to Students at the Beginning of a Test and Measurement Course

Assessment Procedure		Value
Test 1		20%
Test 2		20%
Test 3		20%
Term paper		10%
Final examination		30%
	Total	100%

central aspect of the conference, explaining how each item fits into the grading system. If standardized test results are relevant to the proceedings, the teacher should carefully review the tests and their scoring procedures beforehand in order to present a summary of the results in language clearly understandable to the parents. In subsequent chapters we will address the use and interpretation of standardized tests in school settings.

Summary

In this chapter we focused on the issue of assigning grades based on the performance of students on tests and other assessment procedures. We started by discussing some of the different ways assessment procedures are used in the schools. Formative evaluation involves providing feedback to students whereas summative evaluation involves making evaluative judgments regarding their progress and achievement. We also discussed the advantages and disadvantages of assigning cumulative grades or marks. On the positive side, grades generally represent a fair system for comparing students that minimizes irrelevant characteristics such as gender or race. Additionally, because most people are familiar with grades and their meaning, grades provide an effective and efficient means of providing information about student achievement. On the down side, a grade is only a brief summary of a student's performance and does not convey detailed information about specific strengths and weaknesses. Additionally, although most people understand the general meaning of grades, there is variability in what grades actually mean in different classes and schools. Finally, student competition for grades may become more important than actual achievement, and students may have difficulty separating their personal worth from their grades, both undesirable situations.

Next we discussed some of the more practical aspects of assigning grades. For example, we recommended that grades be assigned solely on the basis of academic achievement. Other factors such as class behavior and attitude are certainly important, but when combined with achievement in assigning grades they blur the meaning of grades. Another important consideration is what frame of reference to use when assigning grades. Although different frames of references have been used and promoted, we recommend using either a relative (i.e., norm-referenced) or an absolute (i.e., criterion-referenced) grading approach, or some combination of the two.

We also provided a discussion with illustrations of how to combine grades into a composite or cumulative grade. When assigning grades, teachers typically wish to take a number of assessment procedures into consideration. Although this process may appear fairly simple, it is often more complicated than first assumed. We demonstrated that when forming composites it is necessary to equate scores by correcting for differences in the variance or range of the scores. In addition to equating scores for differences in variability, we also demonstrated how teachers can apply different weights to different assessment procedures. For example, a teacher may want a test to count two or three times as much as a homework assignment. We also provided examples of how these procedures can be applied in the classroom with relative ease. In closing, we presented some suggestions on presenting information about grades to students and parents.

KEY TERMS AND CONCEPTS

Absolute grading, p. 280
Basis for grades, p. 277
Composite scores, p. 283
Criterion-referenced grading,
  p. 280
Formal evaluation, p. 274
Formative evaluation, p. 271

Frame of reference, p. 278
Grades, p. 271
Informal evaluation, p. 274
Letter grades, p. 275
Marks, p. 271
Norm-referenced grading, p. 278
Numerical grades, p. 276

Pass–fail grades, p. 276
Relative grading, p. 278
Score, p. 271
Summative evaluation, p. 272
Verbal descriptors, p. 276

RECOMMENDED READING

Brookhart, S. M. (2004). *Grading.* Upper Saddle River, NJ: Pearson Merrill Prentice Hall. This provides a good discussion of issues related to grading practices.

CHAPTER 12

Standardized Achievement Tests in the Era of High-Stakes Assessment

Depending on your perspective, standardized achievement tests are either a bane or boon to public schools. Many politicians and ordinary citizens see them as a way of holding educators accountable and ensuring students are really learning. On the other hand, many educators feel standardized tests are often misused and detract from their primary job of educating students.

CHAPTER HIGHLIGHTS

Group-Administered Achievement Tests
Individual Achievement Tests
Selecting an Achievement Battery

LEARNING OBJECTIVES

After reading and studying this chapter, students should be able to:

1. Describe the characteristics of standardized tests and explain why standardization is important.
2. Describe the major characteristics of achievement tests.
3. Describe the major uses of standardized achievement tests in schools.
4. Explain what high-stakes testing means and trace the historical development of this phenomenon.
5. Compare and contrast group-administered and individually administered achievement tests.
6. Describe the strengths and weaknesses of group-administered and individually administered achievement tests.
7. Identify the major publishers of group achievement tests and their major tests.
8. Discuss the major issues and controversies surrounding state and high-stakes testing programs.
9. Describe and evaluate common procedures used for preparing students for standardized tests.
10. Describe and be able to apply the appropriate procedures for administering standardized assessments.
11. Describe and be able to apply the appropriate procedures for interpreting the results of standardized assessments.

12. Describe and evaluate the major individual achievement tests.
13. Describe the major factors that should be considered when selecting standardized achievement tests.

In this and subsequent chapters we will be discussing a variety of standardized tests commonly used in the public schools. In this chapter we will focus on standardized achievement tests. A **standardized test** is a test that is administered, scored, and interpreted in a standard manner. Most standardized tests are developed by testing professionals or test publishing companies. The goal of standardization is to ensure that testing conditions are as nearly the same as is possible for all individuals taking the test. If this is accomplished, no examinee will have an advantage over another due to variance in administration procedures, and assessment results will be comparable. An **achievement test** is a test designed to assess a student's knowledge or skills in a content domain in which he or she has received instruction (AERA et al., 1999). Naturally the vast majority of teacher-constructed classroom tests qualify as achievement tests, but they are not standardized. In describing standardized achievement tests, Linn and Gronlund (2000) highlighted the following characteristics:

A *standardized test* is a test that is administered, scored, and interpreted in a standard manner.

Achievement tests are designed to assess students' knowledge or skill in a content domain in which they have received instruction.

- Standardized achievement tests typically contain high-quality items that were selected on the basis of both quantitative and qualitative item analysis procedures.
- They have precisely stated directions for administration and scoring so that consistent procedures can be followed in different settings.
- Many contemporary standardized achievement tests provide both norm-referenced and criterion-referenced interpretations. Norm-referenced interpretation allows comparison to the performance of other students, whereas criterion-referenced interpretation allows comparison to an established criterion.
- The normative data are based on large, representative samples.
- Equivalent or parallel forms of the test are often available.
- They have professionally developed manuals and support materials that provide extensive information about the test; how to administer, score, and interpret it; and its measurement characteristics.

There are many different types of standardized achievement tests. Some achievement tests are designed for group administration whereas others are for individual administration. Individually administered achievement tests must be given to only one student at a time and require specially trained examiners. Some achievement tests focus on a single subject area (e.g., reading) whereas others cover a broad range of academic skills and content areas (e.g., reading, language, and mathematics). Some use selection type items exclusively whereas others contain constructed-response and performance assessments. In addition to coming in a variety of formats, standardized achievement tests have a number of different uses or applications in the schools. These include:

- One of the most common uses is to track student achievement over time or to compare group achievement across classes, schools, or districts.
- Standardized achievement tests are increasingly being used in high-stakes decision making. For example, they may be utilized to determine which students are promoted or allowed to graduate. They may also be used in evaluating and rating teachers, administrators, schools, and school districts.
- Achievement tests can help identify strengths and weaknesses of individual students.
- Achievement tests can be used to evaluate the effectiveness of instructional programs or curricula and help teachers identify areas of concern.
- A final major use of standard achievement tests is the identification of students with special educational requirements. For example, achievement tests might be used in assessing children to determine whether they qualify for special education services.

The current trend is toward more, rather than less, standardized testing in public schools.

The current trend is toward more, rather than less, standardized testing in public schools. For example, Doherty (2002) notes that all 50 states and the District of Columbia currently have statewide testing programs. This trend is largely attributed to the increasing emphasis on educational accountability and **high-stakes assessment.** Popham (2000) notes that although there have always been critics of public schools, calls for increased accountability became more strident and widespread in the 1970s. During this period news reports began to surface that publicized incidences of high school graduates being unable to demonstrate even the most basic academic skills such as reading and writing. Parents, who as taxpayers were footing the bill for their children's education, increasingly began to question the quality of the education being provided and demanded evidence that schools were actually educating their children. In efforts to assuage taxpayers, legislators started implementing statewide minimum-competency testing programs with the intent of guaranteeing that graduates of public schools were able to meet minimum academic standards. Although many students passed these exams, a substantial number of students failed and the public schools were largely blamed for the failures. In this era of increasing accountability, many schools developed more sophisticated assessment programs using both state-developed tests and commercially produced nationally standardized achievement tests. As the trend continued, it became common for local newspapers to rank schools according to their students' performance on these tests with the implication that a school's ranking reflected the effectiveness or quality of teaching.

Currently, the discussion over the use of standardized achievement tests in the public schools continues unabated with the debate over national testing taking center stage. While states continue to use a combination of state-developed tests and commercially developed nationally standardized achievement tests, there is no consistency from state to state. This means there is no way to compare the performance of students (or schools or school districts) in California with those in New York. State-developed tests vary considerably in what content and skills are measured and what level of performance is required to denote competence.

Additionally, although many commercial achievement tests are designed using national samples, different tests are used in different schools and again it is difficult to make comparisons at the national level. This has resulted in some calling for a **national testing program** that will facilitate comparisons at the national level (Boston, 2001). Plans for national testing have been incorporated in the Elementary and Secondary Education Act of 2001 (No Child Left Behind Act). This act requires states to test students annually in grades 3 through 8. Because most states typically administer standardized achievement tests in only a few of these grades, this new law will require more high-stakes testing than is currently in use (Kober, 2002). The debate continues and it is not possible to predict future events with any confidence, but standardized achievement tests will likely continue to play a major role in public schools for the foreseeable future. Regardless of your stance, it will be to your benefit to be familiar with the different types of standardized achievement tests used in our public schools.

The Elementary and Secondary Education Act of 2001 requires states to test students annually in grades 3 through 8.

In the remainder of this chapter we will introduce a number of standardized achievement tests. First we will provide brief descriptions of some major group achievement tests and discuss their applications in schools. We will then describe a number of individual achievement tests that are commonly used in schools. The goal of this chapter is to familiarize you with some of the salient characteristics of these tests and how they are used in schools.

Group-Administered Achievement Tests

Achievement tests can be classified as either individual or group tests. Individual tests are administered in a one-to-one testing situation. One testing professional (i.e., the examiner) administers the test to one individual (i.e., the examinee) at a time. In contrast, **group-administered tests** are those that can be administered to more than one examinee at a time. The main attraction of group administration is that it is an efficient way to collect information about students or other examinees. By efficient, we mean a large number of students can be assessed with a minimal time commitment from educational professionals. As you might expect, group-administered tests are very popular in school settings. For example, most teacher-constructed classroom tests are designed to be administered to the whole class at one time. Accordingly, if a school district wants to test all the students in grades 3 through 8, it would probably be impossible to administer a lengthy test to each student on a one-to-one basis. There is simply not enough time or enough teachers (or other educational professionals) to accomplish such a task without significantly detracting from the time devoted to instruction. However, when you can have one professional administer a test to 20 to 30 students at a time, the task can be accomplished in a reasonably efficient manner.

The main attraction of *group-administered tests* is that they are an efficient way to collect information about students' achievement.

Although efficiency is the most prominent advantage of group-administered tests, at least three other positive attributes of group testing warrant mentioning. First, because the role of the individual administering the test is limited, group tests will typically involve more uniform testing conditions than individual tests. Second, group tests frequently contain items that can be scored objectively, often even by a computer (e.g., selected–response items). This reduces or eliminates the measurement error introduced by the qualitative scoring procedures more common in individual tests. Finally, group tests often have very large standardization or normative samples. Normative samples for professionally developed group tests are often in the range of 100,000 to 200,000, whereas professionally developed **individually administered tests** will usually have normative samples ranging from 1,000 to 8,000 participants (Anastasi & Urbina, 1997).

Naturally, group tests have some limitations. For example, in a group-testing situation the individual administering the test has relatively little personal interaction with the individual examinees. As a result, there is little opportunity for the examiner to develop rapport with the examinees and closely monitor and observe their progress. Accordingly they have limited opportunities to make qualitative behavioral observations about the performance of their students and how they approach and respond to the assessment tasks. Another concern involves the types of items typically included on group achievement tests. Whereas some testing experts applaud group tests for often using objectively scored items, others criticize them because these items restrict the type of responses examinees can provide. This parallels the same argument for and against selected-response items we discussed in earlier chapters. Another limitation of group tests involves their lack of flexibility. For example, when administering individual tests the examiner is usually able to select and administer only those test items that match the examinee's ability level. With group tests, however, all examinees are typically administered all the items. As a result, examinees might find some items too easy and others too difficult, resulting in boredom or frustration and lengthening the actual testing time beyond what is necessary to assess the student's knowledge accurately (Anastasi & Urbina, 1997). It should be noted that publishers of major group achievement tests are taking steps to address these criticisms. For example, to allay concerns about the extensive use of selected-response items, an increasing number of standardized achievement tests is being developed that incorporate more constructed-response items and performance tasks. To address concerns about limited flexibility in administration, online and computer-based assessments are becoming increasingly available.

In this section we will be discussing a number of standardized group achievement tests. Many of these tests are developed by large test publishing companies and are commercially available to all qualified buyers (e.g., legitimate educational institutions). In addition to these commercially available tests, many states have started developing their own achievement tests that are specifically tailored to assess the state curriculum. These are often standards-based assessments used in high-stakes testing programs. For more information on standards-based assessment, see Special Interest Topic 12.1. We will start by briefly introducing some of the major commercially available achievement tests.

Commercially Developed Group Achievement Tests

In this section we will briefly introduce you to some of the most widely used commercially developed group achievement tests. By commercial, we mean these test batteries are developed for use in public schools around the nation and are available for purchase by qualified professionals or institutions. The most popular tests are comprehensive batteries designed to assess achievement in multiple academic areas such as reading, language arts, mathematics,

---

SPECIAL INTEREST TOPIC   12.1
Standards-Based Assessments

AERA et al. (1999) define standards-based assessments as tests that are designed to measure clearly defined content and performance standards. In this context, content standards are statements that specify what students are expected to achieve in a given subject matter at a specific grade (e.g., Mathematics, Grade 5). In other words, content standards specify the skills and knowledge we want our students to master. Performance standards specify a level of performance, typically in the form of a cut score or a range of scores that indicates achievement levels. That is, performance standards specify what constitutes acceptable performance. National and state educational standards have been developed and can be easily accessed via the Internet. Here are a few examples of state educational Internet sites that specify the state standards:

- *California:* Content Standards for California Public Schools
  www.cde.ca.gov/be/st/ss

- *Florida:* Sunshine State Standards
  http://sunshinestatestandards.net

- *New York:* Learning Standards
  www.emsc.nysed.gov/guides

- *Texas:* Texas Essential Knowledge and Skills
  www.tea.state.tx.us/teks/index.html

---

science, and social studies. These comprehensive tests are often referred to as survey batteries. As noted, many school districts use standardized achievement tests to track student achievement over time or to compare performance across classes, schools, or districts. These batteries typically contain multiple subtests that assess achievement in specific curricular areas (e.g., reading, language, mathematics, and science). These subtests are organized in a series of test levels that span different grades. For example, a subtest might have four levels with one level covering kindergarten through the 2nd grade, the second level covering grades 3 and 4, the third level covering grades 5 and 6, and the fourth level covering grades 7 and 8 (Nitko, 2001). The most widely used standardized group achievement tests are produced and distributed by three publishers: CTB McGraw-Hill, Harcourt Assessment, Inc., and Riverside Publishing.

> **The most widely used standardized group achievement tests are produced by CTB McGraw-Hill, Harcourt Assessment, Inc., and Riverside Publishing.**

CTB McGraw-Hill.   CTB McGraw-Hill publishes three popular standardized group achievement tests, the California Achievement Tests, Fifth Edition (CAT/5), the *TerraNova* CTBS, and the *TerraNova* The Second Edition (CAT/6).

California Achievement Tests, Fifth Edition (CAT/5).   The CAT/5, designed for use with students from kindergarten through grade 12, is described as a traditional achievement battery. The CAT/5 assesses content in Reading, Spelling, Language, Mathematics, Study Skills, Science, and Social Studies. It is available in different formats for different applications (e.g., Complete Battery, Basic Battery, Short Form). The CAT/5 can be paired with the Tests of Cognitive Skills, Second Edition (TCS/2), a measure of academic aptitude, to allow comparison of achievement–aptitude abilities (we will discuss the potential benefits of making achievement–aptitude comparisons in the next chapter).

TerraNova *CTBS.* This is a revision of Comprehensive Tests of Basic Skills, Fourth Edition. The *TerraNova* CTBS, designed for use with students from kindergarten through grade 12, was published in 1997. It combines selected-response and constructed-response items that allow students to respond in a variety of formats. The *TerraNova* CTBS assesses content in Reading/Language Arts, Mathematics, Science, and Social Studies. An expanded version adds Word Analysis, Vocabulary, Language Mechanics, Spelling, and Mathematics Computation. The *TerraNova* CTBS is available in different formats for different applications (e.g., Complete Battery, Complete Battery Plus, Basic Battery). The *TerraNova* CTBS can be paired with the Tests of Cognitive Skills, Second Edition (TCS/2), a measure of academic aptitude, to compare achievement–aptitude abilities.

TerraNova *The Second Edition (CAT/6).* The *TerraNova* The Second Edition, or CAT/6, is described as comprehensive modular achievement battery designed for use with students from kindergarten through grade 12 and contains year 2000 normative data. The CAT/6 assesses content in Reading/Language Arts, Mathematics, Science, and Social Studies. An expanded version adds Word Analysis, Vocabulary, Language Mechanics, Spelling, and Mathematics Computation. It is available in different formats for different applications (e.g., CAT Multiple Assessments, CAT Basic Multiple Assessment, CAT Plus). The CAT/6 can be paired with *InView,* a measure of cognitive abilities, to compare achievement–aptitude abilities. Figures 12.1 and 12.2 provide sample score reports for *TerraNova* The Second Edition.

Harcourt Assessment, Inc. Harcourt Assessment, Inc., formerly Harcourt Educational Measurement, publishes the Stanford Achievement Test Series, Tenth Edition (Stanford 10). Originally published in 1923, the Stanford Achievement Test Series has a long and rich history of use.

Stanford Achievement Test Series, Tenth Edition (Stanford 10). The Stanford 10 can be used with students from kindergarten through grade 12 and has year 2002 normative data. It assesses content in Reading, Mathematics, Language, Spelling, Listening, Science, and Social Science. The Stanford 10 is available in a variety of forms, including abbreviated and complete batteries. The Stanford 10 can be administered with the Otis-Lennon School Ability Test, 8th Edition (OLSAT-8). Also available from Harcourt Assessment, Inc. are the Stanford Diagnostic Mathematics Test, Fourth Edition (SDMT 4) and the Stanford Diagnostic Reading Test, Fourth Edition (SDRT 4), which provide detailed information about the specific strengths and weaknesses of students in mathematics and reading.

Riverside Publishing. Riverside Publishing produces three major achievement tests: the Iowa Tests of Basic Skills (ITBS), Iowa Tests of Educational Development (ITED), and Tests of Achievement and Proficiency (TAP).

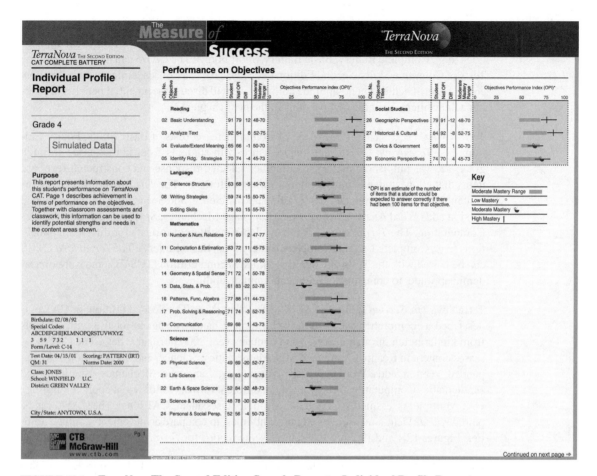

FIGURE 12.1 *TerraNova* **The Second Edition Sample Report—Individual Profile Report**
This figure is similar to the report teachers might receive for their students. By examining the
Key located on the right side of the report, you can interpret the student's performance in
different areas of achievement. For example, this student demonstrated High Mastery in Basic
Understanding and Analyze Text under Reading, but Low Mastery in Science Inquiry,
Physical Science, and Life Science under Science.

Source: Reproduced by permission of The McGraw-Hill Companies, Inc. Copyright 2001 CTB/McGraw-Hill.
All rights reserved.

Iowa Tests of Basic Skills (ITBS).   The ITBS is designed for use with students from kindergarten through grade 8, and as the name suggests is designed to provide a thorough assessment of basic academic skills. The most current ITBS form was published in 2001. The
ITBS assesses content in Reading, Language Arts, Mathematics, Science, Social Studies,
and Sources of Information. The ITBS is available in different formats for different applications (e.g., Complete Battery, Core Battery, Survey Battery). The ITBS can be paired with
the Cognitive Abilities Test (*Cog*AT), Form 6, a measure of general and specific cognitive

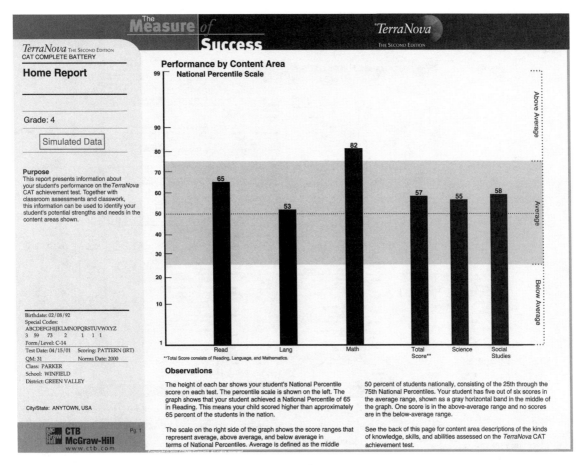

FIGURE 12.2 *TerraNova* **The Second Edition Sample Report—Home Report** This figure is similar to the report parents might receive for their children. The scores are reported in National Percentiles. For example, this student received a National Percentile of 65 in Reading, indicating that she scored better than 65% of the students in the national sample. This performance is in the Average range. Her math National Percentile is 82, indicating that she scored better than 82% of the students in the national sample. This performance is in the Above-Average range.

Source: Reproduced by permission of The McGraw-Hill Companies, Inc. Copyright 2001 CTB/McGraw-Hill. All rights reserved.

skills, to allow comparison of achievement–aptitude abilities. Figures 12.3, 12.4, and 12.5 provide sample score reports for the ITBS and other tests Riverside Publishing publishes.

Iowa Tests of Educational Development (ITED).   The ITED, designed for use with students from grades 9 through 12, was published in 2001 to measure the long-term goals of secondary education. The ITED assesses content in Vocabulary, Reading Comprehension, Language: Revising Written Materials, Spelling, Mathematics: Concepts and Problem

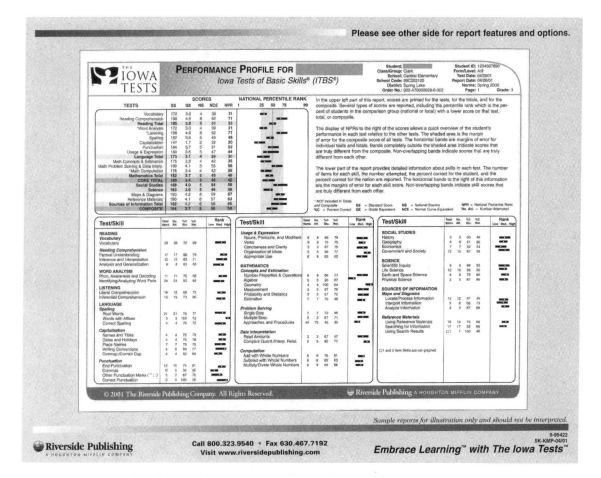

FIGURE 12.3   Performance Profile for Iowa Tests of Basic Skills (ITBS) This figure illustrates a Performance Profile for the Iowa Tests of Basic Skills (ITBS). It is one of the score report formats that Riverside Publishing provides for the ITBS. The display in the upper-left portion of the report provides numerical scores for the individual tests, totals, and overall composite. The National Percentile Rank is also displayed using confidence bands immediately to the right of the numerical scores. The display in the lower portion of the report provides detailed information about the specific skills measured in each test. Riverside Publishing provides an *Interpretive Guide for Teachers and Counselors* that provides detailed guidance for interpreting the different score reports.

Source: Reproduced by permission of the publisher, Riverside Publishing Company. Copyright 2001 The Riverside Publishing Company. All rights reserved.

Solving, Computation, Analysis of Science Materials, Analysis of Social Studies Materials, and Sources of Information. The ITED is available as both a complete battery and a core battery. The ITED can be paired with the Cognitive Abilities Test (*Cog*AT), Form 6, a measure of general and specific cognitive skills, to allow comparison of achievement–aptitude abilities.

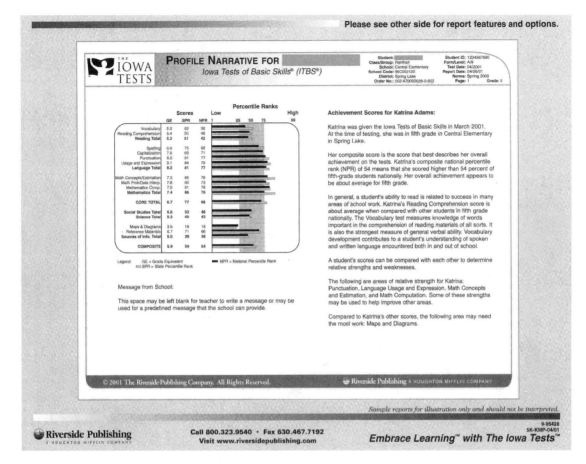

FIGURE 12.4　Profile Narrative for Iowa Tests of Basic Skills (ITBS) This figure illustrates the Profile Narrative report format available for the Iowa Tests of Basic Skills (ITBS). Although this format does not provide detailed information about the skills assessed in each test, as in the Performance Profile shown in Figure 12.3, it does provide an easy-to-understand discussion of the student's performance. This format describes the student's performance on the composite score (reflecting the student's overall level of achievement) and the two reading tests (i.e., Vocabulary and Reading Comprehension). This report also identifies the student's relative strengths and areas that might need attention. This report illustrates the reporting of both state and national percentile ranks.

Source: Reproduced by permission of the publisher, Riverside Publishing Company. Copyright 2001 The River-side Publishing Company. All rights reserved.

Tests of Achievement and Proficiency (TAP). The TAP, designed for use with students from grades 9 through 12, was published in 1996 to measure skills necessary for growth in secondary school. The TAP assesses content and skills in Vocabulary, Reading Comprehension, Written Expression, Mathematics Concepts and Problem Solving, Math Computation, Science, Social Studies, and Information Processing. It also contains an optional Student

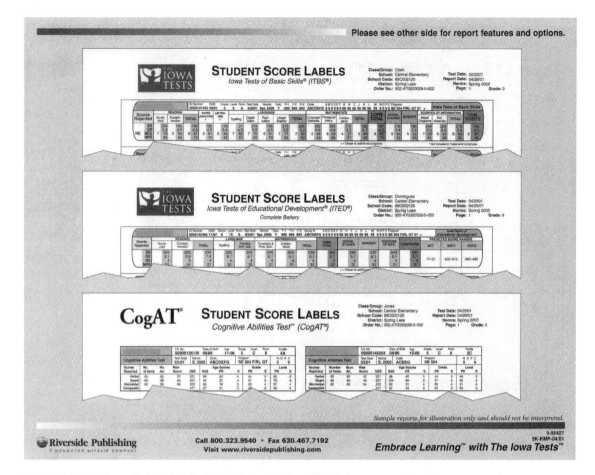

FIGURE 12.5   Score Labels for the Iowa Tests and *Cog*AT This figure presents student score labels for the Iowa Tests of Basic Skills (ITBS), Iowa Tests of Educational Development (ITED), and Cognitive Abilities Test (*Cog*AT). The *Cog*AT is an ability test discussed in the next chapter. These labels are intended for use in the students' cumulative records and allow educators to track student growth over time.

Source: Reproduced by permission of the publisher, Riverside Publishing Company. Copyright 2001 The Riverside Publishing Company. All rights reserved.

Questionnaire that solicits information about attitudes toward school, extracurricular interests, and long-term educational and career plans. The TAP is available as both a complete battery and a survey battery. The TAP can be paired with the Cognitive Abilities Test (*Cog*AT), Form 5, a measure of general and specific cognitive skills, to allow comparison of achievement–aptitude abilities.

Supplemental Constructed-Response and Performance Assessments.   As we discussed in earlier chapters, many educators criticize tests that rely extensively on selected-response items and advocate the use of constructed-response and performance assessments. To address this criticism, many of the survey batteries previously discussed provide open-ended and performance assessments to complement their standard batteries. For example, Riverside Publishing offers the *Performance Assessments for ITBS, ITED,* and *TAP.* These are norm-referenced open-ended assessments in Integrated Language Arts, Mathematics, Science, and Social Studies. These free-response assessments give students the opportunity to demonstrate content-specific knowledge and higher-order cognitive skills in a more life-like context. Other publishers have similar products available that supplement their survey batteries.

Diagnostic Achievement Tests. The most widely used achievement tests have been the broad survey batteries designed to assess the student's level of achievement in broad academic areas. Although these batteries do a good job in this context, they typically have too few items that measure specific skills and learning objectives to be useful to teachers when making instructional decisions. For example, the test results might suggest that a particular student's performance is low in mathematics, but the results will not pinpoint the student's specific strengths and weaknesses. To address this limitation, many test publishers have developed **diagnostic achievement tests.** These diagnostic batteries contain a larger number of items linked to each specific learning objective. In this way they can provide more precise information about which academic skills have been achieved and which have not. Examples of group-administered diagnostic achievement tests include the Stanford Diagnostic Reading Test, Fourth Edition (SDRT 4) and the Stanford Diagnostic Mathematics Test, Fourth Edition (SDMT 4), both published by Harcourt Assessment, Inc. Most other publishers have similar diagnostic tests to complement their survey batteries.

Obviously these have been very brief descriptions of these major test batteries. These summaries were based on information current at the time of this writing. However, these tests are continuously being revised to reflect curricular changes and to update normative data. For the most current information, interested readers should access the Internet sites for the publishing companies (see Table 12.1) or refer to the current edition of the *Mental Measurements*

TABLE 12.1 Major Publishers of Standardized Group Achievement Tests

CTB McGraw-Hill   Web site: http:/ctb.com
California Achievement Tests, Fifth Edition (CAT/5)
TerraNova CTBS
TerraNova The Second Edition (CAT/6)

Harcourt Assessment, Inc.   Web site: harcourtassessment.com
Stanford Achievement Test Series, Tenth Edition (Stanford 10)

Riverside Publishing   Web site: www.riverpub.com
Iowa Tests of Basic Skills (ITBS)
Iowa Tests of Educational Development (ITED)
Tests of Achievement and Proficiency (TAP)

SPECIAL INTEREST TOPIC **12.2**
Finding Information on Standardized Tests

When you want to locate information on a standardized test, it is reasonable to begin by examining information provided by the test publishers. This can include their Internet sites, catalogs, test manuals, specimen test sets, score reports, and other supporting documentation. However, you should also seek out resources that provide independent evaluations and reviews of the tests you are researching. The Testing Office of the American Psychological Association Science Directorate (American Psychological Association, 2004) provides the following description of the four most popular resources:

- *Mental Measurements Yearbook (MMY).* MMY, published by the Buros Institute for Mental Measurements, lists tests alphabetically by title. Each listing provides basic descriptive information about the test (e.g., author, date of publication) plus information about the availability of technical information and scoring and reporting services. Most listings also include one or more critical reviews by qualified assessment experts.
- *Tests in Print (TIP).* TIP, also published by the Buros Institute for Mental Measurements, is a bibliographic encyclopedia of information on practically every published test in psychology and education. Each listing provides basic descriptive information on tests, but does not contain critical reviews or psychometric information. After locating a test that meets your criteria, you can turn to the *Mental Measurements Yearbook* for more detailed information on the test.
- *Test Critiques.* Test Critiques, published by Pro-Ed, Inc., contains a three-part listing for each test that includes Introduction, Practical Applications/Uses, and Technical Aspects, followed by a critical review of the test.
- *Tests.* Tests, also published by Pro-Ed, Inc., is a bibliographic encyclopedia covering thousands of assessments in psychology and education. It provides basic descriptive information on tests, but does not contain critical reviews or information on reliability, validity, or other technical aspects of the tests. It serves as a companion to *Test Critiques.*

These resources can be located in the reference section of most college and larger public libraries. In addition to these traditional references, Test Reviews Online is a Web-based service of the Buros Institute of Mental Measurements (www.unl.edu/buros). This service makes test reviews available online to individuals precisely as they appear in the *Mental Measurements Yearbook.* For a relatively small fee (currently $15), users can download information on any of over 2,000 tests.

Yearbook or other reference resources. See Special Interest Topic 12.2 for information on these resources.

State-Developed Achievement Tests

Standardized achievement tests are increasingly being used in making high-stake decisions at the state level.

As we noted earlier, standardized achievement tests increasingly are being used in making high-stakes decision at the state level (e.g., which students are promoted or graduate; rating teachers, administrators, schools, and school districts). All states now have

statewide testing programs, but different states have adopted different approaches. Some states utilize commercially available achievement batteries such as those described in the previous section. For example, for many years California evaluated its schools based largely on their students' performance on the Stanford Achievement Test Series, Ninth Edition (Stanford 9). One significant limitation of using a commercial off-the-shelf national test for this purpose is that it might not closely match the state's curriculum. In other words, the test might not be valid for the stated purpose. Special Interest Topic 12.3 describes a study that examined the alignment between off-the-shelf commercial achievement tests and state standards and found evidence of inconsistent alignment.

To address this limitation, other states have developed their own achievement batteries that are designed to closely match the state's curriculum (Doherty, 2002). For example, a statewide program in Texas includes the Texas Assessment of Knowledge and Skills (TAKS). The TAKS measures success of students in the state's curriculum in reading (grades 3 through 9), mathematics (grades 3 through 11), writing (grades 4 and 7), English/language arts (grades 10 and 11), science (grades 5, 10, and 11), and social studies (grades 8, 10, and 11). A Spanish TAKS is available for Spanish-speaking students in grades 3 through 6. The decision to promote a student to the next grade may be based on passing the reading and math sections, and successful completion of the TAKS at grade 11 is required for students to receive a high school diploma. The statewide assessment program contains two additional tests. A Reading Proficiency Test in English (RPTE) is administered to limited-English-proficient students to assess annual growth in reading proficiency. Finally, the State-Developed Alternative Assessment (SDAA) can be used with special education students when it is determined that the standard TAKS is inappropriate. All of these tests are designed to measure the educational objectives specified in the state curriculum, the Texas Essential Knowledge and Skills curriculum (TEKS) (see www.tea.state.tx.us).

SPECIAL INTEREST TOPIC **12.3**

Mismatch between State Standards and Off-the-Shelf Achievement Tests?

In an article published in *Education Week,* Boser (1999) describes studies that found that commercial off-the-shelf achievement tests often do not provide adequate coverage of many state content standards. Boser notes that commercial achievement tests typically are not designed to measure the content standards of specific states, but instead reflect an amalgamation of the content of major textbooks, state standards, and national standards. He describes a study commissioned by California's education department that examined a number of commercially available achievement tests to see how they line up with the state's math standards. These studies found that the off-the-shelf tests focused primarily on basic math skills and did not adequately assess whether students had mastered the state's standards. This comes down to a question of the intended use of the assessment. If you are interested in assessing what is being taught in classrooms across the nation, the commercially available group achievement tests probably give you a good measure. However, if you are more interested in determining whether your students are mastering your state's content standards, off-the-shelf achievement tests are less adequate and state-developed content-based assessments are preferable.

Proponents of high-stakes testing programs believe they increase academic expectations and ensure that all students are judged according to the same standards.

Critics of high-stakes testing programs believe too much instructional time is spent preparing students for the tests instead of teaching the really important skills necessary for success in life.

There is considerable controversy concerning statewide testing programs (Doherty, 2002). Proponents of high-stakes testing programs see them as a way of increasing academic expectations and ensuring that all students are judged according to the same standards. They believe these testing programs guarantee that students graduating from public schools have the skills necessary to be successful. They point to recent data showing that achievement scores have improved in recent years and attribute this increase to high-stakes testing programs. Critics of these testing programs argue that these tests emphasize rote learning and often neglect critical thinking, problem-solving, and communication skills. To exacerbate the problem, critics feel that too much instructional time is spent preparing students for the tests instead of teaching the really important skills teachers would like to focus on. Additionally, they argue that these tests are culturally biased and are not fair to minority students (Doherty, 2002). For additional information on high-stakes testing programs, see Special Interest Topics 12.4 and 12.5. This debate is likely to continue for the foreseeable future, but in the meantime these tests will continue to play an important role in public schools. Special Interest Topic 12.6 provides an introduction to value-added assessment, an innovative approach to educational accountability.

Best Practices in Using Standardized Achievement Tests in Schools

As you can see from our discussion of standardized achievement tests to this point, these tests have widespread applications in schools today. As a result, modern teachers are often asked to prepare students for these tests as well as to administer and interpret them. In this section we will briefly discuss some guidelines for completing these tasks. We will start by discussing how teachers can prepare students to take standardized tests. This discussion will focus on group-administered achievement tests, but can actually be generalized to many of the other standardized tests we will be discussing in this and later chapters.

Preparing Students for the Test.   Much has been written in recent years about the proper procedures or practices for preparing students to take standardized achievement tests. As we noted earlier, high-stakes testing programs are in place in every state, and these tests are used to make important decisions such as which students graduate or get promoted, which teachers receive raises, and which administrators retain their jobs. As you might imagine, the pressure to ensure that students perform well on these tests has also increased. Legislators exert pressure on state education officials to increase student performance, who in turn put pressure on local administrators, who in turn put pressure on teachers. An important question is "What **test preparation practices** are legitimate and acceptable, and what practices are unethical or educationally contraindicated?" This is a more complicated question than one might first imagine.

American Educational Research Association (AERA) Position Statement on High-Stakes Testing

The American Educational Research Association (AERA) is a leading organization that studies educational issues. The AERA (2000) presented a position statement regarding high-stakes testing programs employed in many states and school districts. Its position is summarized in the following points:

1. Important decisions should not be based on a single test score. Ideally, information from multiple sources should be taken into consideration when making high-stakes decisions. When tests are the basis of important decisions, students should be given multiple opportunities to take the test.
2. When students and teachers are going to be held responsible for new content or standards, they should be given adequate time and resources to prepare themselves before being tested.
3. Each test should be validated for each intended use. For example, if a test is going to be used for determining which students are promoted *and* for ranking schools based on educational effectiveness, both interpretations must be validated.
4. If there is the potential for adverse effects associated with a testing program, efforts should be made to make all involved parties aware of them.
5. There should be alignment between the assessments and the state content standards.
6. When specific cut scores are used to denote achievement levels, the purpose, meaning, and validity of these passing scores should be established.
7. Students who fail a high-stakes test should be given adequate opportunities to overcome any deficiencies.
8. Adequate consideration and accommodations should be given to students with language differences.
9. Adequate consideration and accommodations should be given to students with disabilities.
10. When districts, schools, or classes are to be compared, it is important to specify clearly which students are to be tested and which students are exempt, and to ensure that these guidelines are followed.
11. Test scores must be reliable.
12. There should be an ongoing evaluation of both the intended and unintended effects of any high-stakes testing program.

These guidelines may be useful when trying to evaluate the testing programs your state or school employs. For more information, the full text of this position statement can be accessed at www.aera.net/about/policy/stakes.htm.

Teaching to the test **has become a popular concept in both the popular media and professional literature.**

A popular phrase currently being used in both the popular media and professional educational literature is **teaching to the test.** This phrase generally implies efforts by teachers to prepare students to perform better on standardized achievement tests. Many writers use "teaching to the test" in a derogatory manner, referencing unethical or **inappropriate preparation practices.** Other writers use

Why Standardized Tests Should Not Be
Used to Evaluate Educational Quality

W. James Popham (2000) provided three reasons why he feels standardized achievement tests should not be used to evaluate educational effectiveness or quality:

1. There may be poor alignment between what is taught in schools and what is measured by the tests. Obviously, if the test is not measuring what is being taught in schools, this will undermine the validity of any interpretations regarding the quality of an education.
2. In an effort to maximize score variance, test publishers often delete items that are relatively easy. Although this is a standard practice intended to enhance the measurement characteristics of a test, it may have the unintended effect of deleting items that measure learning objectives that teachers feel are most important and emphasize in their instruction. He reasons that the items might be easy because the teachers focused on the objectives until practically all of the students mastered them.
3. Standardized achievement tests may reflect more than what is taught in schools. Popham notes that performance on standardized achievement tests reflects the students' intellectual ability, what is taught in school, and what they learn outside of school. As a result, to interpret them as reflecting only what is taught in school is illogical, and it is inappropriate to use them as a measure of educational quality.

the phrase more broadly to reference any instruction designed to enhance performance on a test. As you will see, a wide range of test preparation practices can be applied. Some of these practices are clearly appropriate whereas others are clearly inappropriate. As an extreme example, consider a teacher who shared the exact items from a standardized test that is to be administered to students. This practice is clearly a breach of test security and is tantamount to cheating. It is unethical and educationally indefensible and most responsible educators would not even consider such a practice. In fact, such a breach of test security could be grounds for the dismissal of the teacher, revocation of license, and possible legal charges (Kober, 2002).

Thankfully such flagrantly abusive practices are relatively rare, but they do occur. However, the appropriateness of some of the more common methods of preparing students for tests is less clear. With one notable exception, which we will describe next, it is generally accepted that *any test preparation practice that raises test scores without also increasing mastery of the underlying knowledge and skills is inappropriate.* In other words, if a practice *artificially* increases test performance while failing to increase mastery of the domain of knowledge or skills reflected on the test, the practice is inappropriate. You may recognize that this involves the issue of test validity. Standardized achievement tests are meant to assess the academic achievement of students in specific areas. If test preparation practices increase test scores without increasing the level of achievement, the validity of the test is compromised. Consider the following examples of various test preparation procedures.

SPECIAL INTEREST TOPIC **12.6**

Value-Added Assessment: A New Approach to Educational Accountability

The term *value-added* has been used in business and industry to mean the economic value gain that occurs when material is changed through manufacturing or manipulation. In education this has been interpreted as the change in a student's knowledge that occurs as the result of instruction. In many ways, it can be seen as determining the value of instruction in raising knowledge levels (however, the model does not attempt to determine many benefits of schooling that go beyond knowledge acquisition). One of the most complex models of value-added assessment has been developed in Tennessee (Ceperley & Reel, 1997; Sanders, Saxton, & Horn, 1997). This model also has been implemented in a form in Dallas (Webster & Mendro, 1997). This is a rather complex model, and the basic ideas are presented here in a hypothetical situation.

Consider students who attend Washington School in East Bunslip, New Jersey, in Ms. Jones's 3rd-grade class (all names are made up). These students may be typical or representative of 3rd-grade students, or there may be a substantial proportion of excellent or poor students. Ms. Jones teaches in her style, and the students are given the state achievement test at the end of the year. For this example, let's assume that statewide testing begins in grade 3. The results of the state test, student by student, are used to build a model of performance for each student, for Ms. Jones, for Washington School, and for the East Bunslip school district. One year's data are inadequate to do more than simply mark the levels of performance of each focus for achievement: student, teacher, school, and district.

The next year Ms. Jones's previous students have been dispersed to several 4th-grade classrooms. A few of her students move to different school districts, but most stay in East Bunslip and most stay at Washington School. All of this information will be included in the modeling of performance. Ms. Jones now has a new class of students who enter the value-added assessment system. At the end of this year there is now data on each student who completed 4th grade, although some students may have been lost through attrition (e.g., missed the testing, left the state). The Tennessee model includes a procedure that accounts for all of these "errors." The performance of the 4th-grade students can now be evaluated in terms of their 3rd-grade performance and the effect of their previous teacher, Ms. Jones, and the effect of their current teacher (assuming that teacher also taught last year and there was assessment data for the class taught). In addition a school level effect can be estimated. Thus, the value-added system attempts to explain achievement performance for each level in the school system by using information from each level. This is clearly a very complex undertaking for an entire state's data. As of 1997, Sanders et al. noted that over 4 million data points in the Tennessee system were used to estimate effects for each student, teacher, school, and district.

The actual value-added component is not estimated as a gain, but as the difference in performance from the expected performance based on the student's previous performance, current grade in school effect, sum of current and previous teacher effectiveness, and school effectiveness. When three or more years' data become available, longitudinal trend models can be developed to predict the performance in each year for the various sources discussed.

Student achievement is what it is. A student either passes or fails the state test according to criteria the state establishes. What is unique in the value-added model of accountability is that the focus is on teacher, school, and district effectiveness rather than on individual student performance. The system is intended to (1) guide instructional change through inspection of the teacher and grade level estimates of average performance and (2) evaluate teachers and administrators by examining consistency of performance averages across years. The second purpose is certainly controversial and has its detractors. In particular, teacher evaluation based on state assessments has been criticized due

(continued)

to the limited coverage of the state tests. This, it is argued, has resulted in reduced coverage of content, focus on low-level conceptual understanding, and overemphasis on teaching to the test at the expense of content instruction. Nevertheless, there is continued interest in the value-added models, and their use will likely increase.

Instruction in Generic Test-Taking Skills.   This involves instruction in general test-taking skills such as completing answer sheets, establishing an appropriate pace, narrowing choices on selected-response items, and introductions to novel item formats (e.g., Kober, 2002). This is the "notable exception" to the general rule just noted. Instruction in general test-taking skills does not increase mastery of the underlying knowledge and skills, but it does make students more familiar and comfortable with standardized tests. As a result, their scores are more likely to reflect accurately their true academic abilities and not the influence of deficient test-taking skills (e.g., Linn & Gronlund, 2000; Popham, 1999). This practice enhances the validity of the assessment. This type of instruction is also typically fairly brief and, as a result, not detrimental to other educational activities. Therefore, instruction in generic test-taking skills is an appropriate test preparation practice (see Table 12.2).

Preparation Using Practice Forms of the Test.   Many states and commercial test publishers release earlier versions of their exams as practice tests. Because these are released as practice tests, their use is not typically considered unethical. However, if these tests become the focus of instruction at the expense of other teaching activities, this practice can be harmful. Research suggests that direct instruction using practice tests may produce short-term increases in test

TABLE 12.2   Important Test-Taking Skills to Teach Students

1. Carefully listen to or read the instruction.
2. Carefully listen to or read the test items.
3. Establish an appropriate pace. Do not rush carelessly through the test, but do not proceed so slowly you will not be able to finish.
4. If you find an item to be extremely difficult, do not spend an inordinate amount of time on it. Skip it and come back if time allows.
5. On selected-response items, make informed guesses by eliminating alternatives that are clearly wrong.
6. Unless there is a penalty for guessing, make an effort to complete every item. It is better to try to guess the correct answer than simply leave it blank.
7. Ensure that you carefully mark the answer sheet. For example, on computer-scored answer sheets, make sure the entire space is darkened and avoid extraneous marks.
8. During the test periodically verify that the item numbers and answer numbers match.
9. If time permits, go back and check your answers.

Sources: Based on Linn & Gronlund (2000) and Sarnacki (1979).

scores without commensurate increases in performance on other measures of the test domain (Kober, 2002). Like instruction in generic test-taking skills, the limited use of practice tests may help familiarize students with the format of the test. However, practice tests should be used in a judicious manner to ensure that they do not become the focus of instruction.

Preparation Emphasizing Test-Specific Item Formats.   Here teachers provide instruction and assignments that prepare students to deal exclusively with the specific item formats used on the standardized test. For example, teachers might use classroom tests and homework assignments that resemble actual items on the test (Kober, 2002). If the writing section of a test requires single-paragraph responses, teachers will restrict their writing assignments to a single paragraph. If a test uses only multiple-choice items, the teachers will limit their classroom tests to multiple-choice items. The key feature is that students are given instruction exposing them only to the material as presented and measured on the test. With this approach students will be limited in their ability to generalize acquired skills and knowledge to novel situations (Popham, 1999). Test scores may increase, but the students' mastery of the underlying domain is limited. As a result, this practice should be avoided.

Preparation Emphasizing Test Content.   This practice is somewhat similar to the previous one, but instead of providing extensive exposure to items resembling those on the test, the goal is to emphasize the skills and content most likely to be included on the standardized tests. Kober (2002) notes that this practice often has a "narrowing effect" on instruction. Because many standardized achievement tests emphasize basic skills and knowledge that can be easily measured with selected-response items, this practice may result in teachers neglecting more complex learning objectives such as the analysis and synthesis of information or development of complex problem-solving skills. While test scores may increase, the students' mastery of the underlying domain is restricted. This practice should be avoided.

Preparation Using Multiple Instructional Techniques.   With this approach students are given instruction that exposes them to the material as conceptualized and measured on the test, *but* also presents the material in a variety of different formats. Instruction covers all salient knowledge and skills in the curriculum and addresses both basic and higher-order learning objectives (Kober, 2002). With this approach, increases in test scores are associated with increases in mastery of the underlying domain of skills and knowledge (Popham, 1999). As a result, this test preparation practice is recommended.

Only *test preparation practices* that introduce generic test-taking skills and use multiple instructional techniques can be recommended enthusiastically.

Although this list of test preparation practices is not exhaustive, we have tried to address the most common forms. In summary, only preparation that introduces generic test-taking skills and uses multiple instructional techniques can be recommended enthusiastically. Teaching generic test-taking skills makes students more familiar and comfortable with the assessment process, and as a result enhances the validity of the assessment. The use of multiple instructional techniques results in enhanced test performance that reflects an increased mastery of the content domain. As a result, neither of these practices compromises the validity of the score interpretation as reflecting domain-specific knowledge. Other test preparation practices generally fall short of this goal. For example, practice tests may be useful when used cautiously, but they are often overused and become the focus of instruction with detrimental results. Any procedures that emphasize test-specific content or test-specific item formats should be avoided because they may increase test scores without actually enhancing mastery of the underlying test domain.

Administering Standardized Tests. When introducing this chapter we noted that standardized tests are professionally developed and must be administered and scored in a standard manner. For **standardized scores** to be meaningful and useful, it is imperative to follow these standard procedures precisely. These procedures are explicitly specified so that the tests can be administered in a uniform manner in different settings. For example, it is obviously important for all students to receive the same instructions and same time limits at each testing site in order for the results to be comparable. Teachers are often responsible for administering group achievement tests to their students and as a result should understand the basics of standardized test administration. Here are a few guidelines to help teachers in **standardized test administration** to their students that are based on our own experience and a review of the literature (e.g., Kubiszyn & Borich, 2003; Linn & Gronlund, 2000; Popham, 1999, 2000).

> **For *standardized scores* to be meaningful and useful, it is imperative to follow the test's administration procedures precisely.**

Review the Test Administration Manual before the Day of the Test. Administering standardized tests is not an overly difficult process, but it is helpful to review the administration instructions carefully before the day of the test. This way you will be familiar with the procedures and there should be no surprises. This review will alert you to any devices (e.g., stopwatch) or supporting material (e.g., scratch paper) you may need during the administration. It is also beneficial to do a mock administration by reading the instructions for the test in private before administering it to the students. The more familiar you are with the administration instructions, the better prepared you will be to administer the test. Additionally, you will find the actual testing session to be less stressful.

Encourage the Students to Do Their Best. Standardized achievement tests (and most other standardized tests used in schools) are maximum performance tests and ideally students will put forth their best efforts. This is best achieved by explaining to the students how the test results will be used to their benefit. For example, with achievement tests you might tell the students that the results can help them and their parents track their academic progress and identify any areas that need special attention. Although it is important to motivate students to do their best, it is equally crucial to avoid unnecessarily raising their level of anxiety. For example, you would probably not want to focus on the negative consequences of poor performance immediately before administering the test. This presents a type of balancing act; you want to encourage the students to do their best without making them excessively anxious.

Closely Follow Instructions. As we noted, the reliability and validity of the test results are dependent on the individual administering the test closely following the administration instructions. First, the instructions to students must be read word for word. Do not alter the instructions in any way, paraphrase them, or try to improvise. It is likely that some students will have questions, but you are limited in how you can respond. Most manuals indicate that you can clarify procedural questions (e.g., where do I sign my name?), but you cannot define words or in any other way provide hints to the answers.

Strictly Adhere to Time Limits.   Bring a stopwatch and practice using it before the day of the test.

Avoid Interruptions.   Avoid making announcements or any other types of interruptions during the examination. To help avoid outside interruptions you should post a Testing in Session—Do Not Disturb sign on the door.

Be Alert to Cheating.   Although you do not want to hover over the students to the extent that it makes them unnecessarily nervous, active surveillance is indicated and can help deter cheating. Stay alert and monitor the room from a position that provides a clear view of the entire room. Walk quietly around the room occasionally. If you note anything out of the ordinary increase your surveillance of those students. Document any unusual events that might deserve further consideration or follow-up.

By following these suggestions you should have a productive and uneventful testing session. Nevertheless, be prepared for unanticipated events to occur. Keep the instruction manual close so you can refer to it if needed. It is also helpful to remember you can rely on your professional educational training to guide you in case of unexpected events.

Interpreting Standardized Tests.   Teachers are also often called on to interpret the results of standardized tests. This often involves interpreting test results for use in their own classroom. This can include monitoring student gains in achievement, identifying individual strengths and weaknesses, evaluating class progress, and planning instruction. At other times, teachers are called on to interpret the results to parents or even students. Although report cards document each student's performance in the class, the results of standardized tests provide normative information regarding student progress in a broader context (e.g., Linn & Gronlund, 2000).

The key factor in accurately interpreting the results of standardized tests is being familiar with the type of scores reported.

The key factor in accurately interpreting the results of standardized tests is being familiar with the type of scores reported. In Chapter 3 we presented a review of the major types of test scores major publishers use. As we suggested in that chapter, when reporting test results to parents it is usually best to use percentile ranks. As with all norm-referenced scores, the percentile rank simply reflects an examinee's performance relative to the specific norm group. Percentile ranks are interpreted as indicating the percentage of individuals scoring below a given point in a distribution. For example, a percentile rank of 75 indicates that 75% of the individuals in the standardization sample scored below this score. A percentile rank of 30 indicates that only 30% of the individuals in the standardization sample scored below this score. Percentile ranks range from 1 to 99, and a rank of 50 indicates median performance.

When discussing results in terms of percentile rank, it is helpful to ensure that they are not misinterpreted as "percent correct" (Kamphaus, 1993). That is, a percentile rank of 80 means that the examinee scored better than 80% of the standardization sample, not that he or she correctly answered 80% of the items. Although most test publishers report grade equivalents, we recommend that you avoid interpreting them to parents. In Chapter 3 we discussed many of the problems associated with the use of these scores and why they should be avoided.

Before leaving our discussion of the use of standardized achievement tests in schools, it is appropriate to discuss some factors other than academic achievement that may influence test performance. As we have emphasized in this textbook, it is extremely important to select and use tests that produce reliable and valid scores. It is also important to understand that even with the most psychometrically sound tests, factors other than those we are attempting to measure may influence test performance. Achievement tests are an attempt to measure students' academic achievement in specific content areas. An example of an extraneous factor that might influence performance on a standardized test is the emotional state or mood of the student. If a student is emotionally upset the day of a test, his or her performance will likely be impacted (see Special Interest Topic 12.7 for a personal example). If you can see that a student is upset while taking a test, make a note of this as it might be useful later in understanding his or her performance. Accordingly, a student's level of motivation will also influence performance. Students who do not see the test as important may demonstrate a lackadaisical approach to it. If you notice that a student is not completing the test or is completing it in a haphazard manner, this should also be documented.

SPECIAL INTEREST TOPIC   **12.7**

Deciding Not to Test an Upset Student

A number of years ago when one of our colleagues was working with a private agency, a mother and her young son (approximately 9 or 10 years of age) came in for their appointment. Although he does not remember the specifics of the referral, the primary issue was that the child was having difficulty at school and there was concern that he might have a learning disability. To determine the basis of his school problems, he was scheduled to receive a battery of individual standardized tests. On greeting them it was obvious that the child was upset. He sat quietly crying in the waiting room with his head down. Our colleague asked the mother what was wrong and she indicated his pet cat had died that morning. She was clearly sensitive to her son's grief, but was concerned that it would takes months to get another appointment (this agency was typically booked for months in advance). Our colleague explained to her that he was much too upset to complete the assessment on this day and that any results would be invalid. To ensure that her son received the help he needed in a timely manner, they were able to schedule an appointment in a few weeks. Although teachers may not have this much discretion when scheduling or administering standardized tests, they should be observant and sensitive to the effects of emotional state on test performance.

Individual Achievement Tests

As we noted, standardized achievement tests are also used in the identification, diagnosis, and classification of students with special learning needs. Although some group-administered achievement tests might be used in identifying children with special needs, in many situations individually administered achievement tests are employed. For example, if a student is having learning difficulties and parents or teachers are concerned about the possibility of a learning disability, the student would likely be given a battery of tests, one being an individual achievement test. A testing professional, with extensive training in psychometrics and test administration, administers these tests to one student at a time. Because the tests are administered individually, they can contain a wider variety of item formats. For example, the questions are often presented in different modalities, with some questions presented orally and some in written format. Certain questions may require oral responses whereas some require written responses. In assessing writing abilities, some of these tests elicit short passages whereas others require fairly lengthy essays. Relative to the group tests, individual achievement tests typically provide a more thorough assessment of the student's skills. Because they are administered in a one-to-one context, the examiner can observe the student closely and hopefully gain insight into the source of learning problems. Additionally, because these tests are scored individually, they are more likely to incorporate open-ended item formats (e.g., essay items) requiring qualitative scoring procedures. Although regular education teachers typically are not responsible for administering and interpreting these tests, teachers often do attend special education or placement committee meetings at which the results of these tests are discussed and used to make eligibility and placement decisions. As a result, it is beneficial to have some familiarity with these tests. In this section we will briefly introduce you to some of the most popular individual achievement tests used in the schools.

> **Although some group achievement tests are used in identifying students with special needs, in many situations individually administered achievement tests are used.**

Wechsler Individual Achievement Test—Second Edition (WIAT-II; The Psychological Corporation, 2002). The WIAT-II is a comprehensive individually administered norm-referenced achievement test published by The Psychological Corporation. By comprehensive we mean it covers a broad spectrum of academic skill areas. One desirable feature is its coverage of all of the areas of learning disability recognized in the Education of All Handicapped Children Act of 1975 and its successors. It contains the following composites and subtests:

- *Reading Composite:* composed of the Word Reading subtest (letter knowledge, phonological awareness and decoding skills), Reading Comprehension subtest (comprehension of short passages, reading rate, and oral reading prosody), and Pseudo-word Decoding (phonetic decoding skills).
- *Mathematics Composite:* composed of the Numerical Operations subtest (number knowledge, ability to solve calculation problems and simple equations) and Math Reasoning subtest (ability to reason mathematically including identifying geometric shapes, solving word problems, interpreting graphs, etc.).

- *Written Language Composite:* composed of the Spelling subtest (ability to write dictated letters and words) and Written Language subtest (transcription, handwriting, written word fluency, generate and combine sentences, extended writing sample).
- *Oral Language Composite:* composed of the Listening Comprehension subtest (ability to listen and comprehend verbal information) and Oral Expression subtest (verbal word fluency, repetition, story generation, and providing directions).

The WIAT-II produces a variety of derived scores, including standard scores and percentile ranks. The WIAT-II has excellent psychometric properties and documentation. Additionally, the WIAT-II has the distinct advantage of being statistically linked to the Wechsler intelligence scales. Linkage with these popular intelligence tests facilitates the aptitude–achievement discrimination analyses often used to diagnose learning disabilities (this will be discussed more in the next chapter on aptitude tests).

Woodcock-Johnson III Tests of Achievement (WJ III ACH; Woodcock, McGrew, & Mather, 2001a).   The WJ III ACH is a comprehensive individually administered norm-referenced achievement test distributed by Riverside Publishing. The standard battery contains the following cluster scores and subtests:

- *Broad Reading:* composed of the Letter–Word Identification subtest (identify letters and pronounce words correctly), Reading Fluency subtest (ability to read simple sentences quickly and decide whether the statement is true or false), and Passage Comprehension subtest (ability to read passages and demonstrate understanding).
- *Oral Language:* composed of the Story Recall subtest (ability to recall details of stories presented on an audiotape) and Understanding Directions subtest (ability to follow directions presented on an audiotape).
- *Broad Math:* a comprehensive measure of math skills composed of the Calculation subtest (ability to perform mathematical computations), Math Fluency subtest (ability to solve simple math problems quickly), and Applied Problems subtest (ability to analyze and solve math word problems).
- *Math Calculation Skills:* a math aggregate cluster composed of the Calculation and Math Fluency subtests.
- *Broad Written Language:* a comprehensive measure of writing abilities composed of the Spelling subtest (ability to correctly spell words presented orally), Writing Fluency subtest (ability to formulate and write simple sentences quickly), and Writing Samples subtest (ability to write passages varying in length, vocabulary, grammatical complexity, and abstractness).
- *Written Expression:* a writing aggregate cluster composed of the Writing Fluency and Writing Samples subtests.

Other special-purpose clusters can be calculated using the 12 subtests in the standard battery. In addition, 10 more subtests in an extended battery allow the calculation of supplemental clusters. The WJ III ACH provides a variety of derived scores and has excellent psychometric properties and documentation. A desirable feature of the WJ III ACH is its availability in two parallel forms, which is an advantage when testing a student on more than one occasion because the use of different forms can help reduce carryover effects. Additionally, the WJ III ACH and the Woodcock-Johnson III Tests of Cognitive Abilities (WJ III

COG; Woodcock, McGrew, & Mather, 2001b) compose a comprehensive diagnostic system, the Woodcock-Johnson III (WJ III; Woodcock, McGrew, & Mather, 2001c). When administered together they facilitate the aptitude–achievement discrimination analyses often used to diagnose learning disabilities.

Wide Range Achievement Test 3 (WRAT3). The WRAT3 is a brief achievement test that measures basic reading, spelling, and arithmetic skills. It contains the following subtests:

- *Reading:* assesses ability to recognize and name letters and pronounce printed words.
- *Spelling:* assesses ability to write letters, names, and words that are presented orally.
- *Arithmetic:* assesses ability to recognize numbers, count, and perform written computations.

The WRAT3 can be administered in 15 to 30 minutes and comes in two parallel forms. Relative to the WIAT-II and WJ III ACH, the WRAT3 measures a limited number of skills. However, when only a quick estimate of achievement in word recognition, spelling, and math computation is needed, the WRAT3 can be a useful instrument.

The individual achievement batteries described to this point measure skills in multiple academic areas. As with the group achievement tests, there are individual tests that focus on multiple skill domains. The following two tests are examples of individual achievement tests that focus on specific skill areas.

Gray Oral Reading Test—Fourth Edition (GORT-4). The GORT-4 is a measure of oral reading skills and is often used in the diagnosis of reading problems. The GORT-4 contains 14 passages of increasing difficulty, which students read aloud. The examiner records reading rate and reading errors (e.g., skipping or inserting words, mispronunciation). Additionally, each reading passage contains questions to assess comprehension. There are two parallel forms available.

KeyMath—Revised/NU: A Diagnostic Inventory of Essential Mathematics—Normative Update (KeyMath R/NU). The KeyMath R/NU, published by American Guidance Services, measures mathematics skills in the following areas: Basic Concepts (numeration, rational numbers, and geometry), Operations (addition, subtraction, multiplication, division, and mental computations), and Applications (measurement, time and money, estimation, interpreting data, and problem solving). The KeyMath R/NU is available in two parallel forms.

Selecting an Achievement Battery

Numerous factors should be considered when selecting a standardized achievement battery. If you are selecting a test for administration to a large number of students, you will more than likely need a group achievement test. Nitko (1990, 2001) provides some suggestions for selecting a group achievement battery. He notes that although most survey batteries assess the common educational objectives covered in most curricula, there are some potentially important differences in the content covered. In some instructional areas such as reading and mathematics, there is considerable consistency in the curricula used in different schools. In other areas such as science and social studies, there is more variability. As a

When selecting a standardized achievement test many factors should be considered, including the content covered, its technical properties, and practical issues such as cost and time requirements.

result, potential users should examine any potential battery closely to determine whether its content corresponds with the school, district, or state curriculum. Naturally it is also important to evaluate the technical adequacy of a test. This includes issues such as the adequacy of the standardization sample, the reliability of test scores, and the availability of validity evidence supporting the intended use. This is best accomplished using some of the resources discussed earlier in this chapter (Special Interest Topic 12.2). Finally, it is also useful to consider practical issues such as cost, testing time required, availability of scoring services, and the quality of support materials such as administration and interpretative guides.

Many of the same factors should be considered when selecting an individual achievement test. You should select a test that adequately assesses the specific content areas you are interested in. For example, although a test such as the WRAT3 might be sufficient for screening purposes, it is not adequate for in-depth diagnostic purposes. In testing students to determine whether they have a specific learning disability, it would be important to use a battery such as the WIAT-II, which covers all recognized areas of learning disability.

Summary

In this chapter we focused on standardized achievement tests and their applications in the schools. These tests are designed to be administered, scored, and interpreted in a standard manner. The goal of standardization is to ensure that testing conditions are the same for all individuals taking the test. If this is accomplished, no examinee will have an advantage over another, and test results will be comparable. These tests have different applications in the schools, including:

- Tracking student achievement over time
- Using high-stakes decision making (e.g., promotion decisions; teacher evaluations)
- Identifying individual strengths and weaknesses
- Evaluating the effectiveness of educational programs
- Identifying students with special learning needs

Of these uses, high-stakes testing programs are probably the most controversial. These programs use standardized achievement tests to make such important decisions as which students will be promoted and evaluating educational professionals and schools. Proponents of high-stakes testing programs see them as a way of improving public education and ensuring that students are all judged according to the same standards. Critics of high-stakes testing programs argue that they encourage teachers to focus on low-level academic skills at the expense of higher-level skills such as problem solving and critical thinking.

We next described several of the most popular commercial survey batteries in use today and gave an example of a state-developed achievement test. We also provided some guidelines to help teachers prepare their students for these tests. We noted that any test preparation procedure that raises test scores without also increasing the mastery of the underlying knowledge and skills is inappropriate. After evaluating different test preparation practices, we concluded that preparation that introduces generic test-taking skills and uses multiple instructional techniques can be recommended. These practices should result in improved performance on standardized tests that reflects increased mastery of the underlying content domains. Preparation practices that emphasize the use of practice tests or focus on test-specific content or test-specific item formats should be avoided because they may increase test scores, but may not increase mastery of the underlying test domain. We also provided some suggestions for teachers to help administer and interpret test results. These included:

- Review the test administration manual before the day of the test.
- Encourage students to do their best on the test.
- Closely follow administration instructions.
- Strictly adhere to time limits.
- Avoid interruptions.
- Be alert to cheating.
- Be familiar with the types of derived scores produced by the test.

We concluded the chapter by briefly describing some popular individual achievement tests used in schools. Although teachers are not called on to routinely administer and interpret these individual tests, they often do attend committee meetings at which the results of these tests are discussed and used in making eligibility and placement decisions.

KEY TERMS AND CONCEPTS

Achievement test, p. 292
Appropriate preparation practices, p. 307
Diagnostic achievement tests, p. 303
Group-administered tests, p. 294
High-stakes assessment, p. 293

Inappropriate preparation practices, p. 307
Individually administered tests, p. 295
National testing program, p. 294
Standardized scores, p. 292

Standardized test administration, p. 312
Standardized test, p. 292
Statewide testing programs, p. 305
Teaching to the test, p. 307
Test preparation practices, p. 306

RECOMMENDED READINGS

Nitko, A. J., & Lane, S. (1990). Standardized multilevel survey achievement batteries. In C. R. Reynolds & R. W. Kamphaus (Eds.), *Handbook of psychological and educational assessment of children: Intelligence and achievement* (pp. 405–434). New York: Guilford Press. This chapter provides a good introduction and review of major group achievement tests.

As noted in this chapter, for the most up-to-date information it is recommended that you access the test publisher's Web site and reference resources such as the *Mental Measurements Yearbook*.

The following articles provide interesting commentaries on issues related to the use of standardized achievement tests in the schools:

Boston, C. (2001). The debate over national testing. *ERIC Digest,* ERIC-RIEO. (20010401).

Doherty, K. M. (2002). Education issues: Assessment. *Education Week on the Web.* Retrieved May 14, 2003, from www.edweek.org/context/topics/issuespage.cfm?id=41

Kober, N. (2002). Teaching to the test: The good, the bad, and who's responsible. *Test Talk for Leaders.* (Issue 1). Washington, DC: Center on Education Policy.

13 The Use of Aptitude Tests in the Schools

Conventional intelligence tests and even the entire concept of intelligence testing are perennially the focus of considerable controversy and strong emotion.

—Reynolds & Kaufman, 1990

CHAPTER HIGHLIGHTS

A Brief History of Intelligence Tests
Major Aptitude/Intelligence Tests
College Admission Tests

LEARNING OBJECTIVES

After reading and studying this chapter, students should be able to:

1. Compare and contrast the constructs of achievement and aptitude.
2. Explain how achievement and aptitude can be conceptualized as different aspects of a continuum. Provide examples to illustrate this continuum.
3. Discuss the major milestones in the history of intelligence assessment.
4. Describe the major uses of aptitude and intelligence tests in schools.
5. Explain the rationale for the analysis of aptitude–achievement discrepancies.
6. Describe and evaluate the major group aptitude/intelligence tests.
7. Describe and evaluate the major individual aptitude/intelligence tests.
8. Evaluate and select aptitude/intelligence tests that are appropriate for different applications.
9. Identify the major college admission tests and describe their use.

In Chapter 1, when describing maximum performance tests we noted that they are often classified as either achievement tests or aptitude[1] tests. We defined **achievement tests** as those designed to assess students' knowledge or skills in a content domain in which they

---

[1]In some professional sources the term *aptitude* is being replaced with *ability*. For historical purposes we will use *aptitude* to designate this type of test in this chapter, but we do want to alert readers to this variability in terminology.

Aptitude tests **are designed to measure the cognitive skills, abilities, and knowledge that individuals have accumulated as the result of their overall life experiences.**

have received instruction (AERA, 1999). In contrast, **aptitude tests** are broader in scope than achievement tests and are designed to measure the cognitive skills, abilities, and knowledge that individuals have accumulated as the result of their overall life experiences. In other words, whereas achievement tests are tied to a specific program of instruction, aptitude tests reflect the cumulative impact of life experiences as a whole in concert with an individual's underlying or latent ability to use information.

These introductory comments might lead you to believe there is a clear and universally accepted distinction between achievement and aptitude tests. However, in actual practice this is not the case and the distinction is actually a matter of degree. Many, if not most, testing experts conceptualize both achievement and aptitude tests as tests of developed cognitive abilities that can be ordered along a continuum in terms of how closely linked the assessed abilities are to specific learning experiences. This continuum is illustrated in Figure 13.1. At one end of the continuum you have teacher-constructed classroom tests that are tied directly to the instruction provided in a specific classroom or course. For example, a classroom mathematics test should assess specifically the learning objectives covered in the class during a specific instructional period. This is an example of a test that is linked clearly and directly to specific academic experiences (i.e., the result of curriculum and instruction). Next along the continuum are the survey achievement batteries that measure a fairly broad range of knowledge, skills, and abilities. Although there should be alignment between the learning objectives measured by these tests and the academic curriculum, the scope of a survey battery is considerably broader and more comprehensive than that of a teacher-constructed classroom test. The group-administered survey batteries described in the previous chapter are dependent on direct school experiences, but there is variability in how direct the linkage is. For example, the achievement tests developed by states to specifically assess the state's core curriculum are more directly linked to instruction through the state's specified curriculum than the commercially developed achievement tests that assess a more generic curriculum.

Both achievement and aptitude tests measure developed abilities and can be arranged along a continuum according to how dependent the abilities are on direct school experiences.

Next are intelligence and other aptitude tests that emphasize verbal, quantitative, and visual–spatial abilities. Many traditional intelligence tests can be placed in this category, and even though they are not linked to a specific academic curriculum, they do assess many skills that are commonly associated with academic success. The Otis-Lennon School Ability Test (OLSAT); Stanford-Binet Intelligence Scales—Fifth Edition; Tests of Cognitive

Very Specific ····················	Moderate Specificity ····················		Very General
Teacher-Constructed Classroom Tests	Broad Survey Achievement Batteries	Verbal Intelligence and Aptitude Tests	Cross-Cultural Intelligence Tests

FIGURE 13.1   A Continuum of General Abilities

Note: Modeled after Anastasi & Urbina (1997), Cronbach (1990), and others.

Skills, Second Edition (TCS/2); Wechsler Intelligence Scale for Children—Fourth Edition (WISC-IV); and Reynolds Intellectual Assessment Scales (RIAS) are all examples of tests that fit in this category (these will be discussed later in this chapter). In developing these tests, the authors attempt to measure abilities that are acquired thorough common, everyday experiences; not only those acquired through formal educational experiences. For example, a quantitative section of one of these tests will typically emphasize mental computations and quantitative reasoning as opposed to the developed mathematics skills traditionally emphasized on achievement tests.

Finally, at the most "general" end of the continuum are the nonverbal and cross-cultural intelligence or aptitude tests. These instruments attempt to minimize the influence of language, culture, and educational experiences. They typically emphasize the use of nonverbal performance items and often completely avoid language-based content (e.g., reading, writing, etc.). The Naglieri Nonverbal Ability Test—Multilevel Form (NNAT—Multilevel Form) is an example of a test that belongs in this category. The NNAT—Multilevel Form is a group-administered test of nonverbal reasoning and problem solving that is thought to be relatively independent of educational experiences, language, and cultural background (however, no test is truly culture-free). The NNAT—Multilevel Form (like many nonverbal IQ tests) employs "progressive matrices"—items in which the test taker must find the missing pattern in a series of designs or figures. The matrices in the NNAT—Multilevel Form are arranged in order of difficulty and contain designs and shapes that are not linked to any specific culture. Promoters of the test suggest that this test may be particularly useful for students with limited English proficiency, minorities, or those with hearing impairments.

In summary, both achievement and aptitude tests measure developed cognitive abilities and can be arranged along a continuum according to how dependent the abilities are on direct school experience. As we progress from the specific to the general end of the continuum, test performance becomes less and less dependent on specific learning experiences. The abilities measured by achievement tests are specifically linked to academic instruction or training. In contrast, the abilities measured by aptitude tests are acquired through a broad range of life experiences, including those at school, home, work, and all other settings.

Although we feel it is important to recognize the distinction between achievement and academic tests is not absolute, we also feel the achievement–aptitude distinction is useful. In schools and other settings, achievement and aptitude tests traditionally have been used for different purposes, and these labels help us identify their intended applications. For example, achievement tests typically are utilized to measure what has been learned or "achieved" at a specific point in time. In contrast, aptitude tests usually are used to predict future performance or to reflect an individual's potential in terms of academic or job performance.

Although many sources use the terms *aptitude* and *intelligence* interchangeably, general intelligence tests are not the only type of aptitude test in use today. In addition to intelligence tests, special aptitude tests and multiple aptitude batteries frequently are used in many educational and other settings. Special aptitude tests were developed originally in the context of employment settings to help employers select job applicants based on their aptitudes in specific areas such as mechanical or clerical ability. Subsequently, test developers developed multiple-aptitude batteries to measure a number of distinct abilities. For example, The Psychological Corporation publishes the Differential Aptitude Test for Personnel and Career Assessment (DAT for PCA) as an aid in hiring, training, and counseling job applicants. It assesses the test taker's skills in eight areas related to job performance: Verbal Reasoning, Numerical Ability, Abstract Reasoning, Mechanical Reasoning, Space Relations, Spelling, Language Usage, and Clerical Speed/Accuracy. Although special aptitude tests and multiple aptitude batteries have been used and continue to be used in academic settings, tests of general intelligence have seen the most widespread use.

A Brief History of Intelligence Tests

General intelligence tests historically have been the most popular and widely used aptitude tests in school settings.

General intelligence tests historically have been the most popular and widely used aptitude tests in school settings. While practically everyone is familiar with the concept of **intelligence** and uses the term in everyday conversations, it is not easy to develop a definition of intelligence on which everyone agrees. In fact, the concept of intelligence probably has generated more controversy than any other topic in the area of tests and measurement (see Special Interest Topics 13.1 and 13.2). Although practically all educators, psychologists, and psychometricians have their own personal definition of intelligence, most of these definitions will incorporate abilities such as problem solving, abstract reasoning, and the ability to acquire knowledge (e.g., Gray, 1999). Developing a consensus beyond this point is more difficult. For our present purpose, instead of pursuing a philosophical discussion of the meaning of intelligence, we will focus only on intelligence as measured by contemporary intelligence tests. These tests typically produce an overall score referred to as an **Intelligence Quotient** or **IQ.** By focusing our discussion on intelligence as defined by performance on these tests, we simplify our task considerably.

Intelligence tests actually had their beginning in the schools. In the early 1900s France initiated a compulsory education program. In recognition that not all children had the cognitive abilities necessary to benefit from regular education classes, the minister of education wanted to develop special educational programs to meet the particular needs of these children. To accomplish this, they needed a way of identifying the children who needed special services. **Alfred Binet** and his colleague **Theodore Simon** had been attempting to develop a measure of intelligence for some years, and the French government commissioned them to develop a test that could predict academic performance accurately. The result of their efforts was the first **Binet-Simon Scale,** released in 1905. This test contained problems arranged in the order of their difficulty and assessing a wide range of abilities. The test contained some sensory-perceptual tests, but the emphasis was on verbal items assessing comprehension, reasoning, and judgment. Subsequent revisions of the Binet-Simon Scale were released in 1908 and 1911. These scales gained wide acceptance in France and were soon translated and standardized in the United States by Louis Terman at Stanford University. This resulted in the Stanford-Binet Intelligence Test, which has been revised numerous times and is still a prominent intelligence test in use today. Ironically, Terman's version of the Binet-Simon Scale became even more popular in France and other parts of Europe than the Binet-Simon Scale!

The development and success of the Binet-Simon Scale, and subsequently the Stanford-Binet Intelligence Test, ushered in the era of widespread intelligence testing in the United States. Following the lead of the Stanford-Binet Intelligence Test, other assessment experts

SPECIAL INTEREST TOPIC **13.1**

The Controversial IQ: Knowns and Unknowns

A task force established by the American Psychological Association produced a report titled "Intelligence: Knowns and Unknowns" (Neisser et al., 1996). Its authors summarize the state of knowledge about intelligence and conclude by identifying seven critical questions about intelligence that have yet to be answered. These issues are summarized here.

1. It is widely accepted that there is a substantial genetic contribution to the development of intelligence, but the pathway by which genetic differences are expressed is not known.
2. It is also accepted that environmental factors contribute significantly to the development of intelligence, but no one really knows the mechanism by which they express their influence.
3. The role of nutrition in the development of intelligence is unclear. It is clear that profound early malnutrition is detrimental, but the effects of more subtle nutritional differences in populations that are "adequately fed" are not well understood.
4. Research has revealed significant correlations between information-processing speed and intelligence, but these findings have not resulted in clear theoretical models.
5. The "Flynn Effect" is real! That is, mean IQs are increasing worldwide. No one is really sure what factors are driving these gains.
6. Mean IQ differences between races cannot be attributed to obvious test bias or simply to differences in socioeconomic status. There is also no support for genetic explanations. Simply put, no one really knows the basis of these differences.
7. It is widely accepted that standardized intelligence tests do not measure all aspects of intelligence such as creativity, common sense, and interpersonal finesse. However, we do not know very much about these abilities such as how they relate to more traditional aspects of intelligence or how they develop.

In concluding their report, the Neisser et al. (1996) note:

In a field where so many issues are unresolved and so many questions unanswered, the confident tone that has characterized most of the debate on these topics is clearly out of place. The study of intelligence does not need politicized assertions and recriminations; it needs self-restraint, reflection, and a great deal more research. The questions that remain are socially as well as scientifically important. There is no reason to think them unanswerable, but finding the answers will require a shared and sustained effort as well as the commitment of substantial scientific resources. Just such a commitment is what we strongly recommend. (p. 97)

The development and success of the *Binet-Simon Scale,* and subsequently the Stanford-Binet, ushered in the era of widespread intelligence testing in the United States.

developed and released their own intelligence tests. Some of the tests were designed for individual administration (like the Stanford-Binet Intelligence Test) whereas others were designed for group administration. Some of these tests placed more emphasis on verbal and quantitative abilities whereas others focused more on visual–spatial and abstract problem-solving abilities. As a general rule, research has shown with considerable consistency that contemporary intelligence tests are good predictors of academic success. This is to be expected

SPECIAL INTEREST TOPIC **13.2**

The Controversial IQ: Schools and IQ Tests

Although IQ tests had their origin in the schools, they have been the source of considerable controversy essentially since their introduction. Opponents of IQ tests often argue IQ tests should be banned from schools altogether whereas proponents can hardly envision the schools without them. Many enduring issues contribute to this controversy and we will mention only the most prominent ones. These include the following.

Mean IQ Differences among Ethnic Groups

There is considerable research that documents mean IQ differences among various ethnic groups, and this has often been the source of considerable controversy. Although the basis for these differences has not been identified, there is ample evidence the differences cannot be attributed merely to test bias (something we address in more detail in Chapter 16). Nevertheless, because mean group differences in IQ may result in differential educational treatment and placement, there continues to be the *appearance* of test bias, and this *appearance* promulgates the controversy regarding the use of IQ tests in schools (Canter, 1997). For example, because of the perception of test bias the state of California has prohibited the use of a number of popular IQ tests for making placement decisions with certain ethnic minorities. This is not based on the psychometric properties of the IQ tests, but on public perception and legal cases. Other states have examined the same tests and concluded that the tests are not biased and supported their use with minorities.

Can IQ Be Increased?

Given the importance society places on intelligence and a desire to help children excel, it is reasonable to ask how much IQ can be improved. Hereditarians, those who see genetics as playing the primary role in influencing IQ, hold that efforts to improve it are doomed to failure. In contrast, environmentalists, who see environmental influences as primary, see IQ as being highly malleable. So who is right? In summary, the research suggests that IQ can be improved to some degree, but the improvement is rather limited. For example, adoption studies indicate that lasting gains of approximately 10 to 12 IQ points are the most that can be accomplished through even the most pervasive environmental interventions. The results of preschool intervention programs such as Head Start are much less impressive. These programs may result in modest increases in IQ, but even these gains are typically lost in a few years (Kranzler, 1997). These programs do have other benefits to children, however, and should not be judged only on their impact on IQ.

Do We Really Need IQ Tests in Schools?

Although public debate over the use of IQ tests in schools has typically focused on ethnic differences and the malleability of intelligence, professional educators and psychologists have also debated the usefulness of IQ tests in educational settings. Different terms have been applied to this question over the years. For example, Wigdor and Garner (1982) framed it as the *instructional validity* of IQ test results, Hilliard (1989) referred to it as the *pedagogical utility question,* and Gresham and Witt (1997) indicated it was essentially an issue of *treatment validity.* Whatever label you use, the question is "Does the use of IQ tests result in educational benefits for students?" Proponents of IQ tests highlight evidence that intelligence plays a key role in success in many areas of life, including school achievement. As an extension they argue that information garnered from IQ tests allows educators to tailor instruction so that it meets the specific needs of their students. As a result more students are able to succeed academically. Opponents of IQ tests argue that there is little evidence that the use of

(continued)

IQ tests results in any real improvement in the education of students. A contemporary debate involves the use of IQ tests in the identification of students with learning disabilities. Historically the diagnosis of learning disabilities has been based on a discrepancy model in which students' level of achievement is compared to their overall level of intelligence. If students' achievement in reading, mathematics, or some other specific achievement area is significantly below that expected based on their IQ, they may be diagnosed as having a learning disability (actually the diagnosis of learning disabilities is more complicated than this, but this explanation is sufficient in this context). Currently some researchers are presenting arguments that IQs need not play an essential role in the diagnosis of learning disabilities and are calling for dropping the use of the discrepancy model.

So what does the future hold for IQ testing in the schools? Opponents of IQ tests have predicted for many years that the use of IQ tests in the schools is coming to an end. On the other hand proponents see IQ tests as indispensable. We believe that when used appropriately IQ tests can make a significant contribution to the education of students. As Braden (1997) noted:

> eliminating IQ is different from eliminating intelligence. We can slay the messenger, but the message that children differ in their learning rate, efficiency, and ability to generalize knowledge to new situations (despite similar instruction) remains. (p. 244)

At the same time we recognize that on occasion IQ tests (and other tests) have been used in inappropriate ways that are harmful to students. The key is to be an informed user of assessment results. To this end a professional educator should have a good understanding of the topics covered in this text, including basic psychometric principles and the ethical use of test results.

Due to the often-emotional debate over the meaning of intelligence, many test publishers have adopted more neutral names such as *academic potential, school ability,* and simply *ability* to designate essentially the same construct.

considering this was the precise purpose for which they were initially developed over one hundred years ago. In addition to being good predictors of school performance, research has shown that IQs are fairly stable over time. Nevertheless, these tests have become controversial themselves as a result of the often-emotional debate over the meaning of intelligence. To try and avoid this association and possible misinterpretations, many test publishers have adopted more neutral names such as *academic potential, scholastic ability, school ability, mental ability,* and simply *ability* to designate essentially the same construct.

The Use of Aptitude and Intelligence Tests in Schools

As you can see from the previous discussion, aptitude and intelligence tests have a long history of use in the schools. Their widespread use continues to this day, with major applications including:

- Providing alternative measures of cognitive abilities that reflect information not captured by standard achievement tests or school grades
- Helping teachers tailor instruction to meet a student's unique pattern of cognitive strengths and weaknesses

- Assessing how well students are prepared to profit from school experiences
- Identifying students who are underachieving and may need further assessment to rule out learning disabilities or other cognitive disorders, including mental retardation
- Identifying students for gifted and talented programs
- Helping guide students and parents with educational and vocational planning

Although we have identified the most common uses of aptitude/intelligence tests in the schools, the list clearly is not exhaustive. Classroom teachers are involved to varying degrees with these applications. For example, teachers are frequently called on to administer and interpret many of the group aptitude tests for their own students. School psychologists or other professionals with specific training in administering and interpreting clinical and diagnostic tests typically administer and interpret the individual intelligence and aptitude tests. Even though they are not directly involved in administering individual intelligence tests, it is important for teachers to be familiar with these individual tests. Teachers frequently need to read and understand psychological reports describing student performances on these tests. Additionally, teachers are often on committees that plan and develop educational programs for students with disabilities based on information derived from these tests.

Aptitude–Achievement Discrepancies

One common assessment practice employed in schools and in clinical settings is referred to as *aptitude–achievement discrepancy analysis*.

One common assessment practice employed in schools and in clinical settings is referred to as **aptitude–achievement discrepancy** analysis. This involves comparing students' performance on an aptitude test with their performance on an achievement test. The basic rationale behind this practice is that normally students' achievement scores should be commensurate with their aptitude scores. In other words, students' performance on an aptitude test serves as a type of baseline to compare their performance on an achievement test to, with the expectation that they will be comparable. In the majority of cases this is what you will discover when you compare aptitude–achievement scores. This is not to suggest that the scores will be identical, but that they will be similar, or that there will not be a statistically significant discrepancy. If students' achievement scores are significantly higher than their aptitude scores, they are considered academic overachievers. This may be attributed to a number of factors such as strong motivation and/or an enriched learning environment. This may not necessarily be a reason for concern, but may suggest that while students perform well with the specific skills that are emphasized in school, they have more difficulty solving novel problems and generalizing their skills to new situations. These students may benefit from instructional activities that emphasize transfer of learning, generalization, and creativity (Riverside Publishing, 2002).

If students' achievement scores are significantly lower than their aptitude scores, they may be considered academic underachievers, which may be cause for concern. Academic underachievement may be the result of a number of factors. The student may not be motivated to perform well in school or may have had inadequate opportunities to learn. This could include limited exposure to instruction or an impoverished home environment. It could also reflect cultural or language differences that impact academic achievement.

Naturally a number of medical factors could also be involved, such as impaired hearing or vision. Additionally a number of psychological disorders or factors could be implicated. For example, children with an attention-deficit hyperactive disorder (ADHD) experience attentional problems that may interfere with achievement. Emotional disorders such as depression or anxiety can also detrimentally affect academic performance. Finally, learning disabilities are often characterized by significant discrepancies between aptitude and achievement. In fact, many contemporary definitions of learning disabilities incorporate a significant discrepancy between aptitude and achievement as a diagnostic criterion for the disorder. Although reliance on aptitude–achievement discrepancies to diagnose learning disabilities is currently the focus of considerable debate (e.g., Fletcher, Foorman, Boudousquie, Barnes, Schatschneider, & Francis, 2002), most states continue to use it as an essential element in the diagnosis of learning disabilities.

In practice there are number of methods for determining whether there is a significant discrepancy between aptitude and achievement scores. Reynolds (1985, 1990) developed criteria for conducting aptitude–achievement discrepancy analyses. These included the requirement that correlation and regression analyses, which are used in predicting achievement levels and establishing statistical significance, must be based on representative samples. To help meet this requirement, many of the popular aptitude/intelligence tests are co-normed (i.e., their normative data were based on the exact same sample of children) or linked (i.e., there is some overlap in the standardization sample so that a proportion of the sample received both tests) with a standardized achievement test. This is a desirable situation and whenever possible one should use co-normed or linked aptitude–achievement tests when performing aptitude–achievement analyses. When aptitude–achievement discrepancy analyses are conducted using "nonlinked" tests, the results should be interpreted with caution (The Psychological Corporation, 2002).

Most major group aptitude tests have been co-normed with a major group achievement test to promote more defensible comparisons of ability and school achievement. For example, when the **Otis-Lennon School Ability Test, 8th Edition** (OLSAT 8) is administered concurrently with the Stanford Achievement Test Series, Tenth Edition (Stanford 10), the individual score reports contain scores referred to as Achievement/Ability Comparisons, or AACs. These AACs indicate how an individual student's achievement in specific areas compares to a comparison group of students of the same age, education level, and ability. If students' achievement score is in the top 23% of the comparison group, their ACC is high; if their achievement score is in the middle 54%, their ACC is middle; and if their achievement score is in the bottom 23%, their ACC is low. This gives you a general idea of students' achievement relative to their measured aptitude and can have significant implications for how a teacher interprets school performance and works with the student. For example, a teacher might respond differently to students with poor class grades if their achievement is commensurate with their aptitude, as opposed to a student whose achievement is substantially below that expected based on their aptitude. With the first students (i.e., low achievement scores and low aptitude scores), the teacher might believe the students are performing up to their potential and decide to build on existing strengths and interests and provide a more structured learning environment with more individual guidance and support. With the second students (i.e., low achievement scores relative to aptitude scores), the teacher might believe the students are not performing up to their potential. The teacher not only might try some of the same instructional techniques as with the first students but also might suspect that a learning disability or some other problem is interfering with learning. In this case the teacher might make a referral for additional testing to try and discover the underlying source of the problem. Most major group-administered aptitude and intelligence tests provide comparable methods of making aptitude–achievement comparisons.

Aptitude–achievement comparisons can also be interpreted with individual tests of general intelligence. As we previously noted, many definitions of learning disabilities incorporate a significant discrepancy between ability and achievement as a diagnostic criterion for the disorder. Some of the popular individual intelligence tests have been co-normed with a standardized achievement test to facilitate the calculation of aptitude–achievement comparisons. These comparisons typically involve the identification of a statistically significant discrepancy between ability and achievement. Although approaches differ, the simple-difference method and predicted-achievement method are most commonly used (The Psychological Corporation, 2002). In the brief descriptions of major aptitude/intelligence tests that follow, we will indicate which instruments have been co-normed or linked to achievement tests, and which tests they have been paired with.

Although it is common for educators and clinicians to make aptitude–achievement comparisons, many testing experts criticize the practice.

Before proceeding, we should note that although it is common for educators and clinicians to make ability–achievement comparisons, many testing experts criticize this practice. Critics of this approach argue that ability–achievement discrepancies can usually be attributed simply to measurement error, differences in the content covered, and variations in student attitude and motivation on the different tests (Anastasi & Urbina, 1997; Linn & Gronlund, 2001). Also, as we noted, there is considerable debate about relying on ability–achievement discrepancies to diagnose learning disabilities. Our position can probably be best described as middle of the road. Analysis of ability–achievement discrepancies may help identify children who are experiencing some academic problems, but they should be interpreted cautiously. That is, interpret such discrepancies in the context of other information you have about the student (e.g., school grades, classroom behavior), and if there is reason for concern, pursue additional assessment or consider a referral to a school psychologist or other assessment professional.

Major Aptitude/Intelligence Tests

Group Aptitude/Intelligence Tests

As with the standardized achievement tests discussed in the previous chapter, it is common for schools routinely to administer standardized aptitude/intelligence tests to a large number of students. Also as with standardized achievement tests, the most commonly used aptitude tests are also group administered, largely due to the efficiency of these tests. Finally, similar to group achievement tests, teachers are often called on to help administer and interpret the results of these tests. The guidelines presented in the previous chapter for administering and interpreting standardized tests apply equally well to both achievement and aptitude tests. Currently, the most widely used

The most widely used group aptitude/intelligence tests are produced by CTB McGraw-Hill, Harcourt Assessment, Inc., and Riverside Publishing.

group aptitude/intelligence tests are produced and distributed by three publishers: CTB McGraw-Hill, Harcourt Assessment, Inc., and Riverside Publishing.

Tests of Cognitive Skills, Second Edition (TCS/2).   The **Tests of Cognitive Skills, Second Edition** (TCS/2), published by CTB McGraw-Hill, is designed for use with children in grades 2 through 12. It measures verbal, nonverbal, and memory abilities that are thought to be important for academic success. It includes the following subtests: Sequences (ability to comprehend rules implied in a series of numbers, figures, or letters), Analogies (ability to recognize literal and symbolic relationships), Verbal Reasoning (deductive reasoning, analyzing categories, and recognizing patterns and relationships), and Memory (ability to remember pictures or nonsense words). Although the TCS/2 does not assess quantitative abilities like many other aptitude tests, its assessment of memory abilities is unique. When administered with *TerraNova* The Second Edition, CAT/5, or CTBS/4, anticipated achievement scores can be calculated.

Primary Test of Cognitive Skills (PTCS).   The PTCS, published by CTB McGraw-Hill, is designed for use with students in kindergarten through 1st grade (ages 5.1 to 7.6 years). It has four subtests (Verbal, Spatial, Memory, and Concepts) that require no reading or number knowledge. The PTCS produces an overall Cognitive Skills Index (CSI), and when administered with *TerraNova* The Second Edition, anticipated achievement scores can be calculated.

InView.   *InView,* published by CTB McGraw-Hill, is designed for use with students in grades 2 through 12. It is actually the newest version of the Tests of Cognitive Skills and assesses cognitive abilities in verbal reasoning, nonverbal reasoning, and quantitative reasoning. *InView* contains five subtests: Verbal Reasoning—Words (deductive reasoning, analyzing categories, and recognizing patterns and relationships), Verbal Reasoning—Context (ability to identify important concepts and draw logical conclusions), Sequences (ability to comprehend rules implied in a series of numbers, figures, or letters), Analogies (ability to recognize literal and symbolic relationships), and Quantitative Reasoning (ability to reason with numbers). When administered with *TerraNova* The Second Edition, anticipated achievement scores can be calculated. Figure 13.2 provides an example of an *InView* sample report.

Otis-Lennon School Ability Test, 8th Edition (OLSAT-8).   The OLSAT-8, published by Harcourt Assessment, Inc., is designed for use with students from kindergarten through grade 12. The OLSAT-8 is designed to measure verbal processes and nonverbal processes that are related to success in school. This includes tasks such as detecting similarities and differences, defining words, following directions, recalling words/numbers, classifying, sequencing, completing analogies, and solving mathematics problems. The OLSAT-8 produces Total, Verbal, and Nonverbal School Ability Indexes (SAIs). The publishers note that although the total score is the best predictor of success in school, academic success is dependent on both verbal and nonverbal abilities, and the Verbal and Nonverbal SAIs can provide potentially important information. When administered with the Stanford Achievement Test Series, Tenth Edition (Stanford 10), one can obtain aptitude–achievement comparisons (Achievement/Ability Comparisons, or AACs).

Cognitive Abilities Test (CogAT), Form 6.   The **Cognitive Abilities Test (*CogAT*)**, distributed by Riverside Publishing, is designed for use with students from kindergarten through

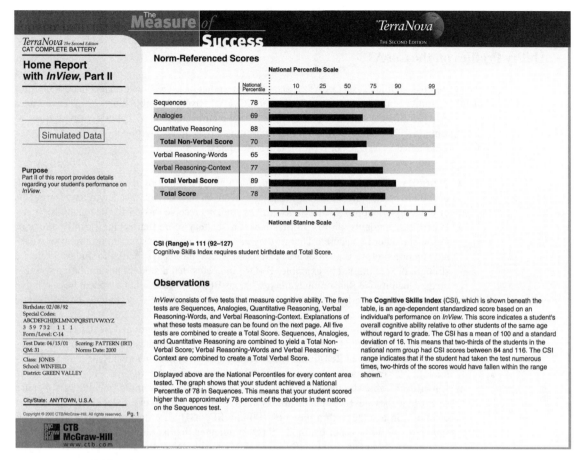

FIGURE 13.2 *InView* **Sample Report—Home Report** This figure is similar to the report parents might receive for their children. The Observations section provides a narrative describing the key aspects of the test and the child's performance.

Source: Reproduced by permission of The McGraw-Hill Companies, Inc. Copyright 2001 CTB/McGraw-Hill. All rights reserved.

grade 12. It provides information about the development of verbal, quantitative, and nonverbal reasoning abilities that are related to school success. Students in kindergarten through grade 2 are given the following subtests: Oral Vocabulary, Verbal Reasoning, Relational Concepts, Quantitative Concepts, Figure Classification, and Matrices. Students in grades 3 through 12 undergo the following subtests: Verbal Classification, Sentence Completion, Verbal Analogies, Quantitative Relations, Number Series, Equation Building, Figure Classification, Figure Analogies, and Figure Analysis. Verbal, quantitative, and nonverbal *battery scores* are provided along with an overall composite score. The publishers encourage educators to focus on an analysis of the profile of the three battery scores rather than the overall composite score. They feel this approach provides the most useful information to teachers regarding how they can tailor instruction to meet the specific needs of students (see Special Interest Topic 13.3 for

Ability Profiles on the *Cog*AT

The Cognitive Abilities Test (*Cog*AT) is an aptitude test that measures the level and pattern of a student's cognitive abilities. When interpreting the *Cog*AT, Riverside Publishing (2002) encourages teachers to focus on the student's performance profile on the three *Cog*AT batteries: Verbal Reasoning, Quantitative Reasoning, and Nonverbal Reasoning. To facilitate interpretation of scores, the profiles are classified as A, B, C, or E profiles, described next.

- **A profiles:** Students with A profiles perform at approximately the s*A*me level on verbal, quantitative, and nonverbal reasoning tasks. That is, they do not have any relative strengths or weaknesses. Approximately one third of students receive this profile designation.
- **B profiles:** Students with B profiles have one battery score that is significantly a*B*ove or *B*elow the other two scores. That is, they have either a relative strength or a relative weakness on one subtest. B profiles are designated with symbols to specify the student's relative strength or weakness. For example, B (Q+) indicates that a student has a relative strength on the Quantitative Reasoning battery, whereas B(V–) indicates that a student has a relative weakness on the Verbal Reasoning battery. Approximately 40% of students have this type of profile.
- **C profiles:** Students with C profiles have *both* a relative strength and a relative weakness. Here the C stands for *C*ontrast. For example, C (V+N–) indicates that a student has a relative strength in Verbal Reasoning and a relative weakness in Nonverbal Reasoning. Approximately 14% of the students demonstrate this profile type.
- **E profiles:** Some students with B or C demonstrate strengths and/or weaknesses that are so extreme they deserve special attention. With the *Cog*AT, score differences of 24 points or more (on a scale with a mean of 100 and SD of 16) are designated as E profiles (*E* stands for *E*xtreme). For example, E (Q–) indicates that a student has an extreme or severe weakness in Quantitative Reasoning. Approximately 14% of students have this type of profile.
- **Level of performance:** In addition to the pattern of performance, it is also important to consider the level of performance. To reflect the level of performance, the letter code is preceded by a number indicating the student's middle stanine score. For example, if a student received stanines of 4, 5, and 6 on the Verbal, Quantitative, and Nonverbal Reasoning batteries, the middle stanine is 5. In classifying stanine scores, Stanine 1 is Very Low, Stanines 2 and 3 are Below Average, Stanines 4–6 are Average, Stanines 7 and 8 are Above Average, and Stanine 9 is Very High.

As an example of a complete profile, the profile 8A would indicate students with relative evenly developed Verbal, Quantitative, and Nonverbal Reasoning abilities with their general level of performance in the Above Average range.

Riverside Publishing (2002) delineates a number of general principles for tailoring instruction to meet the needs of students (e.g., build on strengths) as well as more specific suggestions for working with students with different patterns and levels of performance. *Cog*AT, *Form 6: A Short Guide for Teachers* (Riverside Publishing, 2002), an easy to read and very useful resource, is available online at www.riverpub.com/products/group.cogat6/home.html.

examples). When given with the Iowa Tests of Basic Skills or Iowa Tests of Educational Development, the *Cog*AT provides predicted achievement scores to help identify students whose level of achievement is significantly higher or lower than expected. Figures 13.3, 13.4, and 13.5 provides examples of *Cog*AT score reports. Table 13.1 illustrates the organization of the major group aptitude/intelligence tests.

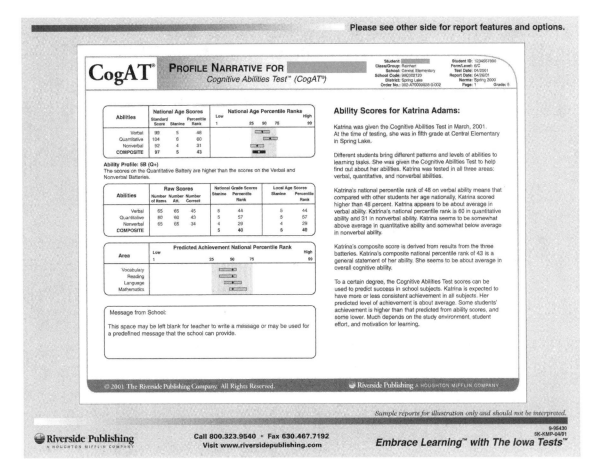

FIGURE 13.3   Profile Narrative for the Cognitive Abilities Test (*Cog*AT) This figure illustrates one of the report formats available from Riverside Publishing for the *Cog*AT. This format provides numerical scores and graphs in the left column and a narrative description of student's performance in the right column. Note that the profile depicted in this figure is identified as 5B (Q+). Please refer to Special Interest Topic 13.3 for information on how *Cog*AT score profiles are coded and how teachers can use this information to customize instruction to meet the needs of individual students.

Source: Reproduced by permission of the publisher, Riverside Publishing Company. Copyright 2001 The Riverside Publishing Company. All rights reserved.

PROFILE NARRATIVE FOR

Iowa Tests of Basic Skills® / CogAT®

	Student:		Student ID: 1234567890
	Class/Group: Rainhart		Form/Level: A/9
	School: Central Elementary		Test Date: 04/2001
	School Code: 99C002120		Report Date: 04/26/01
	District: Spring Lake		Norms: Spring 2000
	Order No.: 002-A70000028-0-002		Page: 1 Grade: 3

NATIONAL PERCENTILE RANK

TESTS	SS	GE	NS	NCE	NPR
Vocabulary	172	3.0	4	39	31
Reading Comprehension	198	4.6	6	62	71
Reading Total	185	3.8	5	51	53
*Word Analysis	172	3.0	4	39	31
*Listening	198	4.6	6	62	71
Spelling	182	3.6	5	49	48
Capitalization	147	1.7	2	22	8
Punctuation	184	3.7	5	51	52
Usage & Expression	180	3.5	5	47	44
Language Total	173	3.1	4	39	30
Math Concepts & Estimation	175	3.3	4	42	35
Math Prob. Solv. & Data Interp.	189	4.1	5	55	59
*Math Computation	176	3.4	4	42	35
Mathematics Total	182	3.7	5	49	48
CORE TOTAL	180	3.4	5	46	42
Social Studies	188	4.0	5	54	58
Science	183	3.6	5	49	49
Maps & Diagrams	183	4.2	6	59	67
Reference Materials	190	4.1	6	57	63
Sources of Info. Total	192	4.2	6	58	65
COMPOSITE	184	3.7	5	50	50

Legend:
SS = Standard Score   NPR = National Percentile Rank
NS = National Stanine   NCE = Normal Curve Equivalent
GE = Grade Equivalent   * Not included in Totals and Composite

Cognitive Abilities Test (CogAT)

	Grade Scores		Age Scores	
	National Stanine	National Percentile Rank	Age Stanine	National Percentile Rank
Verbal	5	44	5	48
Quantitative	5	57	6	60
Nonverbal	4	29	4	31
Composite	5	40	5	43

Profile 5 N(Q+)
The scores on the Quantitative Battery are higher than the scores on the Verbal and Nonverbal Batteries.

Dear Parent or Guardian:

Katrina was given the Iowa Tests of Basic Skills in March 2001. At the time of testing, she was in third grade in Central Elementary in Spring Lake.

Her composite score is the score that best describes her overall achievement on the tests. Katrina's composite national percentile rank of 50 means that she scored higher than 50 percent of third-grade students nationally. Her overall achievement appears to be about average for third grade.

A student's scores can be compared with each other to determine relative strengths and weaknesses. Reading Comprehension and Listening seem to be areas of relative strength for Katrina. Some of these strengths might be used to help improve other areas. Compared to Katrina's other test areas, Capitalization may need the most work.

Different students bring different patterns and levels of abilities to learning tasks. The Cognitive Abilities Test is designed to find out about these abilities. Katrina's national percentile rank of 48 on verbal ability means that, compared with other students her age nationally, Katrina scored higher than 48 percent. Katrina appears to be about average in verbal ability. Katrina's national percentile rank is 60 in quantitative ability and 31 in nonverbal ability. Katrina seems to be somewhat below average in nonverbal ability. Katrina's composite score is derived from results from the three batteries. Katrina's composite national percentile rank of 43 is a general statement of her ability. She seems to be about average in overall cognitive ability.

FIGURE 13.4   Combined Profile Narrative for the Iowa Tests of Basic Skills (ITBS) and the Cognitive Abilities Test (CogAT) This figure illustrates a Profile Narrative depicting a student's performance on both the Iowa Tests of Basic Skills (ITBS) and the Cognitive Abilities Test (CogAT). This format provides numerical scores and graphs in the left column and a narrative description of the student's performance in the right column.

Source: Reproduced by permission of the publisher, Riverside Publishing Company. Copyright 2001 The Riverside Publishing Company. All rights reserved.

Individual Aptitude/Intelligence Tests

As with achievement tests, both group and individual intelligence tests are commonly used in schools. Although teachers are often asked to help administer and interpret the group aptitude tests, school psychologists and other professionals with special training in administering and interpreting clinical and diagnostic tests usually administer and interpret the individual tests. This is not to suggest, however, that teachers do not need to be familiar with these tests. Classroom teachers are being asked more and more frequently to work

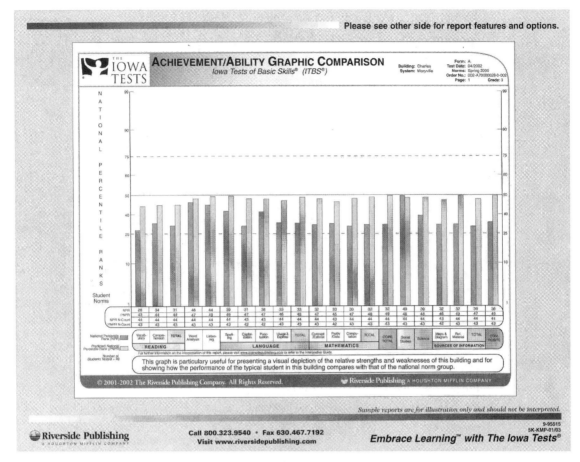

FIGURE 13.5   Achievement–Ability Graphic Comparison of the Iowa Tests of Basic Skills (ITBS) when Combined with the Cognitive Abilities Test (*Cog*AT) This figure presents a visual depiction of the National Percentile Rank for each ITBS test relative to the Predicted National Percentile Rank based on performance on the *Cog*AT. This report illustrates the reporting of group data, in this case the performance of all the 3rd-grade students in one school building.

Source: Reproduced by permission of the publisher, Riverside Publishing Company. Copyright 2001 The Riverside Publishing Company. All rights reserved.

with special education students, and as a result need to be familiar with these tests because they are used in identifying special need students and planning their educational programs (Nitko, 2001).

Wechsler Intelligence Scale for Children—Fourth Edition (WISC–IV).   **The Wechsler Intelligence Scale for Children—Fourth Edition (WISC-IV)** is the fourth edition of the most popular individual test of intellectual ability for children. Empirical surveys of

TABLE 13.1   Organization of Major Group Aptitude/Intelligence Tests

Aptitude Test	Subtests	Composite Scores
Tests of Cognitive Skills, Second Edition (TCS/2)	Sequences Analogies Verbal Reasoning Memory	Verbal ability Nonverbal ability Memory ability
Primary Test of Cognitive Skills (PTCS)	Verbal Spatial Memory Concepts	Cognitive Skills Index (CSI)
InView	Verbal Reasoning—Words Verbal Reasoning—Context Sequences Analogies Quantitative Reasoning	Verbal reasoning Nonverbal reasoning Quantitative reasoning
Otis-Lennon School Ability Test, 8th Edition (OLSAT-8)	Verbal Comprehension Verbal Reasoning Pictorial Reasoning Figural Reasoning Quantitative Reasoning	Verbal School Ability Index Nonverbal School Ability Index Total School Ability Index
Cognitive Abilities Test (*Cog*AT), Form 6 (Levels K, 1, and 2)	Oral Vocabulary Verbal Reasoning Relational Concepts Quantitative Concepts Figure Classification Matrices	Verbal battery score Quantitative score Nonverbal score Overall composite score
Cognitive Abilities Test (*Cog*AT), Form 6 (Levels A–H: Grades 3–12)	Verbal Classification Sentence Completion Verbal Analogies Quantitative Relations Number Series Equation Building Figure Classification Figure Analogies Figure Analysis	Verbal battery score Quantitative score Nonverbal score Overall composite score

Surveys of school psychologists and other assessment personnel have consistently shown that the Wechsler scales are the most popular individual intelligence tests used in clinical and school settings with children.

school psychologists and other assessment personnel have consistently shown that the Wechsler scales are the most popular individual intelligence test used in clinical and school settings with children (e.g., Livingston, Eglsaer, Dickson, & Harvey-Livingston, 2003). The WISC-IV, which takes approximately 1 to 2 hours to administer, must be administered by professionals with extensive training in psychological assessment. Here are brief descriptions of the subtests (Wechsler, 2003):

- *Arithmetic:* The student is presented a set of arithmetic problems to solve mentally (i.e., no pencil and paper) and answer orally. This subtest involves numerical reasoning ability, mental manipulation, concentration, and auditory memory.
- *Block Design:* The student reproduces a series of geometric patterns using red-and-white blocks. This subtest measures the ability to analyze and synthesize abstract visual stimuli, nonverbal concept formation, and perceptual organization.
- *Cancellation:* The student scans sequences of visual stimuli and marks target forms. This subtest involves processing speed, visual attention, and vigilance.
- *Coding:* The student matches and copies symbols that are associated with either objects (i.e., Coding A) or numbers (Coding B). This subtest is a measure of processing speed, short-term visual memory, mental flexibility, attention, and motivation.
- *Comprehension:* The student responds to questions presented orally involving everyday problems or social situations. This subtest is a measure of verbal comprehension and reasoning as well as the ability to apply practical information.
- *Digit Span:* The student is presented sequences of numbers orally to repeat verbatim (i.e., Digits Forward) or in reverse order (i.e., Digits Backwards). This subtest involves short-term auditory memory, attention, and on Digits Backwards, mental manipulation.
- *Information:* The student responds to questions that are presented orally involving a broad range of knowledge (e.g., science, history, geography). This subtest measures the student's general fund of knowledge.
- *Letter–Number Sequencing:* The student reads a list of letters and numbers and then recalls the letters in alphabetical order and the numbers in numerical order. This subtest involves short-term memory, sequencing, mental manipulation, and attention.
- *Matrix Reasoning:* The student examines an incomplete matrix and then selects the item that correctly completes the matrix. This subtest is a measure of fluid intelligence and is considered a largely language-free and culture-fair measure of intelligence.
- *Picture Completion:* The student is presented a set of pictures and must identify what important part is missing. This subtest measures visual scanning and organization as well as attention to essential details.
- *Picture Concepts:* The student examines rows of objects and then selects objects that go together based on an underlying concept. This subtest involves nonverbal abstract reasoning and categorization.
- *Similarities:* Two words are presented orally to the student, who must identify how they are similar. This subtest measures verbal comprehension, reasoning, and concept formation.

- *Symbol Search:* The student scans groups of symbols and indicates whether a target symbol is present. This subtest is a measure of processing speed, visual scanning, and concentration.
- *Vocabulary:* The student is presented a series of words orally to define. This subtest is primarily a measure of word knowledge and verbal conceptualization.
- *Word Reasoning:* The student must identify the underlying or common concept implied by a series of clues. This subtest involves verbal comprehension, abstraction, and reasoning.

Information, Word Reasoning, Picture Completion, Arithmetic, and Cancellation are supplemental subtests whereas the other subtests are core subtests. The administration of supplemental subtests is not mandatory, but they may be used to "substitute" for a core subtest if the core subtest is seen as being inappropriate for a particular student (e.g., due to physical limitation). A supplemental subtest may also be used if a core subtest is "spoiled" or invalidated for some reason (e.g., its administration is interrupted).

The WISC-IV produces four Index Scores, brief descriptions of which follow (Wechsler, 2003):

- *Verbal Comprehension Index (VCI):* The VCI is a composite of Similarities, Vocabulary, and Comprehension. Information and Word Reasoning are supplemental VCI subtests. The VCI reflects verbal reasoning, verbal conceptualization, and knowledge of facts.
- *Perceptual Reasoning Index (PRI):* The PRI is a composite of Block Design, Picture Concepts, and Matrix Reasoning. Picture Completion is a supplemental PRI subtest. The PRI reflects perceptual and nonverbal reasoning, spatial processing abilities, and visual–spatial–motor integration.
- *Working Memory Index (WMI):* The WMI is a composite of Digit Span and Letter–Number Sequencing. Arithmetic is a supplemental WMI subtest. The WMI reflects the student's working memory capacity that includes attention, concentration, and mental control.
- *Processing Speed Index (PSI):* The PSI is a composite of Coding and Symbol Search. Cancellation is a supplemental PSI subtest. The PSI reflects the student's ability to quickly process nonverbal material as well as attention and visual–motor coordination.

This four-index framework is based on factor analytic and clinical research (Wechsler, 2003). Similar index scores have a rich history of clinical use and have been found to provide reliable information about the student's abilities in specific areas (Kaufman, 1994; Kaufman & Lichtenberger, 1999; Wechsler, 2003). Whereas previous Wechsler scales have produced a Verbal IQ, Performance IQ, and Full Scale IQ, the WISC-IV reports only a Full Scale IQ (FSIQ), which reflects the student's general level of intelligence. The organization of the WISC-IV is depicted in Table 13.2. To facilitate the calculation of aptitude–achievement discrepancies, the WISC-IV is statistically linked to the Wechsler Individual Achievement Test—Second Edition (WIAT-II), which was described in the previous chapter on standardized achievement tests. It is also linked to the Adaptive Behavior Assessment System

TABLE 13.2 Organization of the Wechsler Intelligence Scale for Children—Fourth Edition (WISC-IV)

Subtests	Index Scores	IQs
Information Vocabulary Similarities Comprehension Word Reasoning	Verbal Comprehension	
Block Design Picture Completion Matrix Reasoning Picture Concepts	Perceptual Reasoning	Full Scale IQ
Coding Symbol Search Cancellation	Processing Speed	
Digit Span Arithmetic Letter–Number Sequencing	Working Memory	

(ABAS), a measure of adaptive behavior; the Bar-On EQ, a measure of emotional intelligence; the Gifted Rating Scale (GRS), a test used in assessing giftedness; and the Children's Memory Scale (CMS), a test of memory.

The WISC-IV and its predecessors are designed for use with children between the ages of 6 and 16. For early childhood assessment the Wechsler Preschool and Primary Scale of Intelligence—Third Edition (WPPSI-III) is available and is appropriate for children between 2 years 6 months and 7 years 3 months. The Wechsler Adult Intelligence Scale—Third Edition (WAIS-III) is appropriate for individuals between the ages of 16 and 89 years of age.

Stanford-Binet Intelligence Scales, Fifth Edition (SB5).   As we noted, the Stanford-Binet Intelligence Test was the first intelligence test to gain widespread acceptance in the United States. While the Wechsler scales have become the most popular and widely used intelligence tests in schools, the Stanford-Binet scales have continued to have a strong following. The most recent edition of these scales is the **Stanford-Binet Intelligence Scales, Fifth Edition (SB5),** released in 2003. The SB5 is designed for use with individuals from 2 to 85 years of age. It contains 10 subtests, which are combined to produce five factor indexes (i.e., Fluid Reasoning, Knowledge, Quantitative Reasoning, Visual–Spatial Processing, and Working Memory), two domain scores (i.e., Verbal IQ and Nonverbal IQ), and a Full Scale IQ reflecting overall intellectual ability. The organization of the SB5 is depicted in Table 13.3 (Riverside, 2003). A potentially appealing aspect of the SB5 is the availability of an Extended IQ scale that allows the calculation of FSIQs

An appealing aspect of the *Stanford-Binet Intelligence Scales, Fifth Edition* is the availability of an Expanded IQ scale that allows the calculations of IQs higher than 160.

TABLE 13.3   Organization of the Stanford-Binet Intelligence Scales, 5th Edition (SB5)

Subtests	Factor Scores	IQs
Verbal Fluid Reasoning Nonverbal Fluid Reasoning	Fluid Reasoning (FR)	Verbal IQ (composite of 5 verbal subtests)
Verbal Knowledge Nonverbal Knowledge	Knowledge (KN)	
Verbal Quantitative Reasoning Nonverbal Quantitative Reasoning	Quantitative Reasoning (QR)	Nonverbal IQ (composite of 5 nonverbal subtests)
Verbal Visual–Spatial Processing Nonverbal Visual–Spatial Processing	Visual–Spatial Processing (VS)	
Verbal Working Memory Nonverbal Working Memory	Working Memory (WM)	Full Scale IQ (composite of all 10 subtests)

higher than 160. This can be useful in the assessment of extremely gifted individuals. The organization of the SB5 is depicted in Table 13.3.

Woodcock-Johnson III (WJ III) Tests of Cognitive Abilities.   The **Woodcock-Johnson III (WJ III) Tests of Cognitive Abilities** has gained a loyal following and has some unique qualities that warrant mentioning. The battery is designed for use with individuals 2 to 90 years of age. The WJ III Tests of Cognitive Abilities is based on the Cattell-Horn-Carroll (CHC) theory of cognitive abilities, which incorporates Cattell's and Horn's *Gf-Gc* theory and Carroll's three-stratum theory. The CHC theory provides a comprehensive model for assessing a broad range of cognitive abilities, and many clinicians like this battery because it measures such a broad range of abilities. The organization of the WJ III Tests of Cognitive Abilities is depicted in Table 13.4 (Riverside, 2003). The WJ III Tests of Cognitive Abilities is co-normed with the WJ III Tests of Achievement described in the chapter on standardized achievement tests.

Reynolds Intellectual Assessment Scales (RIAS).   The **Reynolds Intellectual Assessment Scales (RIAS)** is a newcomer to the clinician's collection of intelligence tests. It is designed for use with individuals between 3 and 94 years of age and incorporates a co-normed supplemental memory test. One particularly desirable aspect of the RIAS is the ability to obtain a reliable measure of intellectual ability that incorporates both verbal and nonverbal abilities in a relatively brief period (i.e., 20 to 25 minutes). Most other tests that assess verbal and nonverbal cognitive abilities require considerably more time. The supplemental memory tests require about 10 minutes for administration, so a clinician can assess both memory and intelligence in approximately 30 minutes. The organization of the RIAS is depicted in Table 13.5.

One particularly desirable aspect of the *Reynolds Intellectual Assessment Scales (RIAS)* is the ability to obtain a reliable measure of intellectual ability that incorporates both verbal and nonverbal abilities in a relatively brief period (20 to 25 minutes).

TABLE 13.4 Organization of the Woodcock-Johnson III (WJ III) Tests of Cognitive Abilities

Subtests	Factor Scores	IQs
Verbal Comprehension General Information	Comprehension/Knowledge (*Gc*)	
Visual–Auditory Learning Retrieval Fluency Visual–Auditory Learning: Delayed	Long-Term Retrieval (*Glr*)	
Spatial Relations Picture Recognition Planning (*Gv/Gf*)	Visual–Spatial Thinking (*Gv*)	
Sound Blending Auditory Attention Incomplete Words	Auditory Processing (*Ga*)	General Intellectual Ability (GIA)
Concept Formation Analysis–Synthesis Planning (*Gv/Gf*)	Fluid Reasoning (*Gf*)	
Visual Matching Decision Speed Rapid Picture Naming Pair Cancellation	Processing Speed (*Gs*)	
Numbers Reversed Memory for Words Auditory Working Memory	Short-Term Memory (*Gsm*)	

TABLE 13.5 Organization of the Reynolds Intellectual Assessment Scales (RIAS)

Subtests	Factor Scores	IQs
Verbal Reasoning Guess What	Verbal Intelligence Index (VIX)	
Odd-Item Out What's Missing	Nonverbal Intelligence Index (NIX)	Composite Intelligence Index (CIX)
Verbal Memory Nonverbal Memory	Composite Memory Index (CMX)	

TABLE 13.6   Organization of the Universal Nonverbal Intelligence Test (UNIT)

Subtests	Factor Scores	IQs
Symbolic Memory	Memory Quotient (MQ)	
Object Memory		
Spatial Memory	Reasoning Quotient (RQ)	
Analogic Reasoning		Full Scale Intelligence Quotient (FSIQ)
	Symbolic Quotient (SQ)	
Cube Design		
Mazes	Nonsymbolic Quotient (NSQ)	

Note: The Memory Quotient is composed of Symbolic Memory, Object Memory, and Spatial Memory. The Reasoning Quotient is composed of Analogic Reasoning, Cube Design, and Mazes. The Symbolic Quotient is composed of Symbolic Memory, Object Memory, and Analogic Reasoning. The Nonsymbolic Quotient is composed of Spatial Memory, Cube Design, and Mazes.

Universal Nonverbal Intelligence Test (UNIT).   As the name suggests, the **Universal Nonverbal Intelligence Test (UNIT)** is a nonverbal test of general intelligence. It is designed for use with individuals between 5 and 17 years. Although many other nonverbal intelligence tests assess a limited number of abilities (often only matrices), the UNIT incorporates 6 different and varied subtests (see Table 13.6). The UNIT, like all nonverbal intelligence tests, does not assess as broad a range of cognitive abilities as the intelligence tests discussed previously. However, in certain situations a nonverbal test may be desirable. For example, the UNIT and other nonverbal tests are particularly useful when assessing children with different cultural/language backgrounds or speech, language, or hearing impairments (e.g., Riverside, 2003).

Selecting Aptitude/Intelligence Tests

A natural question at this point is "Which of these tests should I use?" There are numerous factors to consider when selecting an aptitude or intelligence test. An initial consideration involves the decision to use a group or individual test. As is the case with standardized achievement tests, group aptitude tests are used almost exclusively for mass testing applications because of their efficiency. Even a relatively brief individual intelligence test typically requires approximately 30 minutes per student to administer. Additionally, assessment professionals with special training in test administration are needed to administer these individual tests. A limited amount of time to devote to testing and a limited number of assessment personnel combine to make it impractical to administer individual tests to a large number of students. However, some situations demand the use of an individual intelligence test. This is often the case when making classification decisions such as identifying students who have learning disabilities or who qualify for gifted and talented programs.

When selecting an intelligence or aptitude test, it is important to consider factors such as how the information will be used and how much time is available for testing.

When selecting an intelligence or aptitude test, it is also important to consider how the information will be used. Are you primarily interested in obtaining a global measure of intellectual ability, or do you need a test that provides multiple scores reflecting different sets of cognitive abilities? As we noted, as a general rule intelligence tests have been shown to be good at predicting academic success. Therefore, if you are simply interested in predicting school success practically any of these tests will meet your needs. If you want to identify the cognitive strengths and weaknesses of your students, you should look at the type of scores provided by the different test batteries and select one that meets your needs from either a theoretical or practical perspective. For example, a teacher or clinician who has embraced the Cattell-Horn-Carroll (CHC) theory of cognitive abilities would be well served using the Woodcock-Johnson III Tests of Cognitive Abilities because it is based on that specific model of cognitive abilities. The key is to select a test that provides the specific type of information you need for your application. Look at the type of factor and intelligence scores the test produces, and select a test that provides meaningful and practical information for your application.

If you are interested in making aptitude–achievement comparisons, ideally you should select an aptitude test that is co-normed with an achievement test that also meets your specific needs. All of the major group aptitude tests we discussed are co-normed or linked to a major group achievement test. When selecting a combination aptitude–achievement battery, you should examine both the achievement test and the aptitude test to determine which set best meets your specific assessment needs. In reference to the individual intelligence tests we discussed, only the WISC-IV and WJ III Tests of Cognitive Abilities have been co-normed with or linked to an individual achievement test battery. While it is optimal to use co-normed instruments when aptitude–achievement comparisons are important, in actual practice many clinicians rely on aptitude and achievement tests that are not co-normed or linked. In this situation, it is important that the norms for both tests be based on samples that are as nearly identical as possible. For example, both tests should be normed on samples with similar characteristics (e.g., age, race, geographic region) and obtained at approximately the same time (Reynolds, 1990).

Another important question involves the population you will use the test with. For example, if you will be working with children with speech, language, or hearing impairments or diverse cultural/language backgrounds, you may want to select a test that emphasizes nonverbal abilities and minimizes cultural influences. Finally, as when selecting any test, you want to examine the psychometric properties of the test. You should select a test that produces reliable scores and has been validated for your specific purposes. All of the aptitude/intelligence tests we have discussed have good psychometric properties, but it is the test user's responsibility to ensure that the selected test has been validated for the intended purposes.

College Admission Tests

A final type of aptitude test that is often used in schools includes those used to make admission decisions at colleges and universities. **College admission tests** were specifically

College admissions tests such as the *SAT* and *ACT* are designed to predict academic performance in college.

designed to predict academic performance in college, and although they are less clearly linked to a specific educational curriculum than most standard achievement tests, they do focus on abilities and skills that are highly academic in nature. Higher education admission decisions are typically based on a number of factors including high school GPA, letters of recommendation, personal interviews, written statements, and extracurricular activities, but in many situations scores on standardized admission tests are a prominent factor. The two most widely used admission assessment tests are the **Scholastic Assessment Test (SAT)** and the **American College Test (ACT).**

Scholastic Assessment Test.   The College Entrance Examination Board (CEEB), commonly referred to as the College Board, was originally formed to provide colleges and universities with a valid measure of students' academic abilities. Its efforts resulted in the development of the first Scholastic Aptitude Test in 1926. The test has undergone numerous revisions and in 1994 the title was changed to Scholastic Assessment Test (SAT). The newest version of the SAT will be administered for the first time in fall 2005 and includes the following three sections: Critical Reading, Mathematics, and Writing. Although the Critical Reading and Mathematics sections assess new content relative to previous exams, the most prominent change is the introduction of the Writing section. This new section contains both multiple-choice questions concerning grammar and a written essay. The SAT is typically taken in a student's senior year. The College Board also produces the Preliminary SAT (PSAT), which is designed to provide practice for the SAT. The PSAT helps students identify their academic strengths and weaknesses so they can better prepare for the SAT. The PSAT is typically taken during a student's junior year. More information about the SAT can be assessed at the College Board's Web site: www.collegeboard.com.

American College Test.   The American College Testing Program (ACT) was initiated in 1959 and is the major competitor of the SAT. The American College Test (ACT) is designed to assess the academic development of high school students and predict their ability to complete college work. The test covers four skill areas—English, Mathematics, Reading, and Science Reasoning—and includes 215 multiple-choice questions. When describing the ACT, the producers emphasize that it is not an aptitude or IQ test, but an achievement test that reflects the typical high school curriculum in English, mathematics, and science. In addition to the four subtests, the ACT also incorporates an interest inventory that provides information that may be useful for educational and career planning. Beginning in the 2004–2005 academic year, the ACT will include an optional 30-minute writing test that assesses an actual sample of students' writing. More information about the ACT can be assessed at the ACT's Web site: www.act.org.

Summary

In this chapter we discussed the use of standardized intelligence and aptitude tests in the schools. We started by noting that aptitude/intelligence tests are designed to assess the cognitive skills, abilities, and knowledge that are acquired as the result of broad, cumulative life experiences. We compared aptitude/intelligence tests with achievement tests that are designed to assess skills and knowledge in areas in which specific instruction has been provided. We noted that this distinction is not absolute, but rather one of degree. Both aptitude and achievement tests measure developed cognitive abilities. The distinction lies with the degree to which the cognitive abilities are dependent on or linked to formal learning experiences. Achievement tests should measure abilities that are developed as the direct result of formal instruction and training whereas aptitude tests should measure abilities acquired from all life experiences, not only formal schooling. In addition to this distinction, achievement tests are usually used to measure what has been learned or achieved at a fixed point in time, whereas aptitude tests are often used to predict future performance. Although the distinction between aptitude and achievement tests is not as clear as one might expect, the two types of tests do differ in their focus and are used for different purposes.

The most popular type of aptitude test used in schools today is the general intelligence test. Intelligence tests actually had their origin in the public schools approximately 100 years ago when Alfred Binet and Theodore Simon developed the Binet-Simon Scale to identify children who needed special educational services to be successful in French schools. The test was well received in France and was subsequently translated and standardized in the United States to produce the Stanford-Binet Intelligence Test. Subsequently other test developers developed their own intelligence tests and the age of intelligence testing had arrived. Some of these tests were designed for group administration and others for individual administration. Some of these tests focused primarily on verbal and quantitative abilities whereas others placed more emphasis on visual–spatial and abstract problem-solving skills. Some of these tests even avoided verbal content altogether. Research suggests that, true to their initial purpose, intelligence tests are fairly good predictors of academic success. Nevertheless, the concept of intelligence has taken on different meanings for different people, and the use of general intelligence tests has been the focus of controversy and emotional debate for many years. This debate is likely to continue for the foreseeable future. In an attempt to avoid negative connotations and misinterpretations, many test publishers have switched to more neutral titles such as *school ability* or simply *ability* to designate the same basic construct.

Contemporary intelligence tests have numerous applications in today's schools. These include providing a broader measure of cognitive abilities than traditional achievement tests, helping teachers tailor instruction to meet students' unique patterns of cognitive strengths and weaknesses, determining whether students are prepared for educational experiences, identifying students who are underachieving and may have learning or other cognitive disabilities, identifying students for gifted and talented programs, and helping students and parents make educational and career decisions. Classroom teachers are involved to varying degrees with practically all of these applications. Teachers often help with the administration and interpretation of group aptitude tests, and although they typically do not administer and interpret individual aptitude tests, they do need to be familiar with the tests and the type of information they provide.

One common practice when interpreting intelligence tests is referred to as aptitude–achievement discrepancy analysis. This simply involves comparing a student's performance on an aptitude test with performance on an achievement test. The expectation is that achievement will be commensurate with aptitude. Students with achievement scores significantly greater than ability scores may be considered academic overachievers whereas those with achievement scores significantly below ability scores may be considered underachievers. There are a number of possible causes for academic underachievement ranging from poor student motivation to specific learning disabilities. We noted that there are different methods for determining whether a significant discrepancy between ability and achievement scores exists and that standards have been developed for performing these analyses. To meet these standards, many of the popular aptitude and achievement tests have been co-normed or statistically linked to permit comparisons. We cautioned that while ability–achievement discrepancy analysis is a common practice, not all assessment experts support the practice. As we have emphasized throughout this text, test results should be interpreted in addition to other sources of information when making important decisions. This suggestion applies when making ability–achievement comparisons.

The chapter concluded with an examination of a number of the popular group and individual aptitude tests. Finally, a number of factors were discussed that should be considered when selecting an aptitude test. These included deciding between a group and individual test, determining what type of information is needed (e.g., overall IQ versus multiple factors scores), determining what students the test will be used with, and evaluating the psychometric properties (e.g., reliability and validity) of the test.

KEY TERMS AND CONCEPTS

Achievement tests, p. 320
Alfred Binet and Theodore Simon, p. 323
American College Test (ACT), p. 344
Aptitude–achievement discrepancies, p. 327
Aptitude tests, p. 321
Binet-Simon Scale, p. 323
Cognitive Abilities Test (CogAT), p. 330
College admission tests, p. 343

Intelligence, p. 323
Intelligence quotient (IQ), p. 323
InView, p. 330
Otis-Lennon School Ability Test, 8th Edition, p. 328
Primary Test of Cognitive Skills, p. 330
Reynolds Intellectual Assessment Scales (RIAS), p. 340
Scholastic Assessment Test (SAT), p. 344

Stanford-Binet Intelligence Scales, Fifth Edition (SB5), p. 339
Tests of Cognitive Skills, Second Edition, p. 330
Universal Nonverbal Intelligence Test (UNIT), p. 342
Wechsler Intelligence Scale for Children—Fourth Edition (WISC-IV), p. 335
Woodcock-Johnson III (WJ III) Tests of Cognitive Abilities, p. 340

RECOMMENDED READINGS

Cronbach, L. J. (1975). Five decades of public controversy over mental testing. *American Psychologist, 36,* 1–14. An interesting and readable chronicle of the controversy surrounding mental testing during much of the twentieth century.
Kamphaus, R. W. (2001). *Clinical assessment of child and adolescent intelligence.* Boston: Allyn & Bacon. This text provides an excellent discussion of the assessment of intelligence and related issues.

14 Assessment of Behavior and Personality

Although educators have typically focused primarily on cognitive abilities, federal laws mandate that schools provide special education and related services to students with emotional disorders. Before these services can be provided, the schools must be able to identify children with these disorders. The process of identifying these children often involves a psychological evaluation completed by a school psychologist or other clinician. Teachers often play an important role in this assessment process.

CHAPTER HIGHLIGHTS

Assessing Behavior and Personality

Behavior Rating Scales

Self-Report Measures

Projective Techniques

LEARNING OBJECTIVES

After reading and studying this chapter, students should be able to:

1. Compare and contrast maximum performance tests and typical response tests.
2. Explain how classroom teachers are involved in the assessment of children with emotional disorders.
3. Define personality as used in assessment and explain why this should be applied cautiously with children and adolescents.
4. Define and give examples of response sets.
5. Explain how test validity scales can be used to guard against response sets and give an example.
6. Describe the strengths and limitations of behavior rating scales.
7. Describe and evaluate the major behavior rating scales.
8. Describe the strengths and limitations of self-report measures.
9. Describe and evaluate the major self-report measures.
10. Explain the central hypothesis of projective techniques.
11. Describe the strengths and limitations of projective techniques.
12. Describe and evaluate the major projective techniques.

In Chapter 1, when describing the different types of tests, we noted that tests typically can be classified as measures of either maximum performance or typical response. Maximum performance tests are often referred to as ability tests. On these tests items are usually scored as either correct or incorrect, and examinees are encouraged to demonstrate the best performance possible. Achievement and aptitude tests are common examples of maximum performance tests. In contrast, **typical response tests** attempt to measure the typical behavior and characteristics of examinees. Typical response tests typically assess constructs such as personality, behavior, attitudes, or interests (Cronbach, 1990). Although maximum performance tests are the most prominent type of test used in schools today, typical response tests are used frequently also.

Typical response tests **usually assess constructs such as personality, behavior, attitudes, or interests.**

Public Law 94-142 and its most current reauthorization, the Individuals with Disabilities Education Act—97 (IDEA 97), mandate that schools provide special education and related services to students with emotional disorders. (As of this writing, the U.S. Senate is actively debating the passage of the next reauthorization of **IDEA;** however, despite a number of proposed changes, the requirement that the schools provide a free, appropriate public education to students with serious emotional disturbance is not expected to change.) These laws compelled schools to identify students with emotional disorders and, as a result, expanded school assessment practices, which had traditionally focused primarily on cognitive abilities, to include the evaluation of personality, behavior, and related constructs. The primary goal of this chapter is to help teachers become familiar with the major instruments used in assessing emotional and behavioral features of children and adolescents and to assist them in understanding the process of evaluating such students because teachers are often called on to provide relevant information on students' behavior. Teachers are involved to varying degrees with the assessment of student behavior and personality. Classroom teachers are often asked to help with the assessment of students in their classroom, for example, by completing behavior rating scales on students in their class. This practice provides invaluable data to school psychologists and other clinicians because teachers have a unique opportunity to observe children in their classrooms. Teachers can provide information on how the child behaves in different contexts, both academic and social. As a result, the knowledge derived from behavior rating scales completed by teachers plays an essential role in the assessment of student behavior and personality. Teachers may also be involved with the development and implementation of educational programs for children with emotional or behavioral disorders. As part of this role, teachers may need to read psychological reports and incorporate these findings into instructional strategies. In summary, although teachers do not need to become experts in the field of psychological assessment, it is vital for them to become familiar with the types of instruments used in assessing children's behavior and personality.

Personality **can be defined as an individual's characteristic way of thinking, feeling, and behaving.**

Before proceeding, it is beneficial to clarify how assessment experts conceptualize personality. Gray (1999) defines **personality** as "the relatively consistent patterns of thought, feeling, and behavior that characterize each person as a unique individual" (p. G12). This definition probably captures most people's concept of personality. In conventional assessment terminology, personality is defined in a similar manner, incorporating a host of emotional, behavioral, motivational, interpersonal, and attitudinal characteristics (Anastasi & Urbina, 1997). In the context of child and adolescent assessment, the term *personality* should be used with some care. Measures of personality and behavior in children demonstrate less stability than comparable measures in adults. This is not particularly surprising given the rapid developmental changes characteristic of children and adolescents. As a result, when using the term *personality* in the context of child and adolescent assessment, it is best to interpret it cautiously and understand that it does not necessarily reflect a fixed construct, but one that is subject to development and change.

Assessing Behavior and Personality

Even though we might not be consciously aware of it, we all engage in the assessment of personality and behavior on a regular basis. When you note that "Johnny has a good personality," "Tommy is a difficult child," or "Susan is extroverted," you are making a judgment about personality. We use these informal evaluations to determine whom we want to associate with and whom we want to avoid. We use these informal evaluations to determine who can be trusted and who cannot.

The development of the first formal instrument for assessing personality is typically traced to the efforts of Robert Woodworth. In 1918, he developed the Woodworth Personal Data Sheet, which was designed to help collect personal information about military recruits. Much as the development of the Binet scales ushered in the era of intelligence testing, the introduction of the Woodworth Personal Data Sheet ushered in the era of personality assessment. Subsequent instruments for assessing personality and behavior took on a variety of forms, but they all had the same basic purpose of helping us to understand the behavior and personal characteristics of ourselves and others. Special Interest Topic 14.1 provides a brief description of an early test of personality.

Response Sets

A *response set* is present when test takers respond in a manner that misrepresents their true characteristics.

Response biases or **response sets** are present when individuals respond on a test in a manner that misrepresents either their own or another person's true characteristics. For example, an individual completing an employment-screening test might attempt to present an overly positive image by answering all of the questions in the most socially appropriate manner possible, even if these responses do not accurately represent the person. On the other hand, a teacher who is hoping to have a disruptive student transferred from his or her class might be inclined to exaggerate the student's misbehavior in order to hasten that student's removal. In both of these situations the individual completing the test or scale responded in a manner that systematically distorted reality. Response sets can be present when completing maximum performance tests. For example, an individual with a pending court case claiming neurological damage resulting from an accident might "fake bad" on an intelligence test in an effort to substantiate the presence of brain damage and enhance his or her legal case. However, response sets are an even bigger

SPECIAL INTEREST TOPIC **14.1**

The Handsome and the Deformed Leg

Sir Francis Galton (1884) related a tale attributed to Benjamin Franklin about a crude personality test. Franklin describes two types of people, those who are optimistic and focus on the positive and those who are pessimistic and focus on the negative. Franklin reported that one of his philosophical friends desired a test to help him identify and avoid people who were pessimistic, offensive, and prone to acrimony.

> In order to discover a pessimist at first sight, he cast about for an instrument. He of course possessed a thermometer to test heat, and a barometer to tell the air-pressure, but he had no instrument to test the characteristic of which we are speaking. After much pondering he hit upon a happy idea. He chanced to have one remarkably handsome leg, and one that by some accident was crooked and deformed, and these he used for the purpose. If a stranger regarded his ugly leg more than his handsome one he doubted him. If he spoke of it and took no notice of the handsome leg, the philosopher determined to avoid his further acquaintance. Franklin sums up by saying, that every one has not this two-legged instrument, but every one with a little attention may observe the signs of a carping and fault-finding disposition. (pp. 9–10)

Source: This tale was originally reported by Sir Francis Galton (1884). Galton's paper was reproduced in Goodstein & Lanyon (1971).

problem on typical performance tests. Because many of the constructs measured by typical performance tests (e.g., personality, behavior, attitudes, beliefs) have dimensions that may be seen as either socially "desirable" or "undesirable," the tendency to employ a response set is heightened. When response sets are present, the validity of the test results may be compromised because they introduce construct-irrelevant error to test scores (e.g., AERA et al., 1999). That is, the test results do not accurately reflect the construct the test was designed to measure. To combat this, many typical performance tests incorporate some type of **validity scale** designed to detect the presence of response sets. Validity scales take different forms, but the general principle is that they are designed to detect individuals who are not responding in an accurate manner. Special Interest Topic 14.2 provides an example of a "fake good" response set.

Assessment of Behavior and Personality in the Schools

The instruments used to assess behavior and personality in the schools can usually be classified as behavior rating scales, self-report measures, or projective techniques. The results of a recent national survey of school psychologists indicated that five of the top ten instruments were behavior rating scales, four were projective techniques, and one was a self-report measure (Livingston, Eglsaer, Dickson, & Harvey-Livingston, 2003; see Table 14.1 for a listing of these assessment instruments). These are representative of the type of instruments school psychologists use to assess children suspected of having an emotional, behavioral, or other type of disorder. These are not the only types of typical performance tests

An Example of a "Fake Good" Response Set

Self-report inventories, despite the efforts of test developers, always remain susceptible to response sets. The following case is an authentic example. In this case the BASC-SRP was utilized.

Maury was admitted to the inpatient psychiatric unit of a general hospital with the diagnoses of impulse control disorder and major depression. She is repeating the seventh grade this school year because she failed to attend school regularly last year. When skipping school, she spent time roaming the local shopping mall or engaging in other relatively unstructured activities. She was suspended from school for lying, cheating, and arguing with teachers. She failed all of her classes in both semesters of the past school year.

Maury's responses to the diagnostic interview suggested that she was trying to portray herself in a favorable light and not convey the severity of her problems. When asked about hobbies, for example, she said that she liked to read. When questioned further, however, she could not name a book that she had read.

Maury's father reported that he has been arrested many times. Similarly, Maury and her sisters have been arrested for shoplifting. Maury's father expressed concern about her education. He said that Maury was recently placed in an alternative education program designed for youth offenders.

Maury's SRP results show evidence of a social desirability or fake good response set. All of her clinical scale scores were lower than the normative T-score mean of 50 and all of her adaptive scale scores were above the normative mean of 50. In other words, the SRP results suggest that Maury is optimally adjusted, which is in stark contrast to the background information obtained.

Maury's response set , however, was identified by the Lie scale of the SRP, where she obtained a score of 9, which is on the border of the caution and extreme caution ranges. Her full complement of SRP scores are:

Clinical Scales		**Adaptive Scales**	
Scale	*T-Score*	*Scale*	*T-Score*
Attitude to School	41	Relations with Parents	53
Attitude to Teachers	39	Interpersonal Relations	57
Sensation Seeking	41	Self-Esteem	54
Atypicality	38	Self-Reliance	52
Locus of Control	38		
Somatization	39		
Social Stress	38		
Anxiety	34		
Depression	43		
Sense of Inadequacy	41		

Source: Clinical Assessment of Child and Adolescent Personality and Behavior (2nd ed.) (Box 6.1, p. 99), by R. W. Kamphaus and P. J. Frick, 2002, Boston, MA: Allyn & Bacon. Copyright 2002 by Pearson Education. Reprinted with permission.

TABLE 14.1   Ten Most Popular Tests of Child Personality and Behavior

Name of Test	Type of Test
1. BASC Teacher Rating Scale	Behavior rating scale
2. BASC Parent Rating Scale	Behavior rating scale
3. BASC Self-Report of Personality	Self-report measure
4. Draw-A-Person	Projective technique
5. Conners Rating Scales—Revised	Behavior rating scale
6. Sentence Completion Tests	Projective technique
7. House-Tree-Person	Projective technique
8. Kinetic Family Drawing	Projective technique
9. Teacher Report Form (Achenbach)	Behavior rating scale
10. Child Behavior Checklist (Achenbach)	Behavior rating scale

Note: BASC = Behavior Assessment System for Children. The Conners Rating Scales—Revised and Sentence Completion Tests actually were tied. Based on a national sample of school psychologists (Livingston et al., 2003).

used in the schools. For example, school guidance counselors often use interest inventories to assess a student's interest in different career options. However, we will be limiting our discussion primarily to tests used in assessing children and adolescents with emotional and behavioral disorders. To this end, we will briefly describe behavior rating scales, self-report measures, and projective techniques in the following sections.

Behavior Rating Scales

A *behavior rating scale* is an inventory that asks an informant to rate a child on a number of dimensions.

A **behavior rating scale** is essentially an inventory that asks an informant, usually a parent or teacher, to rate a child on a number of dimensions. For example, the instructions might ask an informant to rate a child according to the following guidelines:

0 = rarely or never
1 = occasionally
2 = often or almost always

The scale will then present a series of item stems for which the informant rates the child. For example:

1. Has difficulty paying attention:	0	1	2
2. Lies:	0	1	2
3. Plays well with peers:	0	1	2
4. Contributes to class discussion:	0	1	2

Behavior rating scales have a number of positive characteristics (e.g., Kamphaus & Frick, 2002; Piacentini, 1993; Ramsay, Reynolds, & Kamphaus, 2002; Witt, Heffer, & Pfeiffer, 1990). For example, children may have difficulty accurately reporting their own feelings and behaviors due to a number of factors such as limited insight or verbal abilities or, in the context of self-report tests, limited reading ability. However, when using behavior rating scales, information is solicited from the important adults in a child's life. Ideally these adult informants will have had ample opportunities to observe the child in a variety of settings over an extended period of time. Behavior rating scales also represent a cost-effective and time-efficient method of collecting assessment information. For example, a clinician may be able to collect information from both parents and one or more teachers with a minimal investment of time. Most popular behavior rating scales have separate inventories for parents and teachers. This allows the clinician to collect information from multiple informants who observe the child from different perspectives and in various settings. Behavior rating scales can also help clinicians assess the presence of rare behaviors. Although any responsible clinician will interview the child, parents, and hopefully teachers, it is still possible to miss important indicators of behavioral problems. The use of well-designed behavior rating scales may help detect the presence of rare behaviors, such as fire setting and animal cruelty, that might be missed in a clinical interview.

There are some limitations associated with the use of behavior rating scales. Even though the use of adult informants to rate children provides some degree of objectivity, these scales are still subject to response sets that may distort the true characteristics of the child. For example, as a "cry for help" a teacher may exaggerate the degree of a student's problematic behavior in hopes of hastening a referral for special education services. Accordingly, parents might not be willing or able to acknowledge their child has significant emotional or behavioral problems and tend to underrate the degree and nature of problem behaviors. Although behavior rating scales are particularly useful in diagnosing "externalizing" problems such as aggression and hyperactivity, which are easily observed by adults, they are less helpful when assessing "internalizing" problems such as depression and anxiety, which are not as apparent to observers.

In recent years behavior rating scales have gained popularity and become increasingly important in the assessment of children and adolescents.

Over the past two decades, behavior rating scales have gained popularity and become increasingly important in the psychological assessment of children and adolescents (Livingston et al., 2003). It is common for a clinician to have both parents and teachers complete behavior rating scales for one child. This is desirable because parents and teachers have the opportunity to observe the child in different settings and can contribute unique yet complimentary information to the assessment process. As a result, school psychologists will frequently ask classroom teachers to help with student evaluations by completing behavior rating scales on one of their students. Next we will briefly review some of the most popular scales.

Behavior Assessment System for Children—Teacher Rating Scale and Parent Rating Scale (TRS and PRS)

The **Behavior Assessment System for Children** (BASC) is an integrated set of instruments that includes a **Teacher Rating Scale,** a **Parent Rating Scale,** self-report scales, a classroom observation system, and a structured developmental history (Reynolds & Kamphaus, 1992). Although the BASC is a relatively new set of instruments, a 2003 national survey of school psychologists indicates that the TRS and PRS are the most frequently used behavior rating scales in the public schools today (Livingston et al., 2003). Information obtained from the publisher indicates the BASC was used with an estimated more than 1 million children in the United States alone in 2003. The TRS and PRS are appropriate for children from 2½ to 18 years. Both the TRS and PRS provide item stems to which the informant responds *Never, Sometimes, Often,* or *Almost Always.* The TRS is designed to provide a thorough examination of school-related behavior whereas the PRS is aimed at the home and community environment (Ramsay, Reynolds, & Kamphaus, 2002). Table 14.2 depicts the 10 clinical

TABLE 14.2   Composites and Scales in the TRS and PRS

Composite / Scale	Teacher Rating Scales		Parent Rating Scales	
	Child	*Adolescent*	*Child*	*Adolescent*
Externalizing Problems	*	*	*	*
Aggression	*	*	*	*
Hyperactivity	*	*	*	*
Conduct Problems	*	*	*	*
Internalizing Problems	*	*	*	*
Anxiety	*	*	*	*
Depression	*	*	*	*
Somatization	*	*	*	*
School Problems	*	*		
Attention problems	*	*	*	*
Learning problems	*	*		
(Other Problems)				
Atypicality	*	*	*	*
Withdrawal	*	*	*	*
Adaptive Skills	*	*	*	*
Adaptability	*		*	
Leadership	*	*	*	*
Social skills	*	*	*	*
Study skills	*	*		
Behavioral Symptom Index	*	*	*	*

Source: From *Behavior Assessment System for Children (BASC): Manual* (Table 1.1, p. 3), by Cecil R. Reynolds and Randy W. Kamphaus, 1992. Copyright 1992 by the American Guidance Service, Inc., 4201 Woodland Road, Circle Pines, MN 55014-1796. Reproduced with permission of publisher. All rights reserved. www.agsnet.com

scales, 4 adaptive scales, and 6 composites for all the preschool, child, and adolescent versions of both instruments. Reynolds and Kamphaus (1992) describe the individual subscales of the TRS and PRS as follows:

- *Adaptability:* ability to adapt to changes in one's environment.
- *Aggression:* acting in a verbally or physically hostile manner that threatens others.
- *Anxiety:* being nervous or fearful about actual or imagined problems or situations.
- *Attention Problems:* inclination to be easily distracted or have difficulty concentrating.
- *Atypicality:* reflects behavior that is immature, bizarre, or suggestive of psychotic processes (e.g., hallucinations).
- *Conduct Problems:* inclination to display antisocial behavior (e.g., cruelty, destructive).
- *Depression:* reflects feelings of sadness and unhappiness.
- *Hyperactivity:* inclination to be overactive and impulsive.
- *Leadership:* reflects ability to achieve academic and social goals, particularly the ability to work with others.
- *Learning Problems:* reflects the presence of academic difficulties. This scale is only on the TRS.
- *Social Skills:* reflects the ability to interact well with peers and adults in a variety of settings.
- *Somatization:* reflects the tendency to complain about minor physical problems.
- *Study Skills:* reflects skills that are associated with academic success (e.g., study habits, organization skills). This scale is only on the TRS.
- *Withdrawal:* the inclination to avoid social contact.

In addition to these individual scales, the TRS and PRS provide several different composite scores. The authors recommend that interpretation follow a "top-down" approach, by which the clinician starts at the most global level and progresses to more specific levels (e.g., Reynolds & Kamphaus, 1992). The most global measure is the Behavioral Symptoms Index (BSI), which is a composite of the Aggression, Attention Problems, Anxiety, Atypicality, Depression, and Somatization scales. The BSI reflects the overall level of behavioral problems and provides the clinician with a reliable but nonspecific index of pathology. For more specific information about the nature of the problem behavior, the clinician proceeds to the four lower-order composite scores:

- *Internalizing Problems:* This is a composite of the Anxiety, Depression, and Somatization scales. Some authors refer to internalizing problems as "overcontrolled" behavior. Students with internalizing problems experience subjective or internal discomfort or distress, but they do not typically display acting-out or disruptive behaviors (e.g., aggression, impulsiveness). As a result, these children may go unnoticed by teachers and school-based clinicians.
- *Externalizing Problems:* This is a composite of the Aggression, Conduct Problems, and Hyperactivity scales. Relative to the behaviors and symptoms associated with internalizing problems, the behaviors associated with externalizing problems are clearly apparent to observers. Children with high scores on this composite are

typically disruptive to both peers and adults, and usually will be noticed by teachers and other adults.

- *School Problems:* This composite consists of the Attention Problems and Learning Problems scales. High scores on this scale suggest academic motivation, attention, and learning difficulties that are likely to hamper academic progress. This composite is available only for the BASC-TRS.
- *Adaptive Skills:* This is a composite of Adaptability, Leadership, Social Skills, and Study Skills scales. It reflects a combination of social, academic, and other positive skills (Reynolds & Kamphaus, 1992).

The third level of analysis involves examining the 14 clinical (e.g., Hyperactivity, Depression) and adaptive scales (e.g., Leadership, Social Skills). Finally, clinicians will often examine the individual items. Although individual items are often unreliable, when interpreted cautiously they may provide clinically important information. This is particularly true of what is often referred to as "critical items." Critical items, when coded in a certain way, suggest possible danger to self or others. For example, if a parent or teacher reports that a child often "threatens to harm self or others," the clinician would want to determine whether these statements indicate imminent danger to the child or others.

When interpreting the Clinical Composites and Scale scores, high scores reflect abnormality or pathology. The authors provide the following classifications: T-score > 70 is Clinically Significant; 60–69 is At-Risk; 41–59 is Average; 31–40 is Low; and < 30 is Very Low. Scores on the Adaptive Composite and Scales are interpreted differently, with high scores reflecting adaptive or positive behaviors. The authors provide the following classifications: *T*-score > 70 is Very High; 60–69 is High; 41–59 is Average; 31–40 is At-Risk; and < 30 is Clinically Significant. Computer software is available to facilitate scoring and interpretation, and the use of this software is recommended because hand scoring can be challenging for new users. An example of a completed TRS profile is depicted in Figure 14.1.

The TRS and PRS have several unique features that promote their use. First, they contain a validity scale that helps the clinician detect the presence of response sets. As noted previously, validity scales are specially developed and incorporated in the test for the purpose of detecting response sets. Both the parent and teacher scales contain a "fake bad" (F) index that is elevated when an informant excessively rates maladaptive items as *Almost always* and adaptive items as *Never*. If this index is elevated, the clinician should consider the possibility that a negative response set has skewed the results. Another unique feature of these scales is that they assess both negative and adaptive behaviors. Before the advent of the BASC, behavior rating scales were often criticized for focusing only on negative behaviors and pathology. Both the TRS and PRS address this criticism by assessing a broad spectrum of behaviors, both positive and negative. The identification of positive characteristics can facilitate treatment by helping identify strengths to build on. Still another unique feature is that the TRS and PRS provide three norm-referenced comparisons that can be selected depending on the clinical focus. The child's ratings can be compared to a general national sample, a gender-specific national sample, or a national clinical sample composed of children who have a clinical diagnosis and are receiving treatment. In summary, the BASC PRS and BASC TRS are psychometrically sound instruments that have gained considerable support in recent years.

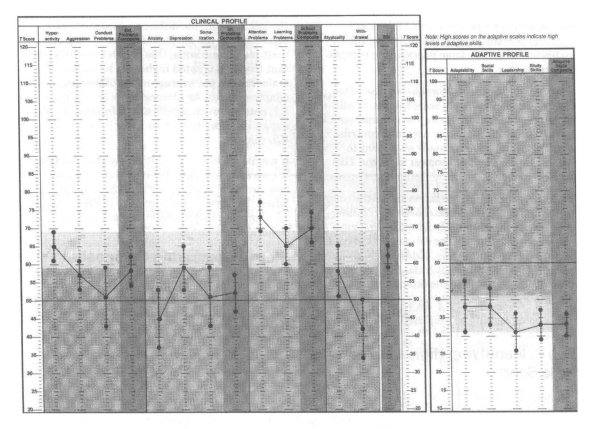

FIGURE 14.1   Completed Clinical and Adaptive Profile Sections of a TRS

Source: From *Behavior Assessment System for Children (BASC): Manual,* by Cecil R. Reynolds and Randy W. Kamphaus, 1992. Copyright 1992 by the American Guidance Service, Inc., 4201 Woodland Road, Circle Pines, MN 55014-1796. Reproduced with permission of publisher. All rights reserved. www.agsnet.com

Conners Rating Scales—Revised (CRS-R)

The **Conners' Rating Scales—Revised (CRS-R)** (Conners, 1997) have a rich history of use in the assessment of children and adolescents, dating back to the late 1960s when the early version of the scales were developed to measure the effectiveness of medication in the treatment of hyperactive children (Kamphaus & Frick, 2002). The current version, the Conners Rating Scales—Revised, includes teacher and parent inventories and is appropriate for children from 3 through 17 years. There are both long forms (e.g., 59 or 80 items) and short forms (27 or 28 items) available. Conners (1997) describes the subscales of the long forms as follows:

- *Oppositional:* a tendency to break rules, be in conflict with authority figures, and be easily angered.
- *Cognitive Problems/Inattention:* characterized by problems with attention, concentration, organization, and difficulty completing projects.

- *Hyperactivity:* reflects a tendency to be overactive, restless, and impulsive.
- *Anxious/Shy:* propensity to be anxious, fearful, and overly emotional.
- *Perfectionism:* inclination to be obsessive and set high standards for themselves.
- *Social Problems:* characterized by feelings of isolation and low self-esteem.
- *Psychosomatic:* tendency to report numerous physical complaints. This scale is only present on the Parent Rating Scale.

The CRS-R produces two index scores, the ADHD Index and the Conners Global Index (CGI). The ADHD Index is a combination of items that have been found to be useful in identifying children who have attention-deficit hyperactivity disorder (ADHD). The CGI, a more general index, is sensitive to a variety of behavioral and emotional problems. The CGI (formerly the Hyperactivity Index) has been shown to be a sensitive measure of medication (e.g., psychostimulants such as Ritalin) treatment effects with children with ADHD. Computer-scoring software is available for the CRS-R to facilitate scoring and interpretation. Specific strengths of the CRS-R include its rich clinical history and the availability of short forms that may be used for screening purposes or situations in which repeated administrations are necessary (e.g., measuring treatment effects; Kamphaus & Frick, 2002).

Child Behavior Checklist and Teacher Report Form (CBCL and TRF)

The **Child Behavior Checklist (CBCL)** and the **Teacher Report Form (TRF)** (Achenbach, 1991a, 1991b) are two components of an integrated system that also includes a self-report scale and a direct observation system. There are two forms of the CBCL, one for children 2 to 3 years and one for children 4 to 18 years. The TRF is appropriate for children from 5 to 18 years. The CBCL and TRF have long played an important role in the assessment of children and adolescents and continue to be among the most frequently used psychological tests in schools today. The scales contain two basic sections. The first section collects information about the child's activities and competencies in areas such as recreation (e.g., hobbies and sports), social functioning (e.g., clubs and organizations), and schooling (e.g., grades). The second section assesses problem behaviors and contains item stems describing problem behaviors. On these items the informant records a response of *Not true, Somewhat true/Sometimes true,* or *Very true/Often true.* The clinical subscales of the CBCL and TRF are:

- *Withdrawn:* reflects withdrawn behavior, shyness, and a preference to be alone.
- *Somatic Complaints:* a tendency to report numerous physical complaints (e.g., headaches, fatigue).
- *Anxious/Depressed:* reflects a combination of depressive (e.g., lonely, crying, unhappy) and anxious (nervous, fearful, worried) symptoms.
- *Social Problems:* reflects peer problems and feelings of rejection.
- *Thought Problems:* evidence of obsessions/compulsions, hallucinations, or other "strange" behaviors.
- *Attention Problems:* reflects difficulty concentrating, attention problems, and hyperactivity.

- *Delinquent Behavior:* evidence of behaviors such as stealing, lying, vandalism, and arson.
- *Aggressive Behavior:* reflects destructive, aggressive, and disruptive behaviors.

The CBCL and TRF provide three composite scores:

- *Total Problems:* overall level of behavioral problems.
- *Externalizing:* a combination of the Delinquent Behavior and Aggressive Behavior scales.
- *Internalizing:* a combination of the Withdrawn, Somatic Complaints, and Anxious/Depressed scales.

Computer-scoring software is available for the CBCL and TRF and is recommended because hand scoring is a fairly laborious and time-consuming process. The CBCL and TRF have numerous strengths that continue to make them popular among school psychologists and other clinicians. They are relatively easy to use, are time efficient (when using the computer-scoring program), and have a rich history of clinical and research applications (Kamphaus & Frick, 2002).

The BASC TRS and PRS, the CBCL and TRF, and the CRS-R are typically referred to as *omnibus rating scales.* This indicates that they measure a wide range of symptoms and behaviors that are associated with different emotional and behavioral disorders. Ideally an omnibus rating scale should be sensitive to symptoms of both internalizing (e.g., anxiety, depression) and externalizing disorders (e.g., ADHD, conduct disorder) to ensure that the clinician is not missing important indicators of psychopathology. This is particularly important when assessing children and adolescents because there is a high degree of comorbidity with this population. Comorbidity refers to the presence of two or more disorders occurring simultaneously in the same individual. For example, a child might meet the criteria for both an externalizing disorder (e.g., conduct disorder) and an internalizing disorder (e.g., depressive disorder). However, if a clinician did not adequately screen for internalizing symptoms, the more obvious externalizing symptoms might mask the internalizing symptoms and result in an inaccurate or incomplete diagnosis. Inaccurate diagnosis typically leads to inadequate treatment.

Although omnibus rating scales play a central role in the assessment of childhood psychopathology, there are a number of *single-domain* or *syndrome-specific* rating scales. These single-domain rating scales resemble the omnibus scales in format, but they focus on a single disorder (e.g., ADHD) or behavioral dimension (e.g., social skills). Although they are limited in scope, they often provide a more thorough assessment of the specific domain they are designed to assess than the omnibus scales. As a result, they can be useful in supplementing more comprehensive assessment techniques (e.g., Kamphaus & Frick, 2002). Examples of single-domain rating scales are the Teacher Monitor Ratings (TMR) and Parent Monitor Ratings (PMR), which are components of the BASC Monitor for ADHD (Kamphaus & Reynolds, 1998). Although these behavior rating scales do contain items related to internalizing disorders, the focus is clearly on behaviors related to ADHD. The BASC Monitor is designed to help parents, teachers, and physicians determine whether medical, behavioral, and educational treatments for ADHD are working (Kamphaus & Frick, 2002).

Self-Report Measures

A *self-report measure* is an instrument completed by individuals that allows them to describe their own subjective experiences, including emotional, motivational, interpersonal, and attitudinal characteristics (Anastasi & Urbina, 1997).

A **self-report measure** is an instrument completed by individuals that allows them to describe their own subjective experiences, including emotional, motivational, interpersonal, and attitudinal characteristics (e.g., Anastasi & Urbina, 1997). Although the use of self-report measures have a long and rich history with adults, their use with children is a relatively new development because it was long believed that children did not have the personal insights necessary to understand and accurately report their subjective experiences. To further complicate the situation, skeptics noted that young children typically do not have the reading skills necessary to complete written self-report tests (e.g., Kamphaus & Frick, 2002). However, numerous self-report measures have been developed and used successfully with children and adolescents. Although insufficient reading skills do make these instruments impractical with very young children, these new self-report measures are being used with older children (e.g., > 7 years) and adolescents with considerable success. Self-report measures have proven to be particularly useful in the assessment of internalizing disorders such as depression and anxiety that have symptoms that are not always readily apparent to observers. The development and use of self-report measures with children is still at a relatively early stage, but several instruments are gaining widespread acceptance. We will now briefly describe some of the most popular child and adolescent self-report measures.

Behavior Assessment System for Children— Self-Report of Personality (SRP)

The **Behavior Assessment System for Children—Self-Report of Personality (SRP)** (Reynolds & Kamphaus, 1992) is a component of the Behavioral Assessment System for Children (BASC) we introduced earlier, and recent research suggests it is the most popular self-report measure among school psychologists. There are two forms of the SRP, one for children 8 to 11 years and one for adolescents 12 to 18 years. The SRP has an estimated 3rd-grade reading level, and if there is concern about the student's ability to read and comprehend the material, the instructions and items can be presented using an audiotape. The SRP contains brief descriptive statements that the children or adolescents mark as either *true* or *false* as it applies to them. Table 14.3 depicts the 10 clinical scales, 4 adaptive scales, and 4 composites available for children and adolescents. Reynolds and Kamphaus (1992) describe the subscales as follows:

- *Anxiety:* feelings of anxiety, worry, and fears and a tendency to be overwhelmed by stress and problems.
- *Attitude to School:* feelings of alienation and dissatisfaction with school.
- *Attitude to Teachers:* feelings of resentment and dissatisfaction with teachers.
- *Atypicality:* unusual perceptions, behaviors, and thoughts that are often associated with severe forms of psychopathology.

TABLE 14.3   Composites and Scales in the SRP

Composite / Scale	Child	Adolescent
Clinical Maladjustment	*	*
Anxiety	*	*
Atypicality	*	*
Locus of control	*	*
Social stress	*	*
Somatization	*	*
School Maladjustment	*	*
Attitude of school	*	*
Attitude of teachers	*	*
Sensation seeking		*
(Other Problems)		
Depression	*	*
Sense of inadequecy	*	*
Personal Adjustment	*	*
Relations with peers	*	*
Interpersonal relations	*	*
Self-esteem	*	*
Self-reliance	*	*
Emotional Symptoms Index	*	*

Source: From *Behavior Assessment System for Children (BASC): Manual* (Table 1.2, p. 3), by Cecil R. Reynolds and Randy W. Kamphaus, 1992. Copyright 1992 by the American Guidance Service, Inc., 4201 Woodland Road, Circle Pines, MN 55014-1796. Reproduced with permission of publisher. All rights reserved. www.agsnet.com

- *Depression:* feelings of rejection, unhappiness, and sadness.
- *Interpersonal Relations:* positive social relationships.
- *Locus of Control:* perception that events in one's life are externally controlled.
- *Relations with Parents:* positive attitude toward parents and feeling of being important in the family.
- *Self-Esteem:* positive self-esteem characterized by self-respect and acceptance.
- *Self-Reliance:* self-confidence and ability to solve problems.
- *Sensation Seeking:* tendency to take risks and seek excitement.
- *Sense of Inadequacy:* feeling unsuccessful in school and unable to achieve goals.
- *Social Stress:* stress and tension related to social relationships.
- *Somatization:* tendency to experience and complain about physical discomforts and problems.

The SRP produces four composite scores. The most global composite is the Emotional Symptoms Index (ESI) composed of the Anxiety, Depression, Interpersonal Relations, Self-Esteem, Sense of Inadequacy, and Social Stress scales. The ESI is an index of global psychopathology, and high scores usually indicate serious emotional problems. The three lower-order composite scores are:

- *Clinical Maladjustment:* This is a combination of the Anxiety, Atypicality, Locus of Control, Social Stress, and Somatization scales. This scale reflects the magnitude of internalizing problems, and clinically significant scores (i.e., T scores > 70) suggest significant problems.
- *School Maladjustment:* This is composed of the Attitude to School, Attitude to Teachers, and Sensation Seeking scales. High scores on this scale suggest a general pattern of dissatisfaction with schools and teachers. Clinically significant scores suggest pervasive school problems, and adolescents with high scores might be at risk for dropping out.
- *Personal Adjustment:* This is composed of the Interpersonal Relationships, Relations with Parents, Self-Esteem, and Self-Reliance scales. High scores are associated with positive adjustment whereas low scores suggest deficits in interpersonal relationships and identity formation.

As with the BASC TRS and PRS, high scores on the SRP Clinical Composites and Scales reflect abnormality or pathology. The authors provide the following classifications: *T*-score > 70 is Clinically Significant; 60–69 is At-Risk; 41–59 is Average; 31–40 is Low; and < 30 is Very Low. Scores on the Adaptive Composite and Scales are interpreted differently, with high scores reflecting adaptive or positive behaviors. The authors provide the following classifications: *T*-score > 70 is Very High; 60–69 is High; 41–59 is Average; 31–40 is At-Risk; and < 30 is Clinically Significant. Computer software is available to facilitate scoring and interpretation. An example of a completed SRP profile is depicted in Figure 14.2.

The SRP has numerous positive features that recommend its use. Possibly the most salient of these features is the inclusion of three validity scales (i.e., F index, L index, and V index). Because self-report measures have historically been criticized for being particularly susceptible to response sets, the detection of response sets is of primary importance. The F index is composed of items that are "infrequently" endorsed in a specific manner in a normal population. For example, very few children or adolescents indicate that they are "*not* a good friend" or that they "often cheat on tests." This type of validity scale is often referred to as an *infrequency index.* If an examinee endorses enough of these items in the keyed direction, his or her F index will be elevated. High scores on the F index can be the result of numerous factors, ranging from reading difficulties to an intentional desire to "fake bad" in order to look more disturbed or pathological. A second SRP validity scale is the L index, which also contains items that are rarely endorsed in a specific manner in a normal population. The distinction is that items on this scale are intended to identify individuals with a "social desirability" response set (i.e., examinees that are trying to "fake good"). For example, few adolescents who are responding honestly will

> **Because self-report measures have long been criticized for being sensitive to response sets, many have incorporated *validity scales* to detect the presence of response sets.**

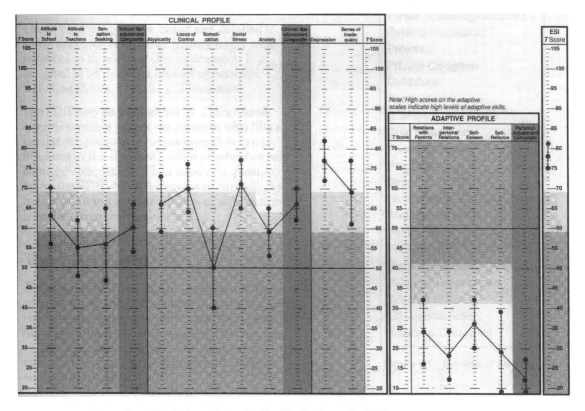

FIGURE 14.2   Completed Clinical and Adaptive Profile Sections of a SRP

Source: From *Behavior Assessment System for Children (BASC): Manual,* by Cecil R. Reynolds and Randy W. Kamphaus, 1992. Copyright 1992 by the American Guidance Service, Inc., 4201 Woodland Road, Circle Pines, MN 55014-1796. Reproduced with permission of publisher. All rights reserved. www.agsnet.com

indicate that "their life is perfect" or that "their teachers are always right." High scores on the L index may suggest that the SRP clinical scales may underestimate any existing emotional or behavioral problems. The final validity scale is the V index, which is composed of nonsensical items that may be endorsed due to carelessness, reading difficulty, or simply a refusal to cooperate. An example of an item that might be included in the V index is "Batman is my best friend." Special Interest Topic 14.2 provides an example of a fake good response set and how the use of the SRP Lie scale helps identify this response set.

Another positive feature of the SRP is its coverage of a relatively broad age range. While most other omnibus self-report measures developed for children were limited to examinees 11 years or older, the SRP extended the age range down to 8 years. An interview version of the SRP is being developed at this time for 6- and 7-year-olds. With the SRP—Interview (SRP-I), the clinician reads the items to the child. Items are phrased appropriately to make them sound as though they are simply part of an interview. The child's responses are then scored according to objective criteria. Another positive aspect of the SRP is that it covers several dimensions or areas that are important to children and adolescents, but have been neglected in other child self-report measures (e.g., attitude toward teachers and school). Finally, the SRP assesses both clinical and adaptive dimensions. This allows the clinician to identify not only problem areas but also areas of strength to build on.

Youth Self-Report (YSR)

The **Youth Self-Report (YSR)** (Achenbach, 1991c) is a component of Achenbach's assessment system that includes the CBCL and TRF described earlier. The YSR can be used with children from 11 to 18 years and closely parallels the format and content of the CBCL and TRF. In fact, it produces the same scales (i.e., Withdrawn, Somatic Complaints, Anxious/ Depressed, Social Problems, Thought Problems, Attention Problems, Delinquent Behavior, and Aggressive Behavior) and composite scores (Externalizing, Internalizing, and Total Problems). This close correspondence with the CBCL and TRF is one of the strengths of the YSR. Additionally, the YSR has an extensive research base that facilitates clinical interpretations and computer-scoring software that eases scoring. The YSR has a strong and loyal following and continues to be a popular instrument used in school settings.

As with behavior rating scales, self-report measures come in omnibus and single-domain formats. Both the SRP and YSR are omnibus self-report measures. An example of a single-domain self-report measure is the Children's Depression Inventory (CDI; Kovacs, 1991). The CDI is a brief, 27-item self-report inventory designed for use with children between 7 and 17 years. It presents a total score as well as five factor scores: Negative Mood, Interpersonal Problems, Ineffectiveness, Anhedonia (loss of pleasure from activities that previously brought pleasure), and Negative Self-Esteem. The CDI is easily administered and scored, is time efficient and inexpensive, and has an extensive research database. As with the other single-domain measures, the CDI does not provide coverage of a broad range of psychological disorders or personality characteristics, but it does give a fairly in-depth assessment of depressive symptoms.

Projective Techniques

Projective techniques **involve the presentation of unstructured or ambiguous stimuli that allows an almost infinite range of responses from the examinee.**

Projective techniques involve the presentation of unstructured or ambiguous materials that allows an almost infinite range of responses from the examinee. For example, the clinician shows the examinee an inkblot and asks: "What might this be?" The central hypothesis of projective techniques is that the examinees will interpret the ambiguous material in a manner that reveals important and often unconscious aspects of their psychological functioning or personality. In other words, the ambiguous material serves as a blank screen on which the examinees "project" their most intimate thoughts, desires, fears, needs, and conflicts (Anastasi & Urbina, 1997; Finch & Belter, 1993). Although extremely popular, the use of projective techniques in the assessment of personality has a long and controversial history. In fact, Chandler (1990) noted that projective techniques have been the focus of controversy practically since they were initially introduced. Proponents of the use of projective techniques claim that they are the richest source of clinical information available and are necessary in order to gain a thorough understanding of the individual. They suggest that behavior rating scales access only surface behavioral patterns, and self-report measures reflect only what the examinee wants to reveal. Whereas behavior rating scales and self-report measures are susceptible to response sets, projective techniques are thought to be relatively free of response sets because the examinee has little idea of what type of responses are expected or are socially appropriate.

Critics of the use of projective techniques note that these procedures typically do not meet even minimum psychometric standards (e.g., having appropriate evidence to support their reliability and validity), and as a result, their use cannot be justified from an ethical or technical perspective. Even if projective techniques are used simply to supplement a psychometrically sound battery of objective measures, their questionable reliability and validity will still detract from the technical soundness of the overall assessment process (Kamphaus & Frick, 2002). Some of the key points of the debate are depicted in Table 14.4.

The debate over the use of projective techniques has been going on for decades. Although there is evidence of a trend for the use of projective techniques to play a diminished role in the assessment of children and adolescents, these techniques are still popular and frequently used

TABLE 14.4   The Projective Debate

Pro	Con
Less structured format allows clinician greater flexibility in administration and interpretation and places fewer demand characteristics that would prompt socially desirable responses from informant.	The reliability of many techniques is questionable. As a result, the interpretations are more related to characteristics of the clinician than to characteristics of the person being tested.
Allows for the assessment of drives, motivations, desires, and conflicts that can affect a person's perceptual experiences but are often unconscious.	Even some techniques that have good reliability have questionable validity, especially in making diagnoses and predicting overt behavior.
Provides a deeper understanding of a person than would be obtained by simply describing behavioral patterns.	Although we can at times predict things we cannot understand, it is rarely the case that understanding does not enhance prediction (Gittelman-Klein, 1986).
Adds to an overall assessment picture.	Adding an unreliable piece of information to an assessment battery simply decreases the overall reliability of the battery.
Helps to generate hypotheses regarding a person's functioning.	Leads one to pursue erroneous avenues in testing or to place undue confidence in a finding.
Nonthreatening and good for rapport building.	Detracts from the time an assessor could better spend collecting more detailed, objective information.
Many techniques have a long and rich clinical tradition.	Assessment techniques are based on an evolving knowledge base and must continually evolve to reflect this knowledge.

Source: From *Clinical Assessment of Child and Adolescent Personality and Behavior* (2nd ed.), (Table 11.1, p. 231) by R. W. Kamphaus and P. J. Frick, 2002, Boston, MA: Allyn and Bacon. Copyright 2002 by Pearson Education. Adapted with permission.

Although some experts have expressed reservations about the use of projective techniques, they continue to play a prominent role in the assessment of children and adolescents.

in schools. For example, a recent national survey of psychological assessment procedures used by school psychologists indicates that four of the ten most popular procedures for assessing personality are projective techniques (Livingston et al., 2003). This debate is apt to continue, but it is highly likely that projectives will continue to play a prominent role in the assessment of children and adolescents for the foreseeable future. Next we will briefly describe a few of the major projective techniques used with children and adolescents.

Projective Drawings

Some of the most popular projective techniques used with children and adolescents involve the interpretation of **projective drawings.** The basis for this popularity is usually attributed to two factors. First, young children with limited verbal abilities are limited in their ability to respond to clinical interviews, objective self-report measures, and even most other projective techniques. However, these young children can produce drawings because this activity is largely nonverbal. Second, because children are usually familiar with and enjoy drawing, this technique provides a nonthreatening "child-friendly" approach to assessment (Finch & Belter, 1993; Kamphaus & Frick, 2002). There are several different projective drawing techniques in use today, including the following.

Draw-A-Person Test (DAP).   The **Draw-A-Person Test (DAP)** is the most widely used projective drawing technique. The child is given a blank sheet of paper and a pencil and asked to draw a whole person. Although different scoring systems have been developed for the DAP, no system has received universal approval. The figure in the drawing is often interpreted as a representation of the "self." That is, the figure reflects how children feel about themselves and how they feel as they interact with their environment (Handler, 1985).

House-Tree-Person (H-T-P).   With the **House-Tree-Person (H-T-P)**, the child is given paper and a pencil and asked to draw a house, a tree, and a person of each gender, all on separate sheets. The clinician then typically asks a standard set of questions for each picture. After these drawings are completed, the child is then given a set of crayons and the process is repeated. The House is typically interpreted as reflecting feelings associated with home life and family relationships. The Tree and Person are thought to reflect aspects of the self, with the Tree representing deep unconscious feelings about the self and the Person reflecting a closer-to-conscious view of self (Hammer, 1985).

Kinetic Family Drawing (KFD).   With the **Kinetic Family Drawing (KFD),** children are given paper and pencil and asked to draw a picture of everyone in their family, including themselves, doing something (hence the term *kinetic*). After completing the drawing the children are asked to identify each figure and describe what each one is doing. The KFD is thought to provide information regarding the children's view of their family and their interactions (Finch & Belter, 1993).

Despite their popularity and appeal to clinicians, little empirical data supports the use of projective drawings as a means of predicting behavior or classifying children by diagnostic type (e.g., depressed, anxious, conduct disordered, etc.). These techniques may provide a non-threatening way to initiate the assessment process and an opportunity to develop rapport, but otherwise they should be used with considerable caution and an understanding of their technical limitations (Finch & Belter, 1993; Kamphaus & Frick, 2002).

Sentence Completion Tests

Sentence completion tests are another popular projective approach used with children and adolescents. These tests typically present incomplete-sentence stems that are completed by the child. The sentence completion forms either can be given to the child to complete independently or can be read aloud to the child and the responses recorded. Examples of possible incomplete sentence stems include "I really enjoy . . ." and "My greatest fear is. . . ." Numerous sentence completion forms are available, and as with the projective drawings, there are different ways of interpreting the results. Because incomplete-sentence stems provide more structure than most projective tasks (e.g., drawings or inkblots), some have argued that they are not actually "projective" in nature, but are more or less a type of structured interview. As a result, some prefer the term *semiprojective* to characterize these tests. Regardless of the classification, relatively little empirical evidence documents the psychometric properties of these tests (Kamphaus & Frick, 2002). Nevertheless, they remain popular, are nonthreatening to children, and in the hands of skilled clinicians may provide an opportunity to enhance their understanding of their clients.

Apperception Tests

Another type of projective technique used with children is **apperception tests.** With this technique the child is given a picture and asked to make up a story about it. Figure 14.3 depicts a picture similar to those used in some apperception tests used with older children and adolescents. These techniques are also sometimes referred to as *thematic* or *storytelling* techniques. Like other projective techniques, children generally find apperception tests inviting and enjoyable. Two early apperception tests, the Thematic Apperception Test (TAT) and the Children's Apperception Test (CAT), have received fairly widespread use with children and adolescents. Like other projective techniques, limited empirical evidence supports the use of the TAT or CAT. A more recently developed apperception test is the Roberts Apperception Test for Children (RATC; McArthur & Roberts, 1982). The unique feature of this instrument is the inclusion of a standardized scoring system and normative data. The standardized scoring approach resulted in increased reliability relative to previous apperception tests. However, the normative data are inadequate and there is little validity evidence available (Kamphaus & Frick, 2002). Nevertheless, the RATC is a step in the right direction in terms of enhancing the technical qualities of projective techniques.

Inkblot Techniques

The final projective approach we will discuss is the **inkblot technique.** With this technique the child is presented an ambiguous inkblot and asked to interpret it in some manner, typically

FIGURE 14.3   A Picture Similar to Those Used on Apperception Tests

Source: From *Psychological Testing: History, Principles, and Applications* (3rd ed.) (Fig. 13.5, p. 505), by Robert J. Gregory, 2000, Boston, MA: Allyn & Bacon. Copyright 2000 by Pearson Education. Reprinted with permission.

FIGURE 14.4   An Inkblot Similar to Those Used on Inkblot Tests

Source: From *Psychological Testing: History, Principles, and Applications* (3rd ed.) (Fig. 13.2, p. 498), by Robert J. Gregory, 2000, Boston, MA: Allyn & Bacon. Copyright 2000 by Pearson Education. Reprinted with permission.

by asking: "What might this be?" Figure 14.4 presents an example of an inkblot similar to those used on inkblot tests. Of all the inkblot techniques, the Rorschach is the most widely used. Different interpretative approaches have been developed for the Rorschach, but the Exner Comprehensive System (Exner, 1974, 1978) has received the most attention by clinicians and researchers in recent years. The Exner Comprehensive System provides an elaborate standardized scoring system that produces approximately 90 possible scores. Relative to other Rorschach interpretive systems, the Exner system produces more reliable measurement and has reasonably adequate normative data. However, evidence of validity is limited, and many of the scores and indexes that were developed with adults have not proven effective with children (Kamphaus & Frick, 2002).

Because there is little empirical data supporting the use of projective techniques as a means of understanding personality or predicting behavior, they should be used with caution.

In summary, in spite of relatively little empirical evidence of the utility of projective techniques, they continue to be popular among psychologists and other clinicians. Our recommendation is to use these instruments cautiously. They should not be used for making important educational, clinical, and diagnostic decisions, but they may have merit in introducing the child to the assessment process, establishing rapport, and developing hypotheses that can be pursued with more technically adequate assessment techniques.

Summary

In this chapter we focused on tests of behavior and personality and their applications in the schools. We noted that Public Law 94-142 and subsequent legislation require that public schools provide special education and related services to students with emotional disorders. Before these services can be provided, the schools must be able to identify children with these disorders. The process of identifying these children often involves a psychological evaluation completed by a school psychologist or other clinician. Teachers often play an important role in this assessment process. For example, teachers often complete rating scales that describe the behavior of students in their class. Teachers are also often involved in the development and implementation of educational programs for these special needs students. As a result, it is beneficial for teachers to be familiar with the types of instruments used to identify students with emotional and behavioral problems.

We noted the three major types of instruments used in assessing personality and behavior in children and adolescents. These include the following.

- *Behavior rating scales:* A behavior rating scale is an inventory completed by an adult informant such as a teacher, parent, or guardian. An advantage of behavior rating scales is that they can be used to collect information from adults who have had many opportunities to observe the child or adolescent in a variety of settings over extended periods of time. Behavior rating scales are efficient, are cost-effective, and are particularly good at assessing externalizing behaviors such as aggression and hyperactivity. Although the use of adult informants provides some degree of objectivity, behavior rating scales are still susceptible to response sets (i.e., a situation in which the individuals completing the test responds in a manner that distorts their own or another person's true characteristics). Although behavior rating scales are particularly useful in diagnosing externalizing problems such as aggression or overt defiance, they are less effective in assessing internalizing behaviors such as depression or anxiety because these problems are not always easily observable.

- *Self-report measures:* A self-report measure is an instrument completed by individuals that allow them to describe their own subjective experiences, including their emotional, motivational, and attitudinal characteristics. The use of self-report measures with children is a relatively recent development because it was long believed that children did not have the personal insights necessary to understand and report their subjective experiences. Although it is true that children must have the reading skills necessary to read and complete these instruments, self-report measures are proving to be useful instruments for assessing emotional and behavioral problems in older children and adolescents. They are particularly useful in the assessment of internalizing disorders such as depression and anxiety, which are not always conspicuous to adults observing the child or adolescent. One prominent limitation of self-report measures is the potential distorting effects of response sets. That is, there is the potential that examinees will respond in a manner that does not accurately reflect their true characteristics. For example, they may answer questions in a way that makes them appear more socially appropriate, even if their responses are not truthful or accurate.

- *Projective techniques:* Projective techniques involve the presentation of an ambiguous task that places little structure or limitation on the examinee's response. A classic example is the presentation of an inkblot followed by the question: "What might this be?" In addition to inkblot tests, projective techniques include projective drawings, sentence completion tests, and apperception (or storytelling) tests. The hypothesis behind the use of projective techniques is that the examinees will respond to the ambiguous stimuli in a manner that reveals basic, often unconscious aspects of their personality. There is considerable controversy over the use of projective techniques. Proponents of their use claim projective techniques represent the richest source of information about the subjective experience of the examinee. Supporters also hold that behavior rating scales and self-report measures are vulnerable to the distorting effects of response sets, whereas projective techniques are relatively free from these effects because it is not obvious what type of response is expected or socially appropriate. In contrast, critics claim that most projective techniques do not meet even minimal psychometric standards and their use cannot be ethically or technically justified. While the use of these projective techniques is vigorously debated in the professional literature, they continue to be among the most popular approaches to assessing the personality of children and adolescents. Our position is that although projective techniques should not be used as the basis for making important educational, clinical, or diagnostic decisions, they may have merit in developing rapport with clients and in generating hypotheses that can be pursued using technically superior assessment techniques.

KEY TERMS AND CONCEPTS

Apperception tests, p. 367

Behavior Assessment System for Children—Parent Rating Scale (PRS), p. 353

Behavior Assessment System for Children—Self-Report of Personality (SRP), p. 360

Behavior Assessment System for Children—Teacher Rating Scale (TRS), p. 353

Behavior rating scale, p. 352

Child Behavior Checklist (CBCL), p. 358

Conners Rating Scales—Revised (CRS-R), p. 357

Draw-A-Person Test (DAP), p. 366

House-Tree-Person (H-T-P), p. 366

Inkblot techniques, p. 367

Kinetic Family Drawing (KFD), p. 366

Personality, p. 348

Projective Drawings, p. 366

Projective techniques, p. 364

Public Law 94-142 / IDEA, p. 348

Response set, p. 349

Self-report measures, p. 360

Sentence completion tests, p. 367

Teacher Report Form (TRF), p. 358

Typical response tests, p. 348

Validity scale, p. 350

Youth Self-Report (YSR), p. 364

RECOMMENDED READINGS

Kamphaus, R. W., & Frick, P. J. (2002). *Clinical assessment of child and adolescent personality and behavior.* Boston: Allyn & Bacon. This text provides comprehensive coverage of the major personality and behavioral assessment techniques used with children and adolescents. It also provides a good discussion of the history and current use of projective techniques.

Reynolds, C. R., & Kamphaus, R. W. (2003). *Handbook of psychological and educational assessment of children: Personality, behavior, and context.* New York: Guilford Press. This is another excellent source providing thorough coverage of the major behavioral and personality assessment techniques used with children. Particularly good for those interested in a more advanced discussion of these instruments and techniques.

15 Assessment Accommodations for Students with Disabilities

Assessment accommodations help students show what they know without being placed at a disadvantage by their disability.

—U.S. Department of Education, 2001, p. 8

CHAPTER HIGHLIGHTS

Major Legislation That Impacts the Assessment of Students with Disabilities

Individuals with Disabilities Education Act (IDEA)

Section 504

The Rationale for Assessment Accommodations

When Are Accommodations Not Appropriate or Necessary?

Strategies for Accommodations

Determining What Accommodations to Provide

Reporting Results of Modified Assessments

LEARNING OBJECTIVES

After reading and studying this chapter, students should be able to:

1. Explain the rationale for making modifications in assessment procedures for students with disabilities.

2. Distinguish between appropriate and inappropriate assessment accommodations and gives examples of both.

3. Identify situations in which assessment accommodations are inappropriate or unnecessary.

4. Identify major legislation that has impacted the provision of educational services to students with disabilities.

5. Trace the history of the Individuals with Disabilities Education Act (IDEA) and describe its impact on the education of students with disabilities.

6. Describe the role of the regular education teacher in providing instructional and assessment services to students with disabilities, and explain why this role is increasing.

7. Identify and briefly describe the categories of disabilities recognized under IDEA.

8. Describe the impact of Section 504 of the Rehabilitation Act of 1973 and explain its relationship to IDEA.

9. Identify and give examples of modifications of the presentation format that might be appropriate for students with disabilities.

10. Identify and give examples of modifications of the response format that might be appropriate for students with disabilities.

11. Identify and give examples of modifications of timing that might be appropriate for students with disabilities.

12. Identify and give examples of modifications of the setting that might be appropriate for students with disabilities.

13. Identify and give examples of adaptive devices and supports that might be appropriate for students with disabilities.

14. Describe and give examples illustrating the use of limited portions of an assessment or an alternate assessment with a student with a disability.

15. Identify and explain the reasoning behind the major principles for determining which assessment accommodations to provide.

16. Briefly describe the current status of research on the selection of assessment accommodations.

17. Explain what is meant by the term *differential effects* in relation to research on assessment accommodation and illustrate how they are studied.

18. Discuss the controversy regarding the reporting of results of modified assessments.

So far in this text we have emphasized the importance of strictly adhering to standard assessment procedures when administering tests and other assessments. This is necessary to maintain the reliability and validity of score interpretations. However, certain times it is appropriate to deviate from these standard procedures. Standard assessment procedures may not be appropriate for students with a disability if the assessment requires the student to use some ability (e.g., sensory, motor, language, etc.) that is affected by their disability, *but is irrelevant to the construct being measured.* To address this, teachers and others involved in assessment may need to modify standard assessment procedures to accommodate the special needs of students with disabilities. In this context, the *Standards* (AERA et al., 1999) note that **assessment accommodations** are changes in the standard assessment procedures that are implemented in order to minimize the impact of student characteristics that are irrelevant to the construct being measured by the assessment. The *Standards* go on to state that the goal of accommodations is to provide the most valid and accurate measurement of the construct of interest. As framed by the U.S. Department of Education (2001), "Assessment accommodations help students show what they know without being placed at a disadvantage by their disability" (p. 8). For example, consider a test designed to assess a student's knowledge of world history. A blind student would not be able to read the material in its standard printed format, but if the student could read Braille, an appropriate accommodation would be to convert the test to the Braille format. In this example, it is important to recognize that reading standard print is incidental to the construct being measured. That is, the test was designed to measure the student's knowledge of world history, not the ability to read standard print. An important consideration when selecting accommodations is that we only want to implement accommodations that preserve the

> **Standard assessment procedures may not be appropriate for a student with a disability if the assessment requires the student to use some ability that is affected by the disability, but is irrelevant to the construct being measured.**

reliability of test scores and the inferences about the meaning of performance on the test (U.S. Department of Education, 2001).

Major Legislation That Impacts the Assessment of Students with Disabilities

More and more often, teachers are being called on to modify their assessments in order to accommodate the special needs of students with disabilities.

More and more often, lawmakers are writing laws that mandate assessment accommodations for students with disabilities. As a result, more and more often, teachers are being called on to modify their assessments in order to accommodate the special needs of students with disabilities. Major laws that address the issue of assessment accommodations include Section 504 of the Rehabilitation Act of 1973; Americans with Disabilities Act (ADA) of 1990; Goals 2000 of 1994; Improving America's Schools Act (the 1994 reauthorization of the Elementary and Secondary Education Act); the 1997 amendments to the Individual with Disabilities Education Act (IDEA 97; as of this writing, the U.S. Senate is debating actively the passage of the next reauthorization of IDEA). Because IDEA in its various revisions and Section 504 are most often applied to students in the public schools, we will briefly address them.

Individuals with Disabilities Education Act (IDEA)

In 1975, Congress passed Public Law 94-142, the Education of All Handicapped Children Act (EAHCA). This law required that public schools provide students with disabilities a **Free Appropriate Public Education (FAPE).** Prior to the passage of this law, it was estimated that as many as one million children with disabilities were being denied a FAPE (e.g., Turnbull, Turnbull, Shank, Smith, & Leal, 2002). In 1986, Public Law 99-457, the Infants and Toddlers with Disabilities Act, was passed to ensure that preschool children with disabilities also received appropriate services. In 1990, the EAHCA was reauthorized and the name was changed to the **Individuals with Disabilities Education Act (IDEA).**

The Education of All Handicapped Children Act required that public schools provide students with disabilities a *Free Appropriate Public Education (FAPE).*

These laws had a significant impact on the way students with disabilities received educational services. The number of children with developmental disabilities in state mental health institutions declined by almost 90%, the rate of unemployment for individuals in their twenties with disabilities was reduced, and the number of young adults with disabilities enrolled in postsecondary education increased. Although this was clearly a step in the right direction, problems remained. Students with disabilities were still dropping out of school at almost twice the rate of students without disabilities, there was concern that minority children were being inappropriately placed in special education, and educational professionals and parents had concerns about the implementation of the law (Kubiszyn & Borich, 2003). To address these and other concerns, the law was reauthorized in 1997 as the Individuals with Disabilities Education Act of 1997 (IDEA 97).

Entire books have been written on IDEA and its impact on the public schools, and it is not our intention to cover this law and its impact in great detail. Because this is a textbook on educational assessment for teachers, we will be limiting our discussion to the effect of IDEA on the assessment practices of teachers. In this context, probably the greatest effect of IDEA has been its requirement that schools provide services to students with disabilities in the general education classroom whenever appropriate. Earlier versions of the act had required that students with disabilities receive instruction in the least restrictive environment. In actual practice students with disabilities were often segregated into resource or self-contained classrooms largely based on the belief that they would not be able to profit from instruction in regular education classrooms. Educational research, however, has shown that students with disabilities demonstrate superior educational and social gains when they receive instruction in regular education classrooms (see McGregor & Vogelsberg, 1998; Stainback & Stainback, 1992). Revisions of IDEA, reflecting this research and prevailing legal and political trends, mandated that public schools educate students with disabilities alongside students who do not have disabilities to the maximum extent possible, an approach often referred to as **inclusion or mainstreaming** (Turnbull et al., 2002). This extends not only to students with mild disabilities but also to those with moderate and severe disabilities. The impact of this on regular education teachers is that they have more students with disabilities in their classrooms. As a result, regular education teachers are increasingly responsible for planning and providing instruction to children with disabilities and for evaluating their progress. This includes helping identify students with disabilities, planning their instruction and assessment, and working with them daily in the classroom.

Research has shown that students with disabilities demonstrate superior educational and social gains when they receive instruction in regular education classrooms.

Central to the provision of services to students with disabilities is the **Individual Education Program (IEP).** The IEP is a written document developed by a committee or team composed of the student's parents, regular education teachers, special education teachers, and other school personnel (e.g., school psychologists, counselors). This committee is typically referred to as the **IEP committee.** When appropriate the students may be invited to participate as well as professionals representing external agencies. At a minimum the IEP should specify the student's present level of academic performance, identify measurable annual goals and short-term objectives, specify their instructional arrangement, and identify the special education and related services the student will receive. In terms of assessment accommodations, the IEP should specify any modifications in classroom tests and other assessments that are deemed necessary, and each of the student's teachers should have a copy of the IEP. Additionally, the IEP should identify any accommodations that are seen as appropriate for state- and district-wide assessment programs. If the committee decides that the student is not able to participate in state and district assessment programs, it should explain why the assessment is not appropriate and how the student's achievement will be measured.

The *Individual Education Program (IEP)* is a written document developed by a committee that specifies a number of factors, including any *assessment accommodations* the student will receive.

As we noted, regular education teachers are becoming increasingly involved in teaching and testing students with disabilities. Mastergeorge and Miyoshi (1999) note that as members of the IEP committee, regular education teachers are involved in:

- Developing, reviewing, and revising the student's IEP
- Developing positive behavioral interventions and supports
- Determining supplementary aids, services, and program modifications (including instructional and assessment modifications or accommodations)
- Determining what type of personnel support is needed to help the child function and progress in the regular education classroom

The involvement of regular education teachers does not stop simply with planning. They are also primarily responsible for implementing the IEP in the classroom. It should be noted that the services and accommodations stipulated in the IEP are not merely suggestions, but legally commit the school to provide the stated modifications, accommodations, services, and so forth.

IDEA Categories of Disabilities

The Education of All Handicapped Children Act and the Individuals with Disabilities Education Act (IDEA) describe a number of categories of disabilities. Teachers play important roles in identifying children with disabilities. In many cases teachers may be the first to recognize that a student is having difficulties that warrant referral for evaluation for special education services. They may also be involved in different aspects of the evaluation process. The assessment of these disorders involves a wide range of assessment activities including interviews with students, parents, and teachers; standardized tests; reviews of existing educational records; reviews of classroom work samples; observations; and reviewing results of medical examinations. Here are brief descriptions of the **IDEA categories of disabilities.**

IDEA defines a learning disability as a disorder that compromises the student's ability to understand or use spoken or written language and is manifested in difficulty in listening, thinking, speaking, reading, writing, spelling, or doing mathematical calculations.

Learning Disabilities. IDEA defines a **learning disability** as a disorder that compromises the student's ability to understand or use spoken or written language and is manifested in difficulty in listening, thinking, speaking, reading, writing, spelling, or doing mathematical calculations. This category includes conditions such as dyslexia, developmental aphasia, and perceptual disabilities, but does not include learning problems that are primarily the result of visual, hearing, or motor deficits, mental retardation, emotional disturbance, or economic/environmental disadvantage. Students with learning disabilities account for approximately 50% of the students receiving special education services (Turnbull et al., 2002).

As we discussed in Chapters 12 and 13, most states base the diagnosis of learning disabilities on the presence of a substantial discrepancy between ability (i.e., intelligence) and achievement. For example, consider a student with a Full Scale IQ on the Wechsler Intelligence Scale for Children—Fourth Edition of 100 and a Reading Comprehension score on the Wechsler Individual Achievement Test, Second Edition of 70. Both of these tests have a mean of 100 and a standard deviation of 15, so there is a discrepancy of 30 points or 2 standard deviations between ability and achievement (i.e., achievement is 2 SDs below ability). Different states have different criteria as to what constitutes a substantial discrepancy. Some use 1 standard deviation as the criteria, some 1.5 standard deviations, and some 2 standard deviations

(Turnbull et al., 2002). Other states use a regression formula to establish the presence of a severe discrepancy. The individual intelligence and achievement tests used in assessing learning disabilities are generally administered by assessment specialists with advanced graduate training in administering and interpreting these tests. Although reliance on ability–achievement discrepancies to diagnose learning disabilities is the most widely accepted methodology, it has become the focus of considerable debate in recent years, and some experts recommend dropping this approach (e.g., Fletcher et al., 2002). As this text goes to print, it appears the next revision of IDEA may drop the requirement of a discrepancy model (but continue to allow its use) for an alternative approach that is still being refined.

Communication Disorders. **Communication disorders** are typically classified as either speech or language disorders. Speech disorders involve problems in the production of speech whereas language disorders involve problems receiving, understanding, and formulating ideas and thoughts. Communication disorders constitute approximately 20% of the students receiving special education services (Turnbull et al., 2002). Speech–language pathologists using a variety of speech and language tests typically take a lead role in the identification of students with communication disorders.

Mental Retardation. **Mental retardation** typically is identified when the student scores more than 2 standard deviations below the mean on an individualized intelligence test and presents significant deficits in two or more areas of adaptive functioning (e.g., communication, self-care, leisure). Additionally, these deficits must be manifested before the age of 18 years (APA, 1994). Students with mental retardation compromise approximately 11% of the special education population (Turnbull et al., 2002). The assessment of students with mental retardation involves the administration of individual intelligence and achievement tests by assessment professionals and also adaptive behavior scales that parents or teachers typically complete.

Emotional Disturbance. Students with emotional disorders comprise approximately 8% of the students receiving special education services (Turnbull et al., 2002). For classification purposes, **emotional disturbance** is defined as follows:

(i) The term means a condition exhibiting one or more of the following characteristics over a long period of time and to a marked degree that adversely affects a student's educational performance:
   (a) An inability to learn that cannot be explained by intellectual, sensory, or other health factors.
   (b) An inability to build or maintain satisfactory interpersonal relationships with peers and teachers.
   (c) Inappropriate types of behavior or feelings under normal circumstances.
   (d) A general pervasive mood of unhappiness or depression.
   (e) A tendency to develop physical symptoms or fears associated with personal or school problems.
(ii) The term includes schizophrenia.

The term does not apply to children who are socially maladjusted, unless it is determined that they have an emotional disturbance. (34 C.F.R. Sec. 300.7(c)(4))

School psychologists typically take a lead role in the identification and assessment of students with an emotional disturbance and use many of the standardized measures of behavior and personality discussed in Chapter 14. When there is concern that students have an emotional disturbance, their teachers will often be interviewed by the school psychologist asked to complete behavior rating scales to better understand the nature and degree of any problems.

Other Health Impaired. IDEA covers a diverse assortment of health conditions under the category of **Other Health Impaired (OHI).** The unifying factor is that all of these conditions involve limitations in strength, vitality, or alertness. Approximately 3.5% of the students receiving special education services have this classification (Turnbull et al., 2002). The health conditions included in this broad category include, but are not limited to, asthma, epilepsy, sickle cell anemia, and cancer. Attention-deficit hyperactivity disorder (ADHD) is also typically classified in this category (but may be served under Section 504 as well). ADHD is characterized by problems maintaining attention, impulsivity, and hyperactivity (APA, 1994). As with the diagnosis of emotional disturbance, when there is concern that students have ADHD, their teachers will often be asked to complete behavior rating scales to acquire a better picture of their functioning in the school setting.

Multiple Disabilities. IDEA defines **multiple disabilities** as concurrent disabilities that cause severe educational impairments. Examples include a student with mental retardation and blindness or mental retardation and a severe orthopedic impairment. Students with multiple disabilities comprise approximately 2% of the population of the students receiving special education services.

Hearing Impairments. IDEA defines **hearing impairments** as hearing loss that is severe enough to negatively impact a student's academic performance. Students with hearing impairments account for approximately 1% of the students receiving special education services (Turnbull et al., 2002). Assessment of hearing impairments will involve an audiologist, but school personnel will typically be involved to help determine the educational ramifications of the impairment.

Orthopedic Impairments. IDEA defines **orthopedic impairments** as orthopedic-related impairments that are the result of congenital anomalies, disease, or other causes. Students with orthopedic impairments comprise approximately 1% of the students receiving special education services. Examples of orthopedic impairments include spina bifida and cerebral palsy. Many educators refer to orthopedic impairments as physical disabilities (Turnbull et al., 2002). Assessment of orthopedic impairments will typically involve a number of medical specialists, with school personnel helping to determine the educational implications of the impairment.

IDEA defines *autism* as a developmental disability that is evident before the age of 3 and impacts verbal and nonverbal communication and social interaction.

Autism. IDEA defines **autism** as a developmental disability that is evident before the age of 3 and impacts verbal and nonverbal communication and social interaction. Students with autism account for approximately 1% of the students receiving special education services (Turnbull et al., 2002). The assessment of autism typically involves a combination of intelligence, achievement, and speech and language tests to assess cognitive abilities as well as behavior rating scales to access behavioral characteristics.

Visual Impairments.   IDEA defines **visual impairment** as impaired vision that even after correction (e.g., glasses) negatively impacts a student's academic performance. Students with visual impairments constitute less than 1% of the students receiving special education services (Turnbull et al., 2002). Assessment of visual impairments will involve an ophthalmologist or an optometrist, but school personnel will typically be involved to determine the educational implications of the impairment.

Traumatic Brain Injury.   IDEA defines **traumatic brain injury** as an acquired brain injury that is the result of external force and results in functional and psychosocial impairments that negatively impact the student's academic performance. Students with traumatic brain injuries constitute less than 1% of the students receiving special education services (Turnbull et al., 2002). The assessment of traumatic brain injuries typically involves a combination of medical assessments (e.g., computerized axial tomography), neuropsychological tests (e.g., to assess a wide range of cognitive abilities such as memory, attention, visual–spatial processing), and traditional psychological and educational tests (e.g., intelligence and achievement). These assessments are often complemented with assessments of behavior and personality.

Developmental Delay.   Kubiszyn and Borich (2003) note that early versions of IDEA required fairly rigid adherence to categorical eligibility procedures that identified and labeled students before special education services could be provided. While the intention of these requirements was to provide appropriate oversight, it had the unintentional effect of hampering efforts at prevention and early intervention. Before student's qualified for special education services, their problems had to be fairly severe and chronic. To address this problem, IDEA 97 continued to recognize the traditional categories of disabilities (i.e., those listed above) and expanded eligibility to children with **developmental delays.** This provision allows states to provide special education services to students between the ages of 3 and 9 with delays in physical, cognitive, communication, social/emotional, and adaptive development. Additionally, IDEA gave the states considerable freedom in how they define developmental delays, requiring only that the delays be identified using appropriate assessment instruments and procedures. The goal of this more flexible approach to eligibility is to encourage early identification and intervention. No longer do educators have to wait until student problems escalate to crisis proportions; they can now provide services early when the problems are more manageable and hopefully have a better prognosis.

Section 504

Section 504 of the Rehabilitation Act of 1973 is another law that had a significant impact on the instruction and assessment of students with disabilities. Section 504 (often referred too simply as **504**) prohibits any discrimination against an individual with a disability in any agency or program that receives federal funds. Because state and local education agencies receive federal funds, Section 504 applies. Although IDEA requires that a student meet spe-

Section 504 **requires that public schools offer students with disabilities reasonable accommodations to meet their specific educational needs.**

cific eligibility requirements in order to receive special education services, Section 504 established a much broader standard of eligibility. Under Section 504, an individual with a disability is defined as anyone with a physical or mental disability that substantially limits one or more life activities. As a result, it is possible that a student may not qualify for special education services under IDEA, but still qualify for assistance under Section 504 (this is often referred to as "504 only"). Section 504 requires that public schools offer students with disabilities reasonable accommodations to meet their specific educational needs. To meet this mandate, schools develop "504 Plans" that specify the instructional and assessment accommodations the student should receive. Parents, teachers, and other school personnel typically develop these 504 Plans. Regular education teachers are involved in the development of these plans and are responsible for ensuring that the modifications and accommodations are implemented in the classroom.

The Rationale for Assessment Accommodations

As we noted earlier, standard assessment procedures may not be appropriate for students with a disability if the assessment requires the students to use some ability that is affected by their disability, but is irrelevant to the construct being measured. Assessment accommodations are modifications to standard assessment procedures that are granted in an effort to minimize the impact of student characteristics that are irrelevant to the construct being measured. If this is accomplished the assessment will provide a more valid and accurate measurement of the student's true standing on the construct (AERA et al., 1999). The goal is not simply to allow the student to obtain a higher score; the goal is to obtain more valid score interpretations. Assessment accommodations should increase the validity of the score interpretations so they more accurately reflect the student's true standing on the construct being measured.

Although some physical, cognitive, sensory, or motor deficits may be readily apparent to teachers (e.g., vision impairment, hearing impairment, physical impairment), other deficits that might undermine student performance are not as obvious. For example, students with a learning disability might not appear outwardly to have any deficits that would impair performance on a test, but might in fact have significant cognitive processing deficits that limit their ability to complete standard assessments. In some situations the student may have readily observable deficits, but have associated characteristics that also need to be taken into consideration. For example, a student with a physical disability (e.g., partial paralysis) may be easily fatigued when engaging in standard school activities. Because some tests require fairly lengthy testing sessions, the student's susceptibility to fatigue, not only the more obvious physical limitations, needs to be taken into consideration when planning assessment accommodations (AERA et al., 1999).

Fairness to all parties is a central issue when considering assessment accommodations.

Fairness to all parties is a central issue when considering assessment accommodations. For students with disabilities, fairness requires that they not be penalized as the result of disability-related characteristics that are irrelevant to the construct being measured by the assessment. For students without disabilities, fairness requires that those receiving accommodations not be given an unjust advantage over those being tested under standard conditions. As you can see, these serious issues deserve careful consideration.

When Are Accommodations *Not* Appropriate or Necessary?

The *Standards* (AERA et al., 1999) specify the following three situations in which accommodations should not be provided or are not necessary.

Accommodations Are Not Appropriate if the Affected Ability Is Directly Relevant to the Construct Being Measured.   For example, it would not be appropriate to give a student with a visual impairment a magnification device if the test were designed to measure visual acuity. Similarly, it would not be appropriate to give a student with a reading disability the use of a "reader" on a test designed to measure reading ability. Even if the test is designed as a measure of reading comprehension (as opposed to decoding or reading fluency), having someone else read the material turns the test into one of listening comprehension, not reading comprehension (Fuchs, 2002). In other words, if the test accommodation changes the construct being measured, the accommodation is inappropriate. Again, the essential question is "Does the assessment require the use of some ability that is affected by the disability, but is *irrelevant* to the construct being measured?"

Accommodations Are Not Appropriate for an Assessment if the Purpose of the Test Is to Assess the Presence and Degree of the Disability.   For example, it would not be appropriate to give a student with attention-deficit hyperactivity disorder (ADHD) extra time on a test designed to diagnose the presence of attention problems. As we indicated earlier, it would not be appropriate to modify a test of visual acuity for a student with impaired vision.

Accommodations Are Not Necessary for All Students with Disabilities.   Not all students with disabilities need accommodations. Even when students with a disability require accommodations on one test, this does not necessarily mean that they will need accommodations on all tests. As we will discuss in more detail later, assessment accommodations should be individualized to meet the specific needs of each student with a disability. There is no specific accommodation that is appropriate, necessary, or adequate for all students with a given disability. As an example, consider students with learning disabilities. Learning disabilities are a heterogeneous group of disabilities that can impact an individual in a multitude of ways. One student with a learning disability may require extended time whereas this accommodation may not be necessary for another student with the same diagnosis.

> **Assessment accommodations should be individualized to meet the specific needs of each student with a disability.**

Strategies for Accommodations

A variety of assessment accommodations have been proposed and implemented to meet the needs of individuals with disabilities. A brief description follows of some of the most widely used accommodations compiled from a number of sources (AERA et al., 1999; King, Baker, & Jarrow, 1995; Mastergeorge & Miyoshi, 1999; Northeast Technical Assistance Center, 1999; U.S. Department of Education, 2001). To facilitate our presentation, we divided these accommodations into major categories. However, these categories are not mutually exclusive and some accommodations may be accurately classified into more than one category.

Modifications of Presentation Format

Modifications of presentation format involve modifying or changing the medium or format used to present the directions, items, or tasks to the student. An example would be the use of Braille or large-print editions for students with visual handicaps (which can be supplemented with large-print or Braille figures). Closed circuit television (CCTV) is an adaptive device that enlarges text and other materials and magnifies them onto a screen (see www.visionaid.com/cctvpage/cctvdeal.htm). For computer-administered tests, ZoomText Magnifier and ScreenReader allows students to enlarge the image on a computer screen and has a screen reader that reads the text on the screen. In some cases the use of oversized monitors may be appropriate. Reader services, which involve listening to the test being read aloud, may also be employed. Here the reader can read directions and questions and describe diagrams, graphs, and other visual material. For students with hearing impairments, verbal material may be presented through the use of sign communication or in writing. Other common modifications to the presentation format include increasing the spacing between items; reducing the number of items per page; using raised line drawings; using language-simplified directions and questions; changing from a written to an oral format (or vice versa); defining words; providing additional examples; and helping students understand directions, questions, and tasks. Table 15.1 provides a listing of these and related accommodations.

Modifications of presentation format involve modifying the medium or format used to present the directions, items, or tasks to the student.

Modifications of Response Format

Modifications of response format allow students to respond with their preferred method of communication. For example, if students are unable to write due to a physical impairment, you can allow them to take the exam orally or provide access to a scribe to write down their responses. A student whose preferred method of communication is sign language could respond in sign language and responses could subsequently be translated for grading. Other common modifications to the response format include allowing the student to point to the correct response; having an aide mark the answers; using a tape recorder to record responses; using a computer or Braillewriter to record responses; using voice-activated computer software; providing increased spacing between lines on the answer sheet; using graph paper for math problems; and allowing the student to mark responses in the test booklet rather than on a computer answer sheet. Table 15.2 provides a summary listing of these and related accommodations.

Modifications of response format allow students to respond with their preferred method of communication.

TABLE 15.1   Accommodations Involving Modifications of Presentation Format

- Braille format
- Large-print editions
- Large-print figure supplements
- Braille figure supplement
- CCTV to magnify text and materials
- For computer-administered tests, devices such as ZoomText Magnifier and ScreenReader to magnify material on the screen or read text on the screen
- Reader services (read directions and questions, describe visual material)
- Sign language
- Audiotaped administration
- Videotaped administration
- Alternative background and foreground colors
- Increasing the spacing between items
- Reducing the number of items per page
- Using raised line drawings
- Using language-simplified questions
- Converting written exams to oral exams; oral exams to written format
- Defining words
- Providing additional examples
- Clarifying and helping students understand directions, questions, and tasks
- Highlighting key words or phrases
- Providing cues (e.g., bullets, stop signs) on test booklet
- Rephrasing or restating directions and questions
- Simplifying or clarifying language
- Using templates to limit amount of print visible at one time

TABLE 15.2   Accommodations Involving Modifications of Response Format

- Oral examinations
- Scribe services (student dictates response to scribe, who creates written response)
- Allowing a student to respond in sign language
- Allowing a student to point to the correct response
- Having an aide mark the answers
- Using a tape recorder to record responses
- Using a computer with read-back capability to record responses
- Using a Braillewriter to record responses
- Using voice-activated computer software
- Providing increased spacing between lines on the answer sheet
- Using graph paper for math problems
- Allowing students to mark responses in the test booklet rather than on a computer answer sheet (e.g., Scantron forms)
- Using a ruler for visual tracking

Modifications of Timing

Extended time is probably the most frequent accommodation provided. Extended time is appropriate for any student who may be slowed down due to reduced processing speed, reading speed, or writing speed. It is also appropriate for students who use other accommodations such as the use of a scribe or some form of adaptive equipment, because these often require more time. Determining how much time to allow is a complex consideration. Research suggests that 50% additional time is adequate for most students with disabilities (Northeast Technical Assistance Center, 1999). Although this is probably a good rule of thumb, be sensitive to special conditions that might demand extra time. Nevertheless, most assessment professionals do not recommend "unlimited time" as an accommodation. It is not necessary, can complicate the scheduling of assessments, and can be seen as unreasonable and undermine the credibility of the accommodation process in the eyes of some educators. Other time-related modifications include providing more frequent breaks or administering the test in sections, possibly spread over several days. For some students it may be beneficial to change the time of day the test is administered to accommodate their medication schedule or fluctuations in their energy levels. Table 15.3 provides a summary listing of these and related accommodations.

Modifications of Setting

Modifications of setting allow students to be tested in a setting that will enable them to perform their best.

Modifications of setting allow students to be tested in a setting that will enable them to perform at their best. For example, for students who are highly distractible this may include administering the test individually or in a small group setting. For other students preferential seating in the regular classroom may be sufficient. Some students will have special needs based on space or accessibility requirements (e.g., a room that is wheelchair accessible). Some students may need special accommodations such as a room free from extraneous noise/distractions, special lighting, special acoustics, or the use of a study carrel to minimize distractions. Table 15.4 provides a summary listing of these and related accommodations.

Adaptive Devices and Supports

There is a multitude of **adaptive devices and supports** that may be useful when testing students with disabilities. These can range from sophisticated high-technology solutions to fairly simple low-technology supports. For individuals with visual impairments, a number

TABLE 15.3   Accommodations Involving Modifications of Timing

- Extended time
- More frequent breaks
- Administering the test in sections
- Spreading the testing over several days
- Changing the time of day the test is administered

TABLE 15.4   Accommodations Involving Modifications of Setting

- Individual test administration
- Administration in a small group setting
- Preferential seating
- Space or accessibility considerations
- Avoidance of extraneous noise/distractions
- Special lighting
- Special acoustics
- Study carrel to minimize distractions
- Alternate sitting and standing

There is a multitude of *adaptive devices and supports* that may be useful when testing students with disabilities.

of companies produce products ranging from handheld magnification devices to systems that automatically enlarge the size of print viewed on a computer screen (e.g., ZoomText Magnifier and ScreenReader, ClearView, Optelec, and Visualtek). There are voice recognition computer programs that allow students to dictate their responses and print out a document containing their text (e.g., Dragon Dictate). Also available are a number of adaptive keyboards and trackball devices (e.g., Intellikeys keyboard, Kensington Trackball mouse, HeadMaster Plus mouse). Auditory amplification devices as well as audiotape and videotape players and recorders may be appropriate accommodations. On the low-tech side, students may benefit from special chairs and large surface desks, earplugs/earphones, colored templates, markers to maintain place, securing the paper to the desk with tape, dark, heavy, or raised lines of pencil grips. It may be appropriate to provide an abacus, math tables, or calculators to facilitate math calculations. Accordingly, in some situations it may be appropriate to provide reference materials such as a dictionary or thesaurus. In many situations the use of aids such as calculators, spell check, and reference materials have become so common, they are being made available to students without disabilities. Table 15.5 provides a summary listing of these and related accommodations.

Using Only a Portion of a Test

In some situations it may be appropriate to **use only a portion of a test** with a student with a disability. In clinical settings clinicians might delete certain subtests of a test battery that are deemed inappropriate for an individual with a disability. For example, when testing a student with a severe visual impairment, a psychologist administering the WISC-IV (see Chapter 13) might delete subtests that require vision (e.g., Block Design, Matrix Reasoning, Picture Concepts) and use only subtests presented and responded to orally (e.g., Vocabulary, Information, Similarities). The same principle can be applied to classroom assessments. That is, a teacher might decide to delete certain items that are deemed inappropriate for certain students with disabilities. Along the same lines, in some situations items will be deleted simply to reduce the length of the test (e.g., to accommodate a student who is easily fatigued). These may be acceptable accommodations in some situations, but it is also possible that using only portions of an assessment will significantly alter the nature of the

TABLE 15.5   Accommodations Involving Adaptive Devices and Supports

- Handheld magnification devices and CCTV
- Systems that enlarge print (e.g., ZoomText Magnifier, ClearView, Optelec, and Visualtek)
- Systems that read text on the screen (ZoomText Magnifier and ScreenReader)
- Voice recognition computer programs that allow students to dictate their responses and print out a document containing their text (e.g., Dragon Dictate)
- Adaptive keyboards and trackball devices (e.g., HeadMaster Plus mouse, Intellikeys keyboard, Kensington Trackball mouse)
- Auditory amplification devices
- Audiotape and videotape players and recorders
- Special chairs and large surface desks
- Earplugs/earphones
- Colored templates or transparencies
- Markers to maintain place, highlighters
- Securing paper to desk with tape
- Dark, heavy, or raised lines of pencil grips
- Abacus, math tables, or calculators (or talking calculators)
- Reference materials such as a dictionary or thesaurus, spell checkers
- Watches or clocks with reminder alarms

construct being measured (AERA et al., 1999). As a result, teachers should use this approach with considerable caution.

Using Alternate Assessments

A final category of accommodations involves replacing the standard test with one that has been specifically developed for students with a disability (AERA et al., 1999). **Using alternate assessments** is often appropriate for students with severe disabilities that prevent them from participating in the standard assessments, even with the use of more common accommodations (U.S. Department of Education, 1997). The use of alternative assessments may be an appealing accommodation because, with careful planning and development, they can produce reliable and valid results. The major limitation with this approach is that it may be difficult to find satisfactory alternate assessments that measure the same construct as the standard assessment (AERA et al., 1999).

Determining What Accommodations to Provide

Determining whether a student needs assessment accommodations and which accommodations are appropriate is not an easy decision. In terms of making this decision, the *Standards* (AERA et al., 1999) state, "the overarching concern is the validity of the inference made from the score on the modified test: fairness to all parties is best served by a decision about test modification that results in the most accurate measure of the construct of interest" (p. 102). The *Standards* go on to emphasize the importance of professional judgment in making this

There is relatively little research on assessment accommodations, and what is available has often produced contradictory results.

decision. There is relatively little research on assessment accommodations, and what is available has often produced contradictory findings (AERA et al., 1999; Fuchs, 2002). As a result, there are few universally accepted guidelines about determining what assessment accommodations should be provided. For example, Fuchs (2002) notes that the accommodations that some states recommend for their statewide assessments are actually prohibited by other states. Nevertheless, here are a few principles that experts working with students with disabilities generally accept.

Accommodations Should Be Tailored to Meet the Specific Needs of the Individual Students.   Do not try to apply a "one-size-fits-all" set of accommodations to students with disabilities, even when they have the same disability. Not all students with any specific type of disability need the same set of accommodations. For example, students with learning disabilities are a heterogeneous group and vary in terms of the nature and severity of their disability. As a result, it would be inappropriate to provide the same set of assessment accommodations to all students with learning disabilities. The *Standards* (AERA et al., 1999) give the example of providing a test in Braille format to all students with visual impairments. This might be an appropriate accommodation for some students with visual impairments, but for others it might be more appropriate to provide large-print testing materials whereas for others it might be preferable to provide a reader or an audiotape with the questions. Look at students individually and determine their specific needs. This information should serve as the basis for decisions about assessment accommodations. Because teachers work with students on a day-to-day basis, they are often the best qualified to help determine what types of assessment accommodations are indicated.

Accommodations That Students Routinely Receive in Their Classroom Instruction Are Generally Appropriate for Assessments.   If an accommodation is seen as being appropriate and necessary for promoting learning during classroom instruction, it is likely that the same accommodation will be appropriate and necessary for assessments. This applies to both classroom assessments and state and district assessment programs. For example, if a student with a visual handicap receives large-print instructional materials in class (e.g., large-print textbook, handouts, and other class materials), it would be logical to provide large-print versions of classroom assessments as well as standardized assessments. A reasonable set of questions to ask is (1) What type of instructional accommodations are being provided in the classroom?, (2) Are these same accommodations appropriate and necessary to allow the students to demonstrate their knowledge and skills on assessments?, and (3) Are any additional assessment accommodations indicated? (Mastergeorge & Miyoshi, 1999).

To the Extent Possible, Select Accommodations That Promote Independent Functioning.   Although you want to provide assessment accommodations that minimize the impact of irrelevant student characteristics, it is also good educational practice to promote the independent functioning of students (King et al., 1995). For example, if a student with a visual handicap can read large-print text, this accommodation would likely be preferable to providing a reader. Similarly, you might want to provide tape-recorded directions/items versus a reader or a word processor with a read-back function versus a scribe. You want to provide the accommodations needed to produce valid and reliable results, but this can often be accomplished while also promoting student independence.

Periodically Reevaluate the Needs of the Student. Overtime the needs of a student may change. In some cases, students will mature and develop new skills and abilities. In other situations there may be a loss of some abilities due to a progressive disorder. As a result, it is necessary to periodically reexamine the needs of the student and determine whether the existing accommodations are still necessary and if any new modifications need to be added.

Typically the determination of assessment accommodations is the responsibility of the IEP committee, and they are specified in the IEP (or with students who are 504 only, in the 504 plan). Teachers, as members of these committees, will have a key role in determining what accommodations are necessary for the student. Again, we emphasize that when determining which accommodations to provide you always want to assure that the reliability and validity of the assessment results are maintained. As noted, we do not always have well-developed research-based information to help us make these decisions, and often we have to base them on professional judgment. In other words, you will have to carefully examine the needs of the student and the intended use of the assessment and make a decision about which accommodations are needed and appropriate. As an example, reading the test items to a student would clearly invalidate an assessment of reading comprehension. In contrast, administering the assessment in a quiet setting would not undermine the validity of the results (U.S. Department of Education, 1997). Table 15.6 provides a summary of factors to consider when selecting assessment accommodations for students. Special Interest Topic 15.1 provides information on research into the effectiveness of assessment accommodations, and Special Interest Topic 15.2 illustrates the assessment accommodations allowed on one statewide assessment.

Reporting Results of Modified Assessments

When clinical and school psychologists modify an individually administered standardized test to accommodate the needs of a student with a disability, they typically document this in the psychological or educational assessment report. This is standard practice and is not the focus of serious debate. In contrast, the way scores of students receiving accommodations on large-scale standardized tests are reported has been the focus of considerable debate. Some assessment organizations will use an asterisk or some other "flag" to denote a score resulting from a nonstandard administration. The *Standards* (AERA et al., 1999) note that this practice is promoted by some but seen as discriminatory by others. Proponents of the practice argue that without **nonstandard administration flags** the scores may be misleading to those

(text continues on p. 390)

TABLE 15.6   Determining Which Accommodations to Provide

- Tailor the modifications to meet the specific needs of the individual student (i.e., no one-size-fits-all accommodations).
- If a student routinely receives an accommodation in classroom instruction, that accommodation is usually appropriate for assessments.
- When possible, select accommodations that will promote independent functioning.
- Periodically reevaluate the needs of the students (e.g., Do they still need the accommodation? Do they need additional accommodations?).

SPECIAL INTEREST TOPIC 15.1
Differential Effects and Assessment Accommodations?

Fuchs (2002) notes that one of the prominent strategies for examining the validity of assessment accommodations is to look for **differential effects** of the accommodation between students with and without disabilities. In these studies, the validity of an accommodation is supported when it increases the performance of students with disabilities substantially more than it increases the performance of students without disabilities. For example, consider the use of the Braille format for students with a visual impairment who can read Braille. It is reasonable to expect that the Braille format will allow students with visual impairments to increase their performance on a test of reading comprehension. However, the use of the Braille format would not result in an increase in performance of students without visual impairments (in fact it would severely hamper their performance). Differential effects are evident and this supports the validity of this assessment accommodation with students with visual impairments.

As we noted, there is relatively little research on the validity of assessment accommodations. To complicate the situation, the research has produced conflicting results. Consider these examples. Runyon (1991) examined the effects of extended time on a reading test among college students. Her results showed that for students with learning disabilities the extra time significantly improved their performance. In contrast, for the students without disabilities the extra time did not result in a significant increase in their performance. In other words, her results demonstrate differential effects and support the validity of extended time as an accommodation with these students. In contrast, Fuchs, Fuchs, Eaton, Hamlett, Binkley et al. (2000) examined the effects of extended time for 4th-grade students with and without disabilities on a reading test. This research did not find evidence of differential effects between students with learning disabilities and students without disabilities. In fact, there was some evidence that students without disabilities benefited more from the extra time relative to students with disabilities. In other words, this research suggests extended time on reading tests benefits all students, not just those with learning disabilities. How do you explain these contradictory results? At this time we do not have enough research to explain these discrepancies. The explanation that appears most promising involves the difference in age. Runyan (1991) examined college students whereas Fuchs, Fuchs, Eaton, Hamlett, Binkley et al. (2000) studied 4th-grade students.

On the positive side, educators and researchers are developing strategies that might help resolve many of these issues. For example, Fuchs and colleagues (Fuchs, 2002; Fuchs, Fuchs, Eaton, Hamlett, Binkley et al., 2000; Fuchs, Fuchs, Eaton, Hamlett, & Karns, 2000) have developed and studied a system called the Dynamic Assessment of Test Accommodations (DATA). When using DATA, teachers administer alternate forms of brief math and reading tests and determine which accommodations produce differential effects relative to normative data obtained from students without disabilities. If the increase a student with a disability receives using a specific accommodation (e.g., extended time) substantially exceeds that observed for students without disabilities, DATA recommends that accommodation for classroom and standardized assessments. If the increase obtained with an accommodation is similar to that observed with students without disabilities, DATA does not recommend that accommodation. The results of preliminary studies of the DATA system are very encouraging, and this system may soon help teachers and other educators make objective decisions about assessment accommodations.

SPECIAL INTEREST TOPIC **15.2**

Allowable Accommodations in a Statewide Assessment Program

The Texas Student Assessment Program includes a number of assessments, the most widely administered being the Texas Assessment of Knowledge and Skills (TAKS). The manual (Texas Education Agency, 2003) notes that accommodations that do not compromise the validity of the test results may be provided. Decisions about what accommodations to provide should be based on the individual needs of the student and take into consideration whether the student regularly receives the accommodation in the classroom. For students receiving special education services, the requested accommodations must be noted on their IEP. The manual identifies the following as allowable accommodations:

- Signing or translating oral instructions
- Signing the prompt on the writing test
- Oral administration of selected tests (e.g., math, social studies, and science)
- The use of colored transparencies or place markers
- Small group or individual administration
- Braille or large-print tests
- Modified methods of response
  - Respond orally
  - Mark responses in test booklet (versus machine-scorable response form)
  - Type responses
  - Tape-record essays then play it back to a scribe while spelling, capitalizing, and punctuating it. The student is then allowed to read the essay and indicate any desired corrections.
- Reference materials (English dictionaries are allowed during certain tests)
- Calculators (allowed during certain tests)

Naturally, the testing program allows individuals to request accommodations that are not included in this list, and these will be evaluated on a one-by-one basis. However, the manual identifies the following as nonallowable accommodations:

- Students may not receive reading assistance on the writing, reading, and language arts tests.
- Use of foreign-language reference materials.
- Use of calculators on certain tests.
- Translation of test items.
- Test questions, passages, prompts, or answer choices may not be clarified or rephrased.
- Any other accommodation that would invalidate the results.

In addition to the TAKS, the State-Developed Alternative Assessment (SDAA) is designed for students who are receiving instruction in the state-specified curriculum but for whom the IEP committee has decided the TAKS is inappropriate. Whereas the TAKS is administered based on the student's assigned grade level, the SDAA is based on the student's instructional level as specified by the IEP committee. The goal of the SDAA is to provide accurate information about the student's annual growth in the areas of reading, writing, and math. In terms of allowable accommodations, the manual (Texas Education Agency, 2003) simply specifies that:

> With the exception of the nonallowable accommodations listed below, accommodations documented in the individual education plan (IEP) that are necessary to address the student's instructional needs

(continued)

based on his or her disability may be used for this assessment. Any accommodation made MUST be documented in the student's IEP and must not invalidate the tests. (p. 111)

The nonallowable accommodations include:

- No direct or indirect assistance that identifies or helps identify the correct answer is allowed.
- Test questions, passages, prompts, or answer choices may not be clarified or rephrased.
- The number of answer choices for an item may not be reduced.
- With the exception of specific prompts, the reading and writing tests may not be read aloud to the student.

Some professionals support the use of "flags" to denote scores resulting from nonstandard assessments, whereas others feel this practice is unfair to students with disabilities and may place them at a disadvantage.

interpreting assessment results. That is, they will assume no accommodations were made when they actually were. Opponents of the practice hold that it unfairly labels and stigmatizes students with disabilities and potentially puts them at a disadvantage. The *Standards* suggest that two principles apply: (1) Important information necessary to interpret scores accurately should be provided, and (2) extraneous information that is not necessary to interpret scores accurately should be withheld. Based on this guidance, if adequate evidence demonstrates that scores are comparable both with and without accommodations, flagging is not necessary. When there is insufficient evidence regarding the comparability of test scores, flagging may be indicated. However, a simple flag denoting the use of accommodations is rather imprecise, and when permissible by law it is better to provide specific information about the accommodations that were provided.

Different agencies providing professional assessment services handle this issue differently. Educational Testing Service (ETS) indicates that when an approved assessment accommodation is thought to possibly affect the construct being measured, it includes a statement indicating that the assessment was taken under nonstandard testing conditions. However, if only minor accommodations are required, the administration can be considered standard and the scores are not flagged. Minor accommodations include providing wheelchair access, the use of a sign language interpreter, or large-print test material. ETS provides information about the testing accommodations it provides at www.ets.org/disability/info.html.

Summary

In this chapter we focused on the use of assessment accommodations with students with disabilities. We noted that standard assessment procedures might not be appropriate for a student with a disability if the assessment requires the students to use an ability that is affected by their disability but is irrelevant to the construct being measured. In these situations it may be necessary for teachers to modify the standard assessment procedures. We gave the example of students with visual handicaps taking a written test of world history. Although the students could not read the material in its standard format, if they could read

SPECIAL INTEREST TOPIC **15.3**

Assessment of Students with Disabilities—Selected Legal Issues

> [A]n otherwise qualified student who is unable to disclose the degree of learning he actually possesses because of the test format or environment would be the object of discrimination solely on the basis of his handicap.
>
> (Chief Justice Cummings, U.S. 7th Circuit Court of Appeals[1])

> Section 504 imposes no requirement upon an educational institution to lower or to effect substantial modifications of standards to accommodate a handicapped person.
>
> (Justice Powell, U.S. Supreme Court[2])

These quotes were selected by Phillips (1993) to illustrate the diversity in legal opinions that have been rendered regarding the provision of assessment accommodations for students with disabilities. Dr. Phillips' extensive writings in this area (e.g., 1993, 1994, & 1996) provide some guidelines regarding the assessment of students with disabilities. Some of these guidelines are most directly applicable to high-stakes assessment programs, but they also have implications for other educational assessments.

Notice

Students should be given adequate notice when they will be required to engage in a high-stakes testing program (e.g., assessments required for graduation). Although this requirement applies to all students, it is particularly important for students with disabilities to have adequate notice of any testing requirements because it may take them longer to prepare for the assessment. What constitutes adequate notice? With regard to a test required for graduation from high school, one court found 1½ years to be inadequate (*Brookhart v. Illinois State Board of Education*). Another court agreed, finding that approximately 1 year was inadequate, but suggested that 3 years was adequate (*Northport v. Ambach*).

Curricular Validity of the Test

If a state is going to implement a high-stakes assessment, it must be able to show that students have had adequate opportunities to acquire the knowledge and skills assessed by the assessment (*Debra P. v. Turlington*). This includes students with disabilities. One way to address this is to include the learning objectives measured by the assessment in the student's Individual Education Program (IEP). One court ruled that parents and educators could decide not to include the skills and knowledge assessed by a mandatory graduation test on a student's IEP, but only if there was adequate time for the parents to evaluate the consequences of their child receiving a certificate of completion in lieu of a high school diploma (*Brookhart*).

Accommodations Must Be Individualized

Both IDEA and Section 504 require that educational programs and assessment accommodations be tailored to meet the unique needs of the individual student. For example, it is not acceptable for educators to decide that all students with a specific disability (e.g., learning disability) will receive the same assessment accommodations. Rulings by the federal Office of Civil Rights (OCR) maintain that decisions to provide specific assessment accommodations must be made on a case-by-case basis.

[1]*Brookhart v. Illinois State Board of Education,* 697 F. 2d 179 (7th Cir. 1983).
[2]*Southeastern Community College v. Davis,* 442 U.S. 397 (1979).
Debra P. v. Turlington, 474 F. Supp. 244 (M.D. FL 1979).

(continued)

SPECIAL INTEREST TOPIC **15.3**   Continued

Invalid Accommodations

Courts have ruled that test administrators are not required to grant assessment accommodations that "substantially modify" a test or that "pervert" the purpose of the test (*Brookhart*). In psychometric terms, the accommodations should not invalidate the interpretation of test scores. Phillips (1994) suggests the following questions should be asked when considering a given accommodation:

1. Will format changes or accommodations in testing conditions change the skills being measured?
2. Will the scores of examinees tested under standard conditions have a different meaning than scores for examinees tested with the requested accommodation?
3. Would nondisabled examinees benefit if allowed the same accommodation?
4. Does the disabled examinee have any capability for adapting to standard test administration conditions?
5. Is the disability evidence or testing accommodation policy based on procedures with doubtful validity and reliability? (p. 104)

If the answer to any of these questions is "yes," Phillips suggests the accommodations are likely not appropriate.

Flagging

"Flagging" refers to administrators adding notations on score reports, transcripts, or diplomas indicating that assessment accommodations were provided (and in some cases what the accommodations were). Proponents of flagging hold that it protects the users of assessment information from making inaccurate interpretations of the results. Opponents of flagging hold that it unfairly labels and stigmatizes students with disabilities, breaches their confidentiality, and potentially puts them at a disadvantage. If there is substantial evidence that the accommodation does not detract from the validity of the interpretation of scores, flagging is not necessary. However, flagging may be indicated when there is incomplete evidence regarding the comparability of test scores. Phillips (1994) describes a process labeled "self-selection with informed disclosure." Here administrators grant essentially any reasonable accommodation that is requested, even if it might invalidate the assessment results. Then, to protect users of assessment results, they add notations specifying what accommodations were provided. An essential element is that the examinee requesting the accommodations must be adequately informed that the assessment reports will contain information regarding any accommodations provided and the potential advantages and disadvantages of taking the test with accommodations. However, even when administrators get informed consent, disclosure of assessment accommodations may result in legal action.

Phillips (1993) notes that at times the goal of promoting valid and comparable test results and the legal and political goal of protecting the individual rights of students with disabilities may be at odds. She recommends that educators develop detailed policies and procedures regarding the provision of assessment accommodations, decide each case on an individual basis, and provide expeditious appeals when requested accommodations are denied. She notes:

> To protect the rights of both the public and individuals in a testing program, it will be necessary to balance the policy goal of maximum participation by the disabled against the need to provide valid and interpretable student test scores. (p. 32)

Braille an appropriate accommodation would be to convert the test to the Braille format. Because the test is designed to measure knowledge of world history, not the ability to read standard print, this would be an appropriate accommodation. The goal of assessment accommodations is not simply to allow the student to obtain a better grade, but to provide the most reliable and valid assessment of the construct of interest. To this end, assessment accommodations should always increase the validity of the score interpretations so they more accurately reflect the student's true standing on the construct being measured.

We noted three situations in which assessment accommodations are not appropriate or necessary (AERA et al., 1999). These are when (1) the affected ability is directly relevant to the construct being measured, (2) the purpose of the assessment is to assess the presence and degree of the disability, and (3) the student does not actually need the accommodation.

A number of federal laws mandate assessment accommodations for students with disabilities. The Individuals with Disabilities Education Act (IDEA) and Section 504 of the Rehabilitation Act of 1973 are the laws most often applied in the schools and we spent some time discussing these. IDEA requires that public schools provide students with disabilities a Free Appropriate Public Education (FAPE) and identifies a number of disability categories. These include learning disabilities, communication disorders, mental retardation, emotional disturbance, other health impaired, multiple disabilities, hearing impairments, orthopedic impairments, autism, visual impairments, traumatic brain injury, and developmental delay. A key factor in the provision of services to students with disabilities is the Individual Education Program (IEP). The IEP is a written document developed by a committee that specifies a number of factors, including the students' instructional arrangement, the special services they will receive, and any assessment accommodations they will receive.

Section 504 of the Rehabilitation Act of 1973, often referred to as Section 504 or simply as 504, prohibits discrimination against individuals with disabilities in any agency or school that receives federal funds. In the public schools, Section 504 requires that schools provide students with disabilities reasonable accommodations to meet their educational needs. Section 504 provides a broad standard of eligibility, simply stating that an individual with a disability is anyone with a physical or mental disability that limits one or more life activities. Because Section 504 is broader than IDEA, it is possible for a student to qualify under Section 504 and not qualify under IDEA. This is sometimes referred to as 504 only.

The following assessment accommodations have been developed to meet the needs of students with disabilities:

- Modifications of presentation format (e.g., use of Braille or large print to replace standard text)
- Modifications of response format (e.g., allow a student to respond using sign language)
- Modifications of timing (e.g., extended time)
- Modifications of setting (e.g., preferential seating, study carrel to minimize distractions)
- Adaptive devices and supports (e.g., magnification and amplification devices)
- Using only a portion of a test (e.g., reducing test length)
- Using alternate assessments (e.g., tests specifically developed for students with disabilities)

We noted that there is relatively little research on assessment accommodations and what is available has produced inconsistent results. As a result, only a few principles about providing assessment accommodations are widely accepted. These include:

- Accommodations should be tailored to meet the specific needs of the individual student.
- Accommodations that students routinely receive in their classroom instruction are generally appropriate for assessments.

- To the extent possible, select accommodations that promote independent functioning.
- Periodically reevaluate the needs of the student.

The final topic we address concerned reporting the results of modified assessments. In the context of individual psychological and educational assessments, it is common for the clinician to report any modifications to the standardized assessment procedures. However, in the context of large-scale standardized assessments, there is considerable debate. Some experts recommend the use of flags to denote a score resulting from a modified administration of a test. Proponents of this practice suggest that without the use of flags, individuals interpreting the assessment results will assume that there was a standard administration and interpret the scores accordingly. Opponents of the practice feel that it unfairly labels and stigmatizes students with disabilities and may put them at a disadvantage.

KEY TERMS AND CONCEPTS

Adaptive devices and supports, p. 383

Assessment accommodations, p. 372

Autism, p. 377

Communication disorders, p. 376

Developmental delays, p. 378

Differential effects, p. 388

Emotional disturbance, p. 376

Free Appropriate Public Education (FAPE), p. 373

Hearing impairments, p. 377

IDEA categories of disabilities, p. 375

IEP committee, p. 374

Inclusion or mainstreaming, p. 374

Individual Education Program (IEP), p. 374

Individuals with Disabilities Education Act (IDEA), p. 373

Learning disability, p. 375

Mental retardation, p. 376

Modifications of presentation format, p. 381

Modifications of response format, p. 381

Modifications of setting, p. 383

Modifications of timing, p. 383

Multiple disabilities, p. 377

Nonstandard administration flags, p. 387

Orthopedic impairments, p. 377

Other Health Impaired (OHI), p. 377

Section 504 of the Rehabilitation Act (504) of 1973, p. 378

Traumatic brain injury, p. 378

Using alternate assessments, p. 385

Using only a portion of a test, p. 384

Visual impairment, p. 378

RECOMMENDED READINGS

American Educational Research Association, American Psychological Association, & National Council on Measurement in Education (1999). *Standards for educational and psychological testing.* Washington, DC: AERA. The *Standards* provide an excellent discussion of assessment accommodations.

Mastergeorge, A. M., & Miyoshi, J. N. (1999). *Accommodations for students with disabilities: A teacher's guide* (CSE Technical Report 508). Los Angeles: National Center for Research on Evaluation, Standards, and Student Testing. This guide provides some useful information on assessment accommodations specifically aimed toward teachers.

Phillips, S. E. (1994). High-stakes testing accommodations: Validity versus disabled rights. *Applied Measurement in Education, 7*(2), 93–120. An excellent discussion of legal cases involving assessment accommodations for students with disabilities.

Thurnlow, M., Hurley, C., Spicuzza, R., & El Sawaf, H. (1996). *A review of the literature on testing accommodations for students with disabilities* (Minnesota Report No. 9). Minneapolis: University of Minnesota, National Center on Educational Outcomes. Retrieved April 19, 2004, from http://education. umn.edu/NCEO/OnlinePubs/MnReport9.html

Turnbull, R., Turnbull, A., Shank, M., Smith, S., & Leal, D. (2002). *Exceptional lives: Special education in today's schools.* Upper Saddle River, NJ: Merrill Prentice Hall. This excellent text provides valuable information regarding the education of students with disabilities.

16 The Problem of Bias in Educational Assessment

Test bias: In God we trust; all others must have data.
—Reynolds (1983)

CHAPTER HIGHLIGHTS

What Do We Mean by Bias?

Past and Present Concerns: A Brief Look

The Controversy over Bias in Testing:
   Its Origin, What It Is, and What It Is Not

Cultural Bias and the Nature
   of Psychological Testing

Objections to the Use of Educational and
   Psychological Tests with Minority Students

The Problem of Definition in Test
   Bias Research: Differential Validity

Cultural Loading, Cultural Bias,
   and Culture-Free Tests

Inappropriate Indicators of Bias:
   Mean Differences and Equivalent Distributions

Bias in Test Content

Bias in Other Internal Features of Tests

Bias in Prediction and in Relation
   to Variables External to the Test

LEARNING OBJECTIVES

After reading and studying this chapter, students should be able to:

1. Explain the cultural test bias hypothesis.

2. Describe alternative explanations for observed group differences in performance on aptitude and other standardized tests.

3. Describe the relationship between bias and reliability.

4. Describe the major objections regarding the use of standardized tests with minority students.

5. Describe what is meant by cultural loading, cultural bias, and culture-free tests.

6. Describe the mean difference definition of test bias and its current status.

7. Describe the results of research on the presence of bias in the content of educational and psychological tests.

8. Describe the results of research on the presence of bias in other internal features of educational and psychological tests.

9. Describe the results of research on bias in prediction and in relation to variables that are external to the test.

10. Explain what is implied by homogeneity of regression and describe the conditions that may result when it is not present.

Groups of people, who can be defined on a qualitative basis such as gender or ethnicity (and are thus formed using a nominal scale of measurement as was discussed in Chapter 2), do not always show the same mean level of performance on various educational and psychological tests. For example, on tests of spatial skill, requiring visualization and imagery, men and boys tend to score higher than do women and girls. On tests that involve written language and tests of simple psychomotor speed (such as the rapid copying of symbols or digits), women and girls tend to score higher than men and boys (see Special Interest Topic 16.1 for additional information). Ethnic group differences in test performance also occur and are most controversial and polemic.

There is perhaps no more controversial finding in the field of psychology than the persistent 1 standard deviation (about 15 points) difference between the intelligence test performance of Black and White students taken as a group. Much effort has been expended to determine why group differences occur (and there are many, many such group differences on various measures of specialized ability and achievement), but we do not know for certain why they exist. One major, carefully studied explanation is that the tests are biased in some way against certain groups. This is referred to as the **cultural test bias hypothesis**.

Much effort has been expended to determine why group differences occur on standardized aptitude tests, but we do not know for certain why.

The *cultural test bias hypothesis* maintains that group differences on mental tests are due to inherent, artifactual biases that exist within the tests.

The cultural test bias hypothesis represents the contention that any gender, ethnic, racial, or other nominally determined group differences on mental tests are due to inherent, artifactual biases produced within the tests through flawed psychometric methodology. Group differences are believed then to stem from characteristics of the tests and to be totally unrelated to any actual differences in the psychological trait, skill, or ability in question. The resolution or evaluation of the validity of the cultural test bias hypothesis is one of the most crucial scientific questions facing psychology today.

Bias in mental tests has many implications for individuals including the misplacement of students in educational programs; errors in assigning grades; unfair denial of admission to college, graduate, and professional degree programs; and the inappropriate denial of employment. The scientific implications are even more substantive. There would be dramatic implications for educational and psychological research and theory if the cultural test bias hypothesis were correct. The principal research of the past one hundred years in the psychology of human differences would have to be dismissed as confounded and largely artifactual because much of the work is based on standard psychometric theory and testing technology. This would in turn create major upheavals in applied psychology, because the foundations of clinical, counseling, educational, industrial, and school psychology are all strongly tied to the basic academic field of individual differences.

Teachers, be they in the elementary and secondary schools or colleges and universities, assign grades on the basis of tests or other more subjective evaluations of learning, and

SPECIAL INTEREST TOPIC   **16.1**

Sex Differences in Intelligence

Research has shown that although there are no significant sex differences in overall intelligence scores, substantial differences exist with regard to specific cognitive abilities. Females typically score higher on a number of verbal abilities whereas males perform better on visual–spatial and (starting in middle childhood) mathematical skills. It is believed that sex hormone levels and social factors both influence the development of these differences. As is typical of group differences in intellectual abilities, the variability in performance within groups (i.e., males and females) is much larger than the mean difference between groups (Neisser et al., 1996). Diane Halpern (1997) has written extensively on gender differences in cognitive abilities. This table briefly summarizes some of her findings.

Selected Abilities on Which Women Obtain Higher Average Scores

Type of Ability	Examples
Rapid access and use of verbal and other information in long-term memory	Verbal fluency, synonym generation, associative memory, spelling, anagrams
Specific knowledge areas	Literature and foreign languages
Production and comprehension of prose	Writing and reading comprehension
Fine motor tasks	Matching and coding tasks, pegboard, mirror tracing
School performance	Most subjects

Selected Abilities on Which Men Obtain Higher Average Scores

Type of Ability	Examples
Transformations of visual working memory, moving objects, and aiming	Mental rotations, dynamic spatiotemporal tasks, accuracy in throwing
Specific knowledge areas	General knowledge, mathematics, science, and geography
Fluid reasoning	Proportional, mechanical, and scientific reasoning; SAT Math and GRE Quantitative

Note: This table was adopted from Halpern (1997), Appendix (p. 1102).

make decisions regarding promotion or perhaps even professional certification on much the same criteria. Bias in this process that produces adverse impact because of someone's race, sex, or other unrelated factor is clearly serious and unacceptable. If professionally designed tests subjected to lengthy developmental research and tryout periods and held up to the most

If well-constructed and properly standardized tests are biased, then classroom tests are almost certain to be at least as biased and probably more so.

stringent of psychometric and statistical standards turn out to be culturally biased when used with native-born American ethnic minorities, what about the teacher-made test in the classroom and more subjective evaluation of work samples (e.g., performance assessments)? If well-constructed and properly standardized tests are biased, then classroom measures are almost certain to be at least as biased and probably more so. As the reliability of a test or evaluation procedure goes down, the likelihood of bias goes up, the two being inversely related. A large reliability coefficient does not eliminate the possibility of bias, but as reliability is lowered, the *probability* that bias will be present increases.

The purpose of this chapter is to address the issues and findings surrounding the cultural test bias hypothesis in a rational manner and evaluate the validity of the hypothesis, as far as possible, on the basis of existing empirical research. This will not be an easy task because of the controversial nature of the topic and strong emotional overtones. Prior to turning to the reasons that test bias generates highly charged emotions and reviewing some of the history of these issues, it is proper to engage in a discussion of just what we mean by the term *bias*.

What Do We Mean by Bias?

Bias carries many different connotations for the lay public and for professionals in a number of disciplines.

In terms of assessment, bias denotes systematic error that occurs in the estimation of some value or score.

Bias carries many different connotations for the lay public and for professionals in a number of disciplines. To the legal mind, bias denotes illegal discriminatory practices while to the lay mind it may conjure up notions of prejudicial attitudes. Much of the rancor in psychology and education regarding proper definitions of **test bias** is due to the divergent uses of this term in general but especially by professionals in the same and related academic fields. Contrary to certain other opinions that more common or lay uses of the term *bias* should be employed when using *bias* in definitions or discussions of bias in educational and psychological tests, bias as used in the present chapter will be defined in its widely recognized, but distinct statistical sense. As defined in the *Standards* (AERA et al., 1999), bias is "a systematic error in a test score" (p. 172). Therefore, a biased assessment is one that systematically underestimates or overestimates the value of the variable it is designed to measure. If the bias is a function of a nominal cultural variable (i.e., ethnicity or gender), then the test has a **cultural bias.** As an example, if an achievement test produces different mean scores for different ethnic groups, and there actually are true differences between the groups in terms of achievement, the test is not biased. However, if the observed differences in achievement scores are the result of the test underestimating the achievement of one group or overestimating the achievement of another, then the test is culturally biased.

Other uses of the term *bias* in research on the cultural test bias hypothesis or cross-group validity of tests are unacceptable from a scientific perspective for two reasons: (1) The imprecise nature of other uses of bias makes empirical investigation and rational inquiry exceedingly difficult, and (2) other uses of the term invoke specific moral value systems that are the subject of intense, polemic, emotional debate without a mechanism for rational resolution. It is imperative that the evaluation of bias in tests be undertaken from the standpoint of scholarly inquiry and debate. Emotional appeals, legal–adversarial approaches, and political remedies of scientific issues appear to us to be inherently unacceptable.

Past and Present Concerns: A Brief Look

Concern about cultural bias in mental testing has been a recurring issue since the beginning of the use of assessment in education. From Alfred Binet in the 1800s to Arthur Jensen over the last 50 years, many scientists have addressed the controversial problem, with varying, inconsistent outcomes. In the last few decades, the issue of cultural bias has come forth as a major contemporary problem far exceeding the bounds of purely academic debate and professional rhetoric. The debate over the cultural test bias hypothesis has become entangled and sometimes confused within the larger issues of individual liberties, civil rights, and social justice, becoming a focal point for psychologists, sociologists, educators, politicians, minority activists, and the lay public. The issues increasingly have become legal and political. Numerous court cases have been brought and New York State even passed "truth-in-testing" legislation that is being considered in other states and in the federal legislature. Such attempts at solutions are difficult if not impossible. Take for example the legal response to the question "Are intelligence tests used to diagnose mental retardation biased against cultural and ethnic minorities?" In California in 1979 (*Larry P. v. Riles*) the answer was "yes" but in Illinois in 1980 (*PASE v. Hannon*) the response was "no." Thus two federal district courts of equivalent standing have heard nearly identical cases, with many of the same witnesses espousing much the same testimony, and reached precisely opposite conclusions. See Special Interest Topic 16.2 for more information on legal issues surrounding assessment bias.

Though current opinion on the cultural test bias hypothesis is quite divergent, ranging from those who consider it to be for the most part unresearchable (e.g., Schoenfeld, 1974) to those who considered the issue settled decades ago (e.g., Jensen, 1980), it seems clear that empirical analysis of the hypothesis should continue to be undertaken. However difficult full objectivity may be in science, we must make every attempt to view all socially, politically, and emotionally charged issues from the perspective of rational scientific inquiry. We must also be prepared to accept scientifically valid findings as real, whether we like them or not.

The Controversy over Bias in Testing: Its Origin, What It Is, and What It Is Not

Systematic group differences on standardized intelligence and aptitude tests may occur as a function of socioeconomic level, race or ethnic background, and other demographic variables. Black–White differences on IQ measures have received extensive investigation over the past 50 or 60 years. Although results occasionally differ slightly depending on the age groups under consideration, random samples of Blacks and Whites show a mean difference

SPECIAL INTEREST TOPIC **16.2**
Courtroom Controversy over IQ Testing in the Public Schools

Largely due to overall mean differences in the performance of various ethnic groups on IQ tests, the use of intelligence tests in the public schools has been the subject of courtroom battles around the United States. Typically such lawsuits argue that the use of intelligence tests as part of the determination of eligibility for special education programs leads to overidentification of certain minorities (traditionally African American and Hispanic children). A necessary corollary to this argument is that the resultant overidentification is inappropriate because the intelligence tests in use are biased, underestimating the intelligence of minority students, and that there is in fact no greater need for special education placement among these ethnic minorities than for other ethnic groups in the population.

Attempts to resolve the controversy over IQ testing in the public schools via the courtroom have not been particularly successful. Unfortunately, but not uncharacteristically, the answer to the legal question "Are IQ tests biased in a manner that results in unlawful discrimination against minorities when used as part of the process of determining eligibility for special education placements?" is, it depends on where you live!

There are four key court cases to consider when reviewing this question, two from California and one each from Illinois and Georgia.

The first case is *Diana v. State Board of Education* (C-70-37 RFP, N.D. Cal., 1970), heard by the same federal judge who would later hear the *Larry P.* case (see later). *Diana* was filed on behalf of Hispanic (referred to as Chicano at that time and in court documents) children classified as EMR, or educably mentally retarded (a now archaic term), based on IQ tests administered in English. However, the children involved in the suit were not native English speakers and when retested in their native language, all but one (of nine) scored above the range designated as EMR. *Diana* was resolved through multiple consent decrees (agreements by the adverse parties ordered into effect by the federal judge). Although quite detailed, the central component of interest here is that the various decrees ensured that children would be tested in their native language, that more than one measure would be used, and that adaptive behavior in nonschool settings would be assessed prior to a diagnosis of EMR.

It seems obvious to us now that whenever persons are assessed in other than their native language, the validity of the results as traditionally interpreted would not hold up, at least in the case of ability testing. This had been obvious to the measurement community for quite some time prior to *Diana,* but had not found its way into practice. Occasionally one still encounters cases of a clinician evaluating children in other than their native language and making inferences about intellectual development—clearly this is inappropriate.

Three cases involving intelligence testing of black children related to special education placement went to trial: *Larry P. v. Riles* (343 F. Supp. 306, 1972; 495 F. Supp. 976, 1979); *PASE v. Hannon* (506 F. Supp. 831, 1980); and *Marshall v. Georgia* (CV 482-233, S.D. of Georgia, 1984). Each of these cases involved allegations of bias in IQ tests that caused the underestimation of the intelligence of black children and subsequently led to disproportionate placement of black children in special education programs. All three cases presented testimony by experts in education, testing, measurement, and related fields, some professing the tests to be biased and others professing they were not. That a disproportionate number of black children were in special education was conceded in all cases—what was litigated was the reason.

In California in *Larry P. v. Riles* (Wilson Riles being superintendent of the San Francisco Unified School District), Judge Peckham ruled that IQ tests were in fact biased against black children and resulted in discriminatory placement in special education. A reading of Peckham's decision reveals a clear condemnation of special education, which is critical to Peckham's logic. He determined that because special education placement was harmful, not helpful, to children, the use of a test (i.e., IQ) that resulted in disproportionate placement was therefore discriminatory. He prohibited (or enjoined) the use of IQ tests with black children in the California public schools.

In *PASE v. Hannon* (PASE being an abbreviation for Parents in Action on Special Education), a similar case to *Larry P.* was brought against the Chicago public schools. Many of the same witnesses testified about many of the same issues. At the conclusion of the case, Judge Grady ruled in favor of the Chicago public schools, finding that although a few IQ test items might be biased, the degree of bias in the items was inconsequential.

In *Marshall v. Georgia*, the NAACP brought suit against rural Georgia school districts alleging bias in the instructional grouping and special education placement associated with IQ testing. Although some of the same individuals testified in this case, several new opinions were offered. However, the judge in *Marshall* eventually ruled in favor of the schools, finding that IQ tests were not in fact biased, and that a greater actual need for special education existed in minority populations.

In the courtroom, we are no closer to resolution of these issues today than we were in 1984 when *Marshall* was decided. However, these cases and other societal factors did foster much research on the issues that have brought us closer to a scientific resolution of the issues. They also prompted the development of new, up-to-date IQ tests and more frequent revisions or updating of older tests. Many challenges remain, especially that of understanding the continued higher failure rates (relative to the majority ethnic population of the United States) of some ethnic minorities in the public schools (while other ethnic minorities have a success rate that exceeds the majority population) and the disproportionate referral rates by teachers of these children for special education placement. The IQ test seems to be only one of many messengers in this crucial educational issue, and bias in the tests does not appear to be the answer.

---

of about 1 standard deviation, with the mean score of the White groups consistently exceeding that of the Black groups. When a number of demographic variables are taken into account (most notably socioeconomic status or SES), the size of the difference reduces to 0.5 to 0.7 standard deviation but remains robust in its appearance. The differences have persisted at relatively constant levels for quite some time and under a variety of methods of investigation. Some recent research suggests that the gap may be narrowing, but this has not been firmly established (Neisser et al., 1996).

Mean differences between ethnic groups are not limited to Black–White comparisons. Although not nearly as thoroughly researched as Black–White differences, Hispanic–White differences have also been documented, with Hispanic mean performance approximately 0.5 standard deviation below the mean of the White group. On the average, Native Americans tend to perform lower on tests of verbal intelligence than Whites. Both Hispanics and Native Americans tend to perform better on visual–spatial tasks relative to verbal tasks. All studies of race/ethnic group differences on ability tests do not show higher levels of performance by Whites. Asian American groups have been shown consistently to perform as well as or better than White groups. Depending on the specific aspect of intelligence under investigation, other race/ethnic groups show performance at or above the performance level of White groups (for a readable review of this research, see Neisser et al., 1996).

It should always be kept in mind that the overlap among the distributions of intelligence test scores for different ethnic groups is much greater than the size of the differences between the various groups. Put another way, there is always more within-group variability in performance on mental tests than between-group variability. Neisser et al. (1996) frame it this way:

> Group means have no direct implications for individuals. What matters for the next person you meet (to the extent that test scores matter at all) is that person's own particular score, not the mean of some reference group to which he or she happens to belong. The commitment to evaluate people on their own individual merit is central to a democratic society. It also makes quantitative sense. The distributions of different groups inevitably overlap, with the range of scores within any one group always wider than the mean differences between any two groups. In the case of intelligence test scores, the variance attributable to individual differences far exceeds the variance related to group membership. (p. 90)

Explaining Mean Group Differences.   Once mean group differences are identified, it is natural to attempt to explain them. Reynolds (2000) notes that the most common explanations for these differences have typically fallen into four categories:

a. The differences primarily have a genetic basis.
b. The differences have an environmental basis (e.g., SES, education, culture).
c. The differences are due to the interactive effect of genes and environment.
d. The tests are defective and systematically underestimate the knowledge and skills of minorities.

The final explanation (i.e., category d) is embodied in the cultural test bias hypothesis introduced earlier in this chapter. Restated, the cultural test bias hypothesis represents the contention that any gender, ethnic, racial, or other nominally determined group differences on mental tests are due to inherent, artifactual biases produced within the tests through flawed psychometric methodology. Group differences are believed then to stem from characteristics of the tests and to be totally unrelated to any actual differences in the psychological trait, skill, or ability in question. Because mental tests are based largely on middle-class values and knowledge, they are more valid for those groups and will be biased against other groups to the extent that they deviate from those values and knowledge bases. Thus, ethnic and other group differences result from flawed psychometric methodology and not from actual differences in aptitude. As will be discussed, this hypothesis reduces to one of differential validity; the hypothesis of differential validity being that tests measure intelligence and other constructs more accurately and make more valid predictions for individuals from the groups on which the tests are mainly based than for those from other groups. The practical implications of such bias have been pointed out previously and are the issues over which most of the court cases have been fought.

> **The hypothesis of differential validity suggests that tests measure constructs more accurately and make more valid predictions for individuals from the groups on which the tests are mainly based than for those from other groups.**

If the cultural test bias hypothesis is incorrect, then group differences are not attributable to the tests and must be due to one of the other factors mentioned above. The model emphasizing the interactive effect of genes and environment (category c, commonly referred to as environment × genetic interaction model) is dominant among contemporary professionals who reject the argument that group differences are artifacts of test bias; however, there is much debate over the relative contributions of genetic and environmental factors (Reynolds, 2000; Suzuki & Valencia, 1997). In addition to the models noted, Williams (1970) and Helms (1992) proposed another model with regard to Black–White differences on aptitude tests, raising the possibility of qualitatively different cognitive structures that require different methods of measurement.

The controversy over test bias should not be confused with that over etiology of any observed group differences.

Test Bias and Etiology. The controversy over test bias is distinct from the question of etiology. Reynolds and Ramsay (2003) note that the need to research etiology is only relevant once it has been determined that mean score differences are real, not simply artifacts of the assessment process. Unfortunately, measured differences themselves have often been inferred to indicate genetic differences and therefore the genetically based intellectual inferiority of some groups. This inference is not defensible from a scientific perspective.

Test Bias and Fairness. Bias and fairness are related, but separate concepts. As noted by Brown, Reynolds, and Whitaker (1999), fairness is a moral, philosophical, or legal issue on which reasonable people can disagree. On the other hand bias is a statistical property of a test. Therefore, bias is a property empirically estimated from test data whereas fairness is a principle established through debate and opinion. Nevertheless, it is common to incorporate information about bias when considering the fairness of an assessment process. For example, a biased test would likely be considered unfair by essentially everyone. However, it is clearly possible that an unbiased test might be considered unfair by at least some. Special Interest Topic 16.3 summarizes the discussion of fairness in testing and test use from the *Standards* (AERA et al., 1999).

Test Bias and Offensiveness. There is also a distinction between test bias and item offensiveness. Test developers often utilize a minority review panel to examine each item for content that may be offensive or demeaning to one or more groups. This is a good procedure for identifying and eliminating offensive items, but it does not ensure that the items are not biased. Research has consistently found little evidence that one can identify, by personal inspection, which items are biased and which are not (for reviews, see Camilli & Shepard, 1994; Reynolds, Lowe, & Saenz, 1999).

Test Bias and Inappropriate Test Administration and Use. The controversy over test bias is also not about blatantly inappropriate administration and usage of mental tests. Administration of a test in English to an individual for whom English is a poor second language is inexcusable both ethically and legally, regardless of any bias in the tests themselves (unless of course, the purpose of the test is to assess English language skills). It is of obvious importance that tests be administered by skilled and sensitive professionals who are aware of the factors that may artificially lower an individual's test scores. That should go without saying, but some court cases involve just such abuses. Considering the use of tests to assign pupils to special education classes or other programs, the question needs to be asked, "What

SPECIAL INTEREST TOPIC   **16.3**
Fairness and Bias—A Complex Relationship

The *Standards* (AERA et al., 1999) present four different ways that fairness is typically used in the context of assessment.

1. *Fairness as absence of bias:* There is general consensus that for a test to be fair, it should not be biased. Bias is used here in the statistical sense: systematic error in the estimation of a value.
2. *Fairness as equitable treatment:* There is also consensus that all test takers should be treated in an equitable manner throughout the assessment process. This includes being given equal opportunities to demonstrate their abilities by being afforded equivalent opportunities to prepare for the test and standardized testing conditions. The reporting of test results should be accurate, informative, and treated in a confidential manner.
3. *Fairness as opportunity to learn:* This definition holds that test takers should all have an equal opportunity to learn the material when taking educational achievement tests.
4. *Fairness as equal outcomes:* Some hold that for a test to be fair it should produce equal performance across groups defined by race, ethnicity, gender, and so on (i.e., equal mean performance).

Many assessment professionals believe that (1) if a test is free from bias and (2) test takers received equitable treatment in the assessment process, the conditions for fairness have been achieved. The other two definitions receive less support. In reference to definition (3) requiring equal opportunity to learn, there is general agreement that adequate opportunity to learn is appropriate in some cases but irrelevant in others. However, disagreement exists in terms of the relevance of opportunity to learn in specific situations. A number of problems arise with this definition of fairness that will likely prevent it from receiving universal acceptance in the foreseeable future. The final definition (4) requiring equal outcomes has little support among assessment professionals. The *Standards* note:

> The position that fairness requires equality in overall passing rates for different groups has been almost entirely repudiated in the professional testing literature . . . unequal outcomes at the group level have no direct bearing on questions of test bias. (pp. 74–76)

In concluding the discussion of fairness, the *Standards* suggest:

> It is unlikely that consensus in society at large or within the measurement community is imminent on all matters of fairness in the use of tests. As noted earlier, fairness is defined in variety of ways and is not exclusively addressed in technical terms; it is subject to different definitions and interpretations in different social and political circumstances. According to one view, the conscientious application of an unbiased test in any given situation is fair, regardless of the consequences for individuals or groups. Others would argue that fairness requires more than satisfying certain technical requirements. (p. 80)

would you use instead?" Teacher recommendations alone are less reliable and valid than standardized test scores and are subject to many external influences. As to whether special education programs are of adequate quality to meet the needs of children, that is an important educational question, but distinct from the test bias one, a distinction sometimes confused.

Bias and Extraneous Factors.   The controversy over the use of mental tests is complicated further by the fact that resolution of the cultural test bias question in either direction will not resolve the problem of the role of nonintellective factors that may influence the test scores of *individuals* from any group, minority or majority. Regardless of any group differences, it is individuals who are tested and whose scores may or may not be accurate. Similarly, it is individuals who are assigned to classes and accepted or rejected for employment or college admission. Most assessment professionals acknowledge that a number of emotional and motivational factors may impact performance on intelligence tests. The extent to which these factors influence individuals as opposed to group performance is difficult to determine.

Cultural Bias and the Nature of Psychological Testing

The question of cultural bias in testing arises from and is continuously fueled by the very nature of psychological and educational processes and how we measure those processes. Psychological processes are by definition internal to the organism and not subject to direct observation and measurement but must instead be inferred from behavior. It is difficult to determine one-to-one relationships between observable events in the environment, the behavior of an organism, and hypothesized underlying mediational processes. Many classic controversies over theories of learning revolved around constructs such as expectancy, habit, and inhibition. Disputes among different camps in learning were polemical and of long duration. Indeed, there are still disputes as to the nature and number of processes such as emotion and motivation. One of the major areas of disagreement has been over the measurement of psychological processes. It should be expected that intelligence, as one of the most complex psychological processes, would involve definitional and measurement disputes that prove difficult to resolve.

There are few charges of bias relating to physical measures that are on absolute scales, whether interval or ratio. Group differences in height, as an extreme example, are not attributed by anyone to any kind of cultural test bias. There is no question concerning the validity of measures of height or weight of anyone in any culture. Nor is there any question about one's ability to make cross-cultural comparisons of these absolute measures.

The issue of cultural bias arises because of the procedures involved in psychological testing. Psychological tests measure traits that are not directly observable, subject to differences in definition, and measurable only on a relative scale. From this perspective, the question of cultural bias in mental testing is a subset, obviously of major importance, of the problem of uncertainty and possible bias in psychological testing generally. Bias might exist not only in mental tests but in other types of psychological tests as well, including personality, vocational, and psychopathological. Making the problem of bias in mental testing even more complex, not all mental tests are of the same quality; some are certainly psychometrically superior to others. There is a tendency for critics and defenders alike to overgeneralize across tests, lumping virtually all tests together under the heading *mental tests* or *intelligence tests*. Professional opinions of mental tests vary considerably, and some of the most widely used tests are not well respected by psychometricians. Thus, unfortunately, the question of bias must eventually be answered on a virtually test-by-test basis.

The question of bias must eventually be answered on a virtually test-by-test basis.

Objections to the Use of Educational and Psychological Tests with Minority Students

In 1969, the Association of Black Psychologists (ABP) adopted the following official policy on educational and psychological testing (Williams, Dotson, Dow, & Williams, 1980):

> The Association of Black Psychologists fully supports those parents who have chosen to defend their rights by refusing to allow their children and themselves to be subjected to achievement, intelligence, aptitude and performance tests which have been and are being used to (a) label Black people as uneducable; (b) place Black children in "special" classes and schools; (c) perpetuate inferior education in Blacks; (d) assign Black children to lower educational tracks than Whites; (e) deny Black students higher educational opportunities; and (f) destroy positive intellectual growth and development of Black people.

Since 1968 the ABP has sought a moratorium on the use of all psychological and educational tests with students from disadvantaged backgrounds. The ABP carried its call for a moratorium to other professional organizations in psychology and education. In direct response to the ABP call, the American Psychological Association's (APA) Board of Directors requested its Board of Scientific Affairs to appoint a group to study the use of psychological and educational tests with disadvantaged students. The committee report (Cleary, Humphreys, Kendrick, & Wesman, 1975) was subsequently published in the official journal of the APA, *American Psychologist.*

Subsequent to the ABP's policy statement, other groups adopted similarly stated policy statements on testing. These groups included the National Association for the Advancement of Colored People (NAACP), the National Education Association (NEA), the National Association of Elementary School Principals (NAESP), the American Personnel and Guidance Association (APGA), and others. The APGA called for the Association of Measurement and Evaluation in Guidance (AMEG), a sister organization, to "develop and disseminate a position paper stating the limitations of group intelligence tests particularly and generally of standardized psychological, educational, and employment testing for low socioeconomic and underprivileged and non-white individuals in educational, business, and industrial environments." It should be noted that the statements by these organizations *assumed* that psychological and educational tests are biased, and that what is needed is that the assumed bias be removed.

Many potentially legitimate objections to the use of educational and psychological tests with minorities have been raised by Black and other minority psychologists. Unfortunately, these objections are frequently stated as facts on rational rather than empirical grounds. The most frequently stated problems fall into one of the following categories (Reynolds, 2000; Reynolds, Lowe, & Saenz, 1999; Reynolds & Ramsay, 2003).

Inappropriate Content

Black and other minority children have not been exposed to the material involved in the test questions or other stimulus materials. The tests are geared primarily toward White middle-class homes, vocabulary, knowledge, and values. As a result of inappropriate content, the tests are unsuitable for use with minority children.

Inappropriate Standardization Samples

Ethnic minorities are underrepresented in standardization samples used in the collection of normative reference data. As a result of the **inappropriate standardization** samples, the tests are unsuitable for use with minority children.

Examiner and Language Bias

Because most psychologists are White and speak only standard English, they may intimidate Black and other ethnic minorities and so **examiner and language bias** result. They are also unable accurately to communicate with minority children—to the point of being insensitive to ethnic pronunciation of words on the test. Lower test scores for minorities, then, may reflect only this intimidation and difficulty in the communication process, not lower ability.

Inequitable Social Consequences

As a result of bias in educational and psychological tests, minority group members, already at a disadvantage in the educational and vocational markets because of past discrimination, are thought to be unable to learn and are disproportionately assigned to dead-end educational tracks. This represents **inequitable social consequences**. Labeling effects also fall under this category.

Measurement of Different Constructs

Related to inappropriate test content mentioned earlier, this position asserts that the tests measure different constructs when used with children from other than the middle-class culture on which the tests are largely based, and thus do not measure minority intelligence validly.

Differential Predictive Validity

Although tests may accurately predict a variety of outcomes for middle-class children, they do not predict successfully any relevant behavior for minority group members. In other words, test usage might result in valid predictions for one group, but invalid predictions in another. This is referred to as **differential predictive validity**. Further, there are objections to the use of the standard criteria against which tests are validated with minority cultural groups. That is, scholastic or academic attainment levels in White middle-class schools are themselves considered by a variety of Black psychologists to be biased as criteria.

Qualitatively Distinct Aptitude and Personality

Minority and majority groups possess aptitude and personality characteristics that are qualitatively different, and as a result test development should begin with different definitions for different groups.

The early actions of the ABP were most instrumental in bringing forward these objections into greater public and professional awareness and subsequently prompted a considerable

The early actions of the ABP were most instrumental in bringing these issues into greater public and professional awareness and subsequently promoted a considerable amount of research.

amount of research. When the objections were first raised, very little data existed to answer these charges. Contrary to the situation decades ago when the current controversy began, research now exists that examines many of these concerns. There is still relatively little research regarding labeling and the long-term social consequences of testing, and these areas should be investigated using diverse samples and numerous statistical techniques (Reynolds, Lowe, & Saenz, 1999).

The Problem of Definition in Test Bias Research: Differential Validity

Arriving at a consensual definition of test bias has produced considerable, as yet unresolved debate among many measurement professionals. Although the resulting debate has generated a number of models from which to examine bias, these models usually focus on the *decision-making system* and not on the test itself. The concept of test bias per se then resolves to a question of the validity of the proposed interpretation of performance on a test and the estimation of that performance level, that is, the test score. Test bias refers to systematic error in the estimation of some "true" value for a group of individuals. As we noted previously, differential validity is present when a test measures a construct differently for one group than for another. As stated in the *Standards* (AERA et al., 1999), bias:

> is said to arise when deficiencies in a test itself or the manner in which it is used result in different meanings for scores earned by members of different identifiable subgroups. (p. 74)

As we discussed in previous chapters, evidence for the validity of test score interpretations can come from sources both internal and external to the test. Bias in a test may be found to exist in any or all of these categories of validity evidence. Prior to examining the evidence on the cultural test bias hypothesis, the concept of culture-free testing and the definition of mean differences in test scores as test bias merit attention.

Cultural Loading, Cultural Bias, and Culture-Free Tests

Cultural loading and *cultural bias* are not synonymous terms, though the concepts are frequently confused even in the professional literature. A test or test item can be culturally loaded without being culturally biased. **Cultural loading** refers to the degree of cultural specificity present in the test or individual items of the test. Certainly, the greater the cultural specificity of a test item, the greater the likelihood of the item being biased when used with individuals from other cultures. Virtually all tests in current use are bound in some way by their cultural specificity. Culture loading must

Cultural loading refers to the degree of cultural specificity present in the test or individual items of the test.

be viewed on a continuum from general (defining the culture in a broad, liberal sense) to specific (defining the culture in narrow, highly distinctive terms).

A number of attempts have been made to develop a culture-free (sometimes referred to as culture fair) intelligence test. However, **culture-free tests** are generally inadequate from a statistical or psychometric perspective (e.g., Anastasi & Urbina, 1997). It may be that because intelligence is often defined in large part on the basis of behavior judged to be of value to the survival and improvement of the culture and the individuals within that culture, a truly culture-free test would be a poor predictor of intelligent behavior within the cultural setting. Once a test has been developed within a culture (a culture loaded test) its generalizability to other cultures or subcultures within the dominant societal framework becomes a matter for empirical investigation.

Inappropriate Indicators of Bias:
Mean Differences and Equivalent Distributions

Differences in mean levels of performance on cognitive tasks between two groups historically (and mistakenly) are believed to constitute test bias by a number of writers (e.g., Alley & Foster, 1978; Chinn, 1979; Hilliard, 1979). Those who support mean differences as an indication of test bias state correctly that there is no valid *a priori* scientific reason to believe that intellectual or other cognitive performance levels should differ across race. It is the inference that tests demonstrating such differences are inherently biased that is faulty. Just as there is no *a priori* basis for deciding that differences exist, there is no *a priori* basis for deciding that differences do not exist. From the standpoint of the objective methods of science, *a priori* or premature acceptance of either hypothesis (differences exist versus differences do not exist) is untenable. As stated in the *Standards* (AERA et al., 1999):

> Most testing professionals would probably agree that while group differences in testing outcomes should in many cases trigger heightened scrutiny for possible sources of test bias, outcome differences across groups do not in themselves indicate that a testing application is biased or unfair. (p. 75)

Some adherents to the "mean differences as bias" position also require that the *distribution* of test scores in each population or subgroup be identical prior to assuming that the test is nonbiased, regardless of its validity. Portraying a test as biased regardless of its purpose or the validity of its interpretations conveys an inadequate understanding of the psychometric construct and issues of bias. The **mean difference definition of test bias** is the most uniformly rejected of all definitions of test bias by psychometricians involved in investigating the problems of bias in assessment (Camilli & Shepard, 1994; Cleary et al. 1975; Cole & Moss, 1989; Hunter, Schmidt, & Rauschenberger, 1984; Reynolds, 1982, 1995, 2000).

Jensen (1980) discusses the mean differences as bias definition in terms of the *egalitarian fallacy*. The egalitarian fallacy contends that

The *mean difference definition of test bias* **is the most uniformly rejected of all definitions of test bias by psychometricians involved in investigating the problems of bias in assessment.**

all human populations are in fact identical on all mental traits or abilities. Any differences with regard to any aspect of the distribution of mental test scores indicate that something is wrong with the test itself. As Jensen points out, such an assumption is totally, scientifically unwarranted. There are simply too many examples of specific abilities and even sensory capacities that have been shown to unmistakably differ across human populations. The result of the egalitarian assumption then is to remove the investigation of population differences in ability from the realm of scientific inquiry, an unacceptable course of action (Reynolds, 1980).

The belief of many people in the mean differences as bias definition is quite likely related to the nature–nurture controversy at some level. Certainly data reflecting racial differences on various aptitude measures have been interpreted to indicate support for a hypothesis of genetic differences in intelligence and implicating one group as superior to another. Such interpretations understandably call for a strong emotional response and are not defensible from a scientific perspective. Although IQ and other aptitude test score differences undoubtedly occur, the differences do not indicate deficits or superiority by any group, especially in relation to the personal worth of any individual member of a given group or culture.

Bias in Test Content

Bias in the content of educational tests has been a popular topic of critics of testing.

Bias in the content of educational and psychological tests has been a popular topic of critics of testing. These criticisms typically take the form of reviewing the items, comparing them to the critics' views of minority and majority cultural environments, and then singling out specific items as biased or unfair because:

- The items ask for information that minority or disadvantaged children have not had equal opportunity to learn; or
- The items require the child to use information in arriving at an answer that minority or disadvantaged children have not had equal opportunity to learn; or
- The scoring of the items is improper, unfairly penalizing the minority child, because the test author has a Caucasian middle-class orientation that is reflected in the scoring criterion. Thus minority children do not receive credit for answers that may be correct within their own cultures but do not conform to Anglocentric expectations; or
- The wording of the questions is unfamiliar to minority children and even though they may "know" the correct answer are unable to respond because they do not understand the question.

These problems with test items cause the items to be more difficult than they should actually be when used to assess minority children. This, of course, results in lower test scores for minority children, a well-documented finding. Are these criticisms of test items accurate? Do problems such as these account for minority–majority group score differences on mental tests? These are questions for empirical resolution rather than armchair speculation, which is certainly abundant in the evaluation of test bias. Empirical evaluation first requires a working definition. We will define a biased test item as follows:

> An item is considered to be biased when it is demonstrated to be significantly more difficult for one group than another item measuring the same ability or construct when the overall level of performance on the test is held constant.

There are two concepts of special importance in this definition. First, the group of items must be unidimensional; that is, they must all be measuring the same factor or dimension of aptitude or personality. Second, the items identified as biased must be differentially more difficult for one group than another. The definition allows for score differences between groups of unequal standing on the dimension in question but requires that the difference be reflected on all items in the test and in an equivalent fashion. A number of empirical techniques are available to locate deviant test items under this definition. Many of these techniques are based on item-response theory (IRT) and designed to detect differential item functioning, or DIF. The relative merits of each method are the subject of substantial debate, but in actual practice each method has led to similar general conclusions, though the specific findings of each method often differ.

With multiple-choice tests, another level of complexity can easily be added to the examination of **content bias**. With a multiple-choice question, typically three or four distracters are given in addition to the correct response. Distracters may be examined for their attractiveness (the relative frequency with which they are chosen) across groups. When distracters are found to be disproportionately attractive for members of any particular group, the item may be defined as biased.

Research that includes thousands of subjects and nearly one hundred published studies consistently finds very little bias in tests at the level of the individual item. Although some biased items are nearly always found, they seldom account for more than 2% to 5% of the variance in performance and often, for every item favoring one group, there is an item favoring the other group.

Earlier in the study of item bias it was hoped that the empirical analysis of tests at the item level would result in the identification of a category of items having similar content as biased and that such items could then be avoided in future test development (Flaugher, 1978). Very little similarity among items determined to be biased has been found. No one has been able to identify those characteristics of an item that cause the item to be biased. In summarizing the research on item bias or differential item functioning (DIF), the *Standards* (AERA et al., 1999) note:

> Although DIF procedures may hold some promise for improving test quality, there has been little progress in identifying the cause or substantive themes that characterizes items exhibiting DIF. That is, once items on a test have been statistically identified as functioning differently from one examinee group to another, it has been difficult to specify the reasons for the differential performance or to identify a common deficiency among the identified items. (p. 78)

It does seem that poorly written, sloppy, and ambiguous items tend to be identified as biased with greater frequency than those items typically encountered in a well-constructed, standardized instrument.

A common practice of test developers seeking to eliminate "bias" from their newly developed educational and psychological tests has been to arrange for a panel of expert minority group members to review all proposed test items. Any item identified as "culturally biased" by the panel of experts is then expurgated from the instrument. Because, as previously noted, no detectable pattern or common characteristic of individual items statistically shown to be biased has been observed (given reasonable care at the item writing stage), it seems reasonable to question the armchair or expert minority panel approach to determining biased items. Several researchers, using a variety of psychological and educational tests, have identified items as being disproportionately more difficult for minority group members than for members of the majority culture and subsequently compared their results with a panel of expert judges. Studies by Jensen (1976) and Sandoval and Mille (1979) are representative of the methodology and results of this line of inquiry.

After identifying the 8 most racially discriminating and 8 least racially discriminating items on the Wonderlic Personnel Test, Jensen (1976) asked panels of 5 Black psychologists and 5 Caucasian psychologists to sort out the 8 most and 8 least discriminating items when only these 16 items were presented to them. The judges sorted the items at a no better than chance level. Sandoval and Mille (1979) conducted a somewhat more extensive analysis using items from the WISC-R. These two researchers had 38 Black, 22 Hispanic, and 40 White university students from Spanish, history, and education classes identify items from the WISC-R that are more difficult for a minority child than a White child and items that are equally difficult for each group. A total of 45 WISC-R items were presented to each judge; these items included the 15 most difficult items for Blacks as compared to Whites, the 15 most difficult items for Hispanics as compared to Whites, and the 15 items showing the most nearly identical difficulty indexes for minority and White children. The judges were asked to read each question and determine whether they thought the item was (1) easier for minority than White children, (2) easier for White than minority children, or (3) of equal difficulty for White and minority children. Sandoval and Mille's (1979) results indicated that the judges were not able to differentiate between items that were more difficult for minorities and items that were of equal difficulty across groups. The effects of the judges' ethnic backgrounds on the accuracy of their item bias judgments were also considered. Minority and nonminority judges did not differ in their ability to identify accurately biased items nor did they differ with regard to the type of incorrect identification they tended to make. Sandoval and Mille's (1979) two major conclusions were that "(1) judges are not able to detect items which are more difficult for a minority child than an Anglo child, and (2) the ethnic background of the judge makes no difference in accuracy of item selection for minority children" (p. 6). Even without empirical support for its validity, the use of expert panels of minorities continues but for a different purpose. Members of various ethnic, religious, or other groups that have a cultural system in some way unique may well be able to identify items that contain material that is offensive, and the elimination of such items is proper.

Content bias **in well-prepared standardized tests is irregular in its occurrence, and no common characteristics of items that are found to be biased can be ascertained by expert judges.**

From a large number of studies employing a wide range of methodology a relatively clear picture emerges. Content bias in well-prepared standardized tests is irregular in its occurrence, and no common characteristics of items that are found to be biased can be ascertained by expert judges (minority or nonminority). The variance in group score differences on mental tests associated with ethnic group membership when content bias has been found is relatively small (typically ranging from 2% to 5%). Although the search for common biased item characteristics will continue, cultural bias in aptitude tests has found no consistent empirical support in a large number of actuarial studies contrasting the performance of a variety of ethnic and gender groups on items of the most widely employed intelligence scales in the United States. Most major test publishing companies do an adequate job of reviewing their assessments for the presence of content bias. Nevertheless, certain standardized tests have not been examined for the presence of content bias, and research with these tests should continue regarding potential content bias with different ethnic groups (Reynolds & Ramsay, 2003).

Bias in Other Internal Features of Tests

There is no single method for the accurate determination of the degree to which educational and psychological tests measure a distinct construct. The defining of bias in construct measurement then requires a general statement that can be researched from a variety of viewpoints with a broad range of methodology. The following rather parsimonious definition is proffered:

Bias exists in regard to construct measurement when a test is shown to measure different hypothetical traits or constructs for one group than another or to measure the same trait but with different degrees of accuracy.

Bias exists in regard to construct measurement when a test is shown to measure different hypothetical traits (psychological constructs) for one group than another or to measure the same trait but with differing degrees of accuracy. (After Reynolds, 1982)

As is befitting the concept of construct measurement, many different methods have been employed to examine existing psychological tests and batteries of tests for potential bias. One of the more popular and necessary empirical approaches to investigating construct measurement is factor analysis. Factor analysis, as a procedure, identifies clusters of test items or clusters of subtests of psychological or educational tests that correlate highly with one another, and less so or not at all with other subtests or items. Factor analysis allows one to determine patterns of interrelationships of performance among groups of individuals. For example, if several subtests of an intelligence scale load highly on (are members of) the same factor, then if a group of individuals score high on one of these subtests, they would be expected to score at a high level on other subtests that load highly on that factor. Psychometricians attempt to determine through a review of the test content and correlates of performance on the factor in question what psychological trait underlies performance; or, in a more hypothesis testing approach, they will make predictions concerning the pattern of factor loadings. Hilliard (1979), one of the more vocal critics of IQ tests on the basis of cultural bias, has pointed out that one of the potential ways of studying bias involves the comparison of factor analytic results of test studies across race.

If the IQ test is a valid and reliable test of "innate" ability or abilities, then the factors which emerge on a given test should be the same from one population to another, since "intelligence" is asserted to be a set of *mental* processes. Therefore, while the configuration of scores of a particular group on the factor profile would be expected to differ, logic would dictate that the factors themselves would remain the same. (p. 53)

Although not agreeing that identical factor analyses of an instrument speak to the "innateness" of the abilities being measured, consistent factor analytic results across populations do provide strong evidence that whatever is being measured by the instrument is being measured in the same manner and is in fact the same construct within each group. The information derived from **comparative factor analysis** across populations is directly relevant to the use of educational and psychological tests in diagnosis and other decision-making functions. Psychologists, in order to make consistent interpretations of test score data, must be certain that the test(s) measure the same variable across populations.

In contrast to Hilliard's (1979) strong statement that factorial similarity across ethnicity has not been reported "in the technical literature," a number of such studies have appeared over the past three decades, dealing with a number of different tasks. These studies have for the most part focused on aptitude or intelligence tests, the most controversial of all techniques of measurement. Numerous studies of the similarity of factor analysis outcomes for children of different ethnic groups, across gender, and even diagnostic groupings have been reported over the past 30 years. Results reported are highly consistent in revealing that the internal structure of most standardized tests vary quite little across groups. Comparisons of the factor structure of the Wechsler Intelligence Scales (e.g., WISC-III, WAIS-III) and the Reynolds Intellectual Assessment Scales (Reynolds, 2002) in particular and other intelligence tests find the tests to be highly factorially similar across gender and ethnicity for Blacks, Whites, and Hispanics. The structure of ability tests for other groups has been researched less extensively, but evidence thus far with Chinese, Japanese, and Native Americans do not show substantially different factor structures for these groups.

As is appropriate for studies of construct measurement, comparative factor analysis has not been the only method of determining whether bias exists. Another method of investigation involves the comparison of internal consistency reliability estimates across groups. As described in Chapter 4, internal consistency reliability is determined by the degree to which the items are all measuring a similar construct. The internal consistency reliability coefficient reflects the accuracy of measurement of the construct. To be unbiased with regard to construct validity, internal consistency estimates should be approximately equal across race. This characteristic of tests has been investigated for a number of popular aptitude tests for Blacks, Whites, and Hispanics with results similar to those already noted.

Many other methods of comparing construct measurement across groups have been used to investigate bias in tests. These methods include the correlation of raw scores with age, comparison of item-total correlations across groups, comparisons of alternate form and test–retest correlations, evaluation of kinship correlation and differences, and others (see Reynolds, 2002, for a discussion of these methods). The general results of research with these methods have been supportive of the consistency of construct measurement of tests across ethnicity and gender.

Construct measurement of a large number of popular psychometric assessment instruments has been investigated across ethnicity and gender with a divergent set of methodologies. No consistent evidence of bias in construct measurement has been found in the many prominent standardized tests investigated. This leads to the conclusion that these psy-

Single-group or differential validity has not been found and likely is not an existing phenomenon with regard to well-constructed standardized educational tests.

chological tests function in essentially the same manner across ethnicity and gender, the test materials are perceived and reacted to in a similar manner, and the tests are measuring the same construct with equivalent accuracy for Blacks, Whites, Hispanic, and other American minorities for both sexes. Differential validity or single-group validity has not been found and likely is not an existing phenomenon with regard to well-constructed standardized psychological and educational tests. These tests appear to be reasonably unbiased for the groups investigated, and mean score differences do not appear to be an artifact of test bias (Reynolds & Ramsay, 2003).

Bias in Prediction and in Relation to Variables External to the Test

Internal analyses of bias (such as with item content and construct measurement) are less confounded than analyses of bias in prediction due to the potential problems of bias in the criterion measure. Prediction is also strongly influenced by the reliability of criterion measures, which frequently is poor. (The degree of relation between a predictor and a criterion is restricted as a function of the square root of the product of the reliabilities of the two variables.) Arriving at a consensual definition of bias in prediction is also a difficult task. Yet, from the standpoint of the traditional practical applications of aptitude and intelligence tests in forecasting probabilities of future performance levels, prediction is the most crucial use of test scores to examine. Looking directly at bias as a characteristic of a test and not a selection model, Cleary et al.'s (1975) definition of test fairness, as restated here in modern times, is a clear direct statement of test bias with regard to **prediction bias:**

From the standpoint of traditional practical applications on aptitude and intelligence tests in forecasting probabilities of future performance levels, prediction is the most crucial use of test scores to examine.

A test is considered biased with respect to prediction when the inference drawn from the test score is not made with the smallest feasible random error or if there is constant error in an inference or prediction as a function of membership in a particular group. (After Reynolds, 1982, p. 201)

The evaluation of bias in prediction under the Cleary et al. (1975) definition (known as the regression definition) is quite straightforward. With simple regressions, predictions take the form $Y_1 = aX + b$, where a is the regression coefficient and b is some constant. When this equation is graphed (forming a regression line), a represents the slope of the regression line and b the Y-intercept. Given our definition of bias in prediction validity, nonbias requires errors in prediction to be independent of group membership, and the regression line formed for any pair of variables must be the same for each group for whom predictions are to be made. Whenever the slope or the intercept differs significantly across groups, there is bias in prediction if one attempts to use a regression equation based on the combined groups. When the regression equations for two (or

When the regression equations are the same for two or more groups, prediction is the same for those groups.

more) groups are equivalent, prediction is the same for those groups. This condition is referred to variously as **homogeneity of regression** across groups, simultaneous regression, or fairness in prediction. Homogeneity of regression is illustrated in Figure 16.1, in which the regression line shown is equally appropriate for making predictions for all groups. Whenever homogeneity of regression across groups does not occur, then separate regression equations should be used for each group concerned.

In actual clinical practice, regression equations are seldom generated for the prediction of future performance. Rather, some arbitrary, or perhaps statistically derived, cutoff score is determined, below which failure is predicted. For school performance, a score of 2 or more standard deviations below the test mean is used to infer a high probability of failure in the regular classroom if special assistance is not provided for the student in question. Essentially then, clinicians are establishing prediction equations about mental aptitude that are *assumed* to be equivalent across race, sex, and so on. Although these mental equations cannot be readily tested across groups, the actual form of criterion prediction can be compared across groups in several ways. Errors in prediction must be independent of group membership. If regression equations are equal, this condition is met. To test the hypothesis of simultaneous regression, **regression slopes** and **regression intercepts** must both be compared.

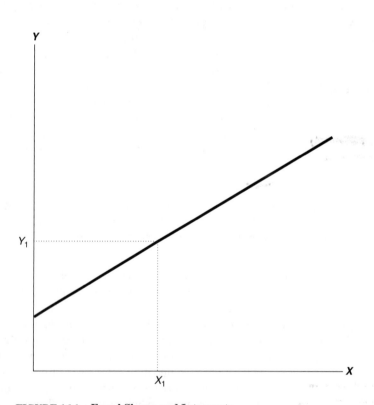

FIGURE 16.1   Equal Slopes and Intercepts

Note: Equal slopes and intercepts result in homogeneity of regression in which the regression lines for different groups are the same.

When homogeneity of regression does not occur, three basic conditions can result: (a) Intercept constants differ, (b) regression coefficients (slopes) differ, or (c) slopes and intercepts differ. These conditions are illustrated in Figures 16.2, 16.3, and 16.4, respectively.

When intercept constants differ, the resulting bias in prediction is constant across the range of scores. That is, regardless of the level of performance on the independent variable, the direction and degree of error in the estimation of the criterion (systematic over- or underprediction) will remain the same. When regression coefficients differ and intercepts are equivalent, the direction of the bias in prediction will remain constant, but the amount of error in prediction will vary directly as a function of the distance of the score on the independent variable from the origin. With regression coefficient differences, then, the higher the score on the predictor variable, the greater the error of prediction for the criterion. When both slopes and intercepts differ, the situation becomes even more complex: Both the degree of error in prediction and the direction of the "bias" will vary as a function of level of performance on the independent variable.

A considerable body of literature has developed over the last 30 years regarding differential prediction of tests across ethnicity for employment selection, college admissions, and school or academic performance generally. In an impressive review of 866 Black–White

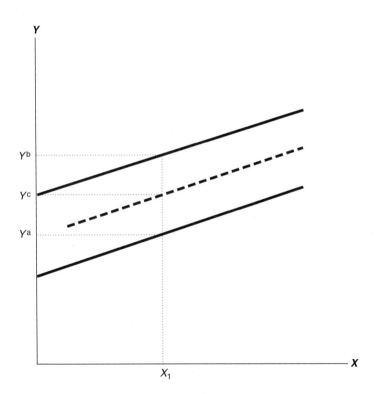

FIGURE 16.2 Equal Slopes with Differing Intercepts

Note: Equal slopes with differing intercepts result in parallel regression lines that produce a constant bias in prediction.

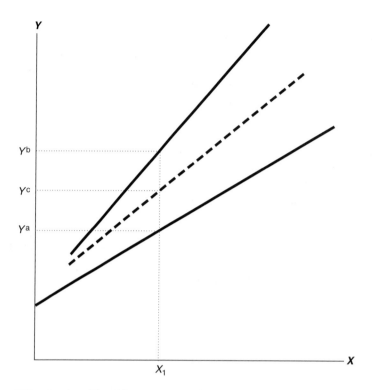

FIGURE 16.3   Equal Intercepts and Differing Slopes

Note: Equal intercepts and differing slopes result in nonparallel regression lines, with the degree of bias depending on the distance of an individual's score from the origin.

prediction comparisons from 39 studies of test bias in personnel selection, Hunter, Schmidt, and Hunter (1979) concluded that there was no evidence to substantiate hypotheses of differential or single-group validity with regard to the prediction of the job performance across race for Blacks and Whites. A similar conclusion has been reached by other independent researchers (e.g., Reynolds, 1995). A number of studies have also focused on differential validity of the Scholastic Aptitude Test (SAT) in the prediction of college performance (typically measured by grade point average). In general these studies have found either no difference in the prediction of criterion performance for Blacks and Whites or a bias (underprediction of the criterion) against Whites. When bias against Whites has been found, the differences between actual and predicted criterion scores, while statistically significant, have generally been quite small.

A number of studies have investigated bias in the prediction of school performance for children. Studies of the prediction of future performance based on IQ tests for children have covered a variety of populations including normal as well as referred children; high-poverty, inner-city children; rural Black; and Native American groups. Studies of preschool as well as school-age children have been carried out. Almost without exception, those studies have produced results that can be adequately depicted by Figure 16.1, that is, equivalent

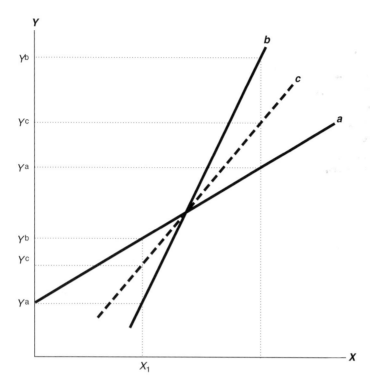

FIGURE 16.4   Differing Slopes and Intercepts

Note: Differing slopes and intercepts result in a complex situation in which the amount and the direction of the bias are a function of the distance of an individual's score from the origin.

prediction for all groups. When this has not been found, intercepts have generally differed resulting in a constant bias in prediction. Yet, the resulting bias has not been in the popularly conceived direction. The bias identified has tended to *overpredict* how well minority children will perform in academic areas and to underpredict how well White children will perform. Reynolds (1995) provides a thorough review of studies investigating the prediction of school performance in children.

With regard to bias in prediction, the empirical evidence suggests conclusions similar to those regarding bias in test content and other internal characteristics. There is no strong evidence to support contentions of differential or single-group validity. Bias occurs infrequently and with no apparently observable pattern, except with regard to instruments of poor reliability and high specificity of test content. When bias occurs, it usually takes the form of small overpredictions for low SES, disadvantaged ethnic minority children, or other low-scoring groups. These overpredictions are unlikely to account for adverse placement or diagnosis in these groups (Reynolds & Ramsay, 2003).

Bias in prediction occurs infrequently and with no apparently observable pattern, except with regard to instruments of poor reliability and high specificity of test content.

Summary

A considerable body of literature currently exists failing to substantiate cultural bias against native-born American ethnic minorities with regard to the use of well-constructed, adequately standardized intelligence and aptitude tests.

A considerable body of literature currently exists failing to substantiate cultural bias against native-born American ethnic minorities with regard to the use of well-constructed, adequately standardized intelligence and aptitude tests. With respect to personality scales, the evidence is promising yet far more preliminary and thus considerably less conclusive. Despite the existing evidence, we do not expect the furor over the cultural test bias hypothesis to be resolved soon. Bias in psychological testing will remain a torrid issue for some time. Psychologists and educators will need to keep abreast of new findings in the area. As new techniques and better methodology are developed and more specific populations examined, the now seen as random, infrequent findings of bias may become better understood and seen to indeed display a correctable pattern.

In the meantime however, one cannot ethnically fall prey to the sociopoliticolegal *Zeitgeist* of the times and infer bias where none exists. Psychologists and educators cannot justifiably ignore the fact that low IQ, ethnic, disadvantaged children are just as likely to fail academically as are their White, middle-class counterparts. Black adolescent delinquents with deviant personality scale scores and exhibiting aggressive behavior need treatment environments as much as their White peers. The potential outcome for score interpretation (e.g., therapy versus prison, special education versus regular education) cannot dictate the psychological meaning of test performance. We must practice *intelligent testing* (Kaufman, 1994). We must remember that it is the purpose of the assessment *process* to beat the prediction made by the test, to provide insight into hypotheses for environmental interventions that prevent the predicted failure or subvert the occurrence of future maladaptive behavior.

Test developers are also going to have to be sensitive to the issues of bias, performing appropriate checks for bias prior to test publication. Progress is being made in all of these areas. However, we must hold to the data even if we do not like it. At present, only scattered and inconsistent evidence for bias exists. The few findings of bias do suggest two guidelines to follow in order to ensure nonbiased assessment: (1) Assessment should be conducted with the most reliable instrumentation available, and (2) multiple abilities should be assessed. In other words, educators and psychologists need to view multiple sources of accurately derived data prior to making decisions concerning individuals. One hopes that this is what has actually been occurring in the practice of assessment, although one continues to hear isolated stories of grossly incompetent placement decisions being made. This is not to say educators or psychologists should be blind to an individual's cultural or environmental background. Information concerning the home, community, and school environment must all be evaluated in individual decisions. As we noted, it is the *purpose* of the assessment process to beat the prediction and to provide insight into hypotheses for environmental interventions that prevent the predicted failure.

Without question, scholars have not conducted all the research that needs to be done to test the cultural test bias hypothesis and its alternatives. A number and variety of criteria need to be explored further before the question of bias is empirically resolved. Many different achievement tests and teacher-made, classroom specific tests need to be employed in future studies of predictive bias. The entire area of differential validity of tests in the affective domain is in need of greater exploration. A variety of views toward bias has been expressed in many sources; many with differing opinions offer scholarly, nonpolemical attempts directed toward a resolution of the issue. Obviously, the fact that such different views are still held indicates resolution lies in the future. As far as the present situation is concerned, clearly all the evidence is not in. With regard to a resolution of bias, we believe that were a scholarly trial to be held, with a charge of cultural bias brought against mental tests, the jury would likely return the verdict other than guilty or not guilty that is allowed in British law—"not proven." Until such time as a true resolution of the issues can take place, we believe the evidence and positions taken in this chapter accurately reflect the state of our empirical knowledge concerning bias in mental tests.

KEY TERMS AND CONCEPTS

Comparative factor analysis, p. 414
Content bias, p. 411
Cultural bias, p. 398
Cultural loading, p. 408
Cultural test bias hypothesis, p. 396
Culture-free tests, p. 409
Differential predictive validity,
    p. 407

Examiner and language bias, p. 407
Homogeneity of regression, p. 416
Inappropriate standardization,
    p. 407
Inequitable social consequences,
    p. 407
Mean difference definition of test
    bias, p. 409

Prediction bias, p. 415
Regression intercepts, p. 416
Regression slopes, p. 416
Test bias, p. 398

RECOMMENDED READINGS

Cleary, T. A., Humphreys, L. G., Kendrick, S. A., & Wesman, A. (1975). *American Psychologist, 30,* 15–41. This is the report of a group appointed by APA's Board of Scientific Affairs to study the use of psychological and educational tests with disadvantaged students—an early and influential article.

Halpern, D. F. (1997). Sex differences in intelligence: Implications for education. *American Psychologist, 52,* 1091–1102. A good article that summarizes the literature on sex differences with an emphasis on educational implications.

Neisser, U., BooDoo, G., Bouchard, T., Boykin, A., Brody, N., Ceci, S., Halpern, D., Loehlin, J., Perloff, R., Sternberg, R., & Urbina, S. (1996). Intelligence: Knowns and unknowns. *American Psychologist, 51,* 77–101. This report of an APA task force provides an excellent review of the research literature on intelligence.

Reynolds, C. R. (1995). Test bias in the assessment of intelligence and personality. In D. Saklofsky & M. Zeidner (Eds.), *International handbook of personality and intelligence* (pp. 545–573). New York: Plenum Press. This chapter provides a thorough review of the literature.

Reynolds, C. R. (2000). Why is psychometric research on bias in mental testing so often ignored? *Psychology, Public Policy, and Law, 6,* 144–150. This article provides a particularly good discussion of test bias in terms of public policy issues.

Reynolds, C. R., & Ramsay, M. C. (2003). Bias in psychological assessment: An empirical review and recommendations. In J. R. Graham & J. A. Naglieri (Eds.), *Handbook of psychology: Assessment psychology* (pp. 67–93). New York: Wiley. This chapter also provides an excellent review of the literature.

Suzuki, L. A., & Valencia, R. R. (1997). Race–ethnicity and measured intelligence: Educational implications. *American Psychologist, 52,* 1103–1114. A good discussion of the topic with special emphasis on educational implications and alternative assessment methods.

17 Best Practices in Educational Assessment

With power comes responsibility!

CHAPTER HIGHLIGHTS

Guidelines for Developing Assessments

Guidelines for Selecting Published Assessments

Guidelines for Administering Assessments

Guidelines for Scoring Assessments

Guidelines for Interpreting, Using, and Communicating Assessment Results

Responsibilities of Test Takers

LEARNING OBJECTIVES

After reading and studying this chapter, students should be able to:

1. Explain why the assessment practices of teachers are held to high professional standards.
2. Identify major professional organizations that have written guidelines addressing educational assessment issues.
3. Describe and give examples of the principles to consider when developing educational assessments.
4. Describe and give examples of the principles to consider when selecting educational assessments.
5. Identify major resources that provide information about published tests and describe the type of information each one provides.
6. Describe and give examples of the principles to consider when administering educational assessments.
7. Describe and give examples of the principles to consider when interpreting, using, and communicating results.
8. Describe and give examples of the primary responsibilities of test takers.
9. Describe the possible consequences for teachers who engage in unethical behavior.

While teachers might not always be aware of it, their positions endow them with considerable power. Teachers make decisions on a day-to-day basis that significantly impact their

It is the teacher's responsibility to make sure that the assessments they use are developed, administered, scored, and interpreted in a technically, ethically, and legally sound manner.

students, and many of these decisions involve information garnered from educational assessments. As a result, it is the teacher's responsibility to make sure that the assessments they use, whether they are professionally developed tests or teacher-constructed tests, are developed, administered, scored, and interpreted in a technically, ethically, and legally sound manner. This chapter provides some guidelines that will help you ensure that your assessment practices are sound.

Much of the information discussed in this chapter has been introduced in previous chapters. We will also incorporate guidelines that are presented in existing professional codes of ethics and standards of professional practice. One of the principal sources is the *Code of Professional Responsibilities in Educational Measurement* that was prepared by the National Council on Measurement in Education (NCME, 1995). This code is presented in its entirety in Appendix B. The *Code of Professional Responsibilities in Educational Measurement* specifies the following general responsibilities for NCME members are involved in educational assessment:

1. protect the health and safety of all examinees;
2. be knowledgeable about, and behave in compliance with, state and federal laws relevant to the conduct of professional activities;
3. maintain and improve their professional competence in educational assessment;
4. provide assessment services only in areas of their competence and experience, affording full disclosure of their professional qualifications;
5. promote the understanding of sound assessment practices in education;
6. adhere to the highest standards of conduct and promote professionally responsible conduct within educational institutions and agencies that provide educational services; and
7. perform all professional responsibilities with honesty, integrity, due care, and fairness. (p. 1)

Although these expectations are explicitly directed toward NCME members, all educational professionals who are involved in assessment activities are well served by following these general guidelines.

The *Code of Professional Responsibilities in Educational Measurement* (NCME, 1995) delineates eight major areas of assessment activity, five of which are most applicable to teachers. These are (1) Developing Assessments, (2) Selecting Assessments, (3) Administering Assessments, (4) Scoring Assessments, and (5) Interpreting, Using, and Communicating Assessment Results. We will use these categories to organize our discussion of best practices in educational assessment, and we will add an additional section, Responsibilities of Test Takers. In addition to the *Code of Professional Responsibilities in Educational Measurement* (NCME, 1995), the following guidelines reflect a compilation of principles presented in the *Standards for Educational and Psychological Testing* (AERA et al., 1999), *The Student Evaluation Standards* (Joint Committee on Standards for Educational Evaluation, 2003), *Code of Fair Testing Practices in Education* (Joint Committee on Testing Practices, 1988), and the *Rights and Responsibilities of Test Takers: Guidelines and Expectations* (JCTP, 1998).

Guidelines for Developing Assessments

Probably the most fundamental right of test takers is to be evaluated with assessments that meet high professional standards and that are valid for the intended purposes (JCTP, 1998).

The Joint Committee on Testing Practices (JCTP, 1998) notes that probably the most fundamental right of test takers is to be evaluated with assessments that meet high professional standards and that are valid for the intended purposes. Accordingly, teachers who are involved in developing their own educational classroom tests and other assessment procedures have a professional responsibility to develop assessments that meet or exceed all applicable technical, ethical, and legal standards (NCME, 1995). The most explicit and comprehensive guidelines for developing and evaluating tests are the *Standards for Educational and Psychological Testing* (AERA et al., 1999). Although these standards apply most directly to professionally developed standardized tests, they may be applied appropriately to less formal assessment procedures such as teacher-constructed tests. Here are a few guidelines for the development of assessments that meet professional standards.

Clearly Specify Your Educational Objectives and Develop a Table of Specifications. When developing classroom tests (or really any test), the first step is to specify the purpose of the test and the construct or domain to be measured. To this end, teachers should begin by explicitly specifying the educational objectives to be measured and developing a table of specifications or test blueprint as described in Chapter 7. The table of specifications should clearly define the content and format of the test and be directly linked to the educational objectives of the instructional unit being assessed. Although the importance of this process is probably obvious, in the day-to-day world of teaching in which teachers have many duties and limited time, it may be tempting to skip these steps and simply start writing the test. However, this is actually one of the most important steps in developing quality tests. If you have not clearly delineated exactly what you want to measure, you are not likely to do a very effective job.

Develop Assessment Procedures That Are Appropriate for Measuring the Specified Educational Outcomes. Once the table of specifications is developed, it should be used to guide the development of items and scoring procedures. Guidelines for developing items of different types were presented in Chapters 8, 9, and 10. Selected-response items, constructed-response items, and performance assessments and portfolios all have their own specific strengths and weaknesses, and are appropriate for assessing some objectives and inappropriate for assessing others. It is the test developer's responsibility to determine which procedures are most appropriate for assessing specific learning objectives. In the past it was fairly common for teachers to use a limited number of assessment procedures (e.g., multiple-choice, true–false, or essay items). However, it has become more widely recognized that no single assessment format can effectively measure the diverse range of educational outcomes emphasized in today's schools. As a result, it is important for teachers to use a diverse array of procedures that are carefully selected to meet the specific purposes of the assessment and to facilitate teaching and achievement (e.g., Linn & Gronlund, 2000).

It has become widely recognized that no single assessment format can effectively measure the diverse range of educational outcomes emphasized in today's schools.

Develop Explicit Scoring Criteria.   Practically all types of assessments require clearly stated criteria for scoring the items. This can range from fairly straightforward scoring keys for selected-response items and short-answer items to detailed scoring rubrics for evaluating performance on extended-response essays and performance assessments. Whatever the format, developing the items and the scoring criteria should be an integrated process guided by the table of specifications. Scoring procedures should be consistent with the purpose of the test and facilitate valid score interpretations (AERA et al., 1999).

Develop Clear Guidelines for Test Administration.   All aspects of test administration should be clearly specified. This includes instructions to students taking the test, time limits, testing conditions (e.g., classroom or laboratory), and any equipment that will be utilized. Teachers should develop administration instructions in sufficient detail so that other educators are able to replicate the conditions if necessary.

When developing assessments, some thought should be given to what types of accommodations may be necessary for students with disabilities.

Plan Accommodations for Test Takers with Disabilities and Other Special Needs.   As discussed in Chapter 15, it is becoming more common for regular education teachers to have students with disabilities in their classroom. When developing assessments, some thought should be given to what types of accommodations may be necessary for these students or other students with special needs.

Carefully Review the Assessment Prior to Administration.   Teachers should carefully review their tests to ensure technical accuracy. To this end it is beneficial to have a trusted colleague familiar with the content area review their test and scoring criteria prior to administration and grading. In addition to reviewing for technical accuracy, assessments should be reviewed for potentially insensitive content or language and evidence of bias due to race, gender, or ethnic backgrounds. Bias in educational assessment is discussed in detail in Chapter 16.

Evaluate the Technical Properties of Assessments.   After administering the test, teachers should use quantitative and qualitative item analysis procedures to evaluate and refine their assessments (discussed in Chapter 6). Teachers should also perform preliminary analyses that will allow them to assess the reliability and validity of their measurements. Reliability and validity were discussed in Chapters 4 and 5. Although it might be difficult for teachers to perform some of the more complex reliability and validity analyses, at a minimum they should use some of the simplified procedures outlined in the appropriate chapters. Table 17.1 presents a summary of these guidelines for developing assessments.

Teachers should perform preliminary analyses regarding the reliability and validity of their measurements.

Guidelines for Selecting Published Assessments

Although teachers develop the majority of the tests administered in schools, professionally developed standardized assessments are playing an increasingly important role in today's schools. Some of these standardized tests are developed by the state and their administration

TABLE 17.1   Checklist for Developing Assessments

1. Have the educational objectives been clearly specified and a table of specifications developed? _____

2. Are the assessment procedures appropriate for measuring the learning outcomes? _____

3. Have explicit scoring criteria been developed? _____

4. Have clear guidelines for test administration been developed? _____

5. Have accommodations for test takers with disabilities and other special needs been planned? _____

6. Has the assessment been reviewed for technical accuracy and potentially insensitive or biased content? _____

7. Have the technical properties of the assessment been evaluated? _____

is mandated. However, teachers are often involved in the selection and administration of other standardized assessment instruments. As a result, they incur numerous responsibilities associated with this role. The guiding principle, as when developing assessments, is to ensure that the assessments meet high professional standards and are valid for the intended purposes. Here are a few guidelines for selecting assessments that meet professional standards.

When selecting standardized assessments, it is of primary importance to select tests that have been validated for the intended purpose.

Select Assessments That Have Been Validated for the Intended Purpose.   As we have emphasized throughout this text, validity is a fundamental consideration when developing or selecting a test (see Chapter 5). Professionally developed assessments should clearly specify the recommended interpretations of test scores and provide a summary of the validity evidence supporting each interpretation. However, in the end it is the person selecting the test who is responsible for determining whether the assessment is appropriate for use in the particular setting (AERA et al., 1999). As an example, in selecting achievement tests it is important that the content of the assessment correspond with the content of the curriculum. The essential questions are "How will the assessment information be used?" and "Has the proposed assessment been validated for those uses?"

Select assessments with normative data that are representative of the type of test takers the test will be used with.

Select Assessments with Normative Data That Are Representative of Correct Target Population.   The validity of norm-referenced interpretations is dependent on the how representative the normative or standardization group is of the target population (see Chapter 3). The fundamental question is "Does the normative sample adequately represent the type of test takers the test will be used with?" It is also important to consider how current the norms are because their usefulness diminishes over time (AERA et al., 1999).

Select Assessments That Produce Reliable Results.   It is important to select assessment procedures that produce reliable results. In Chapter 4, we presented guidelines regarding the levels of reliability recommended for different applications or uses. For example, when making high-stakes decisions it is important to utilize assessment results that are highly reliable (e.g., $r_{xx} > 0.95$).

Select Tests That Are Fair. Although no assessment procedure is absolutely free from bias, efforts should be made to select assessments that have been shown to be relatively free from bias due to race, gender, or ethnic backgrounds. Bias in educational assessment is discussed in detail in Chapter 16.

Select assessments based on a thorough review of the available literature.

Select Assessments Based on a Thorough Review of the Available Literature. The selection of assessment procedures can have significant consequences for a large number of individuals. As a result, the decision should be based on a careful and thorough review of the available information. It is appropriate to begin this review by examining information and material the test publishers provide. This can include catalogs, test manuals, specimen test sets, score reports, and other supporting documentation. However, the search should not stop here and you should seek out independent evaluations and reviews of the tests you are considering. A natural question is "Where can I access information about assessments?" Four of the most useful references are the *Mental Measurements Yearbook, Tests in Print, Tests,* and *Test Critiques.* These resources can be located in the reference section of most college and larger public libraries. The Testing Office of the American Psychological Association Science Directorate (APA, 2004) provides the following description of these resources:

Mental Measurements Yearbook (MMY). Published by the Buros Institute for Mental Measurements, the **Mental Measurements Yearbook (MMY)** lists tests alphabetically by title and is an invaluable resource for researching published assessments. Each listing provides descriptive information about the test, including test author, publication dates, intended population, forms, prices, and publisher. It contains additional information regarding the availability of reliability, validity, and normative data, as well as scoring and reporting services. Most listings include one or more critical reviews by qualified assessment experts.

Tests in Print (TIP). Also published by the Buros Institute for Mental Measurements, **Tests in Print (TIP)** is a bibliographic encyclopedia of information on practically every published test in psychology and education. Each listing includes the test title, intended population, publication date, author, publisher, and references. TIP does not contain critical reviews or psychometric information, but it does serve as a master index to the Buros Institute reference series on tests. In the TIP the tests are listed alphabetically, within subjects (e.g., achievement tests, intelligence tests). There are also indexes that can help you locate specific tests. After locating a test that meets your criteria, you can turn to the *Mental Measurements Yearbook* for more detailed information on the test.

Tests. Published by Pro-Ed, Inc., **Tests** is a bibliographic encyclopedia covering thousands of assessments in psychology and education. It provides a brief description of the tests, including information on the author, purpose, intended population, administration time, scoring method, cost, and the publisher. *Tests* does not contain critical reviews or information on reliability, validity, or other technical aspects of the tests.

Test Critiques.   Also published by Pro-Ed, Inc., **Test Critiques** is designed to be a companion to *Tests. Test Critiques* contains a tripart listing for each test that includes Introduction (e.g., information on the author, publisher, and purposes), Practical Applications/Uses (e.g., intended population, administration, scoring, and interpretation guidelines), and Technical Aspects (e.g., information on reliability, validity), followed by a critical review of the test. Its user-friendly style makes it appropriate for individuals with limited training in psychometrics.

In addition to these traditional references, **Test Reviews Online** is a new Web-based service of the Buros Institute of Mental Measurements (www.unl.edu/buros). This service makes test reviews available online to individuals precisely as they appear in the *Mental Measurements Yearbook.* For a relatively small fee (i.e., currently $15), users can download information on any of over 2,000 tests that includes specifics on test purpose, population, publication date, administration time, and descriptive test critiques. For more detailed information on these and other resources, the Testing Office of the American Psychological Association Science Directorate has prepared an information sheet on "Finding Information on Psychological Tests." This can be requested by visiting its Web site: (www.apa.org/science/faq-findtests.html).

Select and use only assessments that you are qualified to administer, score, and interpret.

Select and Use Only Assessments That You Are Qualified to Administer, Score, and Interpret.   Because the administration, scoring, and interpretation of many psychological and educational tests requires advanced training, it is important to select and use only those tests that you are qualified to use as a result of your education and training. For example, the administration of an individual intelligence test such as the Wechsler Intelligence Scale for Children—Fourth Edition (WISC-IV) requires extensive training and supervision that is typically acquired in graduate psychology and education programs. Most test publication firms have established procedures that allow individuals and organizations to qualify to purchase tests based on specific criteria. For example, Psychological Assessment Resources (2003) has a three-tier system that classifies assessment products according to qualification requirements. In this system, level A products require no special qualifications whereas level C products require an advanced professional degree or license based on advanced training and experience in psychological and educational assessment practices. Before purchasing restricted tests, potential buyers must provide documentation that they meet the necessary requirements.

Guard against Potential Misuses and Misinterpretations.   When selecting assessments, avoid selecting those that are likely to be used or interpreted in an invalid or biased manner. This is a difficult responsibility to discharge. Nitko (2001) suggests that to meet this responsibility you must have a broad knowledge of how assessments are being used in educational settings and their potential misuses and misinterpretations. To this end, he suggests using references such as ***Education Week*** that regularly chronicle the appropriate as well as inappropriate uses of assessment in our schools. *Education Week* is available online at www.edweek.org.

Maintain Test Security.   For assessments to be valid, it is important that **test security** be maintained. Individuals selecting, purchasing, and using standardized assessment have a professional and legal responsibility to maintain the security of assessment instruments. For

Teachers using standardized assessments have a professional and legal responsibility to maintain the security of those instruments.

example, The Psychological Corporation (2003) includes the following principles in its security agreement: (a) Test takers should not have access to testing material or answers before taking the test; (b) assessment materials cannot be reproduced or paraphrased; (c) assessment materials and results can be released only to qualified individuals; (d) if test takers or their parents/guardians ask to examine test responses or results, this review must be monitored by a qualified representative of the organization conducting the assessment; and (e) any request to copy materials must be approved in writing. Examples of breaches in the security of standardized tests include allowing students to examine the test before taking it, using actual items from a test for preparation purposes, making and distributing copies of a test, and allowing test takers to take the test outside of a controlled environment (e.g., allowing them to take the test home to complete it). Table 17.2 provides a summary of these guidelines for selecting published assessments. Special Interest Topic 17.1 provides information about educators who have engaged in unethical and sometimes criminal practices when using standardized assessments.

Guidelines for Administering Assessments

So far we have discussed your professional responsibilities related to developing and selecting tests. Clearly, your professional responsibilities do not stop there. Every step of the assessment process has its own important responsibilities, and now we turn to those associated with the administration of assessments. Subsequently we will address responsibilities related to the scoring, interpreting, using, and communicating assessment results. The following guidelines involve your responsibilities when administering assessments.

TABLE 17.2   Checklist for Selecting Published Assessments

1. Have the desired interpretations of performance on the selected assessments been validated for the intended purpose?	_____
2. Do the selected assessments have normative data that are representative of the target population?	_____
3. Do selected assessments produce reliable results?	_____
4. Are interpretations of the selected assessments fair?	_____
5. Was the selection process based on a thorough review of the available literature?	_____
6. Are you qualified to administer, score, and interpret the selected assessments?	_____
7. Have you screened assessments for likely misuses and misinterpretations?	_____
8. Have steps been taken to maintain test security?	_____

Teachers Cheating?

Over 50 New York City educators may lose their jobs after an independent auditor produced evidence that they helped students cheat on state tests.

(Hoff, 1999)

State officials charge that 71 Michigan schools might have cheated on state tests.

(Keller, 2001)

Georgia education officials suspend state tests after 270 actual test questions were posted on an Internet site that was accessible to students, teachers, and parents.

(Olson, 2003)

Cizek (1998) notes that the abuse of standardized assessments by educators has become a national scandal. With the advent of high-stakes assessment, it should not be surprising that some educators would be inclined to cheat. With one's salary and possibly one's future employment riding on how students perform on state-mandated achievement tests, the pressure to ensure that those students perform well may override ethical and legal concerns for some people. Cannell (1988, 1989) was among the first to bring abusive test practices to the attention on the public. Cannell revealed that by using outdated versions of norm-referenced assessments, being lax with test security, and engaging in inappropriate test preparation practices, all 50 states were able to report that their students were above the national average (this came to be referred to as the Lake Wobegon phenomenon). Other common "tricks" that educators have employed to inflate scores include using the same form of a test for a long period of time so that teachers could become familiar with the content; encouraging low-achieving students to skip school on the day of the test; selectively removing answer sheets of low-performing students; and excluding limited-English and special education students from assessments (Cizek, 1998).

Do not be fooled into thinking that these unethical practices are limited to top administrators trying to make their schools look good; they also involve classroom teachers. Cizek (1998) reports a number of recent cases wherein principals or other administrators have encouraged teachers to cheat by having students practice on the actual test items, and in some cases even erasing and correcting wrong responses on answer sheets. Other unethical assessment practices engaged in by teachers included providing hints to the correct answer, reading questions that the students are supposed to read, answering questions about test content, rephrasing test questions, and sometimes simply giving the students the answers to items. Gay (1990) reported that 35% of the teachers responding to a survey had either witnessed or engaged in unethical assessment practices. The unethical behaviors included changing incorrect answers, revealing the correct answer, providing extra time, allowing the use of inappropriate aids (e.g., dictionaries), and using the actual test items when preparing students for the test.

Just because other professionals are engaging in unethical behavior does not make it right. Cheating by administrators, teachers, or students undermines the validity of the assessment results. If you need any additional incentive to avoid unethical test practices, be warned that the test publishers are watching! The states and other publishers of standardized tests have a vested interest in maintaining the validity of their assessments. As a result, they are continually scanning the results for evidence of cheating. For example, Cizek (1998) reports that unethical educators have been identified as the result of fairly obvious clues such as ordering an excessive number of blank answer sheets or a disproportionate number of erasures, to more subtle clues such as unusual patterns of increased scores. The fact is, educators who cheat are being caught and punished, and the punishment may include the loss of one's job and license to teach!

Provide Information to Students on the Assessment before Administering It. This includes information on (1) when the assessment will be administered, (2) the conditions under which it will be administered, (3) the abilities and content areas that will be assessed, (4) how it will be scored and interpreted, (5) how the results will used, (6) confidentiality issues and who will have access to the results, and (7) how the results are likely to impact the student (AERA et. al., 1999; JCTP, 1998; Nitko, 2001). It is also appropriate to provide information on useful test-taking strategies. For example, if there is a "correction for guessing," students should be made aware of this because it may affect the way they respond to the test. Efforts should be made to make this information available to all students and their parents in an easily understandable format.

Assessments should be administered in a standardized manner to ensure fairness and promote the reliability of scores and the validity of their interpretations.

Administer the Assessments in a Standardized Manner. Assessments should be administered in a standardized manner to ensure fairness and promote the reliability of scores and validity of their interpretations. This implies that all students will take the assessment under the same conditions. For example, all students will receive the same materials and have access to the same resources (e.g., the use of calculators), receive the same instructions, and have the same time limits. Efforts should be made to ensure that the assessment environment is comfortable, quiet, and relatively free from distractions. Students should be given opportunities to ask reasonable questions. Some teachers will answer appropriate questions in front of the entire class so all students will receive the same information. Additional information on preparing students for and administering standardized tests was provided in Chapter 12.

When Appropriate, Modify Administration to Accommodate the Needs of Students with Disabilities. As discussed in Chapter 15, when assessing students with disabilities it is often necessary and appropriate to modify the standard administration procedures to address the special needs of these students. Assessment accommodations are granted to minimize the impact of student characteristics that are irrelevant to the construct being measured by the assessment. A major consideration when selecting accommodations is only to select accommodations that do not undermine the reliability or validity of the assessment results. If assessment accommodations are noted in a special education student's Individual Education Program (IEP), you have a professional and legal obligation to provide these modifications.

Provide Information to Students and Parents about Their Rights and Give Them an Opportunity to Express Their Concerns. Students and parents should have an opportunity to voice concerns about the testing process and receive information about opportunities to retake an examination, have one rescored, or cancel scores. When appropriate they should be given information on how they can obtain copies of assessments or other related information. When an assessment is optional, students and parents should be given this information so they can decide whether they want to take the assessment. If alternative assessments are available, they should also be informed of this. An excellent resource for all test takers is *Rights and Responsibilities of Tests Takers: Guidelines and Expectations* developed by the Joint Committee on Testing Practices (1998). This is reproduced in Appendix D.

Students and parents should have an opportunity to voice concerns about the testing process.

TABLE 17.3   Checklist for Administering Assessments

1. Did you provide information on the assessment before administering it?   _____

2. Was the assessment administered in a standardized and fair manner?   _____

3. When appropriate, was the assessment modified to accommodate the needs of test takers with disabilities? _____

4. Was information provided to students and parents about the rights of test takers?   _____

5. Are you qualified and prepared to administer the assessments?   _____

6. Are proper test security measures being followed?   _____

Administer Only Those Assessments for Which You Are Qualified by Education and Training.   As noted previously, it is important only to select and use tests that you are qualified to use as a result of your education and training. Some assessments require extensive training and supervision before being able to administer them independently.

Maintain Test Security.   As noted previously, it is important for individuals selecting, purchasing, and using standardized assessments to maintain the security of the assessments. Table 17.3 provides guidelines for administering assessments.

Guidelines for Scoring Assessments

Make Sure Assessments Are Scored Properly and the Results Are Reported Accurately.   It is a teacher's professional responsibility to develop reasonable quality control procedures to ensure that the scoring is accurate. With selected-response items this may involve carefully developing a scoring key, double-checking it for errors, and adhering to it diligently (or using computer scoring when possible). With constructed-response items and performance assessments, this typically involves the development of explicit scoring rubrics and strictly following them when scoring the assessments. In Chapters 9 and 10, we provided suggestions for minimizing the effects of irrelevant factors when scoring assessments that involve subjective judgments. It is also possible for errors to occur when recording the grades. This can usually be avoided by simply rechecking your grade book (or spreadsheet) after initially recording the grades.

> Teachers are responsible for developing reasonable quality control procedures to ensure that their scoring is accurate.

Make Sure the Scoring Is Fair.   An aspect of the previous guideline that deserves special attention involves fairness or the absence of bias in scoring. Whenever scoring involves subjective judgment, it is also important to take steps to ensure that the scoring is based solely on performance or content, and is not contaminated by *expectancy effects* related to students. That is, you do not want your personal impressions of the students to influence your evaluation of their performance, in either a positive or negative manner. Again, we provided suggestions for minimizing expectancy effects and other irrelevant factors that can influence scoring in Chapters 9 and 10.

Score the Assessments and Report the Results in a Timely Manner. Students and their parents are often anxious to receive the results of their assessments and deserve to have their results reported in a timely manner. Additionally, to promote learning, it is important that students receive feedback on their performance in a punctual manner. If the results are to be delayed it is important to notify the students, explain the situation, and attempt to minimize any negative effects.

If Scoring Errors Are Detected, Correct the Errors and Provide the Corrected Results in a Timely Manner. If you, or someone else, detect errors in your scoring, it is your responsibility to take corrective action. Correct the errors, adjust the impacted scores, and provide the corrected results in a timely manner.

Students have a right to review their assessments and appeal their scores if they believe there were errors in scoring.

Implement a Reasonable and Fair Process for Appeal. Students have a right to review their assessments and appeal their scores if they believe there were errors in scoring. Although most institutions have formal appeal procedures, it is usually in everyone's best interest to have a less formal process available by which students can approach the teacher and attempt to address any concerns. This option may prevent relatively minor student concerns from escalating into adversarial confrontations involving parents, administrators, and possibly the legal system.

Keep Assessment Results Confidential. It is the responsibility of teachers and others who score assessments to keep the results confidential. Although different standards of confidentiality and privacy exist in different settings, it is a teacher's professional and ethical responsibility to take reasonable steps to maintain the confidentiality of assessment results. Table 17.4 provides a summary of the guidelines for scoring assessments.

TABLE 17.4 Checklist for Scoring Assessments

1. Are procedures in place to ensure that assessments are scored properly and the results are reported accurately? _____

2. Are procedures in place to ensure the scoring is fair? _____

3. Are scores reported in a timely manner?

4. If scoring errors are detected, are the errors corrected and the corrected results provided in a timely manner? _____

5. Is a reasonable and fair process for appeals in place? _____

6. Are assessment results kept confidential? _____

Guidelines for Interpreting, Using, and Communicating Assessment Results

Use assessment results only for the purposes for which they have been validated.

Use Assessment Results Only for Purposes for Which They Have Been Validated.   When interpreting assessment results, the issue of validity is an overriding concern. A primary consideration when interpreting and using assessment results is to determine whether there is sufficient validity evidence to support the proposed interpretations and uses. When teachers use assessment results, it is their responsibility to promote valid interpretations and guard against invalid interpretations.

Be Aware of the Limitations of the Assessment Results.   All assessments contain error, and some have more error than others do. It is the responsibility of teachers and other users of assessment results to be aware of the limitations of assessments and to take these limitations into consideration when interpreting and using assessment results.

Use multiple sources and types of assessment information when making high-stakes educational decisions.

Use Multiple Sources and Types of Assessment Information When Making High-Stakes Educational Decisions.   Whenever you hear assessment experts saying, "multiple-choice items are worthless because they cannot measure higher-order cognitive skills" or "Performance assessments are worthless because they are not reliable," recognize that they are expressing their own personal biases and not being objective. Selected-response items, constructed-response items, and performance assessments all have something to contribute to the overall assessment process. Multiple-choice items and other selected-response formats can typically be scored in a reliable fashion and this is a definite strength. Although we believe multiple-choice items can be written that measure higher-order cognitive abilities, many educational objectives simply cannot be assessed using selected-response items. If you want to measure a student's writing skills, essay items are particularly well suited. If you want to assess a student's ability to engage in an oral debate, a performance assessment is clearly indicated. The point is, different assessment procedures have different strengths and weaknesses, and teachers are encouraged to use the results of a variety of assessments when making important educational decisions. It is not appropriate to base these decisions on the result of one assessment, particularly when it is difficult to take corrective action should mistakes occur.

Take into Consideration Personal Factors or Extraneous Events That Might Have Influenced Test Performance.   This guideline holds that teachers should be sensitive to factors that might have negatively influenced a student's performance. For example, was the student feeling ill or upset on the day of the assessment? Is the student prone to high levels of test anxiety? This guideline also extends to administrative and environmental events that might have impacted the student. For example, were there errors in administration that might have impacted the student's performance? Did any events occur during the administration that might have distracted the student or otherwise undermined performance? If it appears any factors compromised the student's performance, this should be considered when interpreting their assessment results.

With Norm-Referenced Assessment, Take into Consideration Any Differences between the Normative Group and Actual Test Takers.   If there are meaningful differences between the normative groups and the actual test takers, this must be taken into consideration when interpreting and using the assessment results.

Report Results in an Easily Understandable Manner.   Students and their parents have the right to receive comprehensive information about assessment results presented in an understandable and timely manner regarding the results of their assessments. It is the teacher's responsibility to provide this feedback to students and their parents and to attempt to answer all of their questions. Providing feedback to students regarding their performance and explaining the rationale for grading decisions facilitates learning.

Explain to students and parents how they are likely to be impacted by assessment results.

Explain to Students and Parents How They Are Likely to Be Impacted by Assessment Results.   It is the teacher's responsibility to explain to students and their parents both the positive and negative implications of assessment results. Students and their parents have a right to be informed of any likely consequences of the assessments.

Inform Students and Parents How Long the Scores Will Be Retained and Who Will Have Access to the Scores.   Students and their parents have a right to know how long the assessment results will be retained and who will have access to these records.

Develop Procedures so Test Takers Can File Complaints and Have Their Concerns Addressed.   Teachers and school administrators should develop procedures whereby students and their parents can file complaints about assessment practices. As we suggested earlier, it is usually desirable to try to address these concerns in an informal manner as opposed to allowing the problem to escalate into a legal challenge. Table 17.5 provides a summary of these guidelines for interpretating, using, and communicating assessment results.

Responsibilities of Test Takers

So far we have emphasized the rights of students and other test takers and the responsibilities of teachers and other assessment professionals. However, the *Standards* (AERA et al., 1999) note that students and other test takers also have responsibilities. These responsibilities include the following.

Students Are Responsible for Preparing for the Assessment.   Students have the right to have adequate information about the nature and use of assessments. In turn, students are responsible for studying and otherwise preparing themselves for the assessment.

Students Are Responsible for Following the Directions of the Individual Administering the Assessment.   Students are expected to follow the instructions provided by the individual administering the test or assessment. This includes behaviors such as showing up

TABLE 17.5   Checklist for Interpreting, Using, and Communicating Assessment Results

1. Are assessment results used only for purposes for which they
   have been validated?   _____

2. Did you take into consideration the limitations of the
   assessment results?   _____

3. Were multiple sources and types of assessment information
   used when making high-stakes educational decisions?   _____

4. Have you considered personal factors or extraneous events that
   might have influenced test performance?   _____

5. Are there any differences between the normative group and actual
   test takers that need to be considered?   _____

6. Are results communicated in an easily understandable
   and timely manner?   _____

7. Have you explained to students and parents how they are likely
   to be impacted by assessment results?   _____

8. Have you informed students and parents how long the scores
   will be retained and who will have access to the scores?   _____

9. Have you developed procedures so test takers can file complaints
   and have their concerns addressed?   _____

---

on time for the assessment, starting and stopping when instructed to do so, and recording responses as requested.

Students are responsible for acting in an academically honest manner.

Students Are Responsible for Behaving in an Academically Honest Manner.   That is, students should not cheat! Any form of cheating reduces the validity of the test and is unfair to other students. Cheating can include copying from another student, using prohibited resources (e.g., notes or other unsanctioned aids), securing stolen copies of tests, or having someone else take the test for them. Most schools have clearly stated policies on **academic honesty** and students caught cheating may be sanctioned.

Students Are Responsible for Not Interfering with the Performance of Other Students.   Students should refrain from any activity that might be distracting to other students.

Students Are Responsible for Informing the Teacher or Another Professional if They Believe the Assessment Results Do Not Adequately Represent Their True Abilities. If, for any reason students feel that the assessment results do not adequately represent their actual abilities, they should inform the teacher. This should be done as soon as possible so the teacher can take appropriate actions.

Students Should Respect the Copyright Rights of Test Publishers.   Students should not make copies or in any other way reproduce assessment materials.

TABLE 17.6   **Responsibilities of Test Takers**

1. Students are responsible for preparing for the assessment.
2. Students are responsible for following the directions of the individual administering the assessment.
3. Students are responsible for acting is an academically honest manner.
4. Students are responsible for not interfering with the performance of other students.
5. Students are responsible for informing the teacher or another professional if they believe the assessment results do not adequately represent their true abilities.
6. Students should respect the copyright rights of test publishers.
7. Students should not disclose information about the contents of a test.

SPECIAL INTEREST TOPIC   **17.2**
Steps to Prevent Student Cheating

Linn and Gronlund (2000) provide the following suggestions to help prevent cheating in your classroom.

1. Take steps to keep the test secure before the testing date.
2. Prior to taking the test, have students clear off the top of their desks.
3. If students are allowed to use scratch paper, have them turn it in with their tests.
4. Carefully monitor the students during the test administration.
5. When possible provide an empty row of seats between students.
6. Use two forms of the test and alternate forms when distributing (you can use the same test items, just arranged in a different order).
7. Design your tests to have good face validity, that is, so it appears relevant and fair.
8. Foster a positive attitude toward tests by emphasizing how assessments benefit students (e.g., students learn what they have and have not mastered; a fair way of assigning grades).

Students Should Not Disclose Information about the Contents of a Test.   In addition to not making copies of an assessment, students should refrain from divulging in any other manner information about the contents of a test. For example, they should not give other students information about what to expect on a test. This is tantamount to cheating. Table 17.6 provides a summary of the responsibilities of test takers.

Summary

In this chapter we discussed the teacher's responsibility to ensure that the assessments they use, whether professional tests or teacher constructed, are developed, selected, administered, scored, and interpreted in a technically, ethically, and legally sound manner. We provided the following guidelines to help teachers make sure their assessment practices meet these standards:

Guidelines for Developing Assessments

The most fundamental right of test takers is to be evaluated with assessments that meet high professional standards and that are valid for the intended purposes. Because teachers develop most assessments administered in the schools, they must ensure that they develop tests that meet these standards. Specific suggestions for developing assessments include:

- Clearly specify your educational objectives and develop a table of specifications.
- Develop assessment procedures that are appropriate for measuring the specified educational outcomes.
- Develop explicit scoring criteria.
- Develop clear guidelines for test administration.
- Plan accommodations for test takers with disabilities and other special needs.
- Carefully review the assessment prior to administration.
- Evaluate the technical properties of assessments.

Guidelines for Selecting Published Assessments

Teachers are often involved in the selection and administration of published assessment instruments, and as a result they incur numerous responsibilities. Specific suggestions for selecting published assessments include:

- Select assessments that have been validated for the intended purpose.
- Select assessments with normative data that are representative of the correct target population.
- Select assessments that produce reliable results.
- Select tests that are fair.
- Select assessments based on a thorough review of the available literature.
- Select and use only assessment that you are qualified to administer, score, and interpret.
- Guard against potential misuses and misinterpretations.
- Maintain test security.

Guidelines for Administering Assessments

A teacher's professional responsibilities do not end with the development or selection of assessments, but extend to the administration of assessments:

- Provide information to students on the assessment before administering it.
- Administer the assessment in a standardized manner.
- When appropriate, modify administration to accommodate the needs of students with disabilities.
- Provide information to students and parents about their rights and give them an opportunity to express their concerns.

- Administer only those assessments for which you are qualified by education and training.
- Maintain test security.

Guidelines for Scoring Assessments

Guidelines that should be considered when scoring assessments include:

- Make sure the assessments are scored properly and the results are reported accurately.
- Make sure the scoring is fair.
- Score the assessments and report the results in a timely manner.
- If scoring errors are detected, correct the errors and provide the corrected results in a timely manner.
- Implement a reasonable and fair process for appeal.
- Keep assessment results confidential.

Guidelines for Interpreting, Using, and Communicating Results

Guidelines that should be considered when interpreting, using, and communicating results include:

- Use assessment results only for purposes for which they have been validated.
- Be aware of the limitations of the assessment results.
- Use multiple sources and types of assessment information when making high-stakes educational assessments.
- Take into consideration personal factors or extraneous events that might have influenced test performance.
- With norm-referenced assessment, take into consideration any differences between the normative group and the actual test takers.
- Report results in an easily understandable manner.
- Explain to students and parents how they are likely to be impacted by assessment results.
- Inform students and parents how long the scores will be retained and who will have access to the scores.
- Develop procedures so test takers can file complaints and have their concerns addressed.

Responsibilities of Test Takers

Students and other test takers also have responsibilities, including:

- Students are responsible for preparing for the assessment.
- Students are responsible for following the directions of the individual administering the assessment.
- Students are responsible for behaving in an academically honest manner.
- Students are responsible for not interfering with the performance of other students.

- Students are responsible for informing the teacher or another professional if they believe the assessment results do not adequately represent their true abilities.
- Students should respect the copyright rights of test publishers.
- Students should not disclose information about the contents of a test.

KEY TERMS AND CONCEPTS

Academic honesty, p. 436
Code of Fair Testing Practices in Education (JCTP, 1988), p. 423
Code of Professional Responsibilities in Educational Measurement (NCME, 1995), p. 423
Education Week, p. 428

Mental Measurements Yearbook (MMY), p. 427
Rights and Responsibilities of Test Takers: Guidelines and Expectations (JCTP, 1998), p. 423
Standards for Educational and Psychological Testing (AERA et al., 1999), p. 423

The Student Evaluation Standards (JCSEE, 2003), p. 423
Test Critiques, p. 428
Test Reviews Online, p. 428
Tests, p. 427
Test security, p. 428
Tests in Print (TIP), p. 427

RECOMMENDED READINGS

American Educational Research Association, American Psychological Association, & National Council on Measurement in Education (1999). *Standards for educational and psychological testing.* Washington, DC: AERA. This is "the source" for technical information on the development and use of tests in educational and psychological settings.

In addition to the *Standards* (AERA et al., 1999), the codes and guidelines reproduced in the appendixes of this textbook are outstanding resources. These are:

Appendix A: Summary Statements of *The Student Evaluation Standards* (JCSEE, 2003)

Appendix B: *Code of Professional Responsibilities in Educational Measurement* (NCME, 1995)

Appendix C: *Code of Fair Testing Practices in Education* (JCTP, 1988)

Appendix D: *Rights and Responsibilities of Test Takers: Guidelines and Expectations* (JCTP, 1998)

Appendix E: *Standards for Teacher Competence in Educational Assessment of Students* (AFT, NCME, & NEA, 1990)

APPENDIX A

Summary Statements of
The Student Evaluation Standards

Joint Committee on Standards for Educational Evaluation (2003). *The student evaluation standards.* Thousand Oaks, CA: Corwin Press. [Book is available from Corwin Press (www.corwinpress.com) and other book sellers.]

Propriety Standards

The propriety standards help ensure that student evaluations will be conducted legally, ethically, and with due regard for the well-being of the students being evaluated and other people affected by the evaluation results. These standards are as follows:

P1. Service to Students: Evaluations of students should promote sound education principles, fulfillment of institutional missions, and effective student work, so that the educational needs of students are served.

P2. Appropriate Policies and Procedures: Written policies and procedures should be developed, implemented, and made available, so that evaluations are consistent, equitable, and fair.

P3. Access to Evaluation Information: Access to a student's evaluation information should be provided, but limited to the student and others with established legitimate permission to view the information, so that confidentiality is maintained and privacy protected.

P4. Treatment of Students: Students should be treated with respect in all aspects of the evaluation process, so that their dignity and opportunities for educational development are enhanced.

P5. Rights of Students: Evaluations of students should be consistent with applicable laws and basic principles of fairness and human rights, so that students' rights and welfare are protected.

P6. Balanced Evaluation: Evaluations of students should provide information that identifies both strengths and weaknesses, so that strengths can be built upon and problem areas addressed.

P7. Conflict of Interest: Conflicts of interest should be avoided, but if present should be dealt with openly and honestly, so that they do not compromise evaluation processes and results.

Utility Standards

The utility standards help ensure that student evaluations are useful. Useful student evaluations are informative, timely, and influential. Standards that support usefulness are as follows:

U1. Constructive Orientation: Student evaluations should be constructive, so that they result in educational decisions that are in the best interest of the student.

U2. Defined Users and Uses: The users and uses of a student evaluation should be specified, so that the evaluation appropriately contributes to student learning and development.

U3. Information Scope: The information collected for student evaluations should be carefully focused and sufficiently comprehensive, so that the evaluation questions can be fully answered and the needs of students addressed.

U4. Evaluator Qualifications: Teachers and others who evaluate students should have the necessary knowledge and skills, so that the evaluations are carried out competently and the results can be used with confidence.

U5. Explicit Values: In planning and conducting student evaluations, teachers and others who evaluate students should identify and justify the values used to judge student performance, so that the bases for the evaluations are clear and defensible.

U6. Effective Reporting: Student evaluation reports should be clear, timely, accurate, and relevant, so that they are useful to students, their parents/guardians, and other legitimate users.

U7. Follow-Up: Student evaluations should include procedures for follow-up, so that students, parents/guardians, and other legitimate users can understand the information and take appropriate follow-up actions.

Feasibility Standards

The feasibility standards help ensure that student evaluations can be implemented as planned. Feasible evaluations are practical, diplomatic, and adequately supported. These standards are as follows:

F1. Practical Orientation: Student evaluation procedures should be practical, so that they produce the needed information in efficient, nondisruptive ways.

F2. Political Viability: Student evaluations should be planned and conducted with the anticipation of questions from students, their parents/guardians, and other legitimate users, so that their questions can be answered effectively and their cooperation obtained.

F3. Evaluation Support: Adequate time and resources should be provided for student evaluations, so that evaluations can be effectively planned and implemented, their results fully communicated, and appropriate follow-up activities identified.

Accuracy Standards

The accuracy standards help ensure that a student evaluation will produce sound information about a student's learning and performance. Sound information leads to valid interpretations, justifiable conclusions, and appropriate follow-up. These standards are as follows:

A1.   Validity Orientation: Student evaluations should be developed and implemented, so that the interpretations made about the performance of a student are valid and not open to misinterpretation.

A2.   Defined Expectations for Students: The performance expectations for students should be clearly defined, so that evaluation results are defensible and meaningful.

A3.   Context Analysis: Student and contextual variables that may influence performance should be identified and considered, so that a student's performance can be validly interpreted.

A4.   Documented Procedures: The procedures for evaluating students, both planned and actual, should be described, so that the procedures can be explained and justified.

A5.   Defensible Information: The adequacy of information gathered should be ensured, so that good decisions are possible and can be defended and justified.

A6.   Reliable Information: Evaluation procedures should be chosen or developed and implemented, so that they provide reliable information for decisions about the performance of a student.

A7.   Bias Identification and Management: Student evaluations should be free from bias, so that conclusions can be fair.

A8.   Handling Information and Quality Control: The information collected, processed, and reported about students should be systematically reviewed, corrected as appropriate, and kept secure, so that accurate judgments can be made.

A9.   Analysis of Information: Information collected for student evaluations should be systematically and accurately analyzed, so that the purposes of the evaluation are effectively achieved.

A10.   Justified Conclusions: The evaluative conclusions about student performance should be explicitly justified, so that students, their parents/guardians, and others can have confidence in them.

A11.   Metaevaluation: Student evaluation procedures should be examined periodically using these and other pertinent standards, so that mistakes are prevented, or detected and promptly corrected, and sound student evaluation practices are developed over time.

APPENDIX B

Code of Professional Responsibilities in Educational Measurement

Prepared by the NCME Ad Hoc Committee on the Development of a Code of Ethics: Cynthia B. Schmeiser, ACT—Chair; Kurt F. Geisinger, State University of New York; Sharon Johnson-Lewis, Detroit Public Schools; Edward D. Roeber, Council of Chief State School Officers; William D. Schafer, University of Maryland. Copyright 1995 National Council on Measurement in Education. Any portion of this Code may be reproduced and disseminated for educational purposes.

As an organization dedicated to the improvement of measurement and evaluation practice in education, the National Council on Measurement in Education (NCME) has adopted this Code to promote professionally responsible practice in educational measurement. Professionally responsible practice is conduct that arises from either the professional standards of the field, general ethical principles, or both.

The purpose of the Code of Professional Responsibilities in Educational Measurement, hereinafter referred to as the Code, is to guide the conduct of NCME members who are involved in any tinge of assessment activity in education. NCME is also providing this Code as a public service for all individuals who are engaged in educational assessment activities in the hope that these activities will be conducted in a professionally responsible manner. Persons who engage in these activities include local educators such as classroom teachers, principals, and superintendents; professionals such as school psychologists and counselors; state and national technical, legislative, and policy staff in education; staff of research, evaluation, and testing organizations; providers of test preparation services; college and university faculty and administrators; and professionals in business and industry who design and implement educational and training programs.

This Code applies to any type of assessment that occurs as part of the educational process, including formal and informal, traditional and alternative techniques for gathering information used in making educational decisions at all levels. These techniques include, but are not limited to, large-scale assessments at the school, district, state, national, and international levels; standardized tests; observational measures; teacher-conducted assessments; assessment support materials; and other achievement, aptitude, interest, and personality measures used in and for education.

Although NCME is promulgating this Code for its members, it strongly encourages other organizations and individuals who engage in educational assessment activities to endorse and abide by the responsibilities relevant to their professions. Because the Code pertains only to uses of assessment in education, it is recognized that uses of assessments outside of educational contexts, such as for employment, certification, or licensure, may involve additional professional responsibilities beyond those detailed in this Code.

The Code is intended to serve an educational function: to inform and remind those involved in educational assessment of their obligations to uphold the integrity of the manner in which assessments are developed, used, evaluated, and marketed. Moreover, it is expected that the Code will stimulate thoughtful discussion of what constitutes professionally responsible assessment practice at all levels in education.

The Code enumerates professional responsibilities in eight major areas of assessment activity. Specifically, the Code presents the professional responsibilities of those who:

1. Develop Assessments
2. Market and Sell Assessments
3. Select Assessments
4. Administer Assessments
5. Score Assessments
6. Interpret, Use, and Communicate Assessment Results
7. Educate about Assessment
8. Evaluate Programs and Conduct Research on Assessments

Although the organization of the Code is based on the differentiation of these activities, they are viewed as highly interrelated, and those who use this Code are urged to consider the Code in its entirety. The index following this Code provides a listing of some of the critical interest topics within educational measurement that focus on one or more of the assessment activities.

General Responsibilities

The professional responsibilities promulgated in this Code in eight major areas of assessment activity are based on expectations that NCME members involved in educational assessment will:

1. protect the health and safety of all examinees;
2. be knowledgeable about, and behave in compliance with, state and federal laws relevant to the conduct of professional activities;
3. maintain and improve their professional competence in educational assessment;
4. provide assessment services only in areas of their competence and experience, affording full disclosure of their professional qualifications;
5. promote the understanding of sound assessment practices in education;
6. adhere to the highest standards of conduct and promote professionally responsible conduct within educational institutions and agencies that provide educational services; and
7. perform all professional responsibilities with honesty, integrity, due care, and fairness.

Responsible professional practice includes being informed about and acting in accordance with the *Code of Fair Testing Practices in Education* (Joint Committee on Testing Practices, 1988), the *Standards for Educational and Psychological Testing* (American Educational Research Association, American Psychological Association, National Council on Measurement in Education, 1985), or subsequent revisions, as well as all applicable state and federal laws that may govern the development, administration, and use of assessments. Both the *Standards for Educational and Psychological Testing* and the *Code of Fair Testing Practices in Education* are intended to establish criteria for judging the technical adequacy of tests and the appropriate uses of tests and test results. The purpose of this Code is to describe the professional responsibilities of those individuals who are engaged in assessment activities. As would be expected, there is a strong relationship between professionally responsible practice and sound educational assessments, and this Code is intended to be consistent with the relevant parts of both of these documents.

It is not the intention of NCME to enforce the professional responsibilities stated in the Code or to investigate allegations of violations to the Code.

Since the Code provides a frame of reference for the evaluation of the appropriateness of behavior, NCME recognizes that the Code may be used in legal or other similar proceedings.

Section 1: Responsibilities of Those Who Develop Assessment Products and Services

Those who develop assessment products and services, such as classroom teachers and other assessment specialists, have a professional responsibility to strive to produce assessments that are of the highest quality. Persons who develop assessments have a professional responsibility to:

1.1 Ensure that assessment products and services are developed to meet applicable professional, technical, and legal standards.

1.2 Develop assessment products and services that are as free as possible from bias due to characteristics irrelevant to the construct being measured, such as gender, ethnicity, race, socioeconomic status, disability, religion, age, or national origin.

1.3 Plan accommodations for groups of test takers with disabilities and other special needs when developing assessments.

1.4 Disclose to appropriate parties any actual or potential conflicts of interest that might influence the developers' judgment or performance.

1.5 Use copyrighted materials in assessment products and services in accordance with state and federal law.

1.6 Make information available to appropriate persons about the steps taken to develop and score the assessment, including up-to-date information used to support the reliability, validity, scoring and reporting processes, and other relevant characteristics of the assessment.

1.7 Protect the rights to privacy of those who are assessed as part of the assessment development process.

1.8 Caution users, in clear and prominent language, against the most likely misinterpretations and misuses of data that arise out of the assessment development process.

1.9 Avoid false or unsubstantiated claims in test preparation and program support materials and services about an assessment or its use and interpretation.

1.10 Correct any substantive inaccuracies in assessments or their support materials as soon as feasible.

1.11 Develop score reports and support materials that promote the understanding of assessment results.

Section 2: Responsibilities of Those Who Market and Sell Assessment Products and Services

The marketing of assessment products and services, such as tests and other instruments, scoring services, test preparation services, consulting, and test interpretive services, should be based on information that is accurate, complete, and relevant to those considering their use. Persons who market and sell assessment products and services have a professional responsibility to:

2.1 Provide accurate information to potential purchasers about assessment products and services and their recommended uses and limitations.

2.2 Not knowingly withhold relevant information about assessment products and services that might affect an appropriate selection decision.

2.3 Base all claims about assessment products and services on valid interpretations of publicly available information.

2.4 Allow qualified users equal opportunity to purchase assessment products and services.

2.5 Establish reasonable fees for assessment products and services.

2.6 Communicate to potential users, in advance of any purchase or use, all applicable fees associated with assessment products and services.

2.7 Strive to ensure that no individuals are denied access to opportunities because of their inability to pay the fees for assessment products and services.

2.8 Establish criteria for the sale of assessment products and services, such as limiting the sale of assessment products and services to those individuals who are qualified for recommended uses and from whom proper uses and interpretations are anticipated.

2.9 Inform potential users of known inappropriate uses of assessment products and services and provide recommendations about how to avoid such misuses.

2.10 Maintain a current understanding about assessment products and services and their appropriate uses in education.

2.11 Release information implying endorsement by users of assessment products and services only with the users' permission.

2.12 Avoid making claims that assessment products and services have been endorsed by another organization unless an official endorsement has been obtained.

2.13 Avoid marketing test preparation products and services that may cause individuals to receive scores that misrepresent their actual levels of attainment.

Section 3: Responsibilities of Those Who Select Assessment Products and Services

Those who select assessment products and services for use in educational settings, or help others do so, have important professional responsibilities to make sure that the assessments are appropriate for their intended use. Persons who select assessment products and services have a professional responsibility to:

3.1 Conduct a thorough review and evaluation of available assessment strategies and instruments that might be valid for the intended uses.

3.2 Recommend and/or select assessments based on publicly available documented evidence of their technical quality and utility rather than on unsubstantiated claims or statements.

3.3 Disclose any associations or affiliations that they have with the authors, test publishers, or others involved with the assessments under consideration for purchase and refrain from participation if such associations might affect the objectivity of the selection process.

3.4 Inform decision makers and prospective users of the appropriateness of the assessment for the intended uses, likely consequences of use, protection of examinee rights, relative costs, materials and services needed to conduct or use the assessment, and known limitations of the assessment, including potential misuses and misinterpretations of assessment information.

3.5 Recommend against the use of any prospective assessment that is likely to be administered, scored, and used in an invalid manner for members of various groups in our society for reasons of race, ethnicity, gender, age, disability, language background, socioeconomic status, religion, or national origin.

3.6 Comply with all security precautions that may accompany assessments being reviewed.

3.7 Immediately disclose any attempts by others to exert undue influence on the assessment selection process.

3.8 Avoid recommending, purchasing, or using test preparation products and services that may cause individuals to receive scores that misrepresent their actual levels of attainment.

Section 4: Responsibilities of Those Who Administer Assessments

Those who prepare individuals to take assessments and those who are directly or indirectly involved in the administration of assessments as part of the educational process, including teachers, administrators, and assessment personnel, have an important role in making sure that the assessments are administered in a fair and accurate manner. Persons who prepare others for, and those who administer, assessments have a professional responsibility to:

4.1 Inform the examinees about the assessment prior to its administration, including its purposes, uses, and consequences; how the assessment information will be judged or scored; how the results will be kept on file; who will have access to the results; how the results will be distributed; and examinees' rights before, during, and after the assessment.

4.2 Administer only those assessments for which they are qualified by education, training, licensure, or certification.

4.3 Take appropriate security precautions before, during, and after the administration of the assessment.

4.4 Understand the procedures needed to administer the assessment prior to administration.

4.5 Administer standardized assessments according to prescribed procedures and conditions and notify appropriate persons if any nonstandard or delimiting conditions occur.

4.6 Not exclude any eligible student from the assessment.

4.7 Avoid any conditions in the conduct of the assessment that might invalidate the results.

4.8 Provide for and document all reasonable and allowable accommodations for the administration of the assessment to persons with disabilities or special needs.

4.9 Provide reasonable opportunities for individuals to ask questions about the assessment procedures or directions prior to and at prescribed times during the administration of the assessment.

4.10 Protect the rights to privacy and due process of those who are assessed.

4.11 Avoid actions or conditions that would permit or encourage individuals or groups to receive scores that misrepresent their actual levels of attainment.

Section 5: Responsibilities of Those Who Score Assessments

The scoring of educational assessments should be conducted properly and efficiently so that the results are reported accurately and in a timely manner. Persons who score and prepare reports of assessments have a professional responsibility to:

5.1 Provide complete and accurate information to users about how the assessment is scored, such as the reporting schedule, scoring process to be used, rationale for the scoring approach, technical characteristics, quality control procedures, reporting formats, and the fees, if any, for these services.

5.2 Ensure the accuracy of the assessment results by conducting reasonable quality control procedures before, during, and after scoring.

5.3 Minimize the effect on scoring of factors irrelevant to the purposes of the assessment.

5.4 Inform users promptly of any deviation in the planned scoring and reporting service or schedule and negotiate a solution with users.

5.5 Provide corrected score results to the examinee or the client as quickly as practicable should errors be found that may affect the inferences made on the basis of the scores.

5.6   Protect the confidentiality of information that identifies individuals as prescribed by state and federal laws.

5.7   Release summary results of the assessment only to those persons entitled to such information by state or federal law or those who are designated by the party contracting for the scoring services.

5.8   Establish, where feasible, a fair and reasonable process for appeal and rescoring the assessment.

Section 6: Responsibilities of Those Who Interpret, Use, and Communicate Assessment Results

The interpretation, use, and communication of assessment results should promote valid inferences and minimize invalid ones. Persons who interpret, use, and communicate assessment results have a professional responsibility to:

6.1   Conduct these activities in an informed, objective, and fair manner within the context of the assessment's limitations and with an understanding of the potential consequences of use.

6.2   Provide to those who receive assessment results information about the assessment, its purposes, its limitations, and its uses necessary for the proper interpretation of the results.

6.3   Provide to those who receive score reports an understandable written description of all reported scores, including proper interpretations and likely misinterpretations.

6.4   Communicate to appropriate audiences the results of the assessment in an understandable and timely manner, including proper interpretations and likely misinterpretations.

6.5   Evaluate and communicate the adequacy and appropriateness of any norms or standards used in the interpretation of assessment results.

6.6   Inform parties involved in the assessment process how assessment results may affect them.

6.7   Use multiple sources and types of relevant information about persons or programs whenever possible in making educational decisions.

6.8   Avoid making, and actively discourage others from making, inaccurate reports, unsubstantiated claims, inappropriate interpretations, or otherwise false and misleading statements about assessment results.

6.9   Disclose to examinees and others whether and how long the results of the assessment will be kept on file, procedures for appeal and rescoring, rights examinees and others have to the assessment information, and how those rights may be exercised.

6.10   Report any apparent misuses of assessment information to those responsible for the assessment process.

6.11   Protect the rights to privacy of individuals and institutions involved in the assessment process.

Section 7: Responsibilities of Those Who Educate Others about Assessment

The process of educating others about educational assessment, whether as part of higher education, professional development, public policy discussions, or job training, should prepare individuals to understand and engage in sound measurement practice and to become discerning users of tests and test results. Persons who educate or inform others about assessment have a professional responsibility to:

7.1   Remain competent and current in the areas in which they teach and reflect that in their instruction.

7.2   Provide fair and balanced perspectives when teaching about assessment.

7.3 Differentiate clearly between expressions of opinion and substantiated knowledge when educating others about any specific assessment method, product, or service.

7.4 Disclose any financial interests that might be perceived to influence the evaluation of a particular assessment product or service that is the subject of instruction.

7.5 Avoid administering any assessment that is not part of the evaluation of student performance in a course if the administration of that assessment is likely to harm any student.

7.6 Avoid using or reporting the results of any assessment that is not part of the evaluation of student performance in a course if the use or reporting of results is likely to harm any student.

7.7 Protect all secure assessments and materials used in the instructional process.

7.8 Model responsible assessment practice and help those receiving instruction to learn about their professional responsibilities in educational measurement.

7.9 Provide fair and balanced perspectives on assessment issues being discussed by policymakers, parents, and other citizens.

Section 8: Responsibilities of Those Who Evaluate Educational Programs and Conduct Research on Assessments

Conducting research on or about assessments or educational programs is a key activity in helping to improve the understanding and use of assessments and educational programs. Persons who engage in the evaluation of educational programs or conduct research on assessments have a professional responsibility to:

8.1 Conduct evaluation and research activities in an informed, objective, and fair manner.

8.2 Disclose any associations that they have with authors, test publishers, or others involved with the assessment and refrain from participation if such associations might affect the objectivity of the research or evaluation.

8.3 Preserve the security of all assessments throughout the research process as appropriate.

8.4 Take appropriate steps to minimize potential sources of invalidity in the research and disclose known factors that may bias the results of the study.

8.5 Present the results of research, both intended and unintended, in a fair, complete, and objective manner.

8.6 Attribute completely and appropriately the work and ideas of others.

8.7 Qualify the conclusions of the research within the limitations of the study.

8.8 Use multiple sources of relevant information in conducting evaluation and research activities whenever possible.

8.9 Comply with applicable standards for protecting the rights of participants in an evaluation or research study, including the rights to privacy and informed consent.

Afterword

As stated at the outset, the purpose of the *Code of Professional Responsibilities in Educational Measurement* is to serve as a guide to the conduct of NCME members who are engaged in any type of assessment activity in education. Given the broad scope of the field of educational assessment as well as the variety of activities in which professionals may engage, it is unlikely that any code will cover the professional responsibilities involved in every situation or activity in which assessment is used in education. Ultimately, it is hoped that this Code will serve as the basis for ongoing discussions about what constitutes professionally responsible practice. Moreover, these discussions will undoubtedly identify areas of practice that need further analysis and clarification in subsequent editions of the Code. To the extent that these discussions occur, the Code will have served its purpose.

To assist in the ongoing refinement of the Code, comments on this document are most welcome. Please send your comments and inquiries to:

Dr. William J. Russell
Executive Officer
National Council on Measurement in Education
1230 Seventeenth Street, NW
Washington, DC 20036-3078

Index to the *Code of Professional Responsibilities in Educational Measurement*

This index provides a list of major topics and issues addressed by the responsibilities in each of the eight sections of the Code. Although this list is not intended to be exhaustive, it is intended to serve as a reference source for those who use this Code.

APPENDIX C

Code of Fair Testing Practices in Education

The Code of Fair Testing Practices in Education states the major obligations to test takers of professionals who develop or use educational tests. The Code is meant to apply broadly to the use of tests in education (admissions, educational assessment, educational diagnosis, and student placement). The Code is not designed to cover employment testing, licensure or certification testing, or other types of testing. Although the Code has relevance to many types of educational tests, it is directed primarily at professionally developed tests such as those sold by commercial test publishers or used in formally administered testing programs. The Code is not intended to cover tests made by individual teachers for use in their own classrooms.

The Code addresses the roles of test developers and test users separately. Test users are people who select tests, commission test development services, or make decisions on the basis of test scores. Test developers are people who actually construct tests as well as those who set policies for particular testing programs. The roles may, of course, overlap as when a state education agency commissions test development services, sets policies that control the test development process, and makes decisions on the basis of the test scores.

The Code has been developed by the Joint Committee on Testing Practices, a cooperative effort of several professional organizations, that has as its aim the advancement, in the public interest, of the quality of testing practices. The Joint Committee was initiated by the American Educational Research Association, the American Psychological Association, and the National Council on Measurement in Education. In addition to these three groups the American Association for Counseling and Development/Association for Measurement and Evaluation in Counseling and Development, and the American Speech-Language-Hearing Association are now also sponsors of the Joint Committee.

This is not copyrighted material. Reproduction and dissemination are encouraged. Please cite this document as follows: Code of Fair Testing Practices in Education. (1988). Washington, D.C.: Joint Committee on Testing Practices. (Mailing Address: Joint Committee on Testing Practices, American Psychological Association, 1200 17th Street, NW, Washington, D.C. 20036.)

The Code presents standards for educational test developers and users in four areas:

A. Developing/Selecting Appropriate Tests
B. Interpreting Scores
C. Striving for Fairness
D. Informing Test Takers

Organizations, institutions, and individual professionals who endorse the Code commit themselves to safeguarding the rights of test takers by following the principles listed. The Code is intended to be consistent with the relevant parts of the *Standards for Educational and Psychological Testing* (AERA, APA, NCME, 1985). However, the Code differs from the *Standards* in both audience and purpose. The Code is meant to be understood by the general public; it is limited to educational tests; and the primary focus is on those issues that affect the proper use of tests. The Code is not meant to add new principles over and above those in the *Standards* or to change the meaning of the *Standards*. The goal is rather to represent the spirit of a selected portion of the *Standards* in a way that is meaningful to test takers and/or their parents or guardians. It is the hope of the Joint Committee that the Code will also be judged to be consistent with existing codes of conduct and standards of other professional groups who use educational tests.

A. Developing/Selecting Appropriate Tests*

Test developers should provide the information that test users need to select appropriate tests.

Test users should select tests that meet the purpose for which they are to be used and that are appropriate for the intended test taking populations.

Test Developers Should:

1. Define what each test measures and what the test should be used for. Describe the population(s) for which the test is appropriate.

2. Accurately represent the characteristics, usefulness, and limitations of tests for their intended purposes.

3. Explain relevant measurement concepts as necessary for clarity at the level of detail that is appropriate for the intended audience(s).

4. Describe the process of test development. Explain how the content and skills to be tested were selected.

5. Provide evidence that the test meets its intended purpose(s).

6. Provide either representative samples or complete copies of test questions, directions, answer sheets, manuals, and score reports to qualified users.

7. Indicate the nature of the evidence obtained concerning the appropriateness of each test for groups of different racial, ethnic, or linguistic backgrounds who are likely to be tested.

8. Identify and publish any specialized skills needed to administer each test and to interpret scores correctly.

Test Users Should:

1. First define the purpose for testing and the population to be tested. Then, select a test for that purpose and that population based on a thorough review of the available information.

2. Investigate potentially useful sources of information, in addition to test scores, to corroborate the information provided by tests.

3. Read the materials provided by test developers and avoid using tests for which unclear or incomplete information is provided.

4. Become familiar with how and when the test was developed and tried out.

5. Read independent evaluations of a test and of possible alternative measures. Look for evidence required to support the claims of test developers.

6. Examine specimen sets, disclosed tests or samples of questions, directions, answer sheets, manuals, and score reports before selecting a test.

7. Ascertain whether the test content and norm group(s) or comparison group(s) are appropriate for the intended test takers.

8. Select and use only those tests for which the skills needed to administer the test and interpret scores correctly are available.

*Many of the statements in the Code refer to the selection of existing tests. However, in customized testing programs test developers are engaged to construct new tests. In those situations, the test development process should be designed to help ensure that the completed tests will be in compliance with the Code.

B. Interpreting Scores

Test developers should help users interpret scores correctly.

Test users should interpret scores correctly.

Test Developers Should:

9. Provide timely and easily understood score reports that describe test performance clearly and accurately. Also, explain the meaning and limitations of reported scores.

10. Describe the population(s) represented by any norms or comparison group(s), the dates the data were gathered, and the process used to select the samples of test takers.

11. Warn users to avoid specific, reasonably anticipated misuses of test scores.

12. Provide information that will help users follow reasonable procedures for setting passing scores when it is appropriate to use such scores with the test.

13. Provide information that will help users gather evidence to show that the test is meeting its intended purpose(s).

Test Users Should:

9. Obtain information about the scale used for reporting scores, the characteristics of any norms or comparison group(s), and the limitations of the scores.

10. Interpret scores taking into account any major differences between the norms or comparison groups and the actual test takers. Also take into account any differences in test administration practices or familiarity with the specific questions in the test.

11. Avoid using tests for purposes not specifically recommended by the test developer unless evidence is obtained to support the intended use.

12. Explain how any passing scores were set and gather evidence to support the appropriateness of the scores.

13. Obtain evidence to help show that the test is meeting its intended purpose(s).

C. Striving for Fairness

Test developers should strive to make tests that are as fair as possible for test takers of different races, gender, ethnic backgrounds, or different handicapping conditions.

Test users should select tests that have been developed in ways that attempt to make them as fair as possible for test takers of different races, gender, ethnic backgrounds, or handicapping conditions.

Test Developers Should:

14. Review and revise test questions and related materials to avoid potentially insensitive content or language.

15. Investigate the performance of test takers of different races, gender, and ethnic backgrounds when samples of sufficient size are available. Enact procedures that help to ensure that differences in performance are related primarily to the skills under assessment rather than to irrelevant factors.

16. When feasible, make appropriately modified forms of tests or administration procedures available for test takers with handicapping conditions. Warn test users of potential problems in using standard norms with modified tests or administration procedures that result in noncomparable scores.

Test Users Should:

14. Evaluate the procedures used by test developers to avoid potentially insensitive content or language.

15. Review the performance of test takers of different races, gender, and ethnic backgrounds when samples of sufficient size are available. Evaluate the extent to which performance differences may have been caused by the test.

16. When necessary and feasible, use appropriately modified forms or administration procedures for test takers with handicapping conditions. Interpret standard norms with care in the light of the modifications that were made.

D. Informing Test Takers

Under some circumstances, test developers have direct communication with test takers. Under other circumstances, test users communicate directly with test takers. Whichever group communicates directly with test takers should provide the information described below.

Test Developers or Test Users Should:

17. When a test is optional, provide test takers or their parents/guardians with information to help them judge whether the test should be taken, or if an available alternative to the test should be used.

18. Provide test takers with the information they need to be familiar with the coverage of the test, the types of question formats, the directions, and appropriate test-taking strategies. Strive to make such information equally available to all test takers.

Under some circumstances, test developers have direct control of tests and test scores. Under other circumstances, test users have such control.

Whichever group has direct control of tests and test scores should take the steps described below.

Test Developers or Test Users Should:

19. Provide test takers or their parents/guardians with information about rights test takers may have to obtain copies of tests and completed answer sheets, retake tests, have tests rescored, or cancel scores.

20. Tell test takers or their parents/guardians how long scores will be kept on file and indicate to whom and under what circumstances test scores will or will not be released.

21. Describe the procedures that test takers or their parents/guardians may use to register complaints and have problems resolved.

Note: The membership of the Working Group that developed the Code of Fair Testing Practices in Education and of the Joint Committee on Testing Practices that guided the Working Group was as follows: Theodore P. Bartell, John R. Bergan, Esther E. Diamond, Richard P. Duran, Lorraine D. Eyde, Raymond D. Fowler, John J. Fremer (Co-chair, JCTP and Chair, Code Working Group), Edmund W. Gordon, Jo-Ida C. Hansen, James B. Lingwall, George F. Madaus (Co-chair, JCTP), Kevin L. Moreland, Jo-Ellen V. Perez, Robert J. Solomon, John T. Stewart, Carol Kehr Tittle (Co-chair, JCTP), Nicholas A. Vacc, and Michael J. Zieky. (Debra Boltas and Wayne Camara of the American Psychological Association served as staff liaisons.)

Additional copies of the Code may be obtained from the National Council on Measurement in Education, 1230 Seventeenth Street, NW, Washington, D.C. 20036. Single copies are free.

APPENDIX D

Rights and Responsibilities of Test Takers: Guidelines and Expectations

Preamble

The intent of this statement is to enumerate and clarify the expectations that test takers may reasonably have about the testing process, and the expectations that those who develop, administer, and use tests may have of test takers. Tests are defined broadly here as psychological and educational instruments developed and used by testing professionals in organizations such as schools, industries, clinical practice, counseling settings and human service and other agencies, including those assessment procedures and devices that are used for making inferences about people in the above-named settings. The purpose of the statement is to inform and to help educate not only test takers, but also others involved in the testing enterprise so that measurements may be most validly and appropriately used. This document is intended as an effort to inspire improvements in the testing process and does not have the force of law. Its orientation is to encourage positive and high quality interactions between testing professionals and test takers.

The rights and responsibilities listed in this document are neither legally based nor inalienable rights and responsibilities such as those listed in the United States of America's Bill of Rights. Rather, they represent the best judgments of testing professionals about the reasonable expectations that those involved in the testing enterprise (test producers, test users, and test takers) should have of each other. Testing professionals include developers of assessment products and services, those who market and sell them, persons who select them, test administrators and scorers, those who interpret test results, and trained users of the information. Persons who engage in each of these activities have significant responsibilities that are described elsewhere, in documents such as those that follow (American Association for Counseling and Development, 1988; American Speech-Language-Hearing Association, 1994; Joint Committee on Testing Practices, 1988; National Association of School Psychologists, 1992; National Council on Measurement in Education, 1995).

In some circumstances, the test developer and the test user may not be the same person, group of persons, or organization. In such situations, the professionals involved in the testing should clarify, for the test taker as well as for themselves, who is responsible for each aspect of the testing process. For example, when an individual chooses to take a college admissions test, at least three parties are involved in addition to the test taker: the test developer and publisher, the individuals who administer the test to the test taker, and the institutions of higher education who will eventually use the information. In such cases a test taker may need to request clarifications about their rights and responsibilities. When test takers are young children (e.g., those taking standardized tests in the schools) or are persons who spend some or all their time in institutions or are incapacitated, parents or guardians may be granted some of the rights and responsibilities, rather than, or in addition to, the individual.

Perhaps the most fundamental right test takers have is to be able to take tests that meet high professional standards, such as those described in *Standards for Educational and Psychological Testing* (American Educational Research Association, American Psychological Association, & National Council on Measurement in Education, 1999) as well as those of other appropriate professional asso-

456

ciations. This statement should be used as an adjunct, or supplement, to those standards. State and federal laws, of course, supersede any rights and responsibilities that are stated here.

References

American Association for Counseling and Development (now American Counseling Association) & Association for Measurement and Evaluation in Counseling and Development (now Association for Assessment in Counseling). (1989). *Responsibilities of users of standardized tests: RUST statement revised.* Alexandria, VA: Author.

American Educational Research Association, American Psychological Association, & National Council on Measurement in Education. (1999). *Standards for educational and psychological testing.* Washington, DC: American Educational Research Association.

American Speech-Language-Hearing Association. (1994). Protection of rights of people receiving audiology or speech-language pathology services. *ASHA* (36), 60–63.

Joint Committee on Testing Practices. (1988). *Code of fair testing practices in education.* Washington, DC: American Psychological Association.

National Association of School Psychologists. (1992). *Standards for the* provision of school psychological services. Author: Silver Springs, MD.

National Council on Measurement in Education. (1995). *Code of professional responsibilities in educational measurement.* Washington, DC: Author.

The Rights and Responsibilities of Test Takers: Guidelines and Expectations, Test Taker Rights and Responsibilities Working Group of the Joint Committee on Testing Practices, August, 1998

As a Test Taker, You Have the Right To:
Be informed of your rights and responsibilities as a test taker.

Be treated with courtesy, respect, and impartiality, regardless of your age, disability, ethnicity, gender, national origin, religion, sexual orientation or other personal characteristics.

Be tested with measures that meet professional standards and that are appropriate, given the manner in which the test results will be used.

Receive a brief oral or written explanation prior to testing about the purpose(s) for testing, the kind(s) of tests to be used, if the results will be reported to you or to others, and the planned use(s) of the results. If you have a disability, you have the right to inquire and receive information about testing accommodations. If you have difficulty in comprehending the language of the test, you have a right to know in advance of testing whether any accommodations may be available to you.

Know in advance of testing when the test will be administered, if and when test results will be available to you, and if there is a fee for testing services that you are expected to pay.

Have your test administered and your test results interpreted by appropriately trained individuals who follow professional codes of ethics.

Know if a test is optional and learn of the consequences of taking or not taking the test, fully completing the test, or canceling the scores. You may need to ask questions to learn these consequences.

Receive a written or oral explanation of your test results within a reasonable amount of time after testing and in commonly understood terms.

Have your test results kept confidential to the extent allowed by law.

Present concerns about the testing process or your results and receive information about procedures that will be used to address such concerns.

As a Test Taker, You Have the Responsibility To:

Read and/or listen to your rights and responsibilities as a test taker.

Treat others with courtesy and respect during the testing process.

Ask questions prior to testing if you are uncertain about why the test is being given, how it will be given, what you will be asked to do, and what will be done with the results.

Read or listen to descriptive information in advance of testing and listen carefully to all test instructions. You should inform an examiner in advance of testing if you wish to receive a testing accommodation or if you have a physical condition or illness that may interfere with your performance on the test. If you have difficulty comprehending the language of the test, it is your responsibility to inform an examiner.

Know when and where the test will be given, pay for the test if required, appear on time with any required materials, and be ready to be tested.

Follow the test instructions you are given and represent yourself honestly during the testing.

Be familiar with and accept the consequences of not taking the test, should you choose not to take the test.

Inform appropriate person(s), as specified to you by the organization responsible for testing, if you believe that testing conditions affected your results.

Ask about the confidentiality of your test results, if this aspect concerns you.

Present concerns about the testing process or results in a timely, respectful way, if you have any.

The Rights of Test Takers: Guidelines for Testing Professionals

Test takers have the rights described below. It is the responsibility of the professionals involved in the testing process to ensure that test takers receive these rights.

Because test takers have the right to be informed of their rights and responsibilities as test takers, it is normally the responsibility of the individual who administers a test (or the organization that prepared the test) to inform test takers of these rights and responsibilities.

Because test takers have the right to be treated with courtesy, respect, and impartiality, regardless of their age, disability, ethnicity, gender, national origin, race, religion, sexual orientation, or other personal characteristics, testing professionals should:

Make test takers aware of any materials that are available to assist them in test preparation. These materials should be clearly described in test registration and/or test familiarization materials.

See that test takers are provided with reasonable access to testing services.

Because test takers have the right to be tested with measures that meet professional standards that are appropriate for the test use and the test taker, given the manner in which the results will be used, testing professionals should:

Take steps to utilize measures that meet professional standards and are reliable, relevant, useful given the intended purpose and are fair for test takers from varying societal groups.

Advise test takers that they are entitled to request reasonable accommodations in test administration that are likely to increase the validity of their test scores if they have a disability recognized under the Americans with Disabilities Act or other relevant legislation.

Because test takers have the right to be informed, prior to testing, about the test's purposes, the nature of the test, whether test results will be reported to the test takers, and the planned use of the results (when not in conflict with the testing purposes), testing professionals should:

Give or provide test takers with access to a brief description about the test purpose (e.g., diagnosis, placement, selection, etc.) and the kind(s) of tests and formats that will be used (e.g., individual/group, multiple-choice/free response/performance, timed/untimed, etc.), unless such information might be detrimental to the objectives of the test.

Tell test takers, prior to testing, about the planned use(s) of the test results. Upon request, the test taker should be given information about how long such test scores are typically kept on file and remain available.

Provide test takers, if requested, with information about any preventative measures that have been instituted to safeguard the accuracy of test scores. Such information would include any quality control procedures that are employed and some of the steps taken to prevent dishonesty in test performance.

Inform test takers, in advance of the testing, about required materials that must be brought to the test site (e.g., pencil, paper) and about any rules that allow or prohibit use of other materials (e.g., calculators).

Provide test takers, upon request, with general information about the appropriateness of the test for its intended purpose, to the extent that such information does not involve the release of proprietary information. (For example, the test taker might be told, "Scores on this test are useful in predicting how successful people will be in this kind of work" or "Scores on this test, along with other information, help us to determine if students are likely to benefit from this program.")

Provide test takers, upon request, with information about re-testing, including if it is possible to re-take the test or another version of it, and if so, how often, how soon, and under what conditions.

Provide test takers, upon request, with information about how the test will be scored and in what detail. On multiple-choice tests, this information might include suggestions for test taking and about the use of a correction for guessing. On tests scored using professional judgment (e.g., essay tests or projective techniques), a general description of the scoring procedures might be provided except when such information is proprietary or would tend to influence test performance inappropriately.

Inform test takers about the type of feedback and interpretation that is routinely provided, as well as what is available for a fee. Test takers have the right to request and receive information regarding whether or not they can obtain copies of their test answer sheets or their test materials, if they can have their scores verified, and if they may cancel their test results.

Provide test takers, prior to testing, either in the written instructions, in other written documents or orally, with answers to questions that test takers may have about basic test administration procedures.

Inform test takers, prior to testing, if questions from test takers will not be permitted during the testing process.

Provide test takers with information about the use of computers, calculators, or other equipment, if any, used in the testing and give them an opportunity to practice using such equipment, unless its unpracticed use is part of the test purpose, or practice would compromise the validity of the results, and to provide a testing accommodation for the use of such equipment, if needed.

Inform test takers that, if they have a disability, they have the right to request and receive accommodations or modifications in accordance with the provisions of the Americans with Disabilities Act and other relevant legislation.

Provide test takers with information that will be of use in making decisions if test takers have options regarding which tests, test forms or test formats to take.

Because that test takers have a right to be informed in advance when the test will be administered, if and when test results will be available, and if there is a fee for testing services that the test takers are expected to pay, test professionals should:

Notify test takers of the alteration in a timely manner if a previously announced testing schedule changes, provide a reasonable explanation for the change, and inform test takers of the new schedule. If there is a change, reasonable alternatives to the original schedule should be provided.

Inform test takers prior to testing about any anticipated fee for the testing process, as well as the fees associated with each component of the process, if the components can be separated.

Because test takers have the right to have their tests administered and interpreted by appropriately trained individuals, testing professionals should:

Know how to select the appropriate test for the intended purposes.

When testing persons with documented disabilities and other special characteristics that require special testing conditions and/or interpretation of results, have the skills and knowledge for such testing and interpretation.

Provide reasonable information regarding their qualifications, upon request.

Insure that test conditions, especially if unusual, do not unduly interfere with test performance. Test conditions will normally be similar to those used to standardize the test.

Provide candidates with a reasonable amount of time to complete the test, unless a test has a time limit.

Take reasonable actions to safeguard against fraudulent actions (e.g., cheating) that could place honest test takers at a disadvantage.

Because test takers have the right to be informed about why they are being asked to take particular tests, if a test is optional, and what the consequences are should they choose not to complete the test, testing professionals should:

Normally only engage in testing activities with test takers after the test takers have provided their informed consent to take a test, except when testing without consent has been mandated by law or governmental regulation, or when consent is implied by an action the test takers have already taken (e.g., such as when applying for employment and a personnel examination is mandated).

Explain to test takers why they should consider taking voluntary tests.

Explain, if a test taker refuses to take or complete a voluntary test, either orally or in writing, what the negative consequences may be to them for their decision to do so.

Promptly inform the test taker if a testing professional decides that there is a need to deviate from the testing services to which the test taker initially agreed (e.g., should the testing professional believe it would be wise to administer an additional test or an alternative test), and provide an explanation for the change.

Because test takers have a right to receive a written or oral explanation of their test results within a reasonable amount of time after testing and in commonly understood terms, testing professionals should:

Interpret test results in light of one or more additional considerations (e.g., disability, language proficiency), if those considerations are relevant to the purposes of the test and performance on the test, and are in accordance with current laws.

Provide, upon request, information to test takers about the sources used in interpreting their test results, including technical manuals, technical reports, norms, and a description of the comparison group, or additional information about the test taker(s).

Provide, upon request, recommendations to test takers about how they could improve their performance on the test, should they choose or be required to take the test again.

Provide, upon request, information to test takers about their options for obtaining a second interpretation of their results. Test takers may select an appropriately trained professional to provide this second opinion.

Provide test takers with the criteria used to determine a passing score, when individual test scores are reported and related to a pass–fail standard.

Inform test takers, upon request, how much their scores might change, should they elect to take the test again. Such information would include variation in test performance due to measurement error (e.g., the appropriate standard errors of measurement) and changes in performance over time with or without intervention (e.g., additional training or treatment).

Communicate test results to test takers in an appropriate and sensitive manner, without use of negative labels or comments likely to inflame or stigmatize the test taker.

Provide corrected test scores to test takers as rapidly as possible, should an error occur in the processing or reporting of scores. The length of time is often dictated by individuals responsible for processing or reporting the scores, rather than the individuals responsible for testing, should the two parties indeed differ.

Correct any errors as rapidly as possible if there are errors in the process of developing scores.

Because test takers have the right to have the results of tests kept confidential to the extent allowed by law, testing professionals should:

Insure that records of test results (in paper or electronic form) are safeguarded and maintained so that only individuals who have a legitimate right to access them will be able to do so.

Should provide test takers, upon request, with information regarding who has a legitimate right to access their test results (when individually identified) and in what form. Testing professionals should respond appropriately to questions regarding the reasons why such individuals may have access to test results and how they may use the results.

Advise test takers that they are entitled to limit access to their results (when individually identified) to those persons or institutions, and for those purposes, revealed to them prior to testing. Exceptions may occur when test takers, or their guardians, consent to release the test results to others or when testing professionals are authorized by law to release test results.

Keep confidential any requests for testing accommodations and the documentation supporting the request.

Because test takers have the right to present concerns about the testing process and to receive information about procedures that will be used to address such concerns, testing professionals should:

Inform test takers how they can question the results of the testing if they do not believe that the test was administered properly or scored correctly, or other such concerns.

Inform test takers of the procedures for appealing decisions that they believe are based in whole or in part on erroneous test results.

Inform test takers, if their test results are under investigation and may be canceled, invalidated, or not released for normal use. In such an event, that investigation should be performed in a timely manner. The investigation should use all available information that addresses the reason(s) for the investigation, and the test taker should also be informed of the information that he/she may need to provide to assist with the investigation.

Inform the test taker, if that test taker's test results are canceled or not released for normal use, why that action was taken. The test taker is entitled to request and receive information on the types of evidence and procedures that have been used to make that determination.

The Responsibilities of Test Takers:
Guidelines for Testing Professionals

Testing Professionals should take steps to ensure that test takers know that they have specific responsibilities in addition to their rights described above.

Testing professionals need to inform test takers that they should listen to and/or read their rights and responsibilities as a test taker and ask questions about issues they do not understand.

Testing professionals should take steps, as appropriate, to ensure that test takers know that they:

Are responsible for their behavior throughout the entire testing process.

Should not interfere with the rights of others involved in the testing process.

Should not compromise the integrity of the test and its interpretation in any manner.

Testing professionals should remind test takers that it is their responsibility to ask questions prior to testing if they are uncertain about why the test is being given, how it will be given, what they will be asked to do, and what will be done with the results. Testing professionals should:

Advise test takers that it is their responsibility to review materials supplied by test publishers and others as part of the testing process and to ask questions about areas that they feel they should understand better prior to the start of testing.

Inform test takers that it is their responsibility to request more information if they are not satisfied with what they know about how their test results will be used and what will be done with them.

Testing professionals should inform test takers that it is their responsibility to read descriptive material they receive in advance of a test and to listen carefully to test instructions. Testing professionals should inform test takers that it is their responsibility to inform an examiner in advance of testing if they wish to receive a testing accommodation or if they have a physical condition or illness that may interfere with their performance. Testing professionals should inform test takers that it is their responsibility to inform an examiner if they have difficulty comprehending the language in which the test is given. Testing professionals should:

Inform test takers that, if they need special testing arrangements, it is their responsibility to request appropriate accommodations and to provide any requested documentation as far in advance of the testing date as possible. Testing professionals should inform test takers about the documentation needed to receive a requested testing accommodation.

Inform test takers that, if they request but do not receive a testing accommodation, they could request information about why their request was denied.

Testing professionals should inform test takers when and where the test will be given, and whether payment for the testing is required. Having been so informed, it is the responsibility of the test taker to appear on time with any required materials, pay for testing services, and be ready to be tested. Testing professionals should:

Inform test takers that they are responsible for familiarizing themselves with the appropriate materials needed for testing and for requesting information about these materials, if needed.

Inform the test taker, if the testing situation requires that test takers bring materials (e.g., personal identification, pencils, calculators, etc.) to the testing site, of this responsibility to do so.

Testing professionals should advise test takers, prior to testing, that it is their responsibility to:

Listen to and/or read the directions given to them.

Follow instructions given by testing professionals.

Complete the test as directed.

Perform to the best of their ability if they want their score to be a reflection of their best effort.

Behave honestly (e.g., not cheating or assisting others who cheat).

Testing professionals should inform test takers about the consequences of not taking a test, should they choose not to take the test. Once so informed, it is the responsibility of the test taker to accept such consequences, and the testing professional should so inform the test takers. If test takers have questions regarding these consequences, it is their responsibility to ask questions of the testing professional, and the testing professional should so inform the test takers.

Testing professionals should inform test takers that it is their responsibility to notify appropriate persons, as specified by the testing organization, if they do not understand their results, or if they believe that testing conditions affected the results. Testing professionals should:

Provide information to test takers, upon request, about appropriate procedures for questioning or canceling their test scores or results, if relevant to the purposes of testing.

Provide to test takers, upon request, the procedures for reviewing, re-testing, or canceling their scores or test results, if they believe that testing conditions affected their results and if relevant to the purposes of testing.

Provide documentation to the test taker about known testing conditions that might have affected the results of the testing, if relevant to the purposes of testing.

Testing professionals should advise test takers that it is their responsibility to ask questions about the confidentiality of their test results, if this aspect concerns them.

Testing professionals should advise test takers that it is their responsibility to present concerns about the testing process in a timely, respectful manner.

Members of the JCTP Working Group on Test Taker Rights and Responsibilities:

   Kurt F. Geisinger, PhD (Co-Chair)

   William Schafer, EdD (Co-Chair)

   Gwyneth Boodoo, PhD

   Ruth Ekstrom, EdD

   Tom Fitzgibbon, PhD

   John Fremer, PhD

   Joanne Lenke, PhD

   Sharon Goldsmith, PhD

   Kevin Moreland, PhD

   Julie Noble, PhD

   James Sampson Jr., PhD

   Douglas Smith, PhD

   Nicholas Vacc, EdD

   Janet Wall, EdD

Staff liaisons: Heather Fox, PhD, and Lara Frumkin, PhD

APA Science HOME is

   American Psychological Association
   Science Directorate
   750 First Street, NE
   Washington, DC 20002-4242
   Phone: 202-336-6000 • Fax: 202-336-5953
   E-mail: Science Directorate
   PsychNET®
   © 2003 American Psychological Association

A P P E N D I X E

Standards for Teacher Competence in Educational Assessment of Students

Developed by the American Federation of Teachers, National Council on Measurement in Education, and National Education Association. This is not copyrighted material. Reproduction and dissemination are encouraged. 1990.

The professional education associations began working in 1987 to develop standards for teacher competence in student assessment out of concern that the potential educational benefits of student assessments be fully realized. The Committee[1] appointed to this project completed its work in 1990, following reviews of earlier drafts by members of the measurement, teaching, and teacher preparation and certification communities. Parallel committees of affected associations are encouraged to develop similar statements of qualifications for school administrators, counselors, testing directors, supervisors, and other educators in the near future. These statements are intended to guide the preservice and inservice preparation of educators, the accreditation of preparation programs, and the future certification of all educators.

A standard is defined here as a principle generally accepted by the professional associations responsible for this document. Assessment is defined as the process of obtaining information that is used to make educational decisions about students; to give feedback to students about their progress, strengths, and weaknesses; to judge instructional effectiveness and curricular adequacy; and to inform policy. The various assessment techniques include, but are not limited to, formal and informal observation, qualitative analysis of pupil performance and products, paper-and-pencil tests, oral questioning, and analysis of student records. The assessment competencies included here are the knowledge and skills critical to a teacher's role as educator. It is understood that there are many competencies beyond assessment competencies that teachers must possess.

By establishing standards for teacher competence in student assessment, the associations subscribe to the view that student assessment is an essential part of teaching and that good teaching cannot exist without good student assessment. Training to develop the competencies covered in the standards should be an integral part of preservice preparation. Further, such assessment training should be widely available to practicing teachers through staff development programs at the district and building levels. The standards are intended for use as:

- a guide for teacher educators as they design and approve programs for teacher preparation
- a self-assessment guide for teachers in identifying their needs for professional development in student assessment

[1]The Committee that developed this statement was appointed by the collaborating professional associations: James R. Sanders (Western Michigan University) chaired the Committee and represented NCME along with John R. Hills (Florida State University) and Anthony J. Nitko (University of Pittsburgh). Jack C. Merwin (University of Minnesota) represented the American Association of Colleges for Teacher Education, Carolyn Trice represented the American Federation of Teachers, and Marcella Dianda and Jeffrey Schneider represented the National Education Association.

- a guide for workshop instructors as they design professional development experiences for in-service teachers
- an impetus for educational measurement specialists and teacher trainers to conceptualize student assessment and teacher training in student assessment more broadly than has been the case in the past.

The standards should be incorporated into future teacher training and certification programs. Teachers who have not had the preparation these standards imply should have the opportunity and support to develop these competencies before the standards enter into the evaluation of these teachers.

The Approach Used to Develop the Standards

The members of the associations that supported this work are professional educators involved in teaching, teacher education, and student assessment. Members of these associations are concerned about the inadequacy with which teachers are prepared for assessing the educational progress of their students, and thus sought to address this concern effectively. A committee named by the associations first met in September 1987 and affirmed its commitment to defining standards for teacher preparation in student assessment. The committee then undertook a review of the research literature to identify needs in student assessment, current levels of teacher training in student assessment, areas of teacher activities requiring competence in using assessments, and current levels of teacher competence in student assessment.

The members of the committee used their collective experience and expertise to formulate and then revise statements of important assessment competencies. Drafts of these competencies went through several revisions by the Committee before the standards were released for public review. Comments by reviewers from each of the associations were then used to prepare a final statement.

The Scope of a Teacher's Professional Role
and Responsibilities for Student Assessment

There are seven standards in this document. In recognizing the critical need to revitalize classroom assessment, some standards focus on classroom-based competencies. Because of teachers' growing roles in education and policy decisions beyond the classroom, other standards address assessment competencies underlying teacher participation in decisions related to assessment at the school, district, state, and national levels.

The scope of a teacher's professional role and responsibilities for student assessment may be described in terms of the following activities. These activities imply that teachers need competence in student assessment and sufficient time and resources to complete them in a professional manner.

Activities Occurring Prior to Instruction
(a) Understanding students' cultural backgrounds, interests, skills, and abilities as they apply across a range of learning domains and/or subject areas;
(b) Understanding students' motivations and their interests in specific class content;
(c) Clarifying and articulating the performance outcomes expected of pupils; and
(d) Planning instruction for individuals or groups of students.

Activities Occurring during Instruction
(a) Monitoring pupil progress toward instructional goals;
(b) Identifying gains and difficulties pupils are experiencing in learning and performing;
(c) Adjusting instruction;

(d) Giving contingent, specific, and credible praise and feedback;

(e) Motivating students to learn; and

(f) Judging the extent of pupil attainment of instructional outcomes.

Activities Occurring after the Appropriate Instructional Segment (e.g. lesson, class, semester, grade)

(a) Describing the extent to which each pupil has attained both short- and long-term instructional goals;

(b) Communicating strengths and weaknesses based on assessment results to students, and parents or guardians;

(c) Recording and reporting assessment results for school-level analysis, evaluation, and decision making;

(d) Analyzing assessment information gathered before and during instruction to understand each students' progress to date and to inform future instructional planning;

(e) Evaluating the effectiveness of instruction; and

(f) Evaluating the effectiveness of the curriculum and materials in use.

Activities Associated with a Teacher's Involvement in School Building and School District Decision Making

(a) Serving on a school or district committee examining the school's and district's strengths and weaknesses in the development of its students;

(b) Working on the development or selection of assessment methods for school building or school district use;

(c) Evaluating school district curriculum; and

(d) Other related activities.

Activities Associated with a Teacher's Involvement in a Wider Community of Educators

(a) Serving on a state committee asked to develop learning goals and associated assessment methods;

(b) Participating in reviews of the appropriateness of district, state, or national student goals and associated assessment methods; and

(c) Interpreting the results of state and national student assessment programs.

Each standard that follows is an expectation for assessment knowledge or skill that a teacher should possess in order to perform well in the five areas just described. As a set, the standards call on teachers to demonstrate skill at selecting, developing, applying, using, communicating, and evaluating student assessment information and student assessment practices. A brief rationale and illustrative behaviors follow each standard.

The standards represent a conceptual framework or scaffolding from which specific skills can be derived. Work to make these standards operational will be needed even after they have been published. It is also expected that experience in the application of these standards should lead to their improvement and further development.

Standards for Teacher Competence in Educational Assessment of Students

1. Teachers should be skilled in choosing assessment methods appropriate for instructional decisions. Skills in choosing appropriate, useful, administratively convenient, technically adequate, and fair assessment methods are prerequisite to good use of information to support instructional decisions.

Teachers need to be well-acquainted with the kinds of information provided by a broad range of assessment alternatives and their strengths and weaknesses. In particular, they should be familiar with criteria for evaluating and selecting assessment methods in light of instructional plans.

Teachers who meet this standard will have the conceptual and application skills that follow. They will be able to use the concepts of assessment error and validity when developing or selecting their approaches to classroom assessment of students. They will understand how valid assessment data can support instructional activities such as providing appropriate feedback to students, diagnosing group and individual learning needs, planning for individualized educational programs, motivating students, and evaluating instructional procedures. They will understand how invalid information can affect instructional decisions about students. They will also be able to use and evaluate assessment options available to them, considering among other things, the cultural, social, economic, and language backgrounds of students. They will be aware that different assessment approaches can be incompatible with certain instructional goals and may impact quite differently on their teaching.

Teachers will know, for each assessment approach they use, its appropriateness for making decisions about their pupils. Moreover, teachers will know of where to find information about and/ or reviews of various assessment methods. Assessment options are diverse and include text- and curriculum-embedded questions and tests, standardized criterion-referenced and norm-referenced tests, oral questioning, spontaneous and structured performance assessments, portfolios, exhibitions, demonstrations, rating scales, writing samples, paper-and-pencil tests, seatwork and homework, peer- and self-assessments, student records, observations, questionnaires, interviews, projects, products, and others' opinions.

2.   Teachers should be skilled in developing assessment methods appropriate for instructional decisions. Although teachers often use published or other external assessment tools, the bulk of the assessment information they use for decision making comes from approaches they create and implement. Indeed, the assessment demands of the classroom go well beyond readily available instruments.

Teachers who meet this standard will have the conceptual and application skills that follow. Teachers will be skilled in planning the collection of information that facilitates the decisions they will make. They will know and follow appropriate principles for developing and using assessment methods in their teaching, avoiding common pitfalls in student assessment. Such techniques may include several of the options listed at the end of the first standard. The teacher will select the techniques that are appropriate to the intent of the teacher's instruction.

Teachers meeting this standard will also be skilled in using student data to analyze the quality of each assessment technique they use. Because most teachers do not have access to assessment specialists, they must be prepared to do these analyses themselves.

3.   The teacher should be skilled in administering, scoring, and interpreting the results of both externally produced and teacher-produced assessment methods. It is not enough that teachers are able to select and develop good assessment methods; they must also be able to apply them properly. Teachers should be skilled in administering, scoring, and interpreting results from diverse assessment methods. Teachers who meet this standard will have the conceptual and application skills that follow. They will be skilled in interpreting informal and formal teacher-produced assessment results, including pupils' performances in class and on homework assignments. Teachers will be able to use guides for scoring essay questions and projects, stencils for scoring response-choice questions, and scales for rating performance assessments. They will be able to use these in ways that produce consistent results. Teachers will be able to administer standardized achievement tests and be able to interpret the commonly reported scores: percentile ranks, percentile band scores, standard scores, and grade equivalents. They will have a conceptual understanding of the summary indexes commonly reported with assessment results: measures of central tendency, dispersion, relationships, reliability, and errors of measurement.

Teachers will be able to apply these concepts of score and summary indices in ways that enhance their use of the assessments that they develop. They will be able to analyze assessment results to identify pupils' strengths and errors. If they get inconsistent results, they will seek other explanations for the discrepancy or other data to attempt to resolve the uncertainty before arriving at a decision. They will be able to use assessment methods in ways that encourage students' educational development and that do not inappropriately increase students' anxiety levels.

4.   **Teachers should be skilled in using assessment results when making decisions about individual students, planning teaching, developing curriculum, and school improvement.** Assessment results are used to make educational decisions at several levels: in the classroom about students, in the community about a school and a school district, and in society, generally, about the purposes and outcomes of the educational enterprise. Teachers play a vital role when participating in decision making at each of these levels and must be able to use assessment results effectively.

Teachers who meet this standard will have the conceptual and application skills that follow. They will be able to use accumulated assessment information to organize a sound instructional plan for facilitating students' educational development. When using assessment results to plan and/or evaluate instruction and curriculum, teachers will interpret the results correctly and avoid common misinterpretations, such as basing decisions on scores that lack curriculum validity. They will be informed about the results of local, regional, state, and national assessments and about their appropriate use for pupil, classroom, school, district, state, and national educational improvement.

5.   **Teachers should be skilled in developing valid pupil grading procedures that use pupil assessments.** Grading students is an important part of professional practice for teachers. Grading is defined as indicating both a student's level of performance and a teacher's valuing of that performance. The principles for using assessments to obtain valid grades are known and teachers should employ them.

Teachers who meet this standard will have the conceptual and application skills that follow. They will be able to devise, implement, and explain a procedure for developing grades composed of marks from various assignments, projects, inclass activities, quizzes, tests, and/or other assessments that they may use. Teachers will understand and be able to articulate why the grades they assign are rational, justified, and fair, acknowledging that such grades reflect their preferences and judgments. Teachers will be able to recognize and to avoid faulty grading procedures such as using grades as punishment. They will be able to evaluate and to modify their grading procedures in order to improve the validity of the interpretations made from them about students' attainments.

6.   **Teachers should be skilled in communicating assessment results to students, parents, other lay audiences, and other educators.** Teachers must routinely report assessment results to students and to parents or guardians. In addition, they are frequently asked to report or to discuss assessment results with other educators and with diverse lay audiences. If the results are not communicated effectively, they may be misused or not used. To communicate effectively with others on matters of student assessment, teachers must be able to use assessment terminology appropriately and must be able to articulate the meaning, limitations, and implications of assessment results. Furthermore, teachers will sometimes be in a position that will require them to defend their own assessment procedures and their interpretations of them. At other times, teachers may need to help the public to interpret assessment results appropriately.

Teachers who meet this standard will have the conceptual and application skills that follow. Teachers will understand and be able to give appropriate explanations of how the interpretation of student assessments must be moderated by the student's socioeconomic, cultural, language, and other background factors. Teachers will be able to explain that assessment results do not imply that such background factors limit a student's ultimate educational development. They will be able to communicate to students and to their parents or guardians how they may assess the student's educational progress. Teachers will understand and be able to explain the importance of taking measurement errors into account when using assessments to make decisions about individual students. Teachers will be able to explain the limitations of different informal and formal assessment methods. They will be able to explain printed reports of the results of pupil assessments at the classroom, school district, state, and national levels.

7. Teachers should be skilled in recognizing unethical, illegal, and otherwise inappropriate assessment methods and uses of assessment information. Fairness, the rights of all concerned, and professional ethical behavior must undergird all student assessment activities, from the initial planning for and gathering of information to the interpretation, use, and communication of the results. Teachers must be well-versed in their own ethical and legal responsibilities in assessment. In addition, they should also attempt to have the inappropriate assessment practices of others discontinued whenever they are encountered. Teachers should also participate with the wider educational community in defining the limits of appropriate professional behavior in assessment.

Teachers who meet this standard will have the conceptual and application skills that follow. They will know those laws and case decisions that affect their classroom, school district, and state assessment practices. Teachers will be aware that various assessment procedures can be misused or overused resulting in harmful consequences such as embarrassing students, violating a student's right to confidentiality, and inappropriately using students' standardized achievement test scores to measure teaching effectiveness.

Invitation to Users

The associations invite comments from users that may be used for improvement of this document. Comments may be sent to:

Teacher Standards in Student Assessment
American Federation of Teachers
555 New Jersey Avenue, NW
Washington, DC 20001

Teacher Standards in Student Assessment
National Council on Measurement in Education
1230 Seventeenth Street, NW
Washington, DC 20036

Teacher Standards in Student Assessment
Instruction and Professional Development
National Education Association
1201 Sixteenth Street, NW
Washington, DC 20036

APPENDIX F

Proportions of Area under the Normal Curve

Table F.1 Proportions of Area Under the Normal Curve

(a) Value of ±z	(b)	(c)	(a) Value of ±z	(b)	(c)	(a) Value of ±z	(b)	(c)
.00	.0000	.5000	.28	.1103	.3897	.56	.2123	.2877
.01	.0040	.4960	.29	.1141	.3859	.57	.2157	.2843
.02	.0080	.4920	.30	.1179	.3821	.58	.2190	.2810
.03	.0120	.4880	.31	.1217	.3783	.59	.2224	.2776
.04	.0160	.4840	.32	.1255	.3745	.60	.2257	.2743
.05	.0199	.4801	.33	.1293	.3707	.61	.2291	.2709
.06	.0239	.4761	.34	.1331	.3669	.62	.2324	.2676
.07	.0279	.4721	.35	.1368	.3632	.63	.2357	.2643
.08	.0319	.4681	.36	.1406	.3594	.64	.2389	.2611
.09	.0359	.4641	.37	.1443	.3557	.65	.2422	.2578
.10	.0398	.4602	.38	.1480	.3520	.66	.2454	.2546
.11	.0438	.4562	.39	.1517	.3483	.67	.2486	.2514
.12	.0478	.4522	.40	.1554	.3446	.68	.2517	.2483
.13	.0517	.4483	.41	.1591	.3409	.69	.2549	.2451
.14	.0557	.4443	.42	.1628	.3372	.70	.2580	.2420
.15	.0596	.4404	.43	.1664	.3336	.71	.2611	.2389
.16	.0636	.4364	.44	.1700	.3300	.72	.2642	.2358
.17	.0675	.4325	.45	.1736	.3264	.73	.2673	.2327
.18	.0714	.4286	.46	.1772	.3228	.74	.2704	.2296
.19	.0753	.4247	.47	.1808	.3192	.75	.2734	.2266
.20	.0793	.4207	.48	.1844	.3156	.76	.2764	.2236
.21	.0832	.4168	.49	.1879	.3121	.77	.2794	.2206
.22	.0871	.4129	.50	.1915	.3085	.78	.2823	.2177
.23	.0910	.4090	.51	.1950	.3050	.79	.2852	.2148
.24	.0948	.4052	.52	.1985	.3015	.80	.2881	.2119
.25	.0987	.4013	.53	.2019	.2981	.81	.2910	.2090
.26	.1026	.3974	.54	.2054	.2946	.82	.2939	.2061
.27	.1064	.3936	.55	.2088	.2912	.83	.2967	.2033

(continued)

TABLE F.1   Continued

(a) Value of +z / −z	(b)	(c)	(a) Value of +z / −z	(b)	(c)	(a) Value of +z / −z	(b)	(c)
.84	.2995	.2005	1.53	.4370	.0630	2.22	.4868	.0132
.85	.3023	.1977	1.54	.4382	.0618	2.23	.4871	.0129
.86	.3051	.1949	1.55	.4394	.0606	2.24	.4875	.0125
.87	.3078	.1922	1.56	.4406	.0594	2.25	.4878	.0122
.88	.3106	.1894	1.57	.4418	.0582	2.26	.4881	.0119
.89	.3133	.1867	1.58	.4429	.0571	2.27	.4884	.0116
.90	.3159	.1841	1.59	.4441	.0559	2.28	.4887	.0113
.91	.3186	.1814	1.60	.4452	.0548	2.29	.4890	.0110
.92	.3212	.1788	1.61	.4463	.0537	2.30	.4893	.0107
.93	.3238	.1762	1.62	.4474	.0526	2.31	.4896	.0104
.94	.3264	.1736	1.63	.4484	.0516	2.32	.4898	.0102
.95	.3289	.1711	1.64	.4495	.0505	2.33	.4901	.0099
.96	.3315	.1685	1.65	.4505	.0495	2.34	.4904	.0096
.97	.3340	.1660	1.66	.4515	.0485	2.35	.4906	.0094
.98	.3365	.1635	1.67	.4525	.0475	2.36	.4909	.0091
.99	.3389	.1611	1.68	.4535	.0465	2.37	.4911	.0089
1.00	.3413	.1587	1.69	.4545	.0455	2.38	.4913	.0087
1.01	.3438	.1562	1.70	.4554	.0446	2.39	.4916	.0084
1.02	.3461	.1539	1.71	.4564	.0436	2.40	.4918	.0082
1.03	.3485	.1515	1.72	.4573	.0427	2.41	.4920	.0080
1.04	.3508	.1492	1.73	.4582	.0418	2.42	.4922	.0078
1.05	.3531	.1469	1.74	.4591	.0409	2.43	.4925	.0075
1.06	.3554	.1446	1.75	.4599	.0401	2.44	.4927	.0073
1.07	.3577	.1423	1.76	.4608	.0392	2.45	.4929	.0071
1.08	.3599	.1401	1.77	.4616	.0384	2.46	.4931	.0069
1.09	.3621	.1379	1.78	.4625	.0375	2.47	.4932	.0068
1.10	.3643	.1357	1.79	.4633	.0367	2.48	.4934	.0066
1.11	.3665	.1335	1.80	.4641	.0359	2.49	.4936	.0064
1.12	.3686	.1314	1.81	.4649	.0351	2.50	.4938	.0062

z			z			z		
1.13	.3708	.1292	1.82	.4656	.0344	2.51	.4940	.0060
1.14	.3729	.1271	1.83	.4664	.0336	2.52	.4941	.0059
1.15	.3749	.1251	1.84	.4671	.0329	2.53	.4943	.0057
1.16	.3770	.1230	1.85	.4678	.0322	2.54	.4945	.0055
1.17	.3790	.1210	1.86	.4686	.0314	2.55	.4946	.0054
1.18	.3810	.1190	1.87	.4693	.0307	2.56	.4948	.0052
1.19	.3830	.1170	1.88	.4699	.0301	2.57	.4949	.0051
1.20	.3849	.1151	1.89	.4706	.0294	2.58	.4951	.0049
1.21	.3869	.1131	1.90	.4713	.0287	2.59	.4952	.0048
1.22	.3888	.1112	1.91	.4719	.0281	2.60	.4953	.0047
1.23	.3907	.1093	1.92	.4726	.0274	2.61	.4955	.0045
1.24	.3925	.1075	1.93	.4732	.0268	2.62	.4956	.0044
1.25	.3944	.1056	1.94	.4738	.0262	2.63	.4957	.0043
1.26	.3962	.1038	1.95	.4744	.0256	2.64	.4959	.0041
1.27	.3980	.1020	1.96	.4750	.0250	2.65	.4960	.0040
1.28	.3997	.1003	1.97	.4756	.0244	2.66	.4961	.0039
1.29	.4015	.0985	1.98	.4761	.0239	2.67	.4962	.0038
1.30	.4032	.0968	1.99	.4767	.0233	2.68	.4963	.0037
1.31	.4049	.0951	2.00	.4772	.0228	2.69	.4964	.0036
1.32	.4066	.0934	2.01	.4778	.0222	2.70	.4965	.0035
1.33	.4082	.0918	2.02	.4783	.0217	2.71	.4966	.0034
1.34	.4099	.0901	2.03	.4788	.0212	2.72	.4967	.0033
1.35	.4115	.0885	2.04	.4793	.0207	2.73	.4968	.0032
1.36	.4131	.0869	2.05	.4798	.0202	2.74	.4969	.0031
1.37	.4147	.0853	2.06	.4803	.0197	2.75	.4970	.0030
1.38	.4162	.0838	2.07	.4808	.0192	2.76	.4971	.0029
1.39	.4177	.0823	2.08	.4812	.0188	2.77	.4972	.0028
1.40	.4192	.0808	2.09	.4817	.0183	2.78	.4973	.0027
1.41	.4207	.0793	2.10	.4821	.0179	2.79	.4974	.0026
1.42	.4222	.0778	2.11	.4826	.0174	2.80	.4974	.0026
1.43	.4236	.0764	2.12	.4830	.0170	2.81	.4975	.0025
1.44	.4251	.0749	2.13	.4834	.0166	2.82	.4976	.0024
1.45	.4265	.0735	2.14	.4838	.0162	2.83	.4977	.0023
1.46	.4279	.0721	2.15	.4842	.0158	2.84	.4977	.0023
1.47	.4292	.0708	2.16	.4846	.0154	2.85	.4978	.0022
1.48	.4306	.0694	2.17	.4850	.0150	2.86	.4979	.0021
1.49	.4319	.0681	2.18	.4854	.0146	2.87	.4979	.0021
1.50	.4332	.0668	2.19	.4857	.0143	2.88	.4980	.0020
1.51	.4345	.0655	2.20	.4861	.0139	2.89	.4981	.0019
1.52	.4357	.0643	2.21	.4864	.0136	2.90	.4981	.0019

(continued)

TABLE F.1 Continued

Value of +z (−z)	(b)	(c)	Value of +z (−z)	(b)	(c)	Value of +z (−z)	(b)	(c)
2.91	.4982	.0018	3.18	.4993	.0007	3.45	.4997	.0003
2.92	.4982	.0018	3.19	.4993	.0007	3.46	.4997	.0003
2.93	.4983	.0017	3.20	.4993	.0007	3.47	.4997	.0003
2.94	.4984	.0016	3.21	.4993	.0007	3.48	.4997	.0003
2.95	.4984	.0015	3.22	.4994	.0006	3.49	.4998	.0002
2.96	.4985	.0015	3.23	.4994	.0006	3.50	.4998	.0002
2.97	.4985	.0014	3.24	.4994	.0006	3.51	.4998	.0002
2.98	.4986	.0014	3.25	.4994	.0006	3.52	.4998	.0002
2.99	.4986	.0013	3.26	.4994	.0006	3.53	.4998	.0002
3.00	.4987	.0013	3.27	.4995	.0005	3.54	.4998	.0002
3.01	.4987	.0013	3.28	.4995	.0005	3.55	.4998	.0002
3.02	.4987	.0013	3.29	.4995	.0005	3.56	.4998	.0002
3.03	.4988	.0012	3.30	.4995	.0005	3.57	.4998	.0002
3.04	.4988	.0012	3.31	.4995	.0005	3.58	.4998	.0002
3.05	.4989	.0011	3.32	.4995	.0005	3.59	.4998	.0002
3.06	.4989	.0011	3.33	.4996	.0004	3.60	.4998	.0002
3.07	.4989	.0011	3.34	.4996	.0004	3.61	.4998	.0002
3.08	.4990	.0010	3.35	.4996	.0004	3.62	.4999	.0001
3.09	.4990	.0010	3.36	.4996	.0004	3.63	.4999	.0001
3.10	.4990	.0010	3.37	.4996	.0004	3.64	.4999	.0001
3.11	.4991	.0009	3.38	.4996	.0004	3.65	.4999	.0001
3.12	.4991	.0009	3.39	.4997	.0003	3.66	.4999	.0001
3.13	.4991	.0009	3.40	.4997	.0003	3.67	.4999	.0001
3.14	.4992	.0008	3.41	.4997	.0003	3.68	.4999	.0001
3.15	.4992	.0008	3.42	.4997	.0003	3.69	.4999	.0001
3.16	.4992	.0008	3.43	.4997	.0003	3.70	.4999	.0001
3.17	.4992	.0008	3.44	.4997	.0003			

APPENDIX G

Answers to Practice Problems

Chapter 2

1. Calculate the mean, variance, and standard deviation for the following score distributions.

Distribution 1	*Distribution 2*	*Distribution 3*
Mean = 7.267	Mean = 5.467	Mean = 5.20
Variance = 3.3956	Variance = 5.182	Variance = 4.427
SD = 1.8427	SD = 2.276	SD = 2.104

2. Calculate the Pearson Correlation Coefficient for the following pairs of scores.

   Sample 1: $r = 0.631$

   Sample 2: $r = 0.886$

   Sample 3: $r = 0.26$

Chapter 3

1. Transform the following raw scores to the specified standard score formats. The raw score distribution has a mean of 70 and a standard deviation of 10.

   a. Raw score = 85 z-score = 1.5 T-score = 65
   b. Raw score = 60 z-score = −1.0 T-score = 40
   c. Raw score = 55 z-score = −1.5 T-score = 35
   d. Raw score = 95 z-score = 2.5 T-score = 75
   e. Raw score = 75 z-score = 0.5 T-score = 55

2. Convert the following z-scores to T-scores and CEEB scores.

   a. z-score = 1.5 T-score = 65   CEEB score = 650
   b. z-score = −1.5 T-score = 35   CEEB score = 350
   c. z-score = 2.5 T-score = 75   CEEB score = 750
   d. z-score = −2.0 T-score = 30   CEEB score = 300
   e. z-score = −1.70 T-score = 33   CEEB score = 330

Chapter 4

1. Calculating KR 20:

	Item 1	Item 2	Item 3	Item 4	Item 5	Total Score
Student 1	0	1	1	0	1	3
Student 2	1	1	1	1	1	5

(continued)

475

	Item 1	Item 2	Item 3	Item 4	Item 5	Total Score
Student 3	1	0	1	0	0	2
Student 4	0	0	0	1	0	1
Student 5	1	1	1	1	1	5
Student 6	1	1	0	1	0	3
p_i	0.6667	0.6667	0.6667	0.6667	0.5	$SD^2 = 2.1389$
q_i	0.3333	0.3333	0.3333	0.3333	0.5	
$p_i \times q_i$	0.2222	0.2222	0.2222	0.2222	0.25	

$$\sum p_i \times q_i = 0.2222 + 0.2222 + 0.2222 + 0.2222 + 0.25$$

$$\sum p_i \times q_i = 1.1388$$

$$\begin{aligned} KR\ 20 &= 5/4 \times (2.1389 - 1.1388/2.139) \\ &= 1.25 \times (1.0001/2.1389) \\ &= 1.25 \times (0.4675) \\ &= 0.58 \end{aligned}$$

2. Calculating Coefficient alpha:

	Item 1	Item 2	Item 3	Item 4	Item 5	Total Score
Student 1	4	5	4	5	4	23
Student 2	3	3	2	3	2	13
Student 3	2	3	1	2	1	9
Student 4	4	4	5	5	4	22
Student 5	2	3	2	2	3	12
Student 6	1	2	2	1	3	9
SDi^2	1.2222	0.8889	1.8889	2.3333	1.6667	$SD^2 = 32.89$

$$\begin{aligned} \text{Coefficient alpha} &= 5/4 \times \left(1 - \frac{1.2222 + 0.8889 + 1.8889 + 2.3333 + 1.6667}{32.89}\right) \\ &= 1.25 \times (1 - 8/32.89) \\ &= 1.25 \times (1 - 0.2432) \\ &= 1.25 \times (0.7568) \\ &= 0.946 \end{aligned}$$

REFERENCES

Achenbach, T. M. (1991a). *Manual for the Child Behavior Checklists/4–18 and 1991 profile.* Burlington: University of Vermont, Department of Psychiatry.

Achenbach, T. M. (1991b). *Manual for the Teacher's Report Form and 1991 profile.* Burlington: University of Vermont, Department of Psychiatry.

Achenbach, T. M. (1991c). *Manual for the Youth Self-Report and 1991 profile.* Burlington: University of Vermont, Department of Psychiatry.

Aiken, L. R. (1982). Writing multiple-choice items to measure higher-order educational objectives. *Educational & Psychological Measurement, 42,* 803–806.

Aiken, L. R. (2000). *Psychological testing and assessment.* Boston: Allyn & Bacon.

Alley, G., & Foster, C. (1978). Nondiscriminatory testing of minority and exceptional children. *Focus on Exceptional Children, 9,* 1–14.

American Educational Research Association (2000). *AERA position statement concerning high-stakes testing in preK–12 education.* Retrieved September 13, 2003, from www.aera .net/about/policy/stakes.htm

American Educational Research Association, American Psychological Association, & National Council on Measurement in Education (1999). *Standards for educational and psychological testing.* Washington, DC: American Educational Research Association.

American Federation of Teachers, National Council on Measurement in Education, & National Education Association (1990). *Standards for teacher competence in educational assessment of students.* Washington, DC: American Federation of Teachers.

American Psychiatric Association (1994). *The diagnostic and statistical manual of mental disorders* (4th ed.). Washington, DC: Author

American Psychological Association (1954). Technical recommendations for psychological tests and diagnostic techniques. *Psychological Bulletin, 51*(2, pt. 2).

American Psychological Association (1966). *Standards for educational and psychological tests and manuals.* Washington, DC: Author.

America Psychological Association (1993, January). Call for book proposals for test instruments. *APA Monitor, 24,* 12.

American Psychological Association, American Educational Research Association, & National Council on Measurement in Education (1974). *Standards for educational and psychological testing.* Washington, DC: Author.

American Psychological Association, American Educational Research Association, & National Council on Measurement in Education (1985). *Standards for educational and psychological testing.* Washington, DC: Author.

Amrein, A. L., & Berliner, D. C. (2002). High-stakes testing, uncertainty, and student learning. *Education Policy Analysis Archives, 10*(18). Retrieved May 11, 2003, from http://epaa .asu.edu/epaa/v10n18.

Anastasi, A., & Urbina, S. (1997). *Psychological testing* (7th ed.). Upper Saddle River, NJ: Prentice Hall.

American Psychological Association (2004). Testing and assessment: FAQ/Finding information about psychological tests [On-line]. Retrieved December 1, 2004, from www.apa.org/ science/faq-findtests.html#findinfo

Beck, M. D. (1978). The effect of item response changes on scores on an elementary reading achievement test. *Journal of Educational Research, 71,* 153–156.

Bloom, B., Englehart, M., Furst, E., Hill, W., & Krathwohl, D. (1956). *Taxonomy of educational objectives: The classification of educational goals. Handbook I: Cognitive domain.* White Plains, NY: Longman.

Boser, U. (1999). Study finds mismatch between California standards and assessments. *Education Week, 18,* 10.

Boston, C. (2001). The debate over national testing. (Report No. EDO-TM-01-02). College Park, MD: ERIC Clearinghouse on Assessment and Evaluation. (ERIC No. ED 458214).

Braden, J. P. (1997). The practical impact of intellectual assessment issues. *School Psychology Review, 26,* 242–248.

Brookhart, S. M. (2004). *Grading.* Upper Saddle River, NJ: Pearson Merrill Prentice Hall.

Brown, R. T., Reynolds, C. R., & Whitaker, J. S. (1999). Bias in mental testing since "Bias in Mental Testing." *School Psychology Quarterly, 14,* 208–238.

Camilli, G., & Shepard, L. A. (1994). *Methods for identifying biased test items.* Thousand Oaks, CA: Sage.

Campell, D. T., & Fiske, D. W. (1959). Convergent and discriminant validation by the multitrait-multimethod matrix. *Psychological Bulletin, 56,* 546–553.

Cannell, J. J. (1988). Nationally normed elementary achievement testing in America's public schools: How all 50 states are above average. *Educational Measurement: Issues and Practice, 7,* 5–9.

Cannell, J. J. (1989). *The "Lake Wobegon" report: How public educators cheat on standardized achievement tests.* Albuquerque, NM: Friends for Education.

Canter, A. S. (1997). The future of intelligence testing in the schools. *School Psychology Review, 26,* 255–261.

Ceperley, P. E., & Reel, K. (1997). The impetus for the Tennessee value-added accountability system. In J. Millman (Ed.), *Grading teachers, grading schools,* (pp. 133–136). Thousand Oaks, CA: Corwin Press.

Chan, D., Schmitt, N., DeShon, R. P., Cluase, C. S., & Delbridge, K. (1997). Reaction to cognitive ability tests: The relationship between race, test performance, face validity, and test-taking motivation. *Journal of Applied Psychology, 82,* 300–310.

Chandler, L. A. (1990). The projective hypothesis and the development of projective techniques for children. In C. R. Reynolds

& R. Kamphaus (Eds.), *Handbook of psychological and educational assessment of children: Personality, behavior, and context* (pp. 55–69). New York: Guilford Press.

Chase, C. (1979). The impact of achievement expectations and handwriting quality on scoring essay tests. *Journal of Educational Measurement, 16,* 39–42.

Chinn, P. C. (1979). The exceptional minority child: Issues and some answers. *Exceptional Children, 46,* 532–536.

Chipman, S., Nichols, P., & Brennan, R. (1995). Introduction. In P. Nichols, S. Chipman, & R. Brennan (Eds.), *Cognitively diagnostic assessment* (pp. 1–18). Hillsdale, NJ: Erlbaum.

Cizek, G. J. (1998). Filling in the blanks: Putting standardized tests to the test. *Fordham Report, 2*(11).

Cleary, T. A., Humphreys, L. G., Kendrick, S. A., & Wesman, A. (1975). Educational uses of tests with disadvantaged students. *American Psychologist, 30,* 15–41.

Coffman, W. (1972). On the reliability of ratings of essay examinations. *NCME Measurement in Education, 3,* 1–7.

Coffman, W., & Kurfman, D. (1968). A comparison of two methods of reading essay examinations. *American Educational Research Journal, 5,* 99–107.

Cohen, J. (1988). *Statistical power analysis for the behavioral sciences* (2nd ed.). Hillsdale, NJ: Erlbaum.

Cohen, R. C., & Swerdlik, M. E. (2002). *Psychological testing and assessment: An introduction to tests and measurement.* New York: McGraw-Hill.

Cole, N. S., & Moss, P. A. (1989). Bias in test use. In R. L. Linn (Ed.), *Educational measurement* (3rd ed., pp. 201–219). Upper Saddle River, NJ: Merrill Prentice Hall.

Conners, C. K. (1997). *Conners' Rating Scales—Revised.* North Tonawanda, NY: Multi-Health Systems.

Costin, F. (1970). The optimal number of alternatives in multiple-choice achievement tests: Some empirical evidence for a mathematical proof. *Educational & Psychological Measurement, 30,* 353–358.

Cronbach, L. J. (1950). Further evidence on response sets and test design. *Educational & Psychological Measurement, 10,* 3–31.

Cronbach, L. J. (1951). Coefficient alpha and the internal structure of tests. *Psychometrika, 16,* 297–334.

Cronbach, L. J. (1990). *Essentials of psychological testing* (5th ed.). New York: HarperCollins.

Cronbach, L. J., & Furby, L. (1970). How we should measure change—Or should we? *Psychological Bulletin, 52,* 281–302.

Cronbach, L. J., & Gleser, G. C. (1965). *Psychological tests and personnel decisions* (2nd ed.). Champaign: University of Illinois Press.

CTB/Macmillan/McGraw-Hill. (1993). *California Achievement Tests/5.* Monterey, CA: Author.

Deiderich, P. B. (1973). *Short-cut statistics for teacher-made tests.* Princeton, NJ: Educational Testing Service.

Doherty, K. M. (2002). Education issues: Assessment. *Education Week on the web.* Retrieved May 14, 2003, from www.edweek.org/context/topics/issuespage.cfm?id=41

Ebel, R. L. (1970). The case for true–false items. *School Review, 78,* 373–389.

Ebel, R. L. (1971). How to write true–false items. *Educational & Psychological Measurement, 31,* 417–426.

Educational Testing Services (1973). *Making the classroom test: A guide for teachers.* Princeton, NJ: Author.

Engelhart, M. D. (1965). A comparison of several item discrimination indices. *Journal of Educational Measurement, 2,* 69–76.

Exner, J. E. (1974). *The Rorschach: A comprehensive system, I.* New York: Wiley.

Exner, J. E. (1978). *The Rorschach: A comprehensive system, II.* New York: Wiley.

Feldt, L. (1997). Can validity rise when reliability declines? *Applied Measurement in Education, 10,* 377–387.

Feldt, L. S., & Brennan, R. L. (1989). Reliability. In R. L. Linn (Ed.), *Educational measurement* (3rd ed., pp. 105–146). Upper Saddle River, NJ: Merrill Prentice Hall.

Finch, A. J., & Belter, R. W. (1993). Projective techniques. In T. H. Ollendick and M. Hersen (Eds.), *Handbook of child and adolescent assessment* (pp. 224–238). Boston: Allyn & Bacon.

Flaugher, R. L. (1978). The many definitions of test bias. *American Psychologist, 33,* 671–679.

Fletcher, J. M., Foorman, B. R., Boudousquie, A., Barnes, M. A., Schatschneider, C., & Francis, D. J. (2002). Assessment of reading and learning disabilities: A research based intervention-oriented approach. *Journal of School Psychology, 40,* 27–63.

Flynn, J. R. (1998). IQ gains over time: Toward finding the causes. In U. Neisser (Ed.), *The rising curve: Long-term gains in IQ and related measures,* pp. 25–66. Washington, DC: American Psychological Association.

Friedenberg, L. (1995). *Psychological testing: Design, analysis, and use.* Boston: Allyn & Bacon.

Frisbie, D. A. (1992). The multiple true–false format: A status review. *Educational Measurement: Issues and Practice, 11,* 21–26.

Fuchs, L. S. (2002). Best practices in providing accommodations for assessment. In A. Thomas & J. Grimes (Eds.), *Best practices in school psychology* (Vol. IV, pp. 899–909). Bethesda, MD: National Association of School Psychologists.

Fuchs, L. S., Fuchs, D., Eaton, S. B., Hamlett, C., Binkley, E., & Crouch, R. (2000). Using objective data sources to enhance teacher judgments about test accommodations. *Exceptional Children, 67,* 67–81.

Fuchs, L. S., Fuchs, D., Eaton, S. B., Hamlett, C. L., & Karns, K. M. (2000). Supplemental teacher judgments of mathematics test accommodations with objective data sources. *School Psychology Review, 29,* 65–85.

Galton, F. (1884). Measurement of character. *Fortnightly Review, 42,* 179–185. (Reprinted in *Readings in personality assessment,* by L. D. Goodstein & R. I. Lanyon, Eds., 1971, New York: Wiley.)

Gay, G. H. (1990). Standardized tests: Irregularities in administering the test effects test results. *Journal of Instructional Psychology, 17,* 93–103.

Ghiselli, E. E., Campbell, J. P., & Zedeck, S. (1981). *Measurement theory for the behavioral sciences.* San Francisco: W. H. Freeman.

Godshalk, F., Swineford, F., Coffman, W., & Educational Testing Service (1966). *The measurement of writing ability.* New York: College Entrance Examination Board.

Goodstein, L. D., & Lanyon, R. I. (1971). *Readings in personality assessment.* New York: Wiley.

Gorsuch, R. L. (1983). *Factor analysis* (2nd ed.). Hillsdale, NJ: Erlbaum.

Gray, P. (1999). *Psychology.* New York: Worth.

Green, B. F. (1981). A primer of testing. *American Psychologist, 36,* 1001–1011.

Greir, J. B. (1975). The number of alternatives for optimum test reliability. *Journal of Educational Measurement, 12,* 109–113.

Gresham, F. M., & Witt, J. C. (1997). Utility of intelligence tests for treatment planning, classification, and placement decisions. Recent empirical findings and future directions. *School Psychology Quarterly, 12,* 146–154.

Gronlund, N. E. (1998). *Assessment of student achievement* (6th ed.). Boston: Allyn & Bacon.

Gronlund, N. E. (2000). *How to write and use instructional objectives* (6th ed.). Upper Saddle River, NJ: Merrill/Prentice Hall.

Gronlund, N. E. (2003). *Assessment of student achievement* (7th ed.). Boston: Allyn & Bacon.

Gulliksen, H. (1950). *Theory of mental tests.* New York: Wiley.

Haak, R. A. (1990). Using the sentence completion to assess emotional disturbance. In C. R. Reynolds & R. W. Kamphaus (Eds.), *Handbook of psychological and educational assessment of children: Personality, behavior, and context* (pp. 147–167). New York: Guilford Press.

Haak, R. A. (2003). The sentence completion as a tool for to assessing emotional disturbance. In C. R. Reynolds & R. W. Kamphaus (Eds.), *Handbook of psychological and educational assessment of children: Personality, behavior, and context* (2nd ed., pp. 159–181). New York: Guilford Press.

Hakstian, A. (1971). The effects of study methods and test performance on objective and essay examinations. *Journal of Educational Research, 64,* 319–324.

Hales, L., & Tokar, E. (1975). The effect of quality of preceding responses on the grades assigned to subsequent responses to an essay question. *Journal of Educational Measurement, 12,* 115–117.

Halpern, D. F. (1997). Sex differences in intelligence: Implications for education. *American Psychologist, 52,* 1091–1102.

Hammer, E. (1985). The House-Tree-Person Test. In C. Newmark (Ed.), *Major psychological assessment instruments* (pp. 135–164). Boston: Allyn & Bacon.

Handler, L. (1985). The clinical use of the Draw-A-Person Test (DAP). In C. Newmark (Ed.), *Major psychological assessment instruments* (pp. 165–216). Boston: Allyn & Bacon.

Harrow, A. J. (1972). *A taxonomy of the psychomotor domain.* New York: David McKay.

Hays, W. (1994). *Statistics* (5th ed.). New York: Harcourt Brace.

Helms, J. E. (1992). Why is there no study of cultural equivalence in standardized cognitive ability testing? *American Psychologist, 47,* 1083–1101.

Hembree, R. (1988). Correlates, causes, effects, and treatment of test anxiety. *Review of Educational Research, 58,* 47–77.

Hilliard, A. G. (1979). Standardization and cultural bias as impediments to the scientific study and validation of "intelligence." *Journal of Research and Development in Education, 12,* 47–58.

Hilliard A. G. (1989). Back to Binet: The case against the use of IQ tests in the schools. *Diagnostique, 14,* 125–135.

Hoff, D. J. (1999). N.Y.C. probe levels test-cheating charges. *Education Week, 19,* 3.

Hoff, D. J. (2003). California schools experiment with deletion of D's. *Education Week, 32,* 5.

Hopkins, K. D. (1998). *Educational and psychological measurement and evaluation* (8th ed.). Boston: Allyn & Bacon.

Hughes, D., Keeling, B., & Tuck, B. (1980). The influence of context position and scoring method on essay scoring. *Journal of Educational Measurement, 17,* 131–135.

Hunter, J. E., Schmidt, F. L., & Hunter, R. (1979). Differential validity of employment tests by race: A comprehensive review and analysis. *Psychological Bulletin, 86,* 721–735.

Hunter, J. E., Schmidt, F. L., & Rauschenberger, J. (1984). Methodological, statistical, and ethical issues in the study of bias in mental testing. In C. R. Reynolds & R. T. Brown (Eds.), *Perspectives on bias in mental testing* (pp. 41–101). New York: Plenum Press.

James, A. (1927). The effect of handwriting on grading. *English Journal, 16,* 180–205.

Jensen, A. R. (1976). Test bias and construct validity. *Phi Delta Kappan, 58,* 340–346.

Jensen, A. R. (1980). *Bias in mental testing.* New York: Free Press.

Johnson, A. P. (1951). Notes on a suggested index of item validity: The U-L index. *Journal of Educational Measurement, 42,* 499–504.

Joint Committee on Standards for Educational Evaluation (2003). *The student evaluation standards.* Arlen Gullickson, Chair. Thousand Oaks, CA: Corwin Press.

Joint Committee on Testing Practices (1988). *Code of fair testing practices in education.* Washington, DC: American Psychological Association.

Joint Committee on Testing Practices (1998). *Rights and responsibilities of test takers: Guidelines and expectations.* Washington, DC: American Psychological Association.

Kamphaus, R. W. (1993). *Clinical assessment of children's intelligence: A handbook for professional practice.* Boston: Allyn & Bacon.

Kamphaus, R. W. (2001). *Clinical assessment of child and adolescent intelligence.* Boston: Allyn & Bacon.

Kamphaus, R. W., & Frick, P. J. (2002). *Clinical assessment of child and adolescent personality and behavior.* Boston: Allyn & Bacon.

Kamphaus, R. W., & Reynolds, C. R. (1998). *Behavior Assessment System for Children (BASC) ADHD Monitor.* Circle Pines, MN: American Guidance Service.

Kaufman, A. S. (1994). *Intelligent testing with the WISC-III.* New York: Wiley.

Kaufman, A. S., & Lichtenberger, E. O. (1999). *Essentials of WAIS-III assessment.* New York: Wiley.

Keith, T. Z., & Reynolds, C. R. (1990). Measurement and design issues in child assessment research. In C. R. Reynolds & R. W. Kamphaus (Eds.), *Handbook of psychological and educational assessment of children: Intelligence and achievement* (pp. 29–62). New York: Guilford Press.

Keller, B. (2001). Dozens of Michigan schools under suspicion of cheating. *Education Week, 20,* 18, 30.

Kelley, T. L. (1939). The selection of upper and lower groups for the validation of test items. *Journal of Educational Psychology, 30,* 17–24.

Kerlinger, F. N. (1973). *Foundations of behavioral research.* New York: Holt, Rinehart and Winston.

King, W. L., Baker, J., & Jarrow, J. E. (1995). *Testing accommodations for students with disabilities.* Columbus, OH: Association on Higher Education and Disability.

Kober, N. (2002). Teaching to the test: The good, the bad, and who's responsible. *Test Talk for Leaders* (Issue 1). Washington, DC: Center on Education Policy. Retrieved May 13, 2003, from www.cep-dc.org/testing/testtalkjune2002.htm

Koretz, D., Stecher, B., & Deibert, E. (1993). Lessons from an Evolving System. Interim Report: *The reliability of Vermont portfolio scores in the 1992–93 school year.* Project 3.2 State Accountability Models in Action. Los Angeles: Center for Research on Evaluation, Standards, and Student Testing.

Kovacs, M. (1991). *The Children's Depression Inventory* (CDI). North Tonawanda, NY: Multi-Health Systems.

Kranzler, J. H. (1997). Educational and policy issues related to the use and interpretation of intelligence tests in the schools. *School Psychology Review, 26,* 50–63.

Krathwohl, D., Bloom, B., & Masia, B. (1964). *Taxonomy of educational objectives: Book 2: Affective domain.* White Plains, NY: Longman.

Kubiszyn, T., & Borich, G. (2000). *Educational testing and measurement: Classroom application and practice* (6th ed.). New York: Wiley.

Kubiszyn, T., & Borich, G. (2003). *Educational testing and measurement: Classroom application and practice* (7th ed.). New York: Wiley.

Kuder, G. F., & Richardson, M. W. (1937). The theory of the estimation of reliability. *Psychometrika, 2,* 151–160.

Lawshe, C. H. (1975). A quantitative approach to content validity. *Personnel Psychology, 28,* 563–575.

Linn, R., & Baker, E. (1992, fall). Portfolios and accountability. The CRESST Line: *Newsletter of the National Center for Research on Evaluation Standards and Student Testing,* 1, 8–10. Retrieved December 6, 2004, from www.cse.ucla.edu/products/newsletters/clfall92.pdf

Linn, R. L., & Gronlund, N. E. (2000). *Measurement and assessment in teaching* (8th ed.). Upper Saddle River, NJ: Prentice Hall.

Livingston, R. B., Eglsaer, R., Dickson, T., & Harvey-Livingston, K. (2003). *Psychological assessment practices with children and adolescents.* Paper presented at the 23rd Annual National Academy of Neuropsychology Conference, Dallas, TX.

Lord, F. M. (1952). The relation of the reliability of multiple-choice tests to the distribution of item difficulties. *Psychometrika, 17,* 181–194.

Lowry, R. (2003). *Vassar stats: Cohen's kappa.* Retrieved August 10, 2003, from http://faculty./vassar.edu/lowry/kappa.html

Lyman, H. B. (1998). *Test scores and what they mean.* Boston: Allyn & Bacon.

Madaus, G. F., & Kellaghan, T. (1993). The British experience with "authentic" testing. *Phi Delta Kappan, 74,* 458–459.

Manzo, K. K. (2003). Essay scoring goes digital. *Education Week, 22,* 39–40, 42.

Mastergeorge, A. M., & Miyoshi, J. N. (1999). *Accommodations for students with disabilities: A teacher's guide* (CSE Technical Report 508). Los Angeles: National Center for Research on Evaluation, Standards, and Student Testing.

McArthur, D., & Roberts, G. (1982). *Roberts Apperception Test for Children: Manual.* Los Angeles: Western Psychological Services.

McGregor, G., & Vogelsberg, R. (1998). *Inclusive schooling practices: Pedagogical and research foundations. A synthesis of the literature that informs best practices about inclusive schooling.* Pittsburgh, PA: Allegheny University of the Health Sciences.

Mealy, D. L., & Host, T. R. (1992). Coping with test anxiety. *College Teaching, 40,* 147–150.

Messick, S. (1989). Validity. In R. L. Linn (Ed.), *Educational measurement* (3rd ed., pp. 13–103). Upper Saddle River, NJ: Merrill Prentice Hall.

Messick, S. (1994). The interplay of evidence and consequences in the validation of performance assessments. *Educational Researcher, 23,* 13–23.

Murphey, K. R., & Davidshofer, C. O. (2001). *Psychological testing: Principles and applications* (5th ed.). Upper Saddle River, NJ: Prentice Hall.

Myford, C. M., & Cline, F. (2002). *Looking for patterns in disagreement: A Facets analysis of human raters' and e-rater's scores on essays written for the Graduate Management Admission Test* (GMAT). Paper presented at the annual meeting of the American Educational Research Association, New Orleans, LA.

National Council on Measurement in Education (1995). *Code of professional responsibilities in educational measurement.* Washington, DC: Author.

Neisser, U., BooDoo, G., Bouchard, T., Boykin, A., Brody, N., Ceci, S., Halpern, D., Loehlin, J., Perloff, R., Sternberg, R., & Urbina, S. (1996). Intelligence: Knowns and unknowns. *American Psychologist, 51,* 77–101.

Nitko, A. J. (2001). *Educational assessment of students.* Upper Saddle River, NJ: Merrill Prentice Hall.

Nitko, A. J., & Lane, S. (1990). Standardized multilevel survey achievement batteries. In C. R. Reynolds & R. W. Kamphaus (Eds.), *Handbook of psychological and educational assessment of children: Intelligence and achievement* (pp. 405–434). New York: Guilford Press.

Northeast Technical Assistance Center (1999). Providing test accommodations. *NETAC Teacher Tipsheet.* Rochester, NY: Author.

Nunnally, J. C., & Bernstein, I. H. (1994). *Psychometric theory* (3rd ed.). New York: McGraw-Hill.

Olson, L. (2003). Georgia suspends testing plans in key grades. *Education Week, 22,* 1, 15.

Oosterhof, A. C. (1976). Similarity of various item discrimination indices. *Journal of Educational Measurement, 13,* 145–150.

Phillips, S. E. (1993). Testing accommodations for disabled students. *Education Law Reporter, 80,* 9–32.

Phillips, S. E. (1994). High-stakes testing accommodations: Validity versus disabled rights. *Applied Measurement in Education, 7*(2), 93–120.

Phillips, S. E. (1996). Legal defensibility of standards: Issues and policy perspectives. *Educational Measurement: Issues and Practice, 15*(2), 5–19.

Piacentini, J. (1993). Checklists and rating scales. In T. H. Ollendick and M. Hersen (Eds.), *Handbook of child and adolescent assessment* (pp. 82–97). Boston: Allyn & Bacon.

Pike, L. W. (1979). *Short-term instruction, testwiseness, and the Scholastic Aptitude Test: A literature review with research recommendations.* Princeton, NJ: Educational Testing Service.

Popham, W. J. (1999). *Classroom assessment: What teachers need to know.* Boston: Allyn & Bacon.

Popham, W. J. (2000). *Modern educational measurement: Practical guidelines for educational leaders.* Boston: Allyn & Bacon.

Powers, D. E., & Kaufman, J. C. (2002). *Do standardized multiple-choice tests penalize deep-thinking or creative students?* (RR-02-15). Princeton, NJ: Educational Testing Service

Psychological Assessment Resources (2003). *Catalog of professional testing resources, 26.* Lutz, FL: Author.

The Psychological Corporation (2002). *Examiner's manual for the Wechsler Individual Achievement Test—Second Edition.* San Antonio: Author.

Psychological Corporation (2003). *The catalog for psychological assessment products.* San Antonio, TX: Author.

Ramsay, M., Reynolds, C., & Kamphaus, R. (2002). *Essentials of behavioral assessment.* New York: Wiley.

Reynolds, C. R. (1980). In support of "Bias in Mental Testing" and scientific inquiry. *The Behavioral and Brain Sciences, 3,* 352.

Reynolds, C. R. (1982). The problem of bias in psychological assessment. In C. R. Reynolds & T. B. Gutkin (Eds.), *The handbook of school psychology* (pp. 178–208). New York: Wiley.

Reynolds, C. R. (1983). Test bias: In God we trust; all others must have data. *Journal of Special Education, 17,* 241–260.

Reynolds, C. R. (1985). Critical measurement issues in learning disabilities. *Journal of Special Education, 18,* 451–476.

Reynolds, C. R. (1990). Conceptual and technical problems in learning disability diagnosis. In C. R. Reynolds & R. W. Kamphaus (Eds.), *Handbook of psychological and educational assessment of children: Intelligence and achievement* (pp. 571–592). New York: Guilford Press.

Reynolds, C. R. (1995). Test bias in the assessment of intelligence and personality. In D. Saklofsky & M. Zeidner (Eds.), *International handbook of personality and intelligence* (pp. 545–576). New York: Plenum.

Reynolds, C. R. (1998a). Common sense, clinicians, and actuarialism in the detection of malingering during head injury litigation. In C. R. Reynolds (Ed.), *Detection of malingering during head injury litigation. Critical issues in neuropsychology* (pp. 261–286). New York: Plenum.

Reynolds, C. R. (1998b). Fundamentals of measurement and assessment in psychology. In A. Bellack & M. Hersen (Eds.), *Comprehensive clinical psychology* (pp. 33–55). New York: Elsevier.

Reynolds, C. R. (1999). Inferring causality from relational data and design: Historical and contemporary lessons for research and clinical practice. *The Clinical Neuropsychologist, 13,* 386–395.

Reynolds, C. R. (2000). Why is psychometric research on bias in mental testing so often ignored? *Psychology, Public Policy, and Law, 6,* 144–150.

Reynolds, C. R. (2002). *Comprehensive Trail-Making Test: Examiner's manual.* Austin, TX: PRO-ED.

Reynolds, C. R., & Kamphaus, R. (Eds.). (1990a). *Handbook of psychological and educational assessment of children: Personality, behavior, and context.* New York: Guilford Press.

Reynolds, C. R., & Kamphaus, R. (Eds.). (1990b). *Handbook of psychological and educational assessment of children: Intelligence and achievement.* New York: Guilford Press.

Reynolds, C. R., & Kamphaus, R. W. (1992). *Behavior Assessment System for Children: Manual.* Circle Pines, MN: American Guidance Service.

Reynolds, C. R., & Kamphaus, R. W. (1998). *Behavior Assessment System for Children: Manual.* Circle Pines, MN: American Guidance Services.

Reynolds, C. R., & Kaufman, A. S. (1990). Assessment of children's intelligence with the Wechsler Intelligence Scale for Children—Revised (WISC-R). In C. R. Reynolds & R. W. Kamphaus (Eds.), *Handbook of psychological and educational assessment of children: Intelligence and achievement* (pp. 127–165). New York: Guilford Press.

Reynolds, C. R., Lowe, P. A., & Saenz, A. (1999). The problem of bias in psychological assessment. In T. B. Gutkin & C. R. Reynolds (Eds.), *The handbook of school psychology* (3rd ed., pp. 549–595). New York: Wiley.

Reynolds, C. R., & Ramsay, M. C. (2003). Bias in psychological assessment: An empirical review and recommendations. In J. R. Graham & J. A. Naglieri (Eds.), *Handbook of psychology: Assessment psychology* (pp. 67–93). New York: Wiley.

Reynolds, W. M. (1993). Self-report methodology. In T. H. Ollendick and M. Hersen (Eds.), *Handbook of child and adolescent assessment* (pp. 98–123). Boston: Allyn & Bacon.

Riverside Publishing (2002). *CogAT, Form 6: A short guide for teachers.* Itasca, IL: Author.

Riverside Publishing (2003). *Clinical and special needs assessment catalog.* Itasca, IL: Author.

Roid, G. H. (2003). *Stanford-Binet Intelligence Scales, Fifth Edition.* Itasca, IL: Author.

Runyan, M. K. (1991). The effect of extra time on reading comprehension scores for university students with and without learning disabilities. *Journal of Learning Disabilities, 24,* 104–108.

Sanders, W. L., Saxton, A. M., & Horn, S. P. (1997). The Tennessee value-added assessment system: A quantitative, outcomes-based approach to educational assessment. In J. Millman (Ed.), *Grading teachers, grading schools* (pp. 137–162). Thousand Oaks, CA: Corwin Press.

Sandoval, J., & Mille, M. P. W. (1979, September). *Accuracy judgments of WISC-R item difficulty for minority groups.* Paper presented at the annual meeting of the American Psychological Association, New York.

Sarnacki, R. E. (1979, spring). An examination of test-wiseness in the cognitive domain. *Review of Educational Research, 49,* 252–279.

Sattler, J. M. (1992). *Assessment of children* (revised and updated 3rd ed.). San Diego, CA: Author.

Saupe, J. L. (1961). Some useful estimates of the Kuder-Richardson formula number 20 reliability coefficient. *Educational and Psychological Measurement, 2,* 63–72.

Schoenfeld, W. N. (1974). Notes on a bit of psychological nonsense: "Race differences in intelligence." *Psychological Record, 24,* 17–32.

Shavelson, R., Baxter, G., & Gao, X. (1993). Sampling variability of performance assessments. *Journal of Educational Measurement, 30,* 215–232.

Sheppard, E. (1929). The effect of quality of penmanship on grades. *Journal of Educational Research, 19,* 102–105.

Sidick, J. T., Barrett, G. V., & Doverspike, D. (1994). Three-alternative multiple-choice tests: An attractive option. *Personnel Psychology, 47,* 829–835.

Sireci, S. G. (1998). Gathering and analyzing content validity data. *Educational Assessment, 5,* 299–321.

Sireci, S. G., Thissen, D., & Wainer, H. (1991). On the reliability of testlet-based tests. *Journal of Educational Measurement, 28,* 237–247.

Stainback, S., & Stainback, W. (1992). *Curriculum considerations in inclusive classrooms: Facilitating learning for all students.* Baltimore: Brooks.

Stiggens, R. J. (2001). *Student-involved classroom assessment* (3rd ed.). Upper Saddle River, NJ: Merrill Prentice Hall.

Stiggins, R. J., & Conklin, N. F. (1992). *In teacher's hands: Investigating the practices of classroom assessment.* Albany, NY: State University of New York Press.

Suzuki, L. A., & Valencia, R. R. (1997). Race–ethnicity and measured intelligence: Educational implications. *American Psychologist, 52,* 1103–1114.

Tabachnick, B. G., & Fidel, L. S. (1996). *Using multivariate statistics* (3rd ed.). New York: HarperCollins.

Tatsuoka, K., & Tatsuoka, M. (1997). Computerized cognitive diagnostic adaptive testing: Effect on remedial instruction as empirical validation. *Journal of Educational Measurement, 34,* 3–20.

Texas Education Agency (2003). District and campus coordinator manual: Texas student assessment program.

Thurnlow, M., Hurley, C., Spicuzza, R., & El Sawaf, H. (1996). *A review of the literature on testing accommodations for students with disabilities* (Minnesota Report No. 9). Minneapolis: University of Minnesota, National Center on Educational Outcomes. Retrieved April 19, 2004, from http://education.umn.edu/NCEO/OnlinePubs/MnReport9.html

Tippets E., & Benson, J. (1989). The effect of item arrangement on test anxiety. *Applied Measurement in Education, 2,* 289–296.

Turnbull, R., Turnbull, A., Shank, M., Smith, S., & Leal, D. (2002). *Exceptional lives: Special education in today's schools.* Upper Saddle River, NJ: Merrill Prentice Hall.

U.S. Department of Education (1997). Guidance on standards, assessments, and accountability—II. Assessments. Retrieved November 30, 2004, from www.ed.gov/policy/elsec/guid/standardsassessment/guidance_pg4.html

Videro, D., & Drummond, S. (1998, April 22). Software said to grade essays for content. *Education Week.* Retrieved January 30, 2004, from www.edweek.org/ew/ew_printstory.cfm?slug=32soft.h17

Ward, A. W., & Murray-Ward, M. (1994). Guidelines for the development of item banks: An NCME instructional module. *Educational Measurement: Issues and Practice, 13,* 34–39.

Webster, W. J., & Mendro, R. L. (1997). The Dallas value-added accountability system. In J. Millman (Ed.), *Grading teachers, grading schools* (pp. 81–99). Thousand Oaks, CA: Corwin Press.

Wechsler, D. W. (1991). *Wechsler Intelligence Scale for Children—Third Edition: Manual.* San Antonio, TX: Psychological Corporation.

Wechsler, D. W. (1997). WAIS-III administration and scoring manual. San Antonio, TX: Psychological Corporation.

Wechsler, D. W. (2003). *Wechsler Intelligence Scale for Children—Fourth Edition: Technical and interpretive manual.* San Antonio, TX: Psychological Corporation.

Weiss, D. J. (1982). Improving measurement quality and efficiency with adaptive theory. *Applied Psychological Measurement, 6,* 473–492.

Weiss, D. J. (1985). Adaptive testing by computer. *Journal of Consulting and Clinical Psychology, 53,* 774–789.

Weiss, D. J. (1995). Improving individual difference measurement with item response theory and computerized adaptive testing. In D. Lubinski & R. Dawis (Eds.), *Assessing individual differences in human behavior: New concepts, methods, and findings* (pp. 49–79). Palo Alto, CA: Davies-Black.

Wigdor, A. K., & Garner, W. K. (1982). *Ability testing: Uses, consequences, and controversy.* Washington DC: National Academy Press.

Williams, R. L. (1970). Danger: Testing and dehumanizing Black children. *Clinical Child Psychology Newsletter, 9,* 5–6.

Williams, R. L., Dotson, W., Dow, P., & Williams, W. S. (1980). The war against testing: A current status report. *Journal of Negro Education, 49,* 263–273.

Witt, J., Heffer, R., & Pfeiffer, J. (1990). Structured rating scales: A review of self-report and informant rating processes, procedures, and issues. In C. R. Reynolds & Kamphaus (Eds.), *Handbook of psychological and educational assessment of children: Personality, behavior, and context* (pp. 364–394). New York: Guilford Press.

Woodcock, R. W., McGrew, K. S., & Mather, N. (2001a). *Woodcock-Johnson III (WJ III) Tests of Achievement.* Itasca, IL: Riverside Publishing.

Woodcock, R. W., McGrew, K. S., & Mather, N. (2001b). *Woodcock-Johnson III (WJ III) Tests of Cognitive Abilities.* Itasca, IL: Riverside Publishing.

Woodcock, R. W., McGrew, K. S., & Mather, N. (2001c). *Woodcock-Johnson III (WJ III) Complete Battery.* Itasca, IL: Riverside Publishing.

INDEX